𝔗𝔥𝔢 𝔏𝔦𝔣𝔢 𝔬𝔣 𝔍

For fifty years philanthropist and

scholar in the East

George Smith

Alpha Editions

This edition published in 2019

ISBN : 9789353976651

Design and Setting By
Alpha Editions
email - alphaedis@gmail.com

THE LIFE

OF

JOHN WILSON, D.D. F.R.S.

FOR FIFTY YEARS PHILANTHROPIST AND SCHOLAR IN THE EAST

By GEORGE SMITH, LL.D.

COMPANION OF THE ORDER OF THE INDIAN EMPIRE ;

FELLOW OF THE ROYAL GEOGRAPHICAL AND STATISTICAL SOCIETIES, ETC. ;

AUTHOR OF ' THE LIFE OF ALEXANDER DUFF, D.D. LL.D.'

Οἱ τὴν οἰκουμένην ἀναστατώσαντες οὗτοι καὶ ἐνθάδε πάρεισιν.

SECOND EDITION ABRIDGED

WITH PORTRAIT AND ILLUSTRATIONS

LONDON

JOHN MURRAY, ALBEMARLE STREET

1879

PREFACE TO THE SECOND EDITION.

THE continued demand for the book, even after the rapid sale of the First Edition, has led to its re-publication in a cheaper form. The use of smaller type has made this possible without seriously abridging the text, and with the omission of only a few extracts. On the other hand, a fortunate discovery in the Records of the Foreign Office of the Free Church of Scotland has enabled the author to enrich this Edition with the characteristic letter at page 329 to Dr. Wilson from Dr. Livingstone, which Mr. H. Stanley posted from Aden to Bombay. In its present form the Life of Dr. Wilson is placed within the reach of the people, and more especially of both Asiatic and British youth in colleges and schools.

ISLE OF ARRAN,
    25th August 1879.

PREFACE TO THE FIRST EDITION.

WHEN I was asked by his son to go over the voluminous papers and write the life of Dr. Wilson of Bombay, I at once sacrificed other engagements to the duty. As Editor of the *Calcutta Review* for some time before the Mutiny of 1857, and as Editor of *The Friend of India* and Correspondent of *The Times* for many years after it, I was called to observe and occasionally to discuss the career of the Philanthropist and Scholar of Western India. For forty-seven years as a public man and a missionary he worked, he wrote, he spoke, and in countless ways he joyfully toiled for the people of India. While viceroys and governors, officials and merchants, scholars and travellers, succeeded each other and passed away all too rapidly, he remained a permanent living force, a mediator between the natives and the governing class, an interpreter of the varied Asiatic races, creeds, and longings, to their alien but benevolent rulers. Nor was his work for his own countrymen less remarkable, in its degree, than his life of self-sacrifice for Hindoos and Muhammadans, Parsees and Jews, out-castes and aborigines, and his building up of the indigenous Church of India. His influence maintained an English standard of morality and manners

in society, while he was the centre of a select group of
administrators, not confined to Bombay, like Sir Donald
M'Leod, to mention only the dead. As an Orientalist and
scholar, the power of his memory was only less remarkable
than the ardour of his industry ; his linguistic instinct was
regulated by the philosophy with which his native country
is identified, and all were directed by the loftiest motive
and the purest passion that can inflame the breast. Wealth
and honours he put from him, save when he could make
them also ministers in the work of humanity. From
Central India to Central Africa, and from Cabul to Comorin,
there are thousands who call John Wilson blessed. His
hundreds of educated converts and catechumens are the
seed of the Church of Western India. Every missionary
and student of India Missions must sit at his feet.

From 1864, when I first visited Bombay, to his death
at the close of 1875, I learned to know the man as well as
his work. But he cannot be so well reproduced on the
cold page, for his own writings do not reflect the charm of
his talk, which delighted generations of friends, from Sir
John Malcolm to Lord Mayo and Lord Northbrook, Sir
Bartle Frere and Mr. Grant Duff. My aim is that this
volume may supply the materials, at least, from which his
Country and the Church Catholic, oriental scholars, and
the princes and educated natives of India, shall not only
see what manner of man he was, but be stimulated by his
rare example. I hope also that the sketches of the other
good and great men who worked for a time by his side
may not be without interest ; and that, still more, it may
be seen how the British Government is rising to the height
of our national responsibility for the good of the millions

of Southern Asia, and of the neighbouring Malay, Chinese,
Tatar, Persian, Arab, Abyssinian, and Negro peoples.

This is an English book, and therefore, though it occasionally treats purely scholarly questions, the English
vowels are used to transliterate oriental names and terms.
Save in extracts which demand the preservation of the
original spelling, and in the name which I would fain have
printed "Boodhist," hardly an Asiatic word or phrase will
be found which is not so rendered as to be capable of
correct pronunciation, and of being easily understood.
Scholars who write for scholars only, do well to follow the
Indian and European vowel sounds. Scholars, officials,
and all who desire the English reader to be attracted to,
instead of being repelled from, the study of India and the
East, will use English as uniformly as ineradicable custom
permits.

Besides the acknowledgments made in the course of the
narrative, I have to thank for their assistance his Excellency
Sir Richard Temple, Bart., who, as the present Governor of
Bombay, instructed the departments to supply copies of
some of Dr. Wilson's official correspondence ; Sir Alexander
Grant, Bart., Principal of the University of Edinburgh, who,
as Director of Public Instruction for some years, was closely
associated with Dr. Wilson ; the third Sir Jamsetjee Jeejeebhoy, Bart. ; The Revs. Dhunjeebhoy Nowrojee and R.
Stothert, M.A.; Dr. Birdwood, C.S.I., and Dr. R. Rost, of
the India Office ; Hugh Miller, M.D., Esq. of Broomfield,
Helensburgh; W. P. Jervis, Esq., Turin; Professors
Charteris and Eggeling ; and Professor Weber of Berlin,
who has communicated to me, through Mr. John Muir,
D.C.L., C.I.E., his very high estimate of the scientific

pursuits of Dr. Wilson as an Orientalist who subordinated
scholarly reputation to missionary ends. Only the long
frontier war, and the other cares of his office as Governor
of Cape Colony, have prevented his Excellency Sir Bartle
Frere from contributing reminiscences of his lifelong friend.

SERAMPORE HOUSE, MERCHISTON,
      EDINBURGH, 19th October 1878.

CONTENTS.

CHAPTER IX.

CHAPTER X.

CHAPTER XI.

CHAPTER XII.

CHAPTER XIII.

CHAPTER XIV.

CHAPTER XV.

CHAPTER XVI.

CHAPTER XVII.

CHAPTER XVIII.

ILLUSTRATIONS.

LIFE OF JOHN WILSON, D.D.

CHAPTER I.

1804-1828.

HOME—SCHOOL—UNIVERSITY—VOYAGE TO BOMBAY.

Lauder and Lauderdale—The Border and the Men it has sent to India—The
Wilsons of Lauder—the Burgh Common and the Big Farms—John Wilson,
"The Priest"—Memories of Waterloo—Dr. James Fairbairn on Schoolboy
days and the Dawn of Evangelicalism—John Wilson, Schoolmaster and
Tutor—Early Indian and Bombay Influences—The Arts Course at Edin-
burgh University—The Theological Professors—Rebellion of the Divinity
Students—Founds the University Missionary Society—Earliest Publica-
tions—Ordained—The Bayne Sisters—Marriage—First view of Cape
Comorin and Western India—Arrives at Bombay.

AT a point some twenty-five miles to the south-east of the
city of Edinburgh, the three counties of Edinburgh, Berwick,
and Roxburgh meet. The spot is the summit of Lauder Hill,
which rises between the railway station of Stow and the
royal burgh of Lauder, chief of all the district of Lauderdale.
As we stand on the ancient road, now grass-grown, we survey
perhaps the widest and most quietly beautiful scene that the
Scottish Border can present. From the Lammermoor to the
Cheviot Hills, with the rounded Eildons sprouting at their
base, the breadth of the two border counties, the Merse or
march of Berwick and the fells of Roxburgh, are spread out
before us. Distant Teviot and near Tweed roll down to the
North Sea, watering a land of more historic renown than any
other part of the too long disunited Kingdom. Behind we
have left Gala Water, with its memories of legend and of
song; before us, half hidden by the hill on which we stand,
is the Leader which gives its name to Lauderdale. For more
than twenty miles the stream flows on from the Lammermoors
till it mingles its waters with the Tweed below Melrose

Abbey. Even Scotland presents few valleys so broad, so fertile, as this Lauder dale throughout its long extent. Monk and warrior early chose it for their own, from Dryburgh Abbey where Sir Walter Scott lies, and Erceldoune or Earlston where Thomas the Rhymer sang his prophecies, to Thirlestane Castle where the Maitlands of Lauderdale perpetuate a house well known in Scottish history. Here it was, along the great highway, from the marshalling-ground of the Boroughmuir of Edinburgh to the fords of the Tweed and the field of Flodden, that the Edwards led their invading armies, and the Stewarts their avenging forces; while noble and yeoman on both sides the marches fought for their own hand. Old Thirlestane, near whose ruins the Leader now flows so gently, was long the tower from which " Maitland, with his auld grey beard," whom Gawan Douglas thought worthy of a place in his allegory of the " Palace of Honour," beat back the English. The ballad of " Auld Maitland," as taken down from the lips of Jane Hogg, the Ettrick Shepherd's mother, who had learned it from a blind man of ninety, deserves all the enthusiasm Sir Walter Scott expresses for it. But dearer to the son of the Border is the more modern song of " Leader Haughs and Yarrow," with its quaint poetic catalogue of names and places more familiar to the natives of Lauderdale and Selkirk than those of Homer or of Milton. The old minstrel sighs at the close for the glory that is departed, for he wrote doubtless in the evil days just after the duke built the present castle in 1674—

> " Sing Erlington and Cowdenknowes,
> Where Humes had ance commanding ;
> And Drygrange with the milk-white yowes
> 'Twixt Tweed and Leader standing :
> The bird that flees through Redpath trees
> And Gladswood banks ilk morrow,
> May chaunt and sing sweet Leader Haughs
> And bonnie howms of Yarrow.

> " But minstrel Burne cannot assuage
> His grief, while life endureth,
> To see the changes of his age
> Which fleeting time procureth ;
> For mony a place stands in hard case,
> Where blythe folk kend nae sorrow,
> With Humes that dwelt on Leader-side
> And Scotts that dwelt on Yarrow."

It was at Lauder, too, in the days of the Third James,

that Archibald Douglas " belled the cat," hanging before his
sovereign's eyes five of the low favourites who misled the
royal youth. Nor should it be overlooked that the minister
of Lauder, inducted in 1638, was James Guthrie, the Coven-
anter whom Lauderdale martyred along with the Marquis of
Argyll, the Earl of Tweeddale alone pleading for the milder
sentence of banishment. But modern times have brought
more peaceful associations. Except, perhaps, the Highland
Inverness-shire, no part of Scotland has been so fruitful a
nursery of heroes for the civilisation, if not the conquest of
our Indian Empire. Tweedside and its many dales have, in
the last century, sent forth Kers and Elliots, Douglases and
Riddells, Scotts and Walkers, Malcolms and Grays, Napiers and
Murrays to the noblest work any country has ever done for
humanity. To a governor-general like Lord Minto, a statesman like Sir John Malcolm, a scholar and poet like Dr. Leyden, and an economist like James Wilson, we have now to
add the Christian missionary John Wilson. He was as great
a scholar and as benevolent a philanthropist as the best of
them, or as all of them together ; and he was a more potent
force than they, because he gave himself to the people of India
for a life of continuous service, covering nearly half a century,
and because that service was inspired and fed every hour by
the highest of all motives, the purest of all forms of self-
sacrifice.

John Wilson was born in the Berwickshire burgh of
Lauder on the 11th day of December 1804. He was the
eldest of seven children, four brothers and three sisters, most
of whom still survive. He came of a long-lived stock of small
proprietors and farmers, who for two hundred years inhabited
the thatched, but now enlarged, house in the " Row " of the
town in which he first saw the light. His great-grandfather
reached the age of ninety-eight, his grandfather lived to be
eighty-eight, his father and mother each died at eighty-two.
Physically, he thus inherited a constitution of singular elas-
ticity and power of endurance, under the frequent hardship of
toilsome journeys and malarious disease in the jungles of
Western India, before British railways, or even roads, had
opened them up. His father, Andrew Wilson, was for more
than forty years a councillor of the burgh, and was an elder
in the parish kirk. His mother, Janet Hunter, the eldest of a

family of thirteen, most of whom lived to a good old age, was a woman of great force of character. This, added to the kindly unselfishness which marked her eldest son also, caused her to be in constant request by her neighbours in times of sickness and trouble. Father and mother combined in their rearing the economic conditions of the surrounding district. Lauderdale, to the east of the Leader, is a district of large farms, yielding an average rental of a thousand a year and upwards, even in those days, and worked in the very best style of the *grande culture*. Of James Hunter, the leaseholder of one of the most extensive of these, John Wilson's mother was the eldest daughter. To the west of the stream lie the town and its unusually extensive commonage, covering at the present time 1700 acres, but doubtless larger a century ago. The land is owned by the burgesses, and a very considerable share of it had always been possessed by the Wilsons of the "Row." The old conditions are only now beginning to give place to the same influences which have made the high farming of the Lothians and the Merse famous in the history of agriculture. At last some of the "portioners" have combined to work the common land by the steam plough on a large scale. Yet, till this present year, the greater part of the burgh lands has been little more than fine pasture slopes, to which the cattle have been led daily, under a common herdsman. Of such a stock, and out of the very heart of farmer-life, sprang the thoughtful scholar, the unwearied missionary, the distinguished philanthropist of Bombay.

No love had he, though the eldest of four sons, for the doubly ancestral and honourable calling. From the womb he had a higher vocation. Had he become the apostle of a superstitious mysticism, like Gooroo Nanuk, the founder of the Sikh dissent from Hindooism, the same stories might have been told of the great Christian Gooroo. For Nanuk, too, was the son of the chief "portioner" of the common of a village near Lahore, and he failed to keep his father's buffaloes from the cultivated fields. Nanuk never played like other children, so that the Hindoos said, "Some god is in him." On the second of Andrew Wilson's sons fell the duty of helping in the farm, and of driving the cattle to the nearest fair of St. Boswell's. From infancy John revealed himself as meant for a very different lot. When a baby he almost

alarmed his mother by speaking before he could walk, and
with an intelligence unprecedented in the experience of the
neighbours.   So the Mussulman villagers had said of Nanuk,
"A holy man of God has been born!"   As he grew up John
Wilson was to his schoolfellows "the priest," by which name
he was always known among them.   His early developed
tendencies brought him into trouble.   On one occasion the
boy was found preaching from a hollow tree behind Thirlestane Castle to the people who were sauntering home on the
Sacrament Sunday evening, and was chastised for what seemed
to his parents an offence.   The secret of his life was not one
which mere heredity may explain, though that too will find
data in it.   It is thus stated by himself in a "diary of religious experience" which he began to write on his twentieth
birthday, but did not continue beyond his departure for India:
—"When about the age of three years, I was put to sleep in
the same bed with my aged grandfather by my father's side.
He was the first person, if I remember rightly, who communicated to me any knowledge about God and my soul.   I remember well the effect his instructions, by the blessing of God,
produced upon my mind : the impressions which were then
conveyed to me have never been wholly removed from me.
I can never forget the fervour with which he engaged in his
evening private devotions, and the feeling with which at such
times he repeated the 23d Psalm, especially the concluding
verse—

'Goodness and mercy all my life
Shall surely follow me,
And in God's house for evermore
My dwelling-place shall be.'

"I was very early under conviction of sin, and I trust that
the Lord at an early period of my life took a saving dealing
with my soul.   When about the age of four years I was sent
to a school in Lauder taught by Mr. George Murray, where I
continued about the space of one year.   I then went to the
parish school taught by Mr. Alexander Paterson, where, under
Mr. Paterson's instructions, I made remarkable progress."   It
was an early and it became a fruitful consecration ; even as
that of the prophet of Naioth and the statesman of Ramah.

John Wilson proved to be as fortunate in his teacher and
in his companions as in his early home life.   A new spirit

in truth was abroad over the land, which had long lain under
the spell of what is called "moderatism" in Scotland.   It
was the beginning, too, of that fifty years' period of peace
and reform, in State as well as Church, which the crowning
victory of Waterloo seemed to introduce.   Dr. Wilson used
to tell how, when he was little more than ten years old, the
Edinburgh coach came to Lauder adorned with boughs, and
one who had gone to the place where it stopped, to hear the
news, rushed down the Row shouting "We've just annihilated
them."   In both Lauder and Stow there happened to be
evangelical preachers in the parish churches, Mr. Cosens and
Dr. Cormack, while the "Burgher" or seceding congregations
were everywhere ministered to by earnest men, to whom
many of the surrounding families were driven by the old
"moderates."   The coming of Mr. Paterson to the parish
school at this time affected at once the spiritual condition
of the whole district, and speedily brought within the reach
of evangelical teaching all the hopeful youth of the surrounding country.   Before his death on the 3d January 1879,
the venerable Dr. Fairbairn of Newhaven thus recalled John
Wilson in those days :—

"He was a modest, devout, affectionate, and gentle boy,
always ready to take part with the weakest, and never in a
quarrel or a scrape.   He was, I think, the most diligent and
persevering student in the school, and I can readily understand how he attained to such acquirements and success.   He
was also eminently truthful and sincere.   There was one of
our number (James Runciman) whom our teacher always
characterised as the 'boy who never told a lie,' and he used
to associate John Wilson with him in this honourable distinction.   I remember in one of the intervals of our school
day, a band of us started 'up the burn' for fishing and other
diversions.   Seduced by the summer sunlight (oh how bright
it was in those days!) we heeded not the lapse of time, till
the school hour had passed.   Then came a conference to
determine what we would say for ourselves, and various proposals, savouring, I fear, of diplomacy, were made.   But the
discussion was cut short by John Wilson saying, in a tone
unusually energetic for him, 'I tell you what—we will tell
the truth,' and the truth he told—ay, and continued to tell
it till his dying day.

"I well remember also a very bright and calm summer Sabbath day. As the people went along the road to church, there was a question in every mouth—'Will they be *fechtin'* on sic a day as this?' After sermon there was a fellowship-meeting in the session-room of the Burgher meeting-house, into which my friend John and I contrived to get admission. Again the question went round, 'Will they be *fechtin?*' and the inquiry tinged all the services with unusual solemnity. A venerable white-headed elder, Saunders Downie, the tailor— who has passed long since into the fellowship of the four-and-twenty Elders that sit around the Throne—delivered himself to this effect: 'Surely,' he said, in his godly simplicity, 'surely they'll let the blessed Sabbath ower afore they fecht.' Whether they were 'fechtin,' or whether they let the blessed Sabbath over before doing so, you will judge when I say that that Sabbath day was the 18th of June 1815. Then came a week of anxiety; groups of people stood all the day at the head of the town, in the expectation of hearing the booming of the guns of the distant castle of Edinburgh announcing a victory. At last came the full accounts of the great battle, which filled every mouth and heart for many a long day. I recollect we were both much impressed with all this, and had our minds opened for the first time to the fact that there was a wide world beyond the limits of our little valley, and that it was a world in which much evil abounded, and which stood in great need of improvement.

"Then came a movement on behalf of the first of the evangelistic schemes which succeeded in penetrating to that part of the country. This was the Bible Society; and I recollect a sermon being preached on its behalf in the Burgher meeting-house by the Rev. Dr. Waugh of London, at which my friend and I were present. The matter and manner of the preacher were both deeply impressive; and I rather think that, if the seeds of the evangelistic spirit were not that night sown for the first time in John Wilson's mind, they were, to say the least of it, very copiously and effectually watered. After that we went to the University of Edinburgh, and we arrived there just at the time when evangelical religion began to reassert its power in this country. The old Gospel, which had been 'by Cameron thundered and by Renwick poured,' now flowed forth in the sweet stream of Henry Grey's pathetic eloquence,

or was uttered from the pulpit of St. George's by the mighty
voice of Andrew Thomson. Some of us were not very sure
about it at first. Coming as we did from the country of Thomas
Boston, there was something new to us in the methods of
these great preachers. One of our number indeed, and he not
the least earnest among us, never quite overcame his scruples.
He held it all to be ' sounding brass and a tinkling cymbal,'
and declared that he could only find ' the root of the matter '
in the Secession meeting-house in the Potterrow, then ministered to by the Rev. Mr. Simpson. I must say this incident
has taught me a great lesson of caution in judging of new
religious movements. We soon discovered, however, that a
new-born day of light and truth had at last broken out in this
country ; and this discovery was fully made to us by the
coming of Dr. Robert Gordon to Edinburgh. That was an
era in our spiritual history never to be forgotten. We were
all carried captive by the mighty spell of his eloquence.
John Wilson attached himself to the ministry of Dr. Gordon,
and you know the great power which it exercised over his
mind and history. All my recollections of my beloved school-
fellow are such as to harmonise with his after-life. Truly in
his case ' the child was father of the man.' "

In his fourteenth year John Wilson went to Edinburgh
University, to begin that eight years' course of linguistic,
philosophical, and theological studies by which the Scottish
Churches still wisely produce a well-trained and often cultured
ministry. Two Border youths, from the not very distant
Annandale, had, after similar home and school training,
matriculated at the University at the same age, and had not
long passed out of it when the Lauder boy first entered his
name in that fragment of the old building which occupied
the quadrangle until the present library was completed.
These were Edward Irving and Thomas Carlyle. Very fresh
traditions of the former still circulated among his juniors,
while the latter had just returned from his mathematical
teachership in Kirkcaldy to write for Brewster's Encyclopædia.
Both had been heroes in Sir John Leslie's class, where Wilson
succeeded them in reputation in due time. We cannot say
that the picture, in the autobiography which Carlyle wrote in
1831 as " Sartor Resartus," of " the University where I was
educated," and the " eleven hundred Christian striplings "

turned loose into its "small ill-chosen library," is altogether
a caricature of the facts. At any rate, Carlyle admits that
there were ,some eleven of that number who were eager to
learn, and Wilson was one of them in his time, as Irving and
Carlyle had been in theirs. Like them, too, Wilson took to
teaching. At the close of the first session, the lad conducted
the school of Horndean on the Tweed, laying thus early the
foundation of that educational experience by which, as Vernacular Missionary, Principal of an English College, and
Vice-Chancellor of the University, he was afterwards to
revolutionise society in Western India. One of his sisters
still tells how the boy of fifteen prepared to resist a midnight
attempt to rob him of the school fees on the first occasion
on which he had gained the hard-earned money. At the close
of the second college session, the Rev. Dr. Cormack, of the
neighbouring village of Stow, made the successful student
tutor to his son and nephews, a duty which he discharged in
a manner to endear him to the parents of both almost up to
the time of his departure for India. Dr. Cormack, when
himself tutor in the family of the Roses of Kilravoch, had
married one of the daughters, and her brother, Colonel Rose,
had sent home his sons to be educated in the manse at Stow.
When Colonel, afterwards Sir John, Rose, himself returned
to his family estate in the Highlands, he tried to induce John
Wilson to settle in his family there for some time, and to
accompany his boys to Holland, so highly did he appreciate
the tutor's services. The youths were happy who had such
a guide, himself still young. Even now it is almost pathetic
to read the letters which they wrote to him during his
absence at college and in India, and carefully treasured by
him among his most precious papers. One of the lads is now
Sir John Rose Cormack, a well-known physician in Paris.
The other two went to India in their day, where their old
friend met them sometimes, and where they won a name for
ability in the civil and military services.

A tour which, in the autumn of 1824, the tutor made to
the North with his pupils, called forth a series of letters to his
home in which we find such entries as these. At Kingussie he
visited the periodical fair : "All the people were very merry.
They were mostly all dressed in the Highland dress, and,
speaking Gaelic, they appeared quite comical. I have laughed

this whole fortnight at them." The letters show the same detailed power of observation and genial humour which marked his Indian tours, and made him the most delightful companion on such occasions. In 1827 he reports, " I have been obliged to buy a pair of silver spectacles for myself :" thus early did study begin to tell on him.

To this residence for four years, with college intervals, in Dr. Cormack's family, we must trace the determination, which he early formed, to give his life to the people of India. When afterwards bidding farewell to Dr. Brown, the minister of Langton, he expressed regret that he had to sail before the annual meeting of the Berwickshire Bible Society, for, he said, " My wish was to have stated publicly that it was the reading of your annual reports that first awakened me to the importance of Missions, and led me to resolve to devote myself to the foreign field." But it was the Rose and Cormack influence which directed that resolve to the East, at a time when Scotland had not a missionary there. The first surprise of the young tutor of sixteen, when he began his duties in the manse of Stow, was caused by the Hindostanee which alone the Rose boys spoke, like so many Anglo-Indian children fresh from the influence of native servants. That was one of the first languages he was to master when he began work in Bombay, in order by voice and pen to influence the Muhamma- dans and all who used what is a mere *lingua franca.* He was more or less in an Indian atmosphere, as each irregular mail in those days brought news of Maratha wars and Pindaree raids, of the triumphs of Lord Hastings, of the political exploits of Malcolm, the yeoman's son of the not distant Burnfoot, and of Governor Munro, the Glasgow boy. But more living to the youth than all that was the personal friendship of General Walker, who often drove into Stow from Bowland, his seat on the Gala Water. As political officer in charge of the great Native State of Baroda, with Kathiawar and Kutch, he had won for himself a name as a philanthropist and administrator, by carrying on the work of the old Governor, Jonathan Duncan, for the prevention of female infanticide among the Jadeja Rajpoots. When re- visiting Kathiawar in 1809, before bidding it a final farewell, General Walker had enjoyed the sweet reward of seeing not a few of the children whom he had preserved, and of hearing

one infant voice lisping to him in the Goojaratee tongue—
" Walker Saheb saved me." The entrancing story of humanity
became familiar to Wilson in his youth, for in 1819, at the
very time of his intercourse with him, the retired officer was
engaged in a correspondence with the Court of Directors, in
which he urged them to keep up the preventive system that
had effected so much, but was being neglected by a new
generation of officials. The only result was the General's
appointment as Governor of St. Helena, the small population
of which he sought to benefit with the same kindly wisdom
that he had shown in north Bombay. That work was not
unknown in the country-side, for the minister of Stow had
been its historian. But it was reserved for the young tutor
himself to complete it, alike by stirring up the Bombay Government, and by writing the "History of the Suppression of
Infanticide in Western India" in 1855, and again in 1875.
Thus to the influences of home and of school, of companions
and of minister, there was added, at the time when he was
most susceptible of such impressions, the subtle power of the
society of men like Cormack and Walker, who drew him
unconsciously to the work prepared for him in the then far
off and shadowy East.

In the second of the four years of his theological studies,
or in his twentieth year, Wilson became more closely identified with Edinburgh in both its university life and its literary
and ecclesiastical coteries. He had taken full advantage of
the Arts course, for among the professors of that faculty were
able teachers and accomplished *savants*. Pillans, unjustly
satirised by Byron, had been transferred from the rector's
chair in the High School at Edinburgh, which Dr. Adam had
made illustrious, and which his successor had not dimmed at
least, to the professorship of Humanity or Latin, taking with
him his "dux," John Brown Patterson, the most promising
student of his day, who became warmly attached to Wilson.
Inscriptions on missionary churches and university founda-
tion-stones in the East prove that Wilson retained to the
last all the graceful Latinity which he acquired at Lauder
and Edinburgh. We may pass over the Greek professor,
but the students found ample atonement in the Moral
Philosophy class of Professor Wilson, whose whirlwind of
rhetoric twenty-one Tory and eleven Whig patrons of the

chair had preferred to the massive erudition and the philosophical power of him who became our modern Aristotle — Sir William Hamilton. Had the Lauder student come under the spell of one who did not become professor of Metaphysics for some years afterwards, even he must have gained a more analytic and expository power in those investigations of the hoary philosophies of Vedist and Buddhist, Zoroastrian and Soofee, by which he did much to shake the grim idolatries and subtle pantheism of southern and western Asia. But he enjoyed what was of equal value for such a purpose at that time—the physical researches of Sir John Leslie, Playfair's successor in the chair of Natural Philosophy. There he stood in the front rank, a significant fact, for it is through the clay of the physical error worked up with the iron of speculative falsehood in the systems of the East, that they are first to be shaken and shattered. What of mathematical principles, physical law, and the natural sciences John Wilson then mastered, he developed and applied all through his conflicts with the defenders of the Oriental faiths, and in his discourses and writings, as the first scholar of Western India. In geology, in botany, in the more recondite region of archæology, he kept pace with the most recent researches, to which, in his own province, he largely contributed. Nature came second only to the divine Word, and worked harmoniously along with it in his whole missionary career.

The same cannot be asserted of the Theological Faculty of the University of Edinburgh at that period. It was the dreary time, just before, in 1828 — too late for Wilson — Thomas Chalmers was transferred from St. Andrews, where he had brought to the birth of a more spiritual and intellectual life, men like Robert Nesbit, soon to precede Wilson to Bombay; and Alexander Duff, William S. Mackay, and David Ewart ; destined to follow him, but to Calcutta. The divinity Professors were also parish ministers, who droned through their lectures as through their sermons, while their hearers slept, or attended to their own private affairs. The pamphlets of these days, on Sir John Leslie's case for instance, make strange revelations of academic ineptitude and ecclesiastical incompetence to those who care to rake among them. But for the dawn of the Evangelical party in the pulpits of Gordon in the New North Church, Andrew Thomson in St. George's, and

Henry Grey, and of Thomas M'Crie outside of the kirk, the
men of the next generation would have been worse than their
fathers.   John Wilson, unlike him who was afterwards Principal Cunningham, had taken with him to the Divinity Hall
the living power which had first moved his childish heart,
when, awestruck, he had seen it visibly in his grandfather's
evening prayers.   Now, on 11th December 1824, on entering
his twenty-first year, he began that "review of the Lord's
gracious dealings with my soul," already referred to.   "This
day I have completed my twentieth year, God teach me to
improve the fleeting moments of my existence.   As bought
with a price, even with the precious blood of Christ, may I
devote myself wholly—soul, body, and spirit—to declare and
show forth thy glory to my sinful brethren of mankind."
About this time he seems to have formally signed a " solemn
profession, dedication, and engagement " of himself to God.
The time-stained paper is without date, and is headed, in
pencil of a much later year evidently, "Form, I think, taken
from Willison."   With it are two similar deeds of holiest consecration, in which, on first January 1759, and again at Elgin
on 11th May 1785, an ancestor of his first wife, James Hay,
son of the Rev. Dr. James Hay, vowed himself to the Lord.
In both cases each page, and in some instances paragraph, is
signed by the covenanting person.   All through his life of
threescore and ten, openly, as in those most private papers
which mark his energising in soul, we see how John Wilson
kept the covenant thus made in the fervour of a first love, and
the comparative innocence of an early freedom from the power
of the world.   At college as at school, of full age as when a
child among his companions, he is still "the priest " in the
highest sense—the priest unto God.   From his Journal at
this time we take these further extracts.   He is in the Stow
Manse, in that first year of his theological studies, one of which
years the loose regulations of these days allowed students to
spend out of college if they wrote the necessary exercises.
His heart is set on missionary work, it will be observed.   He
writes to a friend at this time, "The Memoirs of David Brainerd
and Henry Martyn give me particular pleasure " :—

   14th December 1824.—" This day was cheered by the hope
that I had more success in teaching than usual.   Read part of
the life of the Rev. David Brainerd.   What an example of the

power of divine truth! How many his trials! how great his labours! O Lord, fill my soul with a lowly opinion of myself, and sanctify and prepare me for the same work in which he was engaged."

28*th.*—" Rejoiced to hear of the great progress of divine truth from the *Monthly Extracts of the Correspondence of the British and Foreign Bible Society.* What astonishing effects have, by the blessing of the Spirit of God, been produced by the simple reading of the Word of God! Moral miracles are daily attesting the truth of Christianity."

31*st.*—" This day brings another year to a close. Can I dare to appear before the Lord and ask him to deal with me according to my doings in the year which is past? No ; my conscience itself condemns me. It tells me that in myself I am poor, and miserable, and blind, and naked. It reminds me that much of the year which is ready to depart was spent in the service of Satan ; in the cherishing of my lusts ; in the gratification of my evil nature, and in seeking my own destruction."

Thursday, 6th January 1825.—" Read part of *Cecil's Remains.* Felt unhappy in the afternoon from not having had much communion with God during the course of the day. May I always feel unhappy when I do not set the Lord continually before me. May I ever seek to enjoy the light of his countenance, for when he causes this to shine upon me I am rich and comfortable. If I had every earthly comfort at my command, they could do nothing to cheer my mind and support my soul. May I hunger and thirst after righteousness, and be filled with the good things of the kingdom of God."

1st and 2d February.—" Delighted with good news from near and far countries. Read with great pleasure the *London Missionary Chronicle* and *Scottish Missionary Register.* The Lord is doing great things at home and abroad."

Saturday, 6th.—" This day visited my dear parents and friends at Lauder. Mentioned to them my intention of soon offering myself as a missionary candidate to the Scottish Missionary Society, and oh! what a burst of affection did I witness from my dear mother. Never will I forget what occurred this evening. She told me that at present she thought the trial of parting with me, if I should leave her, would be more hard to bear than my death. When I saw her in her tears I cried unto God that he would send comfort to her mind, and that he would make this affair issue in his glory and our good. I entreated my mother to leave the matter to the Lord's disposal ; and I told her that I would not think of leaving her if the Lord should not make my way plain for me, but that at present I thought it my duty to offer my services to the Society. She then embraced me and seemed more calm. My father said little to us on the subject, but seemed to be in deep thought. In the course of the evening the words 'he that saveth his life shall lose it,' and 'he that loveth father or mother more than me is not worthy of me,' came home to my mind, and kept me from making any promise of drawing back in my resolutions to preach the gospel, by the grace of God, to the heathen world. O Lord, do Thou, Who hast the hearts of all men in Thy hands, and Who turnest them according to Thy pleasure, grant that my parents, with faith in Thy word and promises, may joyfully commit me in all things to Thy disposal, and may I willingly obey Thy will in all things, for Christ's sake. Amen."

With this record of a scene often repeated since, when the best and bravest of our youth have gone forth to an Indian career, the Journal closes for that year. When Robert Nesbit had determined to do the same, he could not tell his mother, but asked Wilson to break the tidings for him. Wilson lost no time in offering himself to the directors of the Scottish Missionary Society in the twenty-first year of his age. At the beginning of his second divinity session in November he was formally received into the seminary, as it was called, at 18 St. John Street. He became an inmate of the family of the Rev. W. Brown, M.D., the Secretary, and there spent the three succeeding years till his departure for India. At College he went through the regular course of study and examination for the ministry of the Church of Scotland. His Journal records his reading, his intercourse with his fellows, his self-abasement in the sight of God and of his own conscience, and his breathings after a more perfect communion with the Father in the Son. The Professor who influenced him most was Principal Lee at a later date, and also Dr. Brunton, who taught Hebrew, and with whom, as Convener of the Foreign Mission Committee for many years afterwards, he corresponded by every mail. Dr. Meiklejohn pretended to teach Church History with an efficiency which has been measured by his habit of yawning when praying in public. As to the Professor of Systematic Theology, let this transcript from a yellow scrap of torn paper, marked in red ink more than once by Dr. Wilson with the word "keep," tell what he was :—

> "EDINBURGH COLLEGE, *Monday, 27th November* 1826.
>
> "At a general meeting of the theological students attending the University, the following resolutions were unanimously adopted :—1*st*, That a deputation should be appointed to wait on the Rev. Dr. William Ritchie, S.S.T.P., to inform him, with the greatest tenderness and respect, that, on account of the weakness of his voice, his lectures when read by him are quite inaudible by the students, and to request of him to take into consideration the propriety of appointing a substitute. 2*d*, That Messrs. James Anderson and L. H. Irving should form the deputation, and report the result of their visit to a general meeting, to be held to-morrow at 2 o'clock P.M.
>
> "JOHN WILSON, *Chairman.*"

> "Minutes of a General Meeting of the Theological Students attending the University of Edinburgh, called in order to receive the report of the deputation appointed to wait on the Rev. Dr. Wm. Ritchie :—

> "LADY YESTER'S CHURCH, *Edinburgh, 28th November* 1826.
>
> "Mr. William Cunningham having been called to the chair, and the minutes of the former meeting having been read and approved of, the deputation appointed to wait on the Rev. Dr. Ritchie stated that, having transmitted to him the minutes of the former meeting, enclosed in a most respectful letter, the Rev. Dr. intimated to them his decided refusal to listen to any such application. The students having considered and approved of the conduct of the deputation, resolved (*duobus contradicentibus*) that it was not competent for them to proceed to any ulterior measures at present, except simply to lay before the Town Council and the Presbytery of Edinburgh the minutes of both meetings, and directed the Secretary accordingly to transmit copies of both to the Right Hon. the Lord Provost and the Reverend the Moderator of the Presbytery.   (Signed)   WM. CUNNINGHAM, *Chairman.*"

Thus strangely were associated the future grave, judicious, and academic Vice-Chancellor of the University of Bombay, and the erudite Principal of the New College, both to be Moderators of the General Assembly in their time. And the work they did, or tried to do, is one which it had been well for more university faculties and colleges than that of theology in the University of Edinburgh, then and since, if there were students wise enough to repeat, in the interests of common honesty and sound scholarship. Scotland and its academic institutions, national and non-national, have always been too poor to pension the old, or quietly get rid of the incompetent teachers, with whom the abuses of patronage

or of popular election have saddled successive generations of
students.

With all his gentleness, and often all the more effectually
because of his almost sensitively chivalrous bearing, John
Wilson was the enemy of incompetence and idleness, which
injured his Master's work. In the previous session he had
shown his terrible earnestness by founding "The Edinburgh
Association of Theological Students in aid of the Diffusion of
Christian Knowledge." In 1825, under the date Thursday,
22d December, this remark occurs in his journal—"This has
been one of the happiest days of my life. About three weeks
ago I proposed to Mr. John T. Brown that we should make
some exertions for the purpose of instituting an association of
the theological students for aiding the diffusion of the Gospel.
This object, by the blessing of God, to whose name be the
praise, we were enabled to accomplish this day." Divided
into two by the Disruption of the Established Church in
1843, that Association has ever since been the fruitful nursery
of missionaries, alike in the University and in the New College of Edinburgh. Of the 120 regular students in the
Faculty of Theology at that time, more than sixty became
members. Wilson was the secretary, as he had been the
founder, and read the first essay. Mr. Thomas Pitcairn, afterwards clerk of the General Assembly, was the first president.
The committee were William Cunningham, David Thorburn,
Thomas Brydon, James P. Bannerman, William Scott Mon-
crieff, William Tait, Æneas M'Rate, and Alexander Patterson,
with Lewis H. Irving as treasurer. The name of Robert
Nesbit, St. Andrews, appears as a corresponding member.
For the first three years Wilson was its life. When he left
for India the members sent forth their founder with prayers
and benedictions, and a gift of memorial volumes. For years
after he continued to correspond with the Association as a
means of stimulating young theologians to give themselves
to India. When he paid his farewell visit to Scotland in
1870 his delight was to address not only the New College
Society, but the old Association in the old room in the
University. He organised a library ; he began a correspondence with the great missionary societies then in existence,
that the students might be fed with the latest intelligence
from foreign lands ; and he kept up a series of circular

C

letters with the corresponding students' societies of St.
Andrews, Glasgow, and Aberdeen; Belfast; and Princeton
in the United States; the careful drafts of which testify
to the zeal with which the youth of twenty-one worked.
A fine spirit of catholicity marks all the communications
of the secretary, and in some instances he bursts out with
a protest against the creation of new agencies to compete
unnecessarily with those already at work. Even at this time
he seems to have awoke to the absurdity and the waste
involved in so many ecclesiastical divisions, as he afterwards
did more painfully when in the front of heathenism.

Privately, John Wilson by pen and voice was ever pointing the abler of his student companions to the mission field,
for his ideal was high. His communications from Robert
Nesbit both strengthened his own determination and enabled
him to combat the fears of his fellows, whose mothers held
them back. He published, chiefly for such, an essay on the
motives and encouragements to active missionary exertions.
He prepared, and issued in 1828 anonymously, a little work
now rarely met with, but which did good service in its day,
The Life of John Eliot, the Apostle of the Indians. In that he
traced the work of the Puritan Fathers in New England, in
their propagation of Christianity among the Red Indians.
Very characteristic of his own future policy is his quotation
of Eliot's words : " There is need of learning in ministers who
preach to Indians much more than to Englishmen and gracious
Christians, for these had sundry philosophical questions, which
some knowledge of the arts must help to give answers to, and
without which these would not have been satisfied. Worse
than Indian ignorance hath blinded their eyes that renounce
learning as an enemy to the gospel." All Eliot's scholarship
and devotion to the mastering of the native dialects are carefully noted, no less than the humility of the man who protested against the application to himself of the pre-eminent
title of " The Indian Evangelist." The missionary student
could not have set before himself a better ideal of the kind
than that of the acute Cambridge scholar, whose eighty-six
years of self-sacrifice Cotton Mather has chronicled. When,
towards the close of his university studies in March 1828,
John Wilson received the farewell eulogies of the students,
his reply was an address which rang with new appeals to the

friends of his youth, based on the words just quoted, and on this prediction of the same writer, in his " Essays To Do Good," a century before—" North Britain will be distinguished by irradiations from heaven upon it of such a tendency (to propagate Christianity). There will be found a set of excellent men in that reformed and renowed Church of Scotland, with whom the most refined and extensive essays to do good will become so natural that the whole world will fare the better for them." We who look back on history may see the anticipation partially fulfilled in the movement which gave Wilson, Duff, and their colleagues to India, Morrison to China, and Livingstone and Moffat to Africa. These are the words which the young Wilson left behind him as his legacy to the students of the University of Edinburgh—how have they met them ?

" 'The work of preaching the gospel in foreign lands is attended with trials, dangers, and sacrifices!' Have we forgotten where is now the promise of Christ, 'Lo! I am with you alway, even unto the end of the world'? How is that hundred-fold to be obtained and enjoyed which is promised to those who 'forsake houses, or brethren, or sisters, or father, or mother, for Christ's sake'? Where is faith in the operations of the Spirit of God, which can view the difficulties of the Christian warfare as calculated to render the consolations of the gospel precious to the soul in every circumstance? Is it probable that dependence on the grace of God will not be exercised by the Christian when he must feel that vain is the help of man, that success must be the result of the divine application of the word, and that he is in a great measure deprived of those sources of earthly enjoyment which, from the corruption of human nature, are frequently made the occasions of sin? 'The work of missions is difficult.' But time is short. Soon shall we be freed from all our toils, and anxieties, and griefs, and disappointments ; and if we suffer with Christ, we shall also reign with Him. 'The work of missions is attended with difficulties, trials, and dangers!' Spirits of Eliot and Brainerd, Martyn, and Fisk, and Hall, do you regret that, for the promotion of its interests, you left the lands of your fathers and your youth, and laboured and died in a foreign clime? No ; you declared that when engaged in it you were happy ;—that, when you reviewed your labours in

connection with it you were ashamed that you had not
devoted yourselves to its interests with more zeal and self-
denial; and that, when entering the dark valley of the
shadow of death you ' saw no trials, no sacrifices, nothing but
sins and mercies.' Since you joined the glorious band of
witnesses to the truth you have seen and felt more of its
importance, and your testimony respecting it is, that eternity
can only sufficiently reveal its character. You feel that is
the glory of the song of Moses and the Lamb, that it is sung
by people of every kindred and country and tongue and
nation; and if you were permitted again to visit this world
you would fly, like the angel of the Apocalypse, to preach the
gospel to all that dwell on the face of the earth. In sincerity
and humility of soul let us say, ' Thy vows are upon us, O God ;
we will render praises unto Thee.' "

The young evangelist had a right to use such language,
for had he not given himself ? These were days when India,
little known still in the land that rules it, was less known
than it had been in the previous generation which had seen
Warren Hastings impeached, and burghs bought and sold by
Anglo-Indian nawabs. The dawn of knowledge and zeal
was not to rise for five years yet, with the Charter which
really opened India in 1833. Then such an incident as the
following was only too truly typical : Dr. Wilson had been
meanwhile licensed to preach by his native Presbytery of
Lauder ; and, after some difficulty caused by adherence to a
routine which did not contemplate missions to non-Christian
lands, he had been ordained on " a request in his own name,
and in the name of the directors of the Scottish Missionary
Society." During the first summer after receiving license he
paid two visits to the Manse at Langton. On the first occasion he delivered an impressive discourse on Paul's address at
Mars' Hill. During the evening of that Sabbath the medical
attendant came to see some member of the family, and after
the visit joined the others in the drawing-room. The subject of missions to India was introduced, and as the doctor
had been in the East he took part, expressing strongly the
opinion that it was utterly hopeless to attempt to convert the
natives of India to Christianity. " I remember," writes Mr.
Brown, " the flush which came on Dr. Wilson's face when he
eagerly took up the question, replying to the objections which

had been advanced, and dwelling on the power of the Gospel
to enlighten those that were in darkness. The doctor soon
changed the subject."

At a time when medical missions were unknown, and
eight years before David Livingstone had turned from cotton-
spinning to become a licentiate of the Faculty of Physicians
in Glasgow, with the frustrated hope of becoming a missionary in China, John Wilson would not consider his preparation
for India complete until he had studied medicine. He had
taken a high place in the classes of Physical and Natural
Science. In 1827-8 he passed through classes for Anatomy,
Surgery, and the Practice of Physic. Many a time afterwards, in the jungles of Western India, and the ghauts or
ravines of its hills, did he find his knowledge of the art of
healing a blessing to the wild tribes and simple peasantry.
Much of his own endurance is to be ascribed to such knowledge, although in Bombay itself physicians in and out of the
Service were ever his most attached friends.

But one qualification seemed still wanting to make the
youth of twenty-three, whom, half a century ago, on Mid-
summer's Day 1828, by the imposition of hands, the Presbytery did solemnly ordain and set apart to the office of
the holy ministry, a fully-equipped missionary. So new was
the whole subject of Christianising foreign lands at that time,
that every instance of a Protestant evangelist going forth
raised the question whether he ought to be married. On this
ecclesiastical authorities were much divided. The Scottish
Missionary Society had assigned India as the country of his
labours, a fact thus recorded in his journal :—" O Lord, Thou
hast graciously heard my prayers in this respect. Do Thou
prepare me for preaching Christ crucified with love and with
power ; do Thou provide for me, if agreeable to Thy will, a
suitable partner of my lot ; one who will well encourage me
and labour with me in Thy work. Do Thou, in Thy good
time, convey me in safety to the place of my destination ; do
Thou open up for me a wide and effectual door of utterance ;
do Thou preserve my life for usefulness ; and do Thou make
me successful in winning souls to Christ." " I rejoice when I
think," he wrote to a friend, " that I shall live, and labour,
and die in India." On the 18th December 1827, he had
written to his father and mother : " Dr. Brown intends to

prepare the articles which I am to take with me to India. He asked me to-night if I intended to marry; but I was not able to give him an answer. If I could get a suitable partner now I would have no hesitation in marrying; but it is a matter of extreme difficulty to find a young lady with the piety, zeal, talents, and education which the work I have in view requires." He was soon after introduced to the family of the Rev. Kenneth Bayne of Greenock, who, on their father's death, had settled in 22 Comely Bank, a northern suburb of Edinburgh. The last entry in his journal records the triumphant joy of one of the daughters in the prospect of death. Two more of the sisters met with a sad death by drowning, several years afterwards, and another survived him a short time. The other three formed a remarkable group of accomplished, cultivated, and zealous women, who gave their lives for India, as the pioneers of female education. Margaret, the eldest, had added to the ordinary teaching a course of study in the university city of Aberdeen. She proved equally facile in the exposition of the faiths of the East, in the mastery of the languages of Western India, in the organisation of native female schools, and in the writing of graceful verse, while she was ever the gentle wife and the fond mother, during the too brief six years of her life in Bombay. When she consented to share the then dreaded toils of an Indian evangelist's life with John Wilson, she at once doubled his efficiency.

In the simple Scottish fashion the newly ordained missionary was married to Margaret Bayne, by her minister Dr. Andrew Thomson, of St. George's, on the 12th August 1828. These were busy months for both, with the prospect of a Cape voyage, and the probability of life-long farewells. Incessant preaching and missionary addresses kept him ever about his Father's business. To this day the few old folks who remember it tell, with tears in their eyes, of his farewell sermon in the quaint pulpit of the cruciform kirk of Lauder. The bailies and council of the royal burgh conferred on the lad all the honours they had to bestow, by giving him, on formal parchment, "the haill immunities and privileges of a burgess royal and freeman." On the 30th August the missionary and his wife sailed from the ancient port of Newhaven, on that heavenly quest on which no knight of poetic creation or

fabled purity ever entered with more self-sacrificing ardour.
A thick haze hid Edinburgh from their sight.

The "Sesostris" East Indiaman sailed from Portsmouth,
as was usual then. The long voyage of five months was not
made shorter by the fact that the captain was uncongenial
and arbitrary, and the majority of the passengers had no
sympathy with the missionary and his wife or their object.
But even there the consistent and kindly devotion of both bore
fruit. Opposition nearly disappeared among the passengers ;
the sailors, whom he influenced for good, treated Mr. Wilson
very tenderly amid the high frolic of these days in crossing
the line. The attempt of a piratical vessel to attack the ship,
and a storm off Table Bay, further relieved the monotony of
a Cape passage. Sufficient time was spent at Cape Town—
then, and till the Mutiny of 1857 led to a change in the
furlough rules, a favourite sanitarium for Anglo-Indians—to
enable Mr. and Mrs. Wilson to see a little of its society, and
to visit not only Constantia, of wine-growing fame, but the
Moravian settlement of Grœnenkloof, forty miles in the
interior. After coasting Ceylon, Wilson obtained his first
view of India :—

"On the 1st of February Cape Comorin, the most southern point of India,
appeared in sight, and my feelings were consequently of a very solemn nature.
When I reflected on the present situation of the country, and on my prospects
connected with it, I was constrained to resort to the throne of grace. My
dear Margaret and I united in the prayer that God might prepare us for all
the trials of life, and support us under them ; that He might ever lift on us
the light of His gracious and reconciled countenance ; that He might impart
to us the views, feelings, dispositions, and purposes which are suitable to the
sacred work which we have in view ; that He might enable us to pay the vows
which we have made ; that He might grant us much success in the work of
converting sinners ; and that He might impart to us those rewards of grace
which are promised to those who turn many to righteousness. The character
of the day (Sabbath) was suited to our exercises, and we had great reason to
thank God for the felicity which we experienced. The sentiments of our
hearts were not expressed in the plaintive language of the Psalmist, 'How
shall we sing the Lord's song in a strange land,' but in that of the joyful resolution, 'From the end of the earth will I cry unto Thee, when my heart is
overwhelmed.' We continued for thirteen days sailing along the coasts of
Malabar, Canara, and the Konkan. The country is very mountainous, but in
its appearance very unlike my native Scotland. The towns have a wretched
appearance, but they are very populous. We arrived in Bombay on the evening of the 14th of this month, and next morning the Rev. Mr. Laurie, one of
the ministers of the Scotch Church, came with a boat to take us on shore."

CHAPTER II.

1829.

OLD BOMBAY AND ITS GOVERNORS.

The Tyre and Alexandria of the Far East—Early History of Bombay—Crom-
well, Charles II., and the East India Company--The first Governors—A
Free City and Asylum for the Oppressed—Jonathan Duncan—Mount-
stuart Elphinstone—Sir John Malcolm--Cotton and the Cotton Duties—
India and the Bombay Presidency Statistics in 1829—The Day of Small
Things in Education—First Protestant Missionaries in Bombay—English
Society in Western India--Testimony of James Forbes--John Wilson's
First Impressions of Bombay.

BOMBAY, with the marvellous progress of which, as city and
province, Wilson was to be identified during the next forty-
seven years, has a history that finds its true parallels in the
Mediterranean emporia of Tyre and Alexandria. Like the
Phœnician "Rock" of Baal, which Hiram enlarged and
adorned, the island of the goddess Mumbai or Mahima, "the
Great Mother," was originally one of a series of rocks which
the British Government has connected into a long peninsula,
with an area of 18 square miles. Like the greater port which
Alexander created to take the place of Tyre, and called by his
own name, Bombay carries in its ships the commerce of the
Mediterranean, opened to it by the Suez Canal, but it bears
that also of the vaster Indian Ocean and Persian Gulf.
Although it can boast of no river like the Nile, by which
alone Alexandria now exists, Bombay possesses a natural harbour, peerless alike in West and East, such as all the capital
and the engineering of modern science can never create for
the land of Egypt. Instead of the "low" sands which gave
Canaan its name, and the muddy flats of the Nile delta, Bombay presents ridge after ridge intersecting noble bays, and hill
upon hill, rising up into the guardian range of the Western

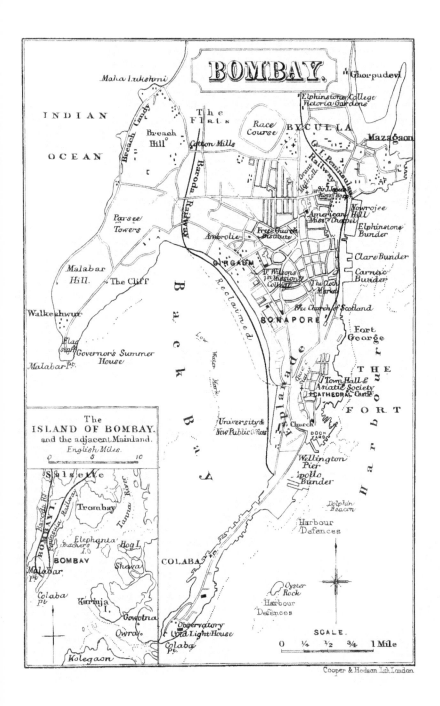

BOMBAY.

"Ghorpudevi"

Maha Lukshmi

Elphinstone College
Victoria Gardens

The
Flats

Race
Course

BYCULLA

Mazagaon

INDIAN

Breach
Hill

Cotton Mills

OCEAN

Baroda Railway

Grand Peninsular Railway

High Coll.

Sir J. Jejeebhoy Hospl.

Nowrojee
Hill

Parsee
Towers

Ambrolie

Free Church
Institute

American
Miss. Chapel

Elphinstone
Bunder

GIRGAUM

Clare Bunder

Malabar
Hill

The Cliff

Dr. Wilson's
1st Mission
College

The Cloth
Market

Carnac
Bunder

Reclaimed

Walkeshwur

SONAPORE

Free Church of Scotland

Fort
George

Flag
Staff

Low Water Mark

Governor's Summer
House

Malabar Pt.

Back Bay

Town Hall &
Asiatic Society
CATHEDRAL Castle

THE

FORT

University &
New Public Offices

Harbour

Esplanade

Church

DOCK
CARGO

Wellington
Pier
Apollo
Bunder

The
ISLAND OF BOMBAY,
and the adjacent Mainland.
English Miles.
0   5   10

Dolphin
Beacon

Salsette

Harbour
Defences

Trombay

COLABA

Elephanta I.
Bruchero I.
I.O
Hog I.

BOMBAY

Malabar
Pt.

Oyster
Rock

Harbour
Defences

Ghowa

Colaba
Pt.

Karinja I.

Gowotna

Owra

Observatory
& Light House
Colaba
Pt.

SCALE.

0   ¼   ½   ¾   1 Mile

Kolegaon

Cooper & Hodson Lith. London

Ghauts. From their giant defiles and green terraces fed by
the periodic rains, the whole tableland of the Indian peninsula
gently slopes eastward to the Bay of Bengal, seamed by
mighty rivers, and covered by countless forts and villages, the
homes of a toiling population of millions. On one fourth, and
that the most fertile fourth, of the two centuries of Bombay's
history, John Wilson, more than any other single influence,
has left his mark for ever.

From the Periplus, and from Marco Polo, we learn the
commercial prosperity and ecclesiastical activity, in the earliest times, of the kingdoms of Broach, Callian, and Tanna,
on the mainland and around Bombay. But, as an island,
Bombay was too exposed to the pirates who, from Abyssinia,
Arabia and India alike, scoured these Eastern seas, to be
other than neglected. Even the Portuguese despised it,
although, as a naval power, they early made a settlement
there, seeing that it lay between their possessions in the
Persian Gulf and their capital of Goa. But they still held
it against the East India Company, whose agents, exposed to
all the exactions of a Mussulman governor in the factory at
Surat, coveted a position where their ships would make them
more independent. Twice they made ineffectual attempts to
take the place, and, in 1654, when Cromwell had given England a vigorous foreign policy, the Directors represented to
him the advantage of asking the Portuguese to cede both
Bombay and Bassein. But although the Protector had exacted a heavy indemnity for all Prince Rupert had done to
injure English commerce, he took hard cash rather than apparently useless jungle. And, although he beheaded the Portuguese ambassador's brother for murder on the very day that
the treaty was signed, there is no evidence that he took any
more interest in the distant and infant settlements in India
than was involved in his general project for a Protestant
Council or Propaganda all over the world. It was left to
Charles II., in 1661, to add Bombay to the British Empire as
part of the Infanta Catherina's dowry; and to present it to
the East India Company in 1668, when the first governor,
Sir Gervase Lucas, who had guarded his father in the flight
from Naseby, had failed to prove its value to the Crown.
For an annual rent of "£10 in gold" the island was made
over to Mr. Goodyer—deputed, with Streynsham Master and

others, by Sir George Oxenden, the President of Surat—" in free and common soccage as of the manor of East Greenwich," along with all the Crown property upon it, cash to the amount of £4879 : 7 : 6, and such political powers as were necessary for its defence and government. Among the commissioners to whom the management of the infant settlement fell on Oxenden's death, is found the name of one Sterling, a Scottish minister, and thus, in some sense, the only predecessor of John Wilson. With the succession of Gerald Aungier, as President of Surat and Governor of the island in 1667, the history of Bombay may be said to have really begun. It is a happy circumstance that the beginning is associated with the names of the few good men who were servants of the Company, in a generation which was only less licentious than that of the Stewarts at home, if the temptations of exile be considered. Oxenden, Aungier, and Streynsham Master were the three Governors of high character and Christian aims, who, at Surat, Bombay and Madras, sought to purify Anglo-Indian society and to evangelise the natives around.

Bombay, which grew to be a city of 250,000 inhabitants when Wilson landed in 1829, and contained 650,000 before he passed away, began two centuries ago with 600 landowners, who were formed into a militia, 100 Brahmans and Hindoos of the trading caste who paid an exemption tax, and the Company's first European regiment of 285 men, of whom only 93 were English. The whole population was little above 5000. A fort was built and mounted with twenty-one guns, and five small redoubts capped the principal eminences around. To attract Hindoo weavers and traders of the Bunya caste, and to mark the new *régime* as the opposite of the intolerant zeal of the Portuguese, notice was given all along the coast, from Diu to Goa, that no one would be compelled to profess Christianity, and that no Christian or Muhammadan would be allowed to trespass within the inclosures of the Hindoo traders for the purpose of killing the cow or any animal, while the Hindoos would enjoy facilities for burning their dead and observing their festivals. Forced labour was prohibited, for no one was to be compelled to carry a burden. Docks were to be made ; manufactures were to be free of tax for a time, and thereafter, when exported, to pay not more than three and a half per cent. The import duties were two and a half per

cent with a few exceptions. Transit and market duties of nine
per cent, that indirect tax on food and clothing which the
people of India in their simplicity prefer to all other imposts,
supplied the chief revenue for the fortifications and administration. And it was needed, for " the flats," which still pol-
lute Bombay between the two ridges, were the fertile seed-
bed of cholera and fever, till in 1864, the first of the many
and still continued attempts at drainage were made. The
result of the first twenty years of the Company's administration was that Bombay superseded Surat. One half of all the
Company's shipping loaded at London direct for the island,
where there was, moreover, no Nawab to squeeze half of the
profits. The revenues had increased threefold. The population consisted of 60,000, of whom a considerable number were
Portuguese, and the " Cooly Christians," or native fishermen,
whom they had baptized as Roman Catholics. In and around
the fort the town stretched for a mile of low thatched houses,
chiefly with the pearl of shells for glass in their windows.
The Portuguese could show the only church. On Malabar
Hill, where Wilson was to die, there was a Parsee tomb. The
island of Elephanta was known not so much for the Cave
Temple which he described, as for the carving of an elephant
which gave the place its name, but has long since disappeared.
At Salsette and Bandora the Portuguese held sway yet a little
longer. From Tanna to Bassein their rich Dons revelled in
spacious country seats, fortified and terraced. The Hidalgos
of Bassein reproduced their capital of Lisbon, with Franciscan
convents, Jesuit colleges, and rich libraries, all of which they
carefully guarded, allowing none but Christians to sleep in
the town.

The tolerant and liberal policy of the English government
of Bombay soon caused all that, and much more, to be absorbed
in their free city, and to contribute to the growth of the
western portion of the new empire. If to some the toleration
promised by Aungier, and amplified by the able though reck-
less Sir John Child, seemed to go too far, till it became virtual
intolerance because indifference towards the faith of the ruling
power, the growing public opinion of England corrected that
in time. For the next century the British island became the
asylum not only of the oppressed peoples of the Indian continent, during the anarchy from the death of Aurungzeb to the

triumph of the two brothers Wellesley and Wellington, but of
persecuted communities of western and central Asia, like the
Parsees and Jews, as well as of slave-ridden Abyssinia and
Africa. Made one of the three old Presidencies in 1708,
under a later Oxenden, and subordinated to Calcutta as the
seat of the Governor-General in 1773, Bombay had the good
fortune to be governed by Jonathan Duncan for sixteen years
at the beginning of this century.

What this Forfarshire lad, going out to India at sixteen,
like Malcolm afterwards, had done for the peace and prosperity, the education and progress of Benares, and the four
millions around it, he did for Bombay at a most critical time.
Not less than Lord William Bentinck does he deserve the
marble monument which covers his dust in the Bombay
Cathedral, where the figure of Justice is seen inscribing on
his urn these words, "He was a good man and a just," while
two children support a scroll, on which is written, "Infanticide
abolished in Benares and Kattywar." Between the thirty-
nine years of his uninterrupted service for the people of
India, which closed in 1811, and the forty-seven years of
John Wilson's not dissimilar labours in the same cause, which
began in 1829, there occurred the administrations, after Sir
Evan Nepean, of the Hon. Mountstuart Elphinstone and Sir
John Malcolm, both of the same great school. Since the
negotiations of the Peshwa Raghoba, in 1775, with the Company, who sought to add Bassein and Salsette to Bombay and
so make it the *entrepôt* of the India and China Seas, the province of Bombay had grown territorially as the power of the
plundering Marathas waned from internal dissension and the
British arms. The first part of India to become British, the
Western Presidency had been the last to grow into dimensions
worthy of a separate government in direct communication with
the home authorities though, in imperial matters controlled
by the Governor-General from Calcutta. Bombay had long
been in a deficit of a million sterling a year or more. But
the final extinction of the Maratha Powers by Lord Hastings
in 1822 enabled Bombay to extend right into Central India
and down into the southern Maratha country, while Poona
became the second or inland capital of the Presidency. The
two men who did most to bring this about, and to settle the
condition of India south of the Vindhyas territorially as it now

is, were Mountstuart Elphinstone and John Malcolm. What
they thus made Bombay Wilson found it, and that it continued to be all through his life, with the addition of Sindh,
to the north, in 1843, and of an exchange of a county with
Madras in the south.

Mountstuart Elphinstone had no warmer admirer than
Wilson, who wrote a valuable sketch of his life for the local
Asiatic Society. A younger son of the eleventh Lord Elphin-
stone, and an Edinburgh High School boy, he went out to
India as a "writer" with his cousin John Adam, who was
afterwards *interim* governor-general. Having miraculously
escaped the 1799 massacre at Benares, he was made assistant
to the British Resident at Poona, then the Peshwa's court.
He rode by the Duke of Wellington's side at the victory of
Assye, as his interpreter, and was told by the then Colonel
Wellesley that he had mistaken his calling, for he was certainly born a soldier. Subsequently, after a mission to Cabul,
on his way from Calcutta to Poona to become Resident, he
made the friendship of Henry Martyn. The battle of Kirkee
in 1817 punished the Peshwa's latest attempt at treachery,
and it became Elphinstone's work to make that brilliant
settlement of the ceded territories which has been the source
of all the happiness of the people since. His report of 1819
stands in the first rank of Indian state papers, and that is
saying much. When, after that, he discovered the plot of
certain Maratha Brahmans to murder all the English in
Poona and Satara, the man who was beloved by the mass of
the natives for his kindly geniality saved the public peace by
executing the ringleaders. His prompt firmness astounded
Sir Evan Nepean, whom he afterwards succeeded as governor,
into advising him that he should ask for an act of indemnity.
The reply was characteristic of his whole career—"Punish
me if I have done wrong; if I have done right I need no act
of indemnity." The eight years' administration of this good
man, and great scholar and statesman, were so marked by
wisdom and success, following a previously brilliant career,
that on his retiring to his native country he had the unique
honour of being twice offered the position of Governor-General.
What he did for oriental learning and education, and how his
nephew afterwards governed Bombay, and became Wilson's
friend in the more trying times of 1857, we shall see.

Sir John Malcolm, too, had his embassage to Persia, and his ,victory in battle—Mahidpore; while it fell to him to complete that settlement of Central India in 1818 with Bajee Rao, which the adopted son, Nana Dhoondopunt, tried vainly to upset in 1857. Malcolm's generosity on that occasion has been much questioned, but it had Elphinstone's approval. His distinguished services of forty years were rewarded by his being made Elphinstone's successor as governor of Bombay in 1827. In the ship in which he returned to take up the appointment was a young cadet, now Sir H. C. Rawlinson, whose ability he directed to the study of oriental literature. He had been Governor for little more than a year when he first received, at his daily public breakfast at Parell, the young Scottish missionary from his own loved Tweedside. Even better than his predecessor, Malcolm knew how to influence the natives, by whom he was worshipped. He continued the administrative system as he found it, writing to a friend—" The only difference between Mountstuart and me is that I have Mullagatawny at tiffin, which comes of my experience at Madras." The Governor was in the thick of that collision with the Supreme Court, forced on him by Sir John Peter Grant's attempt to exercise jurisdiction all over the Presidency—as in Sir Elijah Impey's days in Calcutta. He had just returned from one of those tours through the native States, which the Governor, like Elphinstone before him and the missionary after him, considered "of primal importance" for the well-being of the people. The decision of the President of the Board of Control at home, then Lord Ellenborough, was about to result in the resignation of the impetuous judge. Such was Bombay, politically and territorially, when, in the closing weeks of the cold season of 1828-9, John Wilson and his wife landed from the "Sesostris" East Indiaman.[1]

[1] Our readers will find it useful to refer to this list of the Governors of Bombay just before and during Dr. Wilson's work there—

Governor.	Years.
Jonathan Duncan .	1795
Sir Evan Nepean, Bart. .	1812
The Hon. Mountstuart Elphinstone	1819
Sir John Malcolm, K.C.B. .	1827
Earl of Clare	1831
Sir Robert Grant .	1835

Economically the year 1829 was marked by the first serious attempt on the part of the Directors at home, and the Government on the spot, to extend the cultivation and improve the fibre of the cotton of Western India, which was to prove so important a factor alike in the prosperity and the adversity of Bombay in the coming years. In that review of this three years' administration to 1st December 1830, which Sir John Malcolm wrote for his successors, and published to influence the discussions on the Charter of 1833, under the title of *The Government of India*, this significant sentence occurs :—" A cotton mill has been established in Bengal with the object of underselling the printed goods and yarns sent from England ; but there are, in my opinion, causes which, for a long period, must operate against the success of such an establishment." The period has not proved to be so long as the conservative experience of the Governor led him to believe. In this respect Bombay soon shot ahead of Bengal, which afterwards found a richer trade in jute and tea. But the withdrawal of the last restriction on trade was, when Wilson landed, about to co-operate with a consolidated administration to make Bombay the seat of an enriching commerce, of which its varied native communities obtained a larger share than elsewhere. A society composed of Hindoo, Parsee, Jewish, and even Muhammadan merchant princes, was being brought to the birth, side by side with the great Scottish houses, at the head of which was Sir Charles Forbes. And the man had come to lift them all to a higher level ; to purify them all, in differing degrees, by the loftiest ideal.

Governor.				Years.
Sir James Rivett-Carnac, Bart.	.	.	.	1839
Sir George Arthur, Bart. .	.		.	1842
Sir George Russell Clerk	.		.	1847
Viscount Falkland	.	.	.	1848
Lord Elphinstone, G.C.B. .	.		.	1855
Sir George Russell Clerk (2d time)		.	.	1860
Sir Bartle Frere, Bart.	.	.		1862
Sir Seymour Fitzgerald	.		.	1867
Sir Philip Wodehouse	.	.	.	1872
Sir Richard Temple, Bart.	.	.	.	1877

Sir W. H. Macnaghten was massacred in 1841 when about to leave Cabul to join his appointment as Governor of Bombay. The Honourable Messrs. George Brown in 1811 ; John Romer in 1831 ; James Farish in 1838 ; G. W. Anderson in 1841 ; and L. R. Reid in 1846, were senior members of council, who acted for a short time as *interim* governors.

At this time our Indian Empire was just one third of its present magnitude, but its native army was 186,000 strong, a fourth more than since the Mutiny. Including St. Helena, the area was 514,238 square miles, the population 89½ millions, and the gross revenue £21,695,207. The whole was administered in 88 counties by 1083 British civil officers, and defended by 37,428 white troops. Of the three Presidencies the Western was by far the smallest, but its geographical position gave it an advantage as the centre of action from Cape Comorin to the head of the Persian Gulf, and from Central India to Central Africa. Its area was 65,000 square miles, not much more than that of England and Wales. Its population was 6¼ millions in ten counties, and its gross annual revenue 2½ millions sterling. The whole province was garrisoned by 7728 white troops and 32,508 sepoys, under its own Commander-in-Chief; and it had a marine or navy, famous in its day and too rashly abolished long after, which was manned by 542 Europeans and 618 natives.

Notwithstanding the enlightened action and tolerant encouragement of Mountstuart Elphinstone and Malcolm, public instruction and Christian education were still in the day of small things in Bombay, although it was in some respects more advanced than Bengal, which soon distanced it for a time. In the Presidency, as in Madras and Calcutta, a charity school had been, in 1718, forced into existence by the very vices of the English residents and the conditions of a then unhealthy climate. Legitimate orphans and illegitimate children, white and coloured, had to be cared for, and were fairly well trained by public benevolence, for the Company gave no assistance till 1807. In the Charter of 1813, which Charles Grant and Wilberforce had partially succeeded in making half as liberal as that granted by William III. in 1698, Parliament gave India not only its first Protestant bishop, archdeacons, and Presbyterian chaplains, but a department of public instruction bound to spend at least a lakh of rupees a year, or £10,000, on the improvement of literature, and the promotion of a knowledge of the sciences among the people. In 1815 the Bombay Native Education Society was formed, and opened schools in Bombay, Tanna, and Broach, with the aid of a Government grant. Immediately after Mountstuart Elphinstone's appointment as Governor it extended its operations to

supplying a vernacular and school-book literature.   It recommended the adoption of the Lancasterian method of teaching,
then popular in England, and it continued its useful work till
1840, when it became in name, what it had always been in
fact, the public Board of Education.   Since it failed to provide for the Southern Konkan, or coast districts, Colonel Jervis,
R.E., who became an earnest coadjutor of Wilson, established
a similar society for that purpose in 1823, but that was affili-
ated with the original body.   When Poona became British,
Mr. Chaplin, the Commissioner in the Dekhan, established a
Sanskrit college there, which failed from the vicious Oriental
system on which it was conducted, in spite of its enjoyment
of the Dukshina, or charity fund of Rs. 35,000 a year, which
the Peshwas had established for the Brahmans' education.
The Society's central school in Bombay was more successful,
and is still the principal Government High School.   When
Mountstuart Elphinstone left Bombay in 1827, the native
gentlemen subscribed, as a memorial of him, £21,600, from
the interest of which professorships were to be established " to
be held by gentlemen from Great Britain, until the happy
period arrived when natives shall be fully competent to hold
them."   But no such professors landed till 1835, when they
held, in the Town Hall, classes which have since grown into the
Elphinstone College.   In that year, out of a population of
more than a quarter of a million in the Island of Bombay only
1026 were at school ; in the rest of the province the scholars
numbered 1864 in the Maratha, and 2128 in the Goojaratee
speaking districts, or 5018 in all.   In the four years ending
1830, just before and after Wilson's arrival, the Bombay
Government remarked, "with alarm," that although it had
fixed its annual grant to public instruction at £2000 it had
spent £20,192 in that period.   So apathetic were the natives
that they had subscribed only £471, while the few Europeans
had given £818 for the same purpose.   Truly the system of
a vicious Orientalism was breaking down, as opposed to that
of which Wilson was to prove the apostle—the communication of Western truth on Western methods through the
Oriental tongues so as to elevate learned and native alike.
The almost exclusively Orientalising policy of the Government previous to 1835, left Bombay a *tabula rasa* on which

D

Wilson soon learned to engrave characters of light and life that were never to be obliterated.

Nor had the few missionaries then in Western India anticipated him. Self-sacrificing to an extent for which, save from their great successor, they have rarely got credit, they were lost in the jungle of circumstances. The American missionaries were the first Protestants to take up the work which, in the early Christian centuries, the Nestorians had begun at the ancient port of Kalliana, the neighbouring Callian, which was long the seat of a Persian bishop. In 1813, Dr. Coke sailed for Bombay with the same Colonel Jervis, R.E., who did so much for the Konkan. His successors, for he died at sea, began that work of primary importance in every mission, an improved edition of the New Testament in the vernacular Marathee, for which Mr. Wilson expressed his gratitude soon after his arrival. But when, at a later period, one of their annual reports ignorantly represented the Americans as having been the first to evangelise the Marathas, he felt constrained to publish this statement of the facts.

"The American missionaries first came to Bombay in 1813; but the whole of the New Testament in Marathee had been published by the Serampore missionaries in 1811. Dr. Robert Drummond published his grammar and glossary of the Goojaratee and Marathee languages at the *Bombay Courier* press in 1808. Dr. Carey published his Marathee grammar and dictionary at Serampore in 1810. All these helps were enjoyed by the American missionaries; and though they are by no means so important as those which are now accessible to all students and missionaries, we would be guilty of ingratitude to those who furnished them were we to overlook them. *Suum cuique tribue* should ever be our motto. The Romish Church we know to be very corrupted; but I have seen works composed by its missionaries about two hundred years ago, which could 'give the Marathas the least idea of the true character of God as revealed in the Scripture.' It is too much when the labours of the Romish missionaries are considered, to affirm that 'not a tree in this forest had been felled' till the American missionaries came to this country. There have been some pious Roman Catholics in Europe, and why may there not have been some amongst the eight generations of the 300,000 in the Marathee country? The Seram-

pore missionaries admitted several Marathas to their communion before 1813."

The first American missionaries had their own romance,
like all pioneers. They were driven from Calcutta by the
Government in 1812, and told they might settle in Mauritius.
Judson happily was sent to Burma by Dr. Carey. Messrs.
Hall and Nott took ship to Bombay. Thence the good but
weak Sir Evan Nepean, who had been shocked by Elphin-
stone's firmness in the Poona plot, warned them off; but an
appeal to his Christian principle led him to temporise until
Charles Grant and the charter of the next year restrained the
Company. In 1815 the London Missionary Society repeated
at Surat, and afterwards in Belgaum, an effort to found a
mission, which in 1807 had failed in the island of Bombay.
In 1820, the Church Missionary Society began in Western
India that work which in time bore good fruit for Africa also.
In 1822 the increase of British territory, caused by the ex-
tinction of the Maratha power, led the Scottish Missionary
Society, which since 1796 had been working in West Africa,
to send as its first missionary to Bombay the Rev. Donald
Mitchell, a son of the manse, who, when a lieutenant of infantry at Surat, had been led to enter the Church of Scotland.
He was followed by the Revs. John Cooper; James Mitchell;
Alexander Crawford, whose health soon failed; John Stevenson, who became a chaplain; and, finally, Robert Nesbit,
fellow student of Dr. Duff at St. Andrews University under
Chalmers, and Wilson's early friend. " Desperately afraid of
offending the Brahmans," as a high official expressed it, the
authorities would not allow the early Scottish missionaries to
settle in Poona, which had too recently become British, as
they desired. Had not a native distributor of American tracts
just before been seized, by order, and escorted to the low land
at the foot of the Ghauts? So there, on the fertile strip of
jungly coast, in the very heart of the widow-burning, self-
righteous, intellectually able and proud Maratha Brahmans,
the Scottish evangelists began their work, of sheer necessity,
for they considered that Bombay was already cared for by the
American and English missions. The Governors, Elphinstone
and Malcolm, however, although they would not allow the
good men to be martyred in Poona, as they supposed, with
all the possible political complications, subscribed liberally to

their funds, a thing which no Governor-General dared do till
forty years after, when John Lawrence ruled from Calcutta.
In Hurnee and Bankote, from sixty to eighty miles down the
coast from Bombay, these missionaries had preached in Marathee and opened or inspected primary schools, with small results. So terrible was the social sacrifice involved in the
profession and communion of Christianity, that the first Hindoo convert, in 1823, some weeks after his baptism, rushed
from the Lord's Table when Mr. Hall was about to break the
bread, exclaiming, "No, I will not break caste yet." Long
before this the good James Forbes, father of the Countess de
Montalembert, had given it as his experience of Anglo-Indians
at all the settlements of Bombay, from Ahmedabad to Anjengo,
and dating from 1766, "that the character of the English in
India is an honour to the country. In private life they are
generous, kind, and hospitable ; in their public situations,
when called forth to arduous enterprise, they conduct themselves with skill and magnanimity ; and, whether presiding at
the helm of the political and commercial department, or
spreading the glory of the British arms, with courage, moderation, and clemency, the annals of Hindostan will transmit
to future ages names dear to fame and deserving the applause
of Europe. . . . With all the milder virtues belonging to their
sex, my amiable countrywomen are entitled to their full share
of applause. This is no fulsome panegyric ; it is a tribute of
truth and affection to those worthy characters with whom I
so long associated, and will be confirmed by all who resided
in India." [1] Mr. Forbes finally left India in 1784, when only
thirty-five years of age, but after eighteen years' experience.

The successive Governors had given an improved tone to
Anglo-Indian society, and the few missionaries and chaplains
had drawn around them some of the officials both in the
Council and in the ordinary ranks of the civil and military
services. But the squabbles in the Supreme Court, and the
reminiscences of a Journalist,[2] who has published his memoirs
recently, show that here also the new missionary had a field
prepared for him, which it became his special privilege to
develop and adorn with all the purity of a Christian ideal
and all the grace of a cultured gentleman. What in this way

---

[1] *Oriental Memoirs* (1834), vol. i. page 98.
[2] *The Memoirs of a Journalist*, by J. H. Stocqueler. Bombay, 1873.

he did, unobtrusively and almost unconsciously, in Bombay for forty years, will hardly be understood without a glance at this picture of Bombay in 1830, as drawn by the editor of the *Bombay Courier* :—

"The opportunity of leaving Bombay was not to be regretted. 'Society' on that pretty little island had a very good opinion of itself, but it was in reality a very tame affair. It chiefly consisted of foolish *burra sahibs* (great folks) who gave dinners, and *chota sahibs* (little folk) who ate them. The dinners were in execrable taste, considering the climate. . . . But the food for the palate was scarcely so flavourless as the conversation. Nothing could be more vapid than the talk of the guests, excepting when some piece of scandal affecting a lady's reputation or a gentleman's official integrity gave momentary piquancy to the dialogue. Dancing could hardly be enjoyed with the thermometer perpetually ranging between 80° to 100° Fahrenheit, and only one spinster to six married women available for the big-wigs who were yet to be caged. A quiet tiffin with a barrister or two, or an officer of the Royal Staff who could converse on English affairs, with a game of billiards at the old hotel or one of the regimental messes, were about the only resources, next to one's books, available to men at the Presidency endowed with a trifling share of scholarship and the thinking faculty."

Such was Bombay, the city and the province, when John Wilson thus wrote to the household at Lauder his first impressions of the former :—"Everything in the appearance of Bombay and the character of the people differs from what is seen at home. Figure to yourselves a clear sky, a burning sun, a parched soil, gigantic shrubs, numerous palm trees, a populous city with inhabitants belonging to every country under heaven, crowded and dirty streets, thousands of Hindoos, Muhammadans, Parsees, Buddhists, Jews, and Portuguese ; perpetual marriage processions, barbarous music, etc. etc. ; and you will have some idea of what I observe at present. In Bombay there are many heathen temples, Muhammadan mosques, and Jewish synagogues, several Roman Catholic chapels, one Presbyterian Church, one Episcopal Church, and one Mission Church belonging to the Americans. I preached in the Scotch Church on the first Sabbath after my arrival, and in the Mission Church on Sabbath last."

CHAPTER III.

1829-1836.

ORGANISATION AND FIRST FRUIT OF THE MISSION.

The Languages of the People—If necessary for Officials, much more for
Missionaries — Foundation of Wilson's Oriental Scholarship — Masters
Marathee so as to preach his first Sermon in six Months—Tentative efforts
at Hurnee—First visit to a Hindoo House and Discussion with a Parsee
—Prohibition of Suttee : Letter to Lord William Bentinck—" Plan of
Operations in the Island of Bombay "—His first European Friends—
Establishes the *Oriental Christian Spectator*—Census of Bombay—Wilson
and Duff—Presbyterian Constitution of a Native Church—Transferred
from the Scottish Missionary Society to the General Assembly—Progress
of the Mission to 1836—Letters to Mr. J. Jordan Wilson—The Freeness
of the Gospel.

IF a knowledge of the language of the people, vernacular
and, where possible, classical also, is the indispensable qualification of every official, so that it is carefully provided for by
the competitive examinations in England, and by the professional tests in the four great groups of Provinces in India,
how much more is it required by the foreign missionary. The
assistant-magistrate, even the district officer who rules a
million of people in one of the 200 counties of the Indian
Empire ; the judge who, outside of the three English cities,
hears cases and writes his decisions in the prevailing language
of the province, may be content with a merely official use of
the Marathee or Goojaratee, the Tamul or Telugoo, the
Hindee or Hindostanee, the Bengalee or Oorya, to say nothing
of the Persian and the Sanskrit which enrich all the thirty
languages of our Indian subjects. There is no conscientious
civil or military officer, however, who will not value his linguistic knowledge for the highest social as well as political
ends, in kindly intercourse with all classes ; and there is no
one of scholarly tastes who will be content without some

acquaintance with the learned languages of the East, whether Aryan or Semitic. But as the heart of a people is reached through its mother-tongue, and all that is best worth knowing about a country is to be found in its dialects and literature, the Christian missionary and scholar, above all officials, will master the vernacular as his most precious instrument, and the classical language that feeds it as his most useful storehouse of information and illustration, argument and authority. The Scottish, like the American missionaries who first worked in Western India, were pre-eminent in such studies, following an example fortunately set them and all subsequent preachers and teachers in the East, by the Baptist "cobbler" and most versatile Orientalist of his day,—William Carey. Mr Wilson's student friend especially, Robert Nesbit, who had preceded him to India by sixteen months, was already a fluent speaker of that Marathee of which he became so remarkable a preacher and writer that the natives could not trace even a foreign accent in his pronunciation and use of its idioms. From the first to the last day of his India life Wilson was of opinion that a year or longer should be allowed to every young missionary to acquire the vernacular of his province. He himself had brought to India a more than professional familiarity with Latin and Greek ; he knew French for literary purposes ; and he carried further than his old professor and now friend, Dr. Brunton, a grasp of Hebrew. He had not been a month in Bombay when he and his most apt pupil, his wife, left it for the comparative seclusion of, first Bankote and then Hurnee, that they might, aided by their brethren, and in the midst of the country people, thoroughly learn Marathee, to begin with.

In the eight months of the first hot and rainy seasons, from April to November, Mr. Wilson laid the foundation of his Orientalism with a rapidity, a thoroughness, and a breadth, due alike to his overmastering motive, his previous training, and his Mezzofanti-like memory. He himself shall tell, in the letters and journals of the time, how he set to work after a fashion that may well form the model of every worker in India in whatever position. We find Nesbit thus writing to him at the close of that six months' fruitful apprenticeship :—" I am accused of injuring your health by making you study Marathee and talk with me at night . . . Will the exhortation to take

good care of your health now make any amends ? Get up at
six, by all means ; and, that you may be able to do so, go to
bed at ten." Mr. Wilson thus addressed his directors in
Edinburgh :—

" As a year has passed away since I commenced my studies of the native
languages, it is now my duty to give you a brief account of my progress.
By referring to my journals I find that it was on the 18th of August, being
five months after my arrival in India, that I began to hold consultations with
the Hindoos, and on the 27th of September when I preached my first sermon.
When I was in the Konkan I generally devoted about nine hours to the study
of Marathee. Since I commenced my labours in Bombay I devote, according
to my ability, all the intervals from active missionary duty which I enjoy.
I may mention five hours daily as the average in which I am thus engaged.
During the first two months of my studies I pursued, as far as is practicable,
the Hamiltonian system. Mr. Nesbit during that time kindly furnished me
with the English of my lessons. I afterwards principally depended on my
pundit, who had only a knowledge of Marathee, and on the literary helps
which I could obtain. The books which I used were translations from the
English made by the Native Education Society, native stories, the translation
of the Scriptures, mission tracts, and an account of the Hindoo religion
written by a Brahman in my employment, in reply to queries which I
addressed to him. I kept a writer for four months who furnished me with
lists of words under the different principles of association which I could think
of. I devoted about an hour daily to consideration on the religion, manners,
and customs of the Hindoos, which I regulated according to Mr. Ward's
account.

" In Bombay I have some facilities for study which I did not enjoy in the
Konkan. These principally consist in my being able to get all difficulties
readily and satisfactorily solved, and in my being favoured with the sheets of
Captain Molesworth's and Mr. Candy's Dictionary as they pass through the
press. For the last three months I have devoted the hour between seven and
eight in the morning to the reading of Hebrew with the points. I am very
desirous, for the sake of usefulness among the Jews here, and other important
reasons, to attain to greater proficiency in this ancient language. My teacher,
who is a Rabbi, is an excellent scholar. He is well acquainted with Mr.
Wolff, whom he has frequently seen in Jerusalem ; and he declares, even
among his countrymen, that the Messiah has already appeared. I am not
without hopes of his being a converted man. I expect in a short time to be
able to commence the study of Hindostanee, a language which will enable me
to communicate the truths of the Gospel to many natives in Bombay to whom
at present I cannot find access. "

At Bankote, sixty-eight miles south of Bombay, Mr. Wilson
took his seat in the missionary council. On the first Sabbath
after his arrival he witnessed the baptism of the second
Hindoo convert of the mission, and administered the sacrament to " the children of the East and West, seated together
at the same table." At Hurnee he thus describes his tentative
efforts, after his acquisition of Marathee.

" *November 1st*, 1829. *Sabbath.*—I preached to the natives in the afternoon on the distinguishing characteristics of the children of God. The man whom I met on Friday did not attend the Marathee services.

"*2d.*—I preached to the beggars in the morning, and united with Mr. Cooper in addressing the natives in the afternoon.

"*3d.*—I addressed the natives in the morning.

"*4th, 5th.*—I addressed the servants in the morning, and united with Mr. Cooper in preaching to the natives in the afternoon.

"*6th.*—I addressed the natives in the morning.

"*7th.*—I addressed the natives, and made preparations for the approaching Sabbath.

"*8th. Sabbath.*—I preached to the Europeans on 'The carnal mind is enmity against God.' A lady who heard my discourse appeared to be a good deal affected by it. I observed her in tears. May God unfold to her the knowledge of her state by nature and practice, and lead her to embrace the truth as it is in Jesus.

"*9th.*—I examined the bazaar school, and preached to the beggars in the morning and forenoon. Messrs. Nesbit and Taylor of Belgaum arrived from Bombay, where they had been attending a meeting of the Bombay Missionary Union. Mr. Taylor, who is a highly respected and honoured servant of the Redeemer, communicated some very interesting intelligence to us respecting the spread of the Gospel. He mentioned that he had baptized four criminals lately, who, previously to their death, afforded him a reason to hope that they had been renewed in the spirit of their minds; and showed us a very interesting letter respecting the proceedings of the Baptist Mission in Burma. Dr. Judson baptized ten individuals during the first three months of this year.

"*13th.*—I visited in the morning the schools of Dhapoolie and Jilgao. In the first of these I found twenty-four boys and one girl. Few of them could read. The teacher, like too many of those supported by the Scottish Missionary Society, appears to confine his chief attention to writing and arithmetic, which are taught according to a very careless system.

"*29th November. Sabbath.*—I commenced my ministry among the natives of Bombay by preaching to about twenty individuals in Mr. Laurie's house.

"*30th.*—I wrote out the scrawl copy of a plan of the operations which I intend to pursue in Bombay.

"*2d December.*—I preached to a company of the natives on Colaba.

"*3d.*—I paid the usual respects to the Governor, who has welcomed me to Bombay in the kindest manner, and breakfasted with him; and, along with two of the members of the corresponding committee, looked at several empty houses.

"*4th, 5th.*—I spent these days in the purchase of furniture, and other similar business.

"*6th. Sabbath.*—I preached to the congregation of the Scotch Church in the forenoon; and to twenty-four natives in the afternoon.

"*7th.*—I wrote an advertisement of a short religious Magazine, which is intended principally to contain a record of the progress of the Gospel; and consulted with R. T. Webb, Esq., who, along with myself, Mr. Stone of the American Mission, and R. C. Money, Esq., a member of the corresponding committee, is to be one of the conductors of it, about some matters connected with it.

"*13th. Sabbath.*—I addressed twenty-two natives at Mr. Laurie's house.

"*13th, 14th.*—I engaged with Mr. Laurie in examining and transcribing the accompts of the Mission, and in preparing communications for the directors.

"*15th.*—I visited the house which has been taken for me; conversed with Narayan, who was baptized by Mr. Stevenson, and made arrangements concerning the Mission. In the evening I heard the delightful intelligence that an order for the abolishment of Suttees throughout India had been passed by the Governor General in Council. On account of this measure every Christian must rejoice—(1.) According to a moderate computation it will save three thousand lives annually. (2.) It will tend greatly to the improvement of the moral feelings of the Hindoos. What can be more shocking than the scenes which are witnessed at the funeral pile? Connected with them there is the violation of every principle of humanity, and the exhibition of the most sinful cupidity—the motive by which relations are commonly excited to the encouragement of the horrid deed. (3.) Its tendency will be that of opening the eyes of the Hindoos to the enormities of their religion. It is a testimony from the Government which was greatly needed; and the absence of which, combined with other circumstances, has, I have found, been viewed as an encouragement. When it has been for some time put in force, it will permit the Hindoos, with greater coolness and with less prejudice, to contemplate their Shastres, than at present when they see their most revolting recommendations reduced to practice. The Christian public are undoubtedly bound to return public thanks to Almighty God for the favour which in this respect He has shown to His cause."

The Bombay Missionary Union, consisting of the London, Scottish, and American missionaries in Surat, Belgaum, the Konkan, Poona, and Bombay, afterwards addressed a formal resolution to Lord William Bentinck, accompanied by this letter from Mr. Wilson, as the secretary—" This resolution is · a faint expression of the feelings of those who formed it. It was dictated by the most fervent gratitude, for the measure will immortalise the name of him who carried it into effect, and which will be fraught with unspeakable blessings to the inhabitants of India till the latest generation. The missionaries in the Bombay Presidency have already observed a day of special thanksgiving to God for the abolition of Suttees, and they now beseech Him to shower down His best blessings on the head of your lordship, whom He has honoured to be the instrument of communicating an unspeakable blessing to this benighted land." This was the first-fruit of the determination of the noblest of all the Governors General, who had been but a year in office, to put down with one hand all such crimes against humanity, while with the other he removed the obstacles to the progress of education worthy of the name. For a quarter of a century had the men of Serampore been vainly attacking the English Government's toleration and even encouragement of Suttee. When the new regulation prohibiting it reached Carey, as he was going into his pulpit on Sunday morning, he gave perhaps the most pregnant illustration of the teaching of the " Lord of the Sabbath," by at once

sending for his pundit and completing the translation into
Bengalee before night. So Mr. Marshman, his successor in
the office of Bengalee translator, tells the story. It was a
happy augury for Wilson's work that the news of this first
blow at the crimes sanctioned by Brahmanism — and that
directed according to the teaching of the purest toleration—
should meet him as he began his career of philanthropy in
Bombay. It was long till Suttee was abolished in the feudatory States, where he met with the horror more than once.
But since the Mutiny no chief, however powerful, has gone
unpunished by the government of India who has even con-
nived at a barbarity which the freed conscience of all India
soon learned to condemn. No man, no poor drugged widow
who may yet never have been a wife, dare light the Suttee's
pyre with impunity in the most remote jungle of a native
State, from still Brahman-ridden Travancore to the most
fanatical hamlet of the deserts of Rajpootana.

In June 1830 we find Mr. Wilson writing thus to Dr.
Cormack of Stow : —" We intend soon to take up the subject
of infanticide. Mr. Money (son of W. T. Money, Esq., Mr.
Wilberforce's friend,) told me that he had some thoughts of
memorialising the Supreme Government. Lord W. Bentinck,
you know, has abolished Suttee ; and there is no saying what
he may do. A Jain priest from Kathiawar, who knew General
Walker, is almost daily with me. He speaks very affectionately of him ; but he says that they have allowed the good
bandobast (arrangement) which was made to go to destruction.
I shall give you an account of the movements on this subject."

The closing weeks of the year 1829 were spent in the
organisation of the infant mission, in daily preaching to the
natives, in Sunday sermons to the British sailors in the harbour, for whom Mr. Wilson always cared, and in the Scotch
Church. Till Christmas he was the guest of the chaplain Mr.
Laurie, at his house in the most southerly point of the island
Colaba, itself a separate island at one time. The day after he
moved into his own house in the Fort. This seems to record
his first discussion with Parsees, and his first visit to a Hindoo
house in Bombay.

" 30*th*.—I engaged, with Mr. Allen, in preaching to the
natives. . . . 31*st*. — Some Parsees, with whom we sat for
a considerable time, reprobated the monuments in the English

Church, and accused the English of idolatry. We had a very
curious conversation with them on this subject. I was happy
to inform them that in the Scotch Church there were no
images. I deeply regret that there should be any occasion
for mistake on this and similar subjects. Christianity cannot
be presented to the heathen in too simple a form. Every
practice should be warranted by Scripture ; this is the only
safe principle. I preached for the first time in a Hindoo
house. My audience was larger than could be accommodated."

On the same ground Bishop Cotton long after opposed the
introduction of a reredos with figures into St. Paul's Cathedral,
Calcutta, where it was placed after his death ; defending his
prohibition on the ground of expediency, however, by the fact
that certain Sikh inquirers had been scandalised by the figures
in the painted glass windows of some of the Government
churches. The varied character of his work Mr. Wilson thus
sums up at this early period :—

"*28th January* 1830.—My engagements have been so numerous and
oppressive that I have had no disposition, and scarcely any time, to make
even the shortest entrances in my journal. I will, therefore, give a general
statement of the arrangements which I have made, and on which I am now
acting, and of one or two measures which have been carried into effect. On
Sabbaths I preach to a congregation of natives amounting to between forty
and fifty. About the half of them are servants, who are sent by their masters
for instruction. The remainder are principally led to attend from curiosity,
or from a regard to their worldly interests. Christ himself was called to
address those who followed Him from a view to the loaves and fishes. I
occasionally officiate in the Scotch Church, and once in the three weeks I
preach on board one of the vessels in harbour in connection with the Bombay
Seamen's Friend Association.

"I regularly conduct worship in the Marathee language, and deliver a
short address on some passage of Scripture at nine o'clock in the mornings at
my own house. My audience varies ; but on some occasions it has been
encouraging. At four o'clock in the afternoons I proceed to the streets of the
city to declare the glad tidings of salvation. When I am in a public situation
great numbers come round me ; and when I am in a private one, I have the
advantage of being heard by all those who see me, and of addressing myself
with greater particularity to individuals. On Tuesdays and Fridays I preach,
after the sun has set, in native houses. My services on these occasions,
though attended with many difficulties, afford me considerable comfort. They
are conducted at the time when the impure Shastres and religious stories are
read to the people. On account of the want of circulation of air in the houses
they are not without their danger. I hope, however, that by-and-bye I will
be able to find some places where I may regularly officiate with some degree
of comfort. On Saturday evenings I have a meeting with the Beni-Israelites.
It has hitherto proved encouraging. Marathee is the vernacular language
of this people.

"Three female schools have been instituted by Mrs. Wilson. The progress of the pupils is far from being encouraging. Much patience, attention and consideration will be required to bring them into such a state as will warrant the hope that they will be useful auxiliaries in the mission. The degraded state of those of whom they are composed forms a sufficiently powerful motive for exertion on their behalf. Manuel, who was lately admitted into the Church, is constantly engaged as an inspector. A more regular attendance and efficient discipline, and consequently stricter economy, are secured by this means than could possibly be obtained by another measure. The children are as frequently visited by Mrs. Wilson as her health will permit; and the readers will be required at least once in the week to attend at the house for particular instruction.

"I have established two boys' schools, which, as far as is practicable, are conducted on the principles pursued in the Sessional School of Edinburgh. I have been much disappointed with regard to the number of scholars. The indigenous schools, and the schools of the Native Education Society, are so arranged in Bombay, I find, as to prevent the collecting of any very large number of boys in connection with any of the missions. I do not, however, despair of seeing an improvement. When the discipline of my schools is better understood, and when its fruits become apparent, and when the hostility of neighbouring teachers begins to cool, I expect to see an increase in the number of scholars. Pedro is employed as inspector. One of the schools is under my own roof.

"I have a monthly meeting with some European soldiers. There is every reason to believe that in connection with them the divine blessing has rested on my labours.

"I have been a good deal tried by the conduct of Narayun Shunkur, who was baptized in May last by Mr. Stevenson. He has on more than one occasion shown great aversion to religious ordinances and religious instruction. He is engaged as a printer with Captain Molesworth, who lives in my neighbourhood, and his attendance on me has not accorded with his opportunities. Pedro and Manuel give me great satisfaction.

"A young gentleman in the Civil Service of the Company who was brought under serious impressions during our voyage to India, makes a decided profession of Christianity; and, in the judgment of his pious acquaintances, *adorns* the doctrine of his Lord and Saviour Jesus Christ. I could mention some other facts of a similar nature, which I have no doubt would prove highly gratifying to you. Many reasons, however, will occur to you which will lead you to perceive the propriety of my not mentioning them to you. A weekly meeting is held at my house for prayer and conference on the Scriptures; the average attendance is that of sixteen ladies and gentlemen.

"I am much pleased with Bombay as a missionary station, and when I reflect on the great door of usefulness which has been opened to me, I am much depressed with my insufficiency for the discharge of my duties. The real difficulties of a missionary's life are little known and felt by the religious public. To encounter them and overcome them, much faith, courage, compassion, wisdom, perseverance, and prayerfulness is required. 'Can these dry bones live?' is a question which thrusts itself upon me whenever I am about to deliver the message of salvation. The countenances of my auditors betray pride, stupidity, superstition, unconcern. My addressing them calls forth wrath, folly. My leaving them affords them an opportunity of giving vent to their evil dispositions. When I repeat my visits to them then I see little but aversion. Circumstances are not always of this kind, for there is frequently attention, consideration, and impression manifested by the poor Hindoos; but, when general circumstances are considered, it may be asked 'who is sufficient for these things?' Were it not the consideration that we

are ambassadors for Christ, that the people around us are perishing for lack of
knowledge, that the Word and Spirit of God are omnipotent, and that the
promises of God are on our side, I do not know what could support us or
induce us to declare divine truth. There are, I am happy to say, very
promising appearances in different parts of India. In due season we shall
reap if we faint not."

The experience of country and city, of preaching and
teaching, of creeds and customs, all based on familiarity with
the Marathee tongue, which Mr. Wilson had thus crowded
into the first year of his life in Western India, fitted him to
line out a policy for himself, and to lay the foundations of his
mission deep and broad. He was saved from the errors of
his predecessors, and in confidential communications to the
Society at home he did not hesitate to exercise that independence of judgment and of action which he had claimed
from the first, and without which much that was unique in
his powers and his methods might have been lost to Bombay
in the uniform level of average work. In this passage of such
a letter to the secretary of the Society he anticipates, at that
early date, the mistake which many missionaries have begun
to avoid only in recent years. That is—witness-bearing,
rather than the mere denunciation or exposure of idolatry,
is the key to the hearts and consciences of the natives of
India.

"In reference to the mode of addressing the natives pursued by my brethren, I have been led to entertain and express
the deepest regrets. With one exception, as far as I can form
a judgment, they are too frequently inclined to speak on the
folly of idolatry ; and to neglect the preaching of the unsearchable riches of Christ; and to present divine truth to
the minds of the heathen in any manner which is destitute of
solemnity. I know that their temptations to pursue this
course are great. It is the easiest ; it excites the feelings of
the hearer without any difficulty. It is, however, unprofitable ;
and I believe that it is one of the chief reasons of the comparatively small success of modern missions. It is deceitful ;
a missionary falls into it without his being aware of it, and
perseveres in it at the very time when he declares that an
opposite course is his duty and his aim. It tempts to the use
or inconclusive arguments ; it excites a thousand unprofitable
objections ; it produces a bad impression on the heathen, and
destroys a missionary's temper. It is the bane of our Mission,

and, I believe, is the great cause of the comparatively small success of modern missions.

" The preparations which are made for addressing the heathen are not so regular and extensive as could be wished for. This, I believe, originated in a great degree in the distraction which was produced by the charge of too many schools ; and it is persevered in more from the manner in which the labours are arranged and conducted than from indolence. On this account, however, it ought not to be overlooked. When united with an incorrect pronunciation, proceeding from a want of attention in the early stage of study, or from carelessness on the part of the pundits, and with a violation of the rules of concord, on which the Marathas lay great stress, it forms a serious evil. . . .

" I thank God for enabling me to make much greater progress in Marathee than I expected. I fear, however, that I may have in some degree injured my health. As I did not feel the climate so irksome as I expected, my attention was not directed to this subject till a few weeks ago I received a letter from Mr. Robson, the author of *St. Helena Memoir*, who has been residing at Hurnee, and I found some pain in the region of my heart." It was from that region that his fatal illness proceeded.

The financial affairs of the Scottish Missionary Society were, for local purposes, managed by a corresponding committee, chiefly of laymen, at Bombay. After some hesitation whether he should not begin operations at Poona, that committee had agreed with Mr. Wilson that he should remain in the capital. " I desire," he wrote to the directors at home, " to express my deep-felt gratitude for calling me to labour in a large town. It is evident that cities afford peculiar facilities for missionary exertion. The 'Acts of the Apostles ' leads us to conclude that in the Apostolical age the efforts of the servants of Christ were chiefly directed to them, and from this consideration the word ' pagan ' came to be applied to the heathen." He accordingly drew up, at the end of 1829, the " Plan of operations which I intend to pursue in the island of Bombay." He accompanied it by detailed regulations for the monitors or pupil-teachers, the masters, and the Christian inspectors of his schools. The whole scheme shows a rare foresight as well as the practical experience of the educationist; and it has

indeed, been carried out in more recent times, in most of its
principles, in the village, circle, and other primary vernacular
schools established by the various governments in India by
means of a school-rate.

Of the eight members of the corresponding committee at
that time, all became the fast friends of Mr. Wilson, and all
were distinguished by their high character as officials and
merchants. Besides the Scotch chaplains there were the Hon.
Mr. Farish, who officiated for some time as Governor; Mr. R.
T. Webb of the same civil service; Mr. R. C. Money, Persian
secretary to government, whose name is perpetuated by a
missionary institution; Dr. Maxwell of the Medical Board;
Dr. Smyttan, who became Mr. Wilson's most intimate friend;
and Mr. M'Grigor. With friends and scholars like Captain
Molesworth and Captain Candy, Mr. Hynd from Liverpool,
and the various missionaries, Mr. and Mrs. Wilson soon became
the centre of that gradually extending society of thoughtful
and cultured persons into which, in time, he was to introduce
the native gentlemen of the city. As indispensable to such
varied and aggressive work as he had undertaken, Mr. Wilson
had originated the oldest Christian periodical in India, the
Oriental Christian Spectator. The now rare sets of this monthly
magazine, which was continued for thirty years, form an invaluable record of progress in all forms in Western India and
the adjoining countries. In that appeared the literary fruits
of Wilson's ceaseless labours of every kind.

Thus far the missionary policy of Mr. Wilson does not
seem to have included a high class English school or college.
The central school of the Native Education Society professed
to provide for the increasing number of Hindoos and Parsees
who sought English for commercial or official use; and his
own scheme provided for the Portuguese. As yet Lord
William Bentinck had not moved, Macaulay had not taken
his seat in council as first law member, and Dr. Duff was
only making his way to Calcutta through the perils of repeated shipwreck. But Mr. Wilson had early taken steps
"to begin instructing the natives in the English language."

It was on the 29th March 1832 that the germ of what
became the General Assembly's Institution was established as
the "Ambrolie English School, connected with the Scottish
Mission." "This infant institution," as it is described in the

first year's report, was under the immediate eye of Mr. Wilson as its superintendent. Books as well as teachers had to be created for it, such as Marathee and Goojaratee translations of the *English Instructor*, the *Catechism*, and Dr. A. Thomson's text-books, and a work entitled *Idiomatical Exercises in English and Marathee* " to aid the natives in understanding the structure and vocables of the English language." In the first year the school was attended by 415 Hindoos and 3 Parsees. Fees were exacted, and the Christian character of the education was insisted on from the first. The highest prize was a sum of fifty rupees (£5) for the best essay on the spirituality of God, open to those youths " who attended the Wednesday evening lectures of the Rev. John Wilson."

The population of Bombay, according to the census of 1833, consisted of 18,376 Christians, principally Roman Catholics; 143,298 Hindoos, including Jains; 49,928 Muhammadans, with Arabs and Persians; 20,184 Parsees, and 2246 Jews, including native or Beni-Israelites. The total population, or 234,032, was slightly above that to which Edinburgh and Leith together have grown at the present time. Such was Mr. Wilson's field, and it was to go on increasing threefold as his labours for the good of its varied communities extended.

Calcutta and Bombay, Eastern and Western India, presented in their native communities needs which were supplied from the first by the systems of Duff and Wilson, which differed indeed in the priority of time and importance given to certain methods of operation, but all the more effectually secured the same great end of saturating Asiatic society and government progress with Christian truth conveyed by the most intellectual methods. Duff's instrument was the English language, and it was at first applied exclusively to boys and young men. Wilson's instrument was the vernaculars of a varied population—the Marathee, Goojaratee, Hindostanee, Hebrew, and Portuguese; with Persian, Arabic, and Sanskrit in reserve for the learned classes, which he acquired and fluently used, often in provincial dialects too, in a few years, in preaching and in teaching both girls or women, and boys or young men. But the Calcutta missionary no more neglected Bengalee and even Sanskrit as his college developed, or female education as society advanced in intelligence, than his great

E

Bombay colleague was indifferent to English. It was a happy
adaptation of the men to the conditions which indeed helped
to make them what they became, that English held the first
place with the one, and a purified Orientalism was the most
important weapon of the other. Looking back half a century,
those who know the social and spiritual state of both Eastern
and Western India may fancy that a fuller adoption of
Orientalism in the former, and an earlier use of English for
the highest instruction in the latter, would have been better
for both the missions, and for the advancement of India.
But that is only to forget that such an arrangement would
have paralysed Duff in his fight beside Macaulay with the
fanatical Orientalist party in the government, without whose
defeat progress of any kind would have been impossible ;
while it would have long postponed, if it did not altogether change, that hold which Wilson obtained on the
affections and the intellect of the native communities, which
was due to his oriental lore and his more than Asiatic courtesy
and grace. In truth, the historian of British India who can
estimate causes aright, will put side by side with Duff's
opening of the boys' English school in Calcutta in August
1830, the establishment of Mrs. Wilson's first of many female
schools in Bombay in December 1829. Both were seeds
which have already grown into great trees. Each represented
that side of civilisation without which the other becomes
pernicious. Each reacted on the other. Every succeeding
generation of young men demands educated women in increasing numbers. These bring up better instructed children ;
and in instances no longer rare, present the spectacle, unknown to Asia all through its history, of pure and happy
family life. Mrs. Wilson's organisation and management of
the female schools, her frequent contributions to the *Oriental
Christian Spectator*, and the superintendence of the mission
during her husband's absence on preaching tours, were in-
terrupted only for a time by the birth of four children.

Although laying the foundations of his missionary policy
and machinery broad and deep, and well aware that for
many a day his must be the toil of preparation, Mr. Wilson
from the first expected and worked for baptized converts.
He did not lose himself in his system, nor did he loftily or
vaguely look for a harvest from the seed he was hourly sow-

ing, only in the distant future.   He rather tested, improved,
and extended his system; by the assured belief that the
Divine Spirit would show immediate or speedy fruit such as
his few predecessors had not witnessed in Western India.
He was a man to make and follow his own policy, not theirs ;
while he was too wise and kindly to neglect their experience.
So he formed a native church in Bombay in February 1831,
two years after landing, and a year after evangelising the
island.   He thus announces the fact to his father, himself an
elder of Lauder Kirk, and familiar with the ecclesiastical
organisation :   " I formed a native church on Presbyterian
principles.   Eight members joined it ; and I administered the
Lord's Supper to them and to some Europeans."   The draft
minute of this transaction, the beginning of a church which
he watched and helped till it grew to be what it now is,
worshipping in its own fine ecclesiastical building, has a
peculiar interest as a contribution to these modern ' Acts of
the Apostles.'   In the half-century since those days, when
the number of the Protestant native church in India, in all
its branches, has grown to be nearly half a million, and is
increasing annually, according to the official census, at the rate
of $6\frac{1}{2}$ per cent, contrasted with the half per cent of Hindoos,
all the foreign missionaries have long since agreed that the
Church of India must, as it grows to support itself more
largely, determine its own organisation, free from the divisions
of the Western sects and historical creeds.   This too was Mr.
Wilson's view ; but in 1831 what so well fitted as presbytery
for the infant church ?—

" BOMBAY, 4th February 1831.

"This day, in the house of the Rev. John Wilson, minister of the gospel
in connection with the Church of Scotland, and missionary from Scotland,
amongst some converted Hindoos and others a native church was formed.
John Wilson, the servant of Jesus Christ, stated that he was licensed as a
preacher of the gospel by the Presbytery of Lauder on 6th May 1828 ; that
he was ordained to the office of the ministry in the same place on 24th June
1828, and that he arrived in India on the 13th February 1829.   Mr. Wilson
baptized on the 2d of January in his own house Heer Chund, Ransod, Saha
Wanee, and Dewukee, a Hindoo woman.   He also declared worthy of communion on the same day John Rennie Baptist, an African by descent, who
had been baptized in his youth.   On the 17th January 1831, he baptized
Raghoba Balajee Vaishya.   Along with these Margaret Bayne Wilson, the
sponse of Mr. Wilson, who had been married to him in 1828 ; Rama Chnndra,
formerly a Brahman, who had been baptized at Bankote in 1829, Narayan,
formerly a Shenavee, who had been baptized in Bombay in 1829, and Manuel
Gomes, a Roman Catholic, who had come into the true church in 1830.   All

these persons having declared that they were willing to unite in church fellowship, Mr. Wilson proceeded to explain the nature of church order."

After a detailed account of the Presbyterian organisation, the minute concludes—"All the persons having approved of these statements, Mr. Wilson, in the name of Christ, by prayer constituted them into a church. They agreed to recognise him as their minister, and he gave them suitable instruction. On the 6th of February the Lord's Supper was administered to the church." Thus the organisation of a church followed, in its simplicity and its power, the model of the first gathering of the Eleven in the upper room at Jerusalem, and their successors.

Not so thought the small body, though chiefly Presbyterian ministers, who formed the executive of the Scottish Missionary Society. From the day that he entered their seminary when a student of twenty-one, he had stipulated for a degree of independence which their somewhat extreme rules seemed to forbid. He had hardly landed in India when he found that his colleagues were engaged in a controversy with the directors, the management of which soon fell into his hands. In June 1830 we find him writing to Dr. Cormack of Stow in all the frankness of friendship:—"Our directors in St. John Street have lately sent out to my brethren some very alarming communications. They do not recognise our Presbyterian principles and our ordination vows, and they wish to bring us under a spiritual tyranny. I am sure that you and other worthies of the Church will keep a watch upon them." The controversy we may now speedily dispose of. It was the old one between a strong man—strong in intelligent devotion to his work, and a weak committee—weak by reason of distance from the new condition of things in question, and of the reduction of the strongest among them to the low level of routine uniformity. From the treatment that nearly broke the heart of Carey and his colleagues, against which Andrew Fuller and John Foster in vain protested, down to the present hour, committees have been only necessary evils when interfering with wiser men than themselves. In the infancy of Missions, discretion and charity were especially required on the part of distant directors. Practically it was found that the rules of the Scottish Missionary Society so acted as to clash with the standing and the conscientious duties of the missionaries as ordained ministers of the Church of Scotland. The missionaries, if they were to be merely the paid employés of a committee responsible to an undefined body of contributors, would lose the protection and the efficiency which the perfect representative system of their Church gave them, in common with all its members and office-bearers.

In August 1830, accordingly, Mr. Wilson printed and sent to each of the directors, and to his own friends, a " Memorial addressed to the Directors of the Scottish Missionary Society on their opposition to the practice of Presbytery by the Presbyterian Missionaries." It is a bold and trenchant document, showing a far-sighted regard for the good and the growth of the native church, yet free from all sectarianism in spirit. The result was a reply offering a compromise, under which the Society and its Bombay missionaries, reduced to Messrs. Wilson, Nesbit, and J. Mitchell, worked together for a time. But as the Society's funds declined, and the female schools especially became imperilled, in spite of the growing local support in Bombay itself, the directors began to see that their missionaries had been right. The Church of Scotland had meanwhile been sending out its own missionaries, Duff, Mackay, and Ewart, to Calcutta, by means of the India Mission Committee, of which Mr. Wilson's old professor, Dr. Brunton, was the convener. Before the General Assembly of 1835, accordingly, there was laid a petition from its ministers who were missionaries, and also from the chaplains in Bombay and Poona, which resulted in their transfer from the Society to the Church in its corporate capacity.

Thus pleasantly was the last obstacle to Mr. Wilson's success removed, nor thereafter, either before or after the Disruption of the Church of Scotland in 1843, were his labours impeded by home interference. A new vigour was given to all the operations of the mission, and not least to the English college, to which, after their successful experience in Calcutta, the General Assembly's Committee directed special attention. Mr. Wilson removed it into the Fort, that is, into Bombay proper in those days, as "the situation is the most convenient for the most respectable natives, and in which there is no similar institution." He mentions the rent of the premises, Rs. 120 a month, as "very reasonable, considering the demand for houses in that part of the town." The fact is of economic interest in the light of the speculative mania of 1863-66, and of the present value of property there.

"We have commenced operations with every encouragement, and have now an attendance of 215 boys, who are taught on the intellectual system, and who are making gratifying progress both in literary and religious knowledge, which the parents were expressly informed by me, through the native papers, they would receive, and to the communication of which they have no objection. The pupils form a group as interesting as can be imagined, as far as the variety of tribes is concerned. They have been drawn not only from the different classes of the Hindus, but from among the Pársees, Jains, Mussulmáns, Jews, and native Christians; and their association together, independently of the instructions which they receive, cannot but have a powerful influence in removing those prejudices of caste which so much impede missionary operations in this country.

"Every economy will be studied in reference to the school in Bombay. Unless, however, everything connected with it be arranged on a respectable scale, it will not, while the Native Education Society has such abundant resources from the government, be productive of much good. It is a subject of gratitude that the mission enjoys so much of the confidence of the natives as it actually does, and that even the very individuals who have so zealously but unsuccessfully come forward to the defence of the different systems of superstition, are on the most friendly terms with myself, and frequent in public and private intercourse with me. I lately finished a course of weekly lectures on the evidences and doctrines of natural and revealed religion, which I commenced three years ago. I have begun another course on the propagation of the gospel from the resurrection of Christ to the present day. On this course the *Durpun*, edited by a young Brahman, remarked—'A great many natives were present at the first lecture. The course Mr. Wilson has now commenced cannot but be interesting to them, as not only bringing before them the *data* which must lead to the solution of the most important problem which can engage their attention, but as conveying to them most valuable information on the general history of the world, and the greatest moral revolutions which have taken place on the face of the globe. His avowed object is to *convert* ; but he wishes in the first instance to *inform* and to afford the means of judging.'

"The state of my health is now such that I have felt warranted to resume, though from my multifarious duties I cannot *daily* pursue it, my preaching in the native languages at places of public concourse. My audiences are extremely encouraging. The attendance at the stated services of the mission is greater than I have ever formerly witnessed it. I have seven candidates for baptism. The schools both for boys and girls, in which the native languages are taught, are in much the same state in which they were when I transmitted to you our annual report. I should regret exceedingly to see them diminished, as they are in every respect suitable to the circumstances of the lower orders, the 'poor to whom the gospel is preached,' and from whom the first body of converts may be probably raised in India, as well as in other countries. The English school will, I trust, soon furnish a superior class of teachers for them.

"Though I fear that native missionaries, till they are raised from among the children of converts educated from their earliest days in Christianity and in a Christian atmosphere, will not, generally speaking, prove such efficient labourers as Europeans, and though I believe that we must first show them the example of an apostolic ministration, I enter *with my whole soul* into your views as to the adoption and devising of every practical measure for their training. I have received a very interesting letter from Mr. Mackay. I enter most cordially into the view which he states, that the experience of the two missions will be in many respects mutually advantageous. Mr. Duff's success in the organisation of presbyterial associations in Scotland is truly encouraging to us amidst all our trials and travail in India. The internal spiritual riches of the Church of Scotland will not be diminished, but increased by the most abundant external communication.

"My present salary, exclusive of house rent and travelling expenses, which are included in the general expense of the mission, but inclusive of an allowance for my two children, is £230 per annum. The experience of nearly seven years' residence in Bombay, the expense of which is more than one-third greater than that of out-stations, warrants me to say what both my missionary brethren and members of the corresponding committee of the Scottish Missionary Society long ago urged me to state to my supporters, is inadequate to the comfort and usefulness in the Lord's work which it is desirable I should enjoy, and which, from private sources, I have hitherto enjoyed. I should like it raised to £250. I simply mention this circumstance because you have kindly asked me to be explicit as to the proposed expenditure."

The total cost of the mission in 1836 was £1820, of which one-third was subscribed by the English residents. From first to last Mr. Wilson's income from the mission was insufficient for ordinary requisites, apart from those extensive tours and those social duties which he began to take upon himself, and which gradually became the secret of his power with Oriental, even more than with English society. But nothing save an official demand from the Home Committee ever called forth a reference to his pecuniary affairs. On the contrary, he joyfully devoted such private resources as came to him in subsequent years, and such funds as his friends and admirers entrusted to him personally, to the one work of his life. Mr. J. Jordan Wilson, a wealthy friend of his youth, who was early attracted to him by his student-like zeal and by the belief that there was some slight bond of kinship between them, and above all by close spiritual ties, left him a legacy of a thousand pounds, half of which was for any missionary object he chose, and half for his private use. The letters to his Edinburgh agents, sent in reply to the news of the legacy, directed the expenditure of the whole amount in various ways for the Bombay Mission. The following letter to that gentleman shows how the cares of the mission pressed upon his resources, and how manifold were his labours :—

"BOMBAY, 13th November 1830.

"MY DEAREST FRIEND—I have little leisure, and some of that is spent in connection with the *Oriental Christian Spectator*, which I regularly send to you, and the numbers of which must be viewed by you as letters, as they generally contain something which has proceeded from our own house.   The *Spectator* is very extensively read in India ; and there is reason to believe that it is accomplishing much good by diffusing information on the most important subjects.   I trust that God will honour it in some degree to expose that monstrous system of iniquity, the Hindoo religion, and to aid the servants of the Saviour in proclaiming the gospel.   You will see in the number for November, which I hope will soon reach you, a short paper by myself on the ' Sanscrit and Marathee renderings of Theological Terms.'   I intend to follow up this most important subject, and to make such free remarks on the translations of the Scriptures into the Indian languages as I may conceive calculated to further their improvement.   The paper which follows the article to which I refer, and entitled ' Selected Sanscrit Shloks,' is by a Mr. Law, a young gentleman of the Civil Service.   He is a most extraordinary linguist.   He was brought under serious impressions through our instrumentality during the voyage to India.   He lately stayed a month with us, and we were much pleased with his Christian character.   Our usefulness among Europeans, through the grace of our heavenly Father, continues to extend, particularly among the higher classes.   The old serpent, by stirring up the opposition of bigots, has attempted to defeat and prevent our occasional labours among the sailors and soldiers ; but he has failed.   The true friends of the cause have rallied more closely around us, while our poor countrymen have more highly valued the word of life which they knew had been attempted to be taken from them.

"In your letter you express your wish that I had been connected with the General Assembly's Institution at Calcutta.   I think that it is calculated to be highly useful, and I wish it every success.   I would remark, however, that colleges, though they are admirable instruments in the *instruction* of Christians, are but clumsy instruments in the *making* or *conversion* of Christians.   The preaching of the gospel is the grand means of propagating the gospel, and for every professor at present there should be at least twenty preachers.   The Assembly's operations will have a glorious effect on the Church at home.   Mr. Duff, whom they have sent out, is a pious young man, and he will, I am happy to say, preach as well as profess.   He, like myself, has had toughly to fight, through the newspapers, for religious liberty.   I have two Hindoos under my care, whom I instruct with a view to their being admitted to the office of the ministry.   I have now seven inquirers around me, of most of whom I entertain a favourable opinion.   Five of them are Hindoos, three men and two women ; one is an African, and one a Jew.

"Permit me to make an appeal to your Christian sympathy.   There are many poor people in Bombay in very wretched circumstances.   About two hundred come to me every Monday morning for a little rice, and at that time I endeavour to administer to them the word of life.   On Saturdays I preach to about six hundred of the same description of persons at the house of Captain Molesworth.   For the relief of this class of persons a society, at my suggestion, has been lately formed, and I believe that their wants will be regularly and systematically relieved.   There are other classes, however, for whom I have been able to do nothing, and their circumstances possess peculiar interest.   They are persons who lose employment by inquiring into Christianity, or by embracing it ; they are persecuted Christians (Armenians and Chaldeans), and Jews from Bussora, Baghdad, Tabreez, and other places, who come with the most heartrending accounts of Muhammadan tyranny ; and they are poor Indian Roman Catholics.   My heart is often pained by observing their wants ; and I am not ashamed to say that we have relieved at times beyond our ability.   You know that none of the Missionary Society funds can or ought to be applied to them.   If you and some of the other friends of the Redeemer would in a *quiet* way raise a small sum for them, you would confer a blessing on the cause of humanity and Christianity. By informing me of the sum raised, I could act on the faith of getting it, and tell you how to appropriate it. I would furnish you with an account of the way in which it may be expended.

"My darling wife has six female schools, and she is useful in instructing female inquirers."

In this letter we see the germ of every side of the young missionary's work in and for Bombay, save only the English college. Experiences were soon to teach him that, for preaching and immediate results no less than in that wider work of preparation, the fruit of which comes plenteously after many days and has already begun so to come, the daily instruction of the most intellectual and influential youth by one to whom they become attached, is second to no other agency—is, indeed, for that class superior to all others. But even up to 1836 he had not learned, as he afterwards did, to perfect his own system of Christian aggression on the corrupting civilisations of the East, by the enthusiastic encouragement of the higher education through English. The following letter to Mr. J. Jordan Wilson closes with a statement of spiritual truth, happily familiar enough now, but very rare in Scotland forty years ago. It is the last of a long correspondence covering fifteen years, in which the younger man led the older to a cheerful peace and a joyous self-sacrifice for the cause of Christ. It is the first where we meet with allusions to a friendship with Dr. Duff, and an admiration for him none the less true and hearty because it was discriminating, which continued on both sides all through their Indian lives :—

" " BOMBAY, *7th July* 1836.

"You mention Mr. Duff's elevation to a Doctorship. He is well worthy of his honours, although *some* of his views on the economics of Christian missions are, in my opinion, erroneous. I have just remarked in a letter to a friend to-day as follows :—' Dr. Duff's warm advocacy of the Calcutta Institution has been by far too *exclusive*. I rejoice in the prosperity of the Seminary, and wish it every support ; but he ought not to have advocated its cause by disparaging the direct preaching of the gospel to the natives in their own languages by Europeans, and overlooked female education, and the general education of the natives *through the medium of their own tongues*, which form the readiest key to their hearts. The higher Institutions are well calculated to attract the higher classes of society, and to educate teachers and preachers. We must have a body of Christians, however, from which to *select* these agents. For this body of Christians we must not mainly depend on our Academies. 'To the *poor* the gospel is preached.' 'Of the little flock, and present inquirers at this place,' I also observe to Dr. Brunton, 'some were first impressed by hearing the gospel in the crowded bazaar, some by hearing it at the margin of the sea; some in the church; some in the schoolroom; some in the place in which the Lord of Glory was born when he came on his mission to this world; some in the social circle; some in the private chamber; and some by the perusal of Christian publications. I have thus been encouraged to remember the words of inspiration :—' Blessed are ye that sow beside all waters.' ' In the morning sow thy seed, and in the evening withhold not thine hand : for thou knowest not whether shall prosper, either this or that, or whether they both shall be alike good.' I could not refrain from giving you, who are so much interested in my operations, this brief expression of my views. Were I to visit the Modern Athens, and seek to propagate these opinions, I should, instead of being dubbed a ' Doctor in Divinity,' probably be dubbed a ' Babbler,' like Paul in the Ancient Athens. I have the fullest confidence that the Lord will soon vindicate His own cause : and I am perfectly willing, if I have the means of carrying on my labours, to be personally overlooked and despised. I bless God for what I have already seen as to the diminishment of prejudices against 'highway missionaries.' Six years ago my countrymen laughed at me when they saw me ' haranguing mobs.' These same gentlemen have conferred on me their highest literary honour, and notwithstanding my street preaching propensities, have put me into the chair formerly occupied by these great men Sir James Mackintosh, Sir John Malcolm, etc., and suffered me to ' harangue' *them* as their president ! I had serious thoughts of saying *nolo episcopari ;* but when I thought that I might contribute to shield the whole class of ' Ranters ' from contempt, and use my influence for the Lord's cause, I refrained.

" Would that I could, in reply to your inquiry, speak a word in season to you, as you have done to me ! The foundation of faith is the Gospel offer of salvation to the chief of sinners who will accept it. We must be content to be saved gratuitously. We can neither purchase our justification before we receive it, nor adequately acknowledge it when we have received it. The Saviour is infinitely worthy of our reliance, and the moment we rely upon him we are safe, and may rejoice with joy unspeakable and full of glory. We must seek for comfort by looking to him and his finished work. The eye, as Dr. Chalmers I believe expresses it, must look to the Sun of Righteousness for his light-giving and life-giving beams, and not turn in to gaze upon its internal structure. The work of Christ within us is the evidence of our faith ; but the work of Christ without us is the object of our faith, and the offers of Christ, the warrant of our faith. When Satan says to us, ' You have not believed, else whence all your fears, and all your failings, and offences ? ' we should reply if we cannot give him the direct contradiction, 'I now believe what the Saviour says to me, and I will now give my fears to the winds in spite of all your efforts.' Our struggle with and distress on account of indwelling sin, which is common to us and all the Lord's people, ought to enhance the Saviour in our estimation, and not to detract from our grounds of confidence in him, which are the unchanging graciousness of his character and the unfailing efficacy of his mediation. My little children never imagined that I ceased to be their father when I chode them, or removed them from my presence, or punished them, till I saw in them a proper contrition. Why, then, oh why, should we dishonour God by imagining that he ceases to be our Father ?"

CHAPTER IV.

1830—1836.

PUBLIC DISCUSSIONS WITH LEARNED HINDOOS AND MUHAMMADANS.

How Mr. Wilson became an Orientalist—" Turning the World upside-down " —Ziegenbalg's "Conferences"—First Discussion with Brahmans—Christian Brahman against Hindoo Pundits—" God's Sepoys "—The Ten Incarnations—The Pundits Retire—Morality *versus* Religion—The Second Discussion—The New Champion with Garlands of Flowers — Mr. Wilson's " First Exposure of Hindooism "—The Third Discussion — Mr. Wilson's " Second Exposure of Hindooism " — Parseeism and Muhammadanism enter the Arena — Dr. Pfander's later Treatises — Mr. Wilson's Reply to Hadjee Muhammad Hashim—The Sexualism of the Koran and Slavery— The Sons of Israel in Western India—The Black and White Jews—Joseph Wolff, the Christian Dervish and Protestant Xavier—Visit of Mr. Anthony Groves, Dervish of a different stamp — Mr. Francis W. Newman as a Missionary—Mr. Robert C. Money—Sir John Malcolm—Lord William Bentinck—Sir Robert Grant—Mr. Wilson on the British Sovereignty in India in 1835—Bombay Union of Missionaries—Progress in Kaffraria—Mr. Wilson on Carey and Morrison.

THERE is no recorded instance in the life of any Oriental scholar, whether official or missionary, of such rapid but thorough acquisition of multifarious information regarding the literature and the customs, as well as the languages of the natives, as marked Mr. Wilson's first year's residence in India. Sir William Jones began his purely Indian studies at a later period of life, and carried them on amid comparative leisure and wealth. Colebrooke, the greatest of all Orientalists, laid the foundation of his splendid acquirements so slowly that Sanskrit at first repelled him, though afterwards he would rise from the gaming-table at midnight to study it. Ziegenbalg and Carey had the same overmastering motive as John Wilson, but the former hardly went beyond the one vernacular— Tamul, and the latter was distracted by the hardships of

poverty and a discontented wife; so that he began by working
as an indigo-planter when learning Bengalee.   Mr. Wilson
not only mastered Marathee, but Goojaratee ; to these he soon
added Hindostanee and Persian, while almost his earliest work
in Bombay was the preparation of a Hebrew and Marathee
grammar for the Jews, there known as Beni-Israel.   Thus its
four great communities, Hindoo and Muhammadan, Parsee
and Jewish, he was early prepared to influence, while he had
from the first attained sufficient fluency in Portuguese to care
for the large number of half-caste descendants of our predecessors in the island.   A scholarly knowledge of Arabic he
was later in finding leisure to acquire.   But his advance in
Sanskrit seems to have been parallel with his acquisition of
Marathee, so that we find him from the very first confuting
the Brahmans out of their own sacred books as Paul did in
the case of the Athenians and the Cretans.   This knowledge
he steadily extended to the more obscure and esoteric dialects
of the older Hindoo tongues, in which the various sects of
quasi-dissenters, like the Sikhs and the Vaishnavas, had their
authoritative scriptures.   He was early a collector of Oriental
manuscripts.   Nor was he content with this.   He employed
Brahmans to gather information for him on a definite principle,
and wherever he went he was constant in his cross-examina-
tion of the people and their priests.

The result of the first fifteen months' unwearied toil was
seen in the beginning of a series of discussions on Christianity,
forced on Mr. Wilson, to his great satisfaction, by Hindoo,
Muhammadan, and Parsee apologists in succession.   The
ardent and courageous scholar, having fairly organised his
schools, and his translating and preaching work, was by no
means content to go on in a daily routine, passively believing
that Hindoo and Parsee, Jew and Muhammadan, would come
over to him.   "I have felt it my duty to proceed," he writes
to more than one of his home correspondents in 1831, "somewhat out of the course of *modern* missionary procedure.   The
result of my efforts has more than realised my expectations.
Matters I thought were going on too quietly ; I could see
little of that which is spoken of in the 'Acts of the Apostles'
as a 'turning of the world upside-down,' and nothing of that
stir which attended the labours of the Apostles in the different
cities which they visited.   There was praying and there was

teaching in schools, and there was preaching to some extent, especially by our missionaries ; but there was no attempt to make a general impression on the whole population of a town or province. 'Drive gently' was the maxim. I thought on the days of Paul when he stood on Mars' Hill. I thought on the days of Luther, and Knox, and Calvin, and I began to see that they were right. They announced with boldness, publicly and privately, in the face of every danger, in the midst of every difficulty, to high and low, rich and poor, young and old, and I resolved by divine grace to imitate them. I have consequently challenged Hindoos, Parsees, and Mussulmans to the combat. The former I fight by the mouth principally, and the two latter by the pen. The consternation of many of them I know to be great, and hundreds have heard the gospel in the place of tens. I have had in the idolatrous Bombay, and the still more idolatrous Nasik, 250 miles distant, many hundreds for auditors. At present I am waging war, through the native newspapers, with the Parsees and Mussulmans. They are very indignant ; some of them had got up a petition praying Government to stop me, but this was in vain. They did not present it. They show talent in their communications, but with a bad cause what can they do ? Conscience, the Holy Spirit, the promises of God and the providence of God, are on our side. O for a pentecostal day ! This may not be granted during our sojourn. Perhaps God only wishes, us to be as the voice of one crying in the wilderness, ' Prepare ye the way of the Lord.'"

A year before this, when announcing the first of these debates, he had pronounced it " the first general discussion on the Christian and Hindoo religions which has perhaps taken place in India." This statement is correct, notwithstanding the "conferences" which the Lutheran missionaries of Denmark had held with the Tamul Brahmans and Muhammadans in South India a century before. " Upon the 6th of March 1707," begins the record, " I, Bartholomew Ziegenbalgen, was visited by a grave and learned Brahman ; and, asking him what he proposed to himself by his friendly visit, he replied that he desired to confer with me amicably about the great things and matters of religion." All through the narration there is no sign, at that early time, of the overturning process.

In truth, the good men of that mission, which had Tranquebar
for its head-quarters, from Ziegenbalg to Schwartz, and to
this day, tolerate caste even at the Lord's table, and in all
their converts save ordained natives. Very different was the
"turning upside-down" of Mr. Wilson's Bombay discussions,
and yet in temper and in charity quite as "amicable" on his
part, though terribly in earnest. Thus the first began.

Rama Chundra, the Pooranic Brahman who had been
baptized at Bankote, visited Bombay in May 1830, for the
purpose of declaring to his caste-fellows and priestly colleagues
his reasons for forsaking them. For a time his arguments
failed to prick their apathy. But at last Pundit Lukshmun
Shastree was tempted to defend at great length the teaching of
Hindooism regarding the ten Avatars or incarnations of
Vishnoo, and, in the heat of controversy, to refer the question
to five or six Brahmans. Rama Chundra demanded a fair
public debate. To this the Pundit reluctantly consented, but
himself prepared an advertisement announcing that there
would be a discussion upon the evidences of the Hindoo and
the Christian religion in the house of Mr. Wilson, at four
o'clock on Friday the 21st May; that Rama Chundra, formerly a Pooranic, would defend the Christian religion; and
that Lukshmun, a Pooranic, would, "as he felt disposed," take
up the side of the Hindoo religion. A great crowd assembled
accordingly, and among them upwards of a hundred Brahmans.
Lukshmun being the secular Sanskrit teacher of one of the
American missionaries, and Rama Chundra a convert of the
Scottish missionaries, both missionaries were present. Mr. R.
T. Webb, as a layman and a high official, was asked to keep
order. The interest of the whole lay in the fact that Brahman met Brahman; the one new to the work of Christian
apologetics and exposition, but assisted by Mr. Wilson occasionally; the other also helped by abler reasoners.

Mr. Wilson opened the proceedings, which were in Marathee, with constant quotations of Sanskrit verses, by stating
the advantages of discussion in the attainment of truth, by
exhorting the combatants to observe charity and the audience
to put away prejudice, and by meeting only the initial
assumption that God had established several religions, with
the remark that, as God is the Father of all mankind, he will
not appoint opposing laws for the regulation of his family.

After the first day the Pundit Lukshmun "did not long keep his ground." Rama Chundra, "though he occasionally introduced irrelevant matter, and was too tolerant of the sophistry of his opponents, acquitted himself in a manner which greatly interested many of his auditors." During the next three days, accordingly, the discussion fell into abler hands, Mr. Wilson on the one side, and on the Hindoo side Nirbhaya Rama and Kisundas Joguldas, chief pundit and principal pleader respectively of the highest Government Appellate Court, the Sudder Adawlut. The Brahmans were the first to ask for quarter. The benefit of the discussion was not confined to the crowds who heard it. Two editions of the report in Marathee were speedily exhausted; all Hindoo Bombay talked of it; it stirred up inquiry as nothing else could have done, and the delusion was dispelled that Christianity feared the investigation of the learned. True to his wise, natural, and kindly policy, in this as all through his career, Mr. Wilson took care that what he himself had learned as Western truth, but yet was of Asiatic origin as to its mode, he urged on Orientals in an Eastern form, and so commended it to every man. These extracts from the report, giving the more purely native part of the discussion, will show how it played, then as still, in the East as of late growingly in the West, around the three great questions of the nature of God, the relation of morality to religion, the origin and the means of getting rid of sin, here and hereafter.

Rama Chundra began by declaring that he had abandoned the Hindoo religion because the statements of its scriptures were inconsistent with truth. Finding that the chief pundit, Nirbhaya, demanded proof that there is one God, he pointed to the works of God, and quoted, as binding on his opponent, the sloka of the Bhagavat Geet, to the effect that there is one Supreme Being, the author of birth, life, and death:

"*R. C.* In the Hindoo Shastres it is written that God was at first destitute of qualities, and that afterwards he became possessed of *suttra* (activity), *ruja* (goodness), and *tuma* (darkness). In this statement three difficulties present themselves to my mind. The declaration that God was destitute of qualities tends highly to his dishonour; and I am unable to understand, if he was destitute of power, how he could become possessed of it. I cannot admit that such qualities as ruja and tuma are to be applied to the Divinity. The Avatars (incarnations) of Vishnoo have taken human life and committed other bad actions; on this account I put no faith in them; but not so with the Avatar of Christ; he has obeyed God in all things, and given his life for man. As then the onion and the musk are known by their odour, and the tree is known by its fruits, so are the Avatars to be known by their works. Their works are evil, and therefore I renounce them.

"*Lukshmun.* I ask a question—If a subject commits a crime, is the king to be blamed for punishing him ? Is God to be blamed for taking an Avatar to punish the Rakshusas (demons) ?

"*R. C.* Amongst men a king must punish an offender according to his crime ; but God has established principles, from which men, by their own wickedness, come to evil, and go to hell, therefore there was no occasion for an Avatar to come into the world for that purpose.

"*Nirbhaya.* God was not wholly included in the Avatar, and therefore the sins of the Avatars are not to be laid to God.

"*R. C.* Suppose them to be so far disconnected with God as to be only his messengers—if they are true they will act rightly.

"*Kisundass.* Yes ! the Avatars were God's Sepoys.

"*R. C.* If God's Sepoys, why did they not act according to his will ? If they commit sin, how are they to be known as His Sepoys ?

"*K.* They are known by their badge, and not by their conduct.

"*R. C.* Where is the badge ? Nirbhaya Rama says they are only parts of God ; but if parts, they will be like himself in substance : but God has no parts ; He is everywhere present.

"*—— Shas.* If they are not from God, whence are they ?

"*R. C.* They may have been men, and therefore they are not to be worshipped.

"*K.* But if they are great and powerful, and are sent in the place of God, with power to punish the Rakshusas, they are as kings, who are not to be blamed for punishing offenders.

"*R. C.* Are we then to bow down to all who do any wonderful acts ? Their works prove that they are not part of God. If I have a piece of gold, and break it into many pieces, the qualities in each will still remain the same.

"*K.* In the God you worship you admit three Persons : and why then do you reject ten Avatars ?

"*R. C.* Not so : in the Deity there are three Persons, but one God ; as in the sun,—there is the sun, the light, and the heat, but all included in one sun. I utterly reject the Avatars. Why did they take place ? The object of the Fish Avatar was the discovery of the stolen Vedas. The object of the Tortoise was the placing the newly created earth upon his back to keep it firm. The object of the Boar Avatar was to draw up the earth from the waters, after it was sunken by the Devtya. The object of the Man-lion Avatar was to destroy the rebellious giants, Hirunnyaksha and Hirunyukushipoo. The object of the Dwarf Avatar was the destruction of the religious Bulee. The object of the Purnshoo Rama Avatar was the destruction of the Kshutriyas. The object of the Rama Avatar was the destruction of Ravana. The object of the Krishna Avatar was to destroy the giant Kungshu. These are the Avatars which you say have already taken place. Is there any appearance of God in such acts ? Could He not have accomplished these objects without assuming an Avatar ? Did His taking a form make the work easier ? I maintain, then, the reason for such Avatars is absurd. This is not the case with Christ : He came that the punishment of sin might be endured, and God's hatred of sin manifested.

"*Shukhurama Shastree.* Cannot a king do what he pleases ? Cannot he go into the bazaar and carry off what he pleases ? who can call in question his doings ?

"*Mr. W.* This is one of your other modes of explaining the actions of Krishna. A king, by his power, may prevent inquiry into his conduct ; but he assuredly can sin. If the greatness of Krishna is to be considered, it must be viewed as an aggravation of his faults.   Utterly opposed to these Avatars is that of Christ, in Whom we wish you to trust.   He came into the world to save sinners.   By His miracles he proved His divine mission.   His doctrines were holy ; and His works were holy.   He voluntarily gave His life a ransom for us.   He illustrated the divine mercy, and the divine holiness.   He procured a righteousness for man.   He prays for man in heaven.   He is able to save man.   The books which contain His history are true.   They are not like the Hindoo Shastres.   In them we find no foolish stories, no errors, and no utter want of evidence.   Read them.   Search and pray for wisdom.   Embrace the truth.

"*Shuk.* How can you show that God has forbidden the worship of idols ? for where there is one who does not, there are an hundred who do worship idols.

"*R. C.* All men are sinners, and are inclined to depart from God.

"*Mr. W.* Are the idols like God ?

"*Shuk.* Not so : but if obeisance is made to the shoe of a king in the presence of his servants, and they bear the intelligence to the king that such-a-one has great respect for him, for he every day comes and makes obeisance before his shoe, would you not consider this as paying respect to the king ?—so is it in worshipping the Deity by the idol.

"*Mr. W.* By this reasoning you make God at a distance ; and we say that He is everywhere present, and that He is everywhere propitious. Is God then in the idol ?

"*Shuk.* Yes, in everything.

"*Mr. W.* You say that God is in a particular manner in the idol, and that he is brought in by the Muntras (invocations) ; but if a Mussulman touches it he goes out !—Even your old Shastres say that you are not to worship idols.   The Vedantee philosophers near Calcutta assert this ; and they have produced many passages in support of their opinion.   There is one in the Bhagavat Geet.

"*Luk.* It is said that man cannot approach God ; therefore he must first propitiate Krishna. By Krishna God may be approached, and in no other way.

"*R. C.* You say, then, that Krishna is propitiated by idols, and that through him the Deity. But suppose I am hungry, and have a handful of rice ; if I throw that direct into the fire it will be burnt up, and I shall be deprived of my food ; but I must have a vessel to put it in, that it may be put on the fire and be cooked : but suppose the vessel I select is a dirty one, or a cracked one, then my rice will be spoiled in cooking, or the water will escape, and it will not be cooked ; and in either case I shall remain hungry.   I must then be careful that I select a proper vessel. So must it be with your Avatar —(incarnation).   Take care and get a proper one.

"*K.* We should only follow him if his works are good, and not otherwise.

"*R. C.* Therefore you must see and get a proper mediator.

"*Shuk.* I hold that by the performance of ablution the mind is washed ; for all evil proceeds from evil thoughts ; and by the performance of ablution morning and evening I am brought to think of this, and thereby a check is thrown upon evil thoughts, and so the mind is purified.

"*R. C.* In your own Shastres the inefficiency of these remedies is declared.

"*K.* I allow that unless the mind is firm these austerities are of no avail.

"*A Brahman.* What is sin ?

"*Mr. W.* The breaking of the law of God.

F

"*Brahman.* How did sin get into the world?

"*Mr. W.* How shall sin get out of the world? This should be the great inquiry. When a man is seized with cholera, he does not distress himself by inquiring about the manner in which it came to him; but earnestly seeks a cure. The grand reason why we object to your remedies is, that they all proceed on the principle that man is saved by his own works. Admit this principle and you destroy the kingdom of God."

It is "the immemorial quest, the old complaint." In the Brahmans' conferences with Ziegenbalg the same fixed ideas of the pantheist, the polytheist, the ritualist, ever recur, prefaced always by the assumption which Mr. Wilson put out of the controversy at starting, that to save the European one way and the Hindoo another "is one of the pastimes and diversions of Almighty God," as the Tamul priest of Vishnoo expressed it. The argument of Kisundass, that the nine Avatars or incarnations of Vishnoo—the tenth, Kalki, is to appear as a comet in the sky, on a white horse, with an apocalyptic sword, to restore the righteousness of the golden age—were God's Sepoys, known by their badge and not by their conduct; and that of Shookaram, that as a king God can sin as he pleases, denote the universal belief of the Hindoos that morality and god-worship have different and frequently opposite spheres. Since, about 1864, Sir Henry Maine first brought his study of early institutions and his official task of constant legislation to bear on Hindoo society, this has been recognised, and students of the science of religion, who are at the same time familiar with the social phenomena of native society, have worked it out. Hence missionary and legislator alike, together as well as separately, each in his own sphere, have to act so that the crimes sanctioned by the theology of the Hindoos shall be prohibited by an application of the moral law of Christianity, and the jurisprudence of the civilised nations of the West; while the legislator has to guard against the opposite extreme of seeming to sanction, and of really perpetuating with a new authority, the vast mass of Hindoo religious and therefore civil law, which he must leave untouched. From Lord William Bentinck and Macaulay to Lord Lawrence and Sir Henry Maine, and from Claudius Buchanan and Carey to Duff and Wilson, this double process has gone on, till India enjoys a more humane criminal code and a more perfect toleration of creeds and opinions than Great Britain itself.

The excitement caused by this discussion among the

natives of Bombay had not passed away when, in February
1831, another champion arrived to renew the controversy.
This was Mora Bhatta Dandekara, who thought to succeed
where the pundit Lukshmun and his friends had failed.
Many Brahmans were present. " They brought their chief
champion every day in a carriage, with garlands of flowers
hanging about him. They could not, however, defend their
religion," writes Mr. Wilson to his father. The debate continued during six successive evenings. Mr. Webb again presided at the request of both parties. The Brahman convert,
Rama Chundra, again took part in it, but the chief combatant
for Christianity was Mr. Wilson himself. " The Brahmans
were the first to solicit a cessation of hostilities." It was left
on this occasion to the Hindoos to publish a report of the
proceedings, and several wealthy men subscribed for the purpose. But the Bhatta had not taken notes, and he preferred
to publish as his defence a tract on the *Verification of the Hindoo Religion*, to which he challenged a reply. The debate
had, as on the former occasion, referred principally to the
character of the Divine Being, the means of salvation, the
principles of morals, and the allotment of rewards and
punishments. The *Verification* reiterates the arguments of
the former apologists for Hindooism, but it is of interest from
the attacks it makes on some statements of the Christian
Scriptures which it first perverts. This, for instance, is the
rendering of the opening verse of the fourth Gospel :—" In
the beginning was word. That word was in the heart of
God ; and the same word was manifested in the world in the
form of Christ." The real value of the tract, however, lies in
the fact that it called forth Mr. Wilson's first *Exposure of the
Hindoo Religion*, to which a translation of it by Mr. Nesbit is
prefixed :—" The Bhatta, though he has in some instances
disguised the truth, writes generally in support of what has
been called the exoteric system of Hindooism ; and a little
reflection will show that the attempt to uphold any other can
only be made with the sacrifice of the pretensions to inspiration on the part of the Hindoo scriptures, and with admissions which must prove destructive to the popular superstition. The efforts which have hitherto been made to refine
on the Brahmanical faith have hitherto proved, and must ever
prove, completely abortive. It is essentially distinguished by

exaggeration, confusion, contradiction, puerility, and immorality." Such was Mr. Wilson's earlier impression of a system, with even the innermost recesses of which further study and experience were to make him so familiar, that the Government and the Judges frequently appealed to him as the highest trustworthy authority for political and legal ends.

The Brahmans, thus twice met on the later Pooranic or Brahmanical side, determined to return to the charge, this time on the earlier Vedantic, or what was then called the esoteric ground. One Narayan Rao, English teacher in the Raja of Satara's school, accordingly wrote a reply to the first *Exposure of Hindooism*, under the signature of " An Espouser of his Country's Religion." Mora Bhatta edited the work, and took it to Mr. Wilson. Hence his publication, towards the close of 1834, of *A Second Exposure of the Hindoo Religion*. The title-page bears these lines of Sir William Jones :—

> " Oh ! bid the patient Hindoo rise and live.
> His erring mind that wizard lore beguiles,
> Clouded by priestly wiles,
> To senseless nature bows for Nature's God."

Like its predecessor, this *Exposure* is a model of kindly controversy and lofty courtesy to antagonists. " I beg of them," he writes to the Hindoos in his preface, " to continue to extend credit to me and to my fellow-labourers for the benevolence of our intentions, and to believe that anything which is inconsistent with the deepest charity is not what we would for one moment seek to defend." Both works caused a greater demand for copies than was expected, and called forth many letters from natives assuring the writer that they had been thus led to lose all confidence in the religion of their fathers. The books were translated into Bengalee and other Indian vernaculars, and continued to be long useful in letting light into many a native's mind. Mr. Wilson made good use of the admissions of the Bengalee theist Rammohun Roy, who had at that time written his principal works and had been carefully answered by Carey and Marshman. The *Second Exposure*, dedicated to Mr. James Farish who acted as interim Governor, has a further literary interest, as showing Mr. Wilson's steady as well as rapid advance in his Sanskrit studies, and in the consequent use of the Vedic, Pooranic, and Epic literature, for the demolition of error. His preface thus concludes :—" To several friends I am indebted for the loan of several Sanskrit MSS. which were not in my possession, and which I have used for enabling me to judge of the fidelity of existing translations and opinions, and correctly to make some original extracts. It was my intention at one time to have quoted more liberally from the *Upanishads* than I have done. The inspection of a great number of them led me to perceive that while they abound in metaphysical errors there is a great accordance in the few principles which they respectively unfold, and to which attention should be particularly directed."

At the time of the second of the three discussions with Brahmans on the Christian and Hindoo religions, Mr. Wilson found himself challenged to an encounter on the two very different fields of the Zoroastrianism of the Parsees and the ethics and theology of the Muhammadan Koran. His review of the Armenian *History of the Religious Wars between the Persians and Armenians*, in the *Oriental Christian Spectator* of July and August 1831, tempted the descendants of the persecuting Magi, now peaceable and loyal enough because themselves persecuted exiles, to defend the *Avasta*, their sacred Book. This controversy opens out so wide a field, alike in itself and in Mr. Wilson's career as a scholar and a missionary, that we shall reserve it and its consequences for another chapter. But an expression adverse to Muhammadanism in one of Mr. Wilson's letters to the Parsees, called forth a champion of Muhammad and the Koran, and led to the publication of a *Refutation of Muhammadanism*, in Hindostanee, Goojaratee, and Persian, which may be placed side by side with the two exposures of Hindooism.

"Hadjee Muhammad Hashim of Ispahan," who, as his name shows, had performed the pilgrimage to Mecca, and was the most learned Moulvie in Bombay, "challenged me," writes Mr. Wilson, "to the proof of the licentiousness and imposture of the author of the Koran, and I readily attempted to establish my position. After several letters had appeared in the native newspapers, the Hadjee came forward with a pamphlet of considerable size in Goojaratee and Persian, in which he evinces at once great sophistry and great ability." His *Reply to Hadjee Muhammad Hashim's Defence of the Islamic Faith* is, if we except the necessarily imperfect tract of Henry Martyn, continued by

Dr. Lee, the first controversial treatise of the kind in point of time, as the *Exposures* of Hindooism are. Dr. Pfander had not yet begun that series of Christian apologies in controversy with Muhammadans, which have done more than any other instrument to shake the apparently immovable confidence of the votaries of Islam in Agra and Delhi, in Allahabad and Lucknow, in Lahore and Peshawur, in Constantinople and Cairo, where more than one learned Moulvie now preaches the faith which once he attacked, or even translates the Christian Scriptures. It was Pfander's representation of the need for a biography of the prophet, suitable for the perusal of his followers, that led Sir William Muir, when a busy settlement officer and revenue secretary at Agra, to prepare his *Life of Mahomet*, which is the greatest in the English language, as Sprenger's is in the German. But no one can peruse Mr. Wilson's *Reply* to Muhammad Hashim without remarking how he has, in brief, anticipated Muir in shrewd insight, criticism, and keen exposure of the moral irregularities and shortcomings of Muhammad's Koran and his private life. In twenty-one necessarily condensed chapters Mr. Wilson covered the whole field of the controversy, save on its historical side—which was not raised. But it went very far down into practical life as well as ethical principles, although he does not allude to the almost unmentionable " Mostahil " or temporary husband, so essential a part of the Muhammadan system of divorce, as authoritatively laid down in the " Fatawa-i-Alamgiri." Nor did the attack of the Hadjee lead him to the consideration of a subject which recent treaties have made prominent, the relation of the sexual side of the Koran to the slave-trade and slavery. To the practical efforts in that direction he was soon to be called. But he did not spare the Hadjee in his sixth chapter, " On the mode in which Muhammad procured and treated his wives," a subject on which even Gibbon is severe.

The law of polygamous marriage and treble divorce has never been interferred with by the British Government among the forty millions of its Mussulman subjects in India, while not a few Hindoo criminal practices, like widow-burning, child-murder, hook-swinging, and human sacrifice, all in the name of religion, have been ruthlessly stopped. The result is such a horrible state of society among the Mussulmans of eastern Bengal, as was revealed in an official inquiry in 1873, and

which still goes on corrupting, under the ægis of the Koran
and its expounders.   Mr. Wilson was able to write of this
controversy as of those which preceded it, that it had shaken
the faith of some Muhammadans in different parts of the
country.   The Parsee editor of the newspaper in which it was
at first conducted, summed it up in the brief declaration, " All
the world know that Islamism has been either propagated by
the sword, or embraced on account of its licentiousness."
From far Cochin, and the south, a convert came convinced by
the *Reply*, which was reprinted in other parts of India.   In
October 1833, Mr. Wilson baptized the first Muhammadan of
Bombay who had been received into the Christian Church.
He was a fakeer, or mendicant devotee, whose secession from
Islam infuriated his intolerant brethren.   He was followed by
an inquirer, a very learned Moolla, young and master of several
tongues, who during the controversy was the stoutest opposer
of Christ, but humbly solicited baptism as now convinced of
the truth of Christianity.

It was with a peculiar interest that Mr. Wilson directed his
attention to the Jews of Western India from the very beginning
of his studies in the Konkan.   For it was on that low coast,
and in the country stretching upwards to the high road to
Poona that, according to their own tradition, their ancestors,
seven men and seven women, found an asylum, after shipwreck,
sixteen centuries before.   The little colony increased under the
protection of the Abyssinian Chief who had settled there, and
they came to be recognised as another variety of the Muhammadans.   Destitute of all historical evidence, even of their
own Law, the Beni-Israel, or sons of Israel as they called
themselves, clung all the more tenaciously, generation after
generation, to their paternal customs.   On the mainland they
became industrious agriculturists and oil-sellers.   In the new
settlement of Bombay they found work to do as artizans, and
even shopkeepers and writers.   Not a few of them are Sepoys
in the Bombay army, as many Christians are in the Madras
army.   They differ from the black Jews of Cochin, farther
south, who have sprung of the earliest emigrants from Arabia
and Indian proselytes.   Nor have they any connection with
the so-called white Jews of the same place, whose arrival in
India dates no further back probably than the earliest of those
expulsions from Spain, which, in the same way, afterwards sent

Lord Beaconsfield's ancestors to Venice. The Beni-Israel, re-
pelling the name of Yehudi as a reproach, were probably older
than both, for the Cochin-Jews say that they found them on
their arrival at Rajapoora, in the Konkan. In two careful
and learned papers, written for the Bombay Branch of the
Royal Asiatic Society, Mr. Wilson traced them to Yemen or
Arabia Felix, the Jews of which they resemble, and with
whom they hold intercourse. One of the Rothschild family, Mr.
Samuel, and Mr. Wilson himself afterwards, found the origin of
the Aden Jews in the remnant of the captivity who fled into
Egypt, where, as Jeremiah had warned them, many were sent
captive to Arabia, and where they led the Himyarite King of
Yemen, Toba, to embrace their faith. The Yemen colony was
reinforced after the dispersion, on the fall of Jerusalem, and
again on the defeat of Zenobia ; till Sana, the capital of
Yemen, became a new bulwark of Judaism against the Christians of Ethiopia on the west and the Zoroastrians of Persia
on the east. The Beni-Israel were very near Mr. Wilson's
heart. For them he prepared his first grammar of Hebrew
and Marathee. Long after he ceased to receive support for
them from the home churches he made it his special care to
raise funds on the spot. The transfer of the mission to the
General Assembly he welcomed, among other reasons, because
of the impetus it gave to this department. In 1826 a converted Cochin Jew, Mr. Sargon, had worked among them, and the
American Missionaries also had from the first cared for them.
Of the 1300 children who attended Mr. Wilson's various
schools in 1836, some 250 were Beni-Israel, and of these one
third were girls.

At the end of 1833 Bombay was visited by Joseph Wolff,
the erratic Jew of Prague, who delighted to proclaim himself
the Protestant Xavier, and lamented that he had not altogether
followed that missionary in the matter of celibacy, such was
the sorrow that their separation by his frequent wanderings
had brought on Lady Georgiana and himself. He had the year
before sent Mr. Wilson this communication :—

" CABOOL, 10th May 1832.—The bearers of these lines are the Armenian
Christians of Cabool, whose ancestors were brought to Cabool from Meshed by
Ahmed Shah ; as they had no longer any means of support at Cabool they
were constrained to emigrate from here with their wives and children, and intend now to settle themselves at Jerusalem and round Mount Ararat. As they
are very poor indeed, I cannot but recommend them to my English friends as

worthy objects of their pity and compassion for the sake of our Lord Jesus
Christ, Who will come again in the clouds of heaven in the year 1847 to establish His throne and citadel in the capital of my Jewish ancestors in the city of
Jerusalem—and at that time there shall be neither Armenian nor Englishman,
but all one in Christ Jesus crucified, the King of kings and Lord of lords.—
JOSEPH WOLFF, *Apostle of our Lord Jesus Christ for Palestine, Persia, Bok-
hara, and Balkh.*"

After emerging from Central Asia in a condition more
nearly resembling that of a nude dervish than an Anglican
clergyman, Wolff had attempted to convert Runjeet Singh at
Lahore, had himself been civilised for the time at Simla by
Lord William Bentinck and his noble wife, and had made his
way round and across India by Madras and Goa to the western
capital. Lady William Bentinck had a hard fight to assure
the Governor General's court that Wolff was not mad. " I
have succeeded," she told him, " in convincing all who have
seen and heard you that you are not cracked, but I have not
convinced them that you are not an enthusiast." Wolff
replied, "My dear Lady William, I hope that I am an enthusiast, or, as the Persian Soofees say, that I am drunk with the
love of God. Columbus would never have discovered America
without enthusiasm." And so Wolff afterwards revealed the
true fate of Conolly and Stoddart. In the amusing and by
no means uninstructive *Travels and Adventures*, which, in 1861,
was dedicated "by his friend and admirer" to the Right
Hon. Benjamin Disraeli, we have these glimpses of Bombay
society, and of Mr. Wilson, with whom he afterwards frequently corresponded on mission-work for the Jews and the
eastern Christians. " Wolff arrived in Bombay on the 29th
November, and was received by all classes of denominations
of Christians there with true cordiality and love. He was the
guest of Mr. James Farish, who was several times Deputy-
Governor of Bombay. Lord Clare, the Governor, called, and
heard a lecture which was delivered before a large audience.
Wolff also lectured in Farish's house as well as in the Town
Hall of Bombay, when English, Parsees, Armenians, Mussulmans, Portuguese, and Hindoos were present. One of the
Parsees announced a lecture on the principles of the Parsees,
in which he tried to adopt the style and actions of Joseph
Wolff, but he was dreadfully cut up in the papers. . . . Wolff
had a public discussion with the Muhammadans at Bombay,
when the most distinguished members of the British Govern-

ment were present, both of the military and civil departments, including Farish, Robert Money, and the missionaries Wilson and Nesbit, and also Parsees." Mr. Wilson and Mr. Stevenson introduced him to all departments of their mission-work, but he was especially interested in the Beni-Israel, some of whom he had first seen at Poona. He writes of "those learned, excellent, eloquent, devoted, and zealous missionaries of the Scotch Kirk," and continues,—"Wolff went also with Mr. Wilson to see one of the celebrated Yoghees, who was lying in the sun in the street, the nails of whose hands were grown into his cheek, and a bird's nest upon his head. Wolff asked him, 'How can one obtain the knowledge of God ?' He replied, 'Do not ask me questions ; you may look at me, for I am God !' Wolff indignantly said to him, 'You will go to hell if you speak in such a way.' " The subtle pantheism of the ascetic absorbed into Vishnoo was beyond the Judæo-Christian dervish. He left soon after for Yemen and Abyssinia, whence we shall hear from him again.

A wandering missionary of like zeal but more intensity of spirit visited Bombay in the same year, Mr. Anthony Groves of Exeter, first and most catholic of those who call themselves "The Brethren." Having parted with all he possessed, according to his rendering of Christ's precept—"Lay not up for yourselves treasures on earth," as expounded in a pamphlet on *Christian Devotedness*, he proceeded by St. Petersburg to Baghdad in 1831, and there commenced his mission. He had as his secretary, and the tutor of his children, the deaf lad who afterwards became remarkable as Dr. Kitto. Plague, inundation, and famine, broke up the schools in which he gave a Christian education to eighty children under five masters. His own wife and children fell victims, and in 1833 he visited India to learn lithographic printing, and acquaint himself with the experience of men like Duff and Wilson. But his speculative views were too far advanced for that. He was a dervish of a different type from the buoyant Wolff, but still a dervish. He held that, as the gospel was to be preached for a witness by missionaries supported by the free-will offerings of Christendom, before the end come, no mission should continue in the same place for more than five years. After a visit to England he returned with a considerable reinforcement of coadjutors in 1836. On both occasions Mr. Wilson showed

him that hospitality and did him that social service, which
were already beginning to be drawn upon by all visitors who
could plead any interest of any kind in the East and its
people.

Another type of missionary policy was supplied by Mr.
Francis William Newman, brother of the greater John Henry
Newman, and son of a well-known banker. After giving
brilliant promise, since well redeemed, as Fellow of Balliol up
to 1830, Mr. F. W. Newman drifted away from the Thirty-
Nine Articles into the views of Mr. Groves, whose pamphlet
attracted him also to Baghdad. There he hoped to draw the
Muhammadans to the Arian form at least of Christianity, by
such purely moral evidence of its superiority as the lives of
really disinterested Englishmen might supply. He dreamed
of a colony "so animated by faith, primitive love, and disinterestedness, that the collective moral influence of all might
interpret and enforce the words of the few who preached."
He looked for success "where the natives had gained experience in the characters of the Christian family around them."
This was precisely what Wilson, of all missionaries who have
ever worked in the East, did in Bombay; but he succeeded
where Mr. F. W. Newman soon failed, because he never ceased
to show that a disinterested life and the Christian family sprang
directly out of those "mystical doctrines of Christianity"
which the author of that sadly suggestive book the *Phases of
Faith*,[1] began by postponing. Wolff, Groves, and F. W.
Newman were all on one right track, the superiority of what
is called the internal evidences, of arguments addressed to the
moral and spiritual faculties of heathen and Muhammadan.
So had Wilson begun, and so did he continue all through his
career, from the letter quoted at page 46, to his testimony,
along with that of Bishop French of Lahore, regarding the
importance of witness-bearing, at the Allahabad Conference in
1873. But Wilson did not make the mistake of cutting the
stream off below the fountain-head, and hence the permanent
and developing fruitfulness of his work to all time and among
all creeds and classes. Francis Newman returned to England
in two years, himself partly affected by a Muhammadan car-

---

[1] Compare the "second period" of that book entitled *Strivings after a
more Primitive Christianity* with the greater *Apologia* of his brother, John
Henry Newman, now Cardinal.

penter of Aleppo, to find the Tractarian movement beginning, and his brother and his whole family alienated from him. He would not return to the East; considering the idea of a Christian Church propagating Christianity while divided against itself to be ridiculous. So Ecclesiasticism drove him out, he thinks; and we may admit this much, that Protestant Evangelicalism lost not a little in the brothers Newman, abroad and at home, whoever was to blame. The unity which each has to this day sought they would have found, as John Wilson did, in catholic work for the Master, pursued in loving co-operation with missionaries of all sects in India. The mission in Baghdad and Persia, abandoned by Groves and Newman, he in due time did his best to revive with the only means at his disposal.

In 1835 the society which Mr. Wilson had gradually gathered around him lost its greatest lay ornament in the death of Mr. Robert C. Money, secretary to the Government. The son of Wilberforce's friend, he had ever shown in Bombay all the excellencies of "the Clapham sect," as a devoted member of the Church of England. Under the Charter of 1833 Archdeacon Carr had become the first Bishop of Bombay, and the Church Missionary Society had received a new impetus there. From the first Mr. Money became the attached friend of Mr. Wilson, and co-operated with him in every good work. Men of all classes, native as well as English, united to raise as his memorial the Church of England Institution, or English College, in Bombay, which bears his name. Mr. Wilson was for some time engaged in the preparation for the press of a memoir, and of the papers, of one who, like Mr. Webb and Mr. Law at the same time, and Sir Bartle Frere at a later period, reflected lustre on the Bombay Civil Service.

To the regret of all classes in the Presidency, Sir John Malcolm resigned the office of Governor at the close of 1830, and with that ceased those splendid services to India and Asia right up to the Caspian, which justified Sir Walter Scott's eulogies and the great Duke's friendship. Not the least valued, certainly not the least sincere, of the addresses presented to his Excellency who had come out to India as an infantry cadet at thirteen, was that which Mr. Wilson wrote and signed as Secretary to the Bombay Missionary Union. At a time when the Charter of 1833 had not removed the silly opposi-

tion of the East India Company, these men, some of whom
had been driven from Calcutta and for a time threatened with
expulsion from Bombay, thanked "the Honourable Major-
General Malcolm, G.C.B., Governor of Bombay, for the facilities which he has granted for the preaching of the gospel in
all parts of the Bombay territories, for his favourable exertions
for the abolition of Suttee, and for the kind manner in which
he has countenanced Christian education." His reply was
that of the purely secular but truly tolerant statesman. He
begged Mr. Wilson to assure the missionaries "that it is solely
to their real and Christian humility, combined, as I have ever
found it, with a spirit of toleration and good sense, that I owe
any power I have possessed of aiding them in their good and
pious objects, which . . . must merit and receive the support
of all who take an interest in the promotion of knowledge, the
advancement of civilisation, and the cause of truth." So had
Mountstuart Elphinstone spoken before him. So, and even
still more warmly, did Lord William Bentinck afterwards
reply to a favourable address from the Calcutta missionaries.

    Sir John Malcolm met in Egypt his successor, Lord Clare,
whose Irish blood he found inflamed because of the delay in
the arrival of the steamer at Cosseir. The Earl of Clare was
followed in 1835 by Sir Robert Grant, who keenly sympathised with Mr. Wilson and his work on its highest side. Lord
Clare had, indeed, specially requested Mr. Stevenson to continue to give religious instruction in the Poona School at first
established by that missionary, after it had been transferred
to the Government, and he had privately assisted missions. But
Sir Robert Grant was a man to whom Wilson could, in the
first year of his administration, publicly apply this language
when appropriately dedicating to his Excellency a sermon on
"The British Sovereignty in India." The dedication was
based on "the confidence which I entertain, grounded both
on your well-known sentiments and your actings since your
arrival in this Presidency, that the cause of Christian and
general philanthropy in India, so dear to the heart of your
distinguished father, will ever secure your warmest support
in the high station in which God in his providence has placed
you." Sir Robert Grant, and his elder brother Lord Glenelg,
were sons worthy of Charles Grant, who, from his earliest
experience as a Bengal civilian in 1776, had devoted himself

to the moral and spiritual regeneration of the people of India. Afterwards, as author of the *Observations on the Moral Condition of the Hindoos and the Means of Improving it*, which were written in 1792, and have almost the character of prediction; as chairman of the Court of Directors and member for the county of Inverness, he proved to be the mainspring of all the reforms which were forced by successive charters on the East India Company, up to that of 1833. While his elder son assisted him in the House of Commons, and afterwards as a Cabinet Minister and a peer, it fell to Sir Robert to carry out in Western India the enlightened provisions of that charter. This he did with a wisdom and a success which more than justified Mr. Wilson's eulogy ; while in his private character he became, when at the head of the Bombay Government, the author of those hymns, four of which Lord Selborne has embalmed for ever in his *Book of Praise*, among the four hundred best sacred lyrics of the language. The name of the author of the strains beginning "Saviour, when in dust I lie," and "When gathering clouds around I view," will be always dear to Christendom ; but these hymns were the least of his services to its cause. His last act as Governor of Bombay was to request Mr. Wilson to submit to Government a plan for the practical encouragement of a sound and useful education of the natives, by whomsoever conducted, whether by the State, by missionaries, or by natives themselves.

The sermon on the British Sovereignty in India, which, on the 8th of November 1835, Mr. Wilson preached in St. Andrew's Kirk for the Scottish Mission, marks the broad imperial view which he had already learned to take of our position in Southern India as rulers, and of our relation to the feudatory Princes who have been incorporated with our political system by Lord Canning's patent only since the Mutiny of 1857. The preacher's subject was the not dissimilar mission of Cyrus (Isaiah xlv. 1-4, 6-13). Mr. Wilson spoke at an "epoch-making" time, when the Charter of 1833 had in India just begun to operate in the two directions of opening the trade of the East India Company to the world, and securing the education of the people in the English language, and all that that fact involved. He was too wise and equitable a missionary to exaggerate his success on the one hand, or to argue on the other that the progress of the Christian church in India would have been greater if the State had devoted public funds to it as well as to education.   At a later period, in 1849, he thus wrote : "Though it be devoutly admitted that the exalted Saviour demands the homage of governments and communities as well as of individuals, it is obvious that the professed expression of that homage by the exaction of pecuniary contribution in support even of Christian Institutions, from an unwilling people, may be questioned without any want of loyalty to Christianity itself."

All through this period the Bombay Union of Missionaries showed great activity in the number and variety of the questions which it discussed.   Mr. Wilson was the secretary and the most energetic member.   Now we find him in 1832 submitting a petition, presented by Lord Bexley to the House of Lords, for the amelioration of the Hindoo and Muhammadan laws of property and inheritance as they affected converts to Christianity, which resulted in Lord William Bentinck's first concession on that point, to be completed long after by Lord Dalhousie and Lord Lawrence.   Again he reports on the purchasing and receiving donations of Oriental works for the use of the Union.   Now he gives information regarding the similar Christian Union in China.   Again he seeks light on the delicate questions raised by converts as to marriage and divorce, which he helped Sir Henry Maine and the Legislature to settle half a century after.   Then he proposes such questions as these—'"Are there any instances of a remarkable progress of Christianity among a people without the gospel being previously, generally, and simultaneously, proclaimed among them?"   "How is the statement that Christ is an object of worship in his entire person consistent with the declaration that Christians worship the immaterial God alone?"   " What influences tend to modify and destroy Caste?"   The growing extension of intemperance and drunkenness under the excise and opium laws, among communities who are temperate by climate, custom, and creed, gave at that early period a peculiar interest to the question which was thus decided : " The Union are of the opinion that it is the duty of all Christians in India to promote and encourage the cause of temperance societies ; that these societies should be formed upon the principles of the Bible, and that they should exhibit the prevalence of Christian principles as the grand means of pro-

ducing temperance ; also that they should be formed upon
the principle of entire abstinence from all ardent spirits,
opium, tobacco, and other intoxicating drugs, except when
used as medicines, or in cases of extreme urgency and necessity ; and moderation in the use of fermented and other
liquors."

The spirit of union and co-operation which always marks
the various missionaries abroad in the face of the common foe,
was further illustrated by a communication from the Presbytery of Kaffraria, which expressed a desire for friendly correspondence. To the somewhat narrow remark that Calvinistic
Presbyterian missionaries should be more united than they
are, or than the Churches at home, Mr. Wilson appended the
characteristic note, "We would add in the spirit of gospel
catholicism — and all Christian missionaries." This letter,
dated 4th July 1832, and signed "John Bennie, Moderator,"
describes the work of four missionaries at Chumee and Lovedale, "the two oldest stations, where there is a considerable
population," and Pirie and Burnshill. In the half-century since
we get this glimpse at South Africa, Lovedale has become the
brightest light among its tribes, and the native question has
again and again sought a settlement, in the East Indian sense,
by seven wars.

India itself and China were soon after to lose their two
foremost scholar-missionaries, in the death of Dr. Carey at
Serampore on the 9th June 1834, at the age of seventy-three ;
and of Dr. Morrison at Canton on the 1st August, at the
comparatively early age of fifty-three. Mr. Wilson, who was
still beginning in Western India and Asia the preparatory
work that they had done so well for Eastern and Northern
India, and for China and Eastern Asia, wrote thus of the two
men whose special merits he, of all others, was best fitted to
describe :—

"Dr. Carey, the first of living missionaries, the most hononred and the
most snccessfnl since the time of the apostles, has closed his long and influential career. Indeed his spirit, his life, and his labours were trnly
apostolic. Called from the lowest class of the people, he came to this
country without money, without friends, without learning. He was exposed
to severe persecntion, and forced for some time to labour with his own hands
for his support ; yet then even, in his brief intervals of leisure, he found time
to master the Hebrew and Bengalee langnages, to make considerable progress
in the Sanskrita, and to write with his own hand a complete version of the
Scriptures in the language of the country. The Spirit of God, which was in

him, led him forward from strength to strength, supported him under priva-
tion, enabled him to overcome in a fight that seemed without hope. Like the
beloved disciple, whom he resembled in simplicity of mind, and in seeking to
draw sinners to Christ altogether by the cords of love, he outlived his trials to
enjoy a peaceful and honoured old age, to know that his Master's cause was
prospering, and that his own name was named with reverence and blessing in
every country where a Christian dwelt. Perhaps no man ever exerted a
greater influence for good on a great cause. Who that saw him, poor, and in
seats of learning uneducated, embark on such an enterprise, could ever dream
that, in little more than forty years, Christendom should be animated with the
same spirit, thousands forsake all to follow his example, and that the word of
life should be translated into almost every language, and preached in almost
every corner of the earth ?"

" Dr. Morrison, whose name will be held in everlasting remembrance, died
at Canton on the 1st of August last, at the age of fifty-three. He had
laboured as a missionary for nearly twenty-seven years in China, and (with
the assistance of Dr. Milne in some of the books) translated the Scriptures
into Chinese, compiled and published a copious Chinese dictionary, and several
important philological works, prepared and circulated many Chinese tracts,
founded the Anglo-Chinese College at Malacca, and proved the means of the
conversion and scriptural education of Leang Afa, who is now labouring, with
some success, as a native preacher. He was also for several years interpreter
to the English Factory, and he supported himself, and contributed much to
the cause of missions, from the salary which he received in consequence of the
situation which he thus held."

More than any other missionary in the East, Mr. Wilson
proved to be the successor of these two men. It is a subject
of regret that he could not become the biographer of Carey,
whose life has yet to be worthily written. The Memoir by
Eustace Carey, his nephew, was written avowedly at the
request of the Baptist Missionary Society, which had misunderstood Dr. Carey from the first, and it is unworthy of
the subject. The Lives of the Serampore Missionaries, by
the late John Clark Marshman, C.S.I., is the most valuable
contribution yet made to the history of Christian and social
progress in India, by one who is emphatically the Historian
of British India before the Mutiny ; but its theme is too wide
to represent William Carey in all the details of his unique
career.

CHAPTER V.

1830-1835.

TOURS TO NASIK ; TO JALNA AND ELORA ; TO GOA, KOLHAPORE, AND MAHABLESHWAR.

Man the Missionary's business—Tours of Officials and Missionaries—John
Wilson a delightful companion—*First Tour* with Mr. Farrar—The Glories
of the Ghauts—The Ramoshee Brigands—Brahmanical Opposition at
Nasik—The Sacred Godavery—*Second Tour* to Jalna—Battle of Korigaum
—Ahmedabad—Worship of the Monkey God—Historical Characters—
The Telescope and Hindooism—A Christian Government quoted against
Christianity—Elora—Christ preached in the Cave Temple of Kailas—
Opposition of the Military Authorities at Jalna—Mr. Wilson seriously
injured by a Horse—Strange Iconoclasm—Christian Sectarianism out of
place in India—*Third Tour* to Goa—Old Scenes in the Konkan—Dr.
Claudius Buchanan—The Inquisition at Goa—New and Old Goa—Forged
Romish Vedas—Latin Conversations with Portuguese Priests—A Blushing
Prioress—His Excellency the Vice Rey—The Augustinians and Franciscans
—The Representatives of Sivajee—The Raja of Kolhapore—Satara—
Mahableshwar—A Tiger springs up near Mr. Wilson.

" The business of the missionary is with man," was a saying
of Dr. Chalmers that Mr. Wilson frequently quoted. To
know India, of all countries, is to be familiar with its people ;
to be acquainted with its princes ; and to understand the
relation of the British Government and its administrative
systems to both. For a missionary to know India, he must
add to all that the study, at first hand, of its religions and
their learned men, Brahmanical, Muhammadan, and Non-
Aryan. He must possess the ability to lay a pure and a
historical Christianity alongside both the administrative
systems and the religious philosophies or cultures, so as to
saturate the former with the positive and direct moral spirit
which they necessarily lack from political conditions, and to
overthrow the latter by the more purely spiritual and potent
force of Christ Himself. The ordinary missionary will do well

if he confines his energy to one of the three faiths. As a matter of fact, most Indian missionaries have worked among the Hindoo or the aboriginal communities, who are vast enough. But Mr. Wilson was a pioneer whose deliberate equipment, as well as his evangelic ambition allowed no human or traditional substitute for Christianity to remain unstudied or unattacked. The official, civilian or soldier, however zealous, has to be content with the indirect and frequently unconscious disintegration which has been going on in India ever since Clive obtained the civil government at Benares from the effete emperor, Shah Alum. But, freed from the lower responsibility of political considerations, Mr. Wilson could use all that makes the civilian efficient, and press it home at once with a moral disinterestedness and a spiritual force, which the natives, high and low, were not slow to appreciate. Like the civilian, and to a far greater extent than the average of the eight or nine hundred members of the covenanted civil service who have always governed the millions of India so well, he held the key to the ears and hearts of the people in a knowledge of their languages and hoary civilisations, Aryan and Semitic. Like the district officer and commissioner, too, but with a freedom and over an extent of territory they rarely know, he made his almost annual tours, east, and south, and north, to the very centre of India, to Goa, and again to the far Indus and the courts of Rajpootana, till he knew peasant and prince, rude ascetic, sacerdotal Brahman, and scornful Moulvie, as no one hedged round by officialism could do.

Next to mastering the languages it was his object to mix with the people who spoke them. His model was no lower than " Our Lord and His apostles," with whom he had more than once to silence ignorant critics in England. " Wherever," he wrote, " the objects of their ministry most advantageously presented themselves, they were prepared to fulfil it. The temple, the synagogue, and the private apartment ; the narrow street and the public highway ; the open plain and the lofty mount ; the garden and the wilderness ; the bank of the river and the margin of the sea ; were equally hallowed by these heavenly teachers." And he, like them, was in the East ! " But many say, ' Leave this preaching without doors to native agents, who will be best able to bear the exposure

connected with it.' . . . Even after we have been blessed,
through God's mercy, with native preachers, we must for
some time show them in our own persons the lively example
of an apostolic ministration. . . . Xenophon remarked that
the Asiatics would not fight unless under Greek auxiliaries."
The "exposure" Mr. Wilson ridiculed, although his most
fruitful tours were made at an early period, when even roads
were not, and a paternal government had not doubled its
debt to develop the resources of the country by great public
works.   Rarely did he find a comfortable post-house or even
tolerable resting-place when out of the beaten track of military
stations and civilian hospitalities.   Studying nature as well
as man ; preaching, speaking, examining daily ; keeping up
the correspondence rendered necessary by his supervision of
the still infant Mission in Bombay ; answering references of
all kinds from missionaries, officials, and scholars, he found—
because he made—the tour a holiday.   On such occasions he
carried a few books in an old satchel, manuals, sometimes in
manuscript, of the botany, geology, and political relations with
the feudatory princes, being as indispensable as the bundles
of vernacular and Sanskrit writings which he circulated.
Thus he was never alone, and every tour added to his multifarious collection of objects of natural history and archæology,
to say nothing of Oriental MSS., on which he lectured to his
students and friends.   When accompanied by a brother
missionary, and frequently by survey and settlement officers,
like Colonel Davidson, whom he met in his wanderings, he
proved the most genial of companions.   His stores of information, old and new, interspersed with humorous anecdote and
a child-like fun, turned the frequent mishaps of jungle
journeys into sources of amusement.   And then, when the
travelling or the preaching of the day was done, and the
rough dinner was over at the tent door or in the native
"dhurmsala," or enclosed quadrangle, there went up to
heaven the family supplication for Gentile and Jew, and dear
ones near and far away.   To be on tour in the glorious cold
season of India, from November to March, is to enjoy life in
the purest and most intelligent fashion, whether it be in the
Viceroy's camp or in the more modest tent of the district
civilian.   To be on a missionary tour with one who thus
understands the people and loves them, is to know the highest
form of enjoyment that travel can give.

Mr. Wilson's first tour commenced in the middle of January 1831, after a year of organising work in Bombay. His companion was the Rev. Mr. Farrar,[1] of the Church Missionary Society, who was just beginning to be able to speak to the Marathas. They rode upwards of 400 miles. Their most distant point was the sacred Brahmanical city of Nasik, on the upper waters of the Godavery. They set out by the Bhore Ghaut, now on the Madras line of railway, by Poona, and Ahmednuggur, and returned by the Thull Ghaut, now ascended by the railway to Calcutta. They sailed from Bombay to Panwel, on the mainland, passing the cave-temple islands of Elephanta, Salsette, and Karanja, which Mr. Wilson had previously visited with the civilian scholars Messrs. Law and Webb. At the next village he met with the first specimens of those aboriginal tribes of the jungle for whom he was to do so much, the Katkarees, who prepare catechu. His first view of the glories of the Ghauts of the Syhadree range he thus describes :—" As we rose from the valley a most majestic scene began to unfold itself. When I beheld hill rising upon hill, and mountain upon mountain—the sun setting in glory behind the towering clouds—the distant ocean, forests, rivers, and villages—and when, looking around me, I observed, amid this scene of grandeur, a single stone usurping the place of Jehovah, the Creator of all, I felt and expressed the utmost horror at idolatry, and the baseness, guilt, and stupidity of man."

Some experience of Poona convinced him of the superior importance of Bombay as a centre. On their way to Ahmednuggur one of the servants was attacked by the Ramoshee tribe of robbers, at that time scouring the country under their famous leader Oomajee Naik, compared with whom, writes Mr. Wilson, Rob Roy might be reckoned an honest man. But Nasik was the point of interest, a place of which Mr. Wilson used to say that it first stoned him, and, forty years after, would not allow him to leave Western India for a time without presenting him with a eulogistic and grateful address on parchment from its principal inhabitants of every sect.

[1] Dr Wilson used to tell afterwards how he dandled Mr. Farrar's boy, the present Canon Farrar, on his knee. But of his Anglo-Indian childhood Canon Farrar assures us he has only a dim remembrance.

Nasik was soon after occupied by the Church Missionary Society, who have established there the Christian village of Sharanpoor, an industrial settlement with a congregation of five hundred, of whom some two hundred are communicants, and a training school for freed Africans, who helped Dr. Livingstone. The Godavery river, the scenery on the lower reaches of which Sir Charles Trevelyan, when Governor of Madras, compared to that of the Rhine between Coblentz and Bingen, rises at the village of Trimbuk, only fifty miles from the Indian Ocean at Bombay, and sixteen miles south-west of Nasik. The Maratha Brahmans give out that its source is connected, by a divine underground channel, with that of the Ganges in the snows of the Himalayas. The traditional fountain is a stone platform, approached by a flight of 690 stone steps, on a hill behind Trimbuk village. On to that platform the stream falls from the rock, drop by drop, into the mouth of an idol, out of which the water trickles into a reservoir. Sir Richard Temple, when Chief Commissioner of the Central Provinces, sketched the beauties of the river alike with brush and pen. It has been the scene of the greatest successes as well as the most serious and expensive failures of the Madras school of Irrigation.

Of the second tour, eastward to Jalna and the caves of Elora, in the native State of Hyderabad, the country which the British Government had saved for the Nizam all through the chaos of Maratha, Hyder Ali, and Tippoo wars, we have an account from Mr. Wilson's own pen, in letters to his wife. At a time and in a country for the greater portion of which there were no maps, we find the tour duly marked out in a chart showing the road or track, on one side of it every village with the number of its houses, and on the other the day and date on which each was reached. The Rev. James Mitchell was his companion. After Poona they walked or rode short stages of from ten to fourteen miles a day at first. At Alandi, the first stage onward, they found a great assemblage for the festival of Inanoba, a god of whom Mr. Wilson gives a humorous, but, towards the people, kindly account, published in the *Memoir* of his wife. At the next village, Phulshuhur, he inspected a settlement which was the first of a curious experiment intended to train that most valuable but neglected class, the Eurasians, to agricultural pursuits. Sir John Mal-

colm, in his farewell minute of 1830, had discussed the subject to which the present Governor of Bombay, Sir R. Temple,
has given attention. The record of this tour, like the encounter
with the Ramoshee brigands in that which preceded it, throws
light on the riots and robberies which have again broken out
in the Bombay Dekhan to an alarming extent : —

"THE COLOSSAL PILLAR AT KORIGAUM.—This monument was erected by
the British Government in commemoration of the brave resistance made by
Captain Staunton. The pillar is tastefully constructed. It is in charge of a
Sepoy, who was engaged in the action which it commemorates. He gave us a
plain account of the battle.

"THE HEADMAN OF SHIKRAPOOR.—After we had preached in the village,
and distributed books and tracts, the Patel sent for us. The court of his
house was large, but it bore marks of decay. He received us very kindly, and
invited us into an inner apartment. As soon as we had sat down he brought
out a box containing about twenty very handsome European engravings. He
requested us to translate all their titles into Marathee, and to write them upon
the covers. We complied with his request ; and he told us that never in his
life, advanced now to seventy years, had he met such Sahebs as we. We
preached the gospel to him ; and he furnished us with *pan supári* (betel nut
and a green leaf), according to the native custom. Mr. Mitchell had a great
aversion to chew his offering, and he almost spoilt our discourse by pleading
in excuse the force of habit.

"AHMEDABAD is situated to the westward of Seroor. The village is much
gone to decay, on account of the road to Poona having been changed by the
English. It is remarkable for nothing but the residence of the oldest representative of the once famous house of Pawar, of which an interesting account
is given by Sir John Malcolm. We visited the old man, according to his personal invitation, and were received with much kindness. We were surprised
to find that he was unable to read. He showed us the different buildings
connected with his *wada* (palace), and we endeavoured to engage the interest
of his mind by giving him and his few attendants a simple statement of the
gospel, and by allowing him to view the neighbourhood through the medium
of Mr. Mitchell's telescope.

"WORSHIP OF HANUMAN, THE MONKEY GOD.—In most of the villages of
the Dekhan there is a small temple of Hanuman, under the name of Marwate,
without the principal gate. The images are exceedingly rude. They are
liberally besmeared with red lead : and, alas ! they are viewed as the guardians
and benefactors of the neighbourhood, and frequently resorted to. One of
them fronted the place in which we usually sat at Parner. The votaries generally walked twelve or nineteen times round it, and prostrated themselves before
it, and sometimes refrigerated it with cold water and adorned it with garlands. A great majority of them were females demanding the boon of children. The exercise which they take in connection with their worship may not
be without effect.

"THE CHARACTER OF THE NATIVES of these agricultural districts is almost
daily sinking in my estimation. Falsehood and dishonesty, and, when practicable, incivility, are daily brought before my notice. During the night which
we spent in Jumgaum, we required a guard of two Ramoshees, three Bheels,
and two Mhars ! The latter individuals were always on the watch to give the
alarm. The others, who, as you know, are professed robbers, think it beneath
their dignity to keep their eyes open even when they are paid for their guard-

ianship, and represent it as necessary, as I believe it is, to the safety of travellers. When we arrived at Nimba Dera, on the forenoon of Tuesday the
28th November, we were met by a most impertinent Brahman, who first by
falsehood, and afterwards by passion, endeavoured to drive us from the only
place where we could get shelter from the sun. He was joined by a companion, who without hesitation united with him in wickedness. Nothing but
a severe reprimand, and the threat that we would represent the matter to the
Collector, effected anything.

"FAILURE OF THE CROPS.—In some of the villages through which we
passed on our way to Nimba Dera, we were informed that, on account of the
great drought, the crops of the season had almost entirely failed. Though
the complaints of the natives were conveyed to us in a tone which clearly
intimated to us anything but resignation to the divine will, they were very
heartrending. Starvation appeared to be apprehended by not a few, and,
from the dread of it, many of the inhabitants had departed with their cattle
to the banks of the Godavery and Kandesh. We distributed at several places
a few rupees, and they were received with joy. We endeavoured to improve
the righteous dispensation of divine providence, and we urged upon all the
acknowledgment of the supreme God, who alone can give rain and fruitful
seasons.

"THE UPPER GODAVERY, 1st December.—In the evening we took a walk
on the banks of the Godavery. It is at this place, and even at this season, a
very considerable stream. Numbers of the Brahmans were performing their
evening ablutions at the spot where the river Prawara enters it. They form
a numerous class in the neighbourhood. In Prawara Sangam there are a
hundred houses of them ; in Toka, which is situated on the opposite bank,
there is the same number ; and in Gaigaam, about half a quarter of a mile
farther down the river, there are about ninety houses. Many of them engage
in agriculture, but a great source of their support is the *dakshina* (alms)
which they receive from the pilgrims who come to bathe in the *holy waters*.
This cluster of villages, and Nasik and Paithan, form the only sacred towns
on the Godavery which are situated in the Marathee country. I should think
that their celebrity is on the decline. The progress of knowledge, and the
increasing poverty of the people, contribute principally to the destruction of
the pristine zeal. No true philanthropist can regret the circumstance, for
nothing can be more melancholy than the delusion under which men labour
when they believe that they can wash away their sins in a river, and acquire
a stock of merit by all the trouble, fatigue, and expense which they incur in
the fulfilment of their wishes. In the course of the day we had laboured
much to expose it, and, I trust, with some effect. None of the natives, like
Shookaram Shastree, at the first discussions in Bombay, alluded to any
sacramental use of the waters—a circumstance which is worthy of notice, and
particularly as we had intercourse with the most learned Shastree. The
benefit of ablution was argued to be *positive*, to be an invaluable and
unavoidable blessing to all who use it, according to the many promises and
declarations of the Shastres relative to the virtues of the Ganges. The
Hindoos and Roman Catholics are wonderfully agreed about the efficacy of
rites intrinsically considered. On returning home we saw a very large and
splendid meteor proceeding in a direction horizontal to the earth. It was
visible for a considerable time. The natives assured us that a few days ago
hundreds of a similar nature were seen, and that they were greatly terrified
by the unusual occurrence.

"At Toka we went to the house of Baba Shastree, the richest Brahman in
the place, and we were rather surprised to find him desirous of conducting us
into an inner apartment of the upper story. We were happy to perceive the

liberality of his sentiments and feelings, and we had no objections to gratify him. We found a respectable congregation assembled, and we gave a general view of the Gospel, and of the objections which we commonly urge against Hindooism. We were heard with respect, and nothing was urged in reply to us except the encouragement granted by Europeans to idolatry. Augustus Brookes of Benares, known among the natives as *Gasti Brúk*, it was said, had become a convert to Hindooism. The East India Company was liberal in its donations to temples. The great Saheb, Governor Elphinstone, had distributed money among the Brahmans when he visited Toka, and had given a salaam and Rs.100 to the god. The Collectors were in the habit of employing Brahmans to perform *anusthans* for rain, etc. It was exceedingly difficult to deal with the observations which they made on these subjects. I told them, on the information of the late Dr. Turner, Bishop of Calcutta, communicated to me during his visit to Bombay, that Mr. Brookes had expressed his regret for the countenance which he had given to the delusions of the natives ; that it was not to be concluded that, because the Company had continued the revenue of temples, it approved of these temples, and that I hoped that it would soon see the impropriety and sin of giving any support to them ; that I could not credit the statements given about Mr. Elphinstone, a gentleman who greatly promoted the improvement of the natives, and who subscribed to the propagation of the gospel, and that the Rs.100 were probably placed by the Brahmans without his consent before the idol ; and that, while the *anusthans* were performed to please the natives, the payment of them by the Company, and every other species of encouragement granted to idolatry, was decidedly sinful. I also expressed my hope that the time was at hand when right views on these subjects, and other practices sanctioned without consideration, would generally prevail among Europeans. *All the Brahmans admitted the propriety of the Company, as a Christian Government, giving nothing more than toleration to the Hindoo religion.* Their wishes, I doubt not, were nevertheless what we might expect them to be.

"At half-past nine o'clock he invited us to return to his lodgings, with the view of witnessing a display of fireworks, and the performance of native musicians, etc., which he intended as a compliment to us. We explained our views of the sanctity of the Sabbath ; and it was with great difficulty that he accepted of our refusal. We gave him credit for his intentions ; and I have no doubt that his respect for us was increased by our consistency. I should have mentioned before, that I asked him why he had left the 'holy city' of Kashee (Benares), and come on a journey to Toka in search of merit. He pleaded the respect of his family for the idol at Toka. When I told him that in the Marathee language, the term *kashikare* was equivalent to that of an *arch-villain*, and that the circumstance told little in favour of the 'sacredness' of Varanási, he laughed very heartily.

"ELORA, *4th December.*—After a very fatiguing ride in the sun we arrived at Roza. At this place there is a bungalow belonging to a Mussulman gentleman ; but we found it occupied by two officers. They did not invite us to come in ; and after tying our ponies to a branch of a tree, and engaging in social worship, we stretched ourselves on the stone floor of a large mausoleum, built by the Emperor Aurungzeb. We took our *breakfast* at one o'clock ; and proceeded to make our first visit to *Kailas*, the principal Brahmanical excavation of Elora. We remained in it till after sunset, examining its many wonders and curiosities.

"*5th December.*—We set out very early in the morning to the excavations. We commenced with those situated in the northern part of the hill, and went regularly through them all proceeding to the south. We gave them a very minute examination ; and I wrote down 50 pages of notes on them, of which

the following is a summary :—The caves are situated in a ridge of hills which
runs north and south, with an inclination in the centre towards the east.
They are not far from the base of the hills ; and the entrance to them commands a very extensive and interesting view of the Dekhan towards the west.
The rock out of which they are cut is of the trap formation, and well suited
for their marvellous workmanship. They are undoubtedly of three different
kinds, Jain, Buddhist, and Brahmanical. The Jain caves are situated in the
northern part of the hills, the Brahmanical in the centre, and the Buddhist
in the south. It is difficult to say which of them are the most extensive and
interesting. The Brahmanical excel as works of art. The accounts which
are given of their wonderful structure do not, on the whole, fall beyond the
truth. The Buddhist caves, from the nature of the workmanship, and from
the appearance of the rock, appear to me to be the most ancient.

"I preached the gospel in the temple of Kailas to thirty natives, and Mr.
Mitchell followed me. Little did the formers of this wonderful structure
anticipate an event of this kind. We are in all probability the first messengers of peace who have declared within it the claims of Jehovah, announced
his solemn decree to abolish the idols, and entreated his rebellious children
to accept of the mercy proposed through his Son. Some of our auditors
pointed to the magnificent arches and stupendous figures around us, as the
very works of God's own hand ; but we pointed them to the marks of the
instruments of the mason, to the innumerable proofs of decay everywhere
exhibited, and to the unsuitableness, absurdity, and impiety of the representations. We directed their minds to Him 'who sitteth upon the circle of
the earth, and the inhabitants thereof are as grasshoppers, That stretcheth out
the heavens as a curtain, and spreadeth them out as a tent to dwell in ;' and
we called upon them 'to lift up their eyes on high, and behold Who hath
erected these things, That bringeth out their host by number : Who calleth
them all by names, by the greatness of His might, for that He is strong in
power ; not one faileth.' They could not resist our appeal ; but in all
probability we had not long left them when they would practically deny
their own admissions.

"JILGAUM, 7th December.—We rode through Aurungabad. A great
part of its site is a mere ruin, and a great part of it within the walls seems to
have been used as a burying-ground. From the gate at which we entered to
that at which we came out is a distance of nearly three miles. We arrived at
Jilgaum, distant from Aurungabad about twenty miles, at noon. We had
suffered a great deal from the heat, and we resolved never, without absolute
necessity, to expose ourselves in this manner again. Our luggage did not
come up till about 4 o'clock P.M., and we were not a little anxious on account
of our fatigue and hunger. We have not the consolation that we were
called to endure either in the cause of duty. They were the result of our
own imprudent arrangements.

"JALNA.—At Jalna, which is twenty-one miles east of Jilgaum, we
arrived at ten o'clock. We were received with much warmth and kindly
feeling by Captain Wahab. There are several young officers and their wives,
who are in very hopeful circumstances ; and who may receive much benefit
from our visit. I baptized the child of Lieutenant ——. She is an illegitimate of three years old, and a sweet-looking little girl. I have had much
satisfaction in conversing with the father, who appears a true penitent. I
was asked to-day to baptize another child ; but the father did not meet my
views. To-morrow I intend to baptize the infant of Captain Tomkins. He
is a convert of Henry Martyn, but he dislikes the English form of baptism.
He is an excellent person, and useful as an instructor of the heathen.

"On Tuesday we preached to a large and noisy audience in the bazaar, and distributed a considerable number of books, which were received with much eagerness. One of the tracts, the *Remarks on Muhammadanism*, was handed up to the Colonel commanding the station, by, we ,believe, some European officer ; and his fears have been so much excited by the reports from Bangalore, that he requested us to circulate no more copies at present in the cantonment. We explained the nature of the tract to him, and we told him that in the circumstances of the case we should not continue to distribute it.

"15*th December.*—Since I last wrote to you the enemy of souls has been busy at this station, and he has succeeded in stirring up two or three of his European votaries to represent to the authorities here that our tracts are calculated to excite to sedition, to recall a great number of them and consign them to the flames, and to advise the total prohibition of any further circulation. The consequence is that we have been forbidden to circulate any more, and that, in our present circumstances, we have seen it expedient to dismiss all further applications. I doubt not that in a few days shame will cover those who have thus opposed the work of God. Indeed, they already begin to feel its burnings. You must not imagine from what I have now said that our residence here has become unprofitable or unpleasant. The very contrary is the case. Our pious friends have cleaved more closely than ever ; and even those who were formerly indifferent have been in some degree interested. We have received and accepted an invitation for dinner from one of the informers.

"I received a severe kick from a horse, which has laid me up for a little. I have suffered a great deal of pain from the blow, which was inflicted on the front bone of my right leg below the knee ; but I have reason to be thankful that no serious danger is apprehended. At first I had a few convulsive shocks ; but they soon went off. I am entirely free from sickness, and the injury appears inconsiderable.

"22*d December.*—I am now so well that I write to you upon my chair. *D.V.* I preach to-morrow evening sitting. On Monday I propose to set out for my dearest love. I have engaged twelve porters to carry me down for Rs.112.

"NANDOOR NIMBHA AND SHINGWA, 28*th December.*—We left Shivagaum early in the morning, and proceeded to Nandoor Nimbha. This village is small, and almost all the male inhabitants of it, and a few females, had an opportunity of hearing the Gospel. We offered them Rs.8 for their village gods ; but they said that they were afraid to part with them. We proposed that the power of the idols should be put to the test ; and to our astonishment they consented. The headman handed a large club to Mr. Mitchell, for the purpose of striking them ; and he dealt out three heavy blows upon Hanuman. His lordship received them with great meekness, and without showing the least symptom of displeasure. The villagers stood aghast ; but they immediately destroyed their convictions by alleging that our *virtue* gave us a great power over the gods, which they could never exercise. Death, they said, would be the consequence of *their* inflicting a blow. Thus Satan preserves them in their strong delusions.

"KALLIAN, 9*th January.*—We passed through Rahata on our way to Kallian. The villagers assembled in considerable numbers to hear the Gospel ; but we remarked that the facilities for collecting them are not so great in the Konkan as in the Dekhan. In the latter province the villages are all enclosed within walls, and their houses are not so scattered as those in the villages below the Ghât. In the Dekhan, moreover, there is generally an open space near one of the gates where all business is transacted, and where we can always find auditors without much trouble, and to which there is nothing correspondent in the Konkan. The villages on the sea coast, however, have one advantage. They are on the whole more thriving and populous."

Jalna, where for the hour the military authorities opposed
Mr. Wilson's benevolent work even more effectually than the
Brahmans had done in the previous year at Nasik, has, like
that station, since become the scene of the very successful
mission conducted by the Rev. Narayan Sheshadri, one of
his converts. This tour deserves notice on its European
side. Chaplains, still too few for the wants of the troops,
or so employed that the troops are not cared for first,
were fewer still before the Charter of 1833 enlarged the
ecclesiastical establishment. A sacerdotal conflict between
the Metropolitan of Calcutta and the Government of India
first led Lord William Bentinck to decide, as had been done
in 1813, that the chaplains are the officials of Government,
just as the churches are its property. The English in India
were too few, and heathenism was too strong for sectarian
bigotry to have then shown itself. In the time of Claudius
Buchanan, the author of the ecclesiastical establishment, and
till the arrival of Bishop Middleton and Dr. Bryce in Calcutta,
such a spirit was unknown. Hence Mr. Wilson preached in
the Jalna Church, and in the same service the chaplain from
Secunderabad read prayers previous to the sermon. The
Presbyterian's comment is—"This was very liberal." But
when, soon after, the Bishop, Daniel Wilson, made his first
metropolitan tour after his defeat by Lord William Bentinck,
he forbade this "irregularity" in a general circular to the
chaplains. Long after, his noble successor, Bishop Cotton,
arranged with Government that the ecclesiastical buildings
of the State should be used, when necessary, for Presbyterian
as well as Episcopalian services.

Having thus surveyed the Marathee-speaking country
north-west to Nasik and south-west to Poona, and thence
into the native State of the Muhammadan Nizam of Hydera-
bad, Mr. Wilson gave up the cold season of 1833-34 to the
southern Maratha country and the adjoining settlement of
the Portuguese at Goa. His colleague, the Rev. James
Mitchell, was again his companion. A sea passage of fifteen
hours took them to the old scenes at Hurnee, and thence to
the southern boundary of the former Konkan mission. At
the shrine of the elephant-god Gunesh, endowed with £120
a year, paid at that time through the British Government, an
incident occurred which is a parallel to Cicero's remark on

the two Augurs. An old Brahman, who had come from
Satara to see the god, was reproved because, at the close of a
meal and before he had performed ablution, he had happened
to touch one of the officiating priests. The old man immediately retorted, "Hullo, my religious friend, you have forgotten to wipe the sandal-wood from your forehead"—in
other words, you have either forgotten to-day to purify yourself or to remove the sign of your uncleanness. The priest
confessed that he stood corrected, and he gave a hypocritical
laugh. He had pretended holiness to gain the respect of the
stranger Brahman. At a village farther south, when passing
the tombs usually erected over widows who have burned
with their dead husbands, Mr. Wilson expressed his feelings
to a Brahman, who replied that he approved of Suttee, but
did not find fault with the British Government for abolishing
it. To him, as to the mass of Hindoos, the order of an absolute Government was sufficient to alter or prohibit even a
religious rite, when that was contrary to natural religion or
morality ; just as the teaching of an absolute priesthood had,
by a previous generation, been accepted as an authority for
burning widows who, if childless, otherwise enjoyed the life-
rent of their husbands' estates. The natural spring at this
shrine was believed to come, underground, from the Ganges,
hundreds of miles to the north, wherefore Mr. Wilson read to
the worshippers notes which he had taken of the lectures on
hydrography in the University of Edinburgh. His explanation was confirmed by a young English-speaking Hindoo,
whom he had known in Bombay, and who had come from a
distance of ten miles to pay his respects to the missionary.
Thus already, in four years, the merely scientific truth
radiating out from Bombay, through English, into the jungles
of Maharashtra, and the notes of an Edinburgh lecture-room
were used to overthrow Gunesh with the aid of an educated
Hindoo. Farther on Mr. Wilson saved from the infamy of
their lives, in future, a widow and two daughters who asked
alms for the temple to which they were attached, by arranging
to send them to the destitute girls' school which he had
opened in Bombay. They proved in after years to be
devoted Christians.

The connection between the Government and idolatry was
found at almost every step. At Kampta the town-clerk, a

learned Brahman, " told us that the whole village belonged to Bhagwati (an idol), and that the English Government was so kind as to collect and pay over the revenue to the idol. I expressed my deep regret to him, that, in making the settlement of the country, the Company's servants had fallen into the error and sin of associating themselves with superstition ; and informed him that many of them were aware of the evil, and that it would probably soon be rectified. There is scarcely a temple in this part of the country which has not an allowance from the revenue. The Mahalkaree of Kharipatan showed me a list of the sums granted in his district. I was perfectly thunderstruck on reading it. Even temples that are almost forsaken by the natives are not overlooked. Ten or twelve of this description had an allowance of five or six rupees per annum. I asked how these sums were expended. ' In buying light for the god,' was his reply. ' The allowance,' he added, is ' charitable ; many Brahmans, also, have grants.' I trust that the time is not far distant when all these sums will be profitably employed in promoting the education of the people."

That is the sort of disestablishment which the British Government, as such, can do little directly to bring about as the crowning result of its recent efforts to leave all management of the shrines to the worshippers, and all disputes about the property to the ordinary civil courts. But the time is not so hopelessly distant as may appear at first, when Mr. Wilson's foresight may be justified, by the educated natives themselves insisting on saving from the fraudulent greed of their priests the enormous endowments intended in many cases to act as a poor-law, and transferring them to the education of their children, for which they are now compelled to pay a cess on the land-tax.

At Vingorla, a port to which the frequent famines have led Government to direct their attention recently as likely to be the best on the Western coast, next to Bombay itself, for the import or export of grain, Mr. Wilson and his companion took boat again for Teracol, the first village belonging to the Portuguese. Just a quarter of a century had passed since, in 1808, Goa, the capital of all that was left of the once promising empire of Vasco de Gama and Albuquerque, which Camoens had sung in his *Lusiad*, had been visited by a Christian ecclesiastic whom, in many respects, John Wilson closely

resembled. Claudius Buchanan was the son of an elder of
the Kirk, who was the parish schoolmaster of Cambuslang
during Whitefield's preaching. He was educated at Glasgow
University, was for some time tutor in the old Scottish family
of the Campbells of Dunstaffnage, and was about to become a
preacher of the Church of Scotland, when, fired by the experience of Goldsmith, he determined first to see the world of
Europe. His wanderings ended in the completion of his
studies at Cambridge under Isaac Milner, whence the first of
the Clapham men, Mr. Henry Thornton, sent him out to Calcutta as a Company's chaplain in 1796. There his studies,
his travels, and his researches soon marked him out to Lord
Wellesley and Lord Minto as an adviser on all educational,
philanthropic, and scholarly questions. His writings so influenced public opinion in England, that Parliament in 1813
created the ecclesiastical establishment which Charles Grant
and Wilberforce, though aided by Pitt and Dundas, had failed
to force on the East India Company in the Charter of 1793 ;
that steps were taken to prohibit self-immolation under the
car of Jugganath and the pilgrim-tax ; and that the Inquisition was for ever abolished in Portuguese India in 1812. The
same evangelical charity, the same scholarly research, the same
intellectual breadth of view, the same zeal for the propagation
of Christian truth in the East, marked the two Scotsmen—the
one Episcopalian, the other Presbyterian. Mr. Wilson does
not fail to note, in the Journal of his visit to Goa, that it was
" the first since the days of Claudius Buchanan expressly made
for the circulation of the Scriptures and other missionary operations." Dr. Buchanan's visit to Goa was memorable from his
intercourse with Josephus a Doloribus, one of the Grand In-
quisitors, whose admissions are most important as to the fair-
ness of the account of his two years' sufferings under the order
of the tribunal by the French adventurer and physician Dellon
in 1673-5. In 1808 there were upwards of three thousand
priests belonging to Goa, and those whom Dr. Buchanan saw
declared they would gladly receive copies of the Latin and
Portuguese Vulgate from the hands of the English nation.

Mr. Wilson had one advantage during his visit in 1834.
The recent political changes in the mother country, and the
absence of the Archbishop, made the authorities and priests
more liberal in their intercourse with him.

"TERACOL, 28th Jan. 1834.—We took an early opportunity of visiting the fort. It is in charge of an old officer, Captain de Silva. He has been 44 years in India, and never expects to return to Portugal, which he left when he was 14 years old. We conversed with him about the political affairs of Portugal and other subjects. He told us that Donna Maria had been proclaimed in all the Goanese territories about two weeks ago, and gave us some of the orders of the day to read. He represented the whole province as in a state of perfect quietness. I offered a Portuguese Bible to him. He said that almost the only book which he read was a short treatise on the sufferings of Christ by D'Almeida ; but he intimated his readiness to accept a Bible, provided his padre would allow him. The padre was sent for. I held a long conversation with him in Latin. He granted permission to the Captain to receive the Bible, and on my offering one to himself he said, *Habeo tibi gratias.* He gave me an account of the state of the Romish Church in the territories of Goa, and in return I described to him the state and principles of the Churches of Scotland and England. He showed us his chapel, remarking *parva est.* Pointing to the different figures near the altar, he denominated them *imago Salvatoris, imago mirificæ Virginis, imago Sancti Antonii*, etc. The following conversation then took place. J. W. *Usus imaginum in ecclesia est contra Dei secundum mandamentum.* Padre. *In Novo Testamento imaginum usus permittitur.* J. W. *In quo loco permissio invenitur ?* P. *Nescio, sed hoc scio, Ecclesia Romana permittit.* J. W. *Ecclesia Romana permittit, et Deus interdixit.* P. *Idolatria non est.* J. W. *Sic aiunt Brachmanes.* We parted on good terms, the Padre promising to call upon us in the evening. He kept his word. In the course of our walk I tried to ascertain his theological sentiments. He said that he believed in the doctrine of predestination *ante merita cognita*, agreeably to the principles of Augustine. I expressed my accordance with his views. During our conversation on the celibacy of the clergy, he said, *In hac civitate Pauci Presbyteri muliebribus furtive utuntur.* I urged his admission as a proof of the inexpediency of the vow to observe celibacy made by all the Romish clergy. Few or none of the priests, he observed, knew either Greek or Hebrew. I referred to the Vulgate translation made by St. Jerome as a proof that the Romish Church in the days of old was not averse to the use of the Scriptures in the language best understood by the people. He had not formerly adverted to this circumstance ; and admitted that as the *lingua Latina nunc Romæ non in usu est*, an Italian translation should be made for that place. We compared the proceedings of Romish and Protestant missionaries. I admitted the learning and piety of Francis Xavier. He condemned the use of all violence in the propagation of Christianity, and lamented rash admissions into the visible Church. He expressed his surprise at the audiences with which we are favoured, and remarked, '*Gentiles in hoc regione non audiunt.*' I advised him to study their languages, and to preach the pure doctrines of Christianity.

"Late in the evening, when the padre had retired to the fort, about twenty of the inhabitants of the village came to our lodgings. We examined and addressed them in Marathee, which they speak in rather a corrupted form. We gave a few Portuguese tracts and two Testaments to three or four of them who could read them. One of them brought a large folio volume, which he called a *Purana*, to show to us. It was of Marathee Prakrita, but written in the Roman character. It contained paraphrases of several of the discourses of the apostles, extracts from the Bible, notes on church history, refutations of Hindooism, etc. It is a work of immense labour, and it is creditable to the learning and patience, if not to the piety, of some olden missionary. The owner said that he was in the habit of reading it, in the Brahmanical style, to assemblies at his door."

Was this the work of the Jesuit Stephens, the first Englishman whom we know to have landed in India five years after Francis Xavier's death in October 1579, whose letter to his father, a merchant of London, is found in Hakluyt ? He published a Konkanee Grammar, a History of Christ, and an Account of Christian Doctrine. The Madura Jesuit, Robert de Nobili's " Fifth Veda," which the French called L'Ezour Védam, so far deceived Voltaire that he appealed to it as a proof of the superiority of Hindooism to Christianity ! Taking again to the boat, Mr. Wilson spent the time on the way southward to Goa in reading the Latin Bible " for the sake of facility in conversation," and Cotineau's *Historical Sketch of Goa*.

" *29th January* 1834.—We lay at the mouth of the Goa river, or rather firth, for about half-an-hour, till we obtained permission to go up to Pangim, or New Goa. The aspect of the country, from the appearance of the villages, churches, and forts, is unlike anything which I have seen in India. Our landing at Pangim reminded me much of Cape Town. The houses are, generally speaking, very substantial, and painted white. Many have two stories, and united conical and lofty roofs for every apartment in the upper story. We had not been seated for many minutes, when a great number of persons came to us to offer their services. Some of the proposals which were made to us were calculated to impress us with very unfavourable impressions of the morality of the place, and with the behaviour of our countrymen who came to visit it. We met them with suitable indignation and reproof.

" Two parish priests of Pangim held a discussion with me. They, like the other priests, were anxious to procure books. We gave them, as to all the priests with whom we have had intercourse, a Portuguese Bible, a Latin Bible and New Testament. I offered them a copy of *Calvini Institutiones*. *Non licet nobis libros heretico legere*, was the reply. *Joannes Calvinus vir doctus et pius fuit ; ejus opera legere vos decet*, was my answer. The merits of the Reformation were shortly discussed. The work of the Genevese Reformer was ultimately carried away by those to whom it was proffered. I had a conversation on personal religion with a young lad of twenty, who is at present studying canonical law.

" *1st February.*—The first sight of Goa is magnificent, although it is at once evident that nothing remains but the churches and some other public buildings. The walls of the city are now almost entirely destroyed ; but, like Dr. Claudius Buchanan, we entered the city by the palace gate, over which is the statue of Vasco de Gama, the discoverer of the passage by the Cape, and one of the first ' Vice-reys ' of India. The hero stands aloft, *in vestibus quæ decent tempora antiqua*. The first building which we visited was the Church of the Palace. It is an exact model of St. Peter's at Rome. It is arched in the roof. Its principal altar is decorated in a style surpassing anything which I had formerly seen. Its convent and cloisters are small. It belongs to the Theatins or order of St. Cajetan, who were instituted in Italy by St. Cajetan of Thiena, and by John Caraffa (Pope Paul the Fourth), Bishop of Theato. They were established in Goa in the middle of the seventeenth century. The Italian founders were soon joined by many of the natives. There are at present no Europeans in the convent. No natives but those of Brahmanical descent are admitted. We saw two of the friars seated in confessionals in the

H

church. They were lending ear respectively to a woman, and muttering forgiveness. Several other persons of the female sex were prostrating themselves
in the church, and waiting the appointed time of disburdening their consciences. The Cajetans are the most renowned confessors in the colony.
They live almost entirely on the offerings of the superstitious. They seldom
exceed fifteen in number, and, owing to the unhealthiness of their situation,
are short-lived.

"In passing from St. Cajetan's to the Cathedral, we saw the ruins, or
rather the site, of the Inquisition, which was founded in 1560, and the court
of which was ordered to be suppressed in 1812. The representations of the
British were the cause of its destruction. I cordially assent to the only
remark which Dr. Buchanan makes on the metropolitan church—'It is worthy
of one of the principal cities of Europe.' We went from the Aljuva to the
Monastery of St. Monica. It is the only nunnery in Goa, and was founded by
the infamous Dom Fré Alexo de Menezes, archbishop of Goa, about the year
1600, and by him dedicated to the mother of Augustine. The exterior of the
building has nothing remarkable about it. To the cloister we could of course
have no access. We were directed to the public hall. We found the abbess
and prioress seated in a room adjoining us opposite an iron grating, where
alone they could have communication with us. They were both Europeans,
and very neatly dressed in white, and attended by two or three female servants.
They very readily entered into conversation with us. The abbess entered the
convent when she was fifteen years old, and has resided within its walls for
forty-four years. The prioress entered it in 1818. She blushed when Sr.
Capella jokingly told her that, amidst the political changes which are taking
place, she would be permitted to leave it and to marry. The abbess told us
that, including novices, there are thirty nuns in the establishment at present.
Europeans pay Rs.1000, and natives double that sum, on their entrance. The
funds of the institution are much reduced from the loss of its estates. It
receives Rs.1000 per annum from the Government. The nuns engage in
making rosaries, in knitting, and the preparation of sweetmeats and preserves.
We bought several articles from them. When we offered them a Portuguese
New Testament, the abbess said that she could not take upon herself the
responsibility of accepting it. The prioress, however, seized it besides several
tracts with joy, kissed it, and said that she would always pray for us.

"Precisely at two we saw the doors of the Augustinian Convent thrown
open. The prefect of the Augustinian College, and the prior Fré José, offered
to show us all the buildings, which are nearly as extensive as those of the
University of Edinburgh. 'Few cities in Europe,' says M. Cotineau, 'can
boast of a finer edifice of the kind; the cloisters, pillars, galleries, halls, and
cells, are all most beautiful.' What struck me most was the display of portraits of the martyr missionaries of the order. Many of them are well executed,
and represent the friars in the attitude of death. I could not but think with
admiration of their devotedness, and wish that more of it were exhibited
among Protestants. The view from the turrets is magnificent. We stood
almost entranced on first coming into contact with it. We examined the
library of the college. The books are fast going to decay. They do not
amount, I should think, to more than 1500. Many of them are very old and
valuable. I noticed most of the Roman Catholic Church historians referred to
by Mosheim. I heard the youths of the noviciate of the college read a little
Latin, and put a few questions to them. A European monk followed us with
a very anxious eye. He evidently wished to make some communication to us.
We both felt great compassion for him. The superior of the college was very
free in his communications. He was much pleased to find our pronunciation
of Latin so much like his own. I gave him a Portuguese Bible, and left some

books for the provincial and prior, presented by Mr. J. Wolff and Mr. Farish. Among them was a copy of *Keith on Prophecy*. May the perusal of them be abundantly blessed ! It was in the cloisters of an Augustinian convent that the spark of piety was first kindled in Martin Luther. The Augustinians (twelve in number) came first to Goa in 1572. They have a yearly income of Rs.15,000, independently of an allowance of Rs.1500 made by the Goa Government. They have several missions in the East under their care. Their vestments are white. These were originally black, but were changed on account of the defection of the German Reformer, of whom his friends were greatly ashamed. They are the most respectable monks in the Catholic Church. Leaving the Augustinians, we proceeded to the church of Dom Jesus. It is built in the form of a cross. Though it is a noble edifice we scarcely surveyed it at all. I hastened to the shrine of the celebrated Francis Xavier, of which I had heard much. It surpassed all my expectations, and certainly excels anything of the kind which I had before seen. It is of copper, richly gilt and ornamented, and placed within a silver incasement. It rests upon an altar of Italian marble highly wrought. There is a *vera effigies* of the 'Apostle of India' on the south of the tomb, and a statue of solid silver, which is not exposed to view. He died in the island of Santian, in the Chinese Seas, in 1552. His body was brought to Goa in 1554. It was exposed to public view till 1780, when it was locked up in its present receptacle. Alas that it should now be viewed as the 'sacred dust' of a heathen Buddha !

"We reached the Archbishop's palace at Pannelly about half-past five o'clock. The quaternarian kept his appointment and introduced us to the curator of the library, which I was very anxious to examine. It contained about two thousand volumes. Though they are in a better condition than those in the Augustinian convent, they are rapidly going to decay. Few of them are modern. I observed only three Protestant volumes among the whole of them. I found a MS. translation of the Four Gospels in Arabic, of which it would be well to procure a copy.

"*4th February.*—The secretary introduced us to the Vice-rey, Dom Manuel de Portugal è Castro, at the palace, who received us very politely. He then showed us the portraits of all the Vice-reys of India. Most of them came originally from Portugal. There are not many of them which have not been re-touched by native artists. The portraits with which I was most interested were those of Alfonso de Albuquerque, Vasco de Gama, John de Castro, and Constantine de Braganza. Constantine refused to accept from the king of Pegu the sum of 300,000 cruzados for a monkey's tooth which had been adored at Jaffnapatam as a relic of Buddha. He deserves to be had in remembrance for his firmness and decision, and aversion to countenance idolatry. How different was his conduct from that of the Bengal Governor who sent an ambassador to the Grand Lama to congratulate him on his incarnation ! "

Returning through the jungle of the coast and the forest of the Ghats, where they slept with only a slight covering from the dew, but soundly after the fatigue of their intercourse in Goa, Mr. Wilson and his companion reached the pure Marathee-speaking district of Dharwar, and the London mission station of Belgaum. Here he came on the border line of the Tamul-speaking and the Canarese districts of Madras. In preaching to the English residents he did not,

amid all the claims of India, forget to urge those of the Gaelic
School Society.   He passed through Shunkeswar, the residence of the great *Swami* of Western India, where the annual
fair of the deified reformer Shunkur Acharya was being held
by ten thousand people, and the god was being dragged in a
car forty-five feet high.   After a day's incessant preaching
there, and at other towns and villages, Mr. Wilson thus
writes in his journal :—

"I have often wondered how Whitefield could preach so
frequently in England ; but it is now a considerable time
since I discovered that practice in public speaking makes it
comparatively easy.   Some advocates speak four or five hours
daily at the bar during the press of business ; and we, who
are called to act as ambassadors of Christ to our perishing
fellow men, may well continue our ministrations during a
longer time.   The interest with which we are heard has a
reflex influence in strengthening us for the discharge of our
duties.   The impressions which we produce, though in general
they may not lead to any very striking visible effect, have, I
am persuaded, a powerful influence in weakening the hold of
superstition, and in enlightening and directing the conscience.
When the Gospel is generally preached, as I hope it soon will
be, through the length and breadth of the country, individual
conversions will become more frequent.   It is the *general*
apathy of the unenlightened, which destroys the ardour of
individuals, on whose mind favourable impressions are produced.   I fervently wish that evangelical *agitation* were the
order of the day in India.   Into this agitation I would of
course wish no unholy element to enter.   I would wish it to
be like that of the Apostles and the Reformers."

The town is further remarkable for the first of those interviews with one of the princes of India, to which Mr. Wilson
was afterwards frequently invited.   The house of Sivajee, the
founder of the Maratha power, is now represented only by
the Raja of Kolhapore, the representative of its younger, and
the Raja of Satara, the head of its elder branch.   Bawo Sahib,
who received Mr. Wilson, was "an oppressive and profligate
ruler," who had not many years before been compelled by a
British force to abstain from attacking his brother chiefs.   He
died in 1838, four years after the visit, leaving a son, the
misrule of whose minority again compelled our interference.

But he was faithful in the Mutiny of 1857. On his death, in 1866, we at once recognised his nephew and adopted son, Rajaram. To him a melancholy interest attaches. Well educated he visited England in 1870, a gentle youth who wrote a journal of his experience, presenting a significant contrast to that of his grandfather, to whom Mr. Wilson "opened the Scriptures" in vain, and told the story of the conversion of Britain which these Scriptures had made great. Raja Rajaram died at Florence, and his body was burned with Hindoo rites on the banks of the Arno, the last of that branch of Sivajee's house. To perpetuate it, Lord Mayo's government waived all the usual provisions in a case of adoption, and another Bhonsla boy was searched out in 1871. He is now sixteen years of age, and is being educated to govern some 800,000 tenantry, who pay him annually a revenue of the third of a million sterling.

On reaching the confines of Kolhapore the Scottish missionaries were met by troopers, who attended them. On nearing the town the Captain-General and a few of the troopers and thirty sepoys formed an escort to the banks of the Pandi-Gunga, where their tents had been pitched. There they had presented to them, in the name of the descendant of the mighty Sivajee, "great loads of fruit, sweetmeats, eggs, and chickens," and they found a retinue of liveried servants at their call. After examining the black marble tomb-temples of Shunkur, the reformer, and his first disciple, and preaching for a day, the Sahebs were thus received at an audience :—

"*25th February* 1834.—At four in the afternoon, two of the Sirdars, attended by forty sepoys, came to conduct us to the palace. The streets, as we passed along, were as much lined with people as if the King of England had come to see them. We were vastly ashamed of the honours which they tried to heap upon us. On our arrival at the palace we were received by Haibat Rao Gwaikawar, one of the most respectable of the Sirdars. He conducted us to the great room. We entered it, according to custom, without our shoes. Several hundreds of people, including all the Sirdars, were seated in two rows fronting one another. We were squatted near the *Gádi* (royal cushion). On the entrance of the Raja all the people stood up. He saluted us very kindly and asked us to sit down. After a little commonplace conversation, we directed his attention to the Christian Scriptures and gave him a brief summary of their contents. 1 then presented him with an elegantly bound copy of the New Testament, and of the *Exposure of Hinduism*, and with copies of Matthew bound in silk, and *Exposures* and other tracts for his Sirdars. He expressed his pleasure at receiving them. I told him about the conversion of Britain, and ascribed all its greatness to the book of which I had given him a copy. Mr. Mitchell recommended him to encourage education in his territories. It is to be regretted that he practises polygamy. He has five wives, but only two sons and one daughter.

"10*th March* 1834.—We rose at gun-fire, and, along with Dr. Young, we ascended to the celebrated hill-fort of Satara. It is about 3000 feet above the level of the sea, and its height from the base is about 900 feet. It is strong by nature, as the rocks near the summit are perpendicular. We took about twenty minutes to walk round it. It commands a very fine view of the country. In descending from it, we found the agreeableness of 'the shadow of a great rock in a weary land.' In the afternoon we visited Satara. It is much better laid out than any native town which I have seen. The streets are broad and straight, and the houses are, on the whole, neat and substantial. The English have the credit of forming the plan of some of them. The population may be stated at between fifteen and twenty thousand, and it is reported to be on the increase. The palace is a plain quadrangular building. We should have been introduced to the Raja had he been at home. His high school is also a quadrangular building.

"13*th March.*—We set out for Malcolm-Peth on the Mahableshwar Hills about two hours before sunset ; and we arrived at the Sanitarium, where we were kindly received by Captain Jameson, about nine o'clock. On the top of the ghat, about 4500 feet above the level of the sea, we saw the fern and the willow, and heard the voice of the lark, the thrush, and the blackbird. They called vividly to remembrance our native hills and groves, and made our very souls thrill. We made several calls on European gentlemen throughout the day, and we preached to large congregations of natives. I recognised two of my Bombay native friends among our audience. They were very happy to see me.

"15*th March.*—We proceeded early in the morning to Mahableshwar, which is about three and a half miles distant from the Sanitarium in Malcolm-Peth, or Nehar, as it is called by the natives. Our ride was remarkably pleasant. The tops of the hills and mountains below us were rising above the thick white clouds like islands in the ocean. The appearance of the cottages, roads, and plants reminded us of the scenes in another land. The atmosphere was comparatively cool and bracing. The sun was rising with glory in the east. The birds were offering up their early orisons to Him who formed them. Mahableshwar is a religious establishment, almost on the highest pinnacle of the hills, sacred to Shiva. It has no connection with Wai in the plains below, as has been alleged by some. It is under the direction of Deshast Brahmans, while Wai is under the direction of Konkanasts. There is a considerable spring at the most sacred spot, which is said to be the source of the *Krishnabai, Savitri*, etc., and which is denominated the *Panchaganga.* There is a small tank at the place where it issues from the ground, and which forms the *Tirtha,* to which pilgrims repair. It is surrounded by a small court and shed, in which there are a few idols."

This is our first introduction to the great hill sanitarium of Bombay, which was ceded in 1829 by the Raja of Satara in exchange for other lands. The State lapsed in 1848, but the British Government has continued a pension of £250 a month to the adopted child of the last widow of the Raja, who died in 1874. The concluding extract from Mr. Wilson's journal of this third tour tells of that encounter with a tiger, which some of his Hindoo controversialists declared that he magnified into a miracle !

"18th March 1834.—We set out for Nagotana a little before sunset. On the road I experienced a remarkable deliverance, which should excite my most fervent gratitude to the Father of all mercies. I had got the start of Mr. Mitchell in passing through the jungle, and in order to allow him opportunity of coming to me, I was just about to pull up my horse, when I observed an enormously large tiger about six yards from me. Instead of running from me, he sprang up near my horse ; I then cried out as loud as I could, with the view of frightening him. I had the happiness of seeing him retreat for a little ; and I galloped from him, as fast as my horse could carry me, to Mr. Mitchell, whom I found walking with four or five natives. We passed together the spot where I had the encounter, without seeing our enemy. He was heard, however, among the trees by our horse-keepers. He has been seen by the natives for some days past a short time after sunset, exactly at the place (about six miles from Nagotana) where he appeared to me. The men whom I found with Mr. Mitchell told me that they regularly present offerings for protection from tigers to an image on Wardhan hill. I showed them the vanity of their confidence ; but in their misdirected devotion I saw the call to remember 'the Lord who is my refuge, even the Most High.' "

Some time after this the able civilian, Sir J. P. Willoughby, presented Mr. Wilson with a cottage on Mahableshwar, and there, when more advanced in years, he and his missionary brethren used to recruit their wasted energies during the college vacation in the great heat of May and June in the plains. He became closely identified with the place up to the year of his death, and evangelised among its tribes right down to Poona. When a part of the hill called Sydney Point, after Sir Sidney Beckwith, the Commander-in-Chief, had its name changed to Lodwick Point, he used humorously to resent such tampering with historical and landscape associations. His "bungalow" was another mission centre, like Ambrolie in the native quarter of Bombay. Not a day passed even there without vernacular preaching and examination of schools, while the ever-increasing arrears of his extensive correspondence were cleared off. The climate and the scenery alike tempted to literary labours. To the comparatively small and select society of European officials, civil and military, and to the educated native gentlemen who began to frequent the spot, Mr. Wilson often delivered those lectures which afterwards attracted crowds in the Town Hall of the capital. In close and constant intercourse with the Governor, the Commander-in-Chief, and the members of Council, he brought his wide information and high principles to bear on political questions, especially when these concerned the native princes and people. Thus Mahableshwar became to him the scene not merely of well-deserved rest but of more varied work and wider social influence.

CHAPTER VI.

1835.

TOUR TO SURAT, BARODA, KATHIAWAR, AND SOMNATH.

First Exploration of the Goojaratee Country and its Native States—The Portuguese in Daman—A Catch of Zand MSS.—Surat fruitful in Facts—British Government and Idolatry—Hindoos and Muhammadans denouncing each other—An Eclectic Rationalist—Mr. Wilson's Journal a Love-Offering to his Wife—Baroda Church consecrated by Heber—Audience of the Gaikwar described—Correspondence between the Gaikwar and Mr. Wilson—The Mad Gaikwars—Cambay to Bhownuggur—A Hill of Shrines—Satan's Celestial City—Mr. Wilson's Letter to the Jain Priests—Rajkote—A King punished for murdering his Infant Daughter—Kutch—Work of the Rev. James Gray—A Good Raja—Schwartz and Raja Serfojee—The Land of Krishna—Mr. Wilson anticipates James Prinsep at Girnar—The Historical Temple of Somnath—Death and Separation in the Mission Family of Ambrolie—Mrs. Margaret Wilson's Memoir by her husband.

HAVING now completed such a detailed survey of the central, eastern, and southern districts of the province, including Portuguese Goa, as was possible in three cold weather seasons, Mr. Wilson prepared for the longest and most fruitful of all his early tours, that through the northern half of Bombay. Familiar first of all with the varied elements of the population of a quarter of a million in the capital city itself, he had now carried his elevating message to Hindoo, Muhammadan, and jungle or robber tribe, over the whole Maratha country from sacred Nasik to only less holy Shunkeswar, and from the Jews and Parsees of the Konkan to the Muhammadans of Jalna. All he had studied with a keen interest and a never-failing memory. There remained the Goojaratee country, with its great native States of Baroda, Kathiawar, and Kutch, stretching up to the Indus-washed delta of Sindh and the deserts of Rajpootana. In the rich cotton-fields of Goojarat the Parsees found an asylum before the English attracted them to the island of Bombay, and Mr. Wilson had fairly

given himself to that study of their literature and religion
with which, more than with any other, his name is identified.
Not only there, but in the native States, are the half-Buddhist,
half-Hindoo communities of the Jains to be found, and it was
his task to understand in order that he might influence them.
So the closing weeks of the year 1834 saw him, his wife (as
far as Surat), and his attached friend Dr. Smyttan of the
Government service, set out in that modest "shigram," or one-
horse vehicle, which for half a century was familiar to all
natives and Europeans in Bombay as the great missionary's.
Past Mahim and Bassein, and along the shore washed by the
Arabian Sea to still Portuguese Daman, the travellers crept,
taking a week to accomplish the distance now achieved by
railway in a few hours.   Of Daman, conquered in 1831, we
read in the Journal—"A Parsee gave us no favourable idea
of the Portuguese Government.   The soldiers were represented
as helping themselves to whatever articles they need.   Justice,
it was said, is an article which requires to be purchased at
a dear rate.   The sun of Daman, which Juliao, the late
Miguelite Governor, denominates on a triumphal arch *cele-
berrima urbs in oriente*, appears to have reached its meridian.
There is something very instructive in the decline of the
Portuguese power in India and the rise of that of the British.
Camoens represents Vasco de Gama as describing the whole of
Europe to the lord of Melinda.   The hero makes no mention
of England!   But observe the ways of Divine Providence.
The country which was too contemptible to be noticed three
hundred years ago, is now the most powerful in the world, and
it is under its favour that the Portuguese exercise sovereignty
over their remaining small territories in India."   Here Mr.
Wilson purchased, for Rs.300, a copy of the Vandidad Sadé
and of all the sacred books of the Parsees in the original
Zand, Pahlavi and Pazand tongues, but in the Goojaratee
character, and with a Goojaratee commentary and translation.
Of this work, in five folio volumes, he remarks—"Of its
use to a missionary there can be no doubt.   I procured along
with it copies of all the narratives calculated to throw any
light upon the history of the Zoroastrians in India, and some
other curious pamphlets connected with their religion."
    Continuing their journey northwards, the party passed the
most ancient fire temple in India, at Umarasaree, and inspected

the extensive fire temple of Nausaree, the streets of which
were, at that early time, regularly lighted at night by lamps
with oiled paper shades.   Surat, 177 miles north of the
capital,[1] first of English settlements in India, was found to be
declining as Bombay supplanted it, and the decay has gone
on till the present time, if we may judge from the visit of the
Governor, Sir Richard Temple, to its deserted buildings, and
half-obliterated tombs of Oxenden and others last year.   Mr.
Fyvie was the only (London) missionary there, and he afterwards joined Mr. Wilson on his tour.   But Surat has ever
been marked by the intelligence of its native inhabitants,
whose spirit has shown itself more than once in rioting against
taxes imposed in an unpopular form.   Here Mr. Wilson
collected much information regarding the eighty-four castes
of Goojaratee Brahmans, the early settlements of the Parsee
refugees from Muhammadan intolerance, and the three Bohora
sects of Muhammadans.   He learned that half the great fire
temples of India had been erected only within the previous
twelve years.   The relation of the British Government to
those cults he thus describes :—

"The English Government has still the responsibility, and
a fearful one it is both for rulers and their agents, of directly
and publicly countenancing idolatry and superstition.   The
new moon, except during two months of the year, is regularly
saluted by five guns to please the Mussulmans!   Two
thousand rupees, I was told, are annually contributed to
the same people to assist them in the celebration of their *eeds!*
The chief of Surat, and the British administrator of justice in
its province, commits the cocoa-nut to the river on the day of
the great heathenish procession at the break of the monsoon!
How all this folly originated amidst the ungodliness of many
of the olden servants of the Company I can easily understand ;
but how it has been so long continued I am puzzled to know.
The day was when, I suppose, one would have got a free
passage to Europe, *via* China, for *noticing* it.   I certainly
thought, without making a reference to higher and more
solemn considerations, that after the order came from the
Court of Directors, 'that in all matters relating to their
temples, their worship, their festivals, their religious practices,
and their ceremonial observances, our native subjects be left

---

[1] Pronounced Soorăt, the Sun city of the Ramayun epic.

entirely to themselves,' our late excellent Governor would
have put an extinguisher upon it.   Surely the son of CHARLES
GRANT will perform the right honourable act."

After nine days in the old city, Mr. Wilson was received
at the next stage northwards by Mr. Kirkland, the civilian
in charge, to whom Dr. Chalmers had given him an intro-
ductory note.   The march from the Taptee, which almost
encircles Surat, to the Nerbudda, was spent in discussing
a census of the " Pergunna " or " Hundred " of the district,
from which the fact of the murder of female children became
evident.   A visit to Broach, the ancient Barygaza, the commercial glory of which has given place to a great agricultural
prosperity under British rule, resulted in further work among
the Parsees and Jains, and on the 17th January 1835 Baroda
was reached.   The bruit of the discussions with Hindoos and
Muhammadans in Bombay seemed to have everywhere preceded Mr. Wilson.   At one village belonging to one of the
Gaikwar's feudatories, Mussulmans and Hindoos " commenced
denouncing the faith of each other in no very measured
language," after the statement which they had invited from
the missionary.   Before he could rest on the Saturday of his
arrival at Baroda he had to grapple long with a really earnest
Brahman, who, having become the secretary of a neighbouring Muhammadan Nawab, was an eclectic rationalist, seeking
truth in accordance with reason only, and rejecting his own
scriptures as inspired.   The following very human extract
from one of the letters which generally covered the instal-
ments of his journal, may serve as an introduction to its more
formal narrative.   He preached twice in the English Church
to the European residents, who were rarely visited by chaplain
or missionary.   Bishop Heber had consecrated it ten years
before, when he was " both amused and interested," though a
little fatigued, by his purely ceremonial visit to the Gaikwar,
whose invitation to witness the cruel sport of elephant-baiting
he declined.   The good Bishop's narrative of his visit to
Baroda, in 1826, presents a striking contrast to Mr. Wilson's
Journal in 1835, but the difference is due chiefly to the
knowledge which the Presbyterian " Bishop " had acquired of
the language and religion of the Gaikwar.

"BARODA, 19th January 1835.

"MY DEAREST LOVE—Surely you do not wish me to detain my Journal for the mere purpose of having it accompanied with a letter which I may not always find time to write. You must view the Journal as a communication. I should get on very poorly with it if I had not you in my eye. *It is inter alia* a love-offering. I question if Mrs. Webb had it that she would think of rejecting it. She was very proud about the Journal which her excellent brother Richard Townshend sent to her, and very justly so. Tell *you* her this.

"I write to you from Radical Hall. Captain S—— is over head and ears in an Irish bog; and how he will get out I know not. He has drawn in several young men to him. Irish bogs move, it is said. Do you think that they will ever move to the land of liberty? *I* trow not. I am quite tired of their bawlings. Perhaps I may have done something to stop the spread of the mania.

"Tell Mr. Webb that Bishop Heber consecrated the Baroda Church; and that Bishops Fyvie and Wilson have reconsecrated it. Mr. Fyvie read the prayers of the Church of England in it. Colonel Burford gave the church to us. We had the sacrament *privately* in the evening yesterday, *twelve* communicants including two natives. I thought much of you and the dear children. Surely I may commit you all to the care of Him Who died on the cross for my sins.

"*23d January.*—I spent the morning with Mr. Williams, the Political Commissioner. About eleven o'clock I proceeded with him and Colonel Burford, Dr. Smyttan, Mr. Malet, and Major Morris, to the palace of the Gaikwar. We were all mounted on an elephant, and attended by the guard of honour which accompanies the Political Commissioner on his visit to the king. We were introduced to the Gaikwar at the door of the Durbar; and we walked up with him through the ranks of his courtiers, to the Gadi. Mr. Williams sat next to the great man, and I next to Mr. Williams. After conversing with his Highness for a little on the late frosts, I asked whether or not I should be permitted, as a minister of the Gospel, to give a statement of the principles and evidences of Christianity, the religion professed by the inhabitants of Britain and many other countries, and which demands the acceptance of mankind throughout the world. His Highness informed me that he would be very happy indeed; and I proceeded. I gave a view of the Scripture account of the character of God, of the natural state of man, and of the means of salvation; and contrasted this account with those given in the Hindoo Shastres. When I had concluded, his Highness called upon Venirama, his minister, to come forward, and assist him to form a judgment of what had been said, which was entirely new to him. Venirama obeyed, and declared that Jesus was an incarnation similar to Rama and Krishna, who has received from God as a *war* (boon) the power of saving all those who believe in him. 'Rama and Krishna,' I observed, 'were no incarnations of God at all. They might have been great warriors, like the forefathers of the Gaikwar, who were deified by the poets; but most assuredly their characters forbid the entertainment of the idea that they were incarnations of the divinity. It is evident that they were sinners. Krishna is spoken of in the tenth section of the Bhagavat as having been guilty of murder, adultery, theft, and falsehood; and Rama is described by Valmiki as a person who perjured himself to Mandedari, the wife of Ravana, —who banished his wife, though innocent of the charges brought against her, at a time when she was pregnant, and thus proved himself a bad husband and a bad father; and troubled his poor brother Lukshmun so much that he destroyed himself, and thus proved a bad brother. Christ Jesus, however, committed no sin, and acted in every way suitable to his claims as God manifested in the flesh.'

"Our conversation then proceeded as follows:—*Venirama.* Don't allege that the seeming evil acts of our gods were sinful. God can do what he pleases, and who is to call him to account? *J. W.* God is not responsible to any, but He will act always according to His nature, which is perfectly holy. Even Krishna is represented in the Geeta as admitting the propriety of his regarding moral observances : ' If I were not vigorously to attend to these (the moral duties), all men would presently follow my example, etc.' Judging Krishna by what is here said, I am bound to condemn him. The legend, moreover, says that he felt the effects of his sin. When Jugannath was asked why he had no hands and no feet, he declared that he lost them through his mischief at Gokula. *Venirama.* God *can* sin. He is the author of all sin. *J. W.* Do not blaspheme the Self-existent. *Venirama.* This is. no blasphemy. If God is not the author of sin, pray who is the author of it? *J. W.* The creatures of God are the authors of it. You must admit that God has given a law to men. *Venirama.* I do admit this, and say that this law is good. *J. W.* Now, I make an appeal to his Highness. Will the great king first make laws for his subjects, then give them a disposition to break these laws, and last of all punish them for breaking them ? *Gaikwar* (laughing heartily). Verily I will do nothing of the kind. I am always angry when my subjects break my laws. *J. W.* And is not the King of kings and Lord of lords angry when His laws are broken ? Why does He send disease and death into the world, and why has He prepared hell unless for the punishment of the wicked ? *Venirama.* I know not ; but who is there to sin but God? He is the only entity. *J. W.* So, I suppose, you have no objections to say *Aham Brahmasmi*[1] (I am Brahma). *V.* It is not lawful for me to repeat these sacred words. *J. W.* Not lawful for God to declare His own existence ! You were saying a little while ago that it was lawful for God to do anything, even to sin. *I* think it presumption for any man to declare that he is God in any form of words. Never let the weakness, ignorance, sin, suffering, and change of men, be attributed to God. *V.* God in the form of men is apparently weak, and so forth. Suppose the Divine nature to be a tree. Men are the leaves of that tree. Now, the leaves differ from the branches and the stalk and the root ; and men, growing out from the Godhead, differ in some respects from the Godhead from which they grow. *J. W.* But my position is that men are in no sense part of the Godhead. Their weakness, ignorance, sin, suffering, and so forth, to which I have alluded, prove this. They are the workmanship of God. *V.* But what is the creation but the expansion of God ? *J. W.* It is the product of the Divine word and power. I cannot admit for a moment the theory of God's swelling and contracting, and contracting and swelling. *V.* There are differences in religion you observe. Your religion, I admit, is good for you. *J. W.* My religion professes to be the only one which is given by God, and to be good for all men. God never would give such contradictory accounts of Himself and His will as are to be found in the Christian and Hindoo religions. Both of them cannot be true ; for, in a thousand points which I can enumerate, they are directly opposed to one another. Pray, on what grounds do you believe in Hindooism ? You say that evidence is of four kinds, *pratyash* (sensation), *shabda* (testimony), *anumána* (inference), and *upamána* (analogy). What kind and degree of these species of evidence have you for Hindooism ? *V.* We have our religion as we got it from our forefathers. It was their business to inquire into its evidence. *J. W.* What a strange evasion ! If you be in the wrong, will the errors of your forefathers excuse you for neglecting to seek the truth ? Don't the Bheels plead the custom of their fathers as an excuse for their thefts and robberies ? *Gaikwar* (laughing). Most certainly they do. *J. W.* Surely your minister will not listen to their plea ! *Venirama.* But what have *you* got to say for

---

[1] One of the four great sentences of the Veda.

110 LIFE OF JOHN WILSON. [1835.

Christianity ? *J. W.* Your question is very proper. I have got much to say for it. Suppose the Christian Shastra to be a letter. I peruse it. I find nothing inconsistent with its claims to Divine inspiration. It is in every respect worthy of the holiness and wisdom of God. It bears the impress of the Divinity. I can no more believe it be the unassisted work of man, than I can believe the sun to be the fabrication of a blacksmith. I behold it producing the most marvellous results, particularly in communicating sanctification and happiness to those who believe in it. I find from authentic history that it was published to the world at the time which it alleges ; and that it testifies as to miraculous transactions, which, if unreal, could not have been believed at the time when it was published, etc. I shall be delighted to give you a copy of it, that you may judge for yourselves. The more you peruse it, the more will you discover its excellence. The more that you inquire into its history, the more will you discover its credibility.

"When we had proceeded thus far, his Highness began to compliment me on my *Dakhani boli* (accent), and to declare that he and his ministers, though possessed of a spice of the *rerum terrestrialium prudentia*, knew little about the affairs of the other world. He then turned to Mr. Williams, and told him that he ought to have given him warning, that he might have the Brahmans in readiness. 'There is no lack of Brahmans here,' said Mr. Williams. 'I never dreamt, when you requested leave for the Padre to visit me,' he said, 'that he would act otherwise than the Lord Padre Saheb, who, after looking at every object in the Durbar, went out to see the artillery-yard. This is a *guru vishesha.*'

"After declaring myself unworthy of the compliments which his Highness paid me, I offered him a finely-bound copy of the New Testament in Marathee. This, however, he declined to receive, as he had not yet seen reason to wish to abandon Hindooism. I recommended him to take the earliest opportunity of reflecting on what had been advanced, and stated to him that his acceptance of the Testament was not tantamount to abjuring Hindooism. Mr. Williams sported a joke or two as to his fears, but I thought it proper not to be too importunate, particularly as he would probably not refuse the gift if offered to him privately. The Gaikwar cautioned me against misunderstanding him, and, after again complimenting me, he insisted on my accepting from him, as a token of his good-will, a couple of shawls and a gold ornament. I decidedly refused the offering for some time ; but, on being informed by Mr. Williams that my refusal would probably give offence, I yielded. I then received a letter from the Gaikwar to the authorities at Dwarka ; and, after a little miscellaneous conversation, we took our leave. The Raja, as on our entrance, walked with us through the Durbar. He is rather a good-looking Maratha, and superior in point of talent to most of the great men with whom I have come into contact. His dress was plain, but his ornaments were splendid. His son, a young lad of about sixteen years, who was present during the interview, seemed modest and placid. The Muhammadan Sirdars made rather a good appearance. The Marathas were scarcely to be distinguished from the *plebs* of their tribe.

"Leaving the Durbar, we examined the artillery-yard and other curiosities, and then proceeded homewards. After dining with Mr. Williams, Dr. Smyttan and I proceeded on our journey in the direction of the Gulf of Cambay.

"*24th January.*—We rode from Padrea to Gwasad early in the morning. I distributed, as usual, some tracts, to the natives whom we met on the roads, and preached in the village. We rode to Jambusar in the evening. After our arrival I received the following letter from Mr. Williams relative to the visit to the Gaikwar :—

'Camp Baroda, *January* 24, 1835.

'My dear Sir—His Highness sent for my head clerk this day, and desired him to explain to me that his reason for not accepting the Testament from you yesterday was, that his ministers, relations, and the whole Durbar, would have considered it as a kind of avowal of his inclination to desert his own creed ; that he was very much pleased with what he heard yesterday, and requested that I would send the Testament, and other books, to him by my men. I shall do so, either through the Nawab, or —— , whichever channel his Highness prefers. His Highness further wishes to receive a letter from yourself to his address, stating that you are not offended at his apparent incivility in not receiving the book from your hands when offered to him in the Durbar yesterday ; and desires me to offer you his best wishes, and to say that he has directed all the authorities under him to afford you every aid.'

"*25th January.*—To-day I despatched a Marathee letter, of which the following is a translation, to the Gaikwar :—

'Shri Raja Chhatrapati Akela Praudha Pratap Sayaji Rao Gaiakwad Sena Khas Khel Shamsher Bahadur. To his Highness Sayaji Rao Gaikawad, etc., John Wilson, the Servant of Jesus Christ, with all respect writeth as follows :—

'The illustrious Mr. Williams having communicated to me your Highness's wish to receive a few lines from me, I have the greatest pleasure in addressing you.

'I was much gratified with the interview which I had with your Highness in the Durbar on Friday last, and I am duly sensible of the kindness and condescension which you evinced in granting it to me. I shall always remember it with much satisfaction.

'As the Christian religion appears to me to be possessed of supreme importance, I embraced the opportunity afforded me while in the presence of your Highness, and by your Highness's inquiries, of giving a summary of its principles, and of the evidence on which it rests its claims to universal reception ; and it was with a view to afford your Highness an opportunity of judging of the merits of that religion that I proffered to your Highness a copy of the Christian Shastra. For the patience and interest with which your Highness and your ministers listened, I am truly grateful. Your declining to receive the Christian Shastra in the Durbar, proceeding, as it did, from an apprehension that the public reception of it might be viewed as giving a public testimony in its favour without examination, has given me, I assure you, not the least offence. Nothing is farther from my wish, and that of other Christians, than that Christianity should receive any countenance which does not proceed from the perception of its own merits. We wish it, in every case, to receive the fullest inquiry.

'I return my best thanks to your Highness for the favours given to me in the Durbar, and I shall preserve them as memorials of your kindness.

'Why should I enlarge ? That your Highness may long hold the *chhatra* (umbrella) of protection and shelter over a happy people, and enjoy every blessing in this world and that which is to come, shall ever be my most fervent prayer to Almighty God.   JOHN WILSON.'"

Baroda is one of the three great principalities—Sindia's, Holkar's, and the Gaikwar's—which Maratha soldiers carved out of the débris of the Moghul empire under the flag, first of Sivajee's house, and then of his Mayor of the Palace, the Peshwa. The first Gaikwar, or "cowherd," held the position

of the Peshwa's commander-in-chief till 1721. In the subsequent century the Gaikwars achieved such independence as
was possible under the gradually growing suzerainty of the
East India Company. In 1819 Sayajee Rao, whom Mr.
Wilson describes, had succeeded his brother, and was from
the first, unhappily, left to his own devices under certain
vague guarantees. Misrule, financial insolvency, and dis-
loyalty were the inevitable consequences, till in 1839 he was
threatened with deposition by the paramount power, which
could no longer share the guilt of maintaining his oppression
over a population of two millions, who paid him above a
million sterling a year. Sayajee managed to keep his seat
till his death in 1847, after which the boy whom Mr. Wilson
saw, Gunput Rao, reigned till his death in 1856. He was
succeeded by his brother, Khundee Rao, in 1856, and he by
the youngest brother, Mulhar Rao, in 1870. The maladminis-
tration, which had steadily increased, then became so intolerable and even criminal, that his deportation to Madras
in 1875 was the result, and the succession of a boy adopted
by Khundee Rao's widow. In his Journal, published in the
Oriental Christian Spectator, "specially for the benefit of
the natives," Mr. Wilson gives no indication of the facts
that he learned on the spot regarding the Gaikwar's family
and misrule. But his intimate acquaintance with the whole
history and with the successive Gaikwars, led Lord Northbrook's Government to consult him during the events of
1874-5.[1]

From Daman to Cambay the Gulf of Cambay runs up
into the heart of Goojarat, dividing from Surat and Baroda
the cluster of native States in wild Kathiawar and marshy
Kutch. Mr. Wilson crossed the Gulf to Gogo, the port of
the principality of Bhownuggur, in which State is the famous
Jain hill of temples at Palitana. The great orientalist Colebrooke knew so little of Shatrunjaya as to write of it as
"said to be situated in the west of India." Colonel Tod, of
Rajasthan fame, was the only visitor of note previous to Mr.
Wilson, and that in 1822. The Chinese pilgrim of the
seventh century, Hiuen Thsang, seems to have passed it by,
although he was so near it as Girnar. "The sovereign of
places of pilgrimage," as the old annals call it, was transferred

[1] See Appendix I.

from the Buddhists to their Hindoo friends, the Jains, in
421 A.D. After Mr. Wilson's visit the wealth of the Jain
merchants of the cotton capital covered the hill with fanes,
which even Mr. Fergusson allows to rival the old temples not
only in splendour, but in the beauty and delicacy of their
details ; so that a local writer remarks—" one almost feels
the place a satanic mockery of that fair celestial city into
which naught may enter that defileth ! "

Mr. Wilson prepared the following letter to the Jain
priests of Palitana, and it has ever since been extensively
read by that community :—

"To all the Yatis of Palitana, two Servants of Jesus Christ, the
only Saviour of men, write as follows :—

"Though we have no acquaintance with you we wish your welfare. It is
the desire of our hearts, in the presence of God, that you may be happy in
this world and that which is to come. We have surveyed the splendid
temples which are on the Shatrunji hill ; and however much we admire them
as buildings, we do regret the object for which they have been erected.
They are not, as they ought to have been, places in which God is worshipped.
They are filled with images of *men* whom you suppose to have obtained
Nirwana. These images, or those whom they represent, are the objects of
your supplications ! We do mourn over the errors into which your fathers
fell respecting the divine nature, and from which you have not yet been
delivered. It is lamentable to think that you do not admit a creating and
superintending Providence. You cannot but see in the world on which you
move, and in the worlds above you, decided marks of design and wisdom ;
and, if you reason correctly, you cannot but attribute this design and wisdom
to a being who exercises it. When you look to your own temples, you say
that they have been built. Why do you not admit, when you look to the
temple of the Universe, that *it* must have an Architect, whose wisdom and
power and goodness are infinite ? It is the height of folly to attribute what
you see to a necessitous fate.

" You are wiser than the Brahmans when you say that there is an essential
distinction between matter and spirit. Of neither matter nor spirit, however,
have you correct ideas. All spirit is not, as you imagine, uncreated. God,
whose existence and attributes are proved by his works, is uncreated, but all
other spirit has been created by him, not from his own spirit as the Brahmans
imagine, but from nothing, by his powerful word. In that spirit which has
been created there are essential differences. The spirit of man differs from
that of all the spirits with which we are acquainted on earth. It alone is
capable of knowing, loving, and serving God, and it alone has a moral responsibility in the sight of God. It will continue either in a state of suffering or
of happiness after death, while the spirit of the beasts, etc., shall have perished.
Matter is not, as you imagine, uncreated. God made the whole of it, not
from his own substance, by the word of his power ; and, whenever he pleases,
he can destroy it. To suppose it to exist independently of the creation of
God is to make of it a God."

The letter proceeds to show that the worship of the
twenty-four Tirthankars, and the performance of good works,

cannot remove that sin the existence of which the Jains admit, and it then expounds the salvation offered by Christ. It was largely circulated in the Goojaratee form. Mr. Wilson reasoned with the Raja of the place, and with the Jains of the puritan Dhoondra sect, one of whose religious duties is to keep out of the way of the wind lest it should blow insects into the mouth. Their confidence in their tenderness towards life makes them very conceited. "How many lives are there in a pound of water?" asked Mr. Wilson of a Dhoondra. *D.* "An infinite number." *W.* "How many are there in a bullock?" *D.* "One." *W.* "You kill thousands of lives, then, while the Mussulman butcher kills one." The Hindoos laughed, and the Dhoondras joined them.

At Rajkote, in the heart of the Kathiawar peninsula, Mr. Wilson came fairly face to face with female infanticide. The young Rajpoot chief of the Jhadeja tribe he found under sequestration, because of having been accessory to the murder of his infant daughter. The long-neglected regulations of General Walker had been revived by Sir J. P. Willoughby, who afterwards adorned the Council of the Secretary of State for India. Mr. Wilson expounded to the Raja and his court the Ten Commandments, "not overlooking the sixth, which he has so daringly violated," while regarding him "with deep compassion." This agreement,[1] signed by every Jhadeja chief in General Walker's time, presents a curious contrast to recent legislation on the same subject.

"Whereas the Honourable English Company, and Anund Row Guikwar, Sena Khas Khey! Shamsher Bahadoor, having set forth to us the dictates of the Shastres and the true faith of the Hindoos, as well as that the 'Brumhu Vywurtuk Pooran' declares the killing of children to be a heinous sin, it being written that it is as great an offence to kill an embryo as a Brahman ; that to kill one woman is as great a sin as killing a hundred Brahmans ; that to put one child to death is as great a transgression againt the divine laws as to kill a hundred women ; and that the perpetrators of this sin shall be damned to the hell Kule Sootheeta, where he shall be infested with as many maggots as he may have hairs on his body, be born again a leper, and debilitated in all his members ; we, Jahdeja Dewajee aud Kooer Nuthoo, Zemindars of Gondul (the custom of female infanticide having long prevailed in our caste), do hereby agree for ourselves, and for our offspring for ever, for the sake of our own prosperity, and for the credit of the Hindoo faith, that we shall from this day renounce this practice ; and, in default of this, that we acknowledge ourselves offenders against the Sircars. Moreover, should any

---

[1] Aitchison's *Collection of Treaties, Engagements, and Sunnuds*, vol. iv. p. 129, and also p. 109, second edition, 1876.

one in future commit this offence, we shall expel him from our caste, and he
shall be punished according to the pleasure of the two Governments, and the
rule of the Shastres."

"*22d February—Sabbath.*—I have never travelled on this day since I came
to India, but in order that we might have an opportunity of preaching to our
countrymen in a camp where the face of a minister has not been seen since
the death of Mr. Gray, we rode into Bhooj early in the morning. We found
that arrangements for public worship had been made by Colonel Pottinger,
the Resident, with whom we took up our abode."

The Rev. James Gray—a chaplain worthy as man and
orientalist of Henry Lord, the first of the Company's ecclesiastical establishment at Surat—had died five years before, and
there were 140 Europeans at this remote station. His story
is another added to those romances of an Indian career with
which our history in the East is so plentifully and heroically
strewed. A shoemaker of Dunse, not far from Mr. Wilson's
birthplace, he educated himself to be the second best teacher
of Greek in Scotland, as the senior master of the High School
of Edinburgh. He was the friend of Burns, the tutor of his
boys, the correspondent of Wordsworth, and himself a poet
and classical critic in *Blackwood's Magazine.* His elegy
appears in Hogg's *Queen's Wake* as that of one—

> "Bred on southern shore,
> Beneath the mists of Lammermore."

Intenser views of Christian truth led him to accept an
East Indian chaplaincy, and in the solitude of Bhooj he gave
the close of his life to service to the natives, from the young
Raja whom he taught, to the simple folk whose dialect of
Kutchee, a transition from Goojaratee, he reduced to writing.
These were days when our native feudatories were left to
themselves, and the millions whom they ruled had no such
guarantees against oppression as Lord Dalhousie and Lord
Canning established when the empire became consolidated.
Mr. Gray's good work has often been repeated since, but after
Schwartz he was the first, from 1826 to 1830, to aim at such
an object as this—"I shall be able to make him one of the
most learned kings that ever were in India, as he promises to
be one of the most humane. Oh! that I may be enabled to
impart to his mind a portion of that wisdom that cometh
down from above." A few months after that Mr. Gray passed
away, his death officially declared by Sir John Malcolm to be
" a public loss," and his name associated in the journals with

those of Carey, Leyden, and Morrison. Like Schwartz's royal
pupil, Maharaja Serfojee of Tanjore, the grateful Rao Daisul
of Kutch erected a monument to Mr. Gray. From 1833 to
1860 Rao Daisul ruled his half-million of people with loyalty
to the British Crown, fidelity to the teaching of his Christian
tutor, and the best results to the people. Slavery he abolished
the year after Mr. Wilson's visit. Infanticide he suppressed
by new regulations, so that the proportion of females to males
in the Jhadeja tribe in Kutch rose from 1 to 8 in 1842 to 1
to 1·04 in 1868. His son more recently helped Sir Bartle
Frere to stop the slave trade from Zanzibar to Muscat, which
Kutch capitalists had encouraged ; and his grandson is now a
boy of twelve under training for power at the usual age of
Indian majority, eighteen.

Turning back from Bhooj, the most northerly part of the
tour, Mr. Wilson took boat at its large port of Mandvee for
the famous shrines of Krishna on the south coast of the Gulf
of Kutch. Here, at the island of Beyt and the fortress-
temple of Dwarka, a mixed race of Muhammadans and Hindoos
have long added to the plunder of deluded pilgrims the profits
of organised piracy. Sanguinary wars and sieges, before 1835
and since, have given a horrible notoriety to the Waghurs,
whom their lord and employer, the Gaikwar, failed to control.
The more direct administration of political officers so vigorous
as Colonel Keatinge, has in recent days given peace to the
land of jungle and of idol shrines which forms the most
westerly point of Goojarat. Such merit as temporary absorption into " the prince, the intoxicator "—as Krishna, the lasci-
vious, is called—can give, is now to be obtained without the
risks of 1835 and previously. But the island and the castle
of Krishna, the Lord of Dwarka, are not so attractive as they
were, save for the conch shells which Beyt, " the door of the
shell," exports to supply the uses of every Krishna temple,
and also for purposes of art. Dwarka is to the west what
Pooree, the shrine of Jugganath, the lord of the world, is
to the east of India.

"7th March, POREBUNDER.—We preached, apart from one another, both
morning and evening in the bazaars ; and we had many visitors throughout
the day, whom we addressed and supplied with books. The report of our proceedings in other parts of the province had reached the town, and contributed
not a little to the interest with which our ministrations were viewed. I am
more and more persuaded that long missionary tours are by far the most

beneficial. Had we confined ourselves on this occasion to a small district, there would have been little or none of this ardour, which procures us numerous and interested auditors. 'I must hear,' say many, 'what every person in every place hears.' There has been too much overlooking of human sympathy in the conduct of many Missions. If the Hindoos are to be wrought upon, they must be roused. The ministry of excitement, both of John the Baptist and our blessed Lord, preceded the ministry of conversion through the Apostles in the land of Judæa. Something similar may be the case in India."

Sailing down the coast, Mr. Wilson reached Joonagurh, a Muhammadan principality, in the court of which he had long discussions till past midnight, first with Hindoo and then with Mussulman scholars. He found the Hindoo prime minister well acquainted with Arabic. But his visit has a peculiar interest because of his—the first—attempt, in 1835, to decipher the famous Asoka inscriptions on the granite boulder of Girnar, discussed in a subsequent chapter. The classical hill, ten miles from the town, Mr. Wilson reached through the surrounding jungle at daybreak.

"13th *March.*—The ascent is very difficult, and in some places, from the precipitousness of the mountain, rather trying to the nerves. The rock is of granite, containing, particularly near the summit, a large quantity of mica. There is scarcely any vegetation upon it, and indeed, from its steepness, no possibility of the formation of a soil. The greatest temples are at an elevation, I should think, of about 3000 feet, estimating the greatest height at 3500. They are built of the granite, though some of the steps and staircases are formed of sandstone from the plain below. They are works of prodigious labour, and are executed in excellent taste. They are at present appropriated by the Jains, but the most ancient and remarkable of them appear to me from the Dhagob, and other arrangements, to be undoubtedly Buddhist. The most remarkable Jain images in them are those of Neminatha, not much exceeding the size of a man, black and ornamented with gold, and at present worshipped ; and Rishabhdeva, of a colossal size, of granite covered with white chunam ; and Parasnatha. In the inferior parts there are the images of all the twenty-four Tirthankars. There are numerous cells in the courts of the temples, and places adjoining, which were probably formerly used by the priests. At present the only persons who live on the hill are the sepoys who guard the temples, a few *pujaris* (beadles), and pilgrims who come to worship, and who may sojourn for a night or two. I was allowed to go through all the temples, and even to enter the shrines and measure the idols.

"There are two other peaks on the hill, from one of which the Hindoos who get tired of life throw themselves down in the hope of making a speedy journey of it to heaven. I did not think of visiting them on account of the difficulty of reaching them. There was, however, a staircase leading to them, as to the peak on which I stood. The view from the top of Girnar is one which is not dearly purchased at the expense of ascending it. It embraces the adjoining hills, one of which—the Dhatar—vies with it in height, and an immense range of low country extending in all directions, and, toward the west, reaching the sea. There is much jungle on the lower hills : and cultivation, from the want of water, is not very extensive in the low country. Villages appear scattered only here and there.

"I made as quick a descent of the mountain as possible, that I might reach, before the darkness of night settled upon me, the block of granite near Joonagurh, which contains the ancient inscriptions which, though never deciphered, have attracted much attention. I was able to accomplish the object which I had in view. After examining the block for a little, and comparing the letters with several ancient Sanskrita alphabets in my possession, I found myself able, to my great joy, and that of the Brahmans who were with me, to make out several words, and to decide as to the probable possibility of making out the whole. The taking a copy of the inscriptions, I found, from their extent, to be a hopeless task ; but, as Captain Lang had kindly promised to procure a transcript of the whole for me, I did not regret the circumstance."

But one spot of historical and idolatrous interest remained to be visited—that Somnath which the iconoclast Muhammad of Ghuznee stripped of its treasures, and the so-called gates which Lord Ellenborough dreamed that he would restore as an act of political and religious justice which the Hindoos must appreciate. Having sailed from the port of Joonagurh, Verawul, Mr. Wilson rode two miles to the Phallic shrine of the old temple.

"18th March.—I proceeded to both the new and old temples of Somnath. The former was built by the famous Alya Bai about fifty years ago, and it is now under the care of the Sompada Brahmans, with one of whom I conversed. The latter is that of which the image (a linga) was destroyed by Muhammad of Ghazni, and of which the most extravagant accounts have been published. The greater part of the building (of sandstone) is still standing, and the remains of its external ornaments, though much defaced by the violence of the Mussulmans, show that, as pieces of art, they had been well executed. Some are not very decent, and it is not to be wondered at that the attempt was made to destroy them. The Mussulman conqueror might find treasure about the premises, but most certainly it was not within the god, who had neither head nor belly."

Bombay was safely reached, by sea, on the 20th March, after an absence of above three months. The missionary survey of the whole Province of Bombay proper was now complete.

The one, the only one, intolerable trial of European life in India had already begun to cast its shadow over the otherwise unbroken happiness of the mission family at Ambrolie. Four children had been born to Mr. and Mrs. Wilson, and of these one had died in infancy, while another was soon to follow him. During Mr. Wilson's absence on his tour to Goa in 1834, it had been necessary to send home their eldest boy, Andrew, who has since distinguished himself as a traveller

and author in India, China, and Great Britain. Very pathetic
are the references, in the correspondence of husband and
wife, to these deaths and that separation. But now the close
of the tour of 1835 was to be marked by the greatest blow
of all. Dr. Smyttan had urged Mrs. Wilson to return to
Scotland, after her visit to Surat, as the only means of saving
her life. " It seems worse than death to part from my
husband; but if I must indeed go, the Lord will give me
strength for the hour of trial. Dr. Smyttan has not yet
mentioned it to Mr. Wilson; he is afraid of distressing him,
and he wished me first to give my consent. This I can
never do." On the 8th April she wrote to her boy at home
" the last letter that your dearest mamma will ever write to
you;" and as she laid down the pen exclaimed, "Now I am
ready to die." But not till the struggling spirit had cared
for the Marathee girls also, for she ever spoke in the agony
of dissolution to them, *Anandie, Yeshu Christiavar phar priti
theva*, "O Anandie, I beseech you, greatly love Jesus Christ!"
"The prospect of death is sweet," she could say in her last
words. After that, and on the 19th April, the Sabbath
morning saw her freed from the body.

It is all such a tragedy, and on its human side so common
a tragedy, in the land of which Great Britain has taken possession by the dust of its noblest women as well as bravest
men. But to her it was a triumph. Margaret Wilson was
the first, as she was with Ann Judson the greatest, of that
band of women-missionaries whom Great Britain and America
have ever since given to India, till now they number some
two hundred who are living and dying for its people. Her
sisters soon after took up her work, and her husband published
a very popular Memoir of her life,[1] which the perusal of her
papers enables us to pronounce within the truth in the representations it gives of her intellectual ability and her gracious
force of character. To her, more than to any other, is due
the rapid progress of female education in Bombay, not only
in Christian schools but in Parsee, Hindoo, and even Muhammadan families.

[1] *A Memoir of Mrs. Margaret Wilson*, of the Scottish Mission, Bombay.
Third edition, enlarged. Edinburgh, 1840.

CHAPTER VII.

1836-1842.

ZAND SCHOLARSHIP AND THE PARSEE CONTROVERSY.

WHEN, on the 7th July 1836, Mr. Wilson wrote that pleasant letter to his old friend and benefactor, Mr. J. Jordan Wilson, in which he expressed satisfaction at "Mr. Duff's elevation to a Doctorship" by the vigorous University of Aberdeen, and hinted that his own policy of vernacular preaching would probably lead the Modern Athens to pronounce him a "babbler," like Paul, he was about to be surprised by the receipt of the parchment diploma from his own University of Edinburgh, of D.D., or "Sacrosanctæ Theologiæ Doctor." The learning and the piety of his native country were as ready to mark with academic approval the six years' career of the young scholar who preached and wrote, in season and out of season, to wise and simple, in the vernacular and classical tongues of Western India, as to honour the briefer and more brilliant work of his fellow-missionary who, in Eastern India, had begun an intellectual as well as spiritual revolution which was already affecting even Bombay itself.

Dr. Duff, driven home by an almost fatal disease, was restored to feed the flame of apostolic Evangelism in the churches of great Britain and America, so that soon Bombay and Goojarat, as well as Madras, Nagpore, and Calcutta, were to see the result in new missions and fresh missionaries worthy of such pioneers. Dr. Wilson, in spite of the comparative solitude of bereavement, and not unfrequent sickness from overwork and exposure, was to be enabled to carry on his loved work among the people of India without interruption till the close of 1842. Thus, at every successive period the gifts and the labours of each supplemented those of the other, while specially adapted to the local peculiarities of the provinces and the communities to whom they gave their lives ; and both combined to form an almost perfect ideal of Christian evangelisation among the races of the East.

Certainly the diploma of the University of Edinburgh, as it was given to Wilson after the old fashion, long before the modern and most desirable custom of bestowing such academic degrees personally and in public had originated, well described his previous function as a teacher of divine Theology, and could hardly confer on him any new power or virtue in that capacity. The interest of the already yellow parchment lies rather in the names of some of the men who signed it, among whom we find, besides Principal Baird, such medical professors as Alison and Traill, Ballingall and Syme, and Sir Robert Christison still spared to the city ; Thomas Chalmers and David Welsh ; Sir William Hamilton and James D. Forbes ; Macvey Napier, and that other John Wilson, who taught poetry, criticism, and all the humanities, under the name of Moral Philosophy. Never before, and probably never since, has the honorary degree of Doctor of Divinity, even when conferred by the University of Edinburgh, had so honest a significance as this, which was signed on the 4th of May 1836. He thus acknowledged it, in a letter to Professor Brunton, which also gives us some glimpses of the progress of female education and society :—

"BOMBAY, 16th September 1836.—I received your letter of the 28th May, on the fiftieth day after its date ! I am quite overwhelmed with your kindness ; and I shall not attempt to express my sense of the obligations under which it has placed me. The diploma was unexpected by me ; and I fear that it will prove only a generous payment in advance for work which may never be performed. I desire to view it, however, as a new call to cultivate personal humility, to abound in the proclamation of the Gospel, both by writing and speech, to the perishing multitudes around me, and to unfold for the compassion of the benevolent, as opportunities offer, the systems of transcendental speculation and gross superstition, which exercise such a destructive sway in the regions of Asia. I have already used my new title in a Persian pamphlet which I have just published, entitled *Raddi-i-Din Musalmáni*, or Refutation of Muhammadanism. My grateful acknowledgments are due to the University of Edinburgh.

"The School for Destitute Poor Native Girls now contains fifty-five scholars, who are all making satisfactory progress. The eldest of the two girls connected with it, whom I lately baptized, has been married by me to one of the Brahman converts, and this, the first virtuous union of natives formed in the bosom of the Protestant Church in Bombay, promises to promote the happiness of both the parties. The marriage was honoured by the attendance of several friends of the mission, and by many natives. I embraced the opportunity which it afforded me of entering into a contrast between the injunctions of the Christian Scriptures and the Hindoo Shástres relative to the treatment of females. The Parsee inhabitants of a street in the neighbourhood of the mission-house have placed under me the whole disposal of the juvenile population, including sixteen girls, for instruction through the medium of Goojaratee, a circumstance which has afforded me the highest delight. Altogether, there are upwards of 180 girls educating in connection with the mission."

To his discussions with Brahmans and Moulvies, Jains and Jews, in the central seat of Bombay, and in many of its districts and feudatory principalities, Dr. Wilson had added that which proved to be the most important of all. Alike as a scholar and a missionary, his writings on the Zand language and literature, and his spiritual and social influence among the Parsees, take the highest place. He was the first English scholar to master the original Zand texts, according to the admission of the "irritabile genus" of pure Orientalists, as represented by the late Dr. Haug, who would in no wise give due credit to his German rival, Spiegel, the present able representative of Zand scholarship in Europe. And Dr. Wilson was the first missionary to educate and admit to the Christian Church two converts from the faith of Zoroaster, who still adorn the Free Church of Scotland and the Baptist Church respectively, as ordained ministers.

The Parsees, the people of Pars or Fars which the Greeks called Persis, after having ruled Western Asia from the Black Sea to the Indus from before Kai Khoshru, or Cyrus the Great, fell victims to the same intolerance which they had shown against every other faith, whether idolatrous or Christian as in the case of the long-suffering Armenians. In A.D. 658, Yezdijird III., the last of the Sassanian kings, saw

his army spoiled of its sacred banner, the jewelled apron of
Kawa, on the fatal field of Kadseah.   That palladium gone, a
few years more left the empire of Cyrus extinguished at Naha-
vand, not far from that capital of Hamadan, to which the
Jewess Esther has given an immortality greater than that of
Cyrus or of Artaxerxes her husband.   The mound is still
seen at Toorkman Merv where Yezdijird found a grave after
miserable wanderings, while all of his surviving host who did
not apostatise bore with them the sacred fire to the hills of
Khorassan.   Thence the Kaliph Omar and his successors drove
them south to the sea, to the caves of Ormuz of which Milton
sings, though its wealth and splendour were of later date and
Portuguese origin, on to Diu off Kathiawar, and so to Sanjan
in Goojarat.   There, in 717, they found an aslyum for three
centuries, and became partially Hindooised.   For, explain it
away as their Anglicised descendants may, "the fair, the
fearless, the valiant, and the athletic Parsees," obtained protection from the Rana Jadao by a denial of that very monotheism from which, in its Muhammadan form, they had fled,
and which in controversy they now claim to hold.   In sixteen distichs of corrupt Sanskrit, drawn up after some days
of deliberation, they professed to worship the sun, the five
elements, Hormuzd, chief of the Suras or angels, and the
cow ; and described their ritual and customs.   Regarding
them, evidently, as only another sect of Hindoos, the Rana
assisted them to build their fire-temple, and there they continued to flourish, sending forth settlements to the neighbouring districts.   As the Muhammadan power grew in Western
India their old enemy found them out, and they fled with
their sacred fire to the jungle of Wasanda from the assault
of Sultan Mahmood Begoda of Ahmedabad, in 1507, though
not without showing a courage in defence of their Hindoo
protectors worthy of their fathers.   When the danger passed
by they sought a resting-place in that Goojaratee town of
Nausaree, where Dr. Wilson found their earliest temples and
MSS. during his northern tour.   Surat was not far off, and
thither not a few Parsees carried their intelligence and enterprise to the service of the European traders.   Sir Nicholas
Waite's Parsee broker, for instance, still lives in the early
annals as a clever but by no means honest fellow.   The family
of Ardeshir Dhunjeesha of Surat was founded by a Parsee

whose ability made him the favourite of the Great Moghul at
Agra, and enabled him to obtain commercial privileges for
his English friends. Muncherjee Seth did similar service to
the Dutch. As Surat rose into importance Nausaree became,
what it still is, the city of the Parsee priests. At an early
period the community attracted the attention of Kerridge,
the English Governor of Surat; and in 1616 he urged Henry
Lord, the first English chaplain there, to study thoroughly the
religions of both Hindoos and Parsees. Lord's rare little
quarto was used by Sir Thomas Herbert in his valuable work ;
and by the French traveller Bernier, in his letter to M.
Chaplain, on "Lord's Discovery of Two Foreign Sects."

When Bombay became English, and was opened as a free
city to all the native communities of Western India, Asia,
and Eastern Africa, as we have seen, the Parsees were the
first to take advantage of English rule there. Three years
after its settlement, Dr. Fryer found, on the top of Malabar
Hill, "a Parsee tomb (or tower of silence) lately raised."
Indeed, one Dorabjee Nanabhoy had held office there during
the Portuguese occupation, and his services were found invaluable when the English took possession. His son drove off
the Seedee pirates, and received the hereditary distinction of
Patel or lord of the fishermen whom he led on that occasion,
an honour still valued by the family, who have become great
merchants from China to London. The English shipwright
who built the East India Company's vessels at Bombay
tempted one Lowjee to leave Surat, and his descendants have,
ever since the foundation of the dockyard in 1735, held the
position of master builder. The great and wealthy clans of
Shet Khandans, Dadyshets, and Banajees, still trace their
prosperity to the happy day when their ancestors settled
under the Company's flag in the Fort of Bombay. It was in
1780 that a Dadyshet built the first of the three fire-temples
in the island. The latest census shows that the whole Parsee
community under British rule number 70,000, of whom a
third are in the city of Bombay. There are some in Persia.

For a community with such a history, language, and
sacred literature, whose influence, in spite of their comparatively small number, was half a century ago far beyond that
of the leading men of all the other races and sects in India,
nothing had been done in a high educational sense before Dr

Wilson's arrival in Bombay. Save a few of their priests, they
themselves were ignorant of their sacred books. The little
that Lord had been able to communicate to Europe regarding
them in the beginning of the seventeenth century had been
independently followed up by a Jesuit missionary, whose
undoubtedly rich contributions to early Zand and Sanskrit
scholarship Dr. Haug overlooks in his history of the researches
into the sacred writings and religion of the Parsees. John
Philip Werdin, born of peasant parents in 1748 in South
Austria, went out in 1774 to the Malabar coast as Frater
Paulinus, devoted himself for fourteen years to the study of
Sanskrit and Zand, as well as the languages of South India,
and returned to Rome, from which, when secretary to the
congregation of the Propaganda, he issued at least twenty
great works, mostly quarto volumes, on the classical languages,
literatures and customs of the peoples of India.

Not less a polemic than Paulinus was Anquetil du Perron,
the young theological student of Paris, who first brought the
Zand texts to Europe, and translated them, after a fashion,
into French. Stumbling on a manuscript of the Vandidad in
the king's library, one of the few probably brought to Europe
by Bourchier or Dr. Fraser, he abandoned the church for the
life of a private soldier, that he might find his way out to
India. He sailed in the French expedition of 1745. Knowing Hebrew, Arabic, and Persian, he set himself to Sanskrit,
and such a study of the people as could best be made during
long journeys on foot from Chandernagore to Pondicheri on
the east coast, and from Mahé to Surat on the west coast.
At Surat the support of the French government enabled him
to fee Dustoor Darab, one of the most learned high priests
of the Parsees, to instruct him in both Zand and Pahlavi, and
to sell him manuscripts. Suspecting that he was being
deceived, as later scholars like Wilford were, by the Brahmans, he bribed other priests also, till he was satisfied as to
the honesty of Darab. For six years, during which he
collected a hundred and eighty MSS. in all the sacred
languages of the country, he pursued his researches, and then
he determined to settle at Benares for the composition of a
work on the whole history, literature, and antiquities of India.
The fall of Pondicheri to the English arms forced him to
return to France. He visited Oxford on the way, where he

laid the foundation of a quarrel with Sir William Jones, and
so led the learned of Europe into the error, which Dr. Wilson
was the first completely to dissipate, that Zand, instead of
being the elder sister of the Sanskrit, was that monstrous
impossibility—an invented or forged language. France
honoured the scholar, as, since Colbert, she had always persecuted the soldiers and statesmen who would have given her
an eastern empire, and in 1771 he published his *Zend-Avesta.*
The Revolution drove him into that obscurity which alone
was safety, and when he died in 1805 he was occupied on a
new French edition of the *Viaggio* of his old rival Paulinus.
A century before, Hyde had published his learned apology for
Zoroastrianism, in his *Historia Religionis Veterum Persarum
eorumque Magorum,* but he could not read the MSS. of which
he professed to give a criticism. Du Perron's manuscripts,
the dictations of Darab and the other priests, as still to be
found in the National Library of Paris, and, above all, the
two quartos of his *Zend-Avesta,* became the stream from which
all subsequent scholars drank, till the Danish Rask and the
Scottish Wilson went to the fountain-head.

In the course of a philological tour of Europe, Africa, and
Asia, the Scandinavian scholar Rask visited Bombay to study
Zand. In 1826 he used the collection which he had purchased
for the Copenhagen Library in the production of his small
work on the age and genuineness of the Zand language. In
that he justified by new proofs the conclusions of Paulinus
and Du Perron as to its relation to the Sanskrit, but refused
to follow the latter in his conclusions as to the antiquity of
Zoroaster. For Rask was the first to make out the law of the
transposition of sounds with which Bopp's name is connected.
Five years afterwards Dr. Wilson, prompted by the scholar's
enthusiasm, but, along with that, by the more consuming fire
which inflamed all his life, thus wrote to the secretary of the
Scottish Missionary Society, the first of his draft letters which
we can find specially referring to the Parsees :—

"BOMBAY, 24th *July* 1831. . . . I have now regularly delivered a lecture
on Systematic Theology on Wednesday evenings during the last sixteen weeks.
My audience, which consists partly of Europeans and partly of Natives, has
been respectable. Ten of my lectures were devoted to the consideration of the
testimony which is afforded by the light of Nature to the existence, attributes,
and moral government of God ; and to the duty and destiny of man. Two of
them were occupied in forming an estimate of the discoveries of the light of

Nature, and in evincing the possibility and desirableness of a direct Revelation. I am at present engaged in the consideration of the inquiry, Where is a direct Revelation to be found ? and I have spent four evenings in the discussion of the claims of the Parsee religion. I have been requested to publish my observations upon it ; but I have agreed only to the present printing of such of them as refer to the " Vendidad Sadé," which is the most authoritative work acknowledged by the followers of Zoroaster. I intend, God willing, to comply with the wishes of my friends by preparing a work embracing an analysis of all the sacred books of the Parsees, a particular view of their religious history so far as it can be ascertained, and a description of their manners and customs. I have for a long time been prosecuting inquiries connected with these subjects ; and I have lately procured some documents which throw great light upon them.   When I last wrote to you I had not the intention which I now avow ; but many circumstances have conspired, and especially the encouragement which I have received from some of my friends to whose judgment I bow with deference, the readiness of the natives to make communications to me—the probable usefulness of the work in leading them to inquiry and in assisting future missionaries—which they have hitherto withheld from other Europeans, have led me to come to a determination on the subject.   I have access to most of the books published in Europe which treat of the Parsees.   There is one little work which I cannot find here which I should like to see. It is *The Sacred Oracles of Zoroaster,* published in Greek, at Amsterdam, in 1689.   It is not considered genuine ; but some of the passages which I have seen objected to as inconsistent with the opinions of Zoroaster appear to me to be consonant with them.   If you should see a copy advertised in any of the catalogues, I shall feel much obliged to you if you will purchase it for me."

It was not till 1833 that there appeared the *Commentary on the Yasna,* or Parsee prayer-book, based on Neriosingh's Sanskrit translation, by Eugène Burnouf. Nor was it till 1841 that the other Danish scholar, Westergaard, arrived in Bombay, where he was long Dr. Wilson's guest, and received that self-sacrificing assistance which enabled him to give to the world the first complete edition of the still extant text of the Avasta, "translated with a dictionary grammar, etc.," in 1852-54. There were two men in Bombay on Dr. Wilson's arrival who further stimulated him to vindicate the reputation of the capital in which most of the Parsees were to be found.   Sir John Malcolm, in one of his earliest addresses to the Asiatic Society there, had declared that, in the first instance, Bombay must be specially looked to for an elucidation of the ancient Zoroastrian faith.   Mr. William Erskine, son-in-law of Sir James Mackintosh, and historian of Babar and Hoomayoon, had frequently contributed to its "Transactions" papers on the ancient religion of Persia, which, indeed, had led the king of Denmark to send Professor Rask to India.

The occasion of Dr. Wilson's first encounter with the Parsees was his publication in 1831 of a review of the work of Elisæus on the *History of Vartan and the Battle of the Armenians, containing an Account of the Religious War between the Persians and Armenians*, translated by that accomplished Christian Jew, Karl Friedrich Neumann, who had just visited China, and who died at Berlin a few years ago. It was necessary for the critic to give a very brief and general account of the religious works of the Parsees, and not without the hope that the statement would rouse some apologist on the other side. Two weeks after a Parsee appealed to the editor of the *Samachar*, a respectable Goojaratee newspaper, to say whether, as the writer believed, the account of the Parsee religion was incorrect. " Do the Shets," he asked, the respectable native gentlemen, " and those skilled in the knowledge of our belief, intend to say nothing in refutation ?" The cautious editor declined the challenge for himself, but added, " if it be thought advisable by the intelligent of our tribe, we shall give it a reconsideration." This led Dr. Wilson to acknowledge that he was the author of the review, and to declare his willingness to publish whatever might be written in reply to it. " Tell me your whole mind. . . . You say that we reproach the Hindoo and Parsee religions, but we declare only what is true respecting them. We reason, but we use no violence. We enter into discussion that truth may appear, and we say to all, ' Inquire.' " The unhappy editor did not like the trouble of such rationalism. " Permit us, permit us to follow the road on which we have been travelling, for at last all roads meet in one point ; there is no Redeemer of any," he said. " If our friend the writer, John Wilson (may the grace of God be upon him !), is desirous of drawing us into a discussion of this character, we plainly say to him that it is not suitable to us." But " if any pundit, religious officer, or intelligent person of one of the castes to which he has referred should fulfil his wish, we are perfectly indifferent in the matter, and feel neither joy nor sorrow." In the next number Dr. Wilson slew the slain delusion with the same kindly but uncompromising sympathy that marked all his relations with the natives.

All native Bombay was talking of this new challenge, when a bold printer, who had issued the prospectus of another journal, promised to publish and circulate gratuitously all that should be sent to him on either side till he could establish his paper. So Nowrozjee Mobed Darabjee — a *mobed* being the middle priest, as a *dustoor* is above him and a *herbad* below him—printed on excellent paper a series of pamphlets in royal quarto form. The champion of Zoroaster signed himself, " Nauroz Goosequill," which he changed to " Swanquill," when he realised that he exposed himself to the jocular charge of being a goose. It was sometimes to Dr. Wilson a matter of doubt whether his opponent was in real earnest as regards much which fell from his pen. Goosequill's denial that the Cosmogony, which Dr. Wilson had exposed, was one of the Parsee scriptures, brought down upon him his co-religionists, and the most sacred of all, the Dustoor Eduljee Darabjee, who had translated it into the vernacular Goojaratee. Believing the would-be defender of Parseeism to be a Sadducee of the opposite sect of the Kadmees, the high priest became a challenger in his turn. Goosequill was equal to the work of destruction, and exposed the puerile book in a style which astonished the community, who had accepted it as a popular digest of their faith. It was not difficult for Dr. Wilson to intervene at this stage, and show that all his objections to the Cosmogony applied to the Vandidad. His reply covered sixteen chapters, which appeared in as many numbers of the Goojaratee paper, and these he afterwards condensed into a lecture on the Vandidad, which he delivered to both natives and Europeans, and published at their request.

Had not Gibbon, with all his desire to exalt Zoroastrianism at a time when his knowledge was necessarily imperfect and not derived from the texts themselves, confessed that " in that motley composition, dictated by reason and passion, by enthusiasm and by selfish motives, some useful and sublime truths were disgraced by a mixture of the most abject and dangerous superstition "?

The discussion was now anxiously taken up by the Parsee Sanhedrim, known as the Punchayat—etymologically, council of five — a body of from fifteen to twenty members, empowered by Governor Hornby in 1778 to deal with purely tribal offenders to the extent of beating them with shoes. The Dustoors attacked Dr. Wilson's lecture in the *Jam-i-Jamshid*, the reformers and Dr. Wilson replied in the *Harkārah* and *Vartaman*. The former adopted the position that

the names of the dual principles of good and evil in the
Zoroastrian system, Hormuzd and Ahriman, are purely parabolical : that they have an esoteric meaning not intended for
the ignorant, and that the childish and worse than Talmudic-
miracles ascribed to Zoroaster are as well authenticated as
those of Christ. One of Dr. Wilson's brief rejoinders contains this passage, of striking significance in the light of the
conversion of the two Parsee young men soon after :—

" It appears *wonderful* to the Zoroastrian that God should
have so loved the world as to give His only-begotten Son,
that whosoever believeth in Him should not perish, but have
everlasting life. If he will inquire into the evidences of
Christianity, which are neither few nor small, he will find
that what is wonderful in this instance is also true. If the
Zoroastrian will reflect on the nature of sin, he will perceive
that it is an infinite evil ; that no efforts of his own can of
themselves remove that sin which has been already committed ;
and that, if salvation be obtained at all, it must be through
the merit of a divine substitute. Christ, he will find on inquiry, delivers from the punishment of sin, and saves from
the power of sin, all those who put their trust in His name.
Men's works are imperfect in every case, and in many instances positively sinful ; and if the Zoroastrian looks to *his*
works for his acquittance, he will find himself miserably disappointed. The danger of trusting in our self-righteousness
I have exposed at length in my lecture." The Zoroastrian
boastingly said, " With regard to the conversion of a Parsee
you cannot even dream of the event, because even a Parsee
babe, crying in the cradle, is firmly confident in the venerable
Zartusht." " The conversion of a Parsee," I allow, " is a work
too difficult for *me* to accomplish. The conversion of any
man is a work too difficult for me to accomplish. It is not
too difficult, however, for the Spirit of God. It is my part to
state the truth of God ; and it is God's part to give it his
blessing."

For some five years after these early attacks on Dr. Wilson's Vandidad Lecture the controversy almost ceased. But in
1840 a quarto of 268 pages appeared, bearing this title,
" *Talim-i-Zurtoosht*, or *The Doctrine of Zoroaster*, in the Goojaratee Language, for the Instruction of Parsee Youths, together
with an Answer to Dr. Wilson's Lecture on (the) Vandidad,

compiled by a Parsee Priest." The avowed author was Dosabhoy Sohrabjee, a respectable Moonshee, well known to the native and European communities of Bombay. He confessed himself the hireling of the Parsee sanhedrim. He adopted the old line of representing Ahriman, the evil principle, as a mere personification of the evil qualities inherent in man, and the sacred fire adored in the Yasna ritual as only a centre of worship. His advocacy was soon disowned by the high priest of the large Rasamee sect, Dustoor Edal Daroo. Agreeably to the " orders," and at the expense of Sir Jamsetjee Jeejeebhoy, he published the *Maujazat-i-Zartoshti*, or, *The Undoubted Miracles of Zoroaster*, in 127 quarto pages. The author, who had lived for many years in a state of seclusion at the principal fire-temple, expounded the Zoroastrian faith to aid its followers in their discussions with the Jud-din or Gentiles. Dr. Wilson describes him as having to a considerable extent escaped the untoward march of intellect in his seclusion, but as most creditably preserving his temper.

A third assailant of the Vandidad Lecture, in the same year, 1840, was one who signed himself Kalam Kas, and proposed a series of questions under the title of *Nirang-ha*. So stupid was he that some of the respectable Parsees begged Dr. Wilson not to hold them responsible for the writer's ignorance. The fourth attack, in English as well as Goojaratee, was the *Hadie-Gum-Rahan*, a guide to those who have lost their way, written by Aspandiarjee Framjee in 1841, at the special request of a rich Shet, Jeejeebhoy Dadabhoy, Esq. Of this last Dr. Wilson remarks—

" Its appeals to the Zand writings are pretty numerous, but the translations and interpretations made of them are much more inaccurate than those of Anquetil du Perron, on which, nine years ago, when I published the pamphlet on which its animadversions are made and before I devoted myself seriously to the study of the Zand, I was almost wholly dependent for my knowledge of the sacred books of the Parsees. The author, when he finds my arguments insuperable, generally retreats, like Dosabhoy, into a parabolical sanctuary, which his imagination has called into being as a dernier place of resort for Zoroaster and his foiled followers. In the ruins of this sanctuary, if I mistake not, he has found a place of sepulture."

This is a fair illustration at once of the stage in Zand scholarship reached in 1841 by Dr. Wilson, of the keen yet well-tempered strokes which he dealt at error which debased man and sought to dishonour God, and of the tactics of his priestly assailants. It was not as a scholar, however, but as a Christian apostle, that, as we have before seen, he rejoiced to raise and to engage in the controversies which should let in the true light. Hence, believing it "manifestly desirable that the Parsee system should be exhibited in the light of Christianity, and," as he modestly expresses it, "with a view to aid in this attempt," he left as a legacy to India when illness drove him home at the close of 1842, and he presented to his native country and to Europe, his greatest work, "THE PARSI RELIGION : as contained in the Zand-Avasta, and propounded and defended by the Zoroastrians of India and Persia, Unfolded, Refuted, and Contrasted with Christianity." The volume, long since out of print, was published by the American Mission Press of Bombay from the first Zand and Pahlavi metallic types cast in the East. The Rev. Dr. Allen sent forth from the foundry of that Press for Western India, as Carey, Marshman, and Ward had produced at the Serampore Press long before for all India and China, the first metal types for the regeneration of the East. But it was in 1778 that the earliest critical student of Sanskrit, the Bengal civilian Charles Wilkins, cut with his own hand the types from which the elder Halhed's Grammar was printed, and then a set of Persian types. "He gave to Asia typographic art," may well be written on the tomb of Wilkins, the friend of Sir William Jones.

The Parsi Religion soon brought down on its author, as we shall see, the highest honours of most of the learned societies of Europe, while the lofty honesty, unalterable kindliness and even warm affection of its author for the Parsees as individuals, established his position more firmly than ever in Bombay. Dr. Hyde's Latin work, on the other hand, published more than a century before, though very much an apology for Zoroastrianism, was so ill received that he is said to have boiled his tea-kettle with nearly the whole impression.

In 1833 the " Zoroastrian " controversialist had flung the taunt, that the conversion of a Parsee was not to be even dreamed of. In 1835 the central college of the

General Assembly of the Church of Scotland was opened by Dr. Wilson, then the only Scottish Missionary in Bombay, and in 1839 three Parsee students made their spontaneous and very solemn statements previous to receiving Christian baptism. This was the result of Dr. Wilson's work, and especially of the Vandidad Lecture ; and this accounts for the sudden outburst of controversy against it.

Dhunjeebhoy Nowrojee was sixteen years and a half old, or six months beyond what was supposed to be the legal age of discretion. His mother was living, and his nearest male relative was an uncle. Hormasdjee Pestonjee and Framjee Bahmanjee were above nineteen ; the former was married and the father of one child. The case occurred in the island of Bombay, within the jurisdiction of the purely English law as administered by the Supreme Court and English barrister judges. The most suspicious or hostile could allege no such motives as worldly gain or advancement, for the youths belonged to the best families and were the most intelligent in the college. Altogether, whether we look at the position of the converts, at the character of their teachers, or at the conceited intolerance of the community who believed that a change of religious belief from the doctrines of Zoroaster was as impossible as it would be impious, it was well that the question of religious toleration and civil liberty should thus be tried for the first time in the history of British India and of Asia.

Very slowly had the Court of Directors been compelled by the public voice of England through Parliament to concede, first in 1783, English tribunals with jurisdiction over all within the Presidency cities of Calcutta, Madras, and Bombay, and then in 1813 completed by the charter of 1833, to withdraw the restrictions which prevented the ministers of the Christian faith alone from peaceably preaching and teaching. Now, six years after that charter, and four years after Lord William Bentinck had taken the first step to protect Christian converts from the loss of all their property as well as their families, and the Court of Directors had issued orders that its Government should no longer support Hindoo temples and Muhammadan mosques—which orders were not obeyed—it fell to Dr. Wilson to vindicate the civil and religious rights of the natives of India above sixteen years of age. The similar cases that have occurred since, in the Supreme or High

Courts, as well as in the ordinary territory subject to Indian law, have raised issues of greater moment, and have been on the whole attended with less scandal than are involved in the occasional suits between Roman Catholics and Protestants in this country, as to the rights of conscience of minors. In spite of urgent appeals from both Christians and non-Christians to the Government of India for a declaratory law on the subject, jurists like Sir Henry S. Maine have not found it possible to go beyond the English precedents, which leave it to the judges in each case, after examination of the minor, to decide what is the age or stage of discretion short of sixteen. Unhappily, in states like Mysore, where English precedents are not recognised, oppression of the most atrocious kind may take place without a remedy, as in the case of the well-educated woman, Huchi. Even before the Queen's tribunals there may be a failure of justice from an ignorance of procedure in the lower courts, as in a more recent Lucknow instance, that of the widow Keroda. But in the Dhunjeebhoy trial the age of sixteen was passed, and it only remained for the judge to satisfy himself of the fact. Then too, as in so many other instances, the defeated bigots—for so they must be called while all allowance is made for parental, caste and superstitious feelings—carried off and vilely treated Framjee, so as effectually to prevent his baptism, though not to alter his convictions.

Dhunjeebhoy was not the first Parsee who had sought baptism. Like all the Scottish missionaries, Dr. Wilson kept inquirers longer under observation and instruction than those of a more ritualistic custom think it right to do, thus presenting an extreme contrast to the wholesale baptism of crowds by Xavier as described by that 'apostle' in his letters. Dr. Wilson's official communications to Dr. Brunton thus tell the story :—

"BOMBAY, 6th October 1838.—On the 9th of last month, after I had administered the ordinance of baptism to two children of the converts, I had the satisfaction of enrolling in the list of catechumens the names of five new candidates for admission into the Church—two Mussulmans, one of whom is a Sayad, or reputed descendant of Muhammad; two young Catholic Armenians, and one young Hindoo. A Parsee, the first who has intimated his wish to be baptized in Bombay, appeared along with them, but I declined to allow him to come forward at present on account of his very partial knowledge of Christianity, and my ignorance of his character. I have been obliged, for reasons which will immediately occur to you, to give him shelter in my own house;

but respecting his case in a spiritual point of view, I am not yet able to express a favourable opinion. A short time will probably cast some light on his feelings and motives. I have reason to believe that he is a fair specimen of a considerable class, whose connection for some time past with the Zoroastrians has been maintained more by the strength of their social arrangements than by regard to their religious tenets and practices.

"*1st November* 1838.—You will be deeply interested to learn, what I rejoice with trembling to state to you, that there are several hopeful symptoms of the true conversion to God of one of the most advanced and promising Parsee pupils of our institution. He morning and evening reads the Scriptures and prays with Johannes Essai, our Armenian monitor ; and he has expressed to me his wish to be baptized. He gives a very simple and satisfactory account of the origin and progress of his impressions and convictions. Were we now to receive him into the Church he would immediately be removed from our care and protection. By remaining in his present position he is exposed to many temptations, and he will be in danger when his views and feelings become known to his relatives. A gracious Providence may soon enable us to come to a decision respecting his case. When an open step is taken there will be a great commotion among the Zoroastrians, of whose pride and power you can scarcely form an idea. They are mightily incensed at present on account of the man whose case I mentioned to you last month ; and they have, alas ! succeeded in frightening him into heathen compliances.

"You will see, I doubt not, in the English papers, the declaration of war against Afghanistan and Persia. It is not my province to make on it any comment. I only express the hope that the covenant of offence and defence entered into with Runjeet Singh will ere long prove favourable to the introduction of the Gospel among the independent Sikhs.

"*7th May* 1839.—Intelligence of these defections from the faith of Zarthust having spread among the native community, the clouds began to gather. Our first concern, of course, was the personal safety of our dear children in the faith ; and we lifted up our hearts in prayer that they might be preserved from all danger. On the evening of the 28th of April they were all with me in the mission-house, Ambrolie, engaged in devotional exercises ; and Hormasdjee and Framjee on parting with me said that they had great apprehensions as to their treatment by their connexions. I offered them an asylum should they see reason at any time to place themselves under my protection. Dhunjeebhoy remained with me to assist me in examining some Goojaratee manuscripts, and as it was too late for us when we had concluded our business to proceed to my bungalow on Malabar Hill, where we have generally slept since the commencement of the warm season, and where Dhunjeebhoy had been staying for some days with the view of assisting one of our friends in her studies, we mercifully resolved to rest in the mission-house. All was quiet during the night, but the morning showed too plainly that the elements had been put in motion by the fears and alarms of the families more immediately connected with the youth. One messenger came after another calling on Dhunjeebhoy to return to his friends ; and one attempt after another was made to decoy him from my roof. Different hands began to collect near my premises, and different persons were seen to be on the watch. We were informed that there was great consternation among the Parsees in the Fort ; and we had the most serious apprehensions about Hormasdjee and Framjee, who lived in that locality. When they were at their height the former made his appearance with a man carrying his clothes, and declared that he had heard that Framjee had been put under restraint by his friends, and that he himself had made a narrow escape. I had scarcely given him the promise of protection when two Parsees rushed into the room in which he was sitting, laid violent hands upon him and me, and attempted to carry him off by force. My domestics had some difficulty in overpowering them, but we ultimately succeeded in freeing my house from their unlawful intrusion.

"The baptism of Dhunjeebhoy took place under the protection of the European and native police, on the evening of the 1st of May.   . . Hormasdjee was baptized by me in the mission-house on Sabbath last.   . . On the preceding Saturday I was served with a writ of habeas corpus with reference to Dhunjeebhoy, and a rule *nisi* with reference to Hormasdjee. The affidavits which I lodged apparently completely upset the design of our adversaries, but as they solicited time to answer them my counsel consented. The case will again be heard in about eight days. Thousands of pounds have been subscribed to distress us, and if possible to destroy our glorious cause ; but our righteousness will speedily shine forth clear as the noon-day.

"*20th May* 1839.—Notwithstanding all the wrath, persecution, bribery, and perjury practised by our opponents—of which the enclosed affidavits will give you too sure evidence—a decision has been pronounced in our favour on the writ of habeas corpus commanding me to bring up the body of Dhunjeebhoy Nowrojee ; the rule *nisi*, in the case of Hormasdjee Pestonjee, has been abandoned by the parties in whose behalf it was granted, without a hearing ; and both the interesting converts are now living under my protection, in the undisturbed enjoyment of all the means of grace which are fitted to enlighten, comfort, strengthen, and purify their souls.

"The judgment of Sir John Awdry, you will perceive, decidedly acquits me of ' the imputation of clandestine proceedings ;' and less than this it could not possibly have done. In common with the whole Christian community of Bombay, you will be grieved to observe that in the conclusion of his verdict he has expressed himself so indefinitely regarding the effects of intrusting the education of youth to our charge. What, I doubt not, he intended as a mere statement of his opinion, *supposing* himself, for the moment, to hold the *principles of a Parsee*, has been construed and held up by many of them as an expression of his own view of the right and wrong of the change of religious principle ; and the most injurious effects, which I am sure no man will more regret than Sir John himself, will, I fear, be the consequence.

" We now clearly understand that all questions connected with the personal liberty of the Parsees will be determined, within the bounds of the island of Bombay, by English law and not by Hindoo law or their own variable customs ; and we are far from being sorry to find that this will be the case. The writ of habeas corpus, as in the prosecution now closed, will secure the liberty even of minors when in danger ; the only circumstance which would lead *us* to interfere with the parental control, is actually proved. Another form of prosecution, at the instance of the minors themselves, will secure for them the right of choosing guardians after the age of fourteen years. No very great difficulties will, we trust, be experienced connected with other transactions in which we may be afterwards engaged. Our dispensation of the ordinance of baptism, in any case, must of course stand on moral, and not on legal, grounds, which we see vary in the case of Hindoos, Mussulmans, and Parsees. When we see that the Holy Spirit has performed *His* work in any soul, we must not refuse to acknowledge it by declining to baptize in *His* name, and that of the Father and the Son.

" We have had some tidings, on which we think we may depend, of Framjee Bomanjee, the other dear convert whom the Parsees succeeded in apprehending. On the morning of the 29th of April he was carried before some of the members of the Parsee Punchayat, who used all their influence to induce him to renounce Christianity. That he yielded neither to the threats nor promises which were addressed to him, is proved by the fact that when he returned to his father's residence all the female members of the household were heard beating their breasts and making lamentations as if he had died. It is said that a few days ago he was removed from Bombay, and sent under a convoy along the road to Nausaree, in the south of Goojarat; and that at Banganga he was tied to a date tree and cruelly beaten. I am just about to dismiss a trusty messenger in search of him; and it is not improbable that, if necessary, I myself may go in disguise to the place where he is said to be. He has completed his nineteenth year, and appeared to be much under the influence of divine truth."

The Hon. Mr. Farish was interim Governor, and because of his Christian character and work as a private citizen, he also became an object of suspicion and attack. In a letter to Mr. Poynder, Dr. Wilson thus defended him from misrepresentation :—" Although the Hon. Mr. Farish would not shrink from the responsibility of any of his acts as a private Christian, it so happens that he took no share whatever in the instruction of the Parsee converts; that his class in the Sunday School, which met in the Town Hall before he was Governor, has consisted entirely of professing Christians; and that the troops were called out by the Government on the requisition of the superintendent of the police, who very properly considered his civil establishment inadequate to the preservation of the peace." Sir Charles Forbes laid all the papers in the case before the Court of Directors, which transmitted them to Sir James Rivett Carnac, the new Governor. He was rash enough to declare, on landing at Bombay, that he would give neither official nor private countenance to educational or ministerial labours calculated to interfere with the native religions. Dr. Wilson personally experienced from him, as from all the Governors, "much politeness and attention," and hoped that a knowledge of the country and its needs would make him a successor worthy of Sir Robert Grant, whose sudden death had added private as well as public sorrow to Dr. Wilson's many cares in the year 1839. Anticipating an appeal to the Judicial Committee of the Privy Council against Sir John Awdry's judgment, and desirous that the question should be debated on its merits in both Houses of Parliament, Dr. Wilson submitted the papers to Lord Glenelg, the worthy son of Charles Grant, to Lord Bexley, and to Sir George Sinclair and Mr. J. C. Colquhoun, members of the House of Commons. Meanwhile poor Framjee, after being kept for weeks under restraint by the Mobeds of Nausaree, was allowed to return to Bombay, with the confession that they could not break his attachment to Christianity. There he was strictly watched, so that he could not even write. At last, seven months afterwards, Dr. Wilson informed Dr. Brunton—

"I had an interview with Framjee Bomanjee. He had secreted himself in a cellar below our Institution, and took means to call my attention to him. Our conversation lasted about an hour ; and I received from him a particular account of all the treatment which he has received, and of his present feelings and purposes connected with Christianity. His perils are imminent ; but he says that, through God's grace, he will yet enter the Church. He conveyed to me some special warnings, and I fear that there is too good ground for them. One of the sons-in-law and a nephew of Framjee Cowasjee, one of our principal persecutors, occasionally visits me as a professed inquirer. His case I do not yet understand. There are several very influential Parsees here, in whose friendship I have every confidence ; and they will give our Institution their aid as soon as they can do so with safety."

The Parsee panic spread to Poona, whither Dr. Wilson went for rest, and Mr. J. Mitchell's mission-school there was also emptied for a time. The course which the Punchayat finally resolved on was the most foolish they could have selected. An appeal to the Privy Council would have raised and settled many still undecided questions of importance as to minors, discretion, and the age of majority under English law and for non-European British subjects, which must have led to wise legislation, and have prevented subsequent and still existing cases of persecution and hardship. But, as is usual in such cases, they sought and found an English officer to take payment as their agent in London, and they caused to be drawn up a document which soon proved so notorious as the Anti-Conversion Memorial, that it was scouted by every newspaper in India save their own. To the document, after several months canvassing and misrepresentation, the Parsee priests obtained the signatures of only 2115 persons, who professed to ask Government to prohibit the establishment of missionary schools, to fix the age of discretion for all natives at twenty-one, and to deny to such natives above twenty-one as might become Christians, wife, children, and heritable property, while fining them for the support of the families thus to be denied them. Sir James Rivett Carnac's Bombay Government, and Lord Auckland's Government of India, neither favourable to Christian missionaries, fell back on the position of neutrality, which would have been impregnable if the Bishop of London had not in the previous session of

Parliament shown, amid the applause of the Peers, that the
East India Company was neutral only to Christianity, while
still saluting idols and administering temple and mosque
revenues. The Bombay Government pointed out the inconsistency of the Parsees' request with their professed desire for
education. The Government of India declined to pass enact-
ments at variance with Lord William Bentinck's Regulation
7 of 1832, with the rights of civil and personal liberty, and
the principles of the British Parliament. Dr. Wilson's duty
was difficult; he had to enlighten British opinion, but above
all to reason in the spirit of the very toleration for which he
pled with the misguided leaders of the Parsees. He did both
in an able resumé and exposition of the principles and the
custom of toleration in British India, which may still be read
with advantage side by side with the noble state-paper on the
same subject which Lord Lawrence wrote after the close of
the Mutiny of 1857, when he was Chief Commissioner of the
Punjab.

In a brief Journal, kept for a few weeks at the end of this
conflict, we obtain these glimpses into the daily life of Dr.
Wilson, whose indomitable courage and vigorous constitution
enabled him to pass through depression and sickness, still
abounding in the work of his Master.

"2d *June* 1839.—Considerably indisposed. Letter to Mr. Little on the
improvement of the death of Mr. Graham. Preached at the Poors' Asylum.
Examined the male boarders of the mission. Read account of the persecutions in Persia, given by Socrates and Theodoret, etc. Visited twice the
house of Bai, the convert, to administer medicine and pray. Confined a
good deal to my conch.

"*4th*.—Attended the examination of the Byculla Schools, where Sir
James Carnac delivered his maiden speech, which, as far as missions are
concerned, was very unpromising. When I heard him uttering great swelling
words of vanity on this subject, which he does not understand, I thought of
Him Who has on His vesture and on His thigh a name written, "King of
kings and Lord of Lords," and felt that our cause was safe, even though all
the powers and principalities of earth and hell were to combine against it.
Attended the Institution.

"*5th*.—Attended the Institution. Delivered an address in Marathee to my
domestics and 40 girls of the Schools, in connection with the death of one of
the boarders of the School for Poor and Destitute Native Girls, which took
place in the morning, and delivered a lecture on the Testimony to the Divinity
of Christ furnished by the Old Testament. The girl was six years old, and
distinguished for her intelligence. When I told her to trust in and pray to
Christ, she nodded assent, while the little tears rolled down her cheeks. Her
disease was cholera.

"*6th*.—Much distressed; but obtained some relief after visiting Malabar
Cliff.

" *8th.*—Attended the public levee of Sir James Carnac, because I view it a duty to render him official respect, and because I have no wish to nurse his prejudices against missionaries. Visited my sisters at Malabar Hill, who comforted me much in my afflictions."

The numbers in the schools slowly returned to their former level, and even rose higher, though the Parsees long held aloof. While continuing his aggressive work with no less zeal and courtesy than before, Dr. Wilson soon proved that he had conquered the Parsee community not only by the weapons of discussion but by his lofty charity and his unconquerable disinterestedness. They trusted him; all of them who knew him loved him; and their merchant leaders, and even some of their most sacred priests, were his warm friends to the day of his death. In the field of Truth he knew no compromise; in the region of a courteous charity he was, like a greater, all things to all men that he might win some.

The growth of toleration has been so very slow in Christendom that we need not be surprised if persecution for conscience' sake died hard among the Parsees even under English law and British rule. Not till 1843 did Hormasdjee succeed in rescuing his wife and daughter from the Punchayat. His wife they had married to another man, although she was believed to be desirous to live with her Christian husband. Such a case is now provided for by a law which permits divorce only after two years, during which the convert has failed to influence his wife. As the daughter grew up to girlhood her father applied to the Supreme Court, which at once made her over to him. This raised the ire of the Parsee leaders for the last time. Mr. Nesbit admirably managed the case, for Dr. Wilson had left Bombay on his first furlough. We must follow the course of his history till his departure for Syria and Europe.

CHAPTER VIII.

1836-1842.

DEVELOPMENT OF THE MISSION.

Civilians and Officers raise a special Fund for the College—First and Sixth Public Examination of the College — Domestic Slavery in India — Negro Boys captured from the East African Slavers—An Abyssinian General and his Sons—Joseph Wolff again— Dr. Wilson on the Government College— Two Princes from Joanna—What Converts should be supported by the Mission—First Proposal of a Scottish Mission at Madras—Projected Missions to Runjeet Singh and Independent Sikhs—To Kathiawar by Irish Presbyterian Church—Sir Robert Grant's Death—Dr. Wilson's Report on his Educational System for Lord Elphinstone when Governor of Madras, and for Ceylon—Proposal to send Missionary to the Jews of Arabia and India—First Meeting with Mr. David Sassoon—Female Education and the Misses Bayne—Major Jameson establishes the Ladies' Association in Edinburgh—The Afghan Policy of the Government of India—Intercourse with the Heir-Apparent of Dost Muhammad Khan — Dr. Murray Mitchell arrives—Dr. Duff's Visit—Encouraging Pastoral from the General Assembly —Dr. Wilson's Work as a Translator—Dr. Pfander.

In Bombay, as in Calcutta, the Parsee conversions had established the value of an English college as an agency for evangelising the educated native youth no less than as a means of disintegrating the old faiths of Persia and India.   The English laymen, chiefly officials, who had helped to set up the English school in the Fort in 1832 under Dr. Wilson's superintendence, and who gladly formed the corresponding committee of the General Assembly's Mission in 1835, did not fail to urge the importance of English as the medium of teaching and preaching to this special class.   At the end of 1833 eighteen of the best men and highest officials in Bombay combined to raise a fund for the support of another missionary who should devote his whole attention to this work ; and they instructed Mr. Webb and Captain Candy, who had gone to England, to select a missionary of learning and zeal.   Civilians like

Messrs. Farish, Townsend, and Campbell; scholars like Captains
Molesworth, Shortrede, and Jacob ; and physicians like Drs.
Smyttan and Campbell, with not a few purely military officers
who were an honour to the Bombay army, used these words :
" In gratifying this desire of the natives to learn our language,
we would most solicitously provide against the horrors of
irreligion by communicating and recommending the religion
of God.   We need, for this object, a man qualified for the
instruction of the natives in the English language, and for the
teaching and preaching, through this medium, the Gospel of
Christ.   We need a man qualified to assist the mind now
emerging ; to draw it forth and lead and direct it ; to mould
and form and abidingly fix it.   We need a man devoted to
the Lord ; a man of talent, and intelligence, and general information ; of a vigorous and energetic yet patient mind ; of
a sober and sound judgment, of steady and strong self-
denial; of a prayerful and hopeful spirit, and of great and
catholic love—we want a missionary.   Oh ! how should we
rejoice to behold such a man ; how glowingly should we
welcome him ! "   The transfer of the Scottish Mission to the
Church of Scotland had rendered the need less urgent ; and
Dr. Wilson, while fortunately continuing to hold unshaken
his view of the importance of using the classical and vernacular languages, threw the whole weight of his culture and
energy for a time into the new Institution.   Mr. Nesbit's
absence at the Cape and Ceylon, from ill-health, made the
help of a colleague more than ever necessary, and for this
the special fund was ready.   He studied carefully the experiment of the Baptist missionaries at Serampore, which was of
the same Oriental type as his own, and he was in close correspondence with the Scottish missionaries at Calcutta.

The first examination of Dr. Wilson's college has a curious
interest, as described in the public journals of 1836.   All the
dignitaries of the island were present, even the leading priests
of the Parsee, Hindoo, and Muhammadan communities, for the
conversion case had not yet occurred on its public side.   Dr.
Wilson alluded to the difficulties he had only partially overcome in securing qualified teachers and monitors, and a
sufficient supply of unobjectionable text-books and scientific
apparatus.   He anticipated the time as not far distant when
the knowledge thus communicated would bring many natives

with their children "within the pale of the Church." By the hope of this he defended his connection with the Institution as a missionary, and his determination "to devote to it a large share of my attention without neglecting other important duties which harmonise with its objects." From the reading of the Gospel of Mark in their native tongue by ten Marathee boys selected from the primary schools to be educated as teachers, to a theological examination in the English Shastres, and on natural history and mineralogy by the highest class, the work of the college was passed under review. The same Goojaratee papers, which a few months later denounced the college at the bidding of the sanhedrim because of its necessary and publicly avowed results in the baptism of its students, were unqualified in their eulogies. The *Chabuk* or *Whip* declared that "all were fully satisfied that no such progress as that made by the boys of this school within the eleven months of its existence has ever been exhibited in any institution in this place." A knowledge of the Christian Shastres was liberally put side by side with that of arithmetic, "man, and other objects of natural history." In reporting the examination to Dr. Brunton, Dr. Wilson wrote:—

"10*th November* 1836.— . . . . You will observe that we secure the religious instruction of *all* the pupils, even of the boys who have not made so much progress in English as to use it freely as the medium of communication. It is my intention not to overlook the cultivation of the native languages, which have hitherto, to the great prejudice of English seminaries in India, and to the prevention of their pupils from benefiting their countrymen by translations, been much neglected. The Brahmans here have the greatest contempt for some tolerably good English scholars, because they speak their vernacular tongues like the lowest of the low, and are unable to compare together the native and European science and literature. This, I trust, will not be their feeling in reference to our pupils, if you entertain the view which I have expressed. The natives have already much confidence in our operations. As all their own learning flows through the priesthood, many of them have the idea that all European learning must flow through it also. One of the most influential of their number, and of the class represented by party men as hostile to missions, lately offered me a large sum of money if I would give himself exclusive attention during a part of every day, which I of course declined to do, as it would place me in a wrong position with regard to the natives in general."

With this may be contrasted the facts revealed at the sixth annual examination in March 1842, when 1446 youths were under instruction. Of these 568 were in the girls' vernacular schools, and 723 in the boys' schools. There were

155 in the college, of whom 78 were Hindoos, 38 Jews, 6
Mussulmans, and 33 Christians of the Romanist, Armenian,
and Abyssinian, as well as Reformed Churches. The subjects
and text-books were those of the Scottish Universities, not
excluding Greek and Hebrew. Prize essays were read by
natives on domestic reform and the practice of idolatry.
Geology was the science studied that session. Dr. Wilson
lectured on the evidences of Christianity, Biblical Criticism,
and Systematic Divinity.

So early as 1833 Dr. Wilson directed his attention to the
slave trade from East Africa, and to the character of domestic
slavery among both Hindoos and Muhammadans in India. In
reply to an appeal from T. H. Baber, the Bombay Union of
Missionaries invited the Moravians or United Brethren to
utilise their experience gained in the West Indies and South
Africa, and their knowledge of industrial occupations, in the
formation of a colony in the Upper Wynaad district of South
India, "to reclaim the slaves from their present state of
ignorance and barbarism." The Basel and English missionaries
have since done much in mitigating the oppression of the
casteless races of South India by the native Governments
and Brahminical communities, and that with the aid of the
British Government, while Christianity has won her greatest
numerical triumphs among the simple peoples from the Dekhan
to Cape Comorin. But, till so late a time as 1859, it was the
custom of the civil courts in India, more or less ignorantly, to
register and treat as legal documents contracts for the service
and sale of slaves, which have been prohibited ever since.
Whatever serfdom or domestic slavery exists in India is
beyond the law, and has ever since been discouraged by the
law, as well as by the special efforts of the police directed to
the extirpation of kidnapping, eunuch-making, and other
nameless horrors of the kind. After the interference of
Parliament for the suppression of the African slave-trade the
Indian Navy played its part with a vigour and a humanity
worthy of its reputation, which, till its premature extinction
followed by the revival of a Marine Department, had always
been great in scientific work as well as in maritime warfare.

What was to be done with the captured slaves who were
restored to freedom in Bombay, the head-quarters of the
Navy? The Government at once made over those of school-

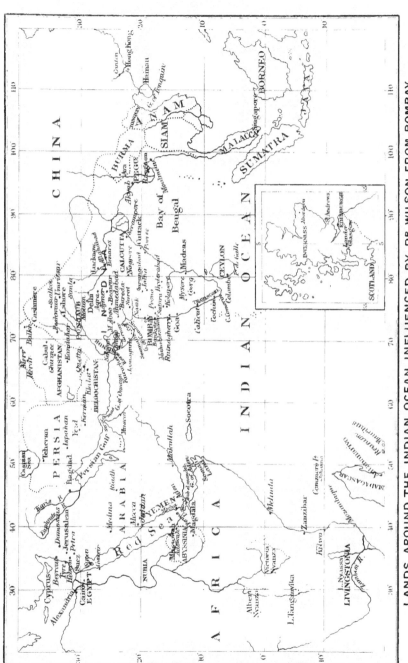

LANDS AROUND THE INDIAN OCEAN, INFLUENCED BY DR. WILSON FROM BOMBAY.

going age to Dr. Wilson, to the number of eight boys and five girls at Bombay, and five boys at Poona, to begin with, in 1836. The problem is not yet solved ; it has assumed proportions since the Zanzibar treaty, secured by Dr. Kirk following Sir Bartle Frere, which must issue in Eastern and Central if not also Western Africa, following the course of the empire created by the East India Company. But the germ of the enterprise, which blossomed out into the expeditions of Dr. Livingstone attended by some of those very slave boys, is to be found in the eighteen youths of whom Dr. Wilson wrote home at the end of 1836 : "There is reason to hope that they may ultimately prove a blessing to the Mission, while their capture will teach the native slavers a salutary lesson."

In April 1837 we find, similarly, the germ of Lord Napier's success in the Abyssinian Expedition. In the course of those almost chronic revolutions from which Abyssinia has been rarely free, Michael Warka, military commander of three towns in Habesh, as it is called, found himself compelled to take refuge with the British Consul at Massowah, along with his two sons Gabru and Maricha. When in power Michael Warka had always shown himself friendly to Mr. Isenberg, Joseph Wolff, and the Church Missionary Society's station at Adowah. The father and sons went on to Bombay, where they became, of course, Dr. Wilson's guests. The boys, then seventeen and twelve years of age, read Amharic and its Tigré dialect with great fluency. Dr. Wilson's polyglott accomplishments had not up to this time extended to the tongue of Ethiopia, but Joseph Wolff accompanied the Abyssinians, and left with him an Amharic and English vocabulary, through which they and their teacher at first learned from each other. " I trust they are not the only Christians connected with the Eastern Churches exterior to India who will be placed under our care," Dr. Wilson wrote. Wolff disappeared *more suo* for America, in order to enter Africa by Liberia, leaving behind him this characteristic letter :—

" BOMBAY, 10*th April* 1836.—MY DEAR WILSON—Knowing that you are a dear brother of mine, I take the liberty of making the following request to you. I don't like to trouble dear Mr. Farish with it, for he does a great deal for me whilst I am with him in his house. My sickness and journey, and the circumstance of having been robbed on my return for Sanaa, obliged me to draw more on Sir Thomas Baring than I think it to be just to draw now. With regard to my dear wife, I gave my word to her worldly brother never to carry on my mission at her expense. I also don't know whether all the money for my book has been sent in. If you, therefore, could procure for my future journey to the Cape some assistance from Christian friends I should be most obliged to you and to the friends. I also wish to consult with the brethren here about my future movements, whether I should pursue my journey to Africa *via* the Cape, or go at once to Kokan and Yarkand *via* Kutch, Kurachee, and Candahar? I think if I could obtain 1200 rupees for either journies it would be abundantly sufficient.—Yours affectionately,

"JOSEPH WOLFF."

In Dr. Wilson's correspondence we find these traces of his own college work, and that of the state institution, the Elphinstone College :—

"*30th November* 1837.—The Elphinstone College, which is in the immediate neighbourhood of our school, and which has most splendid accommodations and large endowment and Government grants, has only at present eight pupils. In order to get the number increased its managers have resolved to found sixteen large scholarships, and to commence an elementary school. Did it not by its constitution and practice exclude Christianity I should wish it success. But while it interdicts the teaching of the words of salvation I must invite the youth of India to those seminaries of learning of which the motto is, ' The fear of the Lord is the beginning of knowledge,' and use all lawful means to induce them to place themselves under their influence. Of the most important of these means, in connection with ourselves, is the procuring of suitable buildings for our Institution.

"*28th February* 1838.—I am happy to state that the Abyssinians have conducted themselves in the most becoming manner, and that the progress which they have made in their studies is most gratifying. Gabru, the elder boy, you would observe particularly noticed in the account of the examination of the seminary. He acquitted himself on that occasion remarkably well, considering the short time that he had been studying English ; and his subsequent advancement has been such as to sustain the hopes which his appearance led us to cherish. He has superior talents and a most commendable thirst after knowledge. His brother, though inferior to him, is also getting on well. I am quite hopeful that good, which may yet prove to be saving, impressions have been made on both their minds. Their father returned to his native country on a visit a few days ago. Had he not been satisfied with the treatment which they are receiving in Bombay he would not have left them even for a season. When I expressed to him the hope that his sons might yet be teachers of primitive Christianity on the mountains of Habesh he seemed much delighted.

" Of the Zanzibarian children rescued from the Arab slavers, there are now with me six boys and six girls. Three boys, and these not the least promising, have been removed by death. Those who remain are learning English. The most advanced of them is a very promising boy. They all wish to be considered Christians, though when they came to me they were Mussulmans. The five boys who are with Mr. Mitchell at Poona are advancing in every respect. For each of the Zanzibarians we receive three rupees monthly from the Government, but about double that sum is needed. The day may be speedily approaching when the interesting objects of our care and solicitude may prove not only the monuments of the divine mercy but the instruments of the divine praise in their native land, or among their benighted countrymen who visit the shores of India.

"Two young princes, aged nineteen and twenty years, nephews of the king of Hinzuan or Joanna, the African island of which an interesting description is given by Sir William Jones, came in their own dhow on a visit to the Government in the month of October. They were first placed with the Kazee of Bombay ; but in their own broken English they said, ' Tat won't do at all. We come from Hinzuan to see white man, and governor send us to stay with black man ;' and leaving the Muhammadan judge to his own meditations they betook themselves to their own vessel in the harbour.   I was then asked to take charge of them, and they became inmates in my house, in which they continued to stay during the three months of their visit.   We felt a great interest in satisfying their curiosity connected with the numerous subjects of their inquiry, and particularly the principles of Christianity ; but though they became acquainted with the truth to a considerable extent, and seemed sometimes to feel the force of the arguments against the Koran, they appeared to the last to cling to their errors.   What the future effects of our intercourse may be no one can tell.   They carried to their homes the word of God in Arabic, which they understand.   Their knowledge of English, picked up principally from shipwrecked seamen and occasional visitors, is considerable ; and even their servants had some acquaintance with it.   From what they stated it would appear that it could be propagated throughout their island without much difficulty.   The language most prevalent with them is the Sowaheli, which is spoken at Zanzibar and through large districts on the coasts of Madima or Africa.   Muhammadanism they represented as making great progress in those quarters, but principally through the violence of the Arab colonists, and the agents of the Imam of Muskat.   Their own hatred of idolatry, though they had not a few superstitions, they made apparent on many occasions. One evening, after they had accompanied me to some of the Hindoo temples, they had a curious discussion with a Hindoo gentleman whom they found in the mission-house on their return : 'We take walk,' they said, 'with Dr. Wilson, but have got great pain in our stomachs (hearts) because all Hindoo men are mad, and make salaam to stone god.   What for got Governor ?   Why not he put you all in prison ?   You come to Joanna, then we flog you.'   The Hindoo, in self-defence, declared that he did not worship idols.   'Then,' pointing to his sectarial mark, said his princely instructors, ' you double-bad ; you come into Englishman's house and say, I wise man, I not worship images ; then you go to your own house and put on Hindoo god's mark just 'bove your eyes there.   You two-faced man !'   With these interesting youths I expect to keep up a correspondence."

The growth of the mission raised such questions as that of " alimenting " or providing for the temporary support of young converts excluded from their Hindoo and Parsee homes, and fit to be trained in the college for missionary or educational work.   From the first Dr. Wilson drew a clear and wise distinction between " promising and select Christian youths while they study English with a view to our subsequent employment of them as agents," and " native Christians who have nearly reached the meridian of life."   Practically, he settled the difficulty in the case of the former by taking them to his own house and table, even up to the end of his life, judging carefully in every case, but with a kindliness that left him

sorely out of pocket. The village and barrack systems for the
occupation and training of converts, must be judged of according to the class to be trained and the state of native society
from which they have come. In every case the very appearance of seeming to hold out a bribe to converts has been carefully eschewed by the Scottish Missions.

In 1832 Dr. Wilson had urged the establishment of a
Scottish Mission at Madras ; offering, on behalf of M. R.
Cathcart of the Civil Service there, £150 a year for a time.
Not till 1836 was the General Assembly, moved by Dr. Duff's
return, able to appoint Mr. Anderson there, soon to be followed
by Mr. Johnston and Mr. Braidwood, the last specially sent
out by the Edinburgh Students' Missionary Association which
Dr. Wilson had established.

The Church of Scotland, influenced by the alliance with
Runjeet Singh, which preceded Lord Auckland's unfortunate
Cabul expedition, projected a mission to the then independent
Sikhs, but Dr. Wilson counselled a first attempt among those
of the protected states of our own territory, such as the Church
Missionary Society and the American Presbyterians afterwards
undertook. He declared his willingness to make a missionary
survey of the Punjab up to the Indus and its tributary streams,
preaching in Hindee and Oordoo or Hindostanee on the way.
" I could perhaps induce some influential natives to betake
themselves to Bombay or Calcutta for their education. I
could furnish you with such a full report, diversified by notices
of the country, people, and prevalent religious systems, as you
could lay before the public for their general information, and
to invite approval and co-operation." Such a survey, and the
consequent action at that time, would have anticipated by
twenty years the Christianising of the land from the deserts
of Rajpootana and Sindh, at which Dr. Wilson's influence
ceased, to the Sutlej immediately, and ultimately to Central
Asia.

What it was not expedient or possible for his own church
to attempt, in the regions beyond the three settled presidencies, as they then were, Dr. Wilson induced other churches to
undertake. The missionary survey which he made of Kathiawar co-operated, with the eloquence of Dr. Duff in Ireland,
to lead the three hundred Presbyterian congregations of the
Synod of Ulster, as the Irish Presbyterian Church was called

in 1839, to establish a mission in India. The Rev. George
Bellis, the secretary, asked Dr. Wilson's counsel in time to
report to the Synod of 1840. He submitted, in reply, an exhaustive report—an apostolic epistle—on the needs and the
advantages of Kathiawar, which thus begins and closes :—

" BOMBAY, 27th November 1839.—About three years ago I had determined
to memorialise the Synod of Ulster about the propriety of its engaging in
foreign missionary operations in its corporate capacity, and with special reference to the great and inviting and promising field to which I am about to
direct your attention, and I was led to delay communicating my views to you
only by observing from one of your missionary reports that you yourselves had
been led to determine to send forth some of your ministers to preach the glad
tidings of salvation to the heathen world, and to make some inquiries—the
result of which I thought it proper to await—at Dr. Philip and some other
individuals, about the particular scene of your operations. When, in April
last, I learned that you had turned your attention to India, I proceeded to
collect some more particular information than I possessed respecting the district the claims of which I had resolved to plead before the bar of your Christian compassion and enlightened benevolence. The arduous duties which I
have been called to discharge, and the great trials in which our mission has
been involved since that time, have hitherto prevented me from accomplishing
my purpose. My procrastination you will easily understand. *Cum ad Maleam
deflexeris, obliviscere quæ sunt domi.*

" . . . . I say nothing about plans of labour, as your dear brethren and
agents ought personally to inspect the field before particular measures are
resolved upon. It will afford me, and the other members of our mission,
unspeakable pleasure to receive them in Bombay, and to introduce them to
the friends of the Redeemer's cause particularly connected with the scene of
their labours. We most cordially invite them to join our ranks, and with us
to fight the battles of the Lord in these high places of the field. Let them
come to us 'full of faith and the Holy Ghost,' and be prepared both to *labour*
and *suffer* agreeably to the Divine will, and the work of the Lord will assuredly prosper in their own souls, and those of multitudes of their fellow-men.
We cannot say to them, ' The fields are already white unto the harvest,' where
the soil is not even broken ; but we can tell them that the field is both large
and unoccupied, and that *when* the seed is sown it will prove incorruptible."

In 1838 Dr. Wilson lost a personal friend in the death of
Sir Robert Grant, the Governor, of whom one of the native
newspapers remarked that his last act had been to subscribe
to the General Assembly's Institution—" the last expression
of his regard to the hallowed cause of education, which ever
lay near his heart, which on various occasions he advocated
with surpassing eloquence, and which many of his public
measures were calculated to advance." In a letter to Miss
Bayne the widowed Lady Grant wrote—" I have much valued
the letter which Dr. Wilson had the kindness to send to me,
and it has interested me often when nothing else could. May

I be enabled to profit by the lessons given in it." Under the
new Charter Act Mr. Farish became Acting-Governor, as senior
member of Council. Soon after Dr. Wilson was pleasantly
associated for the first time with a Governor to whose administration he was destined to render signal services. The
young Lord Elphinstone, nephew of the Hon. Mountstuart
Elphinstone, had been appointed Governor of Madras. One
of his earliest acts was to invite a statement of the experience
of the principal educational institutions in India before introducing reforms into his own Province.

Nor was it only the Madras Government that consulted
Dr. Wilson as to an educational policy. We find in his papers
this extract of a letter which he wrote to the Governor of
Ceylon, the Right Honourable J. A. Stuart Mackenzie, dated
28th April 1841 :—

"It will afford me very great pleasure to write a short epistle to Mr.
Anstruther on the subject of vernacular education, if you will kindly apologise
to him for my intrusion. None of the arrangements connected with the
Indian Governments on the subject of public instruction have given me a tithe
of the gratification which yours in Ceylon have afforded. Our 'boards of education' are by far too exclusive, and they admit no members of practical
experience. They despise and disparage religion, the only available engine of
moral reform; and were their endeavours not in some degree supplemented by
our Christian missions, I should be disposed to question their ultimate safety.
With you all seems right, proper, and judicious ; and it reflects great honour
on Lord John Russell that he has approved of your scheme. There are many
eyes in India placed on Ceylon as a model Government. In saying this, I do
not mean to make any insinuation against the civil officers of the Company,
who as a body are a most honourable, enlightened, and faithful set of public
servants. It is the simple fact of the intervention of a Company, which sometimes appears to me to interpose between this great country and our happy
native land a barrier to the full tide of free and generous British feeling.
Direct responsibility to a chartered corporation—most necessary when infan-
tile adventure required every guarantee against destructive loss—is a very
different thing from direct responsibility to the Sovereign, nobles, and popular
representatives of our own realm. I express this opinion merely as glancing
at the general interests of philanthropy."

Nearly twenty years were to pass before, under the
catholic University and grant-in-aid systems, the Government
of India assumed its proper relation to all educational enterprise, independent as well as under its own departments. But
Dr. Wilson did not confine his energies to India and Ceylon.
His sympathies had been also all along with the Gaelic School
Society, to which he and other Scotsmen were in the habit of
sending remittances. And, in return, he sought to induce

other committees of his Church than that specially charged
with the care of the India Mission, to evangelise the Jews.

"*10th July* 1841.—To ROBERT WODROW, Esq., Glasgow.—It is a joint
Mission to the Jews of Arabia and India, having Bombay as its centre,
which I think in present circumstances most feasible and promising. I will
thank you to direct the particular attention of the General Assembly's Committee to the view which I take of the subject, and also of the friend who has
so generously promised to support a missionary at Aden. I am certain that
his views would be forwarded, and not retarded, by the plan which I venture
to suggest. I think that my friend Dr. Smyttan could easily show the advantages of the scheme which I propose. A missionary for Bombay would require
to direct his particular attention to the Arabic as well as the Marathee language. I called a meeting of the principal Arabian Jews, which was held at
the house of David Sassoon, the most opulent merchant of their body. R. T.
Webb, Esq., Major Jervis, Mr. Mitchell, Mr. Glasgow, and Mr. Kerr were present with me during the greater part of the time that we were together. We
were very politely received, and obtained much of the information which we
asked, as well as the promise of every assistance being granted to a Jew whom
I have employed to commit to writing whatever he can learn of the circumstances of his brethren in Yemen, Bussora, Bombay, and other places.
Towards the close of our interview we entered on the infinitely important
question of the Messiahship of Christ, and had an opportunity of stating the
usual arguments for its establishment. They ordered all their children to leave
the room when we first mentioned the name of the Saviour ; and we could
not help observing how much more reserved they appeared in this matter than
the Beni-Israel. They otherwise evinced, however, no improper feeling ; and
they freely discussed with us the different points to which we adverted. I
told them of the deputation to Palestine, the objects of the General Assembly's
Committee, and its readiness to aid in the instruction of their countrymen ;
and they seemed pleased with the interest which our Church takes in their
welfare. More noble-looking men than they are not to be seen on the streets
of Bombay, where so many tribes of the world have their representatives."

Such was the first love of the Church of Scotland in the
infancy of its missions abroad and its evangelical revival at
home, that it planned enterprises in Arabia, in Persia, and on
the upper Indus,[1] while it stimulated other churches to take up
provinces which its agents had, as pioneers, surveyed. But in
Bombay itself the death of Mrs. Margaret Wilson had left the
many female schools without a head, although a lady teacher
had been speedily sent out to conduct them ; and the development of the College made it imperative that the long-sought-
for colleague, whom the Christian officials desired to help Dr.

[1] Dr. Brunton had written thus to Dr. Wilson :—"EDINBURGH COLLEGE,
2d January 1838.—Allow me to remind you of your promise to send us information about the feasibility of a Mission in the Sikh country. The munificent
patroness of the undertaking is now a widow, and waning fast into the vale of
years. She is the more earnest to learn 'the truth, the whole truth, and nothing
but the truth.'"

Wilson, should be at once found, the more that Mr. Nesbit had
been absent from India for a time seeking health. Accordingly, Dr. Wilson, early in 1836, had summoned to his side
the Misses Anna and Hay Bayne, on whom he pressed the
claims of their sister's work as an inheritance of which they
were bound to take possession. These ladies were to be his
own guests, brought out at his own cost, while retaining their
independence in all things. Towards the end of 1837 the
sisters arrived in Bombay, and at their own charges. Very
tender and beautiful was the family life in the Ambrolie mission home, and occasionally in the country house on Malabar
Hill and in that at Mahableshwar, as revealed by the now
faded correspondence, till Hay was married to Mr. Nesbit only
to carry on her missionary work till her premature death in
1848, and Anna was laid beside her sister Margaret in the
Scottish cemetery, her works following her. Once more did
the fast-increasing class of educated Natives of all sects in
Bombay, as well as the native Christian community, see the
purity, the grace, and the intellectual attraction which cultured women lent to the missionary's home, making it every
year more and more the centre, and largely the source, of
all that was elevating in Bombay society.

Impressed by the importance of the work, a retired Bombay officer who had taken part in it, Major St. Clair Jameson,
brother of Sheriff Jameson, had in 1837 issued an appeal to
the ladies of Scotland, which resulted in the formation of
the Ladies' Society for Female Education in India. That
Association, united in 1865 with a similar agency for Africa,
has ever since worked side by side with the Foreign Mission Committee of the Free Church, and with remarkable
success. At Poona, as well as Bombay, this indispensable
side of a vigorous mission was extended. In a letter to the
Rev. G. White, chaplain of distant Cawnpore, who was successfully conducting a Female Orphan Asylum there, Dr.
Wilson wrote in 1835, "I am more and more convinced that,
in seeking for the moral renovation of India, we must make
greater efforts than we have yet done to operate upon the
female mind. In Christian countries it is, generally speaking,
more on the side of religion than the male mind. In India it
is the stronghold of superstition. Its enlightenment ought to
be an object of first concern with us. You will be happy to

hear that the prejudices against its instruction in Bombay are
fast diminishing among the natives." In a letter to his Edinburgh agent Dr. Wilson gives us a contemporary view of the
then gathering Afghan expedition. He shows himself wise,
as always, in political questions, while, writing to a confidential agent, he expresses his opinion with a frankness rare in
his more public communications. For while he was the citizen
and the statesman, the scholar and the philanthropist, he was
above all things the Christian missionary :—

"I am not by any means satisfied of the *justice* of our invasion of Afghanistan. Shah Shujah (that old cruel monster) has got from our army 6000
volunteers, officered by the Company, to endeavour to reseat him on the throne
of Cabul. Our main army, 13,000 strong, is now assembling on the banks of
the Sutlej, and it is to move to the northward under the command of Sir Henry
Fane. It is entirely composed of Bengal troops. Our army of reserve, 5000
strong, composed of Bombay troops, is now mustering in Kutch. Four of the
Bombay stations, Sholapore, Kaludgee, Belgaum, and Dharwar, are in a few
days to be occupied by Madras troops. The large station of Mhow is to have
Bombay instead of Bengal troops. That we should send an army to *watch*
the movements of Russia, Persia, etc., I fully admit. That we should
dethrone Dost Muhammad Khan I stoutly deny, on the ground of my present
information."

When, three years later, the Afghan iniquity was becoming
a tragedy of a very doleful kind to our arms, our honour, and
our prestige in Asia, and when Dost Muhammad was a state
prisoner on parole in Calcutta, where he might be observed
at his devotions on the Course as the gay world rolled past,
his heir-apparent, Haider Khan, was a frequent visitor at
Ambrolie. On the 1st March 1841 Dr. Wilson thus gossips
in a letter to Dr. Smyttan :—

"We have lately had presented to us a hydro-oxygenic
microscope, which cost Rs. 600. It has been several times
exhibited at my house, and has made a great impression on
the natives. Prince Haider Khan, the son of Dost Muhammad, is coming to see it in a day or two. He and I are great
friends. Should his family ever again be restored to sovereign
power, it will, I think, be favourable to missionary operations.
He sat two hours with Anna and me the other day. He talks
nothing but Persian and Pushtoo. I get on pretty well with
him ; and the Moonshee Abdool Rahman Khan, whom you
will perhaps remember as a companion of Dadoba Pandurang,
makes all clear when I break down. This young man, by the
bye, comes to us every morning to read the Scriptures. He

will, we hope, declare for Christ. What an accession he
would be to our strength!" So grateful was Dost Muhammad
to Dr. Wilson for his kindness to his son when in captivity,
that he declared he would keep the passes open for a visit
from the Padre Saheb, however disturbed the frontier might
be. But Haider Khan never became more than a sensual
Afghan, as described in Colonel Lumsden's confidential report
on the "Mission to Kandahar" in 1856, although he was
always well inclined to the British Government because of
"the manner in which he was treated while a prisoner in
Hindostan." When in Bombay he had an opportunity of
visiting England, of which he afterwards regretted that he
did not avail himself. The late Ameer, Sher Ali, was his
full brother.

The Mr. Mitchell for whom Dr. Wilson wearied, was the
Rev. J. Murray Mitchell, of the University of Aberdeen, which
now followed in the wake of the Universities of Edinburgh
and St. Andrews, and, besides him, gave to India from the
same year's classes the Rev. John Hay, still the able Telugoo
scholar of the London Missionary Society at Vizagapatam,
and the Rev. Dr. Ogilvie, the first missionary of the Established Church of Scotland at Calcutta. Dr. Murray Mitchell,
as in due time he became, took with him the Classical and
Hebrew scholarship with which Aberdeen and Melvin were
associated, while his wife subsequently became a missionary
to the women of Bombay and Calcutta, worthy of her cousins
the Baynes. The arrival of his new colleague towards the end
of 1838 gave Dr. Wilson another proof of the confidence and
affection of the Christian officials, who had raised a special
fund of £1800 for this extension of the college operations.

Having roused the whole of Scotland, the north of Ireland,
and many parts of England by his fiery zeal, Dr. Duff returned
to Calcutta early in the year 1840, by way of Bombay. It
was necessary for the good of the Mission in all three cities
and for the success of the projected Irish Mission, that the two
distinguished men, still young, should consult together—Dr.
Wilson, now almost worn out by eleven years of incessant and
varied work for his Master; Dr. Duff fresh from home, but
also from labours no less abundant. If, in the course of the
many splendid orations which Dr. Duff had spoken and published in the previous five years, he had been led by his Cal-

cutta experience occasionally to seem to Dr. Wilson to under-
estimate the need for female education and instruction in
the vernacular languages which Western India at least had
demanded, all was forgotten or discussed after a most brotherly
fashion when the two held long converse at Ambrolie.

The General Assembly of the subsequent May addressed
an encouraging pastoral letter to its missionaries, ministers,
and elders in India, signed by the moderator, Dr. Makellar,
and the learned Principal Lee, the clerk. Their generous
acknowledgments of the arduous labours of the missionaries,
and co-operation of the chaplains and elders, and the wise
counsels of the document, had so good an effect that a similar
communication might be more frequently sent with the best
results both at home and abroad. After the last Assembly
before the Disruption of 1843, Dr. Welsh, second only to Dr.
Chalmers in the Church of Scotland at that time, addressed
Dr. Wilson, at the request of the Colonial Committee, on the
subject of the scattered settlers in India, for whom no spiritual
provision was made till the establishment of the Anglo-Indian
Union in 1864.

It is difficult to see how, in the midst of all his other
engagements, Dr. Wilson found time for that translation and
publication of books, which formed in his eyes as important a
department as the schools and even the preaching, because
the press fed both.[1] So early as 1833 he had thus justified
his expenditure to the directors of the Scottish Missionary
Society, when they were insisting on restricting operations in
Bombay, where the press cost £128 a year; the Goojaratee
pundit £20; the Hindostanee, £36; and the Sanscrit and
Marathee, £36 :—

"The Pundits whom I have retained for some time have been required by
me not so much for the purpose of aiding me in my studies—though they are

---

[1] "OPERATIONS OF THE PRESS IN 1839.—I published a new edition of my
Idiomatical Exercises, in English and Marathee, which are pretty generally
used as a school-book in this part of India. A Goojaratee tract, addressed by
me to the Jaina priests of Palitana, and an English sermon addressed to the
Parsees, have been new publications. I have spent a considerable time in connection with the Translation Committee of the Bible Society, of which I am
the secretary; and Mr. Nesbit has similarly occupied a part of his leisure.

"The total number of tracts printed is 27,000, and of separate pages
957,000. Most of the tracts belong to the Bombay Tract and Book Society.
The two first were printed at my own expense, but the subsequent sale of
them has almost reimbursed me for the outlay.—J. W."

of course highly useful in this respect—but of aiding me in fulfilling my
engagements with the press.   During the past year I have composed and principally written out with my own hand, in the first instance, upwards of 2000
8vo pages in different languages ; and it will be perceived, when the general
inefficiency of native assistants is considered, that the help which I have
enjoyed has been required for almost merely mechanical purposes. At present
the editing, and in a great degree the translating, of the Marathee Scriptures,
and the editing of the tracts of the Bombay Tract and Book Society, and the
preparation of some pamphlets, have devolved on me.   I have all along paid a
considerable part of my Pundit's wages independently of the Society."

Nor was it in Bombay alone or in its languages that Dr.
Wilson was active.   Dr. Pfander, the Arabic scholar and controversialist, had arrived in Calcutta in 1838, and sought his
aid in printing the three Persian treatises before referred to.
In the work of translating the Scriptures into the various vernaculars all the competent Protestant missionaries in the Province, and scholars like Captains Molesworth and Candy, gladly
gave help.   Until there are native scholars, masters of Greek
and Hebrew as well as of their own classical and vernacular
languages, to become to the races of India what Luther was
to Germany, the translations of the Scriptures by foreigners,
however learned and experienced, will require revision every
generation.   This has been the case in the century since Dr.
Carey began his attempts in northern, and the Lutherans in
southern India.   The difficulties caused by such revisions,
required even in the English Bible, are inevitable, until the
Church of India develops its own organisation and life.

CHAPTER IX.

1836-1842.

TOURS—GAIRSOPPA FALLS—RAJPOOTANA—KATHIAWAR—
THE SOMNATH GATES.

Sun-Worship tested by Arithmetic—Changes in Goa—Gairsoppa and its Falls
Ajunta and the "Possessed" Bangle-Seller—First Tour to Rajpootana—
Farewell to Dr. Duff—Civilisation of Baroda—Dr. Wilson and his Cashmere Shawls—Correcting Bishop Heber—Antiquities of Puttun—The
Potter and the Sword-Maker—The Dewan of Pahlunpore—Native Christians
without a Missionary Teacher—The Bheels and Sir James Outram—Aboo
as it is—First Christian Mission in a Native State—Second Visit to Rajkote
—The Prince's Difficulty about the Existence of Evil—Dr. Wilson's nearly
Fatal Illness—Anna Bayne's Death—Cholera Epidemic of 1842—Persuaded
to take Furlough by prospect of a Tour in Syria—Sir W. Hill's endowment
of the Nagpore Mission—Sir W. H. Macnaghten—Sir George Arthur—Sir
Bartle Frere's First Friendship with Dr. Wilson—The Proclamation of the
Somnath Gates—Macaulay and Lord Ellenborough's Recall.

DR. WILSON'S combined missionary, scientific, and archæological tours in the second period of six years which preceded
his first visit to Europe, were not less thorough and fruitful
in their results than those of the previous six years. February
1837 he devoted to an inspection of the old mission station
of Hurnee and to a second visit to the Portuguese territory
of Goa, his first survey of which had led him to give more
attention to the many Portuguese and their descendants in
Western India, known as Indo-Britons. It was his custom to
examine Government as well as missionary schools at the
request and generally in the presence of the authorities,
wherever he went, as well as to hold services for the scattered
and neglected English communities in distant stations. To
the Government Marathee school of Hurnee, the pupils of
which he found remarkably prompt in arithmetic, he proposed
the question which they readily solved, " If sound travel at

the rate of 1140 feet a second, and the sun be 95,000,000 miles distant from the earth, what time will be required for a man's prayers to reach that luminary?" The Brahmans seemed greatly amazed when they saw the result of a computation which really involved the whole teaching of their system. The examination closed with the suggestion to the Puntojee, or "dominie," that he should extend his cross-examinations to the scope of the passages read as well as to the meaning of each word. The boys were rewarded with books, and their parents crowded to talk with the missionary.

At Goa Dr. Wilson found that a great change had taken place in three years. The Inquisition had been destroyed, but that fact was officially assigned as a reason why no books could be admitted into the settlement without the permission of the Archbishop or the Vicar-General. The number of the clergy had been reduced one-half since the tour of 1834, and all the monastic establishments had been shut up. Their libraries had been sold. The cruel intolerance of Menezes, the Synod of Diamper, and the Inquisition, was avenged. To this day the Archbishop of Goa finds it impossible to assert against the Belgian or French Archbishops of Madras and Bombay, Calcutta and Agra, who are directly subject to the Vatican, his powers under the old Bull, confirmed by two Popes, granting to Portugal in perpetuity whatever lands the great and good Prince Henry and his successors might discover from West Africa to the Indies inclusive. The Vicar-General refused the gift of a Portuguese Bible, alleging that the use of the translation is prohibited. When asked to point out any passages erroneously rendered, he exclaimed, *Plurimi sunt, plurimi sunt*, as he turned the leaves, but could not point out one. Dr. Wilson replied to him in the words of David, *Testimonium Jehovae verax, sapientiam afferens imperito*. The Vicar-General then changed his ground to the charge that this version omitted the Apocrypha. One of the clergy gladly took a Bible, while another presented him with two defences of Roman Catholicism recently published in Colombo, and full of flagrant mis-translations of Scripture. This passage follows in Dr. Wilson's account of the tour :—" A respectable Portuguese officer spent the evening with us. His conversation turned principally on the errors of the Church of Rome, of many of which, like most of the Roman Catholic lay gentlemen whom I have met in India, he seemed to be well aware, and on the immoralities of some of the clergy in the State of Goa. One of them, he mentioned to us there could be little doubt, had been accessary lately to the exposure of his own illegitimate child, the body of which he himself found in the course of being devoured by ravens. The late archbishop he represented as one of the greatest debauchees in the colony. We heard his statements with pain, though we did not much wonder that the Papacy had been tolerant, nay, productive of many of the crimes which he mentioned."

This may be compared with the picture drawn by Meadows Taylor in the last of his vivid romances of Indian life and history, *A Noble Queen*. The professors, 110 students, and resident clergy, at the college of Rachol in Salsette, showed much kindness to Dr. Wilson, and he records that he "particularly prepared" himself for a Latin discussion on the merits of the Vulgate and Portuguese translations of Scripture, which he conducted with two of them. One of his adversaries, taking him aside at the close, confessed his position to be most miserable, and was invited to Bombay. His reply was, *Est mihi voluntas sed valde timeo*. All through Goa the laity showed great eagerness for copies of a tractate containing correspondence between Captain Shortrede and Bishop Prendergast on the heathenism of popery.

But the main interest now of this second tour to Goa lies in the opportunity which it gave Dr. Wilson to visit and describe what has been called the third of the greatest wonders of India, the Gairsoppa Falls, the Himalayas and the Taj Mahal being the other two. The four falls have since become famous in India, but the best English treatises of descriptive or physical geography are still ignorant of them. Some 340 miles south-east of Bombay, in its district of North Canara, the Sheravutty divides into several channels just above the old capital of Gairsoppa, famous three centuries ago for its queen, but plundered successively by the Portuguese, Hyder Ali, and Tippoo Saheb, and taken by assault by General Matthews a century ago. Dr. Wilson, who was accompanied by Dr. Smyttan, sent an account of the falls to his old professor, Dr. Jameson, and it appeared in his *Philosophical Journal*. The water falls eight times the depth of Niagara.

The brief college holiday in January 1838 was devoted to a second tour to Ajuntâ, with its caves, and to Jalna. The incidents are most pleasantly told by Dr. Wilson in letters to the sisters Bayne. The effect on a bangle or bracelet seller of one of the vernacular books distributed in the bazaar, *On the Nature of God*, he describes to have been " such as I have never witnessed."

" *2d February* 1838.—When I was preaching in the evening a man came roaring into the enclosure in such a loud and frantic manner that he frightened the doctor, myself, and all present. He called out to me in the most awful manner which you can imagine, ' It is all true, It is all true, It is all true. You are my Gooroo, You are my Gooroo, You are my Gooroo,' and then threw himself down on the ground with such violence that we feared he had fractured his skull. He quickly recovered himself, caught hold of my feet, and held them with such force that I was obliged to call on the people to extricate me, which with great difficulty they could effect. I tried to calm his mind, but his excitement gained ground notwithstanding all my efforts. His body was greatly convulsed ; and he tossed himself and tore himself in the most fearful manner. On every person but myself he loaded the vilest abuse, and particularly on two of his relatives. To me he gave ascriptions of praise proper to God only, and extolled me as the lord of Pandarpur, and several other idol-shrines. He cried out that he would never leave me till his death, which he declared would take place before the close of the evening. It was now but too evident that he was labouring under temporary derangement, if not under direct possession of the great adversary of souls, which the peculiarities of his case seemed *most* to indicate to us, notwithstanding all our cautious reserve of judgment. I succeeded, with the help of the natives, in getting beyond his grasp for a few moments, when Dr. Smyttan and I anxiously consulted together about what was proper to be done. We agreed to direct our whole efforts to the soothing of his mind ; and to his friends, who ascribed his state to my enchantment, and who were afraid that we should carry him away with us, we gave the assurance that I receive none as disciples but those who are reasonably convinced, and that we should render them every assistance in our power in allaying his excitement. He would listen patiently to none of my counsel or instruction ; but when I found him willing to follow me I took him by the hand and led him to a house in the bazaar, where his friends said he could be accommodated for the night. They held him to the ground, while we, after promising to call upon him in the morning, took our departure. After fighting with them for some time he got quite exhausted, and sank into a profound sleep. They carried him off early next morning before we could hold any communication with him. He belongs to the village of *Shiwanâ*, about six miles from Ajuntâ. He had proceeded about a mile on his return from the bazaar to that place, when he sat down to read the tract ; and he flew to me with the speed of lightning, bursting through all opposition, after his mind began to be affected. He is a man whose reason was never formerly known to be disordered. What his first emotions were on perusing the tract it is impossible to say. The probability from his own language is, that he gave to it his assent at the same time that Satan stirred up the evil feelings of his mind with a view to extinguish his convictions, and to misrepresent our cause in the eyes of the heathen. His case is a most singular one ; and what the result of the whole may be no man can tell. Our prayers ascended to heaven that Christ might say to the waves of his affliction, ' Be still,' and that he might sit meekly at his feet, learn his Gospel, and receive it to the salvation of his soul.   At what I have told you you will no doubt be astonished.   I trust that the occurrence has been blessed to me, as impressing on my mind the fact that we are either the savour of life unto life or death unto death to those to whom we minister. How solemn are our circumstances ! "

Again, at the beginning of 1839, he roamed among the jungles of the mainland, studying the aboriginal tribes, and preparing for a more permanent mission among them, till his stock of provisions was exhausted and his purse was empty. He was to meet a party at the Caves of Elephanta, to which he desired that ammunition for his gun might be sent.   The ardent naturalist writes :—" I wounded an eagle the other day so much that I caught it, and I require to shoot some birds to keep it in life."

To complete his Survey of the Native States around the Province of Bombay, and to seek in the great stone cities and deserts of Upper India forms of Hindooism more ancient and more directly the fruit of its Vedic and Epic times than even the Brahmanism of Maharashtra could afford, Dr. Wilson had resolved to assign the early portion of 1840 to a tour in south-western Rajpootana, with his new colleague Dr. Murray Mitchell.   The visit of Dr. Duff delayed their departure, but they resolved to face the terrors of the hot season, which is, officially, considered to begin on the 15th March, when the cooling *punkah* is for the first time in each year allowed in the public offices.   The tour may well begin with this characteristic letter from its first stage at Tanna, honourable alike to the writer and to Dr. Duff :—

" TANNA, 28*th February* 1840.—MY DEAREST ANNA—I said little to you when I parted with you, because I felt much ; but I offered up to God the fervent prayer that his divine presence might remain with us while we are separated from one another.   My supplication was not that of the moment. It still rises, and will rise from my heart, as I bend my footsteps on this great journey, which the desire of publishing peace to the unsoothed hearts of the inhabitants of Goojarat and Rajpootana has led me to undertake.   You must conceive of me as always addressing the throne of heaven on your behalf ; and I shall have the same realisation of your blessed employment for my sake.   It is only when our desires for our mutual welfare find their expression Godward that we can rest with confidence in the view of all that may await us.

" We went through the fatigues of yesterday wonderfully well ; and I was quite refreshed by Dr. Duff's admiration of the beauties of the Salsitian land-scape, and the interest which he felt in the antiquities of its ancient forests. We rode together in the phaeton to Vehar, where we met with Mr. Nesbit,

M

Dr. Campbell, and Mr. Mitchell ; and after performing the usual operations of conservatism at the table of our old friend Merwanji, we sallied forth on our pilgrimage to the excavated mount. The hamals (bearers) groaned under the weight of their precious load—the apostle of the Ganges ; and two sturdy bullocks, Pandhya and Sona, dragged a crazy chariot containing the carcases encasing the souls of the other constituents of the choice fraternity. We were forced to dismount about a couple of miles from the abodes of the Buddhas, and with staff in hand, and over-canopied with chattris (umbrellas) from the west and the east, we plied our steps to the exalted regions. The sun himself entered into battle with us on the way, and he had nearly over-powered us before we could find refuge in the temple's shade. He applied himself so sturdily to the monk of the Don that he had nearly succeeded in making his visage glow with a radiance as glorious as his own. We congratu-lated ourselves when we arrived at the *terminus ad quem* that we were not reduced to cinders, or melted into minerals, by his furnace heat. Our peram-bulations in the caves followed a second conservative repast, and the echo of our eloquent discourse caused the very hills to shake. The images them-selves told us what they were and what they had been, and pointed to the tombs in which are enshrined the relics of their antitype. We performed *pradakshina* round the Dhagobs, reclined on the living couches of the devotees of Nirwana, traversed the halls of instruction of the primitive intellectualists, peeped into the bowels of the earth, ascended the lofty stairs, and gazed on the beauty and grandeur of the famed isle.

"I cannot tell what I felt when dear Mr. Nesbit, who had kept his inten-tions secret in the chambers of his own individuality during the day, an-nounced that the *moment* had arrived when he and Dr. Duff must proceed to Panwel, and that without the formalities of worship, which the tide, he thought, would not await. We resolved, at all hazards, however, to part calling on the name of God ; and after reading the 20th chapter of the Acts I endeavoured to conduct our devotions. My heart completely failed me when I was praying, but not before many supplications had proceeded from its inmost recesses. Dr. Duff, with whom I was so sorry to part because I felt that I should not again see him till the heavens are no more, addressed to us the words of comfort which his affectionate heart can so well indite, and we solemnly bade each other farewell. My memory will often visit the hallowed spot whence we moved asunder."

This tour extended over a distance of 1525 miles. At Baroda Mr. Sutherland, the Resident, not unassisted by the influence of Dr. Wilson in his former visit to the Gaikwar, was able to announce the abolition of Suttee throughout the extensive territories of his Highness. Dr. Wilson was unable to wait there long enough to accept an invitation to renew his acquaintance with the Gaikwar ; but had much intercourse with his nobles.

"I had a long private interview with the Resident, during which we dis-cussed at considerable length the abolition of Suttee in the native States, the cessation of the Government countenance of idolatry, the propriety of erecting an English school in Baroda, the measures to be adopted for the further suppression of infanticide, etc. He was very free and candid in his communi-cations ; and I am perfectly satisfied that he will do all in his power to forward the cause of philanthropy. I received from him the loan of several

interesting works and documents connected with the country and the native
Governments.   At the Residency I met an important native personage named
Govind Ráo, whose son was adopted by the late Dewánjee of the Baroda
State ; and who, under the new arrangements with our Government, has been
permitted to return to the city as a candidate for high political employment
under the Gáikáwár.   Captain Fawcett, and Mr. Mitchell, Dr. Campbell and
I, went to pay a visit to'him at the Diwanji's Wádì in the evening of the 21st
ult.   My friends were mounted on Mr. Sutherland's elephant, which outstepped
my bearers on the road to the city.   We lost sight of one another in one of
the lanes ; and the wise men who were hearing me took me to the house of
the king instead of to that of his minister !   I had there the pleasure of
seeing two of the Ráuees (queens), whose curiosity introduced them to my
view on one of the staircases.   Having explained the error of the bipeds to
the guards around me, I was quickly transported to what ought to have been
my first destination.   I found the trio sitting in a splendid apartment, and
lost in wonder at the marvels around them.   To me they had little novelty ;
and the delay which had occurred in my movements consumed the time which
should have been devoted to religious conversation.   Alas !   The first movement of the household in reference to our leaving the mansion revealed the
kindness and liberality of its owners.   Govind Ráo rose to present each of us
with a pair of Cashmere shawls and a turban ; and he succeeded in getting us
to accept of them.   The most valuable he set apart for myself ; those next in a
market-reckoning to Mr. Mitchell.   Dr. Campbell, who was last served, fared
worst.   I determined for my own part to manage so as to give a suitable
return ; and when the great man visited us with his followers on the 23d, I
presented his son with an Atlas, phenakistoscope, and several helps to the
acquisition of English which he has begun to study, and himself with several
books.   It was a relief to my feelings to be able to give him an exposition of
Christian doctrine when he waited upon us.   The Bráhmans who attended
him, as well as he himself, were very attentive to what I said.   I must not
forget to mention that he accompanied us to his gardens, which are in
excellent order.   The first fruits of the season were destined for our use ; and
three men followed us home with baskets filled with them."

From Baroda Dr. Wilson and his companion marched
through the level country of Goojarat, by Khaira to which
he sought to induce the Church to send a missionary.   His
journal corrects a few of " the most amusing blunders " of
that very inaccurate but most pleasant book, Bishop Heber's
Narrative.   Here he had much discussion with the Jains, one
of whom proposed to write a reply to his letter to the priests of
Palitana.   Lieutenant Pilfold, " an excellent Sanskrit scholar,"
copied for him Sanskrit inscriptions on his march to Deesa by
Ahmedabad, Khaira, Puttun, and Pahlunpoor.   At Puttun
(" the city "), the ancient capital of Goojarat, they were met
by Captain Lang, the scholarly political agent.   After cross-
examining a young Hindoo ascetic, so as to discover for the
first time that the lengthened hair of these devotees is caused
by twisting to the growth the thinning which is taken from
it, the party proceeded to survey the ruins.

At Pahlunpoor, one of the vassal states of the Gaikwar, the Dewan held a durbar or court for the reception of the missionaries. He was Futh Khan, whom we had put on the throne as the rightful heir of the Afghan Chief first recognised by Akbar, to a principality which the Rajpoot Chief of Jodhpore had reduced to Pahlunpoor and Deesa. He lived till 1854, having been first acknowledged in 1794, and his son still rules after loyal services in the Mutiny. The most interesting visitor, however, was a Muhammadan, who had lived nine years in the Hedjaz of Arabia. He gave Dr. Wilson a description of the *Hajar-as-Swad*, exactly corresponding with the engraving in Burckhardt's travels, but without expressing particular veneration for the sacred stone, the most venerable relic of antiquity in the eyes of Mussulmans. The British cantonment of Deesa, eighteen miles from the Dewan's capital, was next visited, and the Sepoy regimental school was examined through Marathee. Its fifty-five pupils and regimental boys flocked to Dr. Wilson's tent for books, and there he instructed them in Christianity. "Many of the youth in the Army," he writes on this occasion, " in consequence of its discipline and arrangements have had their faith in Hindooism greatly shaken. They are very observant of the walk and conversation of their officers, and they generally respect those of them who are imbued with the spirit of Christianity!" Here Dr. Wilson was surprised by coming into contact with one of the many proofs, apparent to the experienced and unprejudiced observer of Hindoo society, that the leaven of Christianity is working by means and in directions such as no statistics can tabulate nor formal report record. The subsequent history of Christianity in India has revealed many similar cases of quasi-Christian sects, of "almost Christians," of "secret Christians," and of Christian heresies and apostasies, caused by such an admixture of pantheistic speculation with Christ's teaching as Gnosticism, Alexandria, and the early Oriental Churches illustrate.

"*12th April.*—We met three natives at Dr. Robson's door, who said that they had been going about the camp in search of us, in consequence of the report of my having preached in the town of Deesa. To my inquiry, 'Who are you?' they readily and emphatically answered, 'We are *Christians.*' We immediately repaired with them to the bungalow in which we were holding our meetings; and I conversed with them, and addressed them respecting the interests of their immortal souls. The individual who took the lead in the conference with me stated that he is a *Bhagat*, devoted to the service of Christ, that his name is Narottam Ladha, and that his class is that of the Lawana ; one of his companions, that he is a disciple of Narottam, named Daman Deva, and of the Khatree class ; and the other, that he is a Jain Mehta, named Natharam Dalichand, and an inquirer into the doctrine of Christianity, of the truth of which he is thoroughly convinced. Narottam remarked that he teaches Christianity to those who listen to him, and receives the support which they voluntarily afford. His knowledge, he said, he had received from books, and from conversation with a native convert from Bengal, named Kamilakant Rao. His profession of Christianity he had assumed, and his attempts to propagate Christianity he had commenced and carried on without any consultation with Europeans. He had seen the Bishop of Bombay, however, and Mr. Fletcher, on the occasion of their visit to Deesa last year, and is acquainted with Mr. Pemberton, the chaplain, whose services in the church he sometimes attends, with a partial knowledge of what is said though he himself is unable to converse in English. I found, on examination, that he is well acquainted with the principal facts recorded in the New Testament. His views of the offices of the persons of the Holy Trinity appeared, in the first instance, to be obscure, but after I had delivered an exposition to him on the subject, I perceived that they were more extensive and correct than I had supposed. He distinctly ascribed the origination of the plan of human redemption to the Father, its accomplishment to the work and merit of the Son, and its application to the agency of the Spirit, of Whose various operations he spoke in a manner strictly consistent with the divine testimony. Both Mr. Mitchell and myself felt the greatest interest in him and his friends, and we invited him to return to us at the conclusion of English worship in the camp.

"Narottam made his appearance at the time appointed, along with the persons already mentioned, and Jawer, a barber, who represented himself as an 'established believer' in Christ, and Mancharam, a respectable Mehta, who said that he wished himself to be considered as merely in the capacity of an inquirer. The Bhagat, at my request, gave me a particular account of his past history, his present engagements, and the circumstances of his followers. He was born in Bombay about thirty years ago, his father being a native of Bhownuggur, in Kathiawar. Six years ago he received from a soldier in the camp bazaar at Deesa, a copy of a Goojaratee tract, entitled 'The Great Inquiry,' and a Marathee tract superscribed 'The First Book for Children.' He read both of these little publications with the greatest attention, and the consequence of his acquaintance with them was the awakening of great anxiety about the salvation of his soul. Seeing on one of them a notice of different mission stations where information respecting their contents could be found, he determined to betake himself to that which was most accessible. He went on his way to Surat as far as Ahmedabad. He was there assailed by various idolaters, who represented the missionaries to him as too powerful in their influence over the minds of those who come into close contact with them. During his stay at Ahmedabad he met with Jayasingh, the hereditary Kamavisdar of Kadee, a most intelligent gentleman, with whom we had a very agreeable interview on our visit to his native place. Jayasingh's followers said to him, 'There are many Fakeers, Bairagees, Gosavees, etc., in the country, why don't you unite yourself with one of their fraternities ?' but their master, when he had a private opportunity afforded him, said, 'I have as much need of God as you, stay with me ; when I hear of a teacher I will send for him.' This invitation was complied with ; and he to whom it was addressed resided for five months at Kadee, when the failure of the money which he had carried from Deesa, the usual place of his residence, forced him again to proceed northward. About half a year after his return to the camp bazaar he met with Kamilakant, already mentioned, and began to associate with him, and to accompany him occasionally to church. By the perusal of some Goojaratee books, portions of the Bible, and tracts which he obtained, and by conversation with his friend from Bengal, he became convinced that Jesus Christ is the only surety and Saviour of men, and resolved, without consulting with flesh and blood, to devote himself to His service, in which he has now been engaged for a considerable time. He reads and expounds the Scriptures, according to the light which he has obtained, to all who will listen to him. Seven of his acquaintances, he says, have received the truth in the love of it, and avow themselves to be disciples of the Redeemer. About a hundred persons appear to be sincere inquirers. About 20 or 25 of them reside in Deesa, 10 or 15 at Pahlunpoor, 40 at Puttun, 2 at Vijapoor and Kadee, 10 at Baroch, and 5 at Baroda. Many other individuals hold religious intercourse with him ; and there is in various places a growing attachment to the divine word. All his temporal wants are supplied by his followers, and Asharam, a merchant, shows him particular kindness.

"After he had given me this narrative, he asked me to explain to him many passages of the sacred Scriptures which he had found it difficult to . understand. I was surprised at the degree of intelligence which his inquiries evinced, and at the readiness with which he received my expositions. He clearly showed that he reads the Bible with the greatest attention, and that he is no stranger to the analogy of the faith. He had no objection, he said, to be baptized ; but he added that, though not recognised as a teacher by Europeans, he would minister to his native flock as long as its members might choose to attend to him. Some of the rules of the Hindoo devotees he thought it expedient to apply to his services. He wishes to be considered a *Bhagat*, and not a *Gooroo*. 'Gooroos, like yourself,' he said, ' I shall ever attend when I have the opportunity.' Such of his friends as were present expressed the same determination. Though we saw a good deal of superstition in some of their notions, we were rejoiced to find that they were far from being ignorant of the most important truths. I read my letter to the Jain priests to the company, and conversed about some of the topics on which it touches. I then delivered a practical address suited to the circumstances of my audience, and closed our meeting with prayer. The immediate objects of our regard were evidently much affected during the latter exercise, and they grasped my hand in the most tender manner when I ceased to address the Throne of Grace on their behalf. On parting with us they readily acquiesced in a proposal to correspond with our Native Church in Bombay.

"I do not know how you and my other friends in Bombay will receive this intelligence. For my own part, I have no hesitation in saying that the privilege of communicating it is to us a sufficient recompense for the long journey which we have undertaken at this trying season. The simple spread of the knowledge of Christ in this moral wilderness, independently of the hope which this case affords that real conversion may have occurred, demands the fervent gratitude of all His people, and forms a mighty encouragement to the dissemination of the holy Scriptures and religious tracts throughout the length and breadth of the land. The Apostle Paul and his companions met with ' disciples ' in different cities before they had commenced in them their own personal ministrations, and before elders were ordained to watch over their spiritual interests as 'those who must give au account,' and so have we found persons who *appear* to be deserving of the name in a situation where we least expected them." . .

Dr. Wilson had now passed through that wild Bheel

country on the Maheekanta and Rajpootana frontier, which
Sir James Outram had in 1838 pacified and done much to
civilise, but we have no trace of a meeting between men who
must have appreciated each other. It is to be regretted too
that we have here no detailed description of that mountain of
the Jains—Aboo—which in 1840 was purely native. Five
years after his visit the Rao, Sheo Singh, made over to the
British Government lands for a sanitarium, which became the
favourite resort of Sir Henry Lawrence, and of his successors
to the present day. The reigning chief, son of Dr. Wilson's
friend who died a few weeks before the missionary himself,
is now of age, and still insists on the one condition of the
grant, that no kine shall be killed on the holy mount of the
Jains.

Marching forward thus through the country between the
Aboo and Aravullee hills and the wild Bheel land, and
away by Sadra on the Saburmuttee, Dakore, famed in
Hindoo pilgrimage, and the Baria and Champaner jungles,
south-east to the great Nerbudda river, Dr. Wilson and his
companions had to climb the low Satpoora range before
reaching the Maratha-desolated plains of Khandesh. Thence,
by Dhoolia and Malligaum, Bombay was reached in the
middle of June, after a journey unmatched at that time by
any save officials on military or most urgent duty, whether we
look at the terrific heat or at the desert and dangerous lands.
Soon he prepared a series of lectures on a tour which, even
to the few experienced travellers, English and Native, who
had gone over the same route, were full of the highest instruction. It is long since the railway reached Ahmedabad
from Bombay, and the line has already penetrated from
Calcutta to Jeypore for the salt of the Sambhur Lake. It
cannot be long till Ahmedabad and Jeypore are connected by
a line which will follow Dr. Wilson's route away by Aboo to
Palee and Ajmer, to which he afterwards conducted the first
United Presbyterian missionaries.

At the close of February 1841 Dr. Wilson welcomed the
earliest of those bands of missionaries who, of whatever evangelical Church, continued successively, during the next third
of a century, to find in Ambrolie or "The Cliff" on Malabar
Hill the most generous hospitality, the wisest counsel, the
most efficient aid. The first of his tours to bear fruit in the

establishment of a mission by another Church than his own,
was, as we have seen, his exploration of Goojarat and Kathiawar in 1835. To evangelise that, the Synod of Ulster,
daughter of the Scottish Kirk, sent out two missionaries.
The Rev. J. Glasgow and J. Kerr had not been asked to
volunteer for the work, but had been called upon by the
Synod's committee to do it. This course, followed only by
the autocratic organisation of the Church of Rome, was
declared by the very democratic Assembly of the Irish Presbyterian Church "to be a precedent in all time to come." It
may be regretted that the precedent has been so seldom, if
ever since, followed. Certainly few Protestant missions to
people possessed of an ancient civilisation, literature, and
faith, have been so promising, to the present day, as that
conducted by a succession of men of the same stamp as the
Lawrences and Montgomerys of Derry, who, in the civil and
military services, have written their names deepest on the
page of Indian history. The landing of Messrs. Glasgow and
Kerr raised in Government circles, as well as in native society,
a new question : Would they, should they, be allowed to
preach and teach in native States like Baroda and the many
vassal principalities of Kathiawar ?

The East India Company had been compelled, by the
public opinion of Great Britain expressed through Parliament, to tolerate missionaries in their ordinary territory.
But up to this time there had been no instance of a Christian
mission in a native State. And we may be assured that, but
for the pioneering work and influence of Dr. Wilson, the
principalities of Western and Northern India would have
remained closed for many a day. His interviews with chiefs
and people had prepared them as well as the British Government for Christian schools and preachers, a result to which
the earlier example of a chaplain and the increasing number
of Christian officials had contributed. There was some doubt
as to how Sir James R. Carnac, the Governor of Bombay,
would act. He was an " old Indian," who, after experience
as a sepoy officer in the Madras Army, had himself been Resident at Baroda, and then Chairman of the Court of Directors.
One of his first utterances as Governor had seemed hostile to
toleration. But over him also Dr. Wilson's perfect honesty,
fearless character, and fine Christian tact, had had their due

effect. His formal application to the Government produced
this reply, signed by the friendly chief secretary, Sir J. P.
Willoughby, " The Honourable the Governor in Council will
offer no objection to these gentlemen proceeding to and
residing in Kathiawar, so long as they conduct themselves
according to the principles set forth in your communication."
Thus peacefully was established a precedent of which Dr.
Wilson wrote to the Ulster Synod : " The freely accorded
permission of the Government for the establishment of your
mission in Kathiawar, though nothing more than what was
expected in the circumstances of the case, is such as to
demand our fervent gratitude. Though we should not have
refused to enter the province even though the goodwill of
our rulers had not been expressed, the official communication which we have had with the authorities enables us to do
so with the best understanding, and without any apprehen-
sion as to further embarrassments."

The season of the year for tours was past, but now, as
before, Dr. Wilson set the prudent fears of his friends at
defiance, and resolved to spend the hot months in helping his
Irish brethren to establish their mission at Rajkote, Porebunder and Gogo. At all three places Dr. Wilson found that
his former visit had borne fruit in the goodwill and intelligent
interest of the native chiefs in the mission, and in the readiness of the leading inhabitants to send their boys to the
English schools. The Rajkote Chief himself took part in a
public discussion of the comparative merits of Christianity
and Hindooism, propounding the question, " Why does not
God Almighty, who created the world, annihilate sin at once
in the heart of man, and thus instantly save him from evil ? "
This led to a statement of the principles of the moral government of God. Thus, as by some weeks' study of the missionary work in Bombay, were the new missionaries trained.
And not only they, for the Parsee convert, Dhunjeebhoy, was,
for the first time, on this tour the companion of the teacher
to whom he was thenceforth as a son. Hardly had the mission been established in a house in Rajkote when Mr. Kerr
was carried off by jungle fever, which prostrated Dr. Wilson
at the same time. Captain Le Grand Jacob, afterwards a
famous name in Western India, and then acting as Political
Agent, removed his friend from the fatal house, and in the

Residency Dr. Wilson was tenderly nursed by Dhunjeebhoy, while deserted by some of his heathen servants who feared infection.

"Though, when death presented itself to my view, and I called to mind my own waywardness under the teaching of the Lord, and my awful responsibility as a missionary of the Cross to this darkened and unholy country, 'my flesh,' in the first instance, 'trembled for fear of God's judgments,' there was soon imparted to me, through contemplation on the glory and stability of the covenant of grace, and the freeness with which its blessings are bestowed on the humblest and most unworthy believer, a peace and joy the remembrance of which is calculated to excite most fervent and devout gratitude. After I had become in some degree convalescent I was called to experience a most unfavourable relapse. A change of climate affording the only hope of my recovery, I was conveyed, by bearers, from Rajkote to Gogo. I remained about a week at the latter place before the daily paroxysms of fever began to be mitigated ; but as soon as I felt them subsiding I sailed for Bombay, which I reached in safety on the 21st of September.

"Here it pleased the Lord, in his unerring wisdom and unswerving faithfulness, to visit me with other great and sore afflictions. During my voyage I had fondly indulged the hope that my beloved sister and endeared companion Miss Anna Bayne would receive me with her usual affection, and attend to me in my weakness with her wonted care and tenderness. On my arrival at the mission-house, however, I learnt that she was with her sister, Mrs. Nesbit, in the most precarious, nay dangerous state of health. Her appointed days of suffering soon drew to a close ; and on the morning of the 4th of October her ransomed, and justified, and purified soul was called to enter into the joy of its Lord. The triumph of her faith during the whole of her last illness was most remarkable, instructive, animating, and encouraging. She proved a conqueror, and more than a conqueror, through Him that loved her.

"Miss Bayne, though not officially connected with the General Assembly's Mission, was actually much engaged in its service. To comfort and assist me in the work of the Lord, she and her sister Mary, now Mrs. Nesbit, left the land of their fathers. She was the life and charm of my household. To the Parsee converts, and Abyssinian and Native youth, whom I have received into my family, she was a tender and affectionate mother, as they themselves declare and feel, and will long remember. Her visits to the female schools proved very encouraging to the scholars ; and her instruction of the classes in her own room was highly promising of spiritual good. She zealously sought the improvement and conversion of the students of English who visit the mission-house ; and with some of them she regularly read and explained the Scriptures, while with others she regularly corresponded when they were removed from Bombay. In the Christian society in which she moved she was most exemplary and influential ; and both noticed and respected for her gifts and graces. All who enjoyed her friendship admired her kindness, faithfulness, and judiciousness. It was her request, when she came to India, that no mention should be made of her endeavours and exertions in any public report or letter."

The indomitable spirit of Dr. Wilson is apparent in every line of this letter. At Mahableshwar he devoted his returning health to the composition of *The Parsi Religion* and

the renewed study of the aboriginal tribes of the Western
Ghauts.

"I am at present sojourning on the most lovely spot which you can
imagine. The scenery around is the grandest, the most beautiful, and the
most sublime, which I have yet witnessed during my earthly wanderings,
extensive though they have been. The Mahableshwar is part of the great
Western Gháts, and 4700 feet above the level of the sea,—a loftiness considerably surpassing the highest of Caledonia's mountains. The vegetation
partakes of the magnificence of the tropics, but is enchanting to the dwellers
in the climes of the sun, as in some respects resembling that of our beloved
native land. The matériel of the heights is of the trap formation, which by
its basaltic masses and columns, and precipitous scarps, affords the most
wonderful and diversified specimens of nature's architecture, and by its valleys
and ravines, of her gigantic excavation. The province of the Konkan, with
its hills and dales, and exhaustless forests and fruitful fields, stretches below.
At a distance the ocean is seen as a vast mirror of brilliancy, reflecting the
glory of the sky. The clouds baffle all description. Their various and
changing hues, and multifarious forms and motions, as they descend to kiss
the mountain brow, or remain above as our fleecy mantle, or interpose between
us and the luminary of heaven to catch its rays, and to reveal their coloured
splendour, fill the mind with the most intense delight. The whole display
forces us to praise God, and to exclaim, 'Bless the Lord, O my soul. O
Lord my God, Thou art very great, Thou art clothed with honour and
majesty.'

" ' If thus Thy glories gild the span
Of ruined earth and fallen man,
How glorious must the mansion be
Where Thy redeemed shall dwell with thee !'

"MAHABLESHWAR, 27th November 1841.—You have, I suppose, often
seen Sátárá. In my opinion it is the most lovely station in our Presidency.
The valley of the Yená, with its abundant cultivation, and that of the
Krishná, which partly appears, and the mountains to the west, and the hills
to the north and south, presenting, with their basaltic masses and layers, and
columns, and scarps, and towers, the most interesting specimens of nature's
architecture, have a very striking effect on the eye of a spectator. The fort is
curiously formed on the summit of one of the highest elevations, and it is
associated with all the interest and romance of Maráthee history. The
native town is spacious, busy, and regular, to a degree seldom seen in this
country. The camp is very agreeably situated ; and the Residency has a
beautiful neighbourhood.

"We were introduced by Colonel Ovans to the Raja. His Highness was
encamped, with an enormous suite, outside the town, having just arrived from
a pedestrian journey to the shrine of Khandobá at Jejurí. When I intimated
to him the fruitlessness of his pilgrimage by saying Khandobá lakáchyá
bokándin basto, 'Khaudohá seizes folks by the throat,' he laughed most
heartily ; but I have reason to believe that he is really very superstitious.
He has no appearance of the dissipation with which his enemies have charged
him ; and he is noted by the Europeans at present at Sátárá for his benevolence and good nature. Of his own accord he has abolished Suttee and the
sale of children. He has lightened the burdens of his cultivators, and established for the benefit of his subjects an extensive hospital, all the expense of
which—including Rs. 500 monthly to Dr. Erskine for supervision—he himself
discharges. He has increased the efficiency of the school founded by his

brother the ex-Raja, and it is now, as it should be, as much English as it is Oriental. He has greatly extended the roads throughout the country, and he is building two excellent bridges, which I went to see, over the Yená and the Krishná. , I trust that he will be permitted to continue to occupy the throne, for of the guilt of his brother, for which he has been sent to Benares, there ought to be no doubt. You remember what Captain G. told us at Goa, about the horses on which the Capitão General and his suite were riding having been presented to them by the Sátárá State, when the Raja asked the co-operation of the Portuguese in turning the English out of the country. I have seen the letters of Don Manuel de Portugal e Castro, the former Governor of Goa, to the Raja, acknowledging his letters, and identified them by the signature, seal, and other marks. I have also seen the communications of the ex-Raja of Nágpore, and in a similar way identified them. Now, when it is kept in mind that Pratap Singh was bound over by the treaty—ou a breach of which his possessions were to be forfeited—to abstain from *all* correspondence with the different chieftains and States of India not sanctioned by our Government, it must be seen that he has justly been deposed. It is much to be regretted that so many benevolent and excellent men in England have espoused his cause, and seem determined to make it the subject of senatorial and popular agitation, instead of more worthy themes connected with the welfare and amelioration of this great country. In the number of the *Asiatic Journal* of August last you will see a very full report of the debates which have already taken place on the subject before the Court of Proprietors of India stock. Sir R. Campbell quotes a note which I sent to Major Jervis about the Goa affair ; and Mr. George Thompson makes such an absurd and improper comment upon it, that, with my estimate of his Christian worth, I cannot conceive that he had heard the little document read, which he entirely perverts. If he wishes to establish for himself the character of a friendly advocate of the claims of India, he must speak from a perfect knowledge of facts, and not from vague impressions. He seems to insinuate blame against me for presuming to form any judgment in the case at all ; but he ought to have observed that I was brought forward only as a *witness*, and to have remembered that if missionaries do not give notice of any treasonable movements which they may happen to observe, they are altogether unworthy of that protection which is extended to them by the British Government, which, with all its faults, is next to the offer of the Gospel itself—which it facilitates—the greatest blessing ever conferred on India. I have been extremely sorry to observe several speakers impeaching the motives and feelings of the commissioners sent to Sátárá to aid the Bombay Government in its investigations. Colonel Ovans stood in the most disinterested position which can be imagined ; and Mr. Willoughby's benevolence, so well evinced by his most able and persevering efforts to abolish infanticide in Kathiá-wár, not second to those of Walker himself, formed a good guarantee that the claims of mercy would be consulted by him as well as those of justice."

On his return to Bombay at the end of January 1842, he writes :—" I had a most cordial reception, not only from my Christian friends but from great numbers of the natives. The rush of the latter to bid me welcome, and their sincere greetings on my recovery and restoration I am disposed to consider as an indication that they are ready to avail themselves of such ministrations as I may be able to render." He at once announced a new course of lectures on the Parsee

religion, to prepare the community for the appearance of his
book. Dr. Murray Mitchell had vigorously conducted the
Bombay Mission during his absence, a fact which he gratefully reports to Dr. Brunton. On the session of 1842 Dr.
Wilson entered with such vigour that he wrote :—" I have
seldom been able to do more in the mission than during the
last three months." But the season proved to be one of
those periodical years of cholera which was " most extensive
and fearful in its ravages." One of the ladies at the head of
the female schools was struck down by the pestilence ; the
other, the head of the boarding-school, soon followed her, and
that when the loss of Anna Bayne was still fresh.

Dr. Hugh Miller and others so pressed on Dr. Wilson
the duty of taking furlough after thirteen years of toil, that
he agreed to make such arrangements " as will permit me, if
I am preserved, to pay my promised visit to the land of my
fathers." To Dr. Brunton he wrote thus on the 23d May, as
if tempted to a prudent regard for his health and rest only
by the prospect of a far more extended tour, through Syria
and Eastern Europe, than he had yet made in India :—" I
begin already to long to have the privilege of conferring with
you and the committee about our wants and wishes in this
place, and pleading with the public on behalf of this great
country. I wish, however, to look at the Muhammadan
delusion and the Jewish unbelief of Asia near the centre of
their influence as I proceed to the West ; and I know that
you will not consider my movements as aberrations in a missionary point of view, even though they should prove somewhat extended and circuitous." He was not to leave until
enabled by Captain, now Sir W. Hill, to announce the supply
of funds for another Scottish Mission in Nagpore, now the
capital of the Central Provinces, and to plan the organisation
of that mission which was established by Mr. Stephen Hislop
a few years after. And he was summoned, in the last busy
weeks of his preparation for his departure, to the counsels of
the Bombay Government in the matter of Lord Ellenborough
and the proclamation regarding the gates of Somnath. He
had not long before visited the spot. He knew its history
better than any man in India ; he understood, because he
loved, the natives, Hindoo and Muhammadan ; he held familiar
intercourse with the highest English officials. And, in the

Sátara case, he had just proved that his judgment on political questions was as cautious as it was guided by the principles of righteousness in every form.

When, early in the year 1841, Sir James R. Carnac ceased to be Governor of Bombay, the official nominated as his successor was Sir William Hay Macnaghten. Macnaghten was the Calcutta Secretary, whom Lord Auckland and Lord Broughton had found to be the most enthusiastic advocate of the evil policy of interference in Afghanistan. Blameless in life, accomplished as an oriental scholar, for some time a judge of high repute from his knowledge of the natives, and a hard-working secretary, Macnaghten was sent to Cabul as the envoy to carry into execution the mad scheme he had encouraged. During the seven ill-fated weeks when his pre-possessions cheated him, though not those around him, into the belief that that policy had succeeded, he was rewarded by the Governorship of Bombay, and he was arranging to leave Cabul for Western India when the catastrophe came. Sending for the three officers whom he always consulted, though he too often refused to be guided by them, he brusquely directed them to accompany him to a conference with the hostile Akbar Khan, the favourite son of the supplanted ruler Dost Muhammad. Colin Mackenzie, bravest of all the heroes of that time, but the only one of them who, though a Lieutenant-General and C.B., still remains unhonoured by the country he has served so long and so well, remonstrated that it was a plot. "Trust me for that," said the envoy, who had hardly begun to talk when Akbar Khan himself shot him with one of the pistols for which the assassin had just thanked him ; Trevor was also cut down ; and Mackenzie and the third officer, now Sir George Lawrence, escaped alive with difficulty, past a line of excited fanatics.

A new Governor had to be selected, and he proved to be the amiable and useful Sir George Arthur, Bart., who was thus rewarded for services in the Colonies. As his private secretary the new ruler appointed a young civilian, who, eight years before, in 1834, had been admitted to Dr. Wilson's friendship on his presenting a letter of introduction to the missionary at Ambrolie. Henry Bartle Edward Frere had begun to redeem, by his ability and industry in the Revenue Department, the promise which he gave at Haileybury. Over

him, as over so many young officers in both services, Dr. Wilson
exercised a powerful influence, and hence few public men in
high position have so fairly represented the nature and the
importance of missionary work in India and Africa as he.
In his case the intimacy became friendship honourable to
both. When Sir Bartle Frere himself rose to be Governor,
and with all the state of an Indian proconsul would sometimes call on the simple scholar to introduce some native
prince and show the mission college, he used to recall the
day when, as a shy youth, he first ascended the Ambrolie
stair to present his letter to one who was even then beginning
to be regarded with reverence.

The unhappy Lord Auckland had given place to Lord
Ellenborough, as the Governor-General sent out to avenge
and retrieve the disasters of 1838-40. Lord Ellenborough,
in the delirium of a heated and an unequally unprincipled
policy, had with the one hand directed Generals Pollock and
Nott to "retire" without rescuing the noble men and women
who were in captivity, and with the other to bring back the
gates of the Hindoo temple of Somnath, which adorned
Muhammad's tomb at Ghuznee, that he might declare, "the
insult of eight hundred years is at last avenged." On the
5th October the Commander-in-Chief, Sir Jasper Nicholls,
saw the first draft of the precious document known as "The
Proclamation of the Gates," and freely criticised it. Sir
John Kaye, in his best book, *The History of the War in
Afghanistan*, states that it was published in its English form
on the 16th November. But it seems to have been first
referred to the subordinate Governments for opinion, for it
had not appeared in Bombay on the 2d December, as this
note shows :—

"MY DEAR DR. WILSON.—When you were in Kattywar did you visit the
temple of Somnath Puttun, the gates of which are about to be restored by
Lord Ellenborough, and in this case can you afford me any information on the
subject of its present condition, and how it is managed ? The notification
that is about to be published regarding the gates of this pagan temple will
astonish the whole Christian world.—Yours very sincerely, J. WILLOUGHBY.
"2d December 1842."

On the next day Dr. Wilson was officially asked for information to enable the Bombay Government to criticise it.
The temple from which the so-called gates had been taken,

and to which they were to be restored, was in their jurisdiction. In spite of the two months that had passed, and
of all the remonstrances and criticisms of those around him,
it is evident that Lord Ellenborough knew nothing accurately
about the temple, the gates, and their history. His ignorance
was as profound as his conduct was pernicious. Sir Bartle
Frere thus confidentially wrote to Dr. Wilson. Like Carey
when called on to translate the order suppressing Suttee, Dr.
Wilson spent the greater part of a Sunday in meeting this
urgent call in the service of religion and humanity.[1]

"Parell, 3d *December* 1842.—Dear Sir—You are of course aware, that
among the trophies which have been brought away from Afghanistan by the
British army are the 'Somnath Gates' of Sultan Mahmoud's tomb at Guzni ;
and you have probably heard that it is the intention of the Governor-General
that, as a memorial of the triumph of our arms, they shall be restored to the
spot whence they were taken by the Guznivide Sultan 800 years ago. As the
Governor understands that, in the course of your late tour through Kattywar,
you visited the site of Somnath Puttun, and made particular inquiries regarding the history and antiquities of the place, he will feel much obliged if you
will let him know, for the information of the Governor-General, in what state
you found the ruins of the ancient city. How many temples, and of what
kind, are still in existence—which of them is the temple whence the gates are
said to have been taken, and on what kind of evidence the conclusion of its
identity rests—who has charge of or control over it—what is its condition—
who are the 'Poojarees,' or persons who perform the usual ceremonies of
worship, etc.—and of which castes and sects the worshippers are generally
composed ? If your inquiries established any other facts connected with the
history or present state of 'Somnath Puttun,' which you think likely to be of
interest to the Governor, he desires me to say he will feel much obliged by
your communicating them.—Believe me, dear Sir, ever faithfully yours,

"H. B. E. Frere."

So early as October, two months before this, Lord Ellenborough had sent his proclamation privately to the Queen, in
a letter filled with historical mistakes and baseless native
gossip, which thus closed : "The progress of the gates from
Ferozepore to Somnath will be one great national triumph,
and their restoration will endear the Government to the
whole people." Two months after, on the 19th February
1843, he announced to her Majesty, in similarly bombastic
phrases, the arrival of the gates at Delhi under the escort of
five hundred Sikh troopers. "All," he wrote, "consider the
restoration of the gates to be a national not a religious
triumph." His Excellency had been taught by remonstrances
far less courteous than Dr. Wilson's, to abandon the religious

[1] See Appendix II.

argument which he had from the first paraded; while at home the storm was rising, and all the efforts of his personal friend, the Duke of Wellington, could not quell it. To the Governor-General himself the Duke could not write more strongly than this : " I say nothing of the Gates of Somnath, which is, I think, made a *cheval de bataille.*"

The gates never got farther than the Agra arsenal, where they stand to point the sneer against Lord Ellenborough. Mr. Vernon Smith, three months after, faintly expressed public opinion in Europe, when he moved in the House of Commons a resolution condemning the conduct of the Governor-General in this matter as " unwise, indecorous, and reprehensible." The party of the accused, then in power, procured the rejection of the motion; but in spite of all the great Duke's influence, that proclamation soon after led to its author's recall. We cannot altogether regret an act which was the occasion of Macaulay's most famous Philippic; his greatest, at once as a piece of eloquence and a vindication of the principles of religious liberty applied to India.

CHAPTER X.

1836-1842.

ORIENTAL SCHOLARSHIP AND SCHOLARS.

Sir W. Jones founds the Bengal Asiatic Society—Sir James Mackintosh and
   the Bombay Literary Society—The Early Orientalists of Western India—
   Dr. Wilson's first Address as President—Subordinates his Scholarly to his
   directly Missionary Pursuits—Member of the Royal Asiatic Society—The
   first to attempt deciphering of the Fourteen Edicts of Asoka—Colonel
   James Tod at Girnar—James Prinsep's Enthusiasm—Dr. Mill—Prinsep's
   tribute to Dr. Wilson—Girnar as it is—The Second and Thirteenth Edicts,
   and the early successors of Alexander the Great—Dr. Wilson consulted
   by Chief-Justice on Parsee Law and Customs—Congratulatory Letters on
   "The Parsi Religion" from Erskine and Lassen—Dr. Wilson appointed
   Honorary President of the Bombay Asiatic Society—Close of the first period
   of his work in Western India.

WHEN Sir William Jones was sailing across the Indian Ocean,
India itself before him, Persia on his left, and a breeze from
Arabia blowing him on, he tells us that " in the midst of so
noble an amphitheatre, encircled by the vast regions of Asia,"
he resolved to found that greatest successor to the Royal
Society, and the parent of many others—the Asiatic Society
of Bengal. In 1784, encouraged by Warren Hastings who
declined the office of first President in his favour, Sir William
Jones instituted the first " Society for inquiring into the history, civil and national, the antiquities, arts, sciences, and literature of Asia." His translation of *Sakoontala* had revealed to
Europe the virgin mine of Hindoo literature, as Goethe sang.
His greater successor, H. T. Colebrooke, on finally returning
to England, founded the Royal Asiatic Society, as well as the
Astronomical Society.

It was not to be expected that Western India, when it grew
into importance as a Presidency by conquest and diplomacy,

would be allowed by men like the Governor Jonathan Duncan, and Mountstuart Elphinstone and Malcolm afterwards, to remain unrepresented in the republic of letters. What Sir William Jones, with his fresh English energy and Oxford zeal, did for the accomplished officials who surrounded Warren Hastings, Sir James Mackintosh as happily effected among the few who were associated with Jonathan Duncan. An Inverness boy, a medical graduate of Aberdeen, an ethical philosopher, a constitutional lawyer, and a keen politician, Mackintosh leaped into the front rank of the Liberals as they were at the close of last century. He became the worthy adversary of Burke, the warm friend of Robert Hall, the advocate of Peltier who, charged with libelling Napoleon Buonaparte, found in the impetuous Scot a defender whose oration the first Lord Ellenborough pronounced the most eloquent he had ever heard in Westminster Hall. Like Macaulay afterwards, who resembled him in many respects, Mackintosh went out to Bombay as Recorder, was knighted, and remained there for eight years, till his friends thought he had saved enough besides earning a pension. The simple bachelor habits of Jonathan Duncan led him to make over to the new Judge and his family the principal Government house in the island, formerly a Jesuit College, known as Parell. Sir James had not been many months there when, on the 26th November 1804, he summoned a meeting of friends who established the Literary Society of Bombay. His *Discourse* on that occasion mapped out the field of knowledge, moral and physical, which the observers of Western India were called to cultivate. He himself, as President, suggested the first philological and statistical inquiries on a uniform scale, which were not systematically carried out till, in 1862, Lord Canning directed the adoption, for all India, of the extended scheme drawn up by Mr. Claude Erskine, the grandson of Sir James Mackintosh, and by the present writer. That has culminated in the decennial census, the uniform annual *Administration Reports*, and the *Gazetteers* of the whole Empire of India.

The Literary Society of Bombay soon established a reputation from the researches of such members as Mr. William Erskine ; Colonel Boden, founder of the Sanskrit Chair at Oxford ; Colonel Briggs, who succeeded Captain Grant Duff as Resident at Satara ; Colonel Vans Kennedy, and Captain

Basil Hall; besides Elphinstone and Malcolm. Of these
Mackintosh became the literary adviser. To his encouragement we owe such classical works as Wilks's *Mysore,* Elphinstone's *Cabul,* Briggs's *Ferishta,* Dr. John Taylor's *Lilawati,*
and Malcolm's *Political History of India.* Moor, Drummond,
Price, Salt, Colonel Sykes, Sir Charles Forbes, Joseph Hammer,
and the erratic Lord Valentia, also adorned that early group,
each in his own way. Sir James urged on the President of
the Bengal Asiatic Society that co-operation for the publication of translations from the Sanskrit, Arabic, and Persian,
which, in another form, subsequently issued in the " Oriental
Translation Fund," the *Notices des Manuscrits de la Biblio-
thèque du Roi,* and most fully of all, in the *Bibliotheca Indica.*

But his greatest immediate service was the creation of
a Library which, from the nucleus sent out on his return
to England, has grown to be the most useful, alike for the
scholar and the general reader, in all Asia. That Library
gave the Literary Society a new impetus. Besides the papers
which its members contributed to the Bengal and Royal
Asiatic Societies, it published three volumes of *Transactions*
in 1819-1823, and these have recently been reprinted. In
1830 it was incorporated as the Bombay Branch of the Royal
Asiatic Society, and in 1841 it issued independently the first
quarterly number of its *Transactions,* now a goodly series of
volumes. When Dr. Wilson settled in Bombay he thus found
a literary and scholarly home, to which in a few years he
managed to add a museum. Long after, in 1870, he thus
expressed his gratitude :—" I feel that I am under very great
obligations to this Society. I never could have prosecuted
my studies, such as they have been, without access to such a
Library as that which we here possess. I have often had a
hundred volumes from this Library at the same time in my
possession, and though I have now accumulated a very considerable Oriental library for myself, I have still frequently
to refer to these shelves in order to get my inquiries satisfied.
. . . . I have also been much sustained by the literary communion we have here enjoyed. This is not merely the Bombay Branch of the Royal Asiatic Society, but a sort of literary
and scientific club."

But in truth Dr. Wilson had not been a year in Bombay
when he came to be recognised as the most zealous member of

the Society, and soon to be identified with it as almost the
Society itself. In 1830 Sir John Malcolm proposed him as
a member, and from that day his activity was such that, in
1835, the young Scottish missionary was unanimously elected
President in succession to so ripe a scholar as Colonel Vans
Kennedy. Every tour that he made year by year, every
manuscript that he purchased, every oriental book that he
read, contributed material to the Asiatic Society, which
Government royally accommodated in the fine suite of rooms
surrounding the Town Hall of Bombay. Nor did he, in all
this intercourse with scholars, non-Christian as well as Christian, veil for a moment the earnestness of his own convictions,
or restrain his duty as a missionary. With the then distinguished Orientalist whom he succeeded as president, he
had for years conducted a public controversy. In his *Ancient
and Hindu Mythology*, and in his *Treatise on the Vedanta*,
Colonel Vans Kennedy had appeared as something like the
apologist of Vedic and Brahmanical beliefs. While admitting
and even eulogising the ability of these disquisitions as the
most learned up to that time, Dr. Wilson exposed views
which he proved to be as superficial as they were hostile to the
work he had come to India to do. But if his hand was
the hand of iron, he ever used the glove of silk. His
courtesy, even in the impetuosity of youth, was as remarkable
as his gentle chivalry towards all when years and toil began
to weaken his arm.

Dr. Wilson's first address as President, on the 27th January
1836, reviewed the work of the Society and the desiderata of
research, from the similar discourses of Sir James Mackintosh
in 1804 and Sir John Malcolm in 1828, up to that time.
He showed that it had failed to realise the anticipations of
the founder as to Natural History and Statistics. He declared
the condition of the people in the different provinces, as to
language, religion, literature, science, art, means of support,
and manners and customs, to be the paramount object of the
Society's investigation. Beginning with the Parsees, he reviewed the contributions to a study of them made by Malcolm,
Kennedy, Erskine, Rask, Mohl, Shea, Neumann, and Atkinson,
arguing that "should any of the Parsees, of competent attainments, and real and respectable character and influence, ask
membership of this Society, it should be readily accorded."

Such advocacy of the claims of native inquirers and scholars
was characteristic of Dr. Wilson, and it soon bore fruit. He
pointed to Burnouf as the *savant* best fitted to translate faithfully the Vandidad Sadé, but plainly hinted that the work
might be done in Bombay should that great scholar fail from
the disadvantages of his situation in Europe. As to Muhammadanism, he desiderated that fuller account of the state of
Arabia at the time of its origin, which Muir and Sprenger
soon after gave, and of the Bohoras and other sectaries whom
he himself was studying. His observations on researches
into Hindooism may be read with profit even after the forty
years' scholarship of Anglo-Indians, Germans, and Italians.
To H. H. Wilson, who had not long been transferred from
Calcutta to Oxford, he looked for a complete translation of the
Rig Veda, part of which had appeared first in Bombay ; and
of the *Bhagavata Purana*, the greatest practical authority in
the West of India. On the various Hindoo sects, and on the
Jains, he sought for much light, such as he himself afterwards
gave. The despised aborigines, down-trodden by Hindoo and
Muhammadan, and ignored by the ruling class, save by civilians like Sir Donald M'Leod and missionaries, Dr. Wilson
pronounced "particularly worthy of observation by all who
desire to advance their civilisation, and to elevate them from
their present degradation. Description must precede any
considerable efforts made for their improvement—perhaps
leading to important conjectures as to the ancient history of
India." Many of these "have had no connection with Brahmanism except in so far as they may have felt its unhallowed
influence in excluding them from the common privileges of
humanity."

He enlarged on the duty of collecting Sanskrit MSS., a
work not undertaken by Government till a much later date,
but now prosecuted with great zeal and liberality in almost
every province. Such manuscripts, he said, are to be found
in a pure state in the Dekhan more than in any other part of
India, and the poverty of the Brahmans leads them readily to
part with them. After eulogising the work of Mr. William
Erskine, and his own old missionary colleague, Dr. Stevenson,
in their researches into the architecture and inscriptions of
cave temples, Dr. Wilson said :—" We require information as
to the time at which, and the views with which, they were

constructed ; an estimate of them as works of art, or as indicative of the resources of those to whom they are to be ascribed ; and an inquiry into the religious rites and services for which they have been appropriated, and the moral impressions which they seem fitted to make on those resorting to them. Grants of land, engraven on copper plates, are next to them in importance in the advancement of antiquarian research."

We find the key-note of Dr. Wilson's scholarship and erudition in his reference to " The systems of faith which have so long exercised their sway in this country, and the various literary works which, though, unlike those of Greece and Rome, they are of little or no use in the cultivation of taste, are valuable as they illustrate the tendency of those systems in their connection with social and public life ; and as they explain a language the most copious in its vocables and powerful in its grammatical forms, in which any records exist. Destitute of a knowledge of these systems, and the works in which they are embodied, the native character and the state of native society will never be sufficiently understood, a right key obtained to open the native mind, and all desirable facilities enjoyed for the introduction among the people of a body of rational and equitable law, and the propagation of the Gospel, and the promotion of general education. . . . While divine truth must be propagated with unwavering fidelity, and all hopes of its ultimate success rest on its own potency, its suitableness to the general character of man, and the assistance of divine grace, judgment ought to be employed in the mode of its application to those who vary much in their creeds and differ much in their moral practice. Though the great truths proclaimed by the Apostle Paul were the same in all circumstances, they were introduced in very different ways to the Jewish Rabbis and people and to the members of the Athenian Areopagus. I must hold that there is no little unsuitableness in India in addressing a pantheist as a polytheist and *vice versa ;* in speaking to a Jain as to a Brahman ; in condemning that at random which the natives may suppose to be unknown, and in using theological terms and general phrases without any very definite sense of their application by the natives themselves. The more a knowledge of Hindooism and of Hindoo literature is possessed by any teacher, the more patiently and uninterruptedly will he

be listened to by the people, and the more forcibly will he be
enabled, and principally by contrast and concession, to set
forth the authority and the excellence of the doctrines of
Christianity." The address concluded with a reference to
the many Armenians in India, of whom Dr. Wilson remarked,
in allusion to Mr. Dickinson's dissertation on the antiquity
of their language in the Journal of the Royal Asiatic Society,
"There cannot be a doubt that the Armenians can fill up
important blanks in Church history which, to the undue
neglect of the Orientals, is principally formed on the authority
of the Roman and Byzantine Fathers."

The new President's Address called forth a request, proposed and seconded by Mr. Bruce and Mr. Farish, that it
should be printed. Mr. James Prinsep republished it in the
fifth volume of the Bengal Asiatic Society's Journal, with this
introduction—"We make no apology, but rather feel a pride,
in transferring it to our pages entire." It must be taken as
a directory to Dr. Wilson himself of much that he meant to
overtake, and did more than overtake in the wide area of
Orientalism. The immediate effect of the Address, when it
reached Europe, and of the position in which the young missionary had been placed as the successor of Sir James Mackintosh, Mr. William Erskine, Sir John Malcolm, and Vans
Kennedy, was his election as a member of the Royal Asiatic
Society of Great Britain and Ireland, on the 18th of June
1836.

We are now in a position to estimate the exact value of
Dr. Wilson's contribution to the deciphering of the fourteen
edicts graven by the Buddhist Emperor Asoka on the rocks of
Girnar and other places in India, north and east, as well as west.
On the 13th March 1835, Dr. Wilson, hurrying down from
the peak of Girnar before the darkness of the night should
come on, examined "the ancient inscriptions which, though
never deciphered, have attracted much attention." In 1822
Lieutenant-Colonel James Tod had been the first to notice the
antiquities of "the old fort," which Joonagurh means, and
"the noblest monument of Saurashtra, a monument speaking
in an unknown tongue of other times, and calling to the
Frank ' Vedyavan ' or *savant* to remove the spell of ignorance
in which it has been enveloped for ages." But Colonel Tod
had contented himself with directing his old Gooroo, or

pundit, to copy two of the edicts, and a portion of a third, while he speculated quite in the dark as to the author of the inscriptions. Nothing more was heard of the most interesting historical rock-book in all southern Asia, for the next thirteen years, till Dr. Wilson stood before it. " After," he says, " comparing the letters with several Sanskrita alphabets in my possession, I found myself able, to my great joy and that of the Brahmans who were with me, to make out several words, and to decide as to the probable possibility of making out the whole. The taking a copy of the inscriptions I found from their extent to be a hopeless task, but, as Captain Lang had kindly promised to procure a transcript of the whole for me, I did not regret the circumstance." He subsequently wrote thus to James Prinsep :—

"I suggested to Captain Lang a plan for taking a facsimile of the inscriptions. I recommended him to cover the rock with native paper slightly moistened, and to trace with ink the depressions corresponding with the forms of the letters. The idea of using *cloth*, instead of paper, was entirely his own ; and to that able officer, and his native assistants, are we indebted for the very correct facsimile which he presented to me, and which I forwarded to you some months ago for your inspection and use. During the time that it was in Bombay it was mostly with Mr. Wathen, who got prepared for yourself the reduced transcript, and with a native, who, at the request of our Asiatic Society, and with my permission, prepared a copy for M. Jacquet of Paris. I had commenced the deciphering of it when you kindly communicated to me the discovery of your alphabet ; and I at once determined that you, as was most justly due, should have the undivided honour of first promulgating its mysteries. Any little progress which I had made in the attempt to forge a key, was from the assistance which I had received from the alphabets formerly published in your transcendantly able work, Mr. Elliot's Canarese alphabets, and the rigid deductions of VISHNU SHASTRI, my quondam pundit, to whom Mr. Wathen has expressed his obligations in his paper on some ancient copper-plate grants lately sent by him to England. VISHNU's palæographical studies, I may mention, commenced with Dr. Babbington's paper, which I showed to him some years ago ; and they were matured under Mr. WATHEN. I mention these facts from my desire to act according to the maxim *suum cuique tribue.*

"The rock containing the inscriptions, it should be observed, is about half a mile to the eastward of [the present town of] *Junágárh*, and about four miles from the base of *Girnár*, which is in the same direction. It marks, I should think, the extremity of the *Maryádá* of the sacred mountain. The Jainas, as the successors of the Buddhas, greatly honour it. They maintain *pinjarápurs*, or brute hospitals, like the Banyás of Surat, in *many* of the towns both of the peninsula and province of *Gujarát ;* and practise to a great extent the *philopsychy* of the long forgotten, but now restored, edicts of ASOKA."

Dr. Wilson was thus not only the first scholar to report intelligently on the inscriptions, and to cause a copy of them to be carefully taken, but to translate " several words " at

first sight, to "commence the deciphering," and to satisfy
himself that he could probably make out the whole in the
leisure of his study. This his knowledge of Sanskrit, and his
toilsome study of " several ancient Sanskrita alphabets," lists
of which we find in his rough note-books, enabled him to do.
To the last, more brilliant discoverers devoted to this one
work, like James Prinsep and Colonel Mackenzie, were ignorant of Sanskrit. Prinsep modestly confesses that he had
long despaired of deciphering the famous Samudra Gupta's
inscription on the Allahabad pillar, from " want of a competent knowledge of Sanscrit." Priority in time and mastery
of the Sanskrit characters and literature gave Dr. Wilson
an advantage over all the scholars of that day in India.
H. H. Wilson had left Bengal in 1833, and Dr. Mill, on
whom his mantle fell, though translating what General
Cunningham calls "several important inscriptions," resigned
the position of head of Bishop's College, Calcutta, in 1837,
and in his departure Prinsep bewailed an irreparable loss.
General Cunningham ascribes to Professor Lassen the honour
of having been the first to read " any of these unknown
characters," on coins at least. A letter from him to James
Prinsep shows that in 1836 the greatest German Orientalist
of his day had read the Indian Pali legend on the square
copper coins of Agathokles, as *Agathukla Raja*. But Dr.
Wilson's papers prove that he was even then familiar with
the characters on coins, while this letter does not affect the
credit due to him in the matter of the rock inscriptions.

Captain Lang seems to have delayed for a year the
transmission to him of copies of the Girnar inscriptions.
This delay, coupled with Dr. Wilson's unselfish regard for
others, his devotion to truth in all its forms, and the fine
enthusiasm of the young scholar of Bengal—though five years
his senior—led to the despatch of the facsimiles to Prinsep.
The latter was already partially making the Arian Pali
legends of the Bactrian Greek coins tell their historical tale,
and was poring over the Indian Pali legends of the coins of
Surashtra. Mr. Masson had given him the clue through the
Pahlavi signs for *Menandrou, Apollodotou, Erinaiou, Basileōs,*
and *Sotēros*, as he acknowledged in 1835. General Cunningham, his correspondent and friend even in those early days,
admits that " in both of these achievements the first step

towards discovery was made by others." That clue led him
successfully to recognise sixteen of the thirty-three consonants
of the Arian alphabet, and to give a provisional translation of
the rock inscriptions, before, in April 1840, illness induced
by over-work deprived oriental scholarship of its most promising ornament.

Now what does James Prinsep himself say of Dr. Wilson
in this matter of the Girnar inscriptions? The admission of
the missionary scholar's merit, previously made when repub-
lishing his address as President in the Bengal *Journal*, is
almost as modest and courteous as Dr. Wilson's action had
been. It affords a fine example to those orientalists of the
present day who, in Germany, in America, and in England,
have sometimes proved themselves vain controversialists. In
1837 Mr. Wathen had sent to him, and also to M. Jacquet
of Paris—a young orientalist of promise—the reduced copy of
the facsimiles, "which had been taken on cloth by the Rev.
Dr. Wilson." On 7th March 1838 Prinsep read his paper on
the "Discovery of the name of Antiochus the Great in two
of the Edicts of Asoka, King of India," nearly three years
after Dr. Wilson's first partial translation. But he uses this
honourable language—"I should indeed be doing an injustice
to Captain Lang, who executed the cloth facsimile for the
President of the Bombay Literary Society, and to Dr. Wilson
himself, who so graciously placed it at my disposal when,
doubtless, he might with little trouble have succeeded himself in interpreting it much better than I can do, from his
well-known proficiency in the Sanskrit language—it would, I
say, be an injustice to them were I to withhold the publication of what is already prepared for the press, which may be
looked upon as their property and their discovery, and to mix
it with what may hereafter be obtained by a more accurate
survey of the spot."

Prinsep's enthusiasm, as he worked his way through these
rock inscriptions in the weeks of February and March 1838,
and occasionally stumbled over the mutilated portions of the
facsimiles, led him to petition the Governor-General to order
another rubbing to be taken, and the Governor of Bombay
despatched Lieutenant Postans to the spot. That officer
"took infinite pains to secure exactitude, aided by Captain
Lang, who was with him," according to Captain Le Grand

Jacob's account. But, alas! Prinsep was no more when the MSS. and cloth copies reached Calcutta. Not till 1870 did General Cunningham stumble upon the neglected treasures there, although duplicates had been sent to the Royal Asiatic Society. Captain Jacob and Mr. Westergaard made fresh copies to secure more complete accuracy. The Government of Bombay has of late shown an intelligent interest in the priceless antiquities of Western India by appointing an archæo-

THE GIRNAR ROCK.

logical surveyor and reporter so competent as Mr. J. Burgess, M.R.A.S., and long Dr. Wilson's friend. His examination of the Girnar antiquities and his *estampages* of the inscriptions, as described in his second report, were the most careful and thorough of all, and may be regarded as final. He sets at rest the remaining doubts of Professor Weber. After refer-

ring to Dr. Wilson's first transcript, he thus describes the
stone :—

"The Asoka inscription at Girnar covers considerably
over a hundred square feet of the uneven surface of a huge
rounded and somewhat conical granite boulder, rising 12 feet
above the surface of the ground, and about 75 feet in circum-
ference at the base. It occupies the greater portion of the
north-east face, and, as is well known, is divided down the
centre by a vertical line ; on the left, or east side, of which
are the first five edicts or tablets, divided from one another
by horizontal lines ; on the right are the next seven, similarly divided ; the thirteenth has been placed below the fifth

THE SECOND EDICT OF ASOKA.

and twelfth, and is unfortunately damaged ; and the fourteenth is placed to the right of the thirteenth."

We reproduce Westergaard's nearly accurate transcript of
the Second Edict, that our readers may see the characters on
which first Dr. Wilson and then James Prinsep worked. The
Thirteenth Edict follows, in a transliterated form, and as
mutilated by what Tod calls "the magnificent vanity of Sun-
darji, the horse merchant," whose people, when making a
causeway to the spot from Joonagurh, seem to have used a

part of the fifth as well as of the thirteenth tablet. Mr.
Burgess, in 1869, found the precious Rock occupied by "a
lazy, sanctimonious, naked devotee, whose firewood lay
against the sides of the stone, whilst fragments of broken
earthenware covered the top of it." The engraving is from
a photograph, taken under his direction, from the wall of the
causeway. The Joonagurh chief, a Muhammadan, has, at the
request of Government, now protected the stone by a roof.

The latest rendering, by Professor Kern of Leyden, is this:—

"In the whole dominion of King Devânâmpriya Priyadarsin, as also in
the adjacent countries, as Chola (Tanjore), Pandya (Madura), Satyaputra,
Keralaputra (Malabar), as far as Tâmraparnî (Ceylon), the kingdom of Antiochus the Grecian king, and of his neighbour kings, the system of caring for the
sick both of men and cattle, followed by King Devânâmpriya Priyadarsin, has
been everywhere brought into practice ; and at all places where useful healing
herbs for men and cattle were wanting he has caused them to be brought and
planted ; and at all places where roots and fruits were wanting he has caused
them to be brought and planted ; also he has caused wells to be dug and trees
to be planted on the roads for the benefit of men and cattle."

THIRTEENTH EDICT OF ASOKA, TRANSLITERATED.

1 . . de patasa pasamâtam etâhatam haha tâvata kammata tatâ pachhâ
adhunâ ladhesu kalingesu tivo dhammavâyo

2 . . . . vadho va maranam va apavâho va janasata bâdham vedana matacha
ganamatacha Devâ

3 . . . . sâ mâtâ pitari susumsâ guru sumsumsâ mitasamstata
sahâya sa dâsa

4 . .   . . ya ñâtîka vyasanam pâpunoti vata sopi tesam
upaghâto patipati bhago vâsâ sava . . .

0 . . . . mi (?) yato nâsti manusânam ekataramhi pâsamdamhi na
nâma pâsâde yâvakâto jana tada

6 . .   . na yasaka va mitaveyâ vapi ataviyo Devânampiyasa pijite
pâti

7 . .   . . . . sava bhûtânam achhatim cha sayamamcha samam . . . . (?)
cheram cha mâdava cha

8 . . . . . . Yona râjâ paramcha tena chattâro râjano Turamâyo cha Autakâna
cha Magâ cha

9 . . . . . idhe pârimde savata Devânampiyasa dhammânusastim anuva-
tareyata piduti

10 . . . . . vâjayo savathâ puna vijayo pîti raso sâ ladhâ sâ pîti hoti
dhamma vîjayammhi

11 . . . . . yam vijayammâ vijatavyam mam ñâsarasake eva vijayechhâti cha

12 . . . . . . ilokîka cha pâralokikâ cha

This is so mutilated that Professor H. H. Wilson did not
venture to propose a rendering of it while criticising James
Prinsep's. We select these two out of the fourteen Edicts
for purely English readers, because they form the historical

links which connect India with Greece. It is in the Second
Edict that the name of the Yona, Yavan, Ionian or Greek
king Antiochus occurs, that Antiochus II. who died B.C. 247,
in the twelfth year of Priyadarsi's or Asoka's reign. Still
more reliable is the Thirteenth Tablet, damaged though it be,
for it gives us the names of other Greek kings in the eighth
line—Ptolemaios, Antigonus, and Magas ; and of a fourth to
whom Asoka sent embassies which " won from them a victory
not by the sword but by religion."

In the address of the Bombay Asiatic Society to Dr.
Wilson, before his departure for Syria, he was thanked by his
colleagues " for facsimile inscriptions on the Cave Temples at
Karli, of which, aided by Prinsep's monumental alphabet, it
was reserved for your learned associate Dr. Stevenson and
yourself, to be the first decipherers." As Sir William Jones
was the first to introduce into the chaos of Hindoo literature
and history the magical but very real drop of chronological
truth which developed from the Chandragupta of the Mudra
Rakshasa, the Sandrocuptos of Athenæus, or Sandracottus of
Arrian, so Dr. Wilson brought to light the inscriptions, in
which the greater grandson of Chandragupta had engraved on
the rock, twenty centuries before, the names of the successors
of Alexander in Egypt and the East. The Girnar rock must
rank in historical literature with the Rosetta stone, the
Behistun inscription, and the Accadian brick-libraries of
Assyria. Apart from that, in purely Indian literature it
reveals to us, in letters as real and vivid as the printed page,
the character of the great and good Asoka, who, when ruling
over the most extensive empire Hindooism ever saw, from
the eastern uplands of Behar to the Indian Ocean, and from
the snows of Himalaya to the coasts of Malabar, Coromandel,
and Ceylon, was driven by disgust at the sacerdotal tyranny
of the Brahmans to profess and to propagate Buddhism in
the eleventh year of his reign. Tolerant and enlightened,
his edicts alone, as we find them graven on the rocks from
Girnar to Cuttack and the Punjab, justify the title, happily
given to the Constantine of Buddhism by Professor Kern, of
Asoka the Humane.

From the time that he was nominated President of the
Bombay Asiatic Society, Dr. Wilson kept up a somewhat constant correspondence with the scholars of France and Ger-

many, who looked to him in India for new facts and materials. Greatest of them all in France, if not throughout Europe, was the accomplished and accurate Eugène Burnouf, Professor of Sanskrit in the Collège de France, who for the first half of this century was without a rival in the department of Zand. He was the friend, also, of Mr. Brian Hodgson. In 1840 another French scholar, M. Theodore Pavie, of L'Ecole des Langues Orientales in Paris, visited Bombay, passing on thence to Madras and Calcutta, from which, in imperfect English, he addressed to Dr. Wilson a letter of gratitude for learned counsel and the gift of a MS. of one of Kalidasa's dramas. About the same time Mr. Turnour, the greatest Pali scholar in the East, and afterwards translator of the *Mahawanso*, "The Genealogy of the Great," was introduced to Dr. Wilson. They must have had much to talk of, for it was Turnour who first identified the Priyadarsi of the Edicts with Asoka, by "throwing open the hitherto sealed page of the Buddhist historian to the development of Indian monuments and Puranic records," as Prinsep expressed it.

No Government, not even that of the country which rules India, has shown so enlightened an interest in its literature and religions as that of Denmark. It was the first to send Protestant missionaries to the Hindoos, the first to protect the English missionaries whom the East India Company persecuted at the end of last century, and the first to despatch its scholars to the East. Thus Rask had taken from Bombay the rich collection of MSS., Zand and Pahlavi, which he deposited in Copenhagen. And in 1841, after mastering these, Professor Westergaard prepared himself for his critical edition of the *Zand-avasta* by visiting Bombay where he was Dr. Wilson's guest, and exploring both Western India and Persia in a literary sense.

Colonel Dickinson, one of his colleagues in the Asiatic Society, and a valued servant of the State, offered generous aid to Dr. Wilson in the purchase of Oriental MSS., while he himself, in letters to his Edinburgh publisher and to Dr. Brunton, was planning new literary undertakings in aid or rising out of his missionary work. These were—'The Conversion of India and the Means of its Accomplishment ;' 'The Tribes of Western India, with Notices of Missionary Labour ;' 'Poetical Pieces by Anna Bayne, with a Biographical Sketch

of the Author;' 'Memoir of R. C. Money, Esq.' To Dr. Brunton he thus wrote on 19th July 1842, of a scheme afterwards taken up by English biblical scholars and travellers :
—" I have long been talking to our friends here about the propriety of our attempting to found in Britain a society whose express object shall be to collect Oriental illustrations of the Scriptures, and to render available to Europeans the treasures of Church History which are to be found in the Syriac, Armenian, and other Eastern languages. Had leisure permitted, you might ere this have received from me a short memoir on the subject, directing attention to what has occurred respecting it, and offering a few remarks on the intimations of an international communication between the Jews and ancient Persians, which are contained in the writings in the possession of the Zoroastrians of India and of Yezd and Kerman."

In 1836 there seems to have been made to Dr. Wilson the first of those references by the Judges of the Supreme Court as well as the Executive Government, which afterwards became so frequent and honourable to both, as well as conducive to the good administration of the country. The Parsees in India believe that, on their expatriation,* their ancient code of laws as well as their other religious books were lost. They were governed internally by their own Punchayat, under rules recognised by the Government in 1778, which gave that committee the power of beating offenders with the shoe. But as sectarian divisions spread, and as civil suits involving religious questions came before the Supreme Court, the necessity for legislation by the British Government became apparent. Not till 1865 could all parties agree to such a civil code of marriage, divorce, and inheritance at least as would be satisfactory. In one of the numerous disputes in 1835 Dr. Wilson's knowledge of the Parsee literature and customs was appealed to by the Chief Justice, who directed the thanks of the Court to be conveyed to him " for the clear, concise, and lucid manner in which you have framed your answers to the queries submitted to you."

Dr. Wilson now began to prepare for his homeward tour ; for new duty in the midst of holiday recreation. We may here, most appropriately, give some of the letters of congratulation addressed to him by the greatest Orientalists of the day. The learned and amiable William Erskine, who had translated the *Memoirs of the Emperor Baber*, and was engaged on the *History of the House of Taimur* which he was not to live to complete, thus wrote to him, linking on the foundation of the Bombay Literary Society to the more brilliant days of the Asiatic Society :—

"(EDINBURGH), 13 *St. Bernard's Crescent, 14th November* 1843.—MY DEAR SIR—I received with many thanks your valuable researches and remarks on the Parsee religion. Your knowledge of the Zand and Pahlavi, with their cognate languages, has enabled you to do much more, and more correctly, than any of your predecessors, and no person is so well qualified to solve the question of the date of the sacred books of the Parsees and the mode of their composition. You speak more kindly of my surface investigations than they probably deserve. As to the production of Ormuzd by Zerwen, you are no doubt right. Go on and enrich the world of letters, while you think chiefly of the religious world and the religious benefit of the human race. One of the greatest difficulties with Orientals, and especially with close religions like the Hindoo and Parsee, you have in a great measure overcome—that of making them appeal to reason and reasoning. I consider their entering the field of controversy, to fight foot to foot, as the great difficulty overcome. It has always hitherto been the grand obstacle. They have rested in ignorance, regarding even doubt as criminal.

"The address of the Literary Society of Bombay does honour to you and to them. I think, at its first meeting, the present Governor, then Lieutenant Arthur who was with his regiment in India, was made a member, on the motion of Lord Valentia then at Bombay. Believe me, with much esteem, my dear Sir, yours very truly,   WM. ERSKINE."

"BONN, 1st *of September* 1845.—DEAR SIR—I have had the gratification of receiving the valuable present of your learned and important book on the Parsee Religion, and beg to offer you my sincere thanks for this token of your attention. Having devoted much time and labour to the study of the Zand language and the remains of its literature, I need hardly assure you that I have taken a deep interest in your discussions with the Parsees. I trust that your labours will mainly contribute to enlighten the descendants of an ancient people that at present are sunk into such a deep ignorance of their religion. Believe me, dear Sir, your most obliged and obedient Servant,
                                                  "CHR. LASSEN."

On the 30th December 1842 Dr. Wilson gave in his resignation of President of the Bombay Branch of the Royal Asiatic Society, which he had filled for seven years. He presented it with a copy of *The Parsi Religion*, which he dedicated to its office-bearers and members in token of gratitude "for the warm interest which many of them individually have taken in my labours to disseminate useful, but more especially divine, knowledge among the natives of this great country, whose present social and moral condition, as well as past history, it is one of the principal objects of this Society to investigate and unfold." He gave it also the two octavo volumes of the *Vandidad* in Zand, with Goojaratee

translation, lithographed from his own MS., as containing the
doctrinal standards of the Parsees, and two Cufic inscriptions
from the south of Arabia. "It is not without emotion," he
wrote, "I sever this link which has bound me to office with
the Society."   He was made Honorary President.

The Parsee editors and controversialists were not soothed
by the publication of Dr. Wilson's book.   His almost simul-
taneous departure gave them full scope for criticism without
fear, and for attack without the possibility of rejoinder.   In
his edition of Dr. Haug's *Essays*, Dr. E. W. West correctly
states that "any personal ill-feeling which Dr. Wilson may
have occasioned by his book soon disappeared; but it was
many years before his habitual kindliness and conscientious
efforts for the improvement of the natives of India, regained
the confidence of the Parsees.   On his death, however, in 1875,
no one felt more deeply than the Dastoors themselves that
they had lost one of their best friends, and that in controversy with them he had only acted as his duty compelled him."

The controversy, and the political, educational, and social
influences that preceded it, had done much to teach the whole
community such lessons of toleration, free discussion, and
public virtue, as were embodied and recognised in Sir
Jamsetjee Jeejeebhoy, who was created a baronet in 1857.
The day after Dr. Wilson sailed from Bombay, all the worthy
of the island, Native and European, united to lay the foundation of the noble hospital, which bears this inscription:—
"This Edifice was erected as a testimony of devoted loyalty
to the Young Queen of the British Isles, and of unmingled
respect for the just and paternal British Government in India;
also, in affectionate and patriotic solicitude for the welfare of
the poor classes of all races among his countrymen, the British
Subjects of Bombay, by Sir Jamsetjee Jeejeebhoy, Knight,
the first Native of India honoured with British Knighthood,
who thus hoped to perform a pleasing duty towards his
government, his country, and his people: and, in solemn
remembrance of blessings bestowed, to present this, his
offering of religious gratitude to Almighty God, the Father in
Heaven of the Christian, the Hindoo, the Mahommedan, and
the Parsee; with humble, earnest prayer for His continued
care and blessing upon his Children, his Family, his Tribe,
and his Country."

CHAPTER XI.

1843.

HOME BY CAIRO, SINAI, JERUSALEM, DAMASCUS, CONSTANTINOPLE AND PESTH.

Reluctant Farewell to India for a time—Address from Non-Christian Students —Parsee and Abyssinian Youths, his Companions—Makulla and its Slave Atrocities—Aden and the Jews of Yemen—Cairo—Lepsius—Dr. Wilson's Caravan of forty-seven Camels—Jebel Musa and the true Sinai—The first snow seen for fifteen years—The Petra Excavations and the Rock-cut Temples of India—Hebron and a Jewish Greeting—Damascus—The Samaritans and their Pentateuch—Jacob's Well and Dr. A. Bonar's Bible— Smyrna and Polycarp—Constantinople and St. Sophia—Guest of Sir Stratford Canning—Turks, Bulgarians and Servians—A Police Welcome to Christendom—Pesth—Rabbi Duncan, Saphir and the Free Church Mission —Interpreting the Gypsies—Presburg and the Prince Palatine—Colonel Sykes—Edinburgh at last.

FOR fourteen years Dr. Wilson had been doing a work which, in its variety, permanence, and, above all, unselfish energy, had made him, while still under forty years of age, the most prominent public man in Western India. Governors, commanders-in-chief, and judges, had come and gone from Bombay. Governors-General and members of Council had, one after the other, striven to leave their mark at Calcutta on the progress of the empire politically and territorially. The brief span of the five years' term of office, however, allowed to all, then as still more perniciously now, broke the continuity of progress, and silently fostered that disbelief in the inevitable growth and stability of British rule, the outburst of which took civilisation by surprise in 1857. But Wilson, like Carey before him and Duff on the other side of India, had gone on steadily mapping out the decaying fields of anti-Christian and non-Christian error, and, in the exercise of a faith which was strong in proportion to his own labours, taking possession of

CONTINUITY OF DR. WILSON'S WORK.

them for his Master. Not with him, as with successive
Viceroys, Presidents of the Board of Control, and occupants
of the Directors' chairs, did the pendulum swing from side
to side, now violently and again at rest altogether. Coorg
conquests, Afghan wars and Sindh robberies, might go on;
the far-seeing philanthropy of a Bentinck might be neutralised
by the stupid reaction of an Auckland, or imperilled by the
meteor-like madness of an Ellenborough, till massacre, debt,
and unrighteousness stained the annals of England as no
event in her foreign history had done. But the missionary,
master of the literature, the languages, the history, and
therefore the heart, of the peoples of different faiths, and
fired with a divine enthusiasm which no policy of man however exalted can give, had laid the foundations of the Church
of Western India; had grappled with Brahmanism, Muhammadanism, and Parseeism on their chosen ground; had added
to his own direct work in the Konkan, Poona, and Bombay,
the Irish Mission in Goojarat and the beginnings of the Free
Church Mission in Central India and Gondwana; had prepared
the means of evangelising the Jews and the Arabs, the
Armenians and the Nestorians, the Abyssinians and the
Negroes around the Arabian Sea; had proved as salt to the
English society of his own province, and had set in motion
spiritual and social forces which continue to work with
increasing momentum. Can we wonder that, when the hour
came to leave it all, though only for a time, there was more
than the regret which every true worker for and lover of the
people of India experiences, in spite of the attractions of
home and the pains of exile? The conviction that he was
only continuing his work on a wider area was required to
second the commands of the physicians whose warnings had
been long unheeded. There were showered on the departing
philanthropist the farewells of loving and respectful admiration
from public and private friends, in a land where the Anglo-
Indian has more than caught the brotherhood-hospitality of
the Oriental. Every community, not excepting individual
Parsees, vied with the other in its demonstrations, while the
Government of Sir George Arthur supplied letters to the
authorities of the countries through which the traveller wished
to pass. Among many others, Mr. Frere begged his distinguished uncle at Malta to show him all honour.

More highly even than the address of the Asiatic Society, did Dr. Wilson value that of the native and non-Christian students of the Institution which he had established in 1832 as an English school. They had again increased in number from 155 in 1841 to 203, of whom 98 were Hindoos, 8 Muhammadans, 28 Parsees, Israelites, and Jews, and 68 Christians, while 675 boys and 479 girls attended the vernacular schools.

The first day of 1843 was Sunday, when Dr. Wilson concluded his ministrations " by beseeching the little flock of converts from Hindooism, Zoroastrianism, and Muhammadanism, which had been gathered together through my own ministry and that of my fellow-labourers, to let their conversation be as it becometh the Gospel of Christ, that whether I might come and see them, or else be absent, I might hear of their affairs." His own countrymen present he called on " to anticipate the glorious era of the moral renovation of India, when ' all the ends of the world shall remember and turn unto the Lord, and all the kindreds of the nations shall worship before Him.' " Sunset of the next day saw him accompanied to the Palawa or Apollo pier, and on to the deck of the East India Company's steamer ' Cleopatra,' by a regretful crowd of Native and European friends, among them Professor Westergaard, who had been his guest for months. In the infancy of the Overland Route, before the Peninsular and Oriental Company had reduced the distance between Bombay and London to eighteen days, a monthly steamer was run to Aden and Suez by the Indian Navy. So late as 1854 the mail was only fortnightly, and the Bombay portion of it was even then carried by an East India Company's steamer between Aden and Bombay. Among the natives who lingered last on the deck were two who had so far overcome Brahmanical and caste prejudice as to express a desire to travel with Dr. Wilson. These were Atmaram Pandurang, a Brahman gentleman who is still respected as the head of the Prarthna Samaj, corresponding to Baboo Keshub Chunder Sen's Brahmo theists ; and Gunput Lukshmun, of the Prabhoo or writer caste.

Dr. Wilson had prepared for and planned his expedition with a care which, in some degree, every traveller would do well to show. His object was to visit Egypt, Syria, especially the Holy Land and Eastern Europe, not merely for purposes

of scholarly and biblical research, but to report to his Church
on the condition of the Jews, the Samaritans, and the
Eastern Christians. He had accumulated and mastered a
library of all the early travellers in, and writers on, Syria,
such as few public collections possessed at that time, and
much of this he took with him. He had devoted himself
anew to Arabic, and to familiarity with that he gave up all
the leisure of the fortnight's voyage to Suez. Not only by
letters to the Political Residents and Consuls, but by
despatching Mordecai, a Jew, a month or two before him,
he found information awaiting him at Aden and at Cairo.
The friend who was specially his companion in travel, the
late John Smith, Esq., had also gone before him to recruit
his strength by a voyage up the Nile, and to prepare at Cairo
the expedition for the Desert and Syria. All that intelligence, foresight, and learning could do, aided by willing
friends, was done to perfect the success of the expedition.
The Church of Scotland, through both the Foreign and
Jewish Committees, intended it to complete the inquiry
carried out a few years before by Drs. Keith and Black,
Mr. M'Cheyne, and Dr. Andrew Bonar.

Dr. Wilson was accompanied, first of all, by Dhunjeebhoy
Nourojee, whose affection and fidelity he had tested in more
than one of his Indian tours. It was desirable that the first
Parsee convert to Christianity should complete at college in
Scotland those eight years' studies for the office of preacher
which the Scottish Churches wisely demand, that their ministers may have a theological as well as literary education, and
which he had been pursuing in Bombay. Dr. Wilson also
contemplated the publication of a translation into Goojaratee
of his *Parsi Religion*, and he proposed that Dhunjeebhoy
should write that on the lithographic stones in Edinburgh.
Next came the two Abyssinian students, Gabru and Maricha,
who had sat at his table for nearly five years, and were now
returning to their native land to introduce into it the blessings of a pure Christianity and political wisdom. They
parted from their spiritual father at Aden, who prayed " that
to their benighted countrymen they might be the instruments
of great spiritual good, even as Frumentius and Ædesius, the
tender Tyrian youths through whom the Gospel was first
introduced into their native land." We shall see how effect-

ually, but differently from Dr. Wilson's expectations, the
prayer was answered. Finally, the Government Surveyor,
Colonel Dickinson, had recommended as draftsman a Mr.
O'Brien, who did his part of the mission well.

As the 'Cleopatra' skirted the southern coast of Arabia,
Makulla came in sight, recalling the horrors of the slave
trade, of which it continued to be an infamous emporium
till 1873. There Captain Haines had seen seven hundred
Nubian girls at a time, subjected in its slave-market to the
disgusting inspection of the Mussulman sensualist, to be
smuggled into the native states of Kathiawar. Off Makulla
it was that, a few years before, two boats, laden chiefly with
negro children shipped from Zanzibar, had been seized by the
Indian Navy, and the freed youths were distributed among
the Christian Missions of Western India. At Aden, first of
our conquests in the reign of the young Queen Victoria,
Captain Haines, the first Governor, became Dr. Wilson's host,
and aided him in his census and study of the Jewish community. Of 19,938 inhabitants of that extinct volcano, in
1843 there were 590 Jews, 480 Jewesses, and 857 Europeans,
the last chiefly the troops of the garrison. The geological
structure of the vast cinder which was once forced up through
the limestone, so interested Dr. Wilson that, as he collected
specimens of zeolite, chalcedonies, obsidian and vesicular
lava, the simple Somalees who crowded round him declared
he must be searching for gold or hid treasure by magical
arts. His scientific conclusions were confirmed by Dr. Buist,
who had not long before begun his bright literary career in
India, and whom Dr. Wilson described at that time as "one
of the most accomplished mineralogists and geologists in the
East." At Aden the president of the Asiatic Society discussed with Captain Haines those Himyaritic inscriptions
which had begun to attract the attention of the learned. To
complete his study of the Jews, whose settlement in Yemen
had taken place long before the Christian era, Dr. Wilson
was anxious that the steamer should stop at Jeddah on its
way up the Red Sea that he might attempt to reach Mecca.
He had been encouraged to believe that he might report
on the capital of Islam in safety, by Lieutenant Christopher,
I.N., who had been assured by its governor that a European
traveller quietly proceeding from the coast would find no

obstacle.   At Suez the governor showed a keen interest
in our disasters in Afghanistan, in conversation with Dr.
Wilson, who also was surprised when addressed in excellent
English by an Arab, one of the young Fellaheen who had
been sent by Muhammad Ali to Glasgow for education, and
had been there baptized.

At Cairo, after the old and not unpleasant passage of
the desert in vans, Dr. Wilson found the first and greatest
of the present dynasty of Egyptian rulers building his
mosque and palace on the platform of the citadel which
overlooks the Nile valley and the pyramids.   He formed
a hopeful idea of the tolerant but firm rule of the quondam
tobacco-seller of Roumelia, whom—perhaps in an evil hour
—we prevented from remaining master of all Syria and
Arabia.   The Jews, the Copts, the mission of good Mr.
Lieder, the mosques, the tombs, and the pyramids, absorbed
Dr. Wilson's attention for days.   He found himself already
known to the small band of Egyptologists, with some of
whom he had corresponded.   He was unanimously elected an
Honorary Member of the Egyptian Society.   M. Linant de
Bellefonds, in officially communicating the fact, begged him
"to accept this title as the best tribute of respect which the
Society can offer to one so eminently distinguished as yourself in Oriental researches."   Dr. Wilson especially enjoyed
learned intercourse with the great scholar Lepsius, the head
of the commission sent by the King of Prussia to report on
the antiquities of Egypt.   M. Linant, who had accompanied
M. Léon de Laborde to Petra, gave him much information
for his journey to the same place.   With Lepsius he explored
the pyramids and the half-disentombed sphinx.   " When we
were there the body of a child was exhumed.   The coffin had
upon it the cartouche of ' Psammatik ' or Psammitichus.   I
carried part of its contents with me to Cairo, and afterwards
to England, without attributing any great importance to the
possession."   He made considerable purchases of the most
important Arabic, Persian, and Turkish works, published by
Muhammad Ali's press, including the three folios of the
Kámús or *Ocean*, the famous Dictionary translated into
Turkish ; of the Persian *Burhán-i-Kátia* in Turkish he had
the beautiful edition lithographed at Bombay.   His account
of the publications and of the educational system of Egypt at

that time is most favourable to Muhammad Ali. The latter
may be contrasted with that since developed by Mr. Rogers,
formerly H.M. Consul at Cairo. That he might have free
intercourse with the native inhabitants of Cairo, Dr.
Wilson lodged with one Hassan Effendi, teacher of geology in the
Bulák Polytechnic School, who had become a Christian when
in England, and had married an English wife. Cairo is now
as much a French as it is an Oriental city, but the record of
Dr. Wilson's experience correctly describes the impressions
which the capital of Muhammad Ali used to leave on the
Anglo-Indian visitor.

From Cairo Dr. Wilson's expedition made its final start
on the 7th of February 1843. Consisting of nine persons
besides servants, and forty-seven camels, it formed an imposing caravan. Dr. Wilson himself was unanimously installed
as quartermaster-general and interpreter, after the Indian
fashion—that is, he settled arbitrarily all questions connected
with the route and the times of marching and halting. The
whole had been arranged and provisioned by the Bombay
merchant prince, Mr. J. Smith, who, having been already two
months on the Nile, relieved his companions of all care on
this head. Throughout he was paymaster-general, charged to
keep a faithful account of the expenses due by each. The
Rev. H. Sherlock, and Messrs. Allan and Parke, from England, were their companions through the whole of the desert
journey. Mr. O'Brien the artist, Dhunjeebhoy, Mordecai the
Jew, and his little son Abraham, completed the party.
Abdool Futteh, known in Arabia as the "man of the convent," from his frequent visits to the abodes of the monks,
and valued by Colonel Howard Vyse, was Dr. Wilson's servant. Mr. J. Smith engaged Waters, an educated African
who had come from Bombay. The others secured the services
of two assistants, one of whom was Ibraheem, once employed
by Dr. Robinson in his *Biblical Researches*, and again by the
Scottish Mission.

For the first stage, by the Derb El-Basatin and the "valley
of the wanderings" to Sinai, the party had engaged, as its
guide and protector, Mateir, sheikh of the same Aleikat branch
of the Tawarah Arabs who had helped Niebuhr in his explora-
tions in stony Arabia. Guided by local traditions Dr. Wilson
sought to trace the route of the Israelites from the Nile to the

Gulf of Suez, by a track which he believed to harmonise more easily with the narrative of the Exodus than that followed by other travellers. The inscriptions in the Wadi Mukatteb, or valley of the writings, had for him a peculiar interest. He examined the exhausted Pharaonic mines to the northward, and visited Wadi Feiran, "the most beautiful valley in the wilderness, in which the Christianity of the Arabian desert long found a refuge." A careful study of the whole Jebel Musa range led him to hold by the traditional peak as the very "heaven" from which God "talked" with men, in opposition to that of Sufsafah, which Dr. Robinson, and the Ordnance Survey recently, consider to have been the spot where the Lord descended in fire and proclaimed the Law. To a careful examination of both Musa and Sufsafah Mr. J. Smith specially devoted himself. From the top of Musa he ran down to the chapel of Elijah in twelve minutes, and in three-quarters of an hour scrambled up to the top of Sufsafah, climbing the pinnacle on all fours in a serpentine line. He and the Musa party could distinctly hear the call of one another, being at a distance of not more than one geographical mile. The top of Musa was found covered in some places with snow, which Dr. Wilson had not seen since he left the Lammermoors fifteen years before, and the Parsee Dhunjee-bhoy beheld and tasted for the first time.

From this point the party crossed the Tih range into the desert, along the course of Jabal Ajmeh to the Ghadir al Guf. Three of the party went on to Hebron, while Dr. Wilson and Mr. J. Smith made a new arrangement with the Badaween to march to Petra. Having managed, without opposition, to ascend Mount Hor and examine the tomb of Aaron, they "descended into the fearful chasm of Petra by moonlight, and we there found our humble tents and servants ready for our reception." After a quotation from *The Lands of the Bible*, contrasting the rock-cut temples of India with the excavations of Petra, we must send our readers to that elaborate book—in the preparation of which Dr. Wilson spent all his home leisure up to May 1847, when it was published in Edinburgh in two volumes—and turn to his letters to India for a summary of the rest of the tour. That work, dedicated to Dr. Chalmers who showed a keen interest in its preparation, has still a special value in the literature of travel in Bible lands for four reasons : It records the impressions of a learned and observant traveller who approached Syria from the East with a knowledge of many Oriental languages and peoples. It describes several places not previously visited by Europeans. It devotes careful attention to all tribes of Jewish descent or faith, from the Beni-Israel of Bombay and the White and Black Jews of Southern India, to Yemen, Cairo, and Syria. And the work is, to this day, a high authority on many points relating to the Eastern Christian Churches and communities, and should be studied in the light of the great Turkish collapse and Russian extension. Dr. Wilson had undertaken the duty of meeting two Presbyterian missionaries to the Jews, Mr. now Dr. Graham, and Mr. Allan ; and it will be seen that with them he fixed on Damascus as the centre of their labours.

"As efforts of architectural skill the excavations of Petra undoubtedly excel those of the Hindoos, which they also exceed in point of general extent, if we except the wonderful works at Verula or Elora. In individual magnitude they fall short of many of the cave temples, collegiate halls, and monastic cells of the farther East. Their interest, too, is wholly exterior ; while that of those of India, with the exception of the great Brahmanical temple of Kailás, and the porticoes of the Buddhist Vihárs of Sashtí and Karlí, is principally in the multitudinous decorations and fixtures, and gigantic mythological figures of the interior. The sculptures and excavations of Petra have been principally made by individuals, in their private capacity, for private purposes, and the comparatively limited amount of workmanship about them has permitted this to be the case ; while most of those of India, intended for public purposes, and requiring an enormous expenditure of labour and wealth, have mostly been begun and finished by sovereign princes and religious communities. At Petra we have principally the beauty of art applied often legitimately to subdue the terrors of nature in perhaps the most singular locality on the face of the globe, and the cunning of life stamping its own similitude on the mouth of the grave, to conceal its loathsomeness ; but in India we have debasing superstition enshrining itself in gloom, and darkness, and mystery, in order to overawe its votaries, and to secure their reverence and prostration. The moralist, on looking into the empty vaults and tombs of Idumea, and seeing that the very names of 'the kings and counsellors of the earth which constructed these desolate places for themselves' are forgotten, exclaims, 'They are destroyed from morning to evening ; they perish for ever without any regarding it. Doth not their excellency in them go away ? they die even without wisdom.' In entering into the dreary and decaying temples and shrines of India, he thinks of that day when 'a man shall cast his idols of silver and his idols of gold, which they made each one for himself to worship, to the moles and to the bats ; to go into the clefts of the rocks, and into the tops of the ragged rocks, for fear of the Lord and for the glory of His majesty, when He ariseth to shake terribly the earth.'"

"BEYRUT, 30th June.—The Lord has greatly prospered me both in my researches and labours in the Holy Land and Syria. I have an outline of our movements preparing for the youth of our Institution. We have fixed on

Damascus as the headquarters of the Presbyterian mission. It is within the bounds of the Holy Land as drawn by Ezekiel and Zechariah. It has a Jewish population of 5000 souls, many of whom gave us a most cordial welcome. Other places are either already occupied by missionaries or are unsuitable as stations. The Jewish ladies at Damascus say that our ladies must be 'their sisters.' My Oriental dress is that of a Badawee Shaikh, but I seldom wear it. The word *England* is the grand passport both in the wilderness and in the city. Through its might, or rather through the gracious protection of the Lord of hosts, Mr. Graham and I passed about three weeks ago through an encampment of the Badaween, extending over a space of 30,000 camels, after the Turkish authorities at the Jisr Banát Yákab had declared that we should be certainly robbed or destroyed. The appearance of these Badaween, within a day's march of Damascus, has greatly frightened the Pasha there. They are from the great Bariah. They brought vividly to our mind the promise, 'The multitude of camels shall cover thee,' etc. You may tell ———— that ——— is quite full of the project of having a mission established among them and the other Ishmaelitish tribes.

"I have been very busy since our return from Cœle Syria in putting my notes into order. I have gone over all my Arabic collections with a learned man here. I have interesting material for a large volume. The Armenians everywhere are in a most hopeful state. I have been greatly delighted with what I have seen of them."

"BEYRUT, *May* 4.—At the commencement of last month I forwarded to you a few lines from Jerusalem. I omitted to mention in them that, with my fellow-traveller Mr. Smith, I had made a short excursion from the Holy City to Jericho, the Jordan, and the Dead Sea. It afforded us much personal gratification, as well as an opportunity of comparing the present appearance of these and other interesting localities with the sacred narrative, and of making such observations connected with the geography and geology of the country as will enable us, when they are compared with our notes on the Wadi Arabia to the south of the Dead Sea, to hazard an opinion respecting different theories which have been advanced upon the destination of the Jordan previous to the destruction of Sodom and Gomorrah. Since leaving Jerusalem we have more than completed the inland tour of the Holy Land. Every step of our progress has been attended with the most solemn and hallowed associations, and almost inexpressible interest.

"At Náblus or Shechem, we took up our abode with the remnant of the Samaritans, which is now reduced to one hundred and fifty souls; and we received from them much useful information respecting their belief and religious rites and ceremonies. The old priest showed us not only the ancient manuscripts of the Pentateuch, which he is accustomed to exhibit to travellers, but that which is reckoned to be of the highest antiquity, and which he declared had only once been previously unfolded before the eyes of the *Goim*. His eldest son walked with us to the summit of Mount Gerizim, and pointed out to us all its *loca sancta* agreeably to the traditions of his sect. An assembly of all the male adults and of most of the youth convened to meet us. We examined them respecting the views entertained of the Messiah. It was urged by them that the Shiloh of Genesis xlix. 10, was Solomon, to whom all nations either yielded obedience or reverence, and after whose reign the sceptre immediately departed from Judah; and that it is of Joseph that there is to spring the Messiah, 'the shepherd, the stone of Israel.' The son of the priest was much more candid than the father in admitting the force of objections to their method of interpreting the books of Moses; and I am far mistaken if he is not convinced that his people are involved in gross error.

As the Samaritans have preserved the ancient Hebrew character, and have never used the Masoretic points, I was particularly anxious to learn from them their method of reading Hebrew, which, as far as I am aware, has never been inquired into in modern times ; and I carefully noted the peculiarities of their pronunciation, which does not essentially differ from that of the Hebrew Chair of the University of Edinburgh. They are preparing a letter to the Beni-Israel of Bombay, respecting whom they were most minute in their inquiries ; and one of themselves has most strenuously urged me to take him to England, along with his copy of the Pentateuch. I doubt whether he will be permitted to leave his native place. He is an individual of great enterprise ; and, attached to a rope and with a candle in his hand, he descended, under our direction and with our assistance, into Jacob's Well, and recovered from it all that remains of Mr. Bonar's Bible which was dropped into it nearly four years ago. We had a fire kindled in the well, the particular examination of which was the object of our visit to it, and we had it thus lighted throughout. It is exactly seventy-five feet deep, and about three yards in diameter. It is cut out of the solid rock, and has marks about it of the highest antiquity. I have no doubt that it is the well of which the Patriarch drank, and his children, and his cattle ; and at which our Lord held his remarkable interview with the woman of Samaria."

Dr. Wilson paid two visits to Jerusalem, of sixteen days together. Here, as wherever he went, his letters to the British Consuls from the Governor of Bombay opened to him every circle. With Mr. Finn, then our Consul at Jerusalem, he began an intercourse which was long fruitful in good to the Jews of the Holy Land. He was made an honorary member of the Jerusalem Literary Society on its institution a few years after. Very close and beneficial to both was his intimacy with the American missionaries, who have done and are doing so noble a work all over the Turkish dominion. On the 30th June he and Dhunjeebhoy left Beyrut for Constantinople by Smyrna, where, in quarantine, he preached of the church and of Polycarp, and beguiled the week in studying modern Greek. During a fortnight's residence at Constantinople he continued his researches regarding the Eastern Christians, and the Jewish community among whom Mr. Schwartz was the Free Church missionary. To its first fruits, two converts from Judaism, he "simply administered the ordinance of baptism, and pronounced the benediction through the medium of Hebrew." On a visit to St. Sophia he was allowed to walk through the mosque with his boots on and without a covering, though challenged by one of the Moolahs, four words in Persian—"but they are clean"—sufficing to stop opposition. In truth he was under the auspices of the British embassy, being for a time the guest of Sir Stratford

Canning at Buyukdereh.   Among the foreign diplomatists, he
wrote, even at that time, the now venerable Lord Stratford
de Redcliffe " was allowed to be the foremost for ability,
influence, and philanthropy.   His attachés, among whom was
a young nobleman, the name of whose house, that of Napier,
is indissolubly associated with the science and literature of
Scotland, commanded much respect."   There Dr. Wilson
received letters from Professor Westergaard, detailing his visit
to the Gabars of Persia, the tombs of Darius and Xerxes, and
other antiquities.   At Buyukdereh he joined the Austrian
steamer for Varna and Constandjeh, whence, in transit-vans
to Czernavoda for the river steamer, the course lay up the
Danube to Pesth in those pre-railway days.   At Rustchuk
" we observed horses drawing carts, a sight to Dhunjeebhoy
entirely novel, and which I myself had last seen at the Cape
of Good Hope fifteen years ago."   Turks and Bulgarians alike
repelled the observer by their ignorance and filth ; Servia was
pronounced " the smallest State of Turkey in Europe, but the
most advanced in enlightenment and civilisation."

"14th August 1843.—At noon we were as far as Cladova, where the
Danube makes its exit from the Carpathian mountains, through the passage
which it has cut for itself by the might of its waters, as the great drain of
central Europe.   Here we landed, and walked along the right bank of the
river, while the steamer was being dragged up the rapids by oxen.   We had
a delightful romp of it along the mountainous pass ; and I had the satisfaction of pointing out to my Parsee friend from the far East the different bushes
and trees of the European jungle clothing the precipitous bank—the hazel, the
brier, the willow, and the beech, all of which was entirely new to him, and of
directing his attention to the remains of the great road constructed of old by
the Romans, and which formed one of their grandest and most useful works.
We crossed over to Orsova, after a three hours' walk, and we were welcomed
to Christendom, after having passed through the empire of Mnhammadanism
from the straits of Bab el-Mandeb to the rapids of the Iron Bar, by being
put into durance vile, under the farcical name of sanatory gnardianship.   Our
restraint lasted, however, only for a few hours ; and it soon became evident
that it was intended more for political than medical objects.   When the
examination of our passports showed that I was no fugitive Italian outlaw but
a person recognised as a sober subject by a respectable Government, and that
Dhunjeebhoy was not the pioneer of some horde of barbarians from the plains
of central Asia, seeking fresh and green pasturage for their flocks and herds in
the parching months of summer ; and when our deposition had been taken as
to the contents of our boxes, and all our books, with the exception of a Bible,
a Medical Dictionary, and a volume of German Dialogues—which last work we
had much need of studying—had, as was thought, been put by seal and signet
alike beyond our use and that of the public, till their inspection by the censor
at Vienna, eager to peruse a chapter or two of Rabbi Saadi Gaon's dim manuscript of the Pentateuch, or to peep into the secrets of a Samaritan marriage
covenant, and above all to have the satisfaction of repeating, in the original

Zand, a Parsee Nirang for the expulsion of the devil Nesosh from a putrid
corpse, we were set at liberty.   On this occasion Dhunjeehhoy was, as a matter
of course, raised to the rank of an Indian prince, and I degraded to that of his
dragoman or valet, by the intelligent and observant police."

"PESTH, *Sabbath*, 20*th August.*—We were conducted by a young friend,
on the look-out for us, to the house of the Rev. Dr. John Duncan, now
Professor of Oriental Languages in the New College of Edinburgh, and his
associates Messrs. Smith and Wingate, in which we got a most cordial and
affectionate welcome.   We stayed with our friends till the end of the month,
enjoying most delightful fellowship, and witnessing the result of their
endeavours to bring the lost sheep of the house of Israel to the fold of the
Good Shepherd.   We found with them, what we so much wished to see in the
different regions through which we had passed in the East, a living Christianity
shedding its light and love around it, to the enlightenment and quickening, by
the blessing of the Holy Spirit, of the souls both of Jews and Gentiles.   Our
Scottish friends had been there resident only for a few years, and they had
been instrumental in the instruction and conversion of upwards of a score of
individuals belonging to the Jewish community, including Mr. Saphir, a person of excellent education and extensive influence, and all the members of his
family, male and female, old and young.   All this had occurred without the
usual appliances and machinery of modern missions, in connection with the
school, the press, and the pulpit, to which the circumstances of the country
did not permit a resort, and simply by earnest conference, conversation, and
occasional addresses and devotional exercises, animated by sincere piety, illustrated by distinguished biblical learning, and impressed by a holy walk and
conversation.   As the missionaries had not, and sought not, any personal
standing in the country, the converts had been received into the communion
of the Reformed Church of Hungary, the creed of which, as embodied in the
Helvetic Confession, is quite accordant with that of the Protestant Churches
of Britain, and especially of those of the north of the island, approved by the
Presbyterian missionaries themselves, already the agents of the Free Church of
Scotland.

"From several of the inhabitants of Pesth we received much kindness
during our short residence there.   Tasner Antal, the secretary and friend of
the eminently patriotic and liberal nobleman the Count Szechenyi, gave us
much of his time, and effectually aided us in all the inquiries in which we
sought to engage.   He is a gentleman of high literary attainments ; and some
of the institutions of the place have originated in his public spirit.   We were
much interested in a meeting of the Hungarian National Literary Society—
which has a considerable body of active members—to which he introduced us.
The language of the Gypsies—some of whom, attending the fair at Pesth, he
had previously brought to us for examination to Dr. Duncan's—was on that
occasion one of the subjects of our conversation.   It was known to all present
that that language is of Indian origin ; but direct testimony on the subject
was received with much interest.   The governor of Transylvania, who was in
the chair, invited us to visit him, that we might see some of these wanderers
in his province, but our time did not permit us to accept his invitation.
Reference was made to the death in the East of their distinguished member,
Korose Csoma Sandor, who had there wandered far and wide in the fruitless
search for the parent stock of the Magyars, and traces of their language ; to
his unrivalled acquisitions connected with the literature and religion of the
Buddhists ; to his Tibetan grammar and dictionary ; and to the kindness
which he had experienced from the Asiatic Society and the Government in
India.   Mr. Kiss, one of the members resident at Buda, a day or two after

the meeting, exhibited to us his collection of ancient coins and medals, which is rich in the Asiatic department.

" More than one gracious invitation reached us from the palace at Buda, the residence of distinguished goodness as well as greatness. On one occasion, Dhunjeebhoy and I appeared there, by particular request, in our oriental costume, to the great amusement of the young princes and princesses. We bade adieu to Pesth on the 31st of August. Next morning we arrived at Presburg, where the Diet of Hungary was holding its sessions. In the evening we were presented to his Imperial Highness the Archduke Joseph, the Prince Palatine of Hungary. He conversed with us in Latin, the language which he was accustomed to use while presiding over the Diet, and put many questions to us respecting India and the Holy Land, and other countries of the East, with which, it was evident, he had a very extensive and accurate acquaintance, as far as both their sacred and profane history and geography are concerned. He expressed the warm interest which he felt in the progress which Christianity is making in different regions of the earth, and congratulated Dhunjeebhoy on his embracement of the truth. He also spoke in high terms of our friends at Pesth, and of what he had heard of their prudent procedure. He entrusted me with a message to their constituents in Scotland. We formed a high opinion of his intellectual powers and moral feeling, of which his countenance and demeanour, as well as language, were the expression.

" Our onward journey to Britain included in Germany, Vienna, Linz, Ischl, Salzburg, Munich, Augsburg, Stuttgardt, and Carlsruhe. When we got upon the Rhine we were almost at home among the number of countrymen whom we met on board the steamer. Among these was a distinguished officer of the Bombay Presidency, who has reflected the highest honour upon it by his literary and scientific efforts and antiquarian research, and by his wise and liberal counsels in the governing body of India—Colonel Sykes. We stopped with him and his family a night at Mayence, to talk over matters connected with the distant East. From Mayence we went to England by Cologne and Antwerp. We arrived in London on the 23d of September, and in the capital of Scotland on the 4th of November, in my case after an absence of fifteen years from my native land, and a journey of nine months from my adopted home in India. You can imagine the emotions which I experienced, when, after the perils and vicissitudes of a long residence and labour in foreign climes, and a pilgrimage through many lands, both holy and unholy, I found my journeyings for a season brought to a close at the home of Christian affection and love. Only the language of inspiration, as in the hundred and seventh Psalm, can form their expression."

" Any news about the Church of Scotland ?" had been his first question to the boatmen who rowed him ashore at Dover. "They're all out, Sir," was the reply, which Dr. Wilson often afterwards quoted, adding, " My mind was made up. I would have gone out although I had had only half-a-dozen associates."

CHAPTER XII.

1843-1846.

THE MISSIONARY SIDE OF 1843.

Scotland's solution of the Church and State Difficulty—India outside of party strife—Dr. Brunton writes to the Missionaries—The unanimous Response of all Evangelical Anglo-Indians—An equitable Settlement of the Mission Property refused—Dr. Wilson in Jerusalem—Joins the Church of Scotland Free—Letters to Robert Nesbit and Dr. Brunton—General Assembly at Glasgow—Dr. Wilson's Address—First educated Brahman baptized at Bombay—First Caste Expiation—Epistle from American Presbytery of North India—Establishment of the Nagpore Mission—Stephen Hislop—Sir Donald M'Leod—Kaffrarian Mission transferred to Free Church—Dr. Wilson at Oxford—At the May Meetings of 1844, and the Inverness Assembly—Medical Missions—Speech on Turkish Atrocities—Plea for Dhunjeebhoy's Ordination—The Ideal of a Missionary Church.—General Assembly's Farewell.

WHEN Dr. Wilson left Bombay he was appointed a representative of the Church of Scotland in India, in the General Assembly which met in Edinburgh on the 18th of May 1843. On that day, the last of the old historic Kirk, when Dr. Welsh, the Moderator, read the protest of 470 ministers who laid down their livings, and they and he, and Thomas Chalmers, and elders representing a majority of its people, went forth as the Church of Scotland Free, Dr. Wilson was, on camel-back, entering for the second time the city of Jerusalem. The Church's evangelical ministers in Scotland had sacrificed their all, how would its Indian and Jewish missionaries act? The moral grandeur of the spectacle on that 18th day of May, in the Scottish capital, was such as to extort the admiration of judges like Francis Jeffrey and Lord Cockburn,[1] and of many who had no sympathy with the spiritual principles involved, but saw in the protesters the

---

[1] See his *Journal* and *Life of Lord Jeffrey.*

legitimate heirs of, and now the joyous martyrs for, the principles of the Reformation and Revolution Kirk of Scotland. The same party which did the wrong on that day have since sought to undo it, by abolishing what was only an accident of their principles—lay patronage. Although the remnant of the Church as still established has not yet blotted out what are known as the Rescissory Acts, by which it endorsed the wrong and departed from the Reformation and Revolution principle, yet, so recently as last year, by the mouth of its Moderator it expressed admiration of the spiritual heroism of the men whom the Courts and the Legislature drove and the minority of the last General Assembly barred out on that day.   Would the missionaries, then far away, dim or would they increase the lustre of that sacrifice, by adhering to the protest ?   The chaplains of the Church thought it right to cling to their monthly salaries from the Government, and not to forfeit the pensions given by the East India Company.   No one will judge them.   Every missionary, from Pesth and Constantinople to Calcutta and Madras, Bombay and Poona, joined the Church of Scotland Free.   Yet the Kirk's Foreign Mission had owed its origin to Dr. Inglis, father of the present Lord President of the Court of Session, and was directed by Dr. Brunton, both of the "moderate" party.   The grandeur of the testimony was complete.   Missionaries, ministers, and elders united with the people in 1843, under the guidance of Thomas Chalmers, to work out in the vexed question of Church and State the only true solution of the freedom of each within its own proper sphere, yet the respectful alliance of both, which Italy has since accepted ; which Mr. Gladstone of English statesmen has most appreciated ; and which, on the part of a spiritually democratic Church, is as hostile to the sacerdotalism of the Ultramontane as it is a protest against Cæsarism.

During the ten years which preceded the crisis of 1843, all the missionaries and some of the chaplains at Bombay, Calcutta, and Madras, sympathised with the evangelical party whom conscience ultimately forced out.   But they were far removed from the conflict and its excitement.   And they had even higher work to do.   In the face of a common enemy, or league of enemies, like the four great Cults of Hindooism, Parseeism, Muhammadanism, and Fetishism, all non-sacerdotal

missionaries, then and ever since, have formed a union of the
widest catholicity and heartiest co-operation. From the first,
too, foreseeing men like Wilson felt that they were laying the
foundations of the future Church of India, and that it was an
evil thing to introduce into it the purely historical and
sectarian controversies of the warring churches of the West.
The best missionary—he who knows the people best—is still
a foreigner, and he and his translations must in time give
way to an indigenous and self-developing church or churches,
which may a second time illustrate the Christian truth of the
saying, "Ex Oriente Lux." Hence the echoes of the Ten
Years' Conflict, as it is called in Scotland, were somewhat
dull in India, as dull almost as those of the strifes of the home
churches now are to every earnest worker there.   That India
knows no party is as true of ecclesiasticism as of politics.
What the land-tax shall be in a province ? whether it shall
have certain primary schools and village institutions ? how
far the historical creeds and sectarian confessions shall be
bound on the necks of the office-bearers of the native churches ?
—these are questions that affect millions now and hereafter.
Such issues as these are the true politics of India.

Although correspondents kept Dr. Wilson well informed
of the inner life of their Kirk, and a visitor like Dr. Duff in
1840 brought back from Edinburgh the latest tidings, they and
their colleagues, being in the true front of the battle, left the
security of their base to be looked to by others.   And at the
last the crisis in Scotland came with a rush.   The evangelical
party, outraged by a majority of eight to five of the judges,
could not believe for a time that Parliament would set the
seal on such an interpretation of Scottish statutes, Union
contracts, the Revolution Settlement.   Parliament, never very
heroic itself, and affecting a cynical disbelief in the heroism
of others, lent a willing ear to the small band of men of compromise, who, unprepared for sacrifice themselves, scouted the
idea of it in so many of their brethren.   So it came about that,
when Dr. Wilson saw the last of Bombay for a time, as night
settled down on Malabar Hill on the 2d January, he did not
anticipate that his relations with Dr. Brunton were so soon
to cease.   At Cairo, when he heard of the Convocation of 478
of the 1200 ordained ministers, who had consulted all through
a winter week, and resolved to resign their livings if justice

were not done to the principles of the Kirk, he must have
said for the first time, as his colleagues in Bombay expressed
it—" What will remain ?   A Presbyterian Establishment, but
not the Church of Scotland ; nearly all that constitutes
nationality will have vanished." To them Dr. Brunton had
written officially, expressing the anxious wish that all would
continue as they were.   The chaplains, Dr. Stevenson and Mr.
Cook, now Dr. Cook of Borgue, did so.   The missionaries,
Messrs. Nesbit and Murray Mitchell, had kept the public informed of the conflict in Scotland through the *Oriental Christian Spectator*, and the receipt of the mail announcing the
event of the 18th May saw them ministers of the Free Church
of Scotland.   All the elders and a majority of the members
of St. Andrew's kirk also left it.

The missionaries had been in the habit of conducting a
service for Europeans residing at a distance from that church
in the Ambrolie Mission-house.   The congregation, now
greatly increased, found accommodation in the neighbouring
chapel of the American Mission, until it could erect the
building which adorns the Esplanade.   The new college was
about to be occupied, and the missionaries who had struggled
for so many years in the confined and unhealthy rooms of a
native house, had been looking forward with eager eyes to the
building for which they and their friends, chiefly on the spot,
had raised the necessary funds.   They did not enter it.   Not
only so, but at the close of the session of 1843, when Dr.
Brunton's committee established in it a new mission, they had
the pain of making over to the German agent who was sent
to demand the property, the whole library, mathematical,
astronomical, chemical, and other educational apparatus, which
were the fruit of their personal toil and their friends' generosity.   All was quietly given up and carried off, fortunately
without any such scandal as attended a similar act of trans-
ference at Calcutta.   It was well that Dr. Wilson was spared
his share of the pain.   How he viewed the equity of the proceedings his correspondence will show.   On him, at home,
devolved the duty of furnishing the mission anew, and selecting and sending out the first Free Church minister.   In all
this the men who had chosen suffering for conscience sake
made no boast and no complaint—they were Christian gentlemen.   With Dr. Stevenson, who had been their colleague for

some time, their relations had been very close. They did not fail to help their old Institution, as engaged with themselves in the one great contest. And now there is a prospect that both may unite with the other evangelical churches to form a strong and catholic Christian College like Principal Miller's in Madras.

For upwards of two months on the march from Cairo to Jerusalem, Dr. Wilson had been without news. As he sat in the lodging-house of the Greek, Elias of Damascus, in the Via Dolorosa, at the end of March, and devoured his letters and a file of papers sent him by the British Consul, he wrote :—" It would be difficult to say whether, for this day at least, the natural Jerusalem in the land of Israel, or the spiritual Zion in the land of Caledonia, was uppermost in our thoughts and feelings. That the God of Zion reigneth above gave us hope and peace." His second visit to Jerusalem with Dr. Graham, and his distant journey to Damascus, where he left that missionary, caused the time to pass rapidly till he returned to Beyrut, and rested there for a fortnight. On the 2d November 1840 Dr. Brunton had thus written to him :—" Our Church fever is by no means abated. It is carrying its lamentable heats by far too much into private society, but it has not as yet touched at all our committee. Nothing can be more harmonious and united than it continues to be." As the aggression of the Court of Session on the spiritual rights in purely spiritual things guaranteed to the national Church of ministers, elders, and people, continued, it became inevitable that all its members should declare themselves. Thus, on the 28th April 1842, Dr. Brunton met the otherwise pleasing announcement of the proposed foundation of a mission at Nagpore by Sir W. Hill by this response :—" The only ground of doubt is the present state of the Church. I am forced to consider our funds as in a very precarious state. Even if the Establishment escape from the wreck there will be more or less of very embittered secession. Or, though things remain as they are now, a great part of the bounty which used to flow in the various channels of Christian charity is directed to the interminable lawsuits of the Church. Altogether our prospects are anything but cheering. Human aid seems of little avail, but God is able to give deliverance. O may He send it speedily for his own name's sake ! " How it

was sent, and how it continued to be sent, the future of the
Foreign Missions of Scotland will reveal.

Dr. Wilson's first act was to write promptly to his colleague, Mr. Nesbit, at Bombay. When he arrived at Smyrna
he despatched to Dr. Brunton his resignation, in terms most
honourable to both. At the same time he sent on to Dr.
Chalmers, as Moderator, his formal adherence to the Free
Church of Scotland. That document he caused to be published in Bombay also :—

"BEYRUT, 30*th* *June* 1843.—MY DEAR ROBERT—A month before this
can reach you, you will have heard of the rupture which has taken place in
the Church of our beloved native land. It was unavoidable as far as the
faithful ministers of Christ are concerned ; and it will be overruled, I doubt
not, for the great extension of vital religion throughout the country. From
Smyrna—for which I sail to-day in the Austrian steamer—I intend to send
in my adherence as a minister and missionary to the Free Church ; and I
firmly believe that we shall all be found in the same fellowship. Whether
any plan of co-operation with the Moderates may now be practicable or desirable I do not know, though a few weeks ago I dropped a hint to Dr. Brunton
on the subject. One thing is evident, we cannot be divorced from the counsels
and prayers of those whose principles and actings have our conscientious and
strong approbation.

"The question connected with our mission property in Bombay must, I
think, be determined on principles of *equity*. It will be of great consequence
for us to get occupation as soon as possible of the new buildings. The onus
of legal proceedings—should such be resorted to—will rest on the Moderates,
if we are first in possession. I shall propose that we give the Moderates a
fair share of the price should they ask it from us.

"A regard to the souls of the present and future generations of our
countrymen in India demands our decided action in behalf of the Free Church.
Assemble its adherents in Bombay and Poona, promise the continuance of
your services to them till regular pastors be provided, and forthwith petition
for these pastors. I hope that we shall hear of your proceedings before the
meeting of Assembly at Glasgow in October. I shall do all there in my power
in support of your prayer. Tell Captains George and John Jameson, Archie
Graham, Captain Thornbury, Mr. Spencer, Mr. Fallon, Mr. Martin, and Dr.
Malcolmson, etc. etc., that I expect them in particular to be among the first
who will rally round the old flag of the Covenant."

TO DR. BRUNTON

"SMYRNA, *July* 1843.—MY VERY DEAR SIR—The rupture which has
taken place in our beloved Church, which to the last moment I had fondly
thought would have been averted by the Government considering its righteous
claims, or by both parties within the Church agreeing to uphold at least its
spiritual independence, has forced me impartially and prayerfully to consider
to which of the two separated bodies it is my duty to adhere. My decision is
in favour of the free protesting Church ; of the principles professed and advocated by which I have long conscientiously approved.

"In these circumstances it has become my painful duty to intimate, as I
now do, my withdrawal as a minister and missionary from the Established
Church of Scotland, with which I have so long considered it an honour and a
privilege to be connected. I take this momentous step from my desire to bear

and maintain a conscience void of offence toward God and man, and, I trust, without a breach of that charity which it becomes me to cherish towards those with whose judgment my own has been found at variance. I take it with inexpressible regret, as far as it involves the dissolution of that official tie which has so long bound me to yourself, who have ever treated me with more than paternal kindness, and strengthened my hands and encouraged my heart in the work of the Lord more than I can declare. I feel at this moment the unfeigned sorrow of a great bereavement, and it is my humble but fervent prayer that the Lord may comfort us *both* in the afflictive circumstances in which we are placed in His inscrutable providence. To the latest moment of my life I can never forget, or lightly estimate, the multiplied favours which I have experienced at your hands; and if God will that we should soon meet together, I shall tender to you the homage of my unfeigned gratitude.

"Your interest in the continued prosperity of our mission, which you have done so much to advance, will, I am certain, remain undiminished. In a postscript attached to my last letter I expressed the hope that some plan of co-operation between the two sections of our Church might be devised. The terms on which the separation has taken place, however, have for the present annihilated that hope. Had the Residuary Assembly not consented, as I humbly but firmly believe it has done, to the utter overthrow of the scriptural and constitutional liberties of the Church, the case might have been otherwise. —I am, my dearest Sir, yours in the bonds of Christian love and gratitude,

"JOHN WILSON."

"BILSTANEBRAE, 12*th June* 1843.

"MY DEAR DR. WILSON—I have received with great thankfulness your very kind letter from Beyrut. I rejoice to find that you have safely passed a perilous part of your journey without harm, and commit you for the remainder of it to the same protection. Your packets to Dr. Keith I delivered immediately. The opportunity, indeed, came before I had the satisfaction of perusing them. I expect that he will afford me that pleasure still. In the meantime the details of your progress which you have sent to myself will, I am quite sure, awaken in the public the same interest which I felt in reading them.

"The calamity which you anticipate has befallen; and with an extent and an exasperation with which I had by no means laid my account. Our brethren who have left us have announced their purpose to enter immediately on missionary enterprise; I have rejected repeatedly and unhesitatingly declined such a proposal as the one which you suggest. This theme I have uniformly shunned in my correspondence with India, unless perhaps by a hint at its financial bearing, because I could not see how the point in dispute could in the least touch the *status* of our brethren in India. But, of course, after the Disruption took place, I was directed to state to each of the Missions that the Established Church was resolved to go on with all of her schemes as before, and counted in her day of peril on the zealous co-operation of those whom she had found so admirably qualified for their work. Reports are loudly circulated here that my appeal comes too late. I cannot allow myself to believe it. I cannot think that those with whom our intercourse hitherto has been so delightful to us would pledge themselves, as they are said to have done, without giving us the shadow of warning. This would be to peril to an enormous extent the safety of our great cause; as well as, in many other respects, to be a source of very painful feeling. Even now, when it has become necessary to make a direct appeal, I have in no one instance introduced one word of personal pleading; but you will easily understand how painful my personal feelings are. May the Lord Himself direct you to that which is right, and may He who is able to bring good out of evil cause this sore calamity to minister to the advancement of His glory and of the Gospel cause. It is not easy for man to see how this result is to be reached; but with *Him* all things are possible. We are determined, through his blessing, to persevere. So far as human aid avails we have the prospect of abundant funds. But if works of the purest charity are to be henceforward channels for estrangement, and contention, and strife, my whole heart shrinks from what used to be its joy.

"I cannot mix up this subject with any other; indeed I have nothing else that is interesting to communicate. I need not say how very anxious I shall be to hear from you, nor how much I am, yours affectionately,

"ALEX. BRUNTON."

"MUNICH, 14*th September* 1843.

"MY VERY DEAR SIR—On the evening of the day on which I last addressed you, I received your kind letter of the 12th of June. Though it could not alter the decision, which I had intimated to you, of my adherence to the Free Church, I could not peruse it without the deepest emotion. It made me realise in all its extent your exceeding kindness and consideration during the whole period of our official connection, and imparted to me the deepest sorrow. To no individual do I feel a stronger attachment, and for no individual do I cherish a more profound regard than yourself; and could anything of a *personal* nature have prevailed with me in my choice of the ground which I should occupy after the rupture in our beloved Church, I should have been found still ranged by your side in the missionary enterprise.

"I feel it extremely difficult at once to do justice to the credit which I give to those from whom I differ in my judgment as to late events in our Church, and to express the conviction which I feel that my own sentiments are in accordance with the will of Christ. I may be permitted to say, however, that I do think that the Free Church, as far as constitutional principle is concerned, is essentially the Church of Scotland, and that in cleaving to it I am only following out my ordination vows according to my conscientious interpretation of them. In your official correspondence with the missionaries you shunned, as you intimate, all reference to the existing controversies, except in their financial bearing; and my former silence on the subject originated in my respect for your own example, and my reluctance to hold out any threat, however humble, to those with whom I might ultimately be found at variance. Though as a *missionary* employed by both parties I was silent in the discussion, yet as a *member of the Kirk-Session of Bombay* I uniformly supported non-intrusion principles. I constantly opposed premature division in India, and I have a letter from Mr. Cook cordially thanking me for my co-operation and friendship. It was only when the Government proved relentless, and multitudes conspired to overthrow the spiritual liberties and discipline of the Church, that I was compelled as a *missionary* to give in my adherence to the body of whose principles and contendings I approved. Had your own charitable and peaceful remonstrances and pleadings for upholding the authority of the Church prevailed with the body with which you are now associated, the schism I am persuaded would not have occurred.

"Had it appeared that our practical operations in India would likely suffer by our leaving the Establishment, and that it was possible for the Establishment immediately to supply our lack of service, I should have considered it a duty for us to give adequate warning of our intention to forsake that Establishment. I have not yet seen, however, that any of our operations require to be abandoned; and should the Establishment send any faithful missionaries to India, I for one shall most cordially bid them God speed, rejoicing that they preach Christ to the heathen Hindús.

"Perhaps I have erred in thinking these few remarks of explanation called for by your kind letter; if so, I am sure that you will excuse me. I hope very

LIFE OF JOHN WILSON.

soon to see you in Edinburgh ; and I confidently trust that I shall ever
vindicate the sincerity with which I subscribe myself, as of old, yours most
gratefully and affectionately,   JOHN WILSON."
  " Rev. Dr. Brunton. "

The General Assembly of the Free Church of Scotland,
which met at the end of May under Dr. Chalmers, had
necessarily to leave the details of organisation to be worked
out after it rose.   Hence the meeting of a second General
Assembly in the same year, instead of such a " Commission "
of Assembly as holds quarterly meetings every year but with
restricted powers.   At Glasgow, on the 17th October, and
with Dr. Thomas Brown of St. John's, Moderator, this special
Assembly met.   The five months that had passed showed 754
congregations and 730 ministers and preachers.   Of these
465 had given up their livings in the Established Church, and
110 licentiates and others since licensed to preach, their certain appointment to livings.   There remained the twenty-one
missionaries, fourteen in India and seven to the Jews, and in
due time the adherence of all of these was announced.   When
men like the last Marquis of Breadalbane ; Mr. Fox Maule,
afterwards Earl of Dalhousie, who had in vain brought before
the House of Commons "the question of the spiritual independence of the Church and the rights of the Christian people
of Scotland ;" Mr. Murray Dunlop, M.P. ; Dr. Chalmers and
Dr. Candlish had reported arrangements resulting in a response from the country to the amount of £300,000 in that
brief period, Dr. Gordon submitted the statement of the
India Mission.

In answer to those friends of the missionary cause who
had deprecated the long defence of their spiritual rights by
the people of Scotland, on the ground that it was "not a
religious question," he pointed to " the striking fact that the
missionaries of the Church of Scotland, possessing in an
eminent degree the esteem and confidence of the Christian
public both at home and abroad, as holy and devoted men of
God quietly pursuing their pious labours far from the scene
of controversy, and as calm observers watching from a distance the progress. of the conflict, should, the moment that
conflict ended, have unanimously and without hesitation
united themselves to their protesting brethren."   But while
Dr. Chalmers could announce his third of a million, chiefly
due to that unique contribution to ecclesiastical economics,

the Sustentation Fund for the ministers, Dr. Gordon could, at that early stage, when no appeal had been made, report only £327 as the fund with which the Church nevertheless resolved, as Dr. Forbes put it, to continue the "gigantic scheme of Church Extension" among a population which was then estimated at 160 millions, but will be shown, by the second imperial census in 1881, to be nearer 260 millions as British India now is. The fourteen foreign missionaries of 1843-44 have grown in number to forty ordained men, Native and Scottish ; the £327 of October 1843 and £6402 of the whole year, to £30,657 a year in Scotland alone, and nearly double that if the whole annual revenue of the Indian, African, and South Pacific Missions be considered. In the thirty-six years since that time the Church of these fourteen missionaries has given in Scotland alone, £550,000 for foreign missions, and there is not a contributor who does not admit that the amount might have been and will yet be doubled. The conflict of the ten years before 1843, and the struggles of Cameron, the Erskines, and Gillespie before that, will not be exhausted until the three great branches of the Reformation Kirk of John Knox are gathered once again into one reconstructed Church, as free in its own legitimate sphere as the statutes of the Reformation, the treaty of Union and the Revolution Settlement acknowledged it to be. This is, thus far, Scotland's contribution to the question which Pope and Emperor in Italy and Germany are trying to work out on the hopelessly irreconcilable, because intolerant, lines of Ultramontane tyranny and Cæsarist encroachment ; and Dr. Wilson often declared it to be so. The freewill offerings of the members of the Free Church of Scotland every year, for all spiritual purposes at home and abroad, nearly equal £600,000. In all it has raised the sum of thirteen millions sterling[1] side by side with higher moral aims, and as the fruit of a deeper spiritual life.

[1] According to Mr. W. Holms, M.P., himself a member of the Established Church, who stated in the House of Commons debate on the 18th June 1878 : "There are 1517 churches attached to the Free and United Presbyterian Churches against 1390 attached to the Established Church. And these last comprise about 300 Highland charges, most of them very meagrely attended. In regard to the money raised for religious purposes during the year 1877-78, which was not an unfair test of vitality and power, £965,000 had been contributed by Free and United Presbyterians, against £385,000 by the Established Church."

Dr. Wilson's first speech in the General Assembly is remembered to this day for the length as well as the eloquence of its statements of fact and pictures of Oriental superstitions and missionary life. To the attitude of the religions of the East towards the Christian demand for their surrender he happily applied the remark of Tippoo, when the British forces surrounded the last stronghold of Seringapatam—"I am afraid, but afraid not so much of what is seen as of what is unseen." First in the list of the principal means of propagating the Gospel in India he placed those used by the Lord and His apostles, as he had done from the day he took possession of Bombay—"conversation, discussion, public preaching, among all classes of men to whom they could find access, and in all situations in which they could be advantageously practised." After an account of the work of his colleagues, and of the agents of other Churches in every case, he briefly describes his own :—"I have declared the doctrine of the Cross in three languages, the Marathee, Hindostanee, and Goojaratee, from the Shirawutee in Canara to Sirohee in Rajpootana, and from Bombay to Berar." Second in his enumeration of agencies came the translation of the Scriptures into the languages of India, and the publication of works showing the evidence of their truth ; of "plain but affectionate" expositions of their contents ; and of demonstrations of the vanity, falsity, and immorality of the systems of error to which they are opposed. Again, after a generous tribute to the work of others, he briefly stated his own, adding, "It was my privilege to act for twelve years as secretary to the different translation committees of the Bombay Bible Society." Besides the English, Marathee, Goojaratee, Hindostanee, Persian, and Hebrew, in which his own writings had appeared, the missionaries of other societies had translated them into Bengalee, Hindee, Tamul, and Canarese. On the third agency of schools Dr. Wilson gave a fair and full summing-up of a question much disputed in this country, though long set at rest in favour of education, higher and lower, by experienced men of all churches in India, so far as Hindoos, Parsees, Buddhists, and Muhammadans, or the non-aboriginal races, are concerned. This was followed by equally weighty utterances on the two questions which lie at the foundation of the indigenous Church of India, native congregations and native ministers. The Moderator, according to the newspapers of the day, in an eloquent address conveyed the thanks of the General Assembly to Dr. Wilson.

While he was yet speaking there was intelligence on its way from Bombay which gave a new point to the opinions he so emphatically expressed. An educated Brahman youth, now the Rev. Narayan Sheshadri, and long one of the most successful ordained ministers in India, asked to be baptized. He was one of the few Hindoos who had clung to the mission college when the Parsee baptisms in 1839 produced a panic throughout native Bombay. The first *educated* Brahman baptized in the island, he was the direct fruit of the higher Christian education, and a worthy associate of the two Parsees who had anticipated him. Mr. Nesbit's loving gentleness, and Dr. Murray Mitchell's efficient instructions, had continued the good work begun by Dr. Wilson. It seemed likely that both Narayan and his younger brother Shripat would have been allowed to live and study together, holding kindly intercourse with their parents. But the prospect was too much for those who had recently seen toleration triumphant in the case of the two Parsees, and were the more determined "to contest every inch of ground with advancing Christianity." So the appeal was again made not to reason or truth, but to the civil courts, for Shripat was not sixteen years of age. The "age of discretion" rule, the intelligence and sincerity of the youth rather than the age by the horoscope ever difficult to be proved, were pronounced by Sir Erskine Perry to be "not worth a farthing," and Shripat exclaimed, when declared too young to exercise the rights of conscience—"Am I to be compelled to worship idols?"

The scene has often since been repeated in the courts of India, purely English as well as those administering Hindoo and Muhammadan law; and legislation has yet, in this matter alone happily, to complete the little code securing bare toleration, which Bentinck and Dalhousie began, and Sir Henry Maine and Sir James F. Stephen have amplified. "To this sorrowful question of Shripat's," writes an eyewitness, "no answer was returned. Mr. Nesbit was greatly attached to Shripat, and when the weeping boy bade him farewell as they quitted the court-house, he kissed him with much affection, and wept with him." Shripat was never allowed to become a Christian, but it took a long time to shake him by arts such as *Faust* has made the colder West believe to be but the legendary fictions of a dark age.   And since Shripat had eaten with his baptized brother, his case became the first, also, of a long series of gradually weakening concessions by caste, as Christianity practically teaches that God has made of one blood all nations of men.   Not only in Maharashtra, but in the holiest conclave at Benares, and among the most exclusive of the five Koolin clans of Bengal, the very practical question was hotly debated—" Can Shripat be purified and restored to caste ? "   Hindooism was on its trial, for if it yielded now what horror might not come next, till the one last bond was cut in every link ?   A rich minority spent vast sums to develop dogmatically Hindooism into something that would tolerate the *Zeit-Geist*, ease their own consciences, and perhaps connive at their forbidden pleasures. Thus, travelling by railway was afterwards sacerdotally sanctioned, for would not the pilgrim arrive at his journey's end with more in his purse ?   But the year 1843 was too early for the minority, who had got Shripat to swallow the five products of the cow (its urine, etc.), and enriched a priest to conduct the purification.   All who had thus combined were themselves threatened with excommunication, and the priest was as severely handled as if he had been a Christian.   The " liberal " Brahmans publicly confessed their fault, and drank water in which an idol had been washed and ten Brahmans had dipped each his right foot.   For the rest the scandal was hushed up, many feeling it would have been better if Shripat had never been dragged before the English judges. While Narayan and Pestonjee continued their studies for licence and ordination in Bombay, Dhunjeebhoy Nourojee completed his college examinations in Edinburgh, and as a preacher and speaker gave a vivid interest to the missionary cause in Scotland.

The day before the General Assembly sat at Glasgow the Presbytery of Bombay had received a formal letter of sympathy from Allahabad, one of the four presbyteries in north India of the church of the United States.   The brotherly document was signed by the Rev. J. Warren and the Rev. J. Owen, the latter a learned scholar who was long spared to build up the native church.   It has more than a curious interest, as contributing the experience of a Republic which, itself born of the intolerance of the Tudors and the Stewarts, has never found a difficulty in recognising and protecting the legitimate spiritual independence of all churches, even that of Rome. The letter anticipated the time, since realised as to co-operation, when all Presbyterians in India may meet in fellowship, and ultimately in General Assembly.

In his address to the General Assembly Dr. Wilson declared the most clamant need of India to be the establishment of a Christian mission in its Central Provinces. At Nagpore, nearly equidistant from Bombay, Calcutta, and Madras about seven hundred miles, a Raja of the Bhonsla family of Marathas reigned, like the Gaekwar at Baroda, Holkar at Indore, and Sindia at Gwalior. He had been guided by a political Resident so able as Sir Richard Jenkins, and was protected by a combined force of British troops and Madras sepoys at the adjoining cantonment of Kamptee. Stationed there as Deputy Judge-Advocate General, was a Madras officer, Captain, now Sir William Hill, K.C.S.I. He and his wife had long lamented the want of a missionary to evangelise the people. Nor had their desire been fulfilled by the establishment, two hundred miles away, of the industrial or artisan mission of Pastor Gossner of Berlin among the aboriginal Gonds, whose cause Sir Donald M'Leod, when a district officer among them, had long advocated. On the death of his wife Captain Hill resolved to devote her small fortune of £2000, adding to it £500, the whole in three per cents, to the endowment of a mission to the people of Kampthee, Nagpore, and the neighbourhood. He applied to Dr. Wilson, in February 1842, as the missionary best known to him by reputation, offering the amount for a Presbyterian or Church of England Mission. The fruitless result of Dr. Wilson's application to Dr. Brunton has been stated. But his representations to the committee of the Free Church met with such a response that the only difficulty left was to secure a missionary, at a time when every licensed preacher, young and old, was required at home.

Happily Stephen Hislop offered himself; a man, as it proved, after Wilson's own heart. Fresh from a distinguished career at the Universities of Glasgow and Edinburgh and the New College, he was an accurate scholar and a keen naturalist.

.

He proved to be a patient linguist, a worker of rare political insight and administrative power, and, above all, an enthusiast in the spiritual work he had undertaken. All the arrangements at the home end, for fitting out and securing the success of the new mission, fell upon Dr. Wilson, as those in India had devolved upon him in the case of the Irish settlement in Goojarat. But in spite of the need for rest, and the general work of the Church, he and Mr. Hislop so co-operated that, by the end of 1844, the new apostle—in time to prove a martyr by his death in the midst of duty—left for the scene of his labours. We shall hear more of Stephen Hislop. This Nagpore Mission is consecrated by the memory of another Christian official of the civil service, as Sir William Hill was of the military—Sir Donald M'Leod—who, after a brilliant career ending as Lieutenant-Governor of the Punjab, and giving his last days to philanthropic work in London, was killed when attempting to enter a train in motion, on his way to a meeting of the Christian Vernacular Education Society.

Donald M'Leod was the man to whom this double testimony was borne by a Rajpoot and a Sikh. Behari Lal Singh, a Rajpoot official subordinate to him, was led to believe that "Christianity was something living," and ultimately died an ordained missionary of the Presbyterian Church of England, by what he described as "the pious example of this gentleman, his integrity, his disinterestedness, his active benevolence. Here is a man in the receipt of 2000 or 3000 rupees annually ; he spends little on himself, and gives away the surplus for education—the temporal and spiritual welfare of my countrymen. This was the turning-point of my religious history, and led to my conversion." More recently a Sikh declared, "If all Christians were like Sir Donald M'Leod there would be no Hindoos or Muhammadans." Of the M'Leods of Assynt and proprietors of Geanies, one of the three great branches of the old Norwegian clan, young Donald passed from the Edinburgh High School to Putney, where he had Lord Canning and Henry Carre Tucker for schoolfellows ; and to Haileybury, where he first won the admiration of Lord Lawrence. When at his first station of Monghyr in 1831, he learned from his countryman, the Rev. A. Leslie—the Baptist missionary who helped Sir H. Havelock—to adopt the words of Pascal as his own : Religion has " abased me infinitely more than unassisted reason, yet without producing despair; and exalted me infinitely more than pride, yet without puffing up." When he passed to the Thuggee department, created by Lord William Bentinck to put down organised robbery and murder by strangling, and on to the administration of the Saugur and Nerbudda highlands, ceded by the Marathas in 1818, where Seonee was his headquarters, he was soon attracted to Dr. Wilson. From 1836, to his death in 1872, they assisted each other in philanthropic enterprise and scholarly research.

To the India Mission, thus increased, the Free Church added, in 1844, the African stations in Kaffraria, offered to it by the Glasgow Missionary Society; and it soon after sent out two other ministers familiar with Dutch, who for a time conducted missionary operations in Cape Town itself. Thus a new impetus and extension were given to a mission which has made the Lovedale Institution not only the centre and head of all civilising work among the natives of South Africa, in the opinion of observers like Mr. Anthony Trollope and Sir Bartle Frere, but the base of that advance into the Lake Region which has resulted in the establishment of the Livingstonia settlement on Nyassa. The cause of native female education also, in India, made a fresh start. The Ladies' Association was strengthened by the co-operation of the Glasgow Association on behalf of female education in South Africa up to 1865, when both combined to form the present invaluable agency which is carrying light into the Zananas of the most caste-bound families.

Hardly had the Glasgow Assembly risen when Dr. Wilson found himself absorbed for a time in preaching and addressing large audiences of all the evangelical Churches, now on the Free Church of Scotland's assertion of its principles, but more frequently on the missionary claims of India. In November 1843 he opened the new Free Church in his native town of Lauder, to which nearly the whole community flocked to hear the youth who had done such great things in India. His old master, Mr. Paterson, took care that he should preside at the examination of the school, in circumstances very different from those under which he used, on his tours, to stoop under the leafy sheds of the jungle schools of the Konkan, or the low roofs of the bungalows of Bombay and Surat. Invitations to preach flowed in upon him from all parts, from Dr. James

Hamilton of London to Dr. James Lewis and Mr. Thorburn of Leith. It was when Dr. Wilson addressed the children in St. John's, Leith, that his present biographer first saw the even then youthful apostle, and heard the rhythmic roll of his sentences as hundreds learned from him for the first time of the Hindoo idols and the Parsee fire, of the scattered Beni-Israel, and the devil-worshippers and man-sacrificers of the Indian hills.

Dr. Wilson was selected by his Church to accompany Dr. Candlish to England. At Oxford, on the 17th March 1844, he preached to the elite of the University and the Church of England there a sermon on " The Church Glorious before its Lord," from Ephesians v. 25-27. The academic tone of the discourse, and the learning and long self-sacrificing labours of the preacher, combined to call forth a degree of ecclesiastical appreciation as well as missionary sympathy which a local journalist thus expressed when it was published :—" The great movement in Scotland is a new thing under the sun. It is little less than a breaking up and recasting of a nation. It is developing events which mere politicians cannot understand, and which they will be unable to guide. The freedom of the Christian Church in its corporate character has been asserted. And, as we believe, the further assertion of the freedom and equality of Christian men, and of every distinct Christian assembly will follow." At the annual meeting of the Wesleyan Missionary Society, Sir George Rose in the chair, he was introduced by Dr. Bunting ; when, answering the attacks of the late Cardinal Wiseman on Protestant Missions, he made a valuable contribution to that little-known subject—Roman Catholic Missions in India ; referring to such Portuguese authorities as the *Life of Juan de Castro*, one of the earliest Viceroys, and a letter from John I. of Portugal, to be found in that classic. " Dr. Wiseman thinks very little of Protestant efforts," he concluded, " but the Brahmans make a great deal of them. I this morning read a tract written against Christianity and addressed to myself by a Brahman. He tells his countrymen that, unless they act together, all their power and religion are doomed. And, for the sake of the inhabitants of India who have been most marvellously placed under the sway of this Christian country, we wish the doom of Brahmanism. Wishing them good, we must endeavour to save them from the contaminating and ruining power of sin, and prepare them for the glories of heaven. . . . Increase your labourers in India, and look for the divine blessing." Addressing the Baptist Society, over which Mr. W. B. Gurney presided, and the British Society for the Jews, he excited enthusiasm by his fresh and generous descriptions of the labours of their agents, and his appeals for a wide extension of their agencies. "The names of Carey, of Marshman, and of Ward, had been long familiar to me," he said to the former, "before I finished my studies at the University. Dr. Marshman gave me the right hand of fellowship before I proceeded to India; and he was among the first, with a generous heart, to welcome me to its shores."

From his English raid he hurried back to be present as a representative of Bombay at the General Assembly of 1844. There, at its successor, and at the remarkable Assembly of Inverness in August 1845, when Dr. Macdonald of Ferintosh, the Moderator, preached in Gaelic, from Dr. Wilson's familiar text—"Those that have turned the world upside down have come hither also"—the Bombay missionary was true to his calling. At the General Assembly of the Presbyterian Church in Ireland, held in 1844 in Londonderry, he was received with "loud acclamations" as the co-founder of the mission to the two millions of Kathiawar; and he afterwards gave much of his time to providing means for the extension of that mission. At the Birmingham meeting of the Synod of the English Presbyterian Church in 1845, he stood, side by side with Mr. Milne from China, as a deputy with Dr. Beith from the Free Church of Scotland. When, in the same year, addressing the Edinburgh Medical Missionary Society, which has since done much for the people of India, he said—"I recollect being asked by Sir Robert Grant, the late Governor of Bombay, what would be the effect of dissecting a dead body in the Poona Sanskrit College. Why, said I, the first effect certainly would be that the Brahmans would jump out at the windows; and the second effect would be, on their re-entering, that the gods would jump out also; or, in other words, their religious prejudices would take to flight." The Grant Medical College in Western, and the Bengal Medical College in Eastern India, where a Brahman student of Dr. Duff's was one of the first Hindoos to dissect the human subject, have produced great

results. It was in emphatic language that he induced the
Assembly of 1844 to memorialise Her Majesty's Government
on the impotence and misrule of the Ottoman Porte alike in
Asia and in Europe. Nor did he spare Russia's intolerance.

In all Dr. Wilson's correspondence, confidential as well as
public, we have met with no expression of his opinions more
worthy of his whole work for and relation to the Native
Church of India, than a letter on the ordination of
Dhunjeebhoy to Dr. James Buchanan, who had succeeded
Dr. Gordon at the head of the Foreign Missions Committee.
He pleaded, and with success finally, for what at the present
time it is difficult to believe even those most ignorant of India
could have doubted,—the spiritual and ecclesiastical rights of
the educated native converts, in the light of justice and expediency, of the equality of Presbyterianism and the future of
the Indian Church. The Parsee "probationer" himself, who
had already become popular as a preacher all over the country,
intimated that, unless full evangelistic power and liberty were con-
ceded to him, he would not enter the service of the Free Church,
and Dr. Wilson reported to Mr. Nesbit, "his firmness in this respect has been admired. We are for natives being ordained,
after due probation, *as missionaries or evangelists like ourselves.*"

It was well that he and Dr. W. S. Mackay of Calcutta
happened to be in Scotland when their Church, naturally
absorbed in its domestic and internal organisation, was also
called to lay anew the foundations of its Foreign Mission
broad and deep. The missionary buildings at Poona were
not affected by the ecclesiastical changes, and those at Madras
had been rented only. But the property made over to the
Established Church had cost £10,000 at Calcutta and £8000
at Bombay, exclusive of libraries and apparatus. The duty of
raising £20,000 for a new start fell upon Dr. Wilson and Dr.
W. S. Mackay, then on sick leave from Calcutta. How
generously the whole India Mission was aided, not so much
by the public effort as by private and anonymous gifts, the
missionary correspondence of the period reveals. Even more
remarkable was the liberality of Christian men of all sects in
India itself. To that the Free Churches in Bombay and
Calcutta owe their existence.

As the Sustentation Fund, devised by the greatest writer
and most practical worker in the field of Christian and Philan-

thropic Economics, Dr. Chalmers, became consolidated for the
support of the home ministers, it would have been well if a
somewhat similar self-acting and self-developing arrangement
had been then made proportionately for the growing foreign
missions. But Dr. Wilson seems to have attempted the institution of a system which, it is to be hoped, all the churches
will yet adopt in the place of, or in addition to, desultory
offerings. He induced Dr. Candlish and Dr. Gordon to arrange
that St. George's and the New North congregations should
provide the support of the two Parsee missionaries. The former, which gave £63 for the object in 1840, now subscribes
to the Foreign Mission Fund about £700 of its whole annual
contributions of £10,000. If it undertook directly to provide for two missionaries, who would report to it as well as to
the central committee, the congregational life would be completed on its missionary as well as home side; while the
missionaries would be brought into closer contact with the
churches and with their youth, who are to be their successors.
Only where each congregation, able to raise at least £200 a
year in addition to the income of its own minister, thus does
its duty to the Master by sending forth an ordained Native or
European missionary, will the wide fields of Heathenism and
Muhammadanism be adequately overtaken, and the churches
of Christendom prove their spiritual loyalty. When that
union of sects, for which Dr. Wilson longed, comes about, so
that ecclesiastical waste and suicidal divisions shall be reduced
to a minimum, this ideal may be reached.

It was in the year 1844, when he was forty years of age,
that Dr. Wilson sat to Mr. James Caw for that portrait which
has since adorned the walls of the Free Church College in
Bombay. It was painted at the request of the students, and
was pronounced a good likeness of the founder of the mission
there. A fine mezzotint engraving by Mr. Henry Haig was
made for the public at home.

The General Assembly of 1846 formally declared that they
"rejoiced in the prospect of Dr. Wilson's return to Bombay
in renovated health." They recommended all ministers of
the Church, "at least once a year, about the opening of the
college session," to bring the claims of foreign missions specially
before their congregations, and "to enforce upon them the
duties of prayer and self-denial."

CHAPTER XIII.

1845-1847.

AMONG BOOKS—SECOND MARRIAGE—OVER EUROPE TO BOMBAY.

Colonel Jervis, F.R.S., and intercourse with Civil and Military Officers—
Establishment of the *North British Review*—Reception of Dr. Wilson's
Works by the learned of Europe—Elected Fellow of the Royal Society—
Death of Dr. Welsh—Writers in the *North British Review*—Letter to
Hugh Miller, and from Dr. Falconer—Second Marriage—Isabella Dennis-
toun of Dennistoun—Dr. and Mrs. Wilson leave for India—Lassen and
William Erskine at Bonn—Researches in Egypt—Welcomes at Bombay—
Lord Hardinge announces Suppression of Suttee, Infanticide, and Slavery,
in many Native States—George Clerk and Memorial Church of Colaba—
Gaikwar of Baroda dies.

WE have seen how, throughout the first period of Dr. Wilson's
Indian career, he was encouraged and supported in his purely
missionary as well as philanthropic and scientific labours by
laymen, chiefly civil and military officers, who united with
him in dedicating to the very highest ends their intellectual
powers, their social influence, and their Christian culture.
Even at that early time he became the centre and the
stimulus of the best society in Western India. One of the
most remarkable of the officers with whom he formed a very
close friendship was Colonel T. B. Jervis, F.R.S. To his
educational work in the Konkan, and erection of the Bombay
College, transferred on its completion to the Established Kirk,
we have already referred. Born in India, and with a hereditary interest in its people like the majority of the Anglo-
Indian officials under the East India Company, young Jervis
gained extraordinary honours at Addiscombe and entered the
Engineer Corps, became superintending engineer of the
Southern Konkan which had just been made British territory,
and surveyed that large tract of Western India. His maps

still form part of the uncompleted Atlas of India. He made
such a reputation that, when in England in 1837, he was
nominated successor to Sir George Everest as Surveyor-General
of India, an appointment he did not take up. On finally
retiring from the service, shortly before Dr. Wilson's departure
from Bombay, he received a letter of touching farewell, and
a copy of the best edition of the Bible which could then be
procured, " as a small token of Christian affection and gratitude for his admirable design for the General Assembly's
Institution in Bombay."

With no one was Dr. Wilson in such close correspondence
all through his visit to Great Britain, especially on literary
and scientific undertakings for the good of India, as with
Colonel Jervis. While the missionary was striving to devote
every hour he could snatch from ecclesiastical engagements to
the preparation of his elaborate work, *The Lands of the Bible*,
the engineer was projecting a series of Memoirs, Voyages, and
Travels, original and translated, illustrative of the geography
and statistics of Asia. The collection would have formed a
modern Hakluyt, and is still a desideratum in European literature, in spite of similarly fragmentary attempts to supply it
by both German and English editors, for the health and the
resources of Colonel Jervis did not allow him to do more than
issue in 1845 a first volume—Baron Charles Hügel's *Kaschmir
und das Reich der Siek*, in an English dress.

The two friends were farther interested in the success of
the *North British Review*. Evangelical men of all parties in
Scotland had, even before the events of 1843, desired to see
established a Quarterly which, to the literary ability of the
Edinburgh Review and its great rival, would add the discussion
of theological questions which were then beginning to occupy
thoughtful minds—no less in England, where the Tractarian
movement was at its height, than in Scotland. Men like Drs.
Chalmers and Welsh, Cunningham and Fleming, in the Scottish
Universities and Church, and writers like Sir David Brewster,
Isaac Taylor, and Merle D'Aubigné, formed a nucleus to whom
only the leisure of letters was wanting in those stirring times
to make success as lasting as it proved to be brilliant for a
time. For the *North British Review* anticipated that discussion of the deepest theological problems, and of all questions
on the platform of the highest principles, which has of late

marked the higher periodical literature. In the thirty years
of its existence it more than justified the other boast with
which its prospectus was concluded : " The latest discoveries in
mental and physical science will be regularly unfolded by men
themselves of the highest inventive genius. In all departments
individuals of the greatest celebrity in this and other countries
have promised to adorn our pages with their contributions."
Dr. Welsh at once laid hold of Dr. Wilson for his staff. It
should be noted that the same month of May 1844 which saw
the first number of the Scottish Review, witnessed the birth of
another Quarterly which has a history in the East quite as
remarkable as that of the *Edinburgh* in the West—the *Calcutta
Review*, edited, after its fourth number, by Dr. Duff. At a
much later period, and for some time, Dr. Wilson contributed
articles to the *Bombay Quarterly Review* and to the *British and
Foreign Evangelical Review*.

The reputation which Dr. Wilson had gained in the circles
of the learned of Europe by his work on the Parsee Religion
was increased when his *Lands of the Bible* appeared, and,
during his occasional visits to London, caused his society to
be sought by men like Lord Castlereagh, afterwards fourth
Marquis of Londonderry, who had himself been travelling in
the East. In the addresses of 1869 and 1870 to Dr. Wilson,
the public and the Asiatic Society of Bombay thus sum up
contemporary opinions on these two books :—" Your learned
and comprehensive work on the religion of the Parsees, published on the eve of your journey to Europe in 1843, was
recognised by the few scholars then competent to form an
opinion as the most complete investigation into the sacred
writings of the Parsees that had up to that time appeared.
A distinguished Oriental scholar, whose learned labours have
reflected honour on Bombay, Mr. William Erskine, urged you,
in reference to this and other works, ' to go on and enrich
the world of letters, while you think chiefly of the religious
world and religious benefit of the human race ; ' and Professor Westergaard of Copenhagen, whose own valuable labours
in this branch of Oriental research are so well known, thankfully recognised the value of the services you had rendered
himself, which he said he valued the more from the prominent place you hold amongst Oriental philologists, and for
your having signally contributed to the furtherance of ac-

quaintance with the Zoroastrian lore. Your great work, *The Lands of the Bible*, was hailed on its appearance as being in itself a complete storehouse of biblical research, and as abounding in materials illustrating the state of the Christian sects and churches of the East, of the Eastern Jews and Samaritans, of Mahomedanism, and the numerous questions connected with the ancient people and languages of Palestine, Syria, and other parts of the East. The President of the Royal Geographical Society, in directing the attention of the learned to what was new and important in the work specially pertaining to questions of geographical, topographical, and antiquarian research, remarked how much could be done in gleaning what was new in such countries as those you had travelled in, by travellers who enjoyed, as you did, the advantage of understanding the language of the people, and of entering into the spirit of the manners of the East."

Of *The Parsi Religion* the Asiatic Society of Paris thus wrote in their Report of 1843 :—"Tous ces ouvrages sont destinés à servir l'éclaircissement d'une grande controverse qui s'est élevée, à Bombay, entre les missionaires protestants et les Parsis, et qui, dirigée, du côté Chrétien, par un homme savant et intelligent comme M. Wilson, a donné naissance à plusieurs écrits remarquables dont la science doit tirer profit." But the practical criticism which Dr. Wilson valued most was the blue ribband of science in Great Britain. On the 7th February 1845 he was elected a Fellow of the Royal Society.

COLONEL JERVIS TO DR. WILSON.

"12*th February* 1845.—My very dear Friend—I cannot express to you the great delight I experienced, and those also to whom I read it aloud, from the review of my work in the *North British*. You have grasped and epitomised all that was worth knowing on the subject in so masterly and delightful a manner that I have got a far clearer view from it of the Baron's real merit and the happy selection I had made of my preliminary volume than I could ever have hoped for elsewhere. It has given courage to a sinking spirit, and will do more for the recommendation and sale of the work than all the advertisements or exertions I could make.

"I sent you the testimonial (a copy) of your election as Fellow of the Royal Society—and a noble testimonial, and well supported it was, by Dr. Buckland, and Murchison, President of the Geographical Society, and Greenough, President of the Geological Society. I am sorry to say our kind friend Mr. Greenough is laid up with influenza, very severe. On Thursday the Royal Society meeting was put off for the death of the Princess Sophia. To another meeting I went down, and the old dame, the porteress at the door, said, 'Oh dear, Major Jervis, his good majesty Charles the First was martyrised to-day, and you are not the only gentleman who has been disappointed and had a long walk for nothing to Somerset House.' The set day came at length, and I was at my post, Sir John Lubbock in the chair, and rejoiced to communicate to you the tidings of your admission into the long list of 750 Fellows, some eminent for taste and talent, and on the whole the most remarkable men in Europe of the present generation, or perhaps, any in modern times. The honour of your election is mutually yours and that of the great public body, and I always think that a grain of good salt thrown into the leaven will correct many acidities, and tend to give a wholesome zest to the discoveries of intellectual knowledge.

"I have got the view of Bombay, between the hills of Caranja, as seen from the top of Malabar Hill, close to the Rev. Dr. Wilson's bungalow, sketched from nature and painted in oils by Mrs. Jervis. It is a glorious, magnificent scene."

DR. WILSON TO REV. ROBERT NESBIT.

"EDINBURGH, 1st February 1845.—MY DEAR ROBERT—As I am sitting up again a whole night writing letters, you will not expect me to enlarge. The North British Review, No. IV., is sent to you by this mail. The writers of the articles whom I am at liberty to mention to you, are :—1. Dana—Dr. Fleming (Aberdeen). 2. Thornton—Robertson (B.C.S.) 4. Fitchett—J. M. Bell. 5. Arnold—Maitland (Edward). 6. Hügel—John Wilson. 7. Poor Laws — Chalmers. 8. Palestine—Isaac Taylor. 9. Christian Union—Professor Eddye. 10. Jesuits—an Italian. The Review is now established as first-rate. Our Scotch circulation is ahead of the Edinburgh's ; and we are making way in England and on the continent. Westergaard is delighted with it. The Edinburgh prints 5000 copies, and we 3000 for the present.

"I have been strongly urged by friends here to write an essay on the Millennium ; but I can't find time. I grudge every day I am away from my books. I hope that the Encyclopædia Britannica, sent by the Brahman, will reach you safely. Two gigantic globes, with a few volumes, I send off next week. Put one of the globes in the Institution, and keep the other at Ambrolie for native visitors and the female schools.

"Dr. Welsh, our great leader, I grieve to tell you, is threatened with a fatal disease of the liver. Save, O Lord !

"6th March 1845.—I came up to London last week to sign the statutes of the Royal Society, of which, a short time ago, I was elected a member on the recommendation of nine of the great masters of science and literature, of whose unsought patronage I am very unworthy. At the Royal Asiatic Society on Saturday, I reported progress in the decipherment of the Himyaritic inscriptions of the south of Arabia, some of which, the most eminent orientalists here and elsewhere being witnesses, I have now clearly made out. Mr. Foster and Dr. Bird are both wrong. Gesenius was partly right and partly wrong. Rödiger is nearly right. I have not time to tell you how I forged the key.

"I am with Jervis, who is doing great and good things for the East. Yesterday morning he forwarded to Prince Albert, without my knowledge, my proof of the raised map of Palestine. The Prince himself laid it before the Queen, who was much pleased with it, and ordered her private secretary to inform us that Her Majesty will graciously accept the dedication of the map from him and Dr. Wilson."

"5th June 1845.—Our Assembly has passed off well ; but we missed the hallowed form of Welsh. The loss which we have sustained by his death is unspeakably great. Mr. Edward Maitland, advocate, receives charge of the North British Review in the meantime."

DR. WILSON TO HUGH MILLER, Esq.

"*24th July* 1845.—MY DEAR SIR—I have the pleasure of sending for your examination most of the fossils which I brought from Lebanon. The ichthyolites are certainly neither placoids nor ganoids. I have so little practical acquaintance with such remains that I cannot positively say whether they are ctenoids or cycloids, though I am inclined to think that they are the latter. One of the species seems to belong to the salmonidæ. Most of the shells and impressions of shells I picked up in the Jurassic Hills between Jazín and Deir-el-Kamr, south-east of Beyrut. One or two of them are from the under indurated chalk between Deir-el-Kamr and Beyrut. The small packet in white paper is from Ehdur, near the cedars. The recent species of buccinum is for comparison with the largest impression. I send also the specimens of fossil wood which I brought from the Egyptian desert, south-east of Basátín, and from Jebel-el-Tíh, in the Mount Sinai peninsula, north of the granitic range. You will oblige me by asking Mr. Sanderson when he may call upon you, to cut them so as to exhibit a section of them, and to prepare a slip of each for the miscroscope, like those which you yesterday showed to me. You are most welcome to take pieces of them as hand specimens, etc., for yourself. I have a good many other articles here on which I must ask Mr. Sanderson to operate at a future time."

DR. FALCONER TO DR. WILSON.

"BRITISH MUSEUM, *1st May* 1846.—MY DEAR SIR—I commissioned a friend who went out lately to Bombay to send all the information he could gather for me about the Perim island fossils, more especially the Dinotherium and Mastodons. I have received a number of sketches of the specimens in the Bombay Society's Museum, but none of the Dinotherium, and my friend Mr. Winterbottom was informed by Professor Orlebar or Dr. Buist that you had got a cranium of the Dinotherium, and taken it with you to this country. Might I ask the favour of your informing me if such is the case, or if you have any good specimens of Mastodons or Dinotherium teeth from Perim island, and whether I could get access to them for illustrations and description in our 'Fauna Antiqua Sivalensis.' My dear Sir, yours very faithfully,

"H. FALCONER."

Dr. Wilson's second marriage took place in September 1846, to Isabella, second daughter of James Dennistoun of Dennistoun, and of Mary Ramsay, fifth daughter of George Oswald of Scotstoun. For more than twenty years she proved to be a devoted wife, and no less a self-sacrificing missionary than her husband was. Admirably did she fill the place left vacant by the Bayne sisters, alike at the head of the female schools, among the families of the native converts, and in general society. Sprung of a house which, through the alliance of one of its members with Robert the Steward of Scotland, could declare, "kings have come of us, not we of kings," Isabella Wilson ever showed the truest marks of gentle birth and training in the unobtrusive piety and unselfish simplicity of her character.

DR. WILSON TO PROFESSOR WESTERGAARD.

"LONDON, 3d *July* 1847.

"MY DEAR FRIEND—In a box which I forwarded to you to-day, I enclose
a copy of my work on *The Lands of the Bible* for the Royal Society of
Northern Antiquaries at Copenhagen, to the Secretary of whom I have
addressed this note :—' London, 3d July 1847.—My dear Sir—It is only a few
weeks since I received at Edinburgh your letter acquainting me with my election as a founder and member of the Royal Society of Northern Antiquaries at
Copenhagen, even though that letter, and the accompanying diploma, are dated
in the early part of 1843. Your parcel must have lain at some of our public
Institutions without being forwarded to me. Allow me, however late, to
thank your Society for the honour it has done me in electing me a founder,
and also for adding my name to the list of the Collaborateurs des Memoires in
the Asiatic Section. With this editorial committee I shall have pleasure in
co-operating on my return to India, for which I am about to set out.'

"And now, my dear friend Westergaard, I send you *all* my Zand and
Pahlavi MSS. for collation, except a few Zasts which one of my boys has by
mistake put into one of my Indian boxes. They are in eight volumes, viz.—
1. *Parsi Rawayats*, Zand, Pahlavi MSS., etc. 2. *Collection of Zasts*, Zand
MSS. 3. *Great Sirozah and Bazes*, Zand MS. 4. *Sirozahs*, Zand MSS. 5.
Khurda Avasta, MS. 6. *Zand and Pahlavi Minor* MSS. 7. *Nyaishes* Zand
MSS. 8. *Star-Stir*, Zand and Pahlavi MS. You will find my name on them
all. When you have collated them I will thank you to return them to me at
Bombay, where the Parsee may perhaps again fight with me as the wild beasts
with St. Paul at Ephesus."

By lending his MSS. in Scotland as by his personal intercourse and influence in Bombay, he co-operated with the
learned Westergaard in producing what is still, and must long
be, the only complete text of the extant Parsee scriptures. At
the same time we find the then venerable Colonel Briggs
invoking his aid in researches into the development of the
great vernacular languages of Northern and Central India from
the Sanskrit, and their relation to the Dravidian and aboriginal
tongues of the South. About this time Lassen announced to
him his election as a Corresponding Member of the German
Oriental Society.

The month of September 1847 found Dr. and Mrs. Wilson
on their way to India. Their route lay through the north of
France, Belgium, and the Rhine country, Switzerland, Italy,
and Malta, that he might report on the state of religion on the
Continent, and the duty of the Free Church, which supports
many preaching stations there, and aids the indigenous Reformed Churches of France, Italy, and Bohemia. In his letter
to the Rev. J. G. Lorimer, Convener of the committee on the
subject, he describes his meeting with Lassen :—

"In Rhenish Prussia my intercourse with different parties was entirely of a literary character. At Bonn I had the pleasure of seeing Professor Lassen, one of the greatest Orientalists of the Continent. At present he is engaged in the preparation of a truly great work on the History of India, which, I trust, will ere long become well known in our native country as well as in the distant East. It is entitled, *Indische Alterthumskunde*, von CHR. LASSEN. I was favoured with the sheets of the work, so far as it has been printed. After a topographical and ethnographical description of India, the author proceeds to investigate its ancient history. His acquaintance with its sacred language and antiquities gives him advantages, which he turns to a wonderful account. At the same place I met Mr. Erskine, the son-in-law of Sir James Mackintosh. He was one of the founders of our Bombay Asiatic Society, to which he contributed several most able papers on the Pársees and the Cave-temples of India. He has been devoting his attention of late to the Muhammadan History of India, as set forth in its original authorities. He introduced me to Mr. König, who has patronised oriental literature, perhaps more than any other individual of our day, by the publication of many works in the Sanskrit and other languages.'

To Dr. J. Buchanan he wrote :—

"At Cairo I purchased from the Karaim Jews a complete copy of the Hebrew Scriptures, neatly written on 1386 leaves of parchment. Though it is only three hundred and fifty-seven years old, it has peculiar interest as belonging to a recension of which few or no copies are in the hands of Europeans, and as having the text in many places arranged according to the Hebrew poetry. By the help of Mr. Lieder, the esteemed missionary, we were able speedily to equip ourselves for a journey through the land of Goshen, which we were able to accomplish in a very satisfactory manner. At the Tem el-Yehúd, near Thihin, we found undoubted and numerous tokens of an ancient site, and, if we mistake not, traces of the Onion built by Onias in imitation of the Temple of Jerusalem. We successfully explored the Tell el-Yehúd near Belhies, probably the site of the Vicus Judæorum of the Antouinian Itinerary. At the Ten el-Bastá, the Buhastis of the Greeks, and the Pí-Beseth (the first of these syllahles being the Egyptian article), as well as other places, we procured some valuable antiques which have an historical import. We visited a site corresponding with the Thon of the Antoninian Itinerary, and perhaps the Pí-Thom of the Israelites. We examined the site of Heroopolis, the Rameses of the Septuagint ; and we there disinhumed the large image of Rameses II., the Sesostris of the Egyptians. We found what is now generally admitted to be the land of Goshen most minutely accord with the intimations and exigencies of Holy Writ. We went to the Red Sea by a route seldom traversed ; and on its interesting shores we observed fresh proofs of the accuracy of the views which I have ventured to express in *The Lands of the Bible*, on the great question of the passage of the Israelites. We felt very thankful to the Father of mercies when we arrived at our desired haven.

"Our friend Dr. Miller took us on shore early on the morning after we cast anchor in the harbour. We met Mr. Mitchell and Mr. Henderson, and Dhunjeehhoy and Hormasdjee, and then the Abyssinian youth most kindly hastening to bid us welcome, Mr. Neshit, who has since joined us, being then absent from Bombay. Since our establishment in the mission-house we have had crowds of visitors, particularly of all tribes and classes of natives, by many of whom, former acquaintances, we have been received in the most affecting manner. Several of my controversial opponents have proffered their renewed friendship, which is very acceptable, alleging that they never could take offence at what I have written, as I ' uniformly avoided disagreeable personalities.' I have recommenced my usual Sabbath services, both predicatory and catechetical ; and two week-day lectures in English and Marathee, which have hitherto been remarkably well attended.   I am inspecting the educational operations of the mission with a view to the immediate resumption of my duties in that department.   You will ever pray that grace may be given to us all to make full proof of our ministry, incalculably solemn in all circumstances, but especially so in this great land of heathen darkness and death.

"Dhunjeebhoy has set out on an important tour with all juvenile ardour and Christian zeal and humility.   Gabru, one of the two devoted Abyssinian youths, accompanied him as an attendant and assistant.   Hormasdjee is preparing discourses with a view to his ordination, which we hope will soon take place, particularly as, of all the converts in the East, he has endured the greatest trials and suffered the greatest earthly losses in consequence of his embracement of the cause of Christ.   I feel it an unspeakable privilege to be restored to the fellowship of the dear converts."

" Welcome ! welcome again on the Indian shores ! " wrote one whom we may take as representative of all—the Rev. B. Schmidt, of the Church Missionary Society, who had long evangelised the Tamul country, and had returned to India to work among the tribes of the Neilgherry hills.   " I *almost* apprehended that you would find so much to do at home for the mission cause that you would not come out again into the encampment.   But a true Crusader cannot stay at home as long as one Turk is in the field !   Although born in different countries, wearing different uniforms, preaching Christ in different languages, in different provinces, yet we reach each other the right hand of fellowship—we are one in Christ ! " And as, when beginning his mission in Bombay, Dr. Wilson's first privilege was to announce, in the *Oriental Christian Spectator* for January 1830, the suppression of Suttee in what was then British India, so now, on resuming his editorial labours in January 1848, he published the notification, by the Governor-General and Commander-in-Chief Lord Hardinge, that proclamations had been issued by the Maharaja of Kashmere, the notorious Goolab Singh, and a majority of the principal feudatories, prohibiting widow-burning, infanticide, and slavery throughout their States.   " The Governor-General abstains on this occasion from prominently noticing those States in which these barbarous usages are still observed, as he confidently expects at no distant day to hear of the complete renunciation of them in every State in alliance with, or under the protection of, the Paramount Power of India."   That good work was completed a few years afterwards by his successor, the last of the East India Company's Governor-Generals, the Marquis of Dalhousie.

The famous " Political," George Clerk, whose very name had been a tower of strength on our north-west frontier all through the Cabul disasters and the first Sikh War, and at whose feet Sir Henry Lawrence had sat, was now at the close of his first term of office as Governor of Bombay. He laid the foundation-stone of the Colaba Church at its extreme south point, to commemorate our countrymen who had fallen victims to a policy against which many of them had protested, and, as the evangelical bishop of those days expressed it, "to acknowledge the hand of Almighty God, which was equally seen and felt in the victories bestowed. This monumental church will be conspicuously seen by every vessel entering our beautiful and commodious harbour, and our countrymen newly arrived, whether in a civil or a military capacity, will be reminded that although far removed from the land of their fathers, they are still in the land of the God of their fathers." And Dr. Wilson found his old colleagues and some new scholars in the Asiatic Society eagerly discussing those slabs sent to Bombay by Sir Henry Rawlinson, which had been dug up from the ruins of Nineveh. The Governor directed plaster castings to be made from them for his own collection ; and the work, the first of the kind in Bombay, was executed by Abyssinian boys rescued by the Indian Navy from the Arab slavers.

The death, at forty-eight, of his old acquaintance, Syajee Rao, the Gaikwar of Baroda, on the 28th December, drew from Dr. Wilson this public notice of him :—" Sagacity and suspicion were prominent traits in his character ; and it was in consequence of the latter that he sometimes became the dupe of designing men. In 1835, the principles of Christianity were pretty fully unfolded to him at his own request. He heard the communications which were made to him with respect, and stated his objections to some of the arguments advanced by the Brahmans of his Durbar against the Christian missionary."

CHAPTER XIV.

1848-1856.

A NEW PERIOD—TOUR IN SINDH—THE BOMBAY SCHOOL OF THE CATECHUMENS.

Empire of British India territorially completed—Lord Falkland—Satara and
Nagpore become British Districts—The Conquest of Sindh—Stung nearly
to death by Bees—The Sorrows of Missionaries—Non-Christian Teachers
in Mission Schools—Anglo-Indian Society about 1848—Sore sickness—
Missionary survey of Sindh—The Pool of the Crocodiles—Meeting with
Dr. Duff—Through Kutch and Kathiawar to Surat—Bombay Presbytery
to General Assembly on extending Foreign Missions—To Captain Eastwick
on Political and Educational Reform—Almost a Christian—A Gift of
Lionesses—On the Relation of the different Races of India to Christianity
—Bishop Dealtry—Another learned Parsee Inquirer—The Samaritans at
Nablus—Another Habeas Corpus Case—First Fruits from Sindh—Parsee
and Muhammadan Converts from the Government College—Renewed
Excitement and Government Inquiry—Lord Elphinstone—Government
learning the Principles of Toleration—The Goojaratee New Testament and
Native Scholarship—Dr. Wilson on Judson and the Karen Christians.

THE history of British India begins with the Marquis of
Dalhousie. Alike in conquest and in administration, the
work of Clive, Wellesley, and Bentinck, was a foundation—
was a prelude. That of Dalhousie was consolidation—was
completion. The second Sikh War gave the north-west its
natural frontier ; the most foolishly ambitious can never make
Cabul and Quetta, Balkh and Herat, Merv and Meshed, more
than outposts held by subsidised allies. The strategic and
commercial railways, the canals, the roads, the cheap postage,
the telegraph, the schools and universities of Dalhousie, gave
the empire a more secure defence than all the troops, by
withdrawing which prematurely against his protests, the
governments who fought the Crimean War occasioned the
Sepoy mutiny. The lapse from failure of natural heirs of
chaotic States, which we ourselves had created, like Satara
and Nagpore, not only removed centres of disaffection, but

proclaimed the good of the people to be the reason of our existence in India. It also left Lord Canning and Sir Henry Durand a clear space on which to write the new body of international law guaranteeing, by patent, permanence to every feudatory sovereign's house, on the sole conditions of loyalty to the empire and fair administration of their estates. With the last echo of the artillery cannonade of Guzerat on the 22d February 1849, and when Sher Singh and Chutter Singh gave up their swords to General Gilbert on the spot where Alexander the Great had once conquered, British India became what it now is, save only Pegu afterwards forced upon us.

Wellesley and Bentinck were united in the victories of war and of peace which Dalhousie won before he was forty. Henceforth, whether we look at the events of history or the lives of individuals who worked them out each in his own way, like John Wilson, we are in a new atmosphere. Winter is past ; the time of sowing, too, is here and there passing into the blossoming that betokens harvest. Let but the great baptism of blood in 1857 be over, and we shall see the bad as well as some of the good of the Company destroyed—obstruction giving way to rashness sometimes, but always to light ; tradition yielding to fickleness often, so that continuity is sacrificed, but never again choking progress. The Mutiny secured a new start at least, and that in the direction which the missionary, from Carey to Duff and Wilson, had never ceased to demand. In Bombay Sir George Clerk was too soon succeeded by Viscount Falkland, of whom the best that can be said is that he had a clever wife who made society bright, and that he kept the place warm for Lord Elphinstone in 1853. But Lord Falkland had as his principal adviser in council Sir J. P. Willoughby, whose minute on the Satara case, which Lord Dalhousie pronounced the text-book on the law of adoption, gives a mark to the administration.

On the defeat of the last of the Peshwas in 1817 we rescued the representative of their master Sivajee from captivity, and created the principality of Satara for the old man. On investing him Sir James Carnac warned him of the possibility of lapse. When, in spite of his treason, we acknowledged his successor, and that successor died childless, the very considerations which had recommended the creation of

the State justified its extinction as a failure. Apart from
his knowledge of the two Rajàs and the people, Dr. Wilson
had an interest in Satara, for it was during several years the
seat of a branch mission under Mr. Aitken.   Satara, however,
had less interest for him than the fate of Nagpore.   About
the same time Lord Hastings had restored it, and with the
same melancholy results in the misgovernment of the people,
in spite of the control of a Political Resident like Sir R.
Jenkins.   Aided by Sir W. Hill's endowment, Dr. Wilson had
sent out Mr. Hislop to the military station of Nagpore,
Kampthee, and he was afterwards joined by Mr. R. Hunter.
But the new missionaries soon found that toleration was not
recognised in the native State of Nagpore outside of the
British cantonment.   Dr. Wilson had successfully established,
or helped to set up, missions in other States, such as those of
Goojarat, Kathiawar, and Kutch, and was soon to do so in
Rajpootana.   But the imprisonment of a Brahman convert,
afterwards the Rev. Baba Pandurang, in 1848, showed that
in Nagpore the rights of conscience and civil liberty could be
disregarded, till the very existence of a mission became as
impossible as it still is in Russia.   When in 1853, the death
of the Raja after his persistent refusal to adopt an heir left
the fate of Nagpore to the decision of the Government of
India, the substitution of British for native rule, and ultimately of a vigorous Chief Commissioner for an incompetent
subordinate officer, gave the mission the same fair play
which the rest of British India had enjoyed since the Charter
of 1833.

During Dr. Wilson's absence from India the province of
Sindh had been added to the empire as a result of the
Afghan campaigns.   As if the policy of childish interference,
directed by military incapacity, had not at Cabul given a
sufficient blow to the moral prestige of our Government and
the fidelity of its sepoys, Sir Charles Napier was allowed by
Lord Ellenborough to repeat the criminal blunder in the
desert and the delta of the Indus.   Outram's protests were
as vain as the indignation of all whose opinion was worth consideration.   Nor was the conquest all.   No longer a foreign
country, Sindh ceased to be attractive to the sepoys who had
looked there for the batta or extra allowances allowed on
active service beyond the frontier.   First some Bengal and

then some Madras sepoy regiments mutinied because the allowances were refused, and then their immediate commander condoned the heinous offence. The experience of 1857 was anticipated on a scale sufficiently large to warn observers like Sir Henry Lawrence, and to lead Lord Dalhousie afterwards to suggest reforms. But the only effect at the time was, in 1844, to hand Sindh over to Bombay to be garrisoned by its army. It fell to Lord Dalhousie, so soon as he had personally received the submission of the Punjab, a few years after, to visit Sindh that he might provide for those administrative and engineering improvements which promise to make young Egypt one day more than rival old, although the Indus can never equal the Nile.

It was natural that John Wilson should not have been long at his old post in Bombay, without turning his eyes northwards to the new province, in the hope of taking possession of it for his Master. The policies of rulers might be evil or good—and on that question too no man could express a more weighty opinion, or one that these rulers themselves more desired to avail themselves of beforehand. But by whatever means a door was opened, he, or some one stirred up by him, must enter in. He was soon to be the first missionary who had delivered the divine message in Sindh. His companion was Dr. Duff, who, having been consulted whether he would succeed Dr. Chalmers in the New College, had agreed merely to go to Scotland in 1850 to advise regarding the needs of the India Mission. The two apostolic men met at Sehwan, on the Indus. Dr. Tweedie had meanwhile become convener of the Foreign Mission committee in Edinburgh.

STUNG NEARLY TO DEATH BY BEES.

"BOMBAY, 1st April 1848.

"MY DEAR MR. TWEEDIE—Mr. Henderson (he had resigned a Government professorship to join the Mission) and 1 have experienced a painful affliction—associated, however, with many striking mercies—which unfits us for the use of the pen. When we were engaged with a few friends, and some of the pupils, in making researches into the natural history and antiquities of the adjoining island of Salsette, we were attacked by an immense cloud of wild bees, which had received no sensible provocation from any of our party, and nearly stung to death. Mr. Henderson was the first who was attacked. He soon sank, on one of the jungle roads, in the hopeless attempt to guard himself from injury; and he had lain for about forty minutes in a state of almost total insensibility before he was found by our friends and any relief could be extended to him. It was on my joining him, from behind, when he first gave the alarm, that I came in contact with the thousands of infuriated insects. I sprang into a bush for shelter; but there I got no adequate covering. from their onset. In my attempt to free myself from agony and entanglement I immediately slid over a precipice, tearing both my clothes and body among the thorns in the rapid descent of about forty feet. From the number of bees which still encompassed me and multiplied upon me, and my inability to move from them, I had a pretty strong impression upon my mind that, unless God himself specially interposed in my behalf, all my wanderings and journeyings must then have been terminated, though by the humblest agency—the insects of the air. That interposition I experienced! I had kept my hold of a pillow, with which I had gone to Mr. Henderson; and tearing it open on the bushes, when I was unable to rise, I found within it, most unexpectedly, about a couple of square yards of blanket. It was to me, in the circumstances, like a sheet sent down from heaven to cover my head; and, partially protected by it, I lay till the bees left me. When, from the poison of the numerous stings which I had received, violent vomiting and other agitation came on, and my pulse failed and my heart fainted, a native, a Thákoor, one of the aboriginal sons of the forest, who had come up, pulled me into the shade, and made a noise which was heard by our friends, including Mrs. Wilson, who had set out in search of me after they had learned from Mr. Henderson that I had shared in the calamity, and who otherwise would probably never have sought for me in the locality in which I was lying. Among these friends was Dr. Burn, to whose treatment, under God, our resuscitation is in a great measure owing. We were conveyed to our tents, principally in native carts, and on Saturday we were brought to Bombay. Through the kindness of that heavenly Father to whose grace we owe our signal deliverance, we are both doing well, so much so, indeed, that we hope in a few days to be free from all pain, if not inconvenience, arising from this affliction. I have known instances of natives losing their lives by such an attack as we encountered; and our friends from India will explain to you the danger from which we have escaped, nay from which we have been delivered. 'They compassed me about like bees,' is one of the appropriate figures of the Psalmist. The wild bee of India, of a dark chocolate colour, and about an inch and an eighth in length, is of the same variety which I have seen in the Holy Land; and that illustration of the Psalmist has to us an intensity of meaning which we had never before realised. When I was a boy I used to think that John the Baptist's fare of locusts and wild honey was not of a very indifferent character; but I now see that at least it must have been somewhat difficult of acquisition.

"The affliction which I have now mentioned is that of the body; but those of the *soul*, often experienced by Christian missionaries in a heathen land, are still more grievous. One of this latter character I have likewise to bring to your notice. The fond and ardent hopes which we had been led to cherish in connection with the young Parsee whose baptism, in most interesting circumstances at Surat, I brought to your notice in my last letter, have been disappointed. That promising neophyte has, I am most sorry to mention, made shipwreck, for the present at least, of his Christian profession, and returned to the bosom of his caste. This he has done under powerful influences and temptations, arising from Parsees, Hindoos, and Muhammadans confederated together."

NON-CHRISTIAN TEACHERS IN MISSION-SCHOOLS.

"*12th September* 1848.

"My dear Dr. Leith—It is certainly to be expected that there should be a difference of opinion among Christians about many subjects connected with the economy of Christian missions. That to which you refer is one connected with which I myself at one time felt great difficulties, as is sufficiently obvious from the first report which I presented to the public ; and I can well sympathise with any mind still entertaining these difficulties. I do not think them insurmountable, however, when the real order and procedure of our schools is attended to. Our heathen teachers bind themselves to abstain from teaching heathenism in our schools ; and, from the closest inspection of them, I believe that they do so abstain. We use their services only in the mechanical processes of teaching. The Bible, and Bible truth found in our books, are self-defensory, and to a certain extent self-explanatory. Our whole hortative and explicative teaching of Christianity is by ourselves and native Christian assistants ; and it is so full and regular, both at the schools and mission-house, that, in regard to Christian knowledge, our pupils are on a par with the best instructed in our native land. Four of our Bombay teachers have been baptized since the commencement of the Mission, and an encouraging number of the pupils. The young Brahman last baptized by Mr. Mitchell of Poona told me the other day that he owes his first acquaintance with Christianity and good impressions to our vernacular schools in Bombay, and their collateral services."

TO MR. WEBB, C.S., ON THE STATE OF ANGLO-INDIAN SOCIETY.

"*December* 22, 1848.

"MY DEAR FRIEND—I am glad indeed to find that you reserve to yourself the liberty of again returning to India. Relative ties and wants at home will be modified in a few years. India appears to me more than ever to need the presence of faithful witnesses and labourers for Christ. There is a spirit of hostility to true holiness among the majority of our countrymen here, which threatens to have an outbreak. Of this I see many symptoms. The warlike spirit, generated and inflamed by our movements on the frontier since the invasion of Afghanistan, has much deteriorated public sentiment and feeling. Puseyism, by its doctrines of sacramental, ceremonial, and priestly grace, has, in the view of multitudes, obscured the sovereignty of the Father, and the saving work of both the Son and the Holy Spirit, and involved them in mere formalism, imparted to them a delusive peace, and destroyed their charity to those who confide in the Saviour. Plymouthism—the recoil from Puseyism —while gloriously setting forth the sacred duty of every Church availing itself of the gifts and graces of all its members for the edification of the body of Christ, runs counter to Christ's ordinance of a stated ministry, withdraws many from its benefits and blessings who are in great need of them, and sadly neglects the ignorant and perishing multitudes who are ' without.' The disturbances which have occurred, both in the West and East, have intimidated the Government, not resting on the principle that ' righteousness is the strength of a nation,' and made it far more tender and indulgent to heathenism, and inclined to give it support, than it was wont to be even a few years ago. The fruits of the ungodly system of the education of the natives so long pursued by Government, are beginning to be matured in the conceit, pride, infidelity, and insubordination of the more active part of the rising generation. In some Mission Institutions the evangelistic element is in danger of being subordinated to the literary and scientific. The heavenly seed is not so copiously sown at ' all waters ' as the promises and performances of God lead us to expect. Pre-millennarianism is more anxious to get old saints out of their graves than to get new ones."

"MAHABLESHWAR, *27th December* 1848.

"MY DEAR DR. TWEEDIE—As you may easily suppose, I have felt it to be a very heavy affliction to experience, so soon after my visit to Europe, the return of the very serious and dangerous complaint which forced me for a time to leave the shores of India, and when the wants of this great country and varied openings of Providence, and encouragements of Christian friends, seemed to unfold to me a wider and more important sphere of usefulness than ever. What has occurred, however, has not happened without the divine appointment, directing it, we cannot doubt, to most important ends, and leading me I trust more and more to value the unspeakable privilege and grace given me to preach among the Gentiles the unsearchable riches of Christ. It is a matter of gratitude to me, too, that during my illness I was divested entirely of those cares and anxieties by which I am sometimes harassed in the view of the state of our enterprise in this great land; and that I then saw and felt more clearly than ever the warrant of our hope and peace and joy in the accepted sacrifice of Christ, and the glory of that bliss which He has prepared for the humblest and most unworthy sinner who rests in the righteousness of God as thereby manifested.

> ' When languid nature in deep fever burning,
> Feels all her vital springs are parched and dry,
> From side to side still restless, ever turning,
> And scared by phantoms of delirium bye ;
> How sweet, but for a moment's space, to ponder,
> Surrounded by those bitter burning things,
> Where fresh cool life and gushing health flow yonder
> From pure celestial and immortal springs.' "

Accompanied by two of the converts, Bapu Mazda and Malharee, Dr. Wilson reached Kurachee on the first day of 1850, to begin a missionary survey of what he then described as "the Ultima Thule" of British conquest to the north-west of our eastern empire. Two years before one of the American Presbyterian Missionaries to the Protected Sikhs had sailed down the Indus. But Dr. Wilson could, with justice, write thus in his journal: "4th January 1850—I went down early in the morning with Bapu to the bazaar of the native town, and officiated as the first Protestant missionary who has opened his lips in Sindh. Many of the people understood Hindostanee and Goojaratee. We found a Muhammadan and a Brahman able to read the Sindhee in the Nagaree character, and we gave them a copy of the large portion of the Gospel of Matthew as translated by Major Stack. The demand for books in other languages was very considerable." While in the steamer, where the Rev. Mr. Cotes, the first assistant chaplain sent to Sindh, was his fellow-passenger, he had held discussions in Persian with a Muhammadan merchant from Khelat. Of the friends who competed for the pleasure of showing him hospitality Dr. Wilson selected Major Preedy,

the Collector or civil administrator, because he could thus
have access to all the official facts on the country and people,
which, with a map, he set himself at once to compile, as was
his custom. Even in far Kurachee, and at this early period
of British occupation, he found converts and students from the
Christian college of Dr. Duff holding the highest positions and
influencing all around them for good. When examining the
subscription English school near the native town, attended
chiefly by camp-followers and Sindhians proper, and expressing surprise at its efficiency, he discovered the fact thus recorded
in his journal:—"It is rather remarkable that the influence of
both Bengal and Bombay missions is apparent in this school.
Mr. Modoosoodun Seel, the teacher, a convert to Christianity
baptized by the Rev. Mr. Jennings,[1] at Cawnpore, was for
four years a pupil in our Calcutta Institution. One or two of
the books used in the school were composed by our Bombay
missionaries ; while one of the most promising pupils, baptized
by myself, is the grandson of the first Hindoo woman who
was admitted into the church under my ministry, and who,
lately under much trial and affliction, has maintained a consistent Christian profession. She was delighted to see me in
this distant part of the world." With the old chieftain the
Jam of the Jokees, who was on a visit to the new port from
his native hills, and with Naumahal, the most important
Hindoo resident, who had avenged on the Ameers their
forcible circumcision of his father by assisting the English
army at its first appearance on the Indus, Dr. Wilson had
interviews. The former remarked—

"Sir Charles Napier was 'altogether a just man.' If he sincerely holds
this opinion, it is not unlikely that his conscience has responded to this
straightforward epistle which was addressed to him by that distinguished
General on the 15th April 1843 : 'JAM.—You have received the money of
the British for taking charge of the dawk (post) ; you have betrayed your
trust, and stopped the dawks ; and you have also attacked the troops. All
this I forgive you, because the 'Amírs were here, and they were your old
masters. But the 'Amírs are now gone from Sindh for ever. They defied
the British power, and have paid the penalty of so doing. I, as the Governor
of Sindh, am now your immediate master. If you come in and make your
salám, and promise fidelity to the British Government, I will restore to you
your lands and your former privileges, and the superintendence of the dawks.
If you refuse, I will wait till the hot weather has gone past, and then I will

---

[1] This Chaplain baptized Maharaja Dhuleep Singh also, after his training
under the American Presbyterian Mission, and fell in the Delhi massacre of
1857.

carry fire aud sword into your territory, and drive you and all belonging to
you into the mountains ; and if I catch you I will bang you as a rebel. You
have now your choice ; choose. C. J. NAPIER.' Happily for the Jám he
chose submission. It will be a matter of no small difficulty to convey instruction and education to his scattered tribe. ''

In the lack of steamers on the Indus, then about to be supplied by Lord Dalhousie, Dr. Wilson followed a track to the
ancient town of Sehwan, on camels, through the hilly wilderness
which divides Sindh from Beloochistan. At every stage the
geology and natural history of the country were carefully
observed. His first march led him past the Muggur Pool, or
crocodile lake, which is still one of the sights near Kurachee.
It is formed from the water of some hot springs within 150
square yards—" the space of a barn-yard pond,"—and accommodated seventy-five monsters of all sizes, from the baby of
a cubit long, to the patriarch, Mor Saheb, who was eleven
feet long, and was marked with red lead, and worshipped by
the Hindoos. " They seemed quite tame, as they allowed us
to lay hold of their tails, and turned round at the call of the
fakeers, expecting a dainty meal on some unhappy goat. We
found the Mor Saheb asleep, but poked him up with our
sticks. He opened his jaws about a cubit wide, and then
hissed and blew like a pair of smith's bellows. He had lately
had a dreadful duel of it with a competitor for the champion-
ship, and as the battle was a drawn one and threatens to be
renewed, he is kept apart from his fellows. They are all of
the species 'crocodilus communis.' The illiterate keepers
form a community of Muhammadans more remarkable for the
practice of pleasantries than austerities. They both give and
get in marriage, and live quite comfortably with the gardens
and fields which the popular superstition has permitted them
to appropriate, and with the offerings presented at the shrine
of their founder, which they take care to keep in good repair."
They could not read the Injil in Arabic, so that a copy was
not put in their hands.

Having reached Sehwan, on the Indus, he thus wrote on
the 31st January :—" I translated the two first chapters of one
of my tracts into Persian in my tent at the river-side. On
the completion of this exercise I took hold of my telescope,
and sweeping with it the Indus before me to the north, I
discerned what I took to be Dr. Duff's boat gently dropping
down the river and approaching the spot where I was

encamped. My ardent hopes and wishes were realised; and we soon embraced one another with the heart as well as with the hand. The emotions of both of us, meeting at the very ends of the earth after an interval of ten years so eventful to our families, our missions, and our Church, and after multifarious labours and sufferings, and extended travel by land and by sea by both of us, were well nigh overpowering. The gracious and faithful providence of God to us both it was impossible for us to overlook."

By the battlefield of Meeanee and the fort of Haidarabad, where the Governor-General had just before received the homage of the chiefs and landholders of Sindh, the two missionaries went slowly on to Tatta, whence they struck across the delta to Kutch, through the salt desolation of its Runn, and surveyed the Irish mission stations. At Surat they took steamer to Bombay, whence the presbytery sent home to their Church, by Dr. Duff, a powerful appeal for more missionary agents. In his periodical letter to the home committee Dr. Wilson described the speech of Dr. Duff at the annual examination of the college as exciting a controversy on the subject of the purely secular and often antichristian education in the Government schools, which did not subside till it issued in reform in 1854. He also recorded the death of an old student, Madhavarao Moroji, who had won the admiration of the political officers by his influence as tutor of the chief of Jamkhundee. He lived and died like many since, a Christian in all but the name. Through not a few like him the missionary colleges in India are honeycombing Hindoo society.

TO CAPTAIN EASTWICK, C.B.

"BOMBAY, 17*th April* 1850.

"MY DEAR CAPTAIN EASTWICK—I have just returned from an interesting journey in Sindh, the scene of your important political labours in this distant East. I am of opinion that a good deal may yet be made of that province. The people seem to like the English government. This is some consolation to us amidst the misgivings which exist as to our treatment of the Ameers. I read your able speech in their favour, and the two blue books, on the banks of the Indus. I came to the conclusion that the Ameers at last intended to crush us if they could, but that some palliation could have been found in the fact that they were dogged and driven to desperation. I felt, too, that if Pottinger and yourself had been at your quondam posts, this would not have been the issue. I was sorry that I had not your brother's *Dry Leaves* with me during my wanderings and meanderings in Young Egypt. Your friend, the Rev. Mr. Cotes, was my fellow-passenger to Kurachee. He has a very vigorous and energetic mind, and is deeply interested in the improvement and the conversion of the natives, which I always reckon a good sign in a chaplain. I am just sending off a teacher for an English school which he wishes to establish at Haidarabad. I missed both Mr. Pringle and the Governor-General on their descent of the river by a few hours. By the bye, the Governor-General was very reserved in the Durbár he held at Haidarabad, which is rather to be regretted. He gave great satisfaction to the folks in Bombay.

"You will speedily have a great many questions raised in connection with this great country in the prospect of the discussion of the question of a new Charter to the Company. I hope that every question of importance will be settled without party feeling and prejudice. While I am of opinion that the government of the Company should undoubtedly continue, I think that it will be better to shape out a course of administration for it by Acts of Parliament, than to place it under arbitrary control. Encouragement should be given on a large scale to the employment in India of European capital and European enterprise, destitute of which, the country, which may be made so productive, will be involved in fiscal ruin. All the Government contributions to the temples, which are not chartered, I think should be devoted to the support of elementary education through every town and village of the country ; and of education not wholly paid for by Government, but partly supported by the people in private Institutions, provision being made only for the teaching of secular knowledge ; while all should be at liberty, on their own responsibility, to supplement that education by religious instruction as they may please."

In this letter we find one of the too few examples in his correspondence of that political insight as well as information, and those broad economic views regarding European enterprise as well as the prosperity of the natives, with which, in conversation, Dr. Wilson used to delight his friends. These questions, too, no less than his scholarly and scientific researches, he subordinated to the absorbing aims of the Christian missionary and the exacting work of the practical philanthropist. In all respects his programme of reform was soon carried out, save in the disendowment of idol shrines and mosques, but the property rights of these alone are now protected only by the civil courts. The mal-administration of the priestly guardians side by side with the growth of intelligence and Christianity among the people, may yet result in the voluntary application to education of the vast temple lands which cannot be squandered.

The continued success of the mission, and the address on the Christian, as opposed to the purely secular, education of native youth, raised a storm in two quarters. The local press and certain Professors of the Government College waged a bitter controversial warfare against missionaries, urging that these should have nothing to do with education, the effects of

HIS SCHOOL OF THE CATECHUMENS. 251

the positive moral and spiritual elements of which they did not relish. And communities like the Parsees, still resenting the aggressiveness of truth so as to confine their youth to the Government schools, began to find that even there truth pursued the conscience, and would not leave it alone till many became almost, and some had the courage to profess themselves openly altogether, Christians. It was about this time that the fermenting process was seen to work most evidently, as the first generation of educated youth went forth from the Mission college, on the one hand ; and on the other, the persistent discussions, translations of Scripture and other publications, preachings, and tours, began to tell on the varied native communities, already affected by the numerous and often nameless influences of growing western civilisation. Among the educated cases were not unfrequent like that of Victorinus, as described by Simplicianus, the spiritual father of Ambrose, to Augustine. From the unlearned in Bombay, and all the region around the Indian Ocean, of which it is the commercial centre, a small but steady stream of inquirers flowed in to what had become no less a school of the catechumens, spiritually and intellectually, than the famous Didaskaleion Catechumenorum of Pantænus (the first historical missionary to India), Clement and Origen at Alexandria. Nor does the parallel fail on the female side. For just as that Christian institute made the Egyptian Serapeum the last fortress of decaying polytheism, so the Bombay college stirred up the purely Hindoo and Parsee communities to rival efforts in education. Such passages as this are not infrequent in Dr. Wilson's missionary correspondence : When, on 10th May 1850, appealing to his home committee for more liberality, and announcing that Mrs. Wilson had been compelled to add two more female schools to the Ambrolie establishment, he adds :—

"The students of the Elphinstone College have been setting up some schools of their own from which all Christianity is excluded, and they have sought to fill them from our schools by prejudicing the minds of their parents. I have got hold of one of their circulars, with which I could easily expose their system ; but I think it better to allow them to work it to death themselves. Dádobá Pandurang (the president of their society, and superintendent of Government vernacular schools on a salary of Rs. 300 per mensem) called on us the other evening and offered his own daughter, and those of some of his friends, to Mrs. Wilson as pupils, and they now come regularly under the charge of a peon. When Mrs. Wilson congratulated him on having already taught his wife and daughter to read, he said, 'This is all the fruit of what I

myself learned in Ambrolie many years ago.' The knitting and sewing here
are great recommendations to him. He abhors Hinduism and respects Christianity. You must remember him. His companion, Náná Náráyan, is now
English translator to the Gaikwar, on a salary of Rs. 175 a month."

DR. WILSON TO HIS PARENTS.

"*25th July* 1850.—I lately heard from my two young Abyssinian friends,
indeed, I may say, 'sons in the Gospel.' They have given to me the two African lionesses presented to them by the king of their country. These are objects
of great curiosity to the natives of Bombay, hundreds of whom come to see
them in my 'compound.' I find it, however, very expensive to maintain them,
as they devour a goat at a meal. I have been offered a thousand rupees for
them, and I shall soon part with them, devoting the proceeds to the enlightenment of Abyssinia. I must not forget to tell the children with you that they
are very tame. They followed Gabru and Maricha for several days' journey
like dogs. When they came to a bush, when they were tired, they used to get
into it and rest till they were thumped up with clubs to proceed on the march.
Their growl is terrible. I have two other curious animals beside them—a
squirrel about the size of a cat, with a tail like a sweep's brush; and a pan-
golin, or ant-eater, with horny scales lying on its back like a covering of tiles
on a house. I took home a stuffed specimen of the last-mentioned animal,
which some of you may remember to have seen. The natives of this country
call it the 'tiled cat.' These tiles prevent it being stung to death by bees, or
bitten by the ants, on which it lives."

RELATION OF THE DIFFERENT RACES IN INDIA TO CHRISTIANITY.

"I must make a general remark, not unworthy of the attention of the
friends of missions at home. The first races who entered India were undoubtedly from Turania, or the eastern Scythia. They are principally represented at present by the different nations and tribes in India located to the
south of the river Krishna, and speaking the Canarese, Tooloo, Telugoo,
Malayálam, and Támul languages, which have still a great affinity with the
Tartar dialects. The distinctive peculiarity of the religion of these races is
the worship of ghosts and demons whom they seek to conciliate by offerings of
blood. The races which, in the second instance, entered India were from
Ariana, the eastern part of Irán, or Persia, probably the original seat of the
Indo-Teutonic family of nations. They are located in India to the north of
the Krishna; and their languages are all derivatives from the Sanskrit, which
is cognate with the Persian, Gothic, Pelasgic, Greek, Latin, and many other
European languages. Of these last-mentioned races, in their eastern disper-
sions, the 'prayer-bearers,' or 'Brahmans,' by degrees became the hereditary
priests. At first their worship, as developed in the Vedas, was directed to the
personified agents and elements of nature. Afterwards it assumed the monstrous mythological and sublimated spiritual form, which is developed in the
Epics, Law-books, and Puránas. The Aryan tribes in conquering India, urged
by the Brahmans, made war against the Turanian demon-worship, but not
always with complete success. The mountain and forest aboriginal tribes are
still, as far as Brahmanism is concerned, sturdy nonconformists. In many
districts, as in Canara, referred to by Shamráo, Brahmanism has been compelled to make a compromise, and now fattens on the abundant offerings made
to the devils. It is among the Turanian races, and the devil-worshippers, as
in Tinnevelly and other places in the south of India, which have no organised

priesthood and bewitching literature, that the converts to Christianity are most numerous. The day of their merciful visitation seems to be at hand. That of the Brahmanical Aryan tribes, with all their pride of caste and systematic creed, seems to be more distant. No equitable comparison of the results of Christian Missions in India can be made with the forgetfulness of this fact."

MRS. WILSON ON BISHOP DEALTRY.

"AMBROLIE, 16*th November* 1850.

"The two lions at present here are the Nepaulese ambassador and suite (Jung Bahadoor), and the Bishop of Madras with his wife. He is Dr. Dealtry, who was for a long time at Calcutta as Archdeacon. We have met them several times. He is an excellent, evangelical, liberal-minded man, who abhors Puseyism, and takes every opportunity of lifting up his testimony against the prevailing errors of the present times. I hope his visit to Bombay may do good, as nearly all the chaplains are tinged, more or less, with High Church views and feelings. The Bishop and his party breakfasted with us yesterday morning, along with a few other friends. He kindly examined some of the classes of our Institution, and expressed himself as highly pleased with all he heard and saw. We had also a good many of the girls of our schools collected, about one hundred and forty, who were examined, and the Bishop and Mrs. Dealtry were both delighted with them, and seemed quite surprised to see the intelligent countenances of the little things, and to hear the ready manner in which they replied to the questions put to them. Indeed it was not a little gratifying to hear the Bishop say he had seen nothing like it in India, and it was a scene he could never forget. He never says what he does not feel, and he is not afraid to speak out the truth. He is so much opposed to the Government system of education in India (I mean the exclusion of Bible teaching from its seminaries), that he has never visited one of their schools, though again and again requested to do so. We have been asked to accompany the Bishop and a few other friends to Elephanta this afternoon. It will be a smaller and in some respects a more congenial party than on the occasion of our last visit to the caves."

BISHOP DEALTRY TO DR. WILSON.

"BOMBAY, 25*th November* 1850.

"MY DEAR FRIEND—I cannot leave this island without offering our warmest thanks to you and Mrs. Wilson for your Christian kindness and attention to us. We can never forget it, I assure you ; and both Mrs. Dealtry and myself have formed a most sincere Christian attachment to you, and we shall carry such feelings with us until we trust we may meet in the everlasting kingdom of our Heavenly Father. I hope, however, that we may meet again on earth. If you should ever come to Madras you must be our guests, please ; and we shall rejoice to make your stay there as happy, or at least attempt it, as you have made ours here. God bless you, and pour the graces of His grace upon your Mission, and make you the honoured instruments of gathering many precious wandering souls into His fold, and may your crown at last be resplendent with such.—In haste, but ever yours with Christian love,
"T. MADRAS."

This period in the history of the mission was fruitful in such cases, as well as in others. Now a father, who thirteen years before had heard Dr. Wilson at Ajunta, seeks him out at Bombay, unable longer to rest in Hindooism, and returns

to bring not only his family of eight, but a village friend, into
the one fold. Again, his last tour bears fruit at the same
time as this his second, in the baptism of Hadjee, a young
Beloochee, who had been drawn by his words in Sindh, and
becomes "the first fruit of Sindh unto Christ." By the hands
of Mr. Cust he receives an epistle in Old Testament Hebrew
from Amram bin Saleemah, the chief priest of the Nablus
Samaritans, and replies in like style, with none the less ardour
that Dr. M'Gown had reported from Jerusalem the "interesting fact that some of them had lately applied to the Bishop
for admission into the Christian or rather Protestant Church;
that they were first led to inquire after the truth by Dr.
Wilson's instructions when he visited them, and since then
by a Mr. Williams. The Bishop had sent them the Scriptures, and set up schools among them, and hoped soon to do
more to find out how far they really were grounded in the
truth. Dr. M'Gown spoke of Dr. Wilson with the greatest
enthusiasm." This leads Dr. Wilson to write to Dr. Graham,
from whom Sir Henry Havelock had brought him a letter,
projecting a joint tour in Syria to establish a mission in the
Lebanon, such as the Free Church subsequently adopted.
Again, the drawing of the educated native mind towards
Christianity provokes another "habeas corpus" case in the
Supreme Court, in which "Sir Erskine Perry, who had handed
over Shripat Sheshadri to the tender mercies of the intolerant
heathen," is compelled to allow the girl Sai "to go where she
pleases," because her Hindoo father preferred the mission.
The vernacular schools alone are this time temporarily affected
by the native excitement, while nine persons join themselves
to the class of catechumens, and "none of them are idlers."
Nor is the excitement lessened when a Parsee youth of the
wealthiest family, and himself possessor of Rs. 300,000, seeks
spiritual instruction.

So Dr. Wilson year by year followed the greatest of missionaries, Paul, in turning the world upside down. In 1853
the agencies of his Church in Western India embraced
2159 students and pupils, of whom there were 1413 in
Bombay, 546 in Poona, and 200 in Satara. Of the whole
number one-fourth were females; and one-fourth received the
higher education through English as well as the vernaculars.
At this time he prepared a course of lectures for his students

at Bombay, and for the English society both there and at
Mahableshwar, on "The Apostle Paul in Greece ; or Christianity in contact with the Hellenic faith and manners and
the Roman magistracy, compared with Christianity in contact
with the Hindoo faith and manners and the British magistracy." Of the Native Church, consisting of 126 adults, of
whom 55 were communicants and 42 baptized adherents, he
could write that it was in a prosperous spiritual state. In
1855 the value of the college as an evangelising no less than
a pioneering agency, showed itself in the baptism of the best
student, Gunputrao Rhogonath, of the respectable Parbhoo
caste, and of Ismail Ibraim, the first Bohora who had
embraced Christianity in India.

Mrs. Colin Mackenzie, whose journal, *The Camp, the Mission, and the Zenana,* had been received in Europe as revealing
India more fully than any book since Heber's, had sketched
and published lithographs of the converts in Bombay and
Calcutta. Of one of the portraits Dr. Wilson wrote :—" The
serene piety and devotion of Yohan Prem are well brought out
in the likeness. He lives on the word of God and prayer, and
is mighty in the Scriptures. By many of the natives he is
received as a sort of curiosity ; and he finds access to circles
into which others cannot penetrate. He carries the testimony
of Jesus with him wherever he goes, and he brings many
parties to the mission-house for religious converse." Narayan
Sheshadri was soon after ordained, and Dhunjeebhoy, who had
been evangelising in Goojarat among his countrymen, baptized
his first converts from the aboriginal Dheds. In 1854 Dr.
Wilson thus reported the conversion of Baba Pudmanjee, the
ablest Hindoo student of the college : " Though but a young
lad, he is already a Marathee authority of distinction. I know
no native so able to wield the press to advantage. His
modesty is as remarkable as his ability. We have looked, and
laboured and prayed for his conversion for years."

Not till 1855, twelve years after they had built the first
college only to hand it over to others before entering it, were
Dr. Wilson and his colleagues able to take possession of the
present college buildings, erected to accommodate eight hundred students and pupils, at a cost of £6800. But the joy of
the year 1855 was sadly dimmed by the sudden removal by
cholera, on the 26th July, of Robert Nesbit, a few months

after his union to a lady who has ever since given her life to
female education. The most perfect speaker of Marathee, so
that even Brahmans could not detect a foreign accent, with
an uprightness of judgment which the natives regarded as
that of a god, and with a loving fascination which drew all of
every sect and class to his feet, Robert Nesbit, in a few hours
after he closed his last class at the college, was removed by
death. The Rev. Adam White, who was in after years to
meet a like fate in the same sort of self-sacrifice, and then
Mr. W. Gardner, soon arrived from Scotland to take his place.
But who could restore the unique individuality and the
experience which, from St. Andrews University, and youthful
intercourse with John Wilson on the Border hills, grew into
ripeness in the southern Konkan, at the Cape of Good Hope,
and amid the upheaving of Bombay for nigh thirty years?

The East India Company's Government, as well as purely
English judges like Sir Erskine Perry, were to make another
advance in the understanding and practice of toleration. Sir
Erskine had in the last "habeas corpus" case decided that
fourteen was the age of discretion in the case of a woman,
while Shripat Sheshadri had been sent back to Brahmanism
against his will because he was not sixteen. The Company's
Government in every province of India had steadily de-
christianised the English professors, forbidding them, as well
as native teachers, to explain passages in English literature
referring to Christianity. Thus, it was thought, the leaven of
Christianity would be effectually kept out of the State colleges
and schools, while there was no official recognition by grants
in aid of even the secular education in the missionary and
independent colleges, although it was to men like Wilson and
Duff that, as we have seen, the Company owed its educational
stimulus, example, and systems.

In 1854 Lord Elphinstone had become Governor of Bombay after a successful experience of educational reform in
Madras. It was doubtless due to his personal influence that
the Bombay Government in 1856 decided that its teachers
did not violate duty when they gave simple explanations of
references in English text-books to Christianity. Four Parsee
students of the Elphinstone College, in spite of prison bars,
which could not shut out the light, astounded Dr. Wilson and
Mr. White by addressing a letter to them which thus began :—

"We are fully convinced by the grace of God that Parseeism is a *false* religion ; and it consists of VAGUE and EXTRAVAGANT principles. It is the INVENTION of man, not the REVELATION of God. We have found out, after inquiring nearly two or three years after the TRUE RELIGION, that every comfort, joy, hope, success, and every good thing in this world as well as in the world to come, are concentrated in the Lord Jesus. We have now the greatest pleasure to inform you that, as we are fully convinced of the TRUTH of CHRISTIANITY, we wish to be baptized, and to be admitted into the visible Church of Christ. . . . Nothing has led us to join the Christian Church but the pure hope and desire of the salvation of our souls."

Some days after, the youths, all married, appeared at the mission-house, and a legal agent duly noted the circumstances and their ages—from seventeen years and eight months to nineteen years and nine months. A rush of Parsees was made to the spot. For three days the families of the young men, who had free access to them, plied them with the arguments of the devout Zoroastrian, the sober deist, and the arrogant scoffer, in vain. At last the representation that their mothers were dying, and the express pledge that they should have religious liberty at their homes and be allowed to attend the mission for instruction, prevailed at first with Darasha, and a day after with Bhicajee and Nussurwanjee. Bairamjee Kersajee alone remained faithful, and was in due time baptized, but long required the protection of the law on his way to and from the college. The Hindoos and Muhammadans admitted the right of young men of that age to please themselves. The Parsees began to denounce the Government college in this case, as their fathers had attacked the officiating Governor in that of Dhunjeebhoy. They vilified, especially, one of their own tribe as a Christianiser, Professor Ardaseer Framjee. A formal inquiry by Government resulted in justifying him, and in the concession of liberty to the educational service so far as to explain Milton, for instance, to the pupils, hitherto religiously doubtful, or passages of Shakspere ! The result was seen in the next baptisms, those of another Parsee student of the Elphinstone College, Shapoorjee Eduljee, and a Muhammadan class-fellow, Syud Hussan Medinyeh. About the same time a Sikh, from the Punjab, and a Muhammadan moonshee, were admitted to the Church. Syud Hussan's family concealed his conversion from their co-religionists as long as they could, but then openly set their ablest Moulvies to argue with him.

All through this period Dr. Wilson carried on his trans-

lation work, aided by his scholarly converts. He, Dhunjeebhoy, and Hormasdjee, brought out a revision of the Messrs.
Fyvie's translation of the Goojaratee New Testament. " It
contains," he wrote, "such improvements as the progress of
Oriental translation, and the application to it, for the first
time so far as we are aware, of competent native Indian
Christian criticism, have enabled us to effect." As his contribution to the public collection of the British and Foreign
Bible Society, Dr. Wilson sent a MS. copy of the Four Gospels
in Arabic, "evidently prepared for the use of the Eastern
Churches. This valuable document I procured in rather
remarkable circumstances. Some time ago I observed it in
the library of one of the principal fire temples of Bombay, and
on my offering ten pounds for it, the priests allowed me to
have it on condition of my permitting them to make and keep
a copy of it—a proposal on their part in which I immediately
concurred."

To Miss Douglas, who had sent him the *Life of Judson* and
Stier's *Reden Jesu*, he replied—" I am greatly obliged to you
for the *Life of Judson*, which I have found most interesting
in the illustration of his high Christian character and noble
endeavours for the propagation of the truth. I rather wonder
at the rash admissions into the Christian Church by the
Baptist brethren at Burma. This greatly strikes the attention
of a Presbyterian missionary, who knows the ignorance of the
Eastern mind, and its proneness in certain circumstances to
act from impetus, without real and abiding principle, without
the regeneration of the Holy Spirit. Though the apostles
sometimes baptized on sudden professions, their disciples were
tested by providence in an unequivocal manner."

CHAPTER XV.

LITERARY ACTIVITY—THE ROCK-CUT TEMPLES.

1848-1862.

A Missionary-Scholar's Wife—The Rock-cut Temples and Monasteries—Early attempts at an Archæological Survey of India—Dr. Wilson's two Memoirs on the subject—President of the Cave-Temple Commission—Lord Canning's Minute—Necessity of a Corpus Inscriptionum—Colonel Meadows Taylor and Sir Walter Elliot — The first Railway Train — The Peninsular and Oriental Steamers — Declines to be Oriental Translator to Government — "Only a Missionary"—Writes History of Infanticide — New Edition of Marathee Dictionary — Researches into Caste — Most Popular Book on Ancient India—Lectures.

DR. and Mrs. Wilson had, on their return to India, just completed the reorganisation of the Mission in its college and schools, and on its female side at the beginning of 1848, when both threw themselves into the allied work of oriental research. To a correspondent he wrote in May 1849 :—" Mrs. Wilson has enjoyed remarkably good health in India. She has now made great progress in the Marathee language. She has a wide field for usefulness here, as we have upwards of five hundred girls in our native female schools. She is busy translating a paper on the Puranas from the French of Burnouf, which appeared in the *Oriental Christian Spectator.*" This extract from one of Mrs. Wilson's letters further illustrates the duties of a true missionary's wife :—" My labours in the way of teaching are increasing, and I find I require to spend about four hours each day with the girls, that is from twelve to four o'clock, besides previously preparing their work ; in addition to which we have the morning Marathee service for reading and examination of old and young, about ten, and at eleven my moonshee comes for an hour to teach me Hindostanee. I find it easier than Marathee, but I must not expect to get on rapidly, as I have scarcely a moment for private study. I have a class who are learning English, composed of some of our female teachers and some of our day-scholars. I have also the girls of a superior class of natives, who come to me for instruction in sewing and English, and we read the Scriptures in Marathee, and they learn the gospel catechism. They are knitting little boots for their baby brothers, and are much pleased with some pieces of canvas work they have accomplished, of simple patterns. Some of the girls in my school are now very good sewers, and can knit stockings nicely."

To the same correspondent Dr. Wilson announced—" I have just drawn up, what I suppose will ere long be printed, *A Memoir on the Cave-Temples and Monasteries, and other Buddhist, Brahmanical, and Jaina Remains of Western India.* This document I have prepared in connection with the Asiatic Society and the Government." This introduces us to what proved to be intellectually the most fruitful period of his career, from 1848 to 1862. " During my professional journeyings throughout this great country," he wrote in the last published words from his pen, " I have often been brought in contact with its more remarkable antiquarian wonders, which, in a considerable number of instances, I have been among the first to observe and describe, though sometimes with unsatisfied curiosity as well as with qualified information." This is a modest statement, not less of what he was the first to do than of the service which he rendered to Government and the public by collecting all the available facts on the subject in 1848, and by showing the way to such a scientific and complete survey as that which, ever since the Mutiny operations ceased, has been going on.

Such marvels as the fifty large groups of rock-cut temples, monasteries, and cisterns, excavated in the Western Ghauts by Buddhists, Brahmans, and Jains, successively, during the fifteen centuries from Asoka to the inscription of Elora in A.D. 1234, had excited the wonder and the speculations of later Hindoos, the superstitious Portuguese, and the early English travellers. The people saw in them the work of their mythical heroes, the Pandavas ; while the Brahmans pronounced the *dhagob*, or relic-receptacle of their Buddhist foes, to be the filthy *linga*, and the cenobite's rocky chamber to be the abode of the outcast Dhed. The Portuguese his-

torian De Couto magnified the hundred cells and passages of
the hill of Kanha in Salsette into thousands of caverns, reaching as far as the mainland at Cambay, through which a priest
led an expedition for seven days without reaching the end!
Faber, once thought learned, romanced over the *trimurti* of
Elephanta as the cavern of Noah, his three sons and allegorical
consort, reasoning that five heads are equal to three because
two could be imagined. Mr. Henry Salt, the Lichfield artist
who accompanied Lord Valentia in his travels, and was sent
as an envoy to the ruler of Abyssinia, was the first to describe
the Salsette excavations fairly in 1806. But it was not till
Erskine, the "philosophic" son-in-law of Sir James Mackintosh, wrote his *Account of the Cave-Temple of Elephanta* in
1813, that justice was done to the subject, although Niebuhr
had preceded him and had reproached the English for
neglecting works far greater than the Pyramids. The Danish
traveller pronounced the investigation of such antiquities an
undertaking worthy of the patronage of a prince or a nation.
The journals of his tours show how early, and how almost
year by year, Dr. Wilson devoted his little leisure to the
scholarly study not only of the caves but of the inscriptions
which give them a historical as well as architectural value.
Nor was he alone in this. Commercial enterprise had early
sent to Bengal the Ayrshire youth, James Fergusson, who,
after a training in the Edinburgh High School, and ten years'
experience of enterprise and travel among the people of India,
published his *Illustrations of the Rock-Cut Temples* in 1845, and
has ever since been the principal authority on this and allied
subjects.
     When in London, where his knowledge of the character
of the cave and other alphabets enabled him to decipher
certain papers in a concealed Indian hand, which were
essential to adjusting a decision passed by the Admiralty
Court at the Cape, and which had long lain uninterpreted,
Dr. Wilson had pressed his old project of a *Corpus Inscriptionum* in connection with a systematic study of the excavations. Mr. Fergusson was not less zealous, and he was able
to be more persistent. The result seems to have been that
the Royal Asiatic Society in 1844 moved the Court of
Directors to order preliminary arrangements to be made for
conducting antiquarian researches in India, as the phraseology

went. In 1847 the Court finally approved of the detailed
suggestions—"for examining, delineating, and recording some
of the chief antiquities"—sent home by Lord Hardinge, the
Governor-General. In the rest of India very little was done
in those days of Sikh wars, beyond the publication of some
papers by Majors Kittoe and Cunningham, and the enriching
of the old India House in Leadenhall Street with some
antiquities and drawings. But in Western and Central India
Dr. Wilson was ready. The Bombay Government called the
local Asiatic Society to its aid. On the 15th April 1848 it
recommended that "authentic information as to the number
and situation of all the monuments and cave-temples of
antiquity in the territories should be obtained;" it sketched a
plan of operations and urged immediate action. What became known as the Cave-Temple Commission for the next
ten years was accordingly appointed by Government, consisting of Dr. Wilson, president; Dr. Stevenson; Mr. C. J.
Erskine, of the Civil Service; Captain Lynch, of the Indian
Navy; Mr. Harkness, of the Elphinstone College; Venaik
Gungadhur Shastree; and Dr. Carter, secretary of the Society.
Acting throughout with the authorities, and reporting also to
the Society, they engaged Mr. Fallon as artist; Lieutenant
Brett to copy inscriptions, and, at a later period, Captain
Briggs to take photographs; and Vishnoo Shastree, the pundit
of scholars like Mr. Law and Mr. Wathen, of the Supreme Court
translator Mr. Murphy, and of Dr. Wilson himself, to aid in
the translation of the inscriptions. This pioneering work was
arrested by the Mutiny, and soon after a new race of critics,
in ignorance of the past, anonymously attacked the Commission, or rather its native assistant, the Shastree. In the ten
years of its active existence, its whole expenditure did not
much exceed £2350, represented by the paintings, measure-
ments, casts, clearing out of caves, transcripts, and translations. For thirteen years the Commission, and Dr. Wilson
above all his colleagues, gave the work their gratuitous and
zealous labours; and not only they, but coadjutors like Sir
Bartle Frere, Sir Walter Elliot of Madras, Colonel Meadows
Taylor, Mr. Orlebar, and Dr. West, C.E. But to Dr. Wilson
alone is it due that the enlightened orders of Lord Hardinge
and the Directors bore fruit at all. In truth, from the first,
in north-eastern and southern, as well as in western India, a

scholar like the honorary president of the Asiatic Society, or
an architectural authority like Mr. Fergusson, should have
been set apart for the sole duty, with a staff of skilled
assistants, instead of a beggarly expenditure at the rate of
£200 a year.

Hence it became necessary, the moment the state of the
country after 1857 allowed of action, to renew the enterprise,
taught by the experience of the past. When, towards the
end of 1861, engaged at Allahabad in completing his reorganisation of the North-Western government, Lord Canning
resolved to appoint Colonel A. Cunningham Director of the
Archæological Survey of India. From the young Duke of
Wellington's time, at the beginning of the century, the East
India Company had liberally carried out trigonometrical as
well as topographical and revenue surveys of the peninsula.
On the basis of this, now approaching completion, Lord Dalhousie had created a Geological Survey in 1856. And Lord
Canning added to the good work by thus rescuing for all
time the fast perishing memorials which form the only history
of India before the time of our own battle of Hastings, outside of the vague hints of philology and of a literature that
defies historical criticism. The Archæological Survey has
since been extended to Bombay, where it is following up the
investigations of Dr. Wilson and Mr. Fergusson on a uniform
scale, and with the best results.

Dr. Wilson's Memoir on the Cave-Temples and Monasteries,
forming some seventy pages of Volume III. of the *Journal of
the Bombay Asiatic Society,* was circulated by the Government
to all the district and political officers in and around the
province, including great States like the Nizam's country.
These were directed to afford the Commission all the information and assistance in their power in the prosecution of
researches. The result was the publication by Dr. Wilson of
a second Memoir in 1852, recording the new discoveries, for
which Government had offered pecuniary rewards also, and
embodying the results of the Commission's work on the larger
caves like Elephanta. The Memoir had set many observers
to work, with results of the most striking interest, such as
those reported by Colonel Meadows Taylor from the Nizam's
principality of Shorapoor, and by Sir Walter Elliot from
Southern India.

Henceforth, year after year, no new Governor-General, Governor, or Member of Council, landed at Bombay, and no traveller from Europe or America passed through it, without seeking the guidance of Dr. Wilson on a visit to one of the neighbouring groups of excavations. In velvet skull-cap and with long wand, the enthusiastic scholar, with the air of an old knight, would lead his friends through the caves, pouring forth his stores of knowledge with unflagging courtesy, and charming all by the rare combination of goodness and grace, historical and oriental lore, poetic quotation and scientific references, genial remark and childlike humour, till visitors, like the accomplished Lady Canning, declared they had never met such a man. Nor would he allow his guests—for he too often provided the luncheon—to go unprepared by study. He had written a lecture on the subject for the Bombay public, to whom, at the request of the Mechanics' Institute, he delivered it in the Town Hall. By the year 1864, when the present writer for the first time visited Bombay, the manuscript was well worn, and he solicited permission to publish it in the *Calcutta Review*. All were expected, and, as a rule were glad, to master the contents of this popular treatise, of which it was Dr. Wilson's last literary work to prepare a somewhat enlarged edition for the use of the Prince of Wales.

Very different from the debased art of the Brahmanical caves of Elephanta are the excavations at Karla, on the crest of the Western Ghauts, a few miles from Khandalla, near the head of the Bhore Ghaut, where Dr. Wilson heard Sir John Malcolm boast that he had made the first road, and saw not very many years after the magnificent works by which the present railway has ascended the heights on its way to Madras. Standing there, looking down on rich Bombay and round on the plains which stretch away to the Dekhan till they dip into the Bay of Bengal, the traveller, as he recalls the glories of Asoka's reign, feels that in these two thousand years Brahmanism and Muhammadanism have together denied to Southern Asia the splendour and the happiness which Buddhism then vainly promised, and Christianity now renders possible.

TO MR. BUCHAN OF KELLOE.

" BOMBAY, 12*th September* 1853.—During the past year the railway system has been introduced into India. It is certainly calculated to promote the interests of civilisation, but its desecration of the Sabbath is a sad drawback. We are anxious about the improvement of the steam navigation to Bombay, as various disasters have occurred in consequence of bad arrangements, and this monsoon a whole mail was lost on board a pilgrim ship, which went down with the loss of 186 souls. We have had a public meeting on the subject called by the Sheriff, and from the humane aspect of the subject I felt constrained to yield to the request of our merchants that I should take a part in the proceedings. We petition the Lords of the Treasury and the Directors of the East India Company."

Apart from the humane aspect of the question Dr. Wilson was in his right place as a leader in such a meeting, and no similar assembly for discussing questions involving the moral and material good of the people of India or the prosperity of Bombay was held without him. It was in 1773 that a Mr. Holford had navigated the first English ship successfully from its harbour up the Red Sea to Suez. Niebuhr then wrote, "The passage has been found so short and convenient that the regency of Bombay now send their couriers by the way of Suez to England." Not till 1830 did Lord William Bentinck succeed in despatching the small Government steamer, the "Hugh Lindsay," from Bombay to Suez, after the failure of rewards to quicken the Cape voyage and open up the Euphrates route. But even that spent a month during March and April on a voyage which is now done regularly in twelve days, and will soon be accomplished in nine or ten.[1] In 1843 the Peninsular and Oriental Company ran its first steamer from Suez to Calcutta. The development of railway communication in India was more rapid, thanks to Lord Dalhousie, who had been paramount at the Board of Trade during the mania of 1848. What Lord Ellenborough had pronounced "moonshine" in 1843, when Sir M. Stephenson in eastern, Mr. Chapman in western, and Mr. Andrew in north-western India projected the railways which now pay from five to nine per cent, and are revolutionising native society and commerce, became an accomplished fact on the 16th April 1853. Then the first section completed in Asia was opened under a royal salute and the strains of the National Anthem, and the first train ran from Bombay island on to the mainland to Tanna, a distance of twenty-one miles. The twenty-one have now become nearly eight thousand.

[1] The "Kaisar-i-Hind" steamer made the passage in nine days twelve hours with the Bombay mail of 16th December 1878, which reached London in sixteen days twelve hours on the 2d January 1879.

Soon after his return from Great Britain the Bombay Government expressed its anxiety to secure the services of Dr. Wilson as President of the Committee for the examination of civilians and officers in the native languages, vernacular and classical. The request recognised the missionary as the first scholar in Western India, and as better fitted than any of the members of the services, civil or military, for the responsible duty of controlling examinations by which, long before those of the Civil Service Commissioners in this country, promotion and patronage in India had been wisely regulated. " Such an influential position might have been of use to him in various ways," Mrs. Wilson wrote to a friend in 1849, " and the services required would not have been for more than ten or twelve days in a year. However, he has declined, as he wishes to be quite free to give all his time and strength to missionary operations." In 1855 the proposal was received in a different, and to him unobjectionable, because temporary form.

Associated with Major G. Pope and Mr. Harkness, Principal of the Government College, he gave himself to the work of inquiry with characteristic thoroughness before reporting on the Civil and Military Examination Committee. The constitution of the similar Examining Boards in Madras and Calcutta—the latter created by Lord Wellesley, and consisting of Dr. Sprenger, the first Arabic scholar and biographer of Muhammad ; Dr. K. M. Bannerjea, Dr. Duff's first convert ; and Colonel N. Lees—was carefully studied in the light of his experience of the Bombay languages, people, and officials. The result was a report, submitted on the 15th August 1856, which has since regulated the professional examinations of Western India in the Oriental languages and literatures. The document, which called forth an expression of the thanks of Government, contains not only much information regarding such examinations, but a scheme for checking an arbitrary judgment on the part of examiners, which we commend to the Civil Service Commissioners, as sorely needed in the India competitions at least.

 ˙Meanwhile, the Government of 1849 having failed to induce Dr. Wilson to act as official and permanent president of this Examination Committee, the Government of 1854 had thus tried, most honourably, to attract to the public service what would have been the leisure time of most other men. The great Carey had long held a similar office, first as Professor in Lord Wellesley's College of Fort-William, and then as translator and examiner, while the same translatorship is to this hour worthily filled by a Baptist minister, the son of one of his colleagues. Connected with no society, early thrown upon their own resources for the spread of Christianity in Bengal, Carey, Marshman, Ward, and Mr. J. C. Marshman, C.S.I., contributed some £60,000 of their own earnings during half a century for missionary purposes, maintaining at one time so many as twenty-six agents besides themselves. In the case of the Scottish Churches the circumstances are very different, but the temptations held out to the ablest missionaries by the various departments of Government are not less specious and attractive. The Private Secretary thus addressed Dr. Wilson, whose reply may be imagined from his letter to Dr. Tweedie :—

"PARELL, *March* 11, 1854.

"MY DEAR SIR—I am desired by the Governor to acquaint you of his intention, should it be acceptable to you, of appointing you Oriental Translator to Government. The appointment has been created on the occasion of doing away with the Deputy Secretaryship in the Persian Department."

TO DR. TWEEDIE.

"14*th April* 1854.—We have lately had favourable accounts from Abyssinia. Our native converts consider the agency there as primarily *their* mission, contributing to its support to their utmost ability, though it is principally, from their lack of adequate means, dependent on other resources. Their duty of contributing to the spread of the Gospel is amply recognised by them, though most of them are in some capacity or other themselves missionary agents. We are anxious to have an industrial establishment instituted for the converts and catechumens in Bombay, as a counteractive of the combinations and excommunications of caste. A regular source of legitimate missionary revenue in the case of all our Institutions, we see in the encouragement of the natives in general to contribute, partially at least, to the education of their children. In this way we have, from the commencement of our Institution here, got a small sum annually from this source, which we have applied discretionally for its benefit from time to time, especially in providing prizes and school equipments. But something, I am persuaded, of a more systematic nature may easily be accomplished, and that without injury to the distinctly evangelistic feature of our operations. Self-expansion is a desideratum in every Christian institution.

"In connection with what I have now stated to you, I ought perhaps to mention that our new Governor, Lord Elphinstone, within the last few weeks made the offer to me of the superintendence of the work of Government Oriental Translation, which would occupy only a definite portion of my time, without interfering substantially with my missionary engagements, and at the same time secure a remuneration by which I could support a couple of additional missionaries, or enable me to contribute directly to the missionary cause the equivalent of the average annual income of our Auxiliary Society, which receives from us much care, and makes a considerable demand on our time for correspondence with Christian friends in various parts of the country. Without consulting any friend, I at once declined the proposal, with grateful acknowledgment of the kindnesses in which I know it originated. I did this because I believe that it is not the duty of any minister of the Gospel to assume any secular engagement, however productive to the cause of Christ in a pecuniary point of view, while the Christian Church is willing to give him fair support in devoting himself wholly to the ministry of the Word and prayer, and to efforts subordinate and auxiliary to this ministry ; and because I am of opinion that all our exertions in stirring up our brethren to contribute to the missionary cause, even when we could by a partial secularisation of ourselves, maintain or extend the operations already in existence, are themselves of a spiritual character—the calling upon Christian men to discharge a Christian duty. On my mentioning this to Mr. Molesworth—the author of our admirable Marathee Dictionary, one of the most devoted Christians in India, and whose views of Church order generally agree with those of the brethren at Plymouth—he at once said, ' You have done quite right ; no amount of pecuniary compensation can be put in the scale with the entirety of your missionary service.' I think we would be unanimous in our mission in a cause of this kind. For the extension of the missionary enterprise both at home and abroad we must trust to the promises, and providence, and Spirit of God. Though respected brethren in all the Churches may tell us that they ' see a limit ' to their benevolent gifts or the spread of the blessed Gospel, we must, like Nelson, turn our blind eye to this signal of intermission, and act as if it were never made. The more our souls sympathise with the risen and exalted Saviour, who now travails in ceaseless intercession for the accomplishment of the number of His elect and the establishment of His kingdom, the more readily shall we write *Holiness to the Lord* on all our possessions and acquirements. You will see from our report that last year we raised Rs. 7542 for our Bombay Mission. When the contributions for Poona and Satara are added, we perceive that we have had here a missionary income of £1200, exclusive of £400 raised for the purposes of the Free Church congregation to which we minister during the vacancy. Even this liberality may be much increased. It is the principal source of the support of our educational establishments. The permission which you give us, in your last most acceptable letter, of proceeding with the ordination of Mr. Narayan, will be acted upon as soon as possible. What our hopes are in connection with his ministry you well know.''

When alluding to the offer of this appointment in a letter to Miss Douglas, Dr. Wilson wrote, " I declined acceptance, as I wish to be, what I have been since the beginning, *only a missionary.*" Next to his ministrations to the spiritual needs of the people of India, his philanthropic interest in the efforts of the Government to save their bodies came hardly second. From the discovery of the practice of the murder of their female children by the proud and poor Rajkoomars of Benares by Jonathan Duncan in 1789, and the same Governor's attempts to put down the crime in Kathiawar, to which the Greek and Latin writers on India had drawn his attention as prevalent then at Barygaza or Broach, Dr. Wilson had joyously chronicled the facts down to the successful efforts of his early friend Colonel Walker. These had been more recently followed by the measures wisely devised by Sir J. P. Willoughby, Colonels Lang and Le Grand Jacob, and Mr. Malet and other officers, whose humane administration Dr. Wilson was in the habit of illustrating in lectures to the natives and in the press as "gratifying records of British benevolence." Thus he created a healthy native opinion on the crime, and stimulated Government to renewed vigilance, while he did justice to some of the most solid triumphs in the history of philanthropy in the East. On the 27th April 1857 he officially addressed Sir J. P. Willoughby. The result was, as he wrote to Dr. Tweedie, that Lord Elphinstone's Government submitted to impartial Christian review " the whole proceedings from first to last in connection with the great philanthropic, political, and judicial efforts for the suppression of the awful crime of infant murder." The Court of Directors warmly encouraged the undertaking, at a time when the question of what proved to be the last renewal of their Charter—that of 1853—was about to come before Parliament, and works like Sir John Kaye's history of its administration were being prepared in its defence. It was well that the Company enjoyed, on this side at least, the aid of one whose advocacy was all the more effectual that it was purely disinterested and non-political.

The *History of the Suppression of Infanticide in Western India under the Government of Bombay, including notices of the Provinces and Tribes in which the Practice has prevailed,* was published early in 1855, and obtained a wide circulation. When, in 1870, the outbreak of the crime in Northern India led Sir William Muir to prepare, and the Government of India to pass, Act VIII. of that year, and the census of 1871 supplied new facts, Dr. Wilson was invited by the Bombay Government to review the state of the districts to which the preventive legislation was to be applied. A few months before his death he accordingly wrote a preface to Mr. H. R. Cooke's report. In Kathiawar, it was proved, the crime had ceased as a custom of the Jadejas, the proud descendants of the Yadavas of the Mahabharat epic. But the number of girls unbetrothed and unmarried was increasing, because no Rajpoot tribe in India will take a wife from its own proper or paternal clan, and the

Jadejas were unpopular because of occasional intermarriage with Muhammadans. To the advance of an education and a civilisation which recognise the place of unmarried females in well-being and well-doing in the general community, Dr. Wilson looked for a permanent remedy while suggesting local ameliorations. But the only immediate check on the crime must be based on a general registration of births and deaths, such as the coming decennial census of 1881 should make a preliminary attempt to render possible amid so vast and varied and suspicious a population. Sir H. L. Anderson, when secretary to the Bombay Government, expressed to Dr. Wilson the congratulation of the Governor in Council on " the very able and successful" manner in which he had turned to account his access to the records connected with infanticide.

In 1848 Dr. Wilson had been consulted by the Government as to the publication of a revised edition of the Marathee and English dictionary compiled by Mr. Molesworth and George and Thomas Candy twenty years before. In Marathee as in Bengalee, and to a less degree in the other vernaculars of India, the influence of a detailed knowledge of the people, English administration and education, and the progress of scholarship in the classical tongues from which the popular dialects are fed, had developed the vocabularies, and somewhat revealed or modified the grammatical expression of the vernaculars. Dr. Wilson replied that Mr. Molesworth's " unequalled attainments in the Marathee language, his experience in lexicography, and his acquaintance already with some thousands of unrecorded words," pointed him out as best qualified for the undertaking. In truth Dr. Wilson had, in his tours and his intercourse with the peasantry as well as the learned Brahmans of Maharashtra, himself made extensive collections of words new to printed literature, which he had freely communicated to Mr. Molesworth. The result was the appearance in 1857 of the massive quarto which forms the second edition of a work pronounced to stand in the very first rank of dictionaries. Dr. Wilson was the more anxious to see Marathee thus satisfactorily placed among the few languages of men of which a satisfactory lexicon has been made, that the wants of Government and the public in connection with Goojaratee might be supplied. This was done by the Parsee convert Shapoorjee Eduljee eleven years afterwards, in an

octavo volume of some nine hundred pages.   But it should not
be forgotten that in Marathee, as in forty of the languages of
our Indian subjects and Chinese neighbours, Carey had first
provided a dictionary in 1810, as well as a grammar and
translation of the Scriptures.   Besides his indirect contribution to the Marathee Dictionary of nearly a thousand quarto
pages, Dr. Wilson prefaced it with what even the Germans
would pronounce a model monograph, under the title of
"Notes on the Constituent Elements, the Diffusion and the
Application of the Marathee Language."   A wealth of learning and information is scattered over the text and notes, while
the summary with illustrative extracts of the four periods of
Marathee literature is delightfully readable.   He passes in
review the early poetry, associating the popular gods of
Western India with a modified pantheism, which preceded
the rise of Sivajee ; the brilliant era of Tukaram to the rise of
the Peshwas ; the strains of the priestly Moropant and the
beginnings of prose chronicles under the Peshwas ; and finally
the British period, which began in 1818.   As the Serampore
missionaries created a Bengalee language and literature, in the
literary sense, so religion and philanthropy were the moving
powers in generating and extending what may be denominated
the reformed authorship of Maharashtra, from Mountstuart
Elphinstone to his nephew Lord Elphinstone, and the present
day.   "Its most valuable monument " Dr. Wilson declared to
be " the translation of the whole of the Bible, by several hands,
into the language of the people."   The Notes thus conclude
—" The reformed Marathee literature, and the introduction of
typography and lithography into the West of India, have
brought about a reaction in the native mind.   There has been
a *reproduction* of the olden literature.   This result will not
ultimately prove injurious to the cause of truth.   It has furnished the means of comparison and judgment ; and it will
only enhance the victory when, by a higher influence than
that of man, it is eventually secured."

For some time Dr. Wilson had contemplated a new work
on Muhammadanism, to take the place of his early *Refutation ;*
but he seems to have been soon drawn entirely to an attempt
to grapple with the only enemy he had not yet directly
attacked in the press.   At every turn, as a missionary, a
scholar, and a man, in closer social intercourse with the

natives than any other foreigner, he was met by Caste. He
had early set himself to the mastery of its origin and the secret
of its power, and he had in his multifarious reading of the
Hindoo literature noted the passages on the subject, from the
Rig-Veda to the latest *Poorana.* He contemplated the early
publication of an elaborate work on the subject, and in 1857
he was able to put to press the first volume. But his missionary work was too exacting, and his own ideal of an
exhaustive treatment of the question on which Hindooism
hangs in the last resort, was too high to permit him to yield
to the solicitations of his friends not to delay. The prospect
of the taking of the first census of the people of India, finally
accomplished only in 1871-2, was a further reason, to his
mind, for toiling at a work, for the perfecting of which he
maintained a large correspondence with learned Brahmans for
many years, from the venerable Rada Kishn, Runjeet Singh's
pundit at Lahore, to the Namboories of Travancore. The
result was that in publication he was anticipated by other
scholars, notably by Mr. John Muir, D.C.L., in the invaluable
Sanskrit Texts, and death left his work a splendid fragment.
The first volume, virtually prepared and printed at this period,
is a careful review of the origin and development of Caste as.
seen in Sanskrit, Buddhist, and Greek literature. The second
volume, which begins a description of the castes as they are,
does not proceed further than the most important of them all,
the Brahmanical. The criticism of the book by so competent
a writer as Mr. Rhys Davids may be accepted — "The
thoroughness of the work he has done gives rise to the regret
that he should have been unable to complete the inquiry."

What contemporary as well as subsequent criticism, however, has recognised as the ablest of all the publications that
Dr. Wilson threw off as mere bye-works almost every year, is
his *India Three Thousand Years Ago,* or the social state of the
Aryas on the banks of the Indus in the times of the Vedas,
which appeared in 1858. Mr. Max Müller's *Chips* was then
unknown, and his *History of Ancient Sanskrit Literature* was
only promised in the preface to his edition of the *Rig-Veda.*
To the English reading public, both in India and elsewhere,
this popular treatise of some ninety pages was the first revelation of what has long since become commonplace. It was
written with a grace as well as a power which so charmed all,

that the most competent critic, in the *Friend of India* of that day, thus took the author to task—" We wish some of the thousand friends of Dr. Wilson would compel him to do the public and himself a little justice. With a pen of unequalled clearness and learning, of which few are competent to measure the extent, he persists in wasting his strength on erudite little essays. . . . The world is craving for a painting with the details all filled in and bright with life and colour. It is Dr. Wilson's duty to supply the want, and he has no more right to leave the work to inferior artists than Titian to sell studies as finished productions." But Dr. Wilson was so much the Christian philanthropist that even his learning is saturated with his love for man in the highest sense, as expressed sometimes after a curious fashion. This is a note to this very treatise—" The MS. copy of the *Rig-Veda*, in my possession for many years, and which I originally acquired for J. S. Law, Esq., of the Bombay Civil Service, is a Christian trophy surrendered by a Brahman convert to Christianity, baptized at Bankote by the Rev. James Mitchell." Dr. Wilson would never have written his best book but for the public good. He prepared the nucleus of it as one of a course of lectures to the Bombay Mechanics' Institute, projected under " the considerate and vigorous government " of Lord Elphinstone. Other public lectures which belong to this period, but have not yet seen the light in a complete form, are those on the " Progress of Oriental Research in connection with Religious Inquiry," and on " The Six Schools of Indian Philosophy," delivered at the request of the Bombay Dialectic Association.

T

CHAPTER XVI.

1857-1864.

THE MUTINY AND ITS GOOD FRUIT.

The year 1857 a fruitful period—The alleged causes of the Mutiny—Western India quiet in spite of them—The Bombay Rabble—Lord Elphinstone assisted by Dr. Wilson—Deciphering the Treasonable Letters of the Natives—The Massacre of Missionaries at Sialkot—Lord Elphinstone's correspondence with Dr. Wilson—Loyalty of Bombay City—Dr. Wilson's Humiliation and Thanksgiving Lectures—The Government of India constitutionally Christian—United Presbyterian Mission to Rajpootana—Dr. Shoolbred's Narrative of Tour with Dr. and Mrs. Wilson—Timidity of the Authorities—Mrs. Wilson's Letters—Dr. Wilson's Interview with the late Gaikwar : with the Maharaja Tukht Singh of Joudhpore ; with Holkar— The Education Despatch of 1854—The result of co-operation between the Missionaries and Government—Dr. Wilson's Criticism of the new Policy— The three Universities founded in the height of the Mutiny—Dr. Wilson's Influence on the Bombay University Regulations—Appointed Vice-Chancellor—Eulogy of Native Benefactors when laying Foundation-stone of University Hall.

WHETHER it hereafter proves true that the history of the British Empire of India began only with the Mutiny campaigns of 1857-1858, to which the century's conquests and administrative experiments of the East India Company were but a prelude, the *annus tristis* was also the *annus mirabilis* — remarkable for the birth of missionary extension and educational reform from the very womb of massacre and revolt.   From 1857 Christian missions and philanthropy in India received an impetus which they feel to this hour.   Dr. Wilson was the first to guide that to the establishment of the United Presbyterian Church amid the eighteen principalities of Rajpootana.   In the smoke of the Mutiny and its punishment the three Universities were legislatively called into existence, and the seeds of systems of primary education were sown.   The answer of the Christian rulers of India to the brief but bitter madness of its pampered soldiery and pensioned princes was—more light. There may still be doubt how far the administrative changes, politically and financially, of the Government of the Empress are an improvement on the system under which the Company won and built up the empire it bequeathed to the crown. There can be none as to the vast, even infinite, benefit of the new régime on the side of education and of the complete toleration of all religions, not excluding Christianity as the legislation of the Company did in spite of Lord William Bentinck and Lord Dalhousie.

The panic wave of military and political unrest, which swept over Northern India from the Hooghly to the Upper Indus, found and left the great Western Province peaceable and loyal. In none of the eloquent generalisations which he called "history," has the late Sir John Kaye been more unfortunate than in his account of Bombay. According to the obsolete school who see in that very progress, which is the sole justification of our Eastern Empire at all, an excuse for revolt, the causes of mutiny abounded more in the land of the Marathas than in any other. Annexation, lapse, resumption of holdings, confiscation of rent-free tenures, and the proselytism of Christian missionaries with the consent and educational co-operation of the Government—the five causes of the Mutiny according to some short-sighted conservatives—had been altogether more luxuriant in the West of India than in Oudh or the Delhi territory, or anywhere else. Yet it would be easy to prove that it was these very causes—the extinction, legally and equitably, of centres of intrigue ; the care for the peasantry abandoned to irresponsible talookdars ; the intelligence and benevolence of reformers like Dr. Wilson and the authorities whom he stirred up, which kept the panic to the north of the Vindhyas, or to two isolated spots where there was not even the ordinary garrison to keep the peace.

But the temper of the Bombay army, and the intelligence of the Bombay people in and out of the capital, were severely tested. So far as the mutiny assumed a Hindoo aspect it was Bombay in its origin. The infamous Nana Dhoondopunt, whom Sir John Malcolm has been blamed for treating so generously, gave himself out as the political representative of his adoptive father, the last of the Peshwas, and as the head of Hindooism. As he had sent his *quondam* menial Azimoollah to be lionised in London, and to see the weakness of England in the early stages of the Crimean War, so the Satara agent, Rungo Bapoojee, had been active in the old India House. It was to Maharashtra that the ringleaders of the Bengal sepoys looked for the rousing of the whole west and south of India. In reply to a missive from the 75th Bengal Native Infantry a sepoy wrote from Bombay in an intercepted letter—" We are your children ; do with us as it may seem best to you ; in your salvation is our safety. We are all of one mind ; on your intimation we shall come running." Poona and Satara had memories of Sivajee and his generals, of Maratha ambition and Hindoo glories, not second to Delhi in Muhammadan eyes. But Poona and Satara were names to conjure with only in the far-off Ganges valley. Of Western India itself the state-ment of Dr. Wilson at the time is true—" Incipient mutiny in the Bombay army at Kolhapore, Ahmedabad, Kurachee, and some other stations, was early discovered and readily crushed." At two places only did it become overt, Kolhapore and Nurgoond. Of the fifteen hundred English massacred by the sepoys and rabble in 1857-58, of whom 240 were military officers, 4 were chaplains, and 10 were missionaries and their wives, only one fell in Western India—the civilian Mr. Manson. Yet by the three approaches of Rajpootana, of the Vindhyas, and of Nagpore and Hyderabad, the mutineers of the north vainly tried to reach Maharashtra under Tathya Topya and Bala Rao. Instead of their succeeding it was from Bombay that the first help was sent to Lord Canning in the despatch of the troops of the Persian expedition ; and from Bombay that Sir Hugh Rose, at a later period, restored peace right up through central India to the Ganges.

While the Mutiny was purely military in its origin, and owed its opportunity to the reduction of the British troops from thirty-seven to twenty-two regiments for the Crimean and Persian wars, in spite of the unanswered protest of Lord Dalhousie, the sepoys found the vilest confederates and agents in the swashbuckler rabble of the great cities and canton-ments. Bombay was such a city. To this day the fanatical passions of the Parsee and the Muhammadan sometimes blaze up into a conflict, while the Hindoos there are the boldest in all India. Around the three communities whom English law and institutions, born of the Christian faith, have made at once independent and wealthy, there has gradually gathered the scum of Asia and Africa, sailors and traders, adventurers and pilgrims, criminals and loafers, slave-dealers and eunuch or boy and girl kidnappers, such as the polygamous and sexual cults of the East require as their ministrants. A government like that of the Turk would have made of Bombay at this time what Damascus became in the Syrian massacres soon after. But Lord Elphinstone was not only a firm and wise ruler, favouring none, and fair to all of whatever faith : he was a daring statesman, who had the first virtue of a true ruler, that of knowing his agents on the one hand and his duty to his country on the other. He sent away his European troops to Lord Canning. And, whether against the still unknown temper of the sepoys or the mixed multitude of the capital, he trusted the irresponsible missionary, while he made all proper military arrangements.

The Mutiny in Bengal was not many days old when the Government of India determined that the new cheap postal and telegraph arrangements should not become the instruments of intrigue. Accordingly, all the authorities received instructions to intercept native or vernacular letters, and to forward them for examination and translation by confidential and skilled persons named. When found treasonable the letters were submitted to the secretaries to Government. In Bombay letters so intercepted were sent to Dr. Wilson. Just as our beleaguered countrymen and countrywomen in cities like Lucknow, and in sequestered hiding-places, had recourse to French and to the use of the Greek letters in their desperate attempts to communicate with their friends, so the sepoy ringleaders resorted to all sorts of dialects and characters to blind the post-office. No man then in all India was so equal to their resources as the scholar, who for more than twenty years had been translating alphabets and inscriptions for historical and philanthropic ends. In the last edition of his lecture on the "Religious Excavations" he makes this slight reference to a confidential service, of a value which no reward and no honour could adequately recognise. Alluding to James Prinsep's deciphering of the rock inscriptions he writes :—

"The key to the character was found by his tracing backwards—from the current Devanagaree—various forms of older letters, of which the Nagaree is the maturer type, adapted to more rapid writing than the original. Our own assurance respecting it was derived from a comparison of copperplate inscriptions in the hands of Vishnoo Shastree, in which we noticed the accordance in number and position of certain letters and words connected with initial salutations of the gods, and the royal signatures on other legible grants, which betokened an agreement in value in the respective characters, as was found to be the case when they were critically examined and compared. By following out this principle, we were able to make out some of the most difficult letters which came into the hands of our vigilant officials during the late Mutiny. We now see very clearly that the great trouble taken with the adjustment of the cave character would have been unnecessary if we had noticed sufficiently early its correspondence with the Phœnician and Greek alphabets, from a combination of which it is manifestly derived, with most ingenious adaptations to the orthoëpical expression of the Sanskrit and other languages, most creditable to the ingenuity of the Indians, or those by whom they were adapted to those languages."

Thus the whole miserable tragedy of the Mutiny on its western side passed before Dr. Wilson, who, moreover, kept up a close correspondence with the Governor. That was of too confidential a character for Dr. Wilson to have kept even copies of it, but Lord Elphinstone's letters to him reveal an alliance in the interests of order, of civilisation, and of their country's good, of the highest honour to both.

DR. WILSON TO HIS SISTER.

" 30th July 1857.—This mail, like some which have preceded it, conveys very heavy tidings to Britain. The mutiny and revolt of the Bengal sepoys still continues, and their murderous courses are only beginning to be checked. Many of our countrymen—men, women, and children—have been treacherously butchered by them. Five or six missionaries are among the number slain. Among these, I regret to say, is the Rev. Thomas Hunter, of the Church of Scotland's mission at Sialkot in the Punjab (the brother of Mr. Hunter of Nagpore), who was destroyed, along with his wife and infant child, on the 9th of this month. They were in Bombay for a few months before they went to their station. We were acquainted with them, and liked them much. We have not heard of the fate of two converts who were with them. Their station was a new one, and very distant ; and it is to be regretted that they went to it before they were more fully acquainted with the country and its languages. The whole of the native army of the Bombay Presidency (as well as that of Madras) has hitherto remained staunch to the British interests. All, thank God, is very quiet in the city of Bombay. So much is this the case, that at a large meeting of Natives and Europeans held lately in our Town-Hall, and presided over by the Governor, I offered to walk through any of the streets or lanes in the blackest night without a weapon of defence. How long this security may continue is dependent on the will of a gracious Providence. A plot for the murder of the Europeans is suspected to have been formed at Poona, but it has been mercifully detected.

" I enclose copies of some hymns we have used at a prayer-meeting held in Ambrolie in connection with the crisis, and attended by great multitudes. Be sure you let my dear mother know that we are both quite well and safe at present. I hope you all pray for us and for the cause of Christ in India."

TO MISS DOUGLAS.

"*6th May* 1858.—In the pacification of India a good deal remains to
be done, though victory, except in incidental foolish attacks, has in the
mercy of God always followed the movements of our troops. The Bombay
armies, both in Rajpootana and Central India, have done all that was needful
in these important provinces, and much circumscribed the field of action.
Sir Colin Campbell is very careful of the lives of his men, and his plan is evidently that of a gradual advance. I don't think he will be allowed to rest
during the hot and rainy months. It is a great mercy that we have been kept
free from alarm in Bombay, and that all the plots in this Presidency have
been discovered before they could be carried into effect. The plots of the
Satara and Kolhapore nobles are of three or four years' standing, and have
had no connection with the Mutiny, except in so far as one set of evil men
has encouraged another set of evil men.

"You will be glad to hear that the spirit of our Native Church continues
to be most exemplary. The young men and others who joined it last year
are a great accession to it, and all is love and harmony within its enclosure."

LORD ELPHINSTONE TO DR. WILSON.

"*Tuesday, 8th* ——, 1857.

"MY DEAR Dr. WILSON—It was very good of you to remember our conversation about the wild tribes in the North Konkan, and I am much indebted
to you for your little volume on the *Evangelisation of India,* in which you
give an account of these tribes. I have always taken a great interest in those
poor outcasts of humanity, the aboriginal tribes who are scattered throughout
the peninsula of India. I have received with great regret very discouraging
reports on the subject of the attempts which have been made in this Presidency to raise them a little in the scale of humanity. I fear that very little
has been effected in this way, and that we cannot hope for any rapid progress.
The best thing that I have heard was from Mr. Mitchell at Poona, that the
Mhar and Mhang schools at that place were making great progress, and that
a native had taken a great share in the work of establishing and supporting
them.

"Your account of the feelings of the Mussulman population is very satisfactory. I have never given in to the idea of insurrection and conspiracy
which seems to haunt many people. As long as the native army are faithful
there is no fear of a popular rising ; and although unfortunately we have had
one or two cases of mutiny in the Bombay Army, I do not see any signs of
general defection. We may now very shortly expect to receive European
reinforcements, and I hope that the troops we asked the Government of the
Cape to send us are now close at hand. With God's blessing I believe that we
shall be spared the trials and calamities through which our neighbours have
passed, and I am sure that we have great reason to be thankful. I beg to
enclose a draft for my subscription to the native female school, and remain,
my dear Dr. Wilson, very sincerely yours,   ELPHINSTONE."

"I beg to be kindly remembered to Mrs. Wilson. I shall not fail to send
the Notes on the Maratha language to my uncle. He still takes as keen an
interest in all that is passing in this country as ever, but I am afraid that he
is not much more able to appreciate a critical paper on the Maratha than I
am myself !"

"*April* 29, 1859.

"MY DEAR DR. WILSON—I send you Sir Robert Hamilton's memo.
upon Tantia Topey. It appears that his father was a follower of Bajee Rao's,

and that Tantia was a playfellow of the Nana's. Dangan, who has been on
General Mansfield's staff in Oudh, says that they always pronounce Tantia
Topey's name as Sir R. Hamilton spells it, *Topye*, and that they speak of
Nana Sahib as *Nana Rao*.

" I have just received a telegram from Bombay with news from England
up to the 4th. It seems that on that day Lord Derby announced in the
House of Lords, and Mr. Disraeli in the Commons, that as soon as certain
money bills, and bills connected with India, were passed, it was the intention
of Her Majesty's Government to dissolve Parliament. The foreign news does
not look pacific, and I believe that soon India will be the quietest place in
the world, though we may still have little episodes like the Nuggur Parkur
disturbance and Adil Mahomed's party in the Hoshungabad district.—Believe
me, sincerely yours,   ELPHINSTONE."

How accurately Dr. Wilson had gauged the temper of the
various communities of Bombay was soon seen in the united
and loyal movement which they made on the 15th December
1858, in a public meeting summoned to consider the propriety of erecting an Economic and Natural History Museum,
with pleasure gardens, " to be styled, in our Sovereign's
honour, the Victoria Museum and Gardens," presided over by
a Hindoo friend of Dr. Wilson, Mr. Jugganath Sunkersett.
The united Hindoos, Parsees, and Muhammadans determined
to show that they appreciated the blessings of a just Government, under which the city had risen in wealth and importance. The crowd raised fifty thousand rupees on the spot.
But far more important was this language in the mouth of its
chairman : " No Empire has been more consecrated by time,
none more perfectly consolidated, none more great in intellect, more overwhelming in power, more infinite in resources ;
and yet it is not on its awful might that it is founded, nor on
the force of its naval and military greatness, but supremely
in the devotion of its people." Not a few at the Mohurrum
festival of 1857 had distrusted the Muhammadans alone, and
the police commissioner summoned a meeting of the leaders,
at which we meet for the first time in this history with the
name of one who had become second only to Dr. Wilson in
his identification with the interests of the natives of Bombay.
Dr. George Birdwood, now C.S.I., and his father General
Birdwood, had early come under Dr. Wilson's influence ; and
at this, as in all other movements for the good of the natives,
that young member of the Medical Service, and Professor in
the Grant Medical College, was prominent. Even the Wahabee Kazee, or high priest of the Bombay Muhammadans,
offered his services to keep the peace, while the chief native

officer of police was a Wahabee. When the clever detection
of the plot of the sepoys of the Bombay garrison at Sonapore,
to rise and proclaim the sovereignty of the Nana as Peshwa of
the Dekhan, took place, and the mutineers were blown from
guns, all fear of even a local riot was passed. In Lord
Elphinstone's opinion, Bombay city saved Poona and Hyderabad, and even Madras. So did Nagpore, and it must not be
forgotten how well Madras did its duty to the empire by its
European troops under Neill, although the family system and
evil arrangements as to its native officers had long demoral-
ised its sepoy army as a fighting and disciplined force.
While in Bengal there was only one white soldier to twenty-
five sepoys in May 1857, the proportion in Madras was one
to seventeen, and in Bombay one to ten, and in the last many
sepoys were Jews and Christians.

"Shall there be evil in a city and the Lord hath not done
it ?" were the words of Amos from which Dr. Wilson lectured
to the whole Christian community of Bombay, in a sermon
afterwards circulated all over the country under the title of
The Indian Military Revolt viewed in its Religious Aspects. The
calm, impartial, native-loving evangelist looked beyond the
passions the crimes and the follies of the time, and deprecated
" that indiscriminate party and personal inculpation to which
many are too prone to resort in these sad days of trouble and
rebuke." These were the warnings he uttered, against an
under-estimate of the Christian and an over-estimate of the
Gentile character so common among Europeans in India and
at home ; against Caste, the great evil ; against " hedging up
any bodies of our servants or subjects in India from general
enlightenment and Christian instruction ; " against " shortcomings in the supervision, discipline, and employment of our
native army and native officials ; " against a defective Christian
example on our own part ; against failure " in enterprises of
Christian beneficence, and in works calculated to promote the
advancement of European civilisation ; " against forgetfulness
of our dependence in a heathen land on the subduing and
restraining grace of God ; and against the danger of remaining
without a personal interest in the salvation of Christ. Still
better was his sermon on the General Thanksgiving-day on
the prophet Ezekiel's message—" Ye shall know that I am the
Lord, when I have wrought with you for my name's sake."

The events of two years had developed, the Empire had been
proclaimed, and the preacher found these eight causes for
gratitude—the close of such a war ; its restricted limits ; the
marvellous supply of a military and civil agency for the suppression of anarchy ; the safety of Western India ; the steadfastness of the native Church, even to martyrdom ; the
administrative reforms ; the lessons to the natives themselves ;
and the increased zeal in Great Britain for their good.   Dr.
Wilson, like all observers on the spot who knew the facts,
made this admission—" Our highest civil authorities were
asleep when the catastrophe happened."   Lord Canning's own
confession of his fatal mistakes, especially that of not disarming
the Dinapore sepoys and so precipitating the horrors of Cawnpore and delays of Lucknow, is sufficient.   But the incapacity
of his paralysed advisers bore the one good fruit on his part
of an apparently calm clemency, even in the face of the five
stern Acts ; and Dr. Wilson noted with satisfaction, in a letter
to Mr. C. Fraser Tytler, C.S., that the first Sabbath after the
proclamation of the Empire " both Lord and Lady Canning
sent a contribution to the missions at Allahabad," where the
first Viceroy of the Crown then was.   A little later he wrote,
" So they have at last got hold of Tatya ' Topi '—Tokya, I
think it will prove to be, for I know some of his family, as I
opine, at Toka on the Godavery."

The events of 1857 awoke the conscience of the English
in India and at home.   Governors like John Lawrence, and
the Punjab school whom he had reared, became puritans
almost of a Cromwellian stamp, in such public minutes as that
from his pen which reviewed the relation of our Government
to Christianity.   The present Lord Kinnaird had headed an
association to bring about the public and emphatic recognition
of the duty of the Government of India to vindicate its
character as a Christian administration.   When asked to join
in this movement Dr. Wilson's broader knowledge and truer
comprehension of the position led him to return this answer :
While approving of the object he pronounced the movement
inexpedient, because it was better to act on the indisputable
fact that the British Government in all its dependencies *is*
Christian, than to make a mere avowal founded on the apprehension that the Indian authorities questioned this.   Writing
on the 19th May 1860, he said :—

"1. What we ought to do is to assail every act done contrary to our constitutional standing when it occurs. We are stronger, I conceive, in our defiance of all parties violating our constitution than we should be after the most forcible declaration of duty, which might give rise to the surmise that we had doubts of the tenableness of our own position till its principle be reasserted.

"2. Notwithstanding all the sins and shortcomings of the British Government in India, it has not yet ventured to question in any categorical form 'the right, privilege, and duty of every Christian to support and promote the Christian religion, or directly called upon any Christian subject of the British Crown to relinquish his Christian rights and privileges.' I do not see the propriety of our insinuating that it has in any general form denied the existence of the rights and privileges here referred to, however inconsistently it may have acted on particular occasions with the existence of these rights and privileges.

"3. The Government of India has done, and dare do, nothing to prevent its Christian servants giving their private funds to religious societies. An attempt to do something like this by the Directors of the East India Company proved abortive. In the face of Lord Ellenborough we find all the religious Societies in India getting their usual open support from Government officials, even of the highest standing—as for example Lord Elphinstone, who was the official Patron of the Bombay Bible Society, and in his own name a contributor to all the Episcopalian, Presbyterian, Congregational and Lutheran Missions in our neighbourhood. No officials, as far as I know, have been challenged for acting in their private capacity in our evangelistic committees for visiting and examining our mission schools, or of late years for speaking on religious subjects, or distributing bibles, books, or tracts. An unnecessary limit seems to have been hinted at in connection with the attendance of officials at native baptisms, but better seek to remove this limit on its individual demerits by discussions in Parliament and other appliances, than to assail it by a Declaration embracing principles which are yet unchallenged. Even as matters stand, it is just as likely that the Government will take no more notice of the attendance at native baptisms as that any real Christian official will neglect to attend them (when Christian expediency requires him to countenance them) because of the partial restriction of Government.

"4. A Bill is at present before the Legislative Council, the object of which is to free the officials of Government from taking any part as such in the management of Hindoo and Muhammadan endowments. It may be better to watch this bill than to seek subscriptions to a document embracing with various other matters the principle on which it is founded."

Lord Canning had called on Mr. R. N. Cust, then a high civil officer in the Punjab, for an explanation of his presence at the baptism of a sepoy, and had effectually stopped the work of inquiry in the loyal regiment of Muzbee or low-caste Sikhs. But these proved to be the last flickerings of a spirit of antagonism to liberty which was more ignorant or timid than it was malicious. The battle for full toleration and equity, begun when Dr. Wilson landed in Lord William Bentinck's time, was near its close, and such an association as that proposed would only have postponed that close by unnecessarily rousing antagonisms.

Besides the Vernacular Education Society, the special
efforts of the Bible, Tract, and great Missionary Societies,
and the establishment of an American mission in Oudh, as
the results of the Mutiny, the most important and permanently
fruitful enterprise was that of the United Presbyterian Church
of Scotland. Dr. Wilson had by himself, or by the agents he
stimulated, seen the whole field of western and central India,
from Bombay to Kathiawar and Sindh, and from Satara to
Nagpore, mapped out by the Church, while to Mesopotamia,
Arabia, Abyssinia, and eastern Africa, the divine message had
sounded out. He had in desire long before taken possession
of Rajpootana, and now he sent his brother Kirk in Scotland
thither. *This* was for him the outcome of the Mutiny, the
atonement alike for the dark ignorance that prompted and the
swift vengeance that overtook its leaders.

At the close of 1858 the Rev. Dr. Somerville, foreign
secretary of the United Presbyterian Church—which represents the earlier seceders from the Established Kirk, as the
Free Church consists of the later—along with Mr. Cooper, his
old colleague in the Konkan, who had become minister of
Fala, turned to Dr. Wilson for advice and help in the projected
mission to Rajpootana. The case was just that of the Irish
Presbyterian Church in Kathiawar over again. Once more
Dr. Wilson expressed his "peculiar pleasure," and his gratitude to God that this work was to be done at last. With
Rajpootana as a mission field only three others could be
compared, he wrote on the 3d March 1859—the Muhammadan
state of the Nizam, and the Maratha principalities of Sindia
and Holkar, which shut in Rajpootana to the south. But to
their claims of area, population, spiritual destitution and influence on others, Rajpootana added the advantage of a central
field more directly under British rule at that time, while it
was in the line of Presbyterian missions in the west and
north-west of India, "among whom the most friendly relations
and co-operations, if not absolute union, at no distant day will
doubtless exist." The English fear of the hot winds he met
in his own pleasant way, by declaring, from his experience,
that they are not particularly unhealthy or restrictive of
missionary labour.

Then follow, in this and the subsequent correspondence,
exhaustive details, topographical, political, historical, and

ethnological, regarding the Rajpoots and their country. The twenty years' work of the mission which he established at Beawur, side by side with administrative progress and the annual extension of railways and roads, have since incorporated the wild States and warlike princes of the deserts, hills, and small cities of Rajastan, in one now civilised territory. Dr. Wilson's letters remain a proof of his unconquerable zeal, rare self-denial, and statesmanlike breadth of view, which, in language most creditable to it, the Church he assisted again and again strove to acknowledge.

The Rev. Messrs. W. Shoolbred, D.D., and Steel, able students of the University of Edinburgh in their day, were the two missionaries sent forth as pioneers. Dr. Wilson had urged their arrival at Bombay in October, that, going with them, he might introduce them to the Maharaja of Jodhpore, the first king in point of importance in Rajpootana, whose acquaintance he had made in Goojarat in 1840, and who had often referred to the intercourse since ; as well as to Sir George Lawrence, the Governor-General's agent, who had there succeeded his lamented brother Sir Henry. We leave Dr. Shoolbred to describe his intercourse with Dr. and Mrs. Wilson in the tour which they made together by sea to Surat, and thence for thirty marches to Beawur, during which, at Erinpoora, Mr. Steel died, as Mr. Kerr had done under similar circumstances in Kathiawar :—

" From the end of October 1859, till the middle of March 1860, we were thrown constantly together. As Dr. Wilson moved among the élite of the European society of Bombay, or was honoured in the brilliant receptions of native princes, or mingled among the crowds in the native bazaars, or gathered the village peasantry around him that he might tell them of a Saviour ; in the house and by the way, in bright drawing-rooms and dingy dàk bungalows, in health and in sickness, I had abundant opportunities of observing and admiring the true Christian gentleman and devoted missionary of the Cross. In those days, before railways were known or dreamt of in Rajpootana, we made the long journey from Surat to Beawur on horseback or bullock-cart. This in itself involves an amount of hardness and roughness which often severely tries the patience and ruffles the temper even of the most amiable of men. But these trials were greatly intensified during that sad journey by the illness and death of my colleague, Mr. Steel, which protracted the journey, and shed the deepest gloom over the most of its hours. In these trying circumstances, however, the true nobility of his character only shone more clearly out. Never do I remember his temper to have been ruffled or his patience to have given way. His own and his dear wife's deep sympathy with the sufferer, and the affectionate kindness with which they watched over and nursed him, could scarcely have been surpassed by his own parents' loving care. All that their great kindness and cheering presence was to me in that hard beginning of my missionary career I would vainly strive to express.

"What struck me most in Dr. Wilson's character was, perhaps, the rare blending of deep scholarliness with the utmost buoyancy, almost boyishness, of heart. On the literature, philology, and ethnology of India, he was a perfect mine of learning, and delighted to pour out his treasures in the most lavish way into the ear of a sympathising listener. But such was the fresh buoyancy of his nature that a string of pleasantries and puns would succeed a deep disquisition on some obscure philological point, just as the lights and shadows chase each other across the summer hills. I remember his winding up an interesting account of the geology of Elephanta by placing in my hand what, but for its lightness, I would have deemed a specimen of conglomerate rock ; and then, after enjoying my puzzled look, laughingly informing me that it was a piece of Scotch plumcake as it appeared after the long voyage to India. Conversations on graver matters at the breakfast-table were now and again relieved by showers of linguistic puns. Punning on the Marathee names for butter, honey, and sugar, he would smilingly ask, 'Isn't it a strange thing that people in India eat *muck* and *mud* on their bread, and sweeten their tea with *misery?*' And then, when it came to the dessert, and attention was called to the large *pamalo* (a species of shaddock) forming the centre dish, he would propound the conundrum, 'Why is the *pamalo* like William the Third of England ?' To which came the obvious answer, 'Because it is the Prince of Orange.' Thus, too, on the journey, many a trying and anxious moment was relieved by little pleasantries that flowed spontaneously from the depths of a simple and loving heart, which long contact with the world and knowledge of men had failed to rob of its fresh boyishness.

"His devotion to archæological studies was very great, and he never missed an opportunity of prosecuting them. I remember his relating how, when eager to visit the interior of a famous Hindoo temple, he had been almost foiled by the Brahman in charge having insisted on his taking off his boots ; and how he had surmounted the difficulty by getting the Brahman to carry him through the temple on his back for a consideration, and how, as he lingered longer than his sacred ' beast of burden ' bargained for, and the bearer complained of his increasing weight, he easily coaxed him into setting him down, boots and all, on the holy pavement, and was allowed unmolested to pursue his archæological inquiries to a close.

" On our journey up country, when we arrived at the ancient town of Sidhpore, one of the Hindoos' sacred places of pilgrimage, his eagerness to visit the shrines was irrepressible. He would scarcely wait till our early dinner was over, and while the sun was still high and hot he hurried me off with him to the town. With characteristic self-forgetfulness he would have exposed himself and me, unprotected, to the fierce sunshine, had not Mrs. Wilson, with her ever-watchful care, furnished us with umbrellas, and insisted on our using them. The eager archæologist climbed the one hundred and twenty steps leading to the shrines with an alacrity that put to shame his younger companion, and sent my pulse up to fever point. Through the long afternoon and evening he dragged me from shrine to shrine, examining, inquiring, and as often informing those whom he questioned, and finished up by gathering round us a great crowd in the bazaar, and for a full half-hour preaching to these dark idolaters Christ the Saviour, with a power and fervour which his previous labours seemed to have left wholly unexhausted.

" And this leads me to speak of the admirable balance in Dr. Wilson's character, which ever kept him from sinking the missionary in the man of science, or, in his omnivorous eagerness in the pursuit of knowledge, from forgetting the still higher and nobler work of the Christian missionary—the enlightening and saving of heathen souls. I had been delighted, while in Bombay, to see him with his students in the Institution, pouring out to them the treasures of his almost exhaustless knowledge, and seeking earnestly to lead them to the foot of the Cross. Chiefly had I been touched by seeing

how he moved among the members of his Native Church, and
was looked up to by them as a dear and loving father, to
whom they could come with all their griefs and troubles, ever
sure of warm sympathy, consolation, and aid.   No less was I
delighted on the journey by his constant devoted labours as
an evangelist.   Whether in the Raja's palace or beside the
village well, to prince and peasant alike, he eagerly seized
every opportunity of speaking a word for Christ.   And I was
ever and again constrained to admire the ease with which he
adapted his addresses to the character of his audience, and the
readiness with which he won their attention and in many
cases enlisted their sympathies in favour of his message.

"Here I would note another contrast in his character,
no less striking than that to which I have already called
attention.   As a writer or speaker of English Dr. Wilson was
apt to be somewhat stiff and stilted.   His style was heavy and
his periods Johnsonian.   For this reason he was less effective
as an English preacher than his richly varied knowledge and
great ability ought to have made him.   Judging of his power
to persuade solely from his English style, it is not to be
wondered at that Dr. Norman Macleod gave expression to the
opinion, that even a century of such preaching would fail to
make converts.   But had the genial Doctor understood the
Indian vernacular, and heard Dr. Wilson preach in that, he
would have found reason not only to modify but reverse his
judgment.   As a vernacular preacher he was simple, direct,
and effective.   Even with my imperfect knowledge of the
language in those days, I felt this, and could note the effect
which he produced in winning the attention, and not rarely
even the sympathies of his audiences.   During the whole
journey, so long as he could make himself understood in
Hindostanee, he continued to preach in the towns and villages
through which we passed ; and it was only when, after penetrating into Marwar, he found the people with their uncouth
dialects unable to understand him, that he was reluctantly
obliged to desist.   His journal of the tour will show how
eagerly he then devoted himself to the study of the dialectic
varieties of the Marwaree, so as to form the key to its mastery
But his evangelistic efforts were not confined to these more
public ministrations.   He no less eagerly seized every opportunity while conversing with individual natives of turning the

conversation on Christ and His Gospel. With our small guard of Sikh cavalry, and specially with their bright and intelligent Náik, during many a long and weary march he kept up the most lively and interesting conversations on religion as he walked his little hill pony beside their tall and imposing chargers. It was his delight to draw them out about their sacred *Granth* and its tenets, and to show the more excellent way and sure salvation which Christ offers to all who come to him by faith.

"In his whole character and conduct indeed, he seemed to me the *beau idéal* of a Christian missionary—uniting in one the scholar, the gentleman, and the evangelist, and consecrating all his scholarship, his great acquirements, his knowledge of men and of the world, to the cherished and absorbing work of commending his Lord and Master to the hearts and consciences of men. Like the great Apostle of the Gentiles, he was willing to become all things to all men, if by any means he might win some.

"I have already spoken of the great kindness and comfort ministered by Dr. and Mrs. Wilson to my lamented colleague so long as he lived, and to myself. In like manner I could speak at great length of his most valuable services in introducing me to my future field of labour at Beawur ; and in breaking up and smoothing my path by his most judicious and valuable advice and counsel. But feeling that I have already unduly extended my notice, I must forbear. I would only add that the true breadth of the great man's nature came out while initiating an English service at Beawur. Finding that the greater number of English residents at the station were Episcopalians, he at once arranged that their wishes should be met by the commanding officer's reading the Church of England Service, while the missionaries' should comprise a brief Presbyterian service, with preaching at its close. He himself began this mixed service, which has been found to work admirably for many years. I shall ever cherish the memory of Dr. Wilson as one of the greatest and best of men and missionaries. I regard his loss with all the greater regret that such a combination of high qualities as he presented is singularly rare, and that with him, I fear, has passed away the last of a noble type of Christian missionary."

The opening of a Christian Mission among the caste-bound

and native tribes of Rajpootana seemed to some in India a delicate experiment just after the Mutiny, and, indeed, as its fruit. But Sir George Edmonstone, then Lieutenant-Governor of the North-Western Provinces of which Ajmer was a part, did not, demi-officially through Sir George Couper, his secretary and now his successor, do more than write thus of the missionaries, after recommending Nusseerabad instead of Beawur as their headquarters :—" These gentlemen cannot be interfered with, and all that can be done is to beg them to be undemonstrative in their operations ; to refrain from declaring that they are there with the purpose of converting any particular tribe ; and generally, to exercise their functions unobtrusively and with discretion." This called forth from Dr. Wilson an expression of " due appreciation of the kind consideration in which the communication originated," his reasons for preferring Beawur, and a reply to the doubtless unconscious and certainly well-meant attempt of the officials to smuggle the mission into the province. These hints, he wrote, would meet with the respectful attention of Dr. Shool-bred and those who might join him, but " their evangelistic commission is to all classes of the people, whom it is their admitted duty to conciliate and not unreasonably to offend, even while they stand on the basis of that religious toleration and civil protection which are extended to all classes of religionists in this country both in profession and in prose-lytism." Dr. Wilson had fought for this freedom, and had purchased it with the great price of thirty years' toil, and the Mutiny had confirmed the expediency as well as justice of the claim. Colonel Eden was officiating for Sir George Lawrence at the time, March 1860, or no such correspondence would have taken place probably. It has proved to be the last of the kind even in Native States. But cities like Hydera-bad and Gwalior are still without missionaries, although the Rev. Narayan Sheshadri has a prosperous mission at Jalna, in the Nizam's country, and Dr. Valentine has, like Dr. Boughton at the court of the Emperor Shah Jahan, used the physician's art for still nobler ends in the court of Jeypore.

How baseless were even the lurking relics of apprehen-sion in the Lieutenant-Governor's letter was soon proved by the princes of Rajpootana and Indore themselves, in the avidity with which they sought Dr. Wilson's presence and

the honour with which they received the great missionary
and his wife.   At Baroda the Gaikwar, Khunde Rao, whose
brother and successor was recently banished by Lord Northbrook, was most complimentary to Dr. Wilson at a private
audience, especially on the many books the missionary had
written, which his Highness pronounced as " works of great
difficulty."   Dr. Wilson made vain attempts to induce the
Gaikwar to found a secondary school in his capital, and a
system of primary schools throughout the State.

"On Sabbath the 22d January, after preaching in Hindostanee and
Marathee to our servants and others, I baptized in the open air a Brahman,
from the Himalaya mountains, near Kangra, named Chinturám.   This young
man, of twenty-three years of age, has accompanied us from Bombay, where,
for a year and a half residing in the General Assembly's Institution, he had
enjoyed the public services of our mission.   He was educated through the
Hindostanee, both in Government and Mission schools (those of the Church
of England and American Presbyterians in the North-Western Provinces), and
has considerable intelligence.   On the cruel murder by the mutineers of the
Rev. Mr. Hunter and Mrs. Hunter, at Siálkot, where they had been founding
a mission in connection with the Established Church of Scotland, he attached
himself, from motives of benevolence, to a convert who had accompanied them
thither, and assisted in reconducting him to Bombay, where he (Chinturám)
was very anxious to make my personal acquaintance, on account of the
impression which the perusal of my *Exposure of Hindooism* in Hindee had
made on his mind in his first religious inquiries.   He left Bombay with us,
desiring to make a profession of Christianity in his native country ; but
quickened by the divine word which he had often heard from my lips on this
journey, he found that he could no longer delay publicly espousing the cause
of the Lord.   I have a high opinion of his Christian character.

"JODHPORE, 15*th February*.—This Marwar is the darkest province of
India in which I have ever been ; and greatly is it to be regretted that it has
never hitherto been visited by any missionary of the Cross.   I saw much of a
fearful and obscene character at Palee, its commercial capital, and here at its
political capital I find matters in a most extraordinary position both religiously and socially.   The Maharaja Tukht Singh (whom we saw at Ahmednuggur in 1840) is giving me a most kind reception, and has appointed a
grand durbar on my account this evening, at the close of which Mrs. Wilson
and I start again for Palee, which, through relays of bullocks, furnished us by
the Raja, we hope to reach to-morrow forenoon, though the distance over
sandy roads is forty-two miles.   Captain Nixon, the Political Agent, is absent
investigating a case of Traga, in which a Charan has killed his mother,
to bring her blood in a local quarrel upon an opposing party ; but we
are most kindly treated by Mrs. Nixon, with whom we are staying.
Yesterday I spent many hours with the learned men of the durbar.   The
chief Brahman is positively like another Sayana Acharya, interpreting the
Vedas by the ancient helps to their understanding.   The chief Charan has
mastered the *Mahabharata* and all the local chronicles of the Rajpoots, on
which Colonel Tod drew so copiously and credulously.   Both these worthies
think that Hindooism (as 'prophesied') is nearly at its end.   The blood of
all the princes they held to be corrupted by unholy matrimonial alliances,
and a departure from the established institutes of their faith.   Their *achara*

they consider worse than that of Soodras (low castes). They are in possession of rich literary treasures, grammatical and expository, of which Europeans
have yet heard nothing. They were very much interested in the sketch I
gave them of the European investigation of the Vedas, and allowed that it
explains much which they had observed, while it leaves many difficulties
(principally founded on the erroneous idea of the 'eternity' of the Vedas)
unsolved. A report of all that passed between us on Hindooism and Christianity would fill a number of the *Oriental Christian Spectator*. I see that the
Maharaja has a very difficult part to play in the midst of the various *powers*
by which he is surrounded. 'Non-interference' has hitherto been the cruel
and unjust maxim of the British Government with the Rajpoot States. It is
perfectly incompatible with our guarantee to preserve the internal peace of
the provinces. Its corollary is 'Safe Tyranny.'"

MRS. WILSON TO HER SISTERS.

"AMBROLIE, BOMBAY, 11*th April* 1860.—You will be thankful to hear
that, through the goodness of God, we have reached our home in safety after
a most fatiguing journey. We left our kind friends at Beawur on the evening
of the 9th March for Nusseerabad, where we stayed for two days, and on the
12th left by bullock train, *via* Indore, Malligaum, etc. The advantage of
this train is that you can get a change of bullocks every six or eight miles,
which enables you to get over the ground more rapidly than by daily stages
of ten or twenty miles with the same bullocks, as we used to travel. Our
desire was to get home as soon as possible, though the fatigue should be
greater, but I should not like to do it again in similar circumstances, as it
was too trying for my dear husband. We could not get a spring cart, and
were obliged to travel in a common village cart, with a roof of bamboos, and
covered with carpets, in which we had to lie by day and night, as the roof was
too low for us to sit up.

"Between Neemuch and Mhow there are no traveller's bungalows, nor
any place of shelter, so for some days we just halted for some hours in the
middle of the day under some trees, for a little rest and refreshment, quite in
gipsy style. When we got to Mhow we hoped to get a more comfortable cart ;
and we got one much larger and higher in the roof, but it was made of iron,
and was very rough, and the noise it made was something fearful. Sleep in
it was impossible, and Dr. Wilson got quite knocked up and had a good deal
of fever during the last ten days of the journey. I wonder how I stood it so
well, for I could sleep neither by day nor by night, and the heat was great,
in the day time from 95° to 104°, with a high scorching wind, blowing up the
dust in tornadoes, and making us as black as sweeps. We travelled in this
way about 700 miles, and the Lord in His great mercy brought us here, in
peace and safety, on the evening on the 5th. The last forty miles of our
journey was by the railway, and when we got into it the change was most
agreeable and soothing to the brain, and to our bones, which had been sorely
shaken for three weeks.

"We got to Neemuch on 16th March, and spent two days with friends ;
on Sabbath my husband conducted worship in the library. There is neither
a church nor a chaplain there, though the European troops amount to fully
1500. It is very sad to see so many large stations without any means of
grace. Our next halting-place was Indore, where we spent two days, chiefly
with Sir Richmond and Lady Shakespeare. They are very kind, good people.
On the afternoon of Friday there was a grand durbar held, when Holkar had
the right of adoption granted to him, and he was presented with some handsome presents by the Government for his fidelity during the Mutiny. (He
was true to the British, though his loyalty was rather doubtful at the time.)

Dr. Wilson had some conversation with him, but of course that was not the time nor the place for any religious discussion. When we were preparing to leave next day Holkar sent a very urgent request that my husband should meet him in the afternoon at his country palace, as he was most anxious to see him again, and he offered to send us on to Mhow in the evening in his carriage with changes of horses. Dr. Wilson was delighted to have an opportunity of presenting him with a copy of the Bible and other books, and of conversing with him on the Christian religion. I had intended to sit in the carriage in the garden of the palace during the interview, but Holkar very politely sent for me, and begged of me to sit down beside himself and all the learned Brahmans, whom he had assembled to have a discussion with the learned Doctor from Bombay.

"Holkar is a pleasant-looking man about thirty; he was quite plainly dressed, but wore some handsome jewels. He sat in a chair at the end of a long table. At one side sat his prime minister, then Dr. Wilson and myself, and some of his courtiers. On his other side sat a row of learned Pundits and Brahmans, who had been called together for the occasion. At Holkar's request Dr. Wilson and they entered into a discussion on the sacred books of the Hindus and other kindred subjects. They got quite frightened when my husband repeated some Sanskrit quotations, and when they saw how well prepared he was to argue with them, and to point out the absurdities of their system. Holkar and some others who were present seemed to enjoy their discomfiture. We proceeded to Mhow in his carriage (fourteen miles), where we arrived late at night, and were kindly received by Mr. and Mrs. Paton. They were quite strangers to us; he is the chaplain to the 72d Highlanders, he is of the Established Church, and had lately married a lady from Edinburgh. We spent two days with them very pleasantly. He seems to be a good man, and well suited for the work to which he has been called. At six o'clock on Sabbath morning Dr. Wilson preached[1] to about 800 soldiers and officers.

"Our next Sabbath was spent at Malligaum, where my dear husband was very poorly, but he was able to take the Marathee service in a school-room at the request of the missionaries of the Church Mission, two of whom are stationed there. We reached home on the following Thursday evening, when we received such a warm welcome from the dear couverts and others as quite affected us. Their faces beamed with delight on seeing us restored to them after so many trials; and we felt truly thankful to be reunited to them. We feel the soft sea breeze very pleasant, and my dear husband is gradually recovering. He is very busy preparing his reports to go by this mail for the General Assembly.

"Our good friends Dr. and Mrs. Miller leave this evening by the home mail. We shall miss them very much. He has been appointed as elder to the Assembly, and I hope whilst he is at home he may be of use to our mission. There was a large meeting here last evening, a farewell party to the Millers—there were at it about thirty Europeans and a number of converts. After tea an address from the native church to them was read by Mr. Dhunjeebhoy, expressing their gratitude for Dr. Miller's medical aid extended to them, and for many other acts of kindness and sympathy, and they presented him with a very handsome Bible, and Mrs. Miller with Cowper's works."

DR. WILSON TO DR. EDDOWES.

". . . We were often as much covered with dust on the road as the sweeps with soot in chimneys in my young days. Yet we had some pleasant

---

[1] Dr. Wilson had preached to the same 72d Highlanders at Cape Town in 1828.

interludes by the way, as at Chittor, Neemuch, Jawara, Indore, etc. The Nawab of Jawara, and Holkar, and their people, I found very inquisitive on the subject of religion, as I had found some other Rajas. Nothing would satisfy Holkar but a long and formal discussion between his Brahmans and myself. He acted as chairman, and that in an impartial spirit. At the close he said to Mrs. Wilson, who was accommodated near the arena, 'I shall never forget this day; I have got much new light to-day.' He was evidently much disappointed by the appearance made by the Brahmans. They put several questions to me, which the Maharaja declared to be inept; and he himself took their place, boldly asking, 'Why do you kill animals?' My answer was in substance as follows :—'Maharaja, that is a question for yourself as well as for me. You kill all sorts of clean animals for food, except cows. For the same reason that you kill fowls, goats, sheep, etc., I kill cows, getting suitable food from them not forbidden by God. I admire the Sanskrit language. The best word for *man* in it is *manushya*, which means, '*he that has a mind.*' The word for cattle is *pashu* (Latin, *pecu*), 'that which may be tied.' Man is an intellectual and moral being, created for the service of God; cattle are created for the service of man. The Vedas show that the ancient Hindus ate them, and you may eat them too. Death is not to them what it is to us. Even the pain which they suffer at death by violence may be very slight. Dr. Livingstone, when he was overpowered by a lion, from a sort of electrical excitement which he experienced suffered no pain.' 'Yes,' said the Maharaja, 'the question is my own, and you have given a good answer to it. I am always troubled by my friends opposite.' I attribute all the scrupulosity about the use of animal food to the doctrine of the Hindus about birth after birth. I think it would have done the heart of some of our more timid Politicals good to have seen all these go off in good temper on both sides.''

But the new or extended agencies of the Churches of Great Britain, the United States, and Germany, fell short in far-reaching consequences of the catholic system of public instruction which was legislatively established in 1857. That system was directly the work of the missionary party. It was, and is still, the result not of a compromise but of co-operation between the Government or secular State and all non-government or proselytising bodies, Heathen and Christian, who choose to give a sound education to the people in addition to any religious instruction of which the State, as the ruler of millions of men of differing creeds, cults, and customs, can officially take no cognisance at this stage. The State, however, does not ignore natural or even revealed religion. But, calling Universities into existence, and placing them under an executive largely separate from itself, the Government at once puts the higher education in its proper place of self-developing independence, and it provides bodies competent to examine students of all the great religions, as they appear in the literature, the philosophy, the history, the laws,

and in fact the sacred books of each.   Questions long discussed
in the Christian Parliament of the mother country, and not
concluded even yet for Ireland, were in 1857, under far more
conflicting circumstances, settled for ever on the true basis of
complete toleration and fearless confidence in the ultimate
triumph of truth.   And the men who brought that about
were John Marshman, heir of the Serampore men ; Alexander
Duff ; and John Wilson.

Everywhere in India the East India Company first refused
to teach or to tolerate teachers, and when compelled by
Parliament under the influence of Charles Grant, Wilberforce,
and Zachary Macaulay, taught Hindooism and Muhammadanism only, while intolerant to all dissent from either.   By
1835 Dr. Duff, Macaulay, and the Anglicists under Lord
William Bentinck, gradually changed that in Eastern and
Dr. Wilson in Western India.   But till 1854 these and other
educational reformers were discouraged by Government, as
such, because they were also Christian proselytisers.   The
Government and the independent systems of public instruction went on side by side.   All the public money was given
to the former, which was neutral only in profession and
Hindoo-Muhammadan in practice, the latter being maintained
by the Churches of the West so far as it was Christian, and
by a few educated native gentlemen so far as it was aggres-
sively Hindoo.   When in 1853 the Company applied to
Parliament for what proved to be its last charter, the evidence
given by most of the experts, and especially by Dr. Duff and
Mr. Marshman, showed the folly of the rivalry on every side
—of principle, of even secular efficiency, of economy.   Lord
Northbrook, accordingly, when private secretary to the present
Lord Halifax who was then President of the old Board of
Control, drafted a despatch from all the evidence, and also
from the notes of Dr. Duff ; and the Court of Directors sent
that out to Lord Dalhousie, with instructions to carry it into
effect.   That Governor-General, who had been helping Mr.
Thomason with his thousands of primary circle schools in
Upper India, and was maintaining the Bethune girls' school
out of his own pocket, was delighted with this despatch of
July 1854.   At the foundation it placed vernacular schools
for the millions, and then a secondary and partly English
school in every district or county.   Then it recognised exist-

ing colleges, State and independent, Hindoo, Muhammadan, and Christian, Parsee and East Indian ; offering grants in aid to all on the test of secular efficiency, while maintaining its own until endowed, or independent but aided effort as in England, could relieve it of the burden of direct teaching. The whole arch was bound together by the three Universities of Calcutta, Bombay, and Madras, chiefly examining bodies like that of London, but fitted to have Chairs of their own in time, as some now have. The Senate of each consisted of worthy representatives of all educational agencies, of whatever creed. The Syndicate or executive body appointed by the Arts, Law, Medical, and Engineering Faculties of the Senate, regulated the whole education of the country by fixing standards and text-books, and selecting the examiners for degrees. Theoretically the scheme was perfect.

Practically the new policy worked well for a time, because men of the wisdom, experience, and tact as well as principle of Wilson and Duff, were able to preside at the launching of what they had designed. In a letter to their committee in Edinburgh, written by Dr. Wilson and signed also by Mr. Nesbit not long before his death, they reviewed the provisions of the despatch. Unhappily the succession, as Governor, of Sir George Clerk, who with all his merits retained the Company's political prejudices against Christian missions, and the action of Directors and Inspectors of Public Instruction, obstructed the fair working of the new system of grants in aid until the appointment of Sir Alexander Grant as head of the department. But that opposition was temporary, and it did not affect the more independent University and colleges.

"BOMBAY, 16th May 1855.—Your important letter on the Despatch to the Government of India on the subject of Education was duly received, and copies of it have been forwarded by Dr. Wilson to the Dekhan and Nagpore. We rejoice to learn from it that our Committee at home are disposed to concur in our co-operation with Government in carrying its provisions into effect in so far as they may be found to apply to our missionary establishments. The issue of that Despatch, we conceive, constitutes a new and promising epoch in connection with the intellectual and moral enlightenment of this great country. It fully recognises important principles for which we have long and strenuously contended in this Presidency. It forms a discriminative and judicious estimate of the comparative claims of the vernacular and learned languages of India and of English as media of instruction. It makes a very cordial acknowledgment of the benefits derived by India from the missionary enterprise. It makes the Bible accessible for purposes of consultation to inquisitive youth within the walls of the Government seminaries. It permits the communication to them at extra hours of Christian instruction, voluntarily imparted and voluntarily received. It promises certain grants in aid of secular instruction, for certain definite objects, to all private scholastic institutions permitting government inspection and exacting a fee, however small, from the pupils. It proposes the foundation of Universities at the Presidencies, for granting honours and degrees to India youth of requisite attainments. It sanctions the affiliation with these Universities] of all seminaries rightly conducted and furnishing the requisite amount of education. It has our full approbation as far as it goes, and we shall rejoice to find its provisions speedily carried into effect in the spirit in which it has been framed.

"In referring to the moral relations of that Despatch, we must mention, what the members of our Committee cannot have failed to notice, that it offers the same assistance in the communication of sound secular instruction to seminaries founded and conducted on heathen principles that it does to those which are founded and conducted on Christian principles. In doing so, it does not seem to us to recognise any principle of religious latitudinarianism. It simply offers to all a common blessing, without adopting any action with reference to higher blessings on the one hand, or to what may prove an injury and a curse on the other. It leaves its own expression of respect to Christian institutions to remain unmodified by what it proposes to do with reference to those of another character. Sound secular instruction, imparted without any ignoring or depreciating of Christianity, can in no degree favour heathenism or error of any kind. To a certain extent it will be a counteraction of that error. The grants-in-aid will, we hope, be so administered, according to the Despatch, as to go to the encouragement and support only of sound secular knowledge. We do not see that such an appropriation of them will increase the resources of heathenism. To a certain extent it will direct the native resources to what is good, as they will be needed for that effort which is required to secure the progress in secular knowledge which the Government inspection demands. While we make these remarks, we do not in any degree compromise our own views of the supreme importance of the combination of right religious education and training with secular instruction.

"But it is with the probable effects of the Despatch on our missionary undertakings that we have most to do, though we have considered this reference to its general moral bearings essential to our judgment of its acceptability to the Christian community. It will open a wide field to the operation of our Bible and Tract Societies and missionary presses. It will call for an increase of missionary agency, with a view to the hallowing of the secular instruction which it directly encourages. It will do more than this. It will aid the missionary institutions in that department of their labours which embraces secular knowledge. But missionaries and their supporters must vow before God and man not to dilute or diminish their religious instruction in their seminaries on this account. While, as hitherto, they communicate a sound secular instruction, they must never fail to act on the principle of combining this instruction with that of an infinitely higher character.

"To Government inspection, conducted as we trust it will be in a courteous, liberal, and impartial spirit, we cannot object ; while of course we repudiate all right on the part of Government to interfere with the management of our seminaries. Government is entitled to see to the faithful appropriation of its own educational grants.

"To the exaction of a fee from such of our pupils as may be willing and able to pay it, as a condition of our receiving Government help, we do not object. In fact, in a modified form, we have all along acted on this principle to a certain extent in our higher seminary in Bombay. It is our rule to exact an admission fee of one rupee from the pupils for the reasons mentioned at

p. 484 of Dr. Wilson's *Evangelisation of India*. The advanced pupils generally
aid us in instructing the lower classes, partly in compensation for the instruction which they themselves receive in our College Department. We are willing to extend our demands in that Institution and in all our schools, without
excluding from their benefits any who may be unable or unwilling to make a
money payment. The evangelistic feature of our educational establishment
must be preserved. To the poor, who are not the least hopeful in a missionary point of view, the Gospel must be taught in all our schools without money
and without price. We are willing to adopt the principle of payment, as far
as it may be practicable, as a *rule*, but we must have full liberty to make
exceptions whenever they may be proper and expedient. We should never
be excused by our own consciences, or by our Christian brethren at home and
abroad, were we to act otherwise. We hope that Government will give
us full latitude in this matter. At all events, we must follow in regard to it
our own solemn convictions. The Government, we believe, will place the
charitable support which our schools receive in the place, in some instances,
of the fees which are elsewhere exacted. It is perhaps not a matter of much
consequence that *all* our vernacular schools, which are almost wholly devoted
to the communication of scriptural knowledge, should in present circumstances
be connected with the Government scheme."

It was on the 18th July 1857, in the darkest hour of the
Mutiny, that the University of Bombay received its charter.
We applaud the inhabitants of Leyden, said Dr. Wilson
afterwards when speaking as its Vice-Chancellor, who con-
certed measures for founding a University even during the
terrible siege of their town by the Spaniards in 1573, when
6000 of their number perished by famine and pestilence, and
who devoted to that University the remission of taxes offered
them as a reward for their patriotism. Shall we, he asked,
withhold the meed of praise from the Government of India?

Long and detailed were the discussions of the new Senate
in working out regulations for the University. The share
which Dr. Wilson had in these, and the success with which
he secured due recognition of the Christian Philosophy and
Literature, side by side with the non-Christian, and solely on
the ground of confidence in truth and academic fitness, is seen
in the following extracts from letters to Dr. Duff. Dr. Wilson
wrote with the experience not only of one of the founders of
the University, but as a member of the Syndicate, Dean of the
Faculty of Arts, and an examiner in Sanskrit, Persian, Hebrew,
Marathee, Goojaratee, and Hindostance :—

"Had it not been for most strenuous and almost self-destroying efforts
and exertions which I made from day to day during the first discussion of the
bye-laws, there would have been no recognition in them, as subjects of study,
of Moral Philosophy, of Jewish History, and of the Evidences of Christianity
in the case of undergraduates electing them ; and had we not had a good backing

in the addition to the Senate in 1864 of Messrs. Aitken, Dhunjeebhoy, and Stothert, I verily believe that good which has been since effected in other matters might not have been realised. Our combined yet independent action in the frequent meetings of the Senate and in the Faculty to which we belong, is of a most salutary character, while, as calls are made upon us, we can engage in the University examinations without any interruption of our mission work."

"I send you the list of books (independent of those mentioned in our bye-laws) which we have lately chosen in our University, for a cycle of five years in advance of 1870. You will see from it that even in our University studies there is a good foundation for Christian tuition in the case of ardent, judicious, and otherwise competent missionaries. This remark has special reference to the *English* books prescribed, in connection with which the truths of Christianity may be easily and systematically taught. [A lecture which I delivered some three years ago on the Foundational Facts of Milton's *Paradise Lost*, was attended by about 700 students.] In our Sanskrit course, till the B.A. is passed, we have prescribed the *Tarkasangraha*, the fundamental treatise of the Nyaya (the Theistic Philosophy holding, however, the eternity of atoms formed, fashioned, and directed by a Creator). The same Philosophy re-appears in three of the five years in the M.A. course. From the *Vedanta*, which we have admitted for two years, we have eliminated the Brahma Sútras, with the Commentary of that formidable sophist Shankaracharya. The whole Sanskrit course I have all along most profitably contrasted with Christianity. Our Hebrew studies, not yet announced for the cycle, are from the Bible, which can maintain its place spite the Arabic Koran. For our systematic Biblical reading and lecturing we can maintain a due place, by insisting on the *conditions* of our missionary Institutions. It is a fact that the eagerness for graduation is a *temptation* to many young men to confine their attention to the studies prescribed by the Universities; but what would be the consequence if, instead of opposing that temptation, we were to withdraw from the arena? What would soon be the character of the Universities themselves? What would soon be the state of the educated mind of India, which rules the native world? What——? I may go on for hours suggesting most lamentable consequences."

From the first meeting of the Senate to the last which he was able to attend, Dr. Wilson guided the course of the University of Bombay with affectionate solicitude and cultured catholicity of spirit. When the Government appointed the zealous Christian missionary and uncompromising proselytiser, Vice-Chancellor, it at once proclaimed practically the final abandonment of the last relics of the distrust of truth, and won the applause of educated men of all creeds and races in India. The Governor-General had offered the similar honorary but very influential office, of virtual director of the whole education of millions, to the good and the scholarly Bishop Cotton, who too modestly declined it. Had Dr. Duff remained longer in India he would have been nominated by Lord Lawrence. As Vice-Chancellor of Bombay, when, in the resplendent robes of his office, he took the

chief part in the ceremonial of laying the foundation-stone of
the University building designed by Sir Gilbert Scott, he thus
chronicled the endowments presented by his native and non-
Christian friends—endowments to be increased by himself in
the foundation of the John Wilson Chair of Comparative
Philology :

" The personal benevolence which we are required to acknowledge preceded
that of the Government. Mr. Cowasjee Jehanghier Readymoney furnished
the University in 1863 with one lakh of rupees (£10,000), now very considerably increased by accumulated interest, towards the erection of a University
Hall. In 1864 Mr. Premchund Roychund presented us with two lakhs of
rupees for the erection of a Library, and in the same year with another two
lakhs of rupees for the erection of a Tower, to contain a large clock and a set
of joy bells. Independently of the buildings, several most valuable endowments have been conferred on the University, as Rs. 20,000 in four per cent
Government securities, by the Hon. Munguldass Nathoobhoy, for establishing
a travelling fellowship ; Rs. 5000 (£500), by the family of the late Mr.
Manockjee Limjee, for a gold medal to be given for the best English Essay on
a prescribed subject ; Rs. 10,000 by Mr. Bugwandass Purshotumdass, for a
Sanskrit scholarship ; Rs. 5000 by Mr. Homejee Cursetjee Dady Shet, for an
annual gold medal for the best English Poem on a given subject offered in
competition ; an endowment of six Sanskrit scholarships (three of Rs. 25 each,
and three of Rs. 20 each per mensem), amounting altogether to Rs. 30,000,
by Mr. Vinayekrao Jugonnathjee Sunkersett, in memory of his late father,
the Hon. Jugonnath Sunkersett, one of the greatest supporters of education
in the Bombay Presidency ; Rs. 45,000 by His Highness the Jam of Nowa-
nuggur, for an English scholarship to be held by a native of Kathiawar ;
Rs. 5000 in four per cent notes, by Mr. Cowasjee Jehanghier Readymoney,
for founding a Latin Scholarship ; and Rs. 5000 from the members of the
Civil Service and other gentlemen, for an annual gold medal, as a prize in law,
for the commemoration of the accomplishments and worth of the Hon.
Alexander Kinloch Forbes, Judge of the High Court, and Vice-Chancellor of
this University. In all these great and generous gifts, the liberality of
Bombay, according to its wont, has been most distinguished and exemplary.

" Our University, thus auspiciously begun, will, it is confidently believed,
continue to flourish. Under its direction and superintendence the inquisitive and
ingenious Indian youth may effectively study the rich and varied languages,
literature, history, and laws of England, of Italy, of Greece, of Judea, of Arabia,
and of India ; have his mind disciplined and exercised by the sciences of
mathematical demonstration and investigation, and of the dialectic art ; expatiate
in the near and remote, minute and grand regions of physical science ; contemplate what are still more wonderful, the faculties, functions, intuitions, and
phenomena of the human mind ; dwell on the moral relationship of man to his
Maker and to his fellow-creatures ; consider the economy of social and
national government in all its connections ; prepare himself for the practice
of the healing art, for the administration of justice, or for the application of
engineering in all its departments, to the necessities, convenience, and
gratification of the human family ; and train himself for the discharge of the
general duties of life in the most varied circumstances. Its influence on the
intellectual and moral state of its *alumni* on their ultimate position in this
world, and on their prospects with regard to that which is to come, may surely
be expected to be beneficial in no common degree. It is not merely with its

alumni, however, that it will have to do. It will affect through them the whole community of Western India, if not of distant provinces and countries. It will, with the blessing of God, which we implore on its behalf, be for ages an eminent instrumentality in the enlightenment, civilisation, and regeneration of THE EAST."

It was in May 1860 that Bombay lost the services of its Governor, Lord Elphinstone, who had guided the province through perilous times with rare firmness, wisdom, and self-sacrifice. He died soon after, leaving a name worthy to be placed beside that of his greater uncle's, and perpetuated by more than one institution and building in the capital where he ruled so well.

Very beautiful were the relations, of which these glimpses have been given, between the Governor and the Missionary. Good reason had Lord Elphinstone to remark to Dr. H. Miller that to no man was he so indebted personally, for public and private services, as to Dr. Wilson, on whom he could not prevail to accept so much as the value of a shoe-latchet. When, in public meeting, moving the adoption of the farewell address which the province selected him to present to the retiring Governor, Dr. Wilson especially referred to his Excellency's " constant recognition of the great principles of religious toleration and humanity," especially in the suppression of hook-swinging, and in securing to all, out-caste as well as Brahman, access to the public wells and cisterns.

CHAPTER XVII.

1862-1865.

THE KRISHNA ORGIES—DR. WILSON AMONG THE
EDUCATED NATIVES.

Brahmanism opposed to Rational Humanity—The stages of its Corruption—
Krishna Worship—The Four Krishna Reformers—Young Bombay—
Vallabh the Royal Teacher of Deified Adultery—Trade of Bombay taxed
for the Maharajas—A Courageous Editor—The Trial—Mr. Chisholm
Anstey—Dr. Wilson's Evidence—Sir Joseph Arnould's Judgment—Public
Opinion—Advice to Hindoos to travel—Sir Jamsetjee Jeejeebhoy's
Benevolent Institution—Influence of Dr. Wilson in Hindoo and Parsee
Families—Rai Bahadoor Tirmal Rao—"Uncle" Wilson—A Hindoo Lady
learning to read at sixty—Intercourse with Native Princes—Raja Dinkur
Rao—The Converts' Address to Dr. Wilson on the Thirtieth Anniversary
of his Landing—Reviews his Missionary Policy—Building of the Native
Church and Manse—The Drowning of Stephen Hislop.

THE late Canon Mozley, a Christian philosopher who has been
pronounced, with some justice, the Bishop Butler of this generation, published an Essay on "Indian Conversion," twenty years
ago. Writing before the comparatively rapid development of
the Church of India, the Protestant sections of which already
form a varied community of more than three hundred thousand
souls, he argued, on the ground of reason alone, that Brahmanism
will be gradually but completely demolished by the fair and
solid contact of Christianity with it. For Brahmanism is at
disagreement with the original type of rational humanity; with
the religious type and the moral standard in human nature;
with physical truth, and with the ends of society. Not less
convincing is the historical argument; and when both are
looked at together in the light of time, as the factor in the
world's changes, the conclusion is overpowering, apart from
Scripture. From the monotheism and nature-worship of the
early Vedic hymns and Zoroastrian *gathas*, to the polytheism

and sacerdotal caste which provoked the Buddhist reform, what a change! And yet it is spread over, at least, twelve centuries. Arrested for a time by men like Asoka, the Brahmanical corruption leavened the whole lump of Asiatic life, whether Hindoo or Buddhist, till, at the close of the next twelve centuries, the faith of Gautama was wiped out in blood all over the peninsula, and only the conforming Jains remained to tell of the impotence of the creed that had cut its temples and monasteries out of the living rock, that had subdued Tibet and China, Burma and Ceylon. Triumphant Brahmanism entered on the third stage of its descending progress ten centuries ago, with all its evils intensified, and afterwards but little checked by the iconoclastic fanaticism of the Muhammadan invasion. Ceasing to spread, save among the aborigines it had long scorned when it did not reduce them to the worst slavery, Brahmanism was driven in on itself. For nearly a century it found a protection alike against Mussulman intolerance and Christian light in the encouragement of the East India Company, which Charles Grant and Wilberforce first stopped by the Charter of 1833.

After the persecution of Buddhism there arose the latest development of the Hindoo system in the worship of Krishna. Thenceforth Brahmanism was to act on the elastic policy of finding a place for every sect, every sentiment, every god, every deified hero or saint, that would consent, even indirectly, to affiliate itself. Like the Paganism of the Roman empire, the Brahmanism which emerged from the struggle with Buddhism, wounded and wise, would have included Christianity itself, if that had consented to be dragged at its chariot wheels. Krishna, on his best side, it was not difficult to identify with Christ, sufficiently to satisfy the uneducated. The Jesuits of the Madura Mission themselves favoured the identification, and forged Vedas to prove it. So saturated is the Bhagavat Puran of this period with Christian-like sentiment, that it is still a subject of discussion whether the similarity was not designed.

Krishna, the god of love in the Oriental sense of lust, has ever since marked the accelerating corruption of popular Hindooism. At first, like Buddhism, a concession to the discontent with caste, sacerdotalism, exclusiveness, and rigidity, the Krishna worship seems to rest on the idea of brotherhood

including even Muhammadans. From the teaching of
Ramanuj and Ramanand there arose four reformers in the
fifteenth and sixteenth centuries in each of the great provinces
of Hindooism. Kabeer, the weaver, was the Hindee ; Nanuk,
the herd-boy, was the Punjabee or Sikh ; Chaitunya, the Brahman, was the Bengalee ; and Tukaram, the shopkeeper, was
the Marathee teacher, singer, and priest. Each was the Vates
of his countrymen. Dr. Wilson early became familiar with
their teaching, especially with that of Tukaram, a poet who
has of late been frequently translated into English, while the
whole *Adi Granth*, or scriptures of Nanuk, has been recently
turned into English by Dr. Trumpp. All wrote in the vernacular ; all proclaimed the brotherhood of Vishnoo in his
Krishna form ; and all, as developed by their followers, ended
in the deification and practice of lust and intolerant cruelty.
The Jugganath car-worship, on which a lurid light has been
thrown by the trial and banishment to the Andamans of its
deified representative, the Raja of Pooree, for murder by
torture, is of the same reformed school.

Gradually Brahmanism found that its subtle policy of
widening the bonds of Hindooism so as to include all apparently conforming sects, though on the whole successful,
encouraged low-caste fanatics to claim, as pontiffs, the adoration
and very substantial revenues of the people. The Vaishnava
brotherhoods have thus honeycombed the old sacerdotalism
with secret, and generally filthy and execrable, cults all over
India south and west of the Ganges. Their leaders have
established the most frequented shrines, for which whole
armies of debased recruiters tout for pilgrims ; and they have
become wandering popes, who travel with all the pomp and
pride of the gods they represent. The regular Brahmans
resent this, not on moral but on pecuniary grounds, and strive
to compete with their rivals. Thus the deterioration goes
on, till India presents the same state of things which is
so accurately pictured in the second or third century
romance of *The Clementines*, the same crowd of Antinomian
sects, like the Nicolaitans, through which the paganism of
the empire vainly tried to compete with the only Faith that
has ever enforced continence and purity. He who would learn
what Hindooism now is, whether Brahmanical or Vaishnava,
will find the materials in the great treatise of Dr. Norman
Chevers on Medical Jurisprudence in India, and in the collec-

tion of *libri execrandi* in the Bodleian, made by the late Horace Hayman Wilson for his work on *The Religious Sects of the Hindoos.*

Against such teaching and practices there has always been that outraged native opinion which will yet cast forth the whole system responsible for them. So far as the class of educated reformers, in the true sense of the word, has not yet found its way into the Christian Church, but has become known as "Young Bombay" or "Young Bengal," they are indirectly the offspring of the education and influences of the cultured missionaries. In Bombay Dr. Wilson was the teacher, the adviser, the friend, of all such non-Christian or almost Christian natives. To them, in a hundred ways, the most precious portion not only of such morning leisure as he could claim, but of his working hours, was gladly given up. By the press, the college, lectures, the Asiatic Society, public meetings, discussions, social intercourse, and often substantial patronage, he made himself their example and their guide. Poor and rich, low and high caste, pundit and English-speaking, they all knew him; for they, and their fathers, and their children, sat at his feet during nigh half a century. In the light of the future, we believe his work among and for the non-Christian natives who resided in or passed through Bombay, to have exceeded in influence that which created the native church. It extended even where he was not personally known; it returned to him in the most unexpected ways. How he was to the natives as to the Europeans of Bombay a great and recognised moral force, all the more because of his Hindoo and Muhammadan discussions and Parsee controversies, was seen in what is popularly known as the Maharaj libel case.

When, at the end of the fifteenth century, Nanuk was gathering his Sikhs or disciples in the Punjab, Vallabh, son of a Brahman of Bijanuggur, went to the north of India as acharya or religious teacher. "To Krishna," he taught his followers, "dedicate body, soul, and possesions"—*tan, man, dhan*. Krishna is to be worshipped in the person of the gooroo or teacher, who himself becomes the god. The teacher is therefore to be addressed as a King or Maharaj; his followers are to worship him by sexual intercourse, or by witnessing such intercourse. While gods, the Vallabacharyas are also gopees, or herd-women devoted to Krishna, according to the scandalous legend ; and hence they dress as women, with long hair, female ornaments, and toe-rings. The union with the Maharajas of the wives and daughters of the devotees according to the vow of dedication, is union with Krishna, as in the Ras Lila. Hence, like the parallel sect of the Shaktees, or worshippers of the female principle in Bengal, the carnal love-meetings of the married followers, known as Ras Mandalis. Hence every Vallabacharya temple becomes the scene of adultery under so-called divine sanction. This faith is professed, these practices were followed, by the largest and wealthiest of the Hindoo communities of Western India, whose scripture is the tenth book of the Bhagavat Puran, translated from Sanskrit into the Brijabasha dialect as *Prem Sagur*, or the Ocean of Love. The Bhattias, Marwarees, and Lowanas—the men who, as clerks and partners in mercantile houses, as capitalists and shopkeepers, come most closely into contact with Europeans—were the men who adored the Maharajas, and whose wives and daughters were thus publicly debauched. Numbering probably not fewer than half a million in Western India, they paid the Maharajas' dues, according to a fixed tariff, on every article they sold, the real payer being the consumer of course. Thus these pontiffs of Krishna waxed fat with organised adultery and an ever-increasing tax on half the trade of Bombay. The impost of a farthing on every ten pounds' worth of Lancashire goods sold, yielded two temples alone £5300 in one year. Not one important article of trade escaped a similar impost.

The Brahmans of the Island, being beggars chiefly, receive alms from the Vaishnava as well as Shiva sects ; and this the Maharaj pontiffs in 1855 determined to stop, as an interference with their rights. Their followers consented, on the condition of reforms in the temple abuses, such as the cessation by the Maharajas of adulterous intercourse with their females at the winter service at four in the morning, and the pollution of young girls, the ever-increasing extortion, the taking of bribes in cases of arbitration, the summoning of worshippers to the shrines at all hours to attend the idol, and the beating of the crowds to hasten their passage through the temple. The promises were given but never carried out. The ignorant Maharajas were defeated in a public discussion with the

Brahmans who knew Sanskrit ; and their dignity was lowered by the order of the Supreme Court that they must attend when parties in a case, although they objected to sit lower than a European.

Editing the *Satya Prokash*, or "Light of Truth," one of the sixteen Goojaratee newspapers, was a youth Kursundass Mooljee, who was one of their followers and familiar with their practices. He became the centre of the reformers ; and against him the Maharajas hired a Parsee, the editor of our old friend the *Chabook*, or "Whip." Kursundass welcomed the arrival of Judoonath Brizruthunjee from Surat, as a Maharaj who was said to have himself espoused the cause of reform so far as to establish a female school. But one of the reforming party having caught the new-comer in the very act of adultery in the temple, it became necessary to expose that Maharaj also. Formerly the principal men of the community had signed a "slavery bond," vowing to excommunicate Kursundass, and to procure the passing of an Act to exempt the Maharajas from attendance in courts of justice. Only when that had been signed were the temples opened and the enforced fasting ceased. Kursundass then published an article headed "The Primitive Religion of the Hindoos and the present Heterodox Opinions," in which not only the whole sect but Judoonath Maharaj by name was charged with doctrines and practices involving " shamelessness, subtlety, immodesty, rascality, and deceit." This appeared on the 21st October 1860. Seven months after the Maharaj brought an action for libel in the Supreme Court against the editor and printer, laying the damages at Rs. 5000. At the same time he induced his leading followers to refuse to give evidence under pain of excommunication. Two of these were sentenced to heavy fines for conspiracy to defeat the ends of justice, and then the main case proceeded. From the 26th January 1862 it lasted forty days, for twenty-four of which it was before Sir M. Sausse, the Chief Justice, and Sir Joseph Arnould, Puisne Judge.

The success of the defendant, who pleaded justification, was due to two men. Mr. Chisholm Anstey, his senior counsel, supplied the forensic skill with all that persistence which, when not erratic as too often in his case, made him an antagonist to be feared whether in Parliament, at the bar, or

on the bench. Dr. Wilson contributed the learning and the
uprightness required to convict the Maharaj out of his own
books. Some thirty other witnesses on either side were
heard, including Judoonath himself, and the expenses amounted
to £6000, of which he had to pay the greater part. Of
Dr. Wilson's evidence the accomplished Judge remarked—
" Dr. Wilson, who has studied this subject with that comprehensive range of thought (the result of varied erudition)
which has made his name a foremost one among the living
Orientalists of Europe—Dr. Wilson says : ' The sect of Vallabacharya is a new sect, inasmuch as it has selected the
god Krishna in one of his aspects, that of his adolescence,
and raised him to supremacy in that aspect. It is a new
sect in as far as it has established the *pusthti-marg*, or way
of enjoyment, in a natural and carnal sense.' I agree with
Dr. Wilson in thinking that, ' all things considered, the alleged
libel is a very mild expostulation,' involving an ' appeal to
the principle that preceptors of religion, unless they purify
themselves, cannot expect success to attend their labours.' "
And the author of the volume which contains a history of
the whole sect and trial[1] expresses native opinion when he
writes : " Dr. Wilson's labours in this trial deserve special
notice. He placed at the disposal of the defendant his rich
and multifarious stores of learning, which proved of surpassing value. Throughout the whole trial this learned
missionary ably sustained the character which he fills in the
estimation of the natives of India—that of a philanthropist."
All the journals of India, native and European, rejoiced at
the vindication of morality and purity.

Dr. Wilson himself suggested and drew up the appeal
for a public recognition of " the disinterested efforts of Kursundass Mooljee to improve the state of Goojaratee society,
and especially of his courageous conduct, truthfulness, and
singleness of purpose in the management of the Maharaj
libel case." His name is followed by that of the Parsee
reformer, Ardaseer Framjee. Christianity, Hindooism, and
Zoroastrianism were thus seen happily allied in the cause of
morality and humanity. The result, with all that it involved,
was worth Dr. Wilson's thirty years' strivings. On the same

[1] *History of the Sect of the Maharajas or Vallabacharyas in Western
India.* London, 1865.

day he assisted Sir Bartle Frere, the Governor, in examining
the hundreds of Parsee youth, boys and girls, who crowded
the classes of the Benevolent Institution endowed by Sir
Jamsetjee Jeejeebhoy. The learned controversialist, whose
uncompromising but tolerant zeal for his Master had years
before excited a panic among the community when several
of their ablest youths were baptized into Christ, hailing the
pursuit of truth in every form, "referred to the intelligence and enterprise of the Parsee community, who would
not only be patrons of learning in India, like the noble Jeejeebhoy family, but participants of its great advantages."
The Governor followed, congratulating the dowager Lady
Jamsetjee on the results of her encouragement of female
education.

The subtle influence of Dr. Wilson and his teaching, per-
meating generations of non-Christian native society, not only
in the capital but in distant cities and stations, may be best
seen if we select one of the many Hindoo families to whom
he always was, in the childlike language of the grateful
people of India, "Kaka" or Uncle Wilson ; just as soldiers
and administrators like Nicholson, Edwardes, and Abbott, were
among the wild Afghan tribes of our north-west frontier. For
forty years, and with four of its generations whom he
educated, Dr. Wilson and his wife maintained a closer personal intercourse and more affectionate correspondence with
the family of the Hindoo Tirmal Rao, than we have any
example of. The judge, whom in 1836 his father took from
Dharwar in the far south, to be educated in Bombay, tells
the story. This communication is introduced by his son, the
Bombay High Court Interpreter and Senior Canarese and
Marathee Translator, who writes to us—"He knew four
generations of our family. He loved me and my brother
Venkut Rao most tenderly. He very often remarked, in the
meetings of his friends, that our father completed his education under him, that we had been his pupils, and that he
looked upon us as his grandchildren. You heard the same
observation from his lips when he formally introduced us to
you in one of those meetings convened by him for your
sake."

From Rao Bahadoor Tirmal Rao Venkutesh,
    Pensioned Judge and First Class Honorary Magistrate.

"10th *February* 1878.—As my country is situated at the distance of about 350 miles from Bombay, no one in those days sent their children to Bombay to be educated. In 1836 my late father had occasion to go to Bombay on some business, and was struck with the English education that was imparted to the young men in the Government school there, and his European friends advised him to send me to Bombay. It was determined that I should be placed under the care of the then Rev. Dr. J. Wilson, in preference to being put into the Government school. I went to his house to pay my respects to him for the first time. I remember perfectly well how kindly he received me and what encouragement he gave me. He directed me to see him in his house both in the mornings and evenings every day, besides meeting him in the school. For some time Mathematics seemed to me to be a dry and useless study. He therefore, on one occasion, passed his hands over the figure of the 5th proposition of the first book of Euclid in such a peculiar manner, and explained matters to me so clearly, that from that moment I began to take great great liking for Mathematics. He taught me more of Geography, Astronomy, Zoology, general History, and Scripture, in course of his conversations in his house than in the regular classes in the schools. He appointed the late Rev. R. Nesbit to teach me literature specially, in addition to what I learnt in the classes, and permitted me also attend the lectures given in Logic, Geology, Botany, and Chemistry in the Elphinstone College by Professors Orlebar, Harkness, and Bell. Dr. Wilson's mode of teaching was so entertaining that we never felt that we were studying, but we used to think that we were playing with him. He treated us more like our father than any one else. He attended upon us during our sickness personally. In those days my wife was quite illiterate. He impressed upon my mind the advantages of female education, and made me teach her to read and write. At the same time he got his sisters-in-law, the Misses Anna and Hay Bayne, to undertake the education of my wife.

"During nights Dr. Wilson took me out in open air, and made me acquainted with the different planets and constellations. He used daily to pray to God in my behalf, and direct my mind towards God. On Sundays he regularly took me to his church to hear him preach. In fact the trouble that he took to educate me and the students of his classes was really inconceivable. After leaving his school he brought me prominently to the notice of the then Governor, Sir R. Grant, and other officers of the State, and it was in a measure owing to his recommendations that I obtained the offices that I held afterwards. Dr. Wilson always looked upon me as one of his earliest scholars, and loved me to excess. Twenty years afterwards it pleased God to enable me to place several of my children under the personal care of the Rev. Dr. Wilson and his late partner, Mrs. Isabella Wilson, for educational purposes. It would be impossible for me to express adequately the peculiar pleasure with which they undertook the task, and how well they executed it. Dr. Wilson had the charge of the education of the boys, and Mrs. Wilson that of the girls. It was owing wholly to Dr. Wilson's prayers, training, trouble, and exertions that my two boys, Jayasattia Boohrao Tirmal, and Venkutrao Rookmangad (now my legal nephew), have been so well educated. The former now holds a very responsible office in the Honourable the High Court of Judicature at Bombay. The latter obtained the degree of B.A. during Dr. Wilson's lifetime; and it is a pity that the latter did not live long enough to see Venkut Rao become an LL.B. also, which degree the University of Bombay has just conferred upon him.

"The above is a partial account of Dr. Wilson's dealings with my family

alone. He treated several hundreds of other families in a similar manner.
After leaving his college and returning to my country I continued to visit him
once in two years or so, and spent several days with him. The whole of his
time used to be occupied in doing some public good or other. He wrote and
published hundreds of tracts, and several books on religious, educational, historical, and other subjects in English, Marathee, Goojaratee, and other languages. He assisted people of all classes in various ways. His dealings with
all were kind, considerate, and honourable throughout ; so much so that
natives of all classes and creeds feared and honoured him more than they did
any other person. In course of time he had won the hearts of the people
so much that they were convinced that nothing could go wrong with him.
His very name, or, as the natives called him, ' *Wilson Kaka* ' (*i.e.* Uncle Wilson), was sufficient to inspire any one with the fullest confidence.

" He first arrived in India in 1829-30. Since that time, up to his death
in 1875, no less than eighteen Governors ruled over the Western Presidency.
Each, in his turn, did what good lay in his power to the country. There is
no wonder in that, as all of them were invested with official power, and had
at their command money and men. Dr. Wilson was a poor man, without
power or money. Nevertheless, he did more good to India, and still more so
to the Presidency of Bombay, in the way of educating people, composing
books suited to their wants, in various languages and on different subjects,
inducing them to be loyal subjects of the British Crown, collecting ancient
manuscripts and histories of the country, etc. etc., than all the eighteen
Governors put together. He was the father of several religious and educational Institutions. Dr. Wilson was held in the greatest esteem by the successive Governors, Commanders-in-Chief, members of Council, Judges of the
High Court, and almost all the other officers of the State, and the native
nobility. I know of no one to whom greater respect was paid than to Dr.
Wilson. It may be considered that I am exaggerating his virtues and usefulness, but there are thousands and thousands of Europeans and Natives who
would be glad to corroborate my assertions, and I challenge every one and all
to contradict me if they possibly can. Dr. Wilson was an extraordinary
man. Of his learning, travels, and other good deeds in England and elsewhere, I leave it to better hands than myself to describe. I only say what I
have seen and known. It is difficult to find another man like him. I am
really sorry that my knowledge of the English language is so limited that
I am not able to express more vividly the varied learning and usefulness of
Dr. Wilson."

In all the offices of friendship and affection common to
men and women of all countries, save that intercourse from
which Hindoo caste alone shuts out its votaries, Dr. and Mrs.
Wilson, and the Misses Bayne for a time, were one with this
Hindoo family. Children, grandchildren, great-grandchildren,
came successively to the Ambrolie Institution, and to the
Girls' School, while they spent their holiday and leisure hours
in the missionary's home, as English youths would have done.
Of all he wrote in 1857, " I know of no instance of any family
residing at such a distance from the seat of the Western Presidency making such judicious arrangements for the culture
and training of its young members." At the frequent social

gatherings of old students in the mission-house, as in the
grateful support of the college and schools, they were foremost.
When the aged mother of Tirmal Rao passed away, Dr.
Wilson wrote, amid the hurry of his duties in England, to
her son, his student of 1836, "I deeply sympathise with
every one of you. Your mother was no common woman.
It tells much in her favour that she was assiduous in her
endeavours to promote your well-being, and that of all the
members and connections of your family; that she encouraged you all in the acquisition of knowledge; and that
she encouraged the work of female education in India by
learning to read herself, when she had in her life numbered
threescore years. The day must come when we ourselves
must make the great transition and appear before the omnis-
cient and righteous Judge. May God in His mercy impart
to every one of us that salvation from the curse and pollution
of sin of which we stand in need, and which is freely offered
to all who confide in the great atonement of the Son of God.
Of this atonement your dear mother had heard, though not
so fully as you yourself have done." Such cases as this are
by no means rare in the varied transition states of thought
and progress through which India is passing under British
rule and missionary agencies of all kinds. In Bengal whole
families or clans, like the Dutts, have together taken the step
which seals all, and have publicly professed Christ.

Very similar to this among the Parsees were Dr. Wilson's
relations with another Judge, Mr. Manockjee Cursetjee, lasting over forty years. So with Dadoba Pandurang since 1834,
one of the University Examiners and an early reformer. The
Native Princes, Muhammadan and Hindoo, rarely visited the
capital without seeking an interview with one who had been
a welcome preacher in their durbars; and on such occasions
of rejoicing as marriages, they sent him *khureetus*, or letters of
honour, illuminated with the perfect taste of the Oriental,
and delicately besprinkled with gold dust. When a distinguished Native statesman like the Raja Dinkur Rao, who did
so much for Gwalior and for Lord Canning's Administration
in 1858-62, visited Bombay, he carried an introduction to
Dr. Wilson from Sir Richmond Shakespeare. Lord Canning
testified of that astute Marathee:—"Seldom has a ruler been
served in troublous times by a more faithful, fearless, or able

minister," for his counsel saved the Maharaja of Gwalior in 1857. When still more distant potentates, like Sultan Abdou of Joanna, repeated his visit to India, the Government, changed every five years, turned to Dr. Wilson for information regarding him.

But dearest of all to John Wilson were his children in the faith, gathered out of every kindred, and tribe, and tongue ; barbarian, Scythian, bond and free, from all the lands around the Indian Ocean. On the thirtieth anniversary of his landing at Bombay the whole adult community, of more than two hundred souls, presented him with a loving address, and a copy of the *Hexapla*, as best typifying his work and the tie which bound them to him and to each other. The address was signed in their name by the representative Parsee and Brahman now ordained Christian ministers, the Revs. Dhunjeebhoy Nowrojee and Narayan Sheshadri. Its tenor is seen in his reply, which is full of suggestiveness alike to the Church of India and to those Western Churches which have been privileged, all too slowly and coldly, to lay its foundations :

"The love and affection which you have ever borne to me since before my delighted eyes you one by one, and two by two in some instances, passed from the darkness of heathenism and error into the light and grace of the Lord, has, next to your steady and consistent adherence to the cause of Christ and your advancement in usefulness, proved the greatest ministerial solace and comfort which I have enjoyed in the hallowed evangelistic enterprise in which it is my privilege, under a deep sense of personal unworthiness, to engage in this great and promising though still benighted land. I feel that the bond which unites us together in mutual respect and confidence is of a permanent character, and I earnestly pray that it may be more and more sanctified to us all by the spirit of the glorious Saviour by Whom we have been redeemed and Whom we seek to serve.

"You express your belief that good has followed my labours in India. This, as you see and acknowledge, is, to any extent that it may have been realised, the consequence entirely of the divine blessing, which I ever desire to acknowledge with humility and praise. I thank God on all occasions for bringing me to the shores of India, on which my affections were strongly set from my youthful days, though I was ready to be sent as a Missionary of the Cross to any part of the world which might be selected for me by the wisdom of the Church seeking for divine direction. I bless God for my appointment to found the Scottish Missions at the seat of the Western Presidency of India, the peculiar importance of which I had begun to discern before I left my native land, and for the great and effectual door of usefulness which His gracious providence here opened for myself, and for the esteemed brethren in the ministry—particularly my dear brother Mr. Nesbit—who came to my assistance after a considerable number of years had been passed by me in solitary but not unfruitful labours in this mission. I have constantly sought

to use all available instrumentalities and opportunities for the prosecution of
the work in which I have been engaged ; and while I more and more earnestly
pray the Lord to pardon my numerous shortcomings and offences in His
work, I more and more seek to give Him the undivided praise for what has
been accomplished. It is in His name that I have sought to advance His
cause by speech and writing, and by teaching and preaching, both among
young and old, in schools and seminaries of learning both for males and
females, in the lecture-room of this house, and in places of public concourse
both in this city and neighbourhood, and in distant districts of this land. A
similar assurance I can give you in behalf of the Lord's devoted ministerial
servants in Bombay and in the contiguous Presidencies, many of whom we
have been privileged to welcome to this land, and some of whom, as our dear
brethren of the Irish Presbyterian, to introduce in the first instance to the
field of their labours.

"While I thank God for the multitudes near us and afar off in India, who
by the labours of all His servants in this land have become ashamed of the gods
and idols, and doctrines and rites of their varied superstitions ; and while I
see many, particularly of the young in this place and neighbourhood, apparently not far from the kingdom of God, I especially rejoice, with thankfulness
to God, in those who, like yourselves, have altogether entered the Christian
fold, and who by their spirit and temper, as well as their walk and conversation, give good evidence that they belong not only to the visible but invisible
Church of Christ. I view you emphatically as, under God, the hope of this
mission. You are the first fruits into Christ in this locality, and have the
Christian character to exhibit to those who are bone of your bone and flesh of
your flesh. You have the truth of Christ to declare to multitudes from whom,
both privately and publicly, you may obtain a hearing. In this work some
of you, who have been called to the ministry, have been honoured yourselves
to win souls to Christ ; while others of you have brought some of your relations and connections under the sound of the Gospel, and in a good degree
aided in their Christian instruction. In the work of personally endeavouring
to promote the enlightenment and conversion of your countrymen I trust you
will all more and more abound. This work must not be suffered to devolve
wholly, or even principally, on the officials of the Christian Church, necessary
though they be for its advancement. What would you think of a regiment of
soldiers who would be content to trust to its officers for the whole fighting
against the common enemy ? I should be glad to see in you all the activity
and zeal of the Christians of apostolical times, not only in your own mutual
edification and comfort, but in your efforts to convey to those around you the
knowledge of the true God and Jesus Christ whom He has sent.

"My dear brethren Messrs. Dhunjeebhoy and Narayan, in handing me
your address and request, have expressed to me their special gratitude for
what I have from time to time sought to do for the native missionary in the
matters, as I take it, of his being called to labour as an evangelist, set apart
for his great work by the solemnities and vows of ordination—God's own
ordinance, and in his being permitted to share in the common councils and
deliberations of the Christian ministry and mission with which he is connected.
For one to have done less than I have done in this matter would have been to
sacrifice the deepest convictions of my judgment and conscience, both as far
as Christian right and Christian expediency are concerned. You know that
our mission in general fully concurred in the views which I have been led to
take of the questions raised, and that no serious opposition was ever offered
to the principles which they recognised in the headquarters of presbytery in
Scotland. While we seek for the due probation of entrants into the holy
ministry, abroad as well as at home, we must remember that when the proba-

tion has been satisfactorily rendered, all due privileges should not only be greatly but joyfully and thankfully accorded. Probation in such a land as India, filled with people of a strange countenance and a strange tongue, and what is more, a strange heart, is needed certainly as much by the missionaries from the West as those raised up in the field of labour in the East. They cannot, without the greatest injury to themselves and the enterprise in which they are engaged, be free of the judgment and experience of those who may be supposed best to know the people and languages, and creeds and customs of India. A common council is the essential characteristic of presbytery. While it gives full scope to the judgment and conscience of all, it gives the fullest scope to the gifts of all for the information of that judgment and conscience. There is even peculiar potency in its administration, because from time to time it can select its own agencies for work to be done by individuals and committees."

The practical outcome of this address was the erection of that ecclesiastically becoming church, in which the native congregation under a native minister have worshipped since 1869. Aided by friends like Dr. Hugh Miller and Mr. James Burns in the west of Scotland, and themselves contributing ten thousand rupees out of their scanty income, the native church raised the structure at Ambrolie, of which Mr. Emerson was architect, with a manse, at the cost of £6000. In this, as in every Christian and philanthropic movement which he advocated, Dr. Wilson's personal subscriptions were almost lavishly generous, for he knew the force of example. The converts who, as elders and members, bestirred themselves to erect this memorial of their gratitude, were—Manuel Gomes, Mikhail Joseph, Yohan Prem, Baba Pudmanjee, Bapu Mazda, Behramjee Kersajee, Khan Singh, Mattathias Cohen, Kashinath Vishvanath, Wasudeva Pandurang, Shapoorjee Eduljee, and Rewa Ramjee. More significant than any statue of John Wilson is this Christian temple of his converts from many races, on the spot where he lived and laboured for nigh half a century.

In 1863 the Christian civilisation of India suffered a loss second only to that of those other pioneers Wilson and Duff. The Rev. Stephen Hislop of Nagpore had proved himself worthy to stand beside them, alike in the intensity of his devotion and the breadth of his culture. Aided by Mr. Hunter, he had built up the mission to the Hindoos and Gonds of Central India, through all the difficulties of bad feudatory rule, annexation, caste disputes, and the misgovernment even of British officers for a short time. The Rev. J. G. and Mrs. Cooper, who still carry on his work in his spirit,

helped him. How when he was mistaken for another in
1853 he was nearly put to death by a riotous mob in Nagpore,
and how he was the means of preparing the Government
against the mutiny and projected massacre by the sepoys and
Mussulman rabble of Nagpore, Mr. Hunter has told.[1] Were
it becoming so long as some of the actors are alive, we could
add the details of his service which, through the *Friend of
India* and privately, opened the eyes of Lord Canning to the
misrule that followed the Mutiny, and resulted in the creation
of the Central Provinces under Sir R. Temple as first Chief
Commissioner. In all that related to the neglected territory,
its varied people of five tongues, its simple but savage hill
Gonds, its geology and unparalleled mineral resources, its
schools, native officials, and administrative needs, Sir R.
Temple found Hislop his counsellor. The missionary was
more to the country than ten regiments or a whole establishment of civil officers were to it. Dr. Wilson rejoiced in his
work, so like his own—spiritual, scientific, philanthropic.

But all too soon Hislop was removed suddenly, while the
Chief Commissioner and the Bombay philanthropist, each in
his own way, published unavailing lamentations and eulogies.
It was on the 4th September, after a long break in the latter
rain, when Hislop and Sir R. Temple had gone out to study
the Scythian stones at Takulghat, and Hislop remained behind
to examine a Government school, that the missionary disappeared. In the interval between Sir R. Temple crossing a
stream and the missionary reaching it on his way to the camp,
the water had been swollen by sudden rain, and Stephen
Hislop was drowned. His riderless horse told the tale too
late to do more than rescue the dear remains. Another
martyr to duty had his name written in the great roll of
Christian men who have died as well as lived for the people
of India. Foremost among his supporters was the friend of
Judson, Sir Henry Durand, when, for a time, that officer was
the Political Resident at Nagpore.

[1] See the well-written *History of the Missions of the Free Church of Scotland in India and Africa*, by the Rev. Robert Hunter, M.A. 1873.

CHAPTER XVIII.

1865-1868.

NEW BOMBAY—DR. WILSON AMONG THE EUROPEANS—
DR. LIVINGSTONE—THE ABYSSINIAN EXPEDITION.

The Changes in Anglo-Indian Society—Dr. Wilson leaves Ambrolie for "The Cliff"—The Memories of Thirty Years—American Slavery and Bombay Cotton—Rise of prices in India—The Bombay Mania of 1863-66—The Crash in 1867—Dr. Wilson's Letters on the Crisis—His Hospitalities—Distinguished Visitors from 1863 to 1870—Mission in South Arabia—Discoveries in East Africa—Origin of Nyassa Settlement—Lord Elphinstone's Letter—Dr. Livingstone's First Visit—His Organisation of last Expedition—Address in the Town Hall—Chuma and Wykatané—Letter from Dr. Livingstone—The Abyssinian Converts Gabru and Maricha Warka—A Father in Christ—Four Years' Imprisonment of Captives by Theodorus—Sir George Yule's Offer of Rs. 20,000—Military Authorities apply to Dr. Wilson — His Abyssinian Converts become Counsellors of Prince Kassai—The Prince, now King John of Ethiopia—Dr. Wilson entrusted by Government with more Abyssinian Youths—The Light radiating from Bombay.

NOT the least of the results of the Mutiny was a change in Anglo-Indian society. On the one hand the influx of artisans for the railways, and of adventurers from Australia with consignments of horses or in search of employment, was accompanied by the military mistake which disbanded the East India Company's European army, flooded the cities and stations with discontented and injured soldiers, and in too many cases doomed the widows and wives of the men who had regained the empire to a life of shame. The "loafer" class was called into existence, and for the first time in our history white prostitution was seen in India. Now the ablest even of the English authorities who were responsible for the blunder, in spite of the protests of Lord Canning, Sir Henry Durand, and all the experienced officers on the spot, begin to see that the only solution of the difficulty of recruiting

60,000 soldiers for India, is to fall back on a local army
attached to the new organisation of Lord Cardwell. On the
other hand, the ruling class, the civil, military, and mercantile
communities, who emerged from the two years' conflict with
barbarism in its worst form, had lost all confidence in the
permanence not of our rule but of our institutions. They
ceased to trust the natives, to like the country. The "old
Indian " was no more. The change had really begun in 1856,
when the first set of Competition-Wallas arrived, and the
Haileybury monopoly passed away. But when complete
peace once more settled down on the empire with the first
day of 1859, there was a rush home. New furlough rules, the
substitution of England for the Cape of Good Hope as the
furlough sanitarium, more rapid and frequent means of communication, cheaper postage, and finally new men, changed
the whole character of Anglo-Indian society. Whether for
good or evil we shall not here determine, so far as England is
concerned. But the change has not been, either politically or
socially, for the good of the people of India thus far. India is
undoubtedly better ruled so far as systems of administration
are concerned. Is it more wisely governed as to the mode in
which these systems are applied ?

Very much against his will Dr. Wilson had to submit to
the social revolution, which, however, he continued to influence to the last in Bombay. The attendant rise of prices led
the native owner of the Ambrolie mission-house to demand a
rent of Rs. 300 a month. This, wrote Dr. Wilson to Dr.
Tweedie, "is much beyond the ability of both the mission and
myself to give ; " and, accordingly, the home of thirty years
was vacated.

To the adjoining Institution were added sheds, tents, and
other temporary accommodation, and there Dr. and Mrs.
Wilson, his colleague Mr. Stothert, who had brought new
strength to the work some time before, the female schools,
the book depository, and even some of the native catechists,
were accommodated. Twelve years before, when her husband
was subject to frequent attacks of fever, Mrs. Wilson had
urged him to take up his abode permanently in the cottage
given him by Dr. Smyttan on Malabar Hill. She did so,
seconding the orders of the physicians, and pointing out
that the good air of the higher region had made Dr. Stevenson

a new man. But Dr. Wilson had persisted in living among
the natives whom he sought to benefit, all these thirty years,
trusting to his almost annual tour, and an occasional holiday
at Poona or Mahableshwar, for the restoration of such robust-
ness as may be possible in the tropics. Now, when the hot
season of 1862 came on, he was fairly forced to reside in
" The Cliff," which thenceforth became indentified with him.
There, and in a guest chamber which he added, he kept open
house for English and Natives. Thence it was his delight, on
coming up from the day's toil at Ambrolie, or before returning
to it in the morning, to watch the glories of the scene from
the busy harbour away to the Western Ghauts, as he sat at
work in his library, or pointed out to his friends the spots of
historical and scientific interest. The house soon became
more than classical in its associations ;[1] his death made it
sacred.

Hardly had he taken permanent possession of " The Cliff,"
when, on the 9th June 1862, the United States Senate
decreed the abolition of slavery in all territories of the Union.
The secession of South Carolina, eighteen months before, had
another meaning also, which Bombay, of all cities, was the
first to feel, if not intelligently to recognise. For five years
the cotton trade of the world was transferred from the Southern
States of the Union to Western India—from New Orleans
to Bombay. The raw cotton of India rose in price from
threepence to nineteenpence the pound, and the export
gradually doubled in quantity. The normal value of the
export and import trade of the one port of Bombay, in mer-
chandise and treasure, had gradually risen during Dr. Wilson's
residence to forty millions sterling in value, or nearly half
that of all India. In the year 1865-66, when the effect of
the American civil war told most fully, that value was almost
doubled, having risen to £75,693,150, exclusive of Sindh,
which increased it to above eighty millions sterling, equal to
the ordinary sea-board trade of Bengal, Madras, and Burma.
Whereas in 1860-61, the year before that war began to tell,
Bombay received only seven millions sterling for 355½ millions of lbs. of cotton, in the last year of the war she got upwards of thirty millions sterling for little more than the same
quantity, or 380½ million lbs.

1 See page 214 of Maclean's *Guide to Bombay*. 1875.

This was only one, though the chief, of a series of causes which had raised prices in India at a rate disproportionate to that throughout the civilised world. The gold discoveries had been working contemporaneously with the Russian War, which transferred the fibre and seed trade of Europe to Calcutta; with the Mutiny campaigns which poured into India an army and the matériel of war on a scale not witnessed since Napoleon Buonaparte exhausted France; with the progress of public works made from borrowed capital to the amount of a hundred millions sterling; and finally with the Hindostan famine in 1860-61. The consequent rise of prices in a poor country, with only a silver currency, was alarming. First in Eastern India Government had been driven to appoint Mr. H. Ricketts commissioner for the revisal of civil salaries and establishments. Then, when the wave threatened to engulf Bombay in 1863, Sir Bartle Frere nominated a commission to report on " the changes which had taken place during the preceding forty years in the money prices of the principal articles of consumption, in the wages of skilled and unskilled labour, and in house rents at the principal military stations." Their conclusion was this—since 1829 the prices of grain had trebled, and were in 1864 double the average of 1860-63; meat and other necessaries had doubled in price; wages had increased fifty per cent; the hire of carriage had gone up from 200 to 400 per cent. Contrasted with Bengal, Bombay prices were pronounced double or treble, and in some cases at famine rates.

Visiting Bombay, as an outsider, at the height of the mania in 1864-65, and one of the earliest to make the journey by mail-cart across the province and Central India to the railway at Agra, we witnessed a state of things, economic and social, which no report could gauge. In the five years during which the cotton market of the world was transferred from New Orleans to Bombay,[1] Western India received eighty millions sterling over and above the normal price of her produce before and since. So far as this reached the cultivators it was well. That it largely reached them, in spite of their ancestral usurers backed by the civil court procedure, has been unhappily proved by the quantities of silver orna-

---

[1] See the description, from the spot, in the *Times* of 24th January 1865, and subsequently.

ments sent down to the local Mint, in years of enhanced land-tax and repeated scarcity and famine. So far as the sudden profit could be utilised for the public good it was also well. Against the fatal mismanagement of the semi-Government Bank of Bombay must be set Sir Bartle Frere's sale of the land on which the walls of the old fort stood, to form a fund for the creation of New Bombay. But the bulk of the profit was literally thrown into the sea, and with it the reputation and the happiness of not a few of the leading European, Parsee, and Hindoo merchants and bankers of the province. The catastrophe culminated in 1867, in the fall of the old Bank of Bombay, which led even members of the Government of India to recommend the prosecution of the guilty parties in the criminal courts ; in the collapse of the fund for building New Bombay, which necessitated an addition to the ever-increasing Debt of India ; in the flight of speculators like him who, after buying the Government-House at Dapoorie with paper, left an umbrella as his assets ; and in the exposure of countless scandals under the insolvent jurisdiction of the High Court by Mr. Chisholm Anstey, who as an acting Judge was no less pitiless to the gambling traders than he had proved to be to the obscene high priests of Krishna. But England cannot throw a stone at Bombay, for it was in the year before 1867 that Overend, Gurney, and Company had led the panic race.

The millions which might have enriched and beautified Bombay and its varied communities, were early and almost altogether directed to the mania of reclaiming the foreshore of an Island which already covered eighteen square miles. The harbour, beautiful and spacious by nature, was destitute of wharf and jetty accommodation for the necessary commerce. Before the mania there had been undertaken the legitimate and praiseworthy enterprise of removing the reproach by establishing the Elphinstone Company. The prospects and success of this really sound project fired the possessors of the surplus capital of the cotton trade with a dream of the profits to be obtained from reclaiming land. The foreshore of the shallow and useless Back Bay, fit only for fisher craft, became the object of the maddest of the Companies. Just above that, forming the eastern side which shelters it from the great Indian Ocean, rises Malabar Hill, and looking down on the generally peaceful water is "The Cliff." One morning when we happened to be breakfasting with Dr. Wilson, he handed to us a letter received by urgent messenger. "That," he said, "will show you to what we have come in Bombay; but I do not give the mania more than a year to collapse." It was an offer from a substantially rich native speculator, to purchase the cottage and garden for a sum twenty times their original value. He of course put it from him at once; for, all other reasons apart, he was one of the few sane men of Bombay at that time. Officials, chaplains, bankers—none escaped the infection, it was said, save *three*, of whom he was the chief. His entreaties, his counsels, his warnings, especially to his native friends, were in vain. A half share of the Port Canning Company, which threatened to lead away Calcutta also at one time, was assigned to him, but the friend who did so took care not to tell him. When some time after it was sold out and he became aware of the fact for the first time, he devoted the money (Rs. 4194) to those benevolent purposes which had seriously suffered from want of support at such a time.

These are extracts from a journal sent to his wife who had gone to Scotland for six months :—

"*22d May* 1865.—Many of the native firms are in great jeopardy from the time bargains. The Kamas (a Parsee firm) have failed with upwards of three millions sterling of responsibilities, and involve many. This is but the beginning of the evil day, now instant.

"*13th June.*—I breakfasted this morning with the Heycocks. —— was present. Poor fellow! his failure, I hear, is for £100,000. When my work at the Institution was done I went to the Union Press, where our report is printing. I there met Dr. Bháu Dájí. He and his brother, and most of our reforming friends, are ruined in their pecuniary positions by their rash speculations. Even Mr. ————, who had lately a fortune of £300,000, is in great jeopardy. If ———— does not get through (and his liabilities amount to two or three millions) our friend will almost certainly fail. He was lately seized with the share-mania, and acted quite contrary to the advice of all his friends. The close of this month is by the whole city looked forward to with great apprehensions. Mr. ————, your fellow-voyager, has been telegraphed for by his Financial Association. Most of the bankers are in a most perilous position as far as the shareholders (not I believe the deposits) are concerned. The Bombay Bank Shares have been selling at a discount! It is hoped, however, that Government will come to its aid. Back Bay shares have been down to a Rs. 1000 premium, though bought for Rs. 50,000 in some instances.

"*22d June.*—In the *Government Gazette* of this morning the announcement of Sir Alexander Grant as Director of Public Instruction, in succession to Mr. Howard, appears. Mr. Howard remains to practise as a barrister; he has lost much by late speculations. I had the usual Marathee meeting after the Institution work in the evening. David Manaji is now out of employment in consequence of the curtailment of the Back Bay works. I wish our friends would allow us to take him into the employment of the mission, according to his request ; but our prospects for the present year are very low, owing to the great losses following the bursting of the share bubble.

"30th June.—I went through my ordinary duties. Much anxiety felt throughout the city on account of the morrow being settlement day.

"1st July.—My lecture to-day, after my Sanskrit class, was on the History of David. The payments on account of time bargains, etc., have to a good extent been modified or postponed. Our friend —— had (it is said, but I doubt it) £120,000 paid him by one of his creditors, which carries him through his immediate difficulties ; ———— owes him £350,000 for shares, etc. ————'s liabilities are for £2,400,000. His assets are valued at £1,600,000."

TO DR. MURRAY MITCHELL.

"Bombay, 24th July 1867.—Since you left India great changes, both for the better and the worse, have occurred. Bombay has had her day of unequalled madness, and now it has her day of great sadness. The mercantile failures (especially among the natives), and the losses to our banks, have been astounding and far-reaching in their consequences ; and there has been much fraud connected with them, by which the innocent in many cases have suffered. It is scarcely to be wondered at that our religious and philanthropic Institutions have their local resources much curtailed, though it is sad to see retrenchment appearing so prominent in that direction. It is our prayer that the affliction which has fallen upon the city, in the retributive justice of God, not unmingled with mercy, may be sanctified to many. The native mind is certainly more sober at present than it has been for several years. The reforming party (including about one hundred of our mission friends) have founded a meeting for the social worship of God, but they have not yet come to a conclusion about the treatment and practice of idolatry in their own houses. We have some encouragement with the lads in our Institution. The attendance at it is large, but I do not know that our Christian influence over it expands with its extension. In other respects the mission is getting on well. Colonel Tripe of Kamthee, who was much with the converts and inquirers lately, formed a very favourable opinion of them. He presented each of them with a book on practical religion, which he gave them at an entertainment which they provided for him in the Institution. The ordination of Bábá Pudmanjee at Poona is appointed for the 8th of August."

Gradually, after the Mutiny, Bombay became the port of arrival and departure for Anglo-Indians, as the railways extended eastward and westward between it, Madras, and the metropolis of Calcutta. Thus the flow of guests through "The Cliff" steadily increased, till it might be said that its hospitable owner became the best known man in India as well as Bombay. From the first Viceroy Lord Canning, and his truly noble wife, to the visit of the Prince of Wales, he was always in request as guide, philosopher, and friend, amid the antiquities not only of Bombay but of Salsette, Karla, and elsewhere. No distinguished person visited the Governor without seeking an introduction to "the king of Bombay." Of these continuous hospitalities and intercourse we find few traces in his correspondence, for, much as he delighted in them, they were too much a part of his everyday life to demand chronicling, save when, as in Lord Lawrence's case, they crossed his one great work. The thirtieth anniversary of his landing, and the passing of that statesman through Bombay, led him to write thus to Dr. Tweedie :—

"I should require every missionary now coming to India to pass an examination in the vernacular before his induction as a full missionary. The Church Missionary Society is here acting on this principle. It is one the propriety of which cannot for a moment be disputed. I intend to show cause in it to yourself in a distinct letter. I have lately received two letters on the subject from Bengal, but I intend to discuss it entirely free of personal and local considerations. I do not think that the missionaries are always to blame in the matter. We have thrust work prematurely upon them ; and we cannot blame them for neglecting, in the first instance, those studies for which we have left them no leisure.

"To India I feel a growing attachment from year to year, its very woes and miseries, in which I am constantly making new discoveries, increasing the tender regard which I cherish in its behalf. I feel no despair in connection with any of its interests. I see that it is a part, an important part, of the Saviour's purchased inheritance, and I believe that ere long it must become His possession. My only regret is that I can do so little to advance its interests. They will not fail in the hands of Him who has on His vesture and on His thigh a name written, King of kings and Lord of lords. I feel much encouraged, in connection with its present destiny, by a conversation I had last night with Sir John Lawrence, who proceeds to Europe by this mail. He s certainly one of the most courageous of men, both physically and spiritually, his Christian principle regulating and controlling all his movements. His judgment and tact are equal to his courage. The very appearance of such characters on the Indian scene on the day they have been specially wanted, is a pledge from God of His purposes of mercy towards this great and interesting land."

Again, we find him mourning the death of Bishop Carr, in a letter to Mr. Farish ; seeking to comfort the widow when announcing the movement from Serampore to raise a fund in commemoration of the services of the accomplished Dr. Buist; and bidding farewell to old friends on their final departure home, like Mr. Fraser Tytler, Dr. Harkness, and Sir Bartle Frere. To one who has proved himself the most learned and generous of true pundits in his own Edinburgh, as he long was the friend of the Christian education of the Hindoos at Benares and elsewhere, Dr. John Muir, C.I.E., he writes of Sanskrit MSS. Dr. Hanna he welcomes as the new superintendent of the Foreign Missions of his Church at home, and delights him with a report of the success of Mikhail Joseph's mission in South Arabia. All this time, and every year, a stream of visitors passing east and west through Bombay, rested for a time at " The Cliff," from Dr. Livingstone and the Maharaja Dhuleep Singh, to the young missionary and inexperienced traveller who sought counsel. Take this specimen from the Notes of Miss Taylor, Dr. Wilsou's niece :—

1864. *March 8th.*—Maharanee's body burned at Nasik. Dr. and Mrs. Wilson, Miss Taylor, Madame Surtoo, a Native lady, who had been in England with the Maharanee and became a Christian there, her little boy, and the Maharaja, spent the day quietly at the Vehar Lake, Salsette.

12th.—Party in the Institution given by the Maharaja to all the missionaries and Native Christians in Bombay ; 300 Natives were present ; the Maharaja wore the Star of India.

13th.—Maharaja called to say good-bye. He took a very decided stand in Bombay as a Christian.

22d.—Dr. Wilson lectured on board the " Ajdaha," to sailors, on " The Shores of the Red Sea."

June 23d.—Dr. Livingstone called. Dr. Wilson took him over the Institution. Dr. Livingstone came to Bombay for a few days on his way home from Africa. He crossed from Africa in the " Lady Nyassa," a small steamer, 115 feet long and 14 feet broad, built for lake navigation, with a crew of seven Natives who had never seen the sea before. They came down with him to the coast at Zanzibar. He did this in the monsoon, too. Somehow they entered the harbour of Bombay unobserved, and Dr. Livingstone landed with no one to meet him—no one knew he was coming—and found his way in a deluge of rain in an old shigram to Dr. Wilson's. The Governor was in Poona. Dr. Livingstone left with Dr. Wilson, to be educated, two African boys, Chuma and Wykatané. They attended the Institution for a year and a half, and learned a little English. They boarded in a Native Christian family. They were baptized by Dr. Wilson at Dr. Livingstone's request, just before he took them back to Africa, in the end of 1865. Dr. Livingstone thought it would make a good impression on their minds, and be a safeguard to them in their future life. Every one knows how faithfully Chuma kept by Dr. Livingstone to the last, and brought his body to England. Wykatané had been rescued by Bishop Mackenzie and his party from a slave-catching gang, and was a great favourite of Bishop Mackenzie's. On Dr. Livingstone's last journey he became lame, and had to be left behind.

Dec. 23d.—Dr. Wilson went with Sir Bartle Frere to visit the Rajah of Dougurpore. He was staying in Dr. Wilson's old house at Amrholie, and Sir Bartle recalled how he himself had gone there as a young man with a letter of introduction to Dr. Wilson.

1865. *Jan. 16th.*—Dr. Wilson lectured in the Town-Hall on " The Wandering Tribes of India."

Feb. 1st.—Sir Dinkur Rao, ex-minister of Sindhia, called.

Sept. 11th.—Dr. Livingstone arrived from England on his way to make his last journey of discovery in Africa. He called on Dr. Wilson the day after his arrival, but Dr. Wilson was out. He went immediately to Poona to see the Governor, and to Nasik to arrange about some of the African Christians there going with him to Africa.

October 6th.—Dr. Livingstone came from Poona and stayed with Dr. Wilson till the 20th—a fortnight.

7th.—Dr. Wilson and Dr. Livingstone walked to see the temples at Walkeshwar (Malabar Point).

8th.—Dr. Livingstone at the Free Church, and at the Marathee Service in the Native Church.

9th.—Dr. Livingstone called with Sir Bartle Frere on the Sultan of Zanzibar.

10th.—Dr. Livingstone went with Captain Leith to select men from the Marine Battalion to go with him to Africa.

11th.—Durbar in Town-Hall in honour of the Sultan of Zanzibar. Dr. Livingstone there.

12th.—Dr. Livingstone lectured on Africa in the Town-Hall. Dr. Wilson said it was the most enthusiastic meeting he had ever seen in Bombay. The lecture was very simple. Dr. Livingstone said much the same things and in much the same way as he did in conversation. A subscription was begun then which soon realised more than Rs. 7000, to help the expedition. Dr. Livingstone refused to accept it as a personal gift. The Bombay branch of the Geographical Society wished to present him with an address, and Captain Sherard Osborn was to read it, but Dr. Livingstone declined to come forward, and said he would rather have it if he should be spared to come back from Africa.

19th.—Drove through the native town to see the Diwallee illuminations.

Nov. 13th.—Dr. Wilson called on Lord Edward Seymour (eldest son of the Duke of Somerset) at the Governor's bungalow, Malabar Point. Lord E. Seymour went out to travel in India. He visited the Institution, and examined some of the classes himself, and took a great interest in all that he saw. He died soon after, at Belgaum, from the effect of injuries he got when hunting a bear.

14th.—Dr. Wilson, Dr. Livingstone, Lord Edward Seymour, and some others went to Elephanta.

Dec. 6th.—Dr. Wilson, Dr. Livingstone, and a party of gentlemen went to the Kanheri Caves, Salsette. Party was arranged by Mr. Alexander Brown, son of Dr. Charles Brown, Edinburgh.

10th.—Chuma and Wykatané baptized by Dr. Wilson in presence of Dr. Livingstone.

12th.—Large party at Dr. Wilson's to meet Dr. Livingstone.

21st.—Dr. Wilson went to Nagpore to the Exhibition.

1866. *1st Jan.*—Dr. Livingstone and the two boys came to say good-bye.

3d, Wednesday.—Dr. Livingstone sailed for Africa in the "Thule." Dr. Livingstone was engaged most of the time he was in Bombay in preparations for his expedition. He also visited Goojarat. The Rev. Joseph Taylor (son of the Rev. Mr. Taylor, of Belgaum), of the Irish Presbyterian Mission in Goojarat, was at college with Dr. Livingstone, and they lodged together in Glasgow. Dr. Livingstone left for Africa, accompanied by eight or nine Christian Africans from Nasik, the same number, I think, of Sepoys of the Marine Battalion Bombay (they deserted him in Africa, and found their way back to Bombay with a story of his having been murdered), Chuma and Wykatané, and the Africans who had come across with him in 1864. They stayed in Bombay while he was in England, and used to come to Dr. Wilson's to get news of him. Dr. Livingstone wished to have no European companion.

In January 1866 Lady Franklin visited Bombay, and Dr. Wilson saw her a few times. She spent one evening with Dr. and Mrs. Wilson.

Nov.—In this month Dr. Norman Macleod and Dr. Watson arrived in Bombay. They stayed with two young merchants. They spent most of a day with Dr. Wilson, going over the Institution, and another day in the Boarding School and Female Schools, and calling on several native gentlemen. They attended the Marathee service, and sat down with the native congregation at the Communion. Dr. Macleod read *Wee Davie* in the Town-Hall, for the benefit of the Scottish Orphanage.

1868. *March 20th.*—Mr. Clarke of Gya and Dr. Watson called.

23d.—Keshub Chunder Sen came to breakfast.

Oct. 23d.—Dr. Wilson visited the Rajah of Kolhapore.

Dec. 21st —Dr. Wilson attended a reception at Parell for Lord and Lady Mayo and Lord Napier.

29th.—Foundation-stone of University laid by Lord Mayo, Dr. Wilson, Vice-Chancellor. Dr. Wilson, after the ceremony, went to Elephanta with the Government-House party.

1869. *Jan. 28th.*—Native Church opened. First service in the morning at eight.

March 17th.—Dr. Wilson and I started for Calcutta. Lord Napier was a fellow-passenger to Nagpore, on his way to the Durbar at Umballa. We stayed a day or two at Nagpore with the Coopers, then went on to Serampore and Calcutta.

April 3d.—Large party at Mr. Fyfe's, of Europeans and Native Christians, to meet Dr. Wilson.

From Serampore we went to *Benares,* and spent a day with Messrs. Hutton and Blake, London Mission ; next to *Mirzapore,* and stayed with Mr. Sherring ; *Allahabad,* with Mr. and Mrs. Walsh, American Mission ; *Cawnpore, Agra, Umballa,* with Dr. Morrison ; Subathoo, with Dr. Newton, Medical Missionary. At *Simla* Dr. Wilson was the guest of Lord Mayo for about ten days. His old friend, Sir Donald M'Leod, was there at the same time, also Sir Douglas Forsyth.

June 28th.—Dr. Wilson dined with Mr. H. Rivett-Carnac, at the Byculla Club, to meet General Vlangally, Russian ambassador from China.

Aug. 31st.—Lord Napier went home. Dr. Wilson went to say good-bye to him at the Boree Bunder Station.

Nov. 13th.—Bishop of Madras called. Dr. Wilson dined with Mr. Fox to meet him.

16th.—Captain Beaumont and Mr. J. Candlish, M.P. for Sunderland, at breakfast.

29th.—Mr. Shaw called—the traveller who had been a year in Kashgar.

1870.—Dr. Wilson went, in January, to Jalna and Nasik.

22d.—Dr. Wilson called on Dr. Prime, editor of *New York Observer,* travelling with a party round the world. Dr. Elmslie, Cashmere, at tea.

Feb. 1st.—Dr. Wilson lectured in Town-Hall on "Marathee Country and People."

Feb. 3d.—Dr. Wilson at a party given by Chief of Jamkhundee.

17th.—Addresses to students and Native Christians of Bombay.

19th.—Left Bombay for Scotland.

It was a Bombay officer, Richard F. Burton, who, in 1857, set out from Aden to East Africa to find the great lake reported by the Church Missionaries at Zanzibar. That proved to be Tanganika. In 1860 Baron Von der Decken first struck out what has thus far proved a more important route into the lake region of Africa, that to Lake Nyassa from Kilwa.

But it was Dr. Livingstone, in many respects a man like Dr. Wilson, who, after discovering Lake Ngami so early as 1849, and crossing South Africa from the Atlantic to the Zambesi and the Indian Ocean in 1854-5, opened up Lake

Nyassa itself, and pronounced it the spot, of all Africa, for such a missionary settlement as had killed the slave-trade by lawful commerce at Sierra Leone. His great Zambesi expedition, which lasted from 1858 to 1864, confirmed his desire to see Nyassa the centre of light to Eastern Africa. His passing visit to Bombay in June 1864, described by Miss Taylor, was repeated in September 1865, when he returned from England to organise in that capital the greatest of all his journeys of exploration, in which, after seven years, he died. We remember well the enthusiasm which his address, first at Poona and then in Bombay, excited all over India, when he compared Eastern Africa physically to the low Konkan and high Ghauts and uplands of Western India, and declared that all Great Britain was doing for the people of India she must yet do for the negroes of Africa. And there, he said, Nyassa is the spot. How well his vision is being realised, first by Mr. Young, R.N., who went to help him, and then by his companion Dr. Stewart of Lovedale, who together have there established the Livingstonia settlement of the Free Church of Scotland, every year is revealing.

In all the public enthusiasm which bore rich pecuniary fruit for the last expedition, and in organising the details, as in the relaxation of delightful social intercourse, Dr. Wilson was foremost. But perhaps his best gift to Livingstone was the Christian training of the two little slave-boys left with him eighteen months before—Chuma and Wykatané. The baptism was to both the heroic missionaries a joy, and all know the fruit it bore. The beginning of 1866 saw Dr. Livingstone at Zanzibar with a letter of commendation from Sir Bartle Frere to the Sultan, and charged with the pleasant duty of presenting to his Highness the gun-boat "Thule," in which he had crossed the Indian Ocean, as a gift from the Government of Bombay. From that sad hour on the 27th April 1873, when Livingstone made his last note in his Journal, Chuma became leader of the caravan, and brought safely to Lieutenant Cameron the precious remains which find fit resting-place in the nave of Westminster Abbey. To him, and to Susi, Amoda, and the two Nasik boys, his faithful comrades since 1864-5, Mr. Waller, the editor of the *Last Journals*, has expressed the nation's gratitude. And hardly less is due to Wykatané, of whom, in his *Nyassa*, Mr.

Young, R.N., gives us this glimpse, showing how the light from
Bombay had penetrated all the darkness of the slave-boy's life,
and continued to shine, however dimly, as years passed on.
The scene is the jungle at night, near Livingstonia, among the
Maviti ; the time is September 1876.   " I called to Wykatané,
who lay in the next hut, and asked him who was singing : he
replied that it was he.   On telling him to repeat it, I found it
was one of the chants used by the missionaries sixteen years
ago in the hills at Magomero.   Remembering how much pains
Dr. Livingstone had taken with him, and good Dr. Wilson
too, I asked him if he remembered anything of the former
days.   He said, ' This is what Dr. Livingstone taught me :—

> " 'This night I lay me down to sleep,
> I give my soul to Christ to keep,
> If I should die before I wake,
> I pray to God my soul to take.   Amen.'

In the long interval since he had seen white men he had
forgotten nearly all the English he ever knew ; but those
lines, together with some few simple questions and answers
taught him by Dr. Wilson, he could repeat."   When, at the
end of 1864, we presided at the examination of Dr. Wilson's
college, Chuma and Wykatané were prominent in the class of
catechumens gathered from all the natives of the East.
Chuma is now assisting Mr. Thomson, representing the Royal
Geographical Society, in his attempt to reach the head of
Lake Nyassa from Dar-es-Salaam.

During Livingstone's wanderings in the last seven years of
his life he wrote to no friend so frequently as to Dr. Wilson.
This is one of his then confidential communications, which
Dr. Wilson at once submitted both to the Viceroy of India and
to Dr. Duff, in the Free Church Foreign Missions' Office :—

DR. LIVINGSTONE TO DR. WILSON.

" ABOUT TWELVE DAYS EAST OF TANGANYIKA,
"(Private.)   24th January 1872.

"MY DEAR DR. WILSON—This is not my first letter to you, but I have
been in the slave-mart of East Africa, and looked on as a spy, and letters to
and from me have nearly all been destroyed between this and the sea.   All
who have an interest in the slave-trade hate to think of me as sure to expose
their proceedings. The sources of the Nile they know to be a sham, and
what I have seen of the horrid system makes me feel that its suppression
would be of infinitely more importance than all the fountains together ; so my

Arab and Banian friends are not so far wrong. I am now going east to a point called by Speke Kazieh, but by the natives and Arabs Unyanyembe, in order to get the remains of some £500 worth of goods, which were unfortunately entrusted to slaves, and these slaves like jolly fellows have been feasting on my stores ever since the end of October 1870. A precious £500 or £600 worth of goods were also committed to slaves, and at Ujiji the headman sold off all for slaves and ivory for himself. He divined on the Koran and found I was dead ! My friend Dr. Kirk has unintentionally inflicted these losses by going to a Banian for money when my cheques on Bombay were destroyed. He put the affair in the hands of his slaves, and I lost all. The second £500 was half of £1000 sent most kindly by H. M. Government, and this was given by the same Banian, called Sudha, to slaves again. I thought every one knew that our Government is stringently opposed to its officers employing slave labour, but Dr. Kirk—' companion of Livingstone,' Sir Roderick calls him—evidently did not ; so he has, most unwittingly of course, inflicted a loss of two years' time, at least 1800 miles of tramp, and what money I don't exactly know. Sudha probably told him that he could not get pagazi or carriers, but Mr. Stanley, travelling correspondent of the *New York Herald*, was told the same tale by Sudha, and went over to the mainland where my slaves lay and feasted four months, and secured one hundred and forty pagazi in a few days. Mr. Stanley was sent to my aid by James Gordon Bennett junior, at an expense of over £4000, and with the goods he offers I hope to finish up my task. I don't wish to injure Kirk, but I expected better than the ignorance and gross neglect he has displayed. [This was afterwards explained.] Nearly all the slave-trade is carried on by Sudha's and other Banians' money, and they manage adroitly to let the odium rest on their Arab agents, and being English subjects we protect them ; and they instilled it into the minds of all the slaves they sent not to follow but force me back.

"I wish I could give a better report of the Africans I took with me from Bombay. Those from Nassick began by sending me at Bombay an anonymous letter, abusing the teachers who had fed, clothed, and taught them for years. On sending it to Mr. Price for identification, he made a whine about the ' poor boys,' and quashed it. All their desires in Africa were to get back to live in idleness at Nassick ; and to annoy me they reiterated perpetually ' Mr. Price told us lies.' They knew that I could not relish a clergyman being called a liar. On demanding an explanation, they replied that he said that they were first to go to Mozambique and then return and get wives at Nassick. This was so evidently false I let them rave to each other about their benefactor unnoticed. All pretended that they did not know what tribes they came from. I was to leave them with their friends, but they knew that they had all been slaves, and would be treated as slaves again, and forced to work. We met the two uncles of one called Abram or Ibrahim. I advised him to remain with them, but he said, 'I have no mother, no sister here ; I cannot live with my uncles.' The mother and sisters would have cultivated for him, hence his desire to have them. On the desertion of the Johanna men they did pretty fairly, because I employed the country people to do my work ; but on coming in contact with Arab slaves they turned back to their youthful habits of lying, stealing, and every vice. One called Simon Price begged ammunition from some Arab traders when I refused it, and being able to shoot in safety came and reported to me that he had killed two of the men who had been most kind to us. Other two boasted of having committed murder too. Price first bragged of the two slain, then justified himself, then denied it. All showed eagerness to engage uninvited in slave-hunting, and it was mortifying to see them march into the Arab camp, as I did, with captive women. Simon Price and Ibrahim even begged Muhamad Bagharib to make them his slaves.

I was afraid to call Price a Christian carpenter or Ibrahim a blacksmith—one could not cut a piece of wood straight even when chalked out for him ; the blacksmith had never welded iron.   Mr. Price cannot have known this, but if you can inform the Bombay Government privately, and propose a ship anchored in a healthy spot as a school where real *bona fide* work would be taught, it would be a benefit to the community.   Taught to cook, wash, sew, all the jobs sailors can do, and discipline enforced, these poor unfortunates would prove a blessing.   At present the teachers fear them ; they dread their desertion, and bringing an ill name on Nassick school ; and the Africans see it and take full advantage of it either to work or play.—Salaam to Dr. Birdwood and Mrs. Wilson.   DAVID LIVINGSTONE."

                                        "UNYANYEMBE, 13th *March* 1872.
   "This goes off to-morrow by Mr. Stanley, kindly sent to my aid by James Gordon Bennett of New York at an expense of over £4000.   I have got all I need to finish up my work.   Please not to publish this, but keep it for yourself.   D. L.
   " I am obliged to draw on the £645 collected at Bombay.   Thought two years sufficient ; it is now six years, and I am not finished until I see the ancient fountains of Herodotus, if they exist.   What do you say about them ? "

   Still more remarkable than in Chuma's case was the providence which in 1837 led Dr. Wilson unconsciously to prepare two Abyssinian youths for the deliverance of their country by Lord Napier's expedition of 1867.   We have told how, in the former year, Dr. Wolff sent to Bombay for instruction in Dr. Wilson's college, and residence under his roof, Gabru and Maricha Warka, with their father, a high officer in the Abyssinian army.   The two lads became most active catechists, occasionally accompanied Dr. Wilson in his tours, and left him only at Aden, whence, in 1843, he sent them with his benediction to evangelise their own people, and the oldest but most corrupt of Christian Churches.   They found the almost chronic conflict of chief with chief raging, and attempted by personal intercourse and discussion to influence the priests. Very close, and at this time very pathetic, seems their correspondence with Dr. and especially with Mrs. Wilson to have been.   They were at first supported by the kirk-session of the native church in Bombay, which thus early sought to evangelise the regions beyond.   After a visit to the old scenes, on Dr. Wilson's return from Scotland they settled down at Adowah, where for a long time they conducted a vigorous mission school, encouraged by the periodical epistles from Ambrolie.   What a picture this is of the influence of the old mission home, in a letter written by Maricha from Aden on his return to his native country for the second time, in April 1849 :—

"Yes ! it is a dream ; and not only so, but it is a mystery and an awful
dream that troubles my thoughts.   Let me only be thinking of that family
where I was brought up from my childhood, especially when now and then I
think myself to be seated round that family altar ; beside me I see Hormasdjee
and Gabru, and there I see you both—you, Sir, whom we love like a father,
and by you sitting one whom we love like a mother.   I see the large family
Bible and the Psalm-book in your hands.   I see you meeting round that family
altar to offer up a living sacrifice.   I hear you praying, especially for Ethiopia's
soon stretching out her hands unto God.   From upstairs let me take you
down where I used to meet among the different denominations that have come
out from darkness to light, and from the kingdom of Satan to the kingdom of
Christ.   From thence let me convey you to that holy spot, which spot is to be
desired more than all the dwellings of Jacob.   There I hear the harmonious
songs of Zion, that carry the heart, as it were, to the third heaven.   And what
shall I not say more of Zion ? yes, I might tell of the pure doctrines that are
taught Sabbath after Sabbath, but the time will not allow me to do so.
Alas ! is it true that I am to dwell with a people who have no fear of God in
their sight ?   Yes, my soul, thou art no more in that holy society, thou art
no more round that family altar where thou usedst often to sit, where thou
usedst to be glad when they said unto thee, 'Let us go up to the house of
God.'   Now then is the time for thee to cry out with a loud voice, 'My soul
longeth, yea fainteth, for the courts of the Lord ; my heart and my flesh
crieth out for the living God.' "

The years passed as the young men married and carried
on their mission-school, when they suddenly became of vast
importance to the Commander-in-Chief of Bombay and the
Viceroy of India.   From the third day of 1864 the chief
Theodorus, who called himself emperor of Abyssinia, had kept
in confinement Consul Cameron and several German missionaries.   When Mr. Rassam, an Armenian friend of Sir Austen
Layard, along with Dr. Blanc and Lieutenant Prideaux of
the Bombay army, had been sent as an envoy for their release,
they too were put in chains.   Still neither Lord Palmerston
and the one party, nor Lord Stanley and the other party
moved, in spite of the most persistent representations from
the Government of India.   The shame of it was such that,
anonymously at the time, Sir George Yule asked us to publish
his offer of Rs. 20,000 to fit out a volunteer expedition to
rescue the captives who had languished under the power of
a madman for nearly four years.   That was on the 1st August
1867.   The close of that year saw an imperial expedition of
50,000 men, including followers, on the way to Abyssinia, and
the advance guard above the Ghauts at Senafe, whence the
march to Magdala and its fall proved a holiday excursion that
cost several millions sterling.   How much of the facility with
which the work was accomplished was due to the two Abys-

sinian students of Dr. Wilson, may be imagined from these
circumstances. They had risen to be the official councillors
of Kassai, the Prince of Tigré, who steadfastly supported the
British in spite of the urgent overtures of Egypt and Turkey.
In frequent telegrams and despatches Lord Napier of Magdala
warmly acknowledged their services. The special correspondents with the expedition were even more emphatic, the most
experienced of them writing thus :—" The belief that, in connection with the campaign in Abyssinia, England owed more
to the Free Church of Scotland's Mission Institution in Bombay than it does to any institution in the Presidency, the
Government itself and the commissariat department not
excepted, was entertained by not a few."

In truth, when her Majesty's Government had tardily
resolved on the expedition, the first men consulted by Lord,
then Sir Robert Napier, were two missionaries. Mr. Blum-
hardt, half a century before a Church Missionary in the
country, and then in the peaceful Bengalee villages of
Christian Krishnaghur, was asked for information, and was
invited to accompany the force as interpreter. At Lord
Lawrence's request we at once published at Serampore the
Amharic vocabulary which that missionary hastily drew up,
since old age denied him the privilege of going in person.
Dr. Wilson received several letters from the Quartermaster-
General of the army calling into requisition his multifarious
information and experience on all details, from the history of
the ancient church of Ethiopia to a certain breed of camels
well adapted for mountain work. All his replies were submitted to the new Governor, Sir Seymour Fitzgerald, who
had succeeded Sir Bartle Frere.

Lord Napier gladly accepted the Bible Society's gift of
books to the soldiers of the expedition, and to the hospitals.
The result, to himself, of the war, for the humane and bloodless fruits of which, then and since, Dr. Wilson is in a large
sense responsible, was further work for the people of Abyssinia. With the approval of the Government of India
General Merewether entrusted to his training two Anglo-
Abyssinian girls, and two Abyssinian boys, Pedro and Wuldee
Magios, one of whom had helped the captives, while the other
had been presented by Prince Kassai to the conqueror. Lord
Napier desired to place the son of Theodorus under his care,

to fit the boy for a career in Abyssinia hereafter; but the
English authorities decided that the youth should be trained
in England, where he is passing through the Royal Military
College at Sandhurst. So the radius of light and life from
the Bombay mission went on ever extending. The prince
whom Gabru and Maricha counselled so well, has, as *Negoos*
and King Johannes,[1] given to the people of Abyssinia a
degree of peace and prosperity which only the unprovoked
aggression of the late Mussulman Khedive of Egypt broke
for a time.

[1] See that most interesting narrative of travel by E. A. de Cosson, F.R.G.S.,
The Cradle of the Blue Nile: A Visit to the Court of King John of Ethiopia.

CHAPTER XIX.

1867-1871.

SECOND AND LAST VISIT HOME.

The Shadow darkening—Sir Bartle Frere leaves Bombay—Isabella Wilson's Death—Legislation of Sir Henry Maine and Sir Fitzjames Stephen—Acts for Re-marriage of Converts and Marriages between non-Christian Natives —Testimonial from the Inhabitants of Bombay on fortieth Indian Anniversary—Addresses from University and Asiatic Society—Summoned to be Moderator of General Assembly—Addresses to the Assembly—Modern Criticism and Missionary Translators—Work at Home—Portrait—Evidence before Commons' Committee on the Opium and Excise System— Return to Bombay.

THE year 1867 cast over Dr. Wilson the first shadow of that darkness beyond which is the everlasting light. In his long course of nigh forty years he had seen band after band of temporary English settlers in the land come and go ; he had himself trained generations of native youth, and built up a native church, colleges, and schools. As friend departed after friend he bewailed the exodus from a land which needed all their experience and their energy. The last was the Governor whom he had received at Ambrolie fresh from Haileybury, and had admitted to an almost life-long intimacy. Sir Bartle Frere turned from the honours and the applause which attended his departure from Bombay, to spend one of the last days there with the missionary among his schools and college students. Still invested with all the influence of his office, his Excellency, having examined the youth, expressed to them his personal conviction that religion is all important as an element of education. He warmly commended the life-long efforts of Dr. Wilson and others who sought to impart that to the natives of India, to whom it could not fail to be a blessing even when they fell short of embracing Christianity.

As the hot season passed into the rainy time, and the one really intolerable month of the Indian year, September, came round, when wearied humanity pants for the cooling breezes and reviving life of what Europe calls winter, Isabella Wilson was taken away. Her abundant labours of twenty years, in which she had enjoyed only the combined rest and toil of a six months' visit to her sisters in Scotland, precipitated the end. All Bombay, from the Chief Justice and Judges of the High Court to the humblest Native Christian and student, followed to the Scottish cemetery the remains of one whose influence was all the greater that it had been never obtruded yet ever present in all that was good in the place. In her own home, in the native church, in the central native female day school, in the monthly inspection of the district and other girls' schools, in the Beni-Israel school, in the native female boarding-school, in the Ladies' Committee of the Scottish Orphanage, in the Bible-woman's Association, and in other philanthropic institutions of Bombay, she had proved so potent a force that it was difficult to realise how these organisations could prosper without her. Her social intercourse for the highest ends, with Hindoo, Parsee, Jewish, and Muhammadan families, had been closer than that of any other English lady in all India. What she was to her husband in his literary researches and missionary tours, which taxed the courage and resources of the bravest men, we have partially seen. But the purest tribute to her memory was that which the converts rendered, the women and the girls, the catechumens from all the lands of the East from Abyssinia to China, the ordained Natives who, in an eloquent sermon by the Rev. Dhunjeebhoy Nowrojee, expressed the loss of the whole Church of India. Henceforth, to his own last hour, Dr. Wilson is cared for by his niece, Miss Taylor. All this came upon him at the time of the preparations for the Abyssinian Expedition, which, however, gave Lord Napier an opportunity of calling on him to express warm sympathy. His own sorrow he manifested by erecting a female school, as the best memorial of one who had given herself for the women of Bombay.

Soon after his appointment as law member of the Governor-General's Council, Sir Henry Maine had been led by Lord Lawrence to devise a legislative solution of the two questions—What relief should be given, first, to Christian converts whose spouses refuse to join them, or are prevented for years from doing so ; and, secondly, to non-Christian dissidents from Hindooism who have conscientious objections to the idolatrous and suggestively indecent marriage rites of Brahmanism. This second question was afterwards settled by Sir James F. Stephen, so as to satisfy the followers of Keshub Chunder Sen, and even to lead English Comtists to take advantage of an Act under which the parties must declare that they are not Christians. The Converts' Re-marriage Bill had a keen interest for all Christians, however, and called forth ecclesiastical discussion for years. Dr. Wilson was consulted by Government on both difficulties, and the assistance he gave to Sir Henry Maine was warmly acknowledged. Unlike the sacramentarians who hold that a marriage is irrevocable by whomsoever made, even if one of the parties refuses for ever all conjugal duties, Dr. Wilson showed, from the early Fathers down to the Reformers, that Scripture had been consistently interpreted so as to give proper relief. He laid special stress on the opinion of Basilius of Caesareia,[1] because of the great authority of that bishop in the Roman, Greek, Syrian, and Gothic Churches. The result of a learned and sometimes bitter discussion in the Press as well as the Legislative Council of India, was the most equitable Act under which, if a wife persistently refuses to join her converted husband (and *vice versa*) for two years, notwithstanding private opportunities of remonstrance judicially given, the district courts may only then pronounce divorce. The Act has worked extremely well, by affording opportunities to the law to free wives from such restraint as we have seen Brahmanism and Parseeism impose on inquirers, and so to prevent divorce. The great jurist and the experienced scholar were thus happily allied in removing one of the last obstacles to perfect toleration. Nothing now remains to be done by the legislature save the promulgation of a uniform rule or procedure for the protection of the rights of conscience of minors, in a country where marriage takes place at and sometimes before puberty.

As the 14th of February 1869 approached, the leaders of all the communities in Bombay, European and Asiatic, re-

[1] *Epistola* 138, in which Basil cites 1 Cor. vii. 13-16.

solved to honour their foremost man on that, the fortieth
anniversary of his arrival in Western India. Mr. Sassoon,
the Jewish millionnaire, and Dr. Bhau Daji, the most learned
reforming Brahman, were active in the movement, side by side
with Mr. James Taylor, secretary of the Chamber of Commerce
and of the Asiatic Society, and with the secretary of the
committee, Mr. James Douglas. The long roll of subscribers
and signatures in many languages on the parchment sheets,
represents all races, creeds, and classes in the East, and all
varieties of Christian sects. Although New Bombay was
still suffering from the ruin and apprehension that followed
the cotton mania, and the work was rapidly done, upwards of
Rs. 21,000 (£2100) was presented to the missionary on a silver
salver wrought by native artists, and bearing the inscription, in Sanskrit :—" This salver was presented to the Rev.
John Wilson, D.D., F.R.S., at a meeting of the inhabitants of
Bombay, as a mark of esteem for his high personal character,
and in acknowledgment of his great services to India in the
cause of education and philanthropy." The design represents him as a missionary standing under the sacred peepul
tree, a Hindoo temple and a figure of Rama behind, and before
him a crowd of Asiatics of every cult and caste in Western
India, from the learned Brahman to the ignorant peasant.
The Governor, Sir Seymour Fitzgerald, presided at a great
meeting in the Town Hall of Bombay, on the 15th February
1869, and made the presentation. The Chief-Justice, Sir
Richard Couch, assisted. A loving letter was read from Sir
Bartle Frere, and the other speakers were Mr. Sassoon and
Dr. Bhau Daji. Dr. Wilson thus reported the event to Miss
Margaret Dennistoun : — " It is wonderful to think that
gratification has been felt with the issue through the whole
of India. Only one element of my felicitation (I was humbled
rather than exalted) was wanting—the sympathy of her, the
beloved one who was so lately removed from me. I have
been weeping whenever I have been thinking of this depriva-
tion. I always felt that one quiet glance of her loving and
approving eye was better to me than the applause of the·
multitude. Her love was always an emblem to me of that
of the Saviour Himself." It was characteristic of his whole
career and of his unfailing tact, that, agreeing to use the
interest only in his philanthropic and literary labours, he

should designate the capital sum to aid the higher studies
of the youth of Bombay, " in a form which will be agreeable alike to my European and Native friends." The fund
has accordingly devolved on the University of Bombay for
the foundation of the John Wilson Philological Lectureship,
to which his friend and executor, Professor Peterson, was
appointed. Dr. Wilson desired that lectures may thus be
delivered " by a competent European or Native scholar,
annually elected for the purpose, on either of the following classes of languages and the literature in which they
are embodied :—Sanskrit, and the Prakrit languages derived
from it ; Hebrew, and the other Shemitic languages ; Latin
and Greek ; English, viewed in connection with Anglo-Saxon
and its other sources."

The address of the inhabitants of Bombay, followed by
one from the Hindoos and Muhammadans of Nasik, from
which he had been almost expelled in his first missionary
tour, reviewed the whole course of Dr. Wilson's work for the
people, and thus expressed their own special gratitude :—
" As citizens of Bombay we thankfully acknowledge that the
credit of this city has been upheld by the personal courtesy
and learned aid which distinguished foreigners and others,
coming hither as visitors or for purposes of Oriental research
or Christian philanthropy, have always received from you,
as acknowledged by them subsequently in their published
writings or otherwise."

But again, as in 1842, it was left to the Asiatic Society
to review his contributions to scholarship, and to the University to acknowledge his work for the higher education.
Never before in its history had there been such a concourse
of the members of that Society as on the 17th February 1870, when it was known that Dr. Wilson had been
summoned to his native country once more, to fill the highest
office which the democratic Scottish Church can confer, that of
annual Moderator of the General Assembly. The Governor,
who presided, after stating the thanks of Government for his
political services, which, " as regards our relation with the
people in trying times, have been of the utmost value," declared it a happy thing that one who had been able to combine the fearless assertion of what he believed to be true with
a conciliatory demeanour and tender respect for the belief of

others, had been summoned to take the chief part in the government of a religious body who had sacrificed much for the truth at a time when religious discussion too often means animosity and estrangement. Mr. Justice Tucker, Dr. Bhau Daji, Mr. Dhunjeebhoy Framjee, the Portuguese Dr. J. N. Mendonca, Mr. Manockjee Cursetjee, and Messrs. Wedderburn and Connon, told successively what Dr. Wilson had done for scholarship, for literature, for education, for progress of all kinds. Dr. Wilson's reply was more generous to his fellow members than just to his own researches. Two days after he was on his way to Edinburgh. The native journals followed with their eulogies the now venerable apostle, whose delight it had been to spend and be spent in the service of the people, with an unselfishness which all admired, though all did not trace it to Him whom the missionary proclaimed.

The office of Moderator of the General Assembly is filled, as a rule, by the unanimous vote of the six or seven hundred members on the first day of its meeting. But the Moderator is designated some months before by those surviving who have previously filled the chair, is approved of after consultation by the "commisson" of the previous Assembly, and is requested by his immediate predecessor to allow himself to be nominated. In this way Dr. Wilson received a formal invitation from the Rev. Sir Henry Wellwood-Moncreiff, Bart., to come home for the Assembly of May 1870. The Churches, like the country generally, know so little of India till a catastrophe occurs which knowledge might have prevented, that the whole learning and power of Dr. Wilson in his new position proved a surprise to the Free Church of Scotland. Courtesy of the old school; knowledge of men and their public assemblies; promptitude and fluency in expression; learning, rarely obtrusive but always present; and grace of that highest kind which comes down from heaven alone, marked all his public services and official receptions. The time was one when the vexed question was near the embittered stage— Whether the great goal of one reconstructed Kirk of Scotland could best be reached by immediate union with the early seceders of the United and Reformed Presbyterian Churches, or by waiting till the minority of the Established Church atoned for the wrong they have since confessed? To Dr. Wilson, it was well known, the immediate duty of union with

all like-minded who would unite, was plain, but he held the
balance fairly as became one in his judicial position.   So long
before as in 1864 he had moved the Presbytery of Bombay to
"overture" the General Assembly for this possible instalment
of union ; for to one in the distant high places of the field the
still existing divisions look both ludicrous and criminal.   Only
on the one disputed question of the use of hymns in public
worship did he, when he had ceased to be Moderator, let out
the force of his alternate scorn and ridicule for views which
would strike evangelical catholicity out of any Church.

His opening address as Moderator was directed to the
part which Scotland has taken in the reception, propagation,
and conservation of Christianity.   A hearer might have supposed that he had never been out of Scotland, but for the
extent of his knowledge and the breadth of his sympathies.
His vindication of the Westminster Confession of Faith did
justice to the foresight and spirit of its authors, only now
beginning to be acknowledged, while he quoted with a keen
delight the motto of the first Confession of 1560 : "And this
glaid tydingis of the kyngdome sall be precheit through the
haill warld for a witnes unto all natiouns, and then sall the
end cum."   To the then debated question of National Education he gave his support with a confidence since fully justified
by the religious steadfastness of his countrymen.   The narrow,
the sectarian, the purely ecclesiastical found no quarter from
him.   His closing address was no less fair in the tribute to
the lay elders of his Church, and in the remark when alluding
to the rationalism of the great French scholar—"This I say,
without accusing M. Renan of playing false with his own convictions or depreciating his Shemitic scholarship."

When the report on Foreign Missions was read he left the
chair and told the story of his life-work in words which concluded with the declaration that, notwithstanding his forty-
one years' connection with India, if he lived to the age of
Methuselah he would consider it a privilege to devote his life
to its regeneration.   The General Assembly of 1870 appointed
the Rev. W. Robertson Smith, then fresh from the students'
benches but of great reputation, as Professor of Hebrew in
succession to Mr. Sachs at Aberdeen.   Referring to the translations of the Scriptures by the Rev. Dhunjeebhoy Nowrojee
into the Parsee-Goojaratee language, Dr. Wilson said :—

" The missionaries know and take advantage of the results of modern criticism ; not of rash, but devout, intelligent, and reverent criticism, knowing what passages have often been misunderstood. We have to deal in Bombay with languages drawing all their technical terms from the Sanskrit, one of the most wonderful of all languages in regard to its power of expressing human thought. We have great need of able men in India for biblical and other literary work ; and if Mr. Smith, who has this day been appointed a Professor of Hebrew, will come out to India after he has obtained a few years' experience at Aberdeen, he will find there ample scope for his linguistic talents."

If the duties, ecclesiastical and social, devolving on a Moderator are not few during the ten days' sittings of the General Assembly, those which occupy or distract his year of office are formidable. Every cause that needs the preaching of a popular sermon ; every new church that is founded or opened ; every neighbouring Church to which a brotherly deputation has to be sent, in England, Ireland, and on the Continent, looks to the Moderator. To all this, and especially to his own more special work of stimulating missionary zeal, Dr. Wilson gave himself up with an ardour that taxed his waning energies, as time soon showed. The charms of his talk and companionship in private life were universally recognised with a delighted surprise, for who knew anything of Bombay ? Dr. Wilson was as ready to lecture to the theological students of the Established Church in the University Association which he had founded in 1825, as to those of the three New Colleges. And not only to them, for Principal Shairp induced him to delight the students of St. Andrews with a lecture on the Literature and History of the People of India, intended to stir them up to claim their share of appointments in the Services which Scotsmen once almost monopolised.

This growing appreciation led to a movement for securing a portrait of the philanthropist for his native country, since he persisted in his resolution to return to much-beloved Bombay. On the 9th June 1871 he thus wrote to Mr. David Maclagan, who had organised the matter—" The proposal has taken me by surprise, as I feel that I have no claim to be an aspirant to the honours which you and other friends

desiderate on my behalf. In giving my grateful consent to
that proposal, I feel very deeply that it is the judgment of
God and not that of man with which I have mainly to do,
and that I have many grounds for personal humiliation in the
divine presence in connection with my ministrations in all the
places in which they have been conducted." The portrait,
painted by Mr. Norman Macbeth, has since adorned the common hall of the New College, Edinburgh.

The Select Committee of the House of Commons, which
began to take evidence on the financial system of India in
1871, examined Dr. Wilson on the subject of the opium
cultivation of Central and Western India and the excise laws.
Almost from the year of his first landing at Bombay he had,
on the ground of temperance, memorialised Government on
the increase of drunkenness under our rule. He admitted,
from the Vedas and from the state of Poona under the
Marathas, that intoxication had been known in India, both
from drugs and distillation. From his tours, in Rajpootana
especially, he gave much information as to the extent to which
the cultivation of the poppy is absorbing the best lands, de-
moralising the people and killing off their chiefs. He urged
an increase of the spirit duties, the protection of native villages
from the invasion of the drink-sellers caused by our excise
system, and—at least—the conversion of the Bengal opium
monopoly into the Bombay system, for which the Government
and the nation, as such, are not responsible. He testified to
the satisfaction of the natives with British rule as contrasted
with that of their own princes. That Select Committee was
not allowed to give in a final report on the voluminous
evidence which it took. The excise laws and opium monopoly remain unchanged to this day, a blot on our generally
benevolent administration of India, excused but not justified
by financial difficulties.

The toil-worn man of sixty-five, the missionary of forty-
three years' service, might well have been pardoned if he
had chosen to rest where he was. But whether in Scotland
or in India rest could not be for that burning spirit, that
busy mind, that active body. "I go bound in the Spirit to
India to declare the Gospel message," he wrote to Miss
Margaret Dennistoun, when about to step on board the
'Ceylon' at Brindisi. "Nothing but this object sustains my

heart. I am sure you will all earnestly pray for me. My solace is in the Lord."

"*4th October* 1871.—Took leave of my beloved friends at Lauder, who were all deeply affected, not expecting again to see me in the flesh. Though I felt much on parting with them, I was wonderfully supported by the Lord Jesus. I read the 129th and 121st Psalms before engaging in prayer in my own house with the surviving members of our family. They gave me the convoy in the carriage till we got out of sight of the valley of the Leader. Drove to Greenlaw, where I was received with much kindness by Mr. and Mrs. Fairbairn, and Rev. Messrs. Cunningham, Fraser, and Spence, whom they had invited to meet me. Addressed a meeting in the Free Church.

"*5th.*—To Langton, where I addressed Mr. Logan's congregation in the evening. In the afternoon I visited Langton House, to renew my acquaintance with the excellent Lady Hannah Tharpe, who gave me a very kind reception. I had a long talk, too, on the grounds, with Lady Elizabeth Pringle, who has done much for their improvement as well as for that of the mansion. She is a most vigorous and intelligent old lady.

"*6th.*—Driven by Mr. Logan to Dunse, to the Rev. Mr. Miller. After calling on Dr. Ritchie of the United Presbyterian Church I left for Selkirk by rail. I was recognised at Galashiels by Mr. Ovans, son of an old friend, who took me to his house. I posted to Harewood Glen, where James Dennistoun and his family were delighted to see me.

"*8th.*—Driven to Selkirk and preached in the Free Church." Then after a day at Stow, with the Rev. T. N. Brydon, and a visit to Glasgow, he bade farewell to Scotland.

Dr. Guthrie's was the last "kent" face he saw in his native land. Accompanied by his niece he followed his old route by the Rhine to Munich, seeing Professor Christlieb at Bonn, and bitterly lamenting the loss of " my grand walking-cane, the gift of Colonel Davidson." At the Bavarian capital he writes : "I renewed my acquaintance with Dr. Haug, Professor of Sanskrit in the University, and he treated the two of us to a right good German supper in the evening, at which we met not only his wife and son, but Mr. West (now Ph.D.) and Mrs. West, old Bombay friends, much with dearest Isabella and myself.   Dr. Haug offered to introduce me to Dr. Döllinger, the living lion of the place, but I could not spare the needful time." And so, after a day at Trent, and in the cathedral and church of Sta. Maria Maggiore "in which the famous Council intended to defeat the Reformation was held," the last week of November 1871 saw him in the hospitable house of Dr. Yule, the consular chaplain at Alexandria, and soon after on an excursion from Suez to the Wells of Moses. At Aden he and General Irving, R.E., repeated the usual five miles' ride to the town and tanks.   On the 9th December he was welcomed back to Bombay by Dhunjeebhoy and the son of the Nawab of Nasik, who boarded the steamer as it entered the harbour.

CHAPTER XX.

1872-1875.

REST.

A THRILL of feeling[1] like that called forth by the Cawnpore
massacre followed the assassination of the Viceroy, Lord
Mayo, by a fanatical Afghan convict in the penal settlement
of the Andaman Islands, on the 8th February 1872. Not
five months before, a Wahabee traitor had cut down the
blameless Chief Justice, Mr. Norman, as he entered the High
Court in Calcutta. It was difficult, at the time, to believe
that both of these events, unprecedented in our history, were
not the expression of more than the individual blood-
thirstiness of the assassins. But the voice of Dr. Wilson,
who knew well the most excitable Muhammadan communities in India, next at least to the Wahabees and Afghans
on the frontier, was raised again, as in 1857, in deprecation
of sweeping charges against millions of our fellow-subjects.
In a Town Hall meeting, and again at the annual conference
of the British and Foreign Bible Society's branch in Bombay,
he used such language as this of Lord Mayo's assassin : " The
murderer must be prayed for in the spirit of the prayer offered
up by Christ, that we should ask forgiveness for those who

trespass against us. I am thoroughly convinced of the loyalty of the main body of Muhammadans. I believe that many of them are most anxious for the diffusion of knowledge, and even knowledge concerning God." His eulogy of "the benevolent and beneficent Governor-General" was based on the experience he had had of his character and conversation when his guest at Simla. Since that other Irish administrator, the Marquis Wellesley, no ruler had exercised on Native and European alike, such a personal fascination as the upright Peer whose only fault was that he had sometimes too little suspicion of abler intellects directed by lower motives than his own. The missionary's correspondence with Lord Mayo was brief, but it is sufficient to justify the assertion that the Viceroy felt a keen interest in all Christian and philanthropic agencies, "and promised to give all assistance in his power to their efforts amongst the heathen tribes of the land." Soon after, Dr. Wilson was consulted by the authorities on the translation and significance of a treasonable proclamation found in the pulpit of the Jumma Musjeed, the great mosque of Delhi, and in another place.

Lord Northbrook, the successor of Lord Mayo, had hardly taken his seat when he turned to Dr. Wilson for information and counsel as to the working of the University system, in itself and in its influence on the lower and vernacular education. Dr. Murdoch had long called the attention of the various Governments to the idolatrous and obscene passages in Government school-books, from which, nevertheless, Christian allusions were carefully excluded. The new Governor-General instructed each provincial Government to report on the subject, and with his own hand thus wrote to Dr. Wilson on the 3d May 1873 : "The revision of the school-books is intended to extend to the Vernacular as well as the English books, and to give the opportunity of eliminating any indecencies or passages which teach the Hindoo or Muhammadan religions. . . . I did not think it desirable to take any public notice of this part of the question, but I wish to set the matter straight without making a fuss. It is very gratifying to me that you should agree with what I said at the Convocation of the Calcutta University." Lord Northbrook then invited Dr. Wilson's opinion on such vexed questions as the compulsory requirement of an ancient language (Sanskrit, in Bengal) for

University pass degrees, and the establishment of University Professorships. On the latter the Scottish scholar's opinion was most strongly that of Mr. S. Laing when Finance Minister, Mr. C. U. Aitchison, Bishop Cotton, Archdeacon Pratt, Dr. Duff, Principal Miller, and Lord Northbrook himself at last, that the Universities should not be prevented from becoming teaching as well as examining bodies, especially in such subjects common to all, and not involving religious difficulties, as the mathematical and physical sciences. Calcutta and Bombay now possess at least one University Chair.

On the two occasions on which, in 1872 and 1873, Dr. Wilson travelled by railway to Nagpore, to inspect the mission and do presbyterial duty, and to Allahabad to attend the General Missionary Conference, he made something like a triumphal progress. These great cities were the outposts to which his direct influence had extended during the previous forty years. At every station where his advent was known, natives, young and old, converts and non-Christians, crowded to the train to see their teacher once more, while some accompanied him for forty miles to prolong the dearly loved intercourse. His letters show how deeply this affection moved the old man. At Allahabad he was honoured, above all, by the 136 missionaries of 19 societies, Native and European, from all parts of India, who met to discuss the methods and results of the missions in India during the previous decade. In the whole history of foreign missions no such Synod has ever been held, whether we look at the number and varied experience of the members, at the evangelical unity of their faith and love, or at the weight and critical value of their disscussions.[1] Dr. Wilson was one of the daily presidents, and he preached on "The Glory of Christ" on the evening of the united communion service. The subject assigned to him for a paper was "On Preaching to the Hindoos," which he treated not as purely evangelistic, not as only educational, but as the proclamation of the gospel in many forms. His plea for doing justice to the languages of the peoples of India as the grand, though not exclusive, media of Christian instruction—*legendo, scribendo, et loquendo*—was not less emphatic than when he first applied it to himself in 1829. But

---

[1] *Report of the General Missionary Conference held at Allahabad*, 1872-73. London : Seeley, Jackson, and Halliday, 1873.

he advocated English as " an alternative vernacular language, specially adapted to the higher regions of thought and feeling," especially in the great cities. " It is rapidly becoming under the British Government what the Greek became under the Seleucidæ and the Ptolemies and the Latin became under the Roman Consuls. I leave all absolute anti-Anglicists to answer for themselves the question, Why did the wisdom of God choose the Greek language for the New Testament ? " Nowhere will the young Englishman, and especially the preacher and teacher, who goes out to India, find such ripe wisdom and practical counsels as in that paper, and in the subsequent opinions on intercourse with the Muhammadans, the aboriginal tribes, and the advanced Brahmists. The hints are worthy to be placed side by side with, so as to supplement, the famous but now too little known, " Notes of Instructions " to young officials, in Malcolm's *Memoir of Central India.*

To the last, whether in Bombay or elsewhere, Dr. Wilson looked, worked, prayed for true converts, and not in vain. The case of Dhunjeebhoy Nowrojee more than thirty years before, and oft-repeated since, was renewed in 1872. Shapoorjee Dhunjeebhoy Babha, a youth of good family, entered the Surat mission school to learn English. On the second day of his attendance Dr. Wilson happened to visit the school and to distribute copies of his elementary catechism. The simple book issued in Shapoorjee's baptism two years after, in spite of the controversial treatises placed in his hands on the other side, and the frantic declarations of his father that he would destroy himself. The usual persecution followed —kidnapping and imprisonment. But the youth remained firm. He nursed Dr. Wilson in the last hours, and has visited Scotland for the completion of his studies as an ordained medical missionary to his own people.

Again, in 1874, Vithabai, a lady of high caste, sought baptism, and was driven from her home by the violence of her husband, whose treatment of the children was such that the mother had them brought into court on a writ of " habeas corpus." The eldest girl, twelve years of age, vehemently protested her desire to live as a Christian with her mother, but the father's rights were declared absolute, in spite of his acknowledged cruelty. The evidence showed that he had himself placed his daughter in the Free Church female school, and had arranged that she should receive lunch in violation of caste rules ; that when she left the school, a Christian book she took with her led her mother to Christ ; that he then asked the wife of the Rev. Gunputrao Navalkar to teach Christianity in his own house ; and that he himself had even proposed to go over to Christianity with his whole family. Who that knows the little faith and much fearing of his own heart will do more than pity the timidity that prevailed ? In the same year Dr. Wilson wrote to Miss Camilla Dennistoun : " Mission objects are pressing upon me the more that the enterprise expands. Last year I admitted into the Christian Church eighteen individuals of hopeful character, education, and intelligence. This year the harvest promises to be equally extensive."

Statistics are no adequate test of such work as Dr. Wilson's. But the figures for 1877 show that in Bombay and the stations of the Free Church founded by him, 1071 converts had been admitted, on the intelligent profession of their faith, since the beginning of his mission ; while there were 2877 pupils and students in 56 schools. That is but the first-fruit of the harvest which he sowed. We find it in other forms so opposite, as the gift at this time, through Sir Madhava Rao, of Rs. 500 from the Maharaja Holkar, which was devoted to enriching the libraries of the college and schools in vernacular and Sanskrit works ; and in this communication from one who had been long a chaplain in India : " I can never forget that it was at a social meeting at your house in Ambrolie, and while you were engaged in prayer, that a remarkable change, or rather the first step of a remarkable change, passed over my wife. I may say that the life of faith is a different thing to me now from what it was when you and I were first acquainted."

The last of the political services which Dr. Wilson was to be able to render to the Government was called for by Lord Northbrook. As an interpreter between the Oriental and the European mind, as a mediator between the races, he was asked in 1875 for his impressions as to the effect of the recent Baroda trial on the minds of the natives. " The opinion of one occupying your position, with large experience of the country and peculiar opportunities of mixing with all classes, would be very valuable," he was told, as different at once from official reports and the utterances of the Press. His elaborate reply (see Appendix I.) called forth a warm letter of gratitude, and a further request for his opinion on these questions, one of which has since been hastily dealt with :—"Is it desirable to impose any check upon the native Press, or to endeavour to counteract the effect of the disloyal native papers by supporting papers which will put forward correct views?" "Has the time arrived for making those who receive a high English education pay the whole cost of it, limiting the aid of the State to those youths who, by distinguishing themselves in the lower schools, show that they deserve assistance in completing their education, thereby bringing fully into operation the principles expounded in the Educational Despatch of 1854? The leisure for replying to these questions never came, but it is not difficult to say what Dr. Wilson's answer would have been to both. Certainly he would have urged the Governor-General, by arguments no less powerful than those which gave the Despatch of 1854 its force, to remove every obstruction to the development of a policy which would allow all religions, educationally, a fair field, and would permit positive moral and spiritual principle to affect the education of the young, while ceasing to build up and to hedge round pure secularism, and all which that involves, by a State monopoly. It is deeply to be regretted that, in spite of his premature abolition of direct taxation, so that the burdens of India are thrown mainly on the poor, Lord Northbrook did not continue, for at least the usual five years' term of office, to maintain the foreign policy of his great predecessors, and to develop his own wise educational views.

In the mission of Sir Bartle Frere to Africa and the East, to arrange with the Khedive, the Sultan of Zanzibar, and the petty potentates of the littoral from the Persian Gulf west and south to the still slave-trading territory of the Portuguese Government of Mozambique, Dr. Wilson saw the philanthropic efforts of his life approaching that happy issue which our vigorous consul at Zanzibar, Dr. Kirk, soon after reached by treaty. In India itself, as he reviewed the gradual amelioration of Asiatic customs under the East India Company, and the growth of toleration under the Crown, he thus tersely catalogued the bloodless triumphs that had been won on a field where, it may be said, he himself completed what Carey had begun eighty years before :—

HORRORS AND INIQUITIES OF INDIA REMOVED BY GOVERNMENT.

I. MURDER OF PARENTS.
  (*a*) By Suttee.
  (*b*) By exposure on the banks of rivers.
  (*c*) By burial alive. Case in Joudhpore territory, 1860.

II. MURDER OF CHILDREN.
  (*a*) By dedication to the Ganges, to be devoured by crocodiles.
  (*b*) By Rajpoot infanticide, West of India, Punjab, East of India.

III. HUMAN SACRIFICES.
  (*a*) Temple sacrifices.
  (*b*) By wild tribes—Meriahs of the Khonds.

IV. SUICIDE.
  (*a*) Crushing by idol cars.
  (*b*) Devotees drowning themselves in rivers.
  (*c*) Devotees casting themselves from precipices.
  (*d*) Leaping into wells—widows.
  (*e*) By Trága.

V. VOLUNTARY TORMENT.
  (*a*) By hook-swinging.
  (*b*) By thigh-piercing.
  (*c*) By tongue-extraction.
  (*d*) By falling on knives.
  (*e*) By austerities.

VI. INVOLUNTARY TORMENT.
  (*a*) Barbarous executions.
  (*b*) Mutilation of criminals.
  (*c*) Extraction of evidence by torment.
  (*d*) Bloody and injurious ordeals.
  (*e*) Cutting off the noses of women.

VII. SLAVERY.
  (*a*) Hereditary predial slavery.
  (*b*) Domestic slavery.
  (*c*) Importation of slaves from Africa.

VIII. EXTORTIONS.
  (*a*) By Dharaná.
  (*b*) By Trága.

IX. RELIGIOUS INTOLERANCE.
  (*a*) Prevention of Propagation of Christianity.
  (*b*) Calling upon the Christian soldiers to fire salutes at heathen festivals, etc.
  (*c*) Saluting gods on official papers.
  (*d*) Managing affairs of idol temples.

X. SUPPORT OF CASTE BY LAW.
  (*a*) Exclusion of low castes from offices.
  (*b*) Exemption of high castes from appearing to give evidence.
  (*c*) Disparagement of low caste.

But it was ever to the spiritual, the divine, that Dr. Wilson looked as the motive power of all effective philanthropy. Hence, as his end drew near, he longed more and more for the restoration of that unity of the Kirk of Scotland which, when the later Stewarts had failed to wipe it out in blood, the short-sighted advisers of Queen Anne first secretly shattered. His experience during the year of his Moderatorship showed him that, without a united Kirk reconstructed on the historical lines of spiritual but lay independence, as stated by Francis Jeffrey and Henry Cockburn, his country would never do its duty in the Christianisation of India. These were his last letters on that subject, written at a time when he was welcoming back to India the Rev. Narayan Sheshadri " after his most successful campaign in Britain and America," in which the Christian Brahman had pleaded for the depressed tribes and ignorant peasantry for whom he has given his life :—

"*4th September* 1874.—*Nulla vestigia retrorsum* must be the motto of the Free Presbyterian Churches. If others can claim, and receive and maintain their full liberty in Christ, and prove faithful to evangelical truth, let them be received into the advanced fraternity ; but let there be no obscurations, or concessions, or retrogressions, which would endanger or weaken our position or injure our character. The duty of the State now, in the present advanced state of Christian society and the many divisions which exist, is to remove all *imposts* for the support of religion, and to devote all church *property* held by the State to such objects as, in the spirit of its original destination, are not inconsistent with its original consecration, viewed in a general and liberal sense."

"*5th October* 1874.—I am pleased to a certain extent with the Act of Parliament abolishing Patronage, and more particularly because it was sought for by the Established Church of Scotland ; but it does not recognise the essential freedom and autonomy of the Church, and is entirely destitute of Presbyterian Catholicity. *We* are the historical Church of Scotland, and let the Established Churchmen be abreast of us before we unite with them. The hasty comprehensions of the Revolution bear a solemn lesson to us which we should not forget. I am convinced that they are the best friends of the Established Churches of Scotland and England who, in a Christian spirit, seek their disestablishment. Saying or doing nothing in this direction we are responsible for much error and much sin. I express this opinion with much personal regard for thousands of their members and ministers, and with still greater regard for those of our own Church who may not see eye to eye with us in this matter. Much discretion will be needed in the advocacy of the disestablishment cause."

Every year, to the last, seemed to bring with it an increase of Dr. Wilson's social duties and influence, while there was no abatement in his services to the public by frequent lectures on such subjects as " Views of Sin in the Hindoo Books and

in the Bible ;" " Hindoo Philosophy,' etc.   Among the guests
and visitors whom he again and again guided amid the rock-
cut temples around Bombay, while he opened to them its
native, its benevolent and scientific institutions, and delighted
them with his conversation, were, in these last years—Lord
Northbrook, Lady Hobart, Sir Arthur Gordon, Sir Harry
Parkes, Count Cserakotsky, Dr. Hermann Jacobi, Dr. Begg,
General Litchfield, Mr. Grant Duff ; Mr. Maughan and Mr.
Octavius Stone, travellers ; Mr. Seibert, and other United
States astronomers ; Dr. Andreas, sent by the Austrian
Government to study the Parsee religion ; Miss Tucker
(A.L.O.E.) ; M. Minayeff, a Russian traveller ; Professor
Monier Williams ; the Armenian bishop ; the Maharaja
Holkar, Sir Madhava Rao, and the Chief of Jamkhundee ;
Canon Duckworth, and the Rev. Dr. A. N. Somerville.   It
was at the farewell meeting held by that evangelist on
April 7th, 1875, that Dr. Wilson appeared among the non-
Christian natives of Bombay for the last time—a fitting occasion.   On the 22d June he presided at a public meeting for
the reception of E. B. Eastwick, Esq., and spoke with great
animation.   Dr. Templeton closed the long succession of missionaries and friends who had been his guests.   The last time
he gathered his children in the faith around him was on the
18th August, when he opened the "Day-school for Indian
and other Eastern Females," which he had erected in affectionate remembrance of Isabella Wilson, "from a bequest by
herself for any one evangelistic object of his choice."

Mr. Grant Duff has told the world his delight in the
companionship of the missionary :—" We drove round a large
part of the town with Dr. Wilson—a great pleasure, to be
put in the same class as going over Canterbury Cathedral
with the author of the *Memorials*, the Greyfriars Churchyard
with Robert Chambers, or Holyrood with poor Joseph Robertson. . . . I leave Bombay with a much stronger impression
than I had of its great Asiatic as distinguished from its merely
Indian importance.   It is and will be more and more, to all
this part of the world, what Ephesus or Alexandria was to
the eastern basin of the Mediterranean in the days of the
Roman Empire.   I wish I could give it a fortnight, and be
allowed to pick Dr. Wilson's brains all the time."   By the

time that the Prince of Wales landed, and there had been put into his hands the exposition of the "Religious Excavations of Western India," over which Dr. Wilson was to have been his guide, the great missionary was too ill to receive His Royal Highness, who graciously deputed so old a friend as Sir Bartle Frere to visit the dying apostle, and sent him the royal portrait. The Viceroy, Lord Northbrook, sought an interview with him, as Lord Hastings and Lady W. Bentinck had done with Carey when he was sick.

Frequent attacks of fever, after his return to Bombay at the end of 1871, had ended in September 1875 in chronic breathlessness from weakness of the heart. But he could not rest so long as any duty had to be done in the Institution, in the financial affairs of the mission, and in the University, although he had Mr. Stothert and zealous young colleagues to relieve him. On attempting to reach Mahableshwar, after a previous visit to Poona, he was forced by an alarming attack to return from Panchgunny, twelve miles short of the loved sanitarium. Miss Taylor, Dr. Macdonald the medical missionary, and Professor Peterson nursed him with devotion. When again in Bombay under the tender skill of Dr. Joynt, he had ever in his hand, as he sat in the chair to which the disease confined him, a volume of hymns marked at Kelly's "Comfort in Prospect of Death." In the last letter written with his own hand he said : " In the goodness of my Heavenly Father I think I am a little better, but if you saw my difficulty of breathing you would pity me. Let that pity pass into petitions addressed to the Throne of all grace." Ready to die, he yet desired life that he might finish, as he thought, his Master's work. To Mr. Bowen, the American missionary, he said the day before he died : "I have perfect peace, and am content that the Lord should do what seems good to Him." And then he talked of the advance of Christ's kingdom in India, expressing an eager solicitude that during the Prince's tour among its peoples and nobles nothing might be done that should even seem to countenance false religions, or to depart from the Government's attitude of simple toleration. He had lived for the freedom of Truth ; rejoicing in Him Who alone has guaranteed that freedom he died.

At his feet gathered more, and more to him, than prince or viceroy, governor or scholar. The Hindoos were there ;

Tirmal Rao and his two sons came from far Dharwar to seek his blessing. They knelt before him, their turbans on the ground, as they laid the Christian patriarch's hands on their heads; and when he died they—Hindoos—begged his body that they might bury it. The Muhammadans were there. A family greatly attached to him brought their own physician to see him, pleading that a *hukeem* who had healed the Shah of Persia must do him good. The Parsees were represented by Dhunjeebhoy and Shapoorjee, his first and his latest sons in the faith from their tribe. In the wanderings of unconsciousness, the words of Scripture, clearly read, often recalled his soul to follow them.

At five on the evening of 1st December, peacefully, John Wilson entered into his rest. In ten days he would have completed his seventy-first year. The old Scottish Burial Ground, closed by an Act of the Legislature, was opened that his dust might lie in the same grave with that of Margaret and Isabella Wilson. There, too, lie Anna Bayne and Robert Nesbit, of whose wife Hay Bayne, who died at sea, there is a marble record. When we last stood there it was with Dr. Wilson, who said that by the grave which was to open for him he would take possession of India for the Lord. For, he used to remark, the way to Heaven is as short from India as from England. While some may regret that the veteran of threescore and ten did not retire to the leisure and the influence to which his native country invited him, surely there was a dramatic completeness, a spiritual unity, in the death which he died in Bombay. By him such an end was desired, but not as a mere sentiment. In 1849 he had written, "Though for long I thought that missionaries should seek to die in India and not contemplate retiring in any circumstances, observation has led me to qualify my opinion." He would have worked unceasingly anywhere; he desired to go on working long. It is well for the natives he loved and for the Church to which he is an example that he was permitted to fall while still in the front of the battle.

How all Bombay, how half India, made great lamentation for John Wilson, and carried him to his burial, the journals of the day record. Governor, Council, and Judges; University Vice-Chancellor, General, and Sir Jamsetjee Jeejeebhoy; Missionaries, Chaplains, and Portuguese Catholics; the con-

verts, students, and school children ; Asiatics and Africans of
every caste and creed, reverently followed all that was mortal
of the venerated missionary for two hours as the bier was
borne from "The Cliff" along Malabar Hill, and down the road
which sweeps round the head of the Back Bay to the Free
Church on the Esplanade, and then to the last resting-place.

The University of Bombay possesses his library, and a
marble bust of its virtual founder by Mr. J. Adams-Acton. His
countrymen in Scotland have founded memorial scholarships to
stimulate the youth of the Border to follow in his footsteps. Dr.
Norman Macleod's proposal in 1870, that Dr. Wilson's Institution should become the United Christian College of Bombay,
is likely to be carried out. Mr. Vice-Chancellor Gibbs, at the
first convocation of the University afterwards, paid this official
tribute to the learning and reputation of his predecessor :—
"This venerable missionary brought all his power, tempered
by a most catholic spirit, to the service of this University ;
and in every branch of its government, including the office
which I have now the honour to hold, gave it not only his
best and warmest support, but also the incalculable benefit of
his great experience as a teacher and guide of the native youth
of this presidency. He has gone, in the fulness of the age
allotted to man, to his reward and his rest ; the regret we
entertain for his loss is sincere, though perhaps selfish, but all
will, I think, agree in the applicability to him of the often-
quoted sentiment of the Prince of Denmark :—

> "'He was a man, take him for all and all,
> We shall not look upon his like again.'"

Captain R. Mackenzie, I. N., writes to us of his work
among the officers of the Indian Navy :—"Under his usual
calm and placid demeanour there lay a strong current of
genial humour which he often gave vent to in his intercourse
with his more intimate friends. The interest he manifested
in the spiritual welfare of the officers both of the Army and
the Indian Navy soon made Ambrolie Mission House a great
centre of attraction for many in both services ; and the
awakening to spiritual life that manifested itself very decidedly
on the western side, can be traced to the prayers and influence
of Dr. Wilson. Apart from his work among the native community, had he done nothing more than what he was directly

and indirectly instrumental in accomplishing among his own
countrymen of all classes, he would have done enough."

Major-General Ballard, C.B., and his wife enjoyed Dr.
Wilson's friendship for sixteen years, and they were long his
neighbours on Malabar Hill. Mrs. Ballard recalls his care of
the native converts, and his unwearied patience with all their
difficulties. " How often have I watched one after another go
in at his gate, all sure of a welcome, of his courteous attention
and sympathy. No matter how interesting the study in which
he was engaged, he seemed to me to be always ready to lay it
down if he could do the least good to a human soul, or speak
a kind word to a sorrowing heart. He always appealed to
what was best in every man. He fixed his eye steadily, not
on the weaknesses, the inconsistencies of frail human nature,
but on the inherent dignity of the soul, the priceless value of
that for which Christ died. I have heard a Native Christian
of low caste say in a tone that touched my heart, ' Dr. Wilson
believes me ; the Padre Saheb knows I say true ; ' as if hug-
ging to his soul the consciousness that some one trusted him.
I have heard those who were incapable of having even a
glimpse of the nobleness of his nature say with a smile that
he was ' often taken in.' I never could admit that it was a
reproach to say so—not unless it be a reproach to say that a
man's soul is steeped in charity, the charity that thinketh no
evil, that ' beareth all things, believeth all things, and hopeth
all things.' Yes, he was often taken in, and in nothing do I
venerate his memory more. I venerate it, because when he
had been deceived and disappointed, chilled with ingratitude
or wearied with inconsistency, he was able to begin afresh to
love and to pity, to hope and to trust. Few of us are capable
in this sense of being ' often taken in ! '

" But we must not overlook what his life and example
did for many of the natives who felt his elevating influence
though they lacked the moral courage or the strength of conviction to profess his faith. A Parsee gentleman said to me
soon after his death, ' Dr. Wilson did not make me a Christian,
but I hope I am a better man for having known him than
I would otherwise have been.' This may be said of hundreds
in Bombay. There is one class of Dr. Wilson's native friends
that I cannot think of without sadness—the students, numbering hundreds in Bombay, who had the privilege of being

instructed by him ; to whom all the doctrines of Christianity
are familiar ; who are convinced, as many of them acknowledge, of the worthlessness of their own system, but who
outwardly cling to it still.   I never saw Dr. Wilson look so
sad as in speaking of some of these—' They know they ought
to be Christians.'   Surely it cannot be that so much love and
so much labour have been expended in vain !

"I know that there are many missionaries doing noble
work in India who come little into contact with English
society.   They avoid rather than welcome opportunities of
entering into it.   It would not undervalue their labours ; but
it is impossible not to regret that the lesson of their lives is
in a great measure lost upon their own countrymen.   Of
course it may be said that Dr. Wilson possessed special social
gifts, that few have acquired such stores of information, and
few have the same power of imparting it to others.   I do
not think that the secret of his popularity lay in his gifts,
but rather in his ready sympathy, his catholic spirit, and
his genial nature.   He had in a rare degree the power of
imparting knowledge without making others too painfully
conscious of their ignorance.   Then no uncharitable judgments
or injurious reports were ever traced to him.   Every man felt
so safe in talking to him.   Scandal passed him by, the evil
weed found no soil to take root in.   While alive to all that
interested us, our joys and our sorrows, he lived in the world
but not of it.   Dr. Wilson made it a special aim to lead his
countrymen to think justly and kindly of those around them,
and he was often the connecting link between the English and
the natives, helping them to understand each other better.
Many of us have felt that his presence in the midst of us had a
softening effect in our dealings with the natives in our house-
holds, leading us more earnestly to desire to do them good.
When a hasty word rose to our lips, or a severe thought of
them, the remembrance of him seemed to say, ' Hush ! there
is one who would lay down his life to save their souls ! '

"Though he was an attached member of the Free Church
of Scotland, we never found that his ecclesiastical views
chilled his friendship for those of us who adhered to other
communions.   He seemed to belong to all who loved the
Lord Jesus in sincerity.   I remember with what tender regard
he spoke to me of Dr. Douglas, then Bishop of Bombay, and

how deeply he grieved for him at a time of sore bereavement in his family. I believe that regard was reciprocal, and that though they differed widely in some articles of their creed, each recognised and honoured in the other devotion to the same Lord. They see eye to eye now !

"Many look back gratefully to Dr. Wilson's simple but cordial hospitality ; and I believe his liberal charities could only be kept up by the exercise of great personal self-denial. He entered cheerfully into society, and his presence had an elevating influence on conversation. He seemed so much part of Bombay and its interests that every visitor of note made an effort to make his acquaintance, and he took a prominent part on every occasion of public interest there. In the last event of importance, however, during his life he was missed from his wonted place. When Bombay was stirred by loyal enthusiasm on the arrival of the Prince of Wales, our venerable friend was ' wearin' awa' to the land o' the leal ! ' As we drove past his darkened house to join the brilliant gathering the night after the arrival of the Prince, I felt saddened by the thought that, while we were going to a scene which would have been full of interest to him, he was laid on a bed of suffering. I was reminded, however, by Sir Bartle Frere, of the higher view to be taken of his state, and how he was waiting at the entrance-chamber of the King of kings. ' How I have missed Dr. Wilson from his place to-day,' said Sir Bartle. ' But when one thinks of things as they really are, probably there is no man on earth more to be envied at this moment than Dr. Wilson. What must it be to be near the close of such a life ! '

"I stole into the silent bungalow to lay a wreath on his coffin. The sun was rising over the distant hills and tinging the bay with gold. No sound broke the stillness but the rustle of the wind in the dry palm leaves and the dash of the distant wave, until I entered the little study. There a voice of bitter weeping met my ear in the verandah—the Native Christians sorrowing most of all that they should see his face no more. ' We are so glad,' said a Native Christian once to me, ' that Dr. Wilson will never go home. You all go and leave us ; we know you are always looking longingly to England ; but Dr. Wilson will never go home.' Ah ! he had gone Home now."

APPENDIX.

—◆—

I.

DR. WILSON ON NATIVE RULE IN BARODA AND NATIVE OPINION ON BRITISH RULE.

"GOVERNMENT HOUSE, SIMLA, *June* 19*th*, 1875.

" MY DEAR DR. WILSON—Lord Northbrook has desired me to ask you whether you would be so kind as to let him know your impressions as to the effect of recent Baroda events on the minds of the Natives. During the progress of the trial and subsequent proceedings, there was naturally a good deal of excitement, and not a few erroneous impressions as to matters of *fact* got abroad. By this time things have begun to settle down. The truth must be pretty generally known, and opinion is probably beginning to assume its ultimate form. The present, therefore, seems a fitting time to enquire what effect, for good or evil, the general policy of Government has produced on the Native mind.

" The only two main sources of information in our possession are of course official reports and the utterances of the Press. The former are, I have every reason to believe, good and trustworthy as far as they go, but it is obvious that there are many sources of information which are more or less closed to those who occupy an official position. As to the latter—the Press—it is very difficult to judge of the degree of importance which is to be attached to the opinions of any particular journal, European or Native.

" The opinion of one occupying your position, with large experience of the country and peculiar opportunities of mixing with all classes, would, I need hardly say, be very valuable, and Lord Northbrook hopes that you will be willing to express your views to him with complete freedom.—Believe me, yours very truly,

" EVELYN BARING."

"MALABAR HILL, BOMBAY, 3d *August* 1875.

"DEAR SIR—I very readily reply to the inquiries which you
confidentially addressed to me some time ago ; but before doing
this I find it necessary to advert to certain peculiarities in the
Baroda State, and its rulers, which it is needful to bear in mind for
the right understanding of the position of affairs in the West of
India, as I shall to the best of my information and judgment represent them.

"Among the natives of Goojarat the Maratha Government at
Baroda has been unpopular from its very commencement to the
present day. By these it is viewed very much as a foreign Government, differing to a very considerable extent in language and customs, and exercising authority without offering the advantages of
quiet, security, education, enlightened legislation, and protection of
labour and commerce as are presented by the British Government,
and without even generally, even in a subordinate capacity, employing the natives of the province. The fact to which I allude I have
ascertained from varied and unexceptionable testimony, and from
complaints thrust upon me during my journeyings through much of
the Gaikwar's territories, by many respectable natives of Goojarat.
Baroda (in which is to be found much of the refuse of the Maratha
country, both Brahmanical and non-Brahmanical) is considered a
cesspool of moral corruption. Notwithstanding the productiveness
of much of its soil, and the extent of its land revenue, and transit
and other duties, it has seldom, if ever, been free from pecuniary
embarrassments. No proper adjustment, as far as I am aware, has
been made between the claims of the State and those of the ruling
family. Much caprice has been shown in the exactions made from
the agricultural population. The treatment of the wild tribes was
barbarous in the extreme, till the management of them, by mutual
agreement, passed into the hands of the British Government in connection with the Mahee-Kanta agency. The administration of justice
through the Gaikwar's dominions has been most imperfect and partial, leading frequently, I am persuaded, to the injury and cruel
treatment both of the innocent and guilty. I can never forget the
shock which I got the first day of my entrance into the Gaikwar's
territory, now upwards of forty years ago, when the ashes of a fire
(under a tree) were pointed out to me by a friend high in the
Medical Service of the East India Company, over the blazing flames
of which four humble Bheels, suspended by the feet from the branch
of a tree, with their heads nearly reaching the flames, had been executed. My journeyings among jungle tribes, five years afterwards,
led to revelations equally painful. Through these (in 1840) I
learnt, from Mr. James Sutherland, C.S., that he had succeeded in

inducing Sayajee Rao, Gaikwar, to abolish Suttee. I think it right, however, in justice to the Baroda Government, to mention that it has readily concurred with the British Government in the measures proposed by it for the abolition of infanticide among the tributaries of both Governments in Kathiawar, leaving the British authorities free to adopt what action they might please in the exigencies of the case. It is to the credit of the Baroda Government, I also mention, that it has allowed the British Government to collect and pay over to it its share of the Kathiawar tribute, thus avoiding such unhappy collisions as occurred between the Gaikwar and the Peshwa of Poona, whom we succeeded in Kathiawar.

"The Baroda Government has for long received much kindness from the British Government. This, however, it has not sufficiently appreciated and improved. A notable instance of this appeared in the unwillingness of Sayajee Rao to fulfil his engagement to pay, for the support of the cavalry troops he was bound to maintain, the capital and interest of the large sums of money which he had borrowed from Soukars and bankers, on the pledge of the British Government that it should see to the ultimate rectification of the accounts. For this he nearly lost his throne in 1832, when Lord Clare visited Baroda on his way to confer with Lord William Bentinck at Ajmer about this and other exigencies which had arisen. It was only after repeated entreaties, almost tearful, that he ultimately accepted the advice proffered to him by the Resident at his Court, Mr. James Williams, C.S., as I find in a private letter addressed to the brother of Mr. Williams, in my possession. Sayajee Rao, it is admitted, had long had bad native advisers in his employment ; while the British Residents at his Court, in general able and honourable men, too much shrank from interfering with him even by friendly advice, except when the British interests were directly concerned. It is to be regretted that he did not, more frequently than he did, solicit their advice. He bore them no good will ; and his memory is associated with suspicions in connection with the lives of two of them. He did nothing to encourage education among his people, though he took approbatory cognisance on one occasion of two small vernacular schools supported by the officers of the British camp. At a late period of his age he got a qualified teacher for his elder sons from one of the industrial classes of the Marathas, who, if they made but little progress in learning, was not to be blamed on that account. Gunput Rao, who succeeded him on his death, was certainly personally the better of the instructions which he received, though he did not succeed in remedying the grievances of his subjects, or in curtailing the extravagant expenses of his palace. He gave away large sums of money in furnishing and filling the garden palace at the Motee Bagh with expensive gewgaws and toys. He viewed the British Government with respect, and came down to Bombay in 1850 to meet Lord Dalhousie. He died on the 19th November 1856.

"Gunput Rao was succeeded by his brother Khunde Rao, but little fitted to hold the reins of government or to follow good advice when proffered to him. He spoke of his predecessor as a fool, but he had remarkable vagaries of his own. He is said to have spent a lakh and a quarter of rupees (£12,500) on one occasion in reward for a successful wrestler. He was fond of *pashuguddha* as well as of *mallaguddha*—of fighting brutes as well as of men, and spent large sums of money in promoting these oriental sports, happily now not very common. When the Mutiny broke out and extended to serious dimensions, he was greatly afraid, as he well might ; but the sight of the brawny legs and arms of the 92d Highlanders mitigated his fears, and called forth imitations of defence for himself in the formation of a still existent regiment with highlandish habiliments, though without the *cor* or the *corpus* of the valiant Gael. In consideration of his fidelity and friendship to the British, there was remitted to him the payment of the sum of three lakhs of rupees per annum for the payment of the Goojarat Irregular Horse, and the acknowledgment of the right of adoption on the failure of natural heirs. Trusting to the toleration of "the Sirkar," as he denominated the British Government, he had serious thoughts of becoming a Muhammadan, and frequently sat on the bare ground to receive instructions in the doctrines of the Koran from a Brahman convert to Muhammadanism seated before him on a stool. He prepared at an immense expense a pall studded with precious stones and jewels for the tomb of Muhammad at Medina, or failing there, for the tomb of Hassan or Hussein at Kerbela in Mesopotamia, and which, there having been no prospect of acceptance by the Muhammadans, is still at Baroda. At the close of 1859 I had an interview with his Highness in the presence of the Resident, Colonel Wallace ; when, after commending him for the erection of a hospital, I almost succeeded in getting him to found a high school at Baroda for the benefit of his subjects. He came to believe, from suspicious circumstances brought to his notice, and from information which he received, that his brother, Mulhar Rao, had intended to attempt to murder him for his throne ; and he put him into restraint and confinement under this belief. On no account would he suffer him to be set at liberty, even under surveillance. From peculiarities in the temperament and actings of Khunde Rao, at which I have above only gently hinted, considerable sympathy was for a time felt for Mulhar Rao, especially throughout the Maratha country. Nevertheless, it was a mistake to set Mulhar Rao on the throne without an investigation of the charge of attempted fratricide which had been brought against him, more especially as Mulhar Rao had been more than an object of suspicion during the Mutiny, and reckoned from his early days to be altogether untrustworthy and injurious.

" The remarks which I have now to make bear directly on the inquiries which you have confidentially addressed to me. For convenience they will still be made mainly in a narrative form.

" The inefficient and devious administration of Mulhar Rao, and his bad choice of agents, were thought by many both in the Goojarat and Maratha country to be such as would likely bring on a crisis. The appointment of Colonel Phayre, a gentleman well known to possess the highest moral character with very extensive knowledge of the different provinces of Western India, to the Residency of Baroda, rendered the crisis, in the judgment of many, almost certain. The Commission headed by Sir Richard Meade, and its finding, hastened its advent. It was intensified by the marriage of Mulhar Rao of Lukshmibai (illegal in a Hindoo point of view in this *kali yuga*, or iron age), and by the suffering peasantry, sirdars, officers, etc., who, more urgently than ever, sought relief from their grievances and payment of their dues. The Gaikwar, failing in his attempt to corrupt the British officers by bribery, resolved to adopt the desperate measure of destroying Colonel Phayre by poison—a catastrophe which the good providence of God averted.

" The vigorous measures which were adopted by the Government of India to bring the Gaikwar to trial for the heinous crime of which he was suspected, had, notwithstanding the circumstances above alluded to, a stunning effect upon the Marathas, many of them throughout the country fearing that he would be found guilty. I have the strongest belief that the Gaikwar had his agents soon at work on this emergency. The tone of many of the native papers was at once changed for the worse, and many of the educated natives, particularly at Poona, held defiant meetings, at which it was alleged that the British Government had no right to put on his trial an independent prince, as they termed the Gaikwar (forgetful of the subordinate position of his ancestors even in the Maratha empire). The appointment of two princes of high status in India, and a famous administrator, to sit in commission for taking and recording evidence, formed for the time being a quietus to some proud spirits ; but anon the flame of discontent again burst forth, and indignation was felt that any Maratha princes should sanction the principle of sitting in a *quasi*-court for the trial of their peers. The last ' dodge ' was that of getting up a loud protestation of the actual innocence of the Gaikwar, while he and his case were *sub judice*.

Never since I came to this country, upwards of forty-six years ago, have I felt so ashamed and grieved because of our educational proteges, for whom a parental Government has done and is doing so much, devoting their talents and energies, in a spirit of marked ingratitude, to the worst of purposes.

"And yet the affair is to my mind perfectly intelligible. It has long been the ambition of the Maratha Brahmans to assume the direction of the Maratha power. This is perfectly obvious from the usurpation of the Brahman *Peshwas*, who with the Putwurdhans and Rastias, and other Brahmanical warriors, made state prisoners and ciphers of the Rajas of Satara and their Maratha nobles, as so well brought out in Grant Duff's *History*, and the condensed notices of it by Mr. Elphinstone, Sir John Malcolm, Sir Bartle Frere, and others. The young men to whom I now refer, and the partisans whom they have succeeded in acquiring, do not intend rebellion at present, but their object is to depreciate the Paramount Power by plausible mis-representations, to promote a spirit of discontent among the people, which may employ them at present and eventually turn the course of events in the direction of their final aspirations. Their conscious-ness of the depravities of Baroda made them really fear the absorption of that State. Its preservation, under happily devised arrangements, I verily believe is to many of them in a certain sense a disappoint-ment ! Their business of grievance-mongering has had a termina-tion sooner than they expected. They form the same party who go about the country poisoning the minds of the peasantry, and who make them dissatisfied with the terms of their holdings, notwith-standing their visible progress in social prosperity, in the extension of their fields, in the improvement of their dwellings, utensils, and clothing. Many of them I know to be a disappointment and a grief to their aged connections. A worthy old Brahman when speaking of them to me lately said, with tears running down his cheeks, ' They have become ashamed of their parents and abandon them, betaking themselves to vicious courses ; what they may erelong do no man can tell.' In connection with them I would observe, in passing, that we have a *portion* of educated youth of a very different spirit from theirs. At the same time we must have a thorough revision of the educational system. We must give useful instruction to the masses, that they may not be the dupes of the designing ; and leave particular classes, hitherto too highly favoured, to work their way upwards by their own merits. It has been rightly said of Scotland that there is a pathway to the Universities from every parish in the land ; but the youth going to these Universities have generally to pay for their own education.

"In conclusion, keeping your queries in view, I may truthfully say that, after much observation and inquiry, I am convinced that Goojarat has all along had faith in the righteousness and wisdom of the proceedings of the British Government, and that the Maharáshtra, exclusive of a band of self-conceited and mischievous youth (worthy of a term or two in the house of correction), now sees that the Government, though misrepresented for some time as to its motives and endeavours, is really deserving of confidence and praise. The late occurrences at Baroda will occupy a chapter in the history of India of a most instructive character ; and the blessing of God will rest on those who have taught the Princes of India that they have duties to their subjects to discharge, which cannot be overlooked without the endangerment of their own position even with that benign Government which is faithful to the spirit of all its engagements.

" I am, my dear Major BARING, with the greatest respect for His Excellency the VICEROY, yours truly,

" JOHN WILSON."

" GOVERNMENT HOUSE, SIMLA, *August* 7, 1875.

" DEAR DR. WILSON—I am very much obliged to you for your most interesting letter on the subject of the effect of the action taken at Baroda upon native opinions in the Bombay Presidency. It is the more valuable as you have so long an experience, and many means of forming a sound judgment which officers of Government do not possess, or at least do not so fully possess.

" There are two subjects which are raised by the experience we have lately acquired upon which, at your leisure, I should much like to know what you think :—*First,* Is it desirable to impose any check upon the Native Press, or to endeavour to counteract the effect of the disloyal native papers by supporting papers which will put forward correct views ? *Second,* Has the time arrived for making those who receive a high English education pay the whole cost of it, limiting the aid of the State to those youths who, by distinguishing themselves in the lower schools, show that they deserve assistance in completing their education, thereby bringing fully into operation the principles expounded in the Educational Despatch of 1854 ?

" Yours very sincerely,

" NORTHBROOK."

II.

DR. WILSON ON THE SOMNATH GATES.

TO SIR BARTLE FRERE.

" *5th December* 1842.—My dear Sir—I have much pleasure
in replying to your letter of the 3d instant ; and I beg you to assure
the honourable the Governor, that any reference of a similar character will at any time meet with my promptest attention. It was
in the year 1835 that I repaired to Puttun Somnath with a view to
an investigation of its antiquities and traditions ; and since that
time I have had many opportunities of comparing the result of my
observations and inquiries with the notices which I have observed
in the Muhammadan histories, and the narratives of other visitors.
Mr. Westergaard, a learned Dane who has been sent to this country
on a literary mission under the auspices of his Sovereign, and who
is at present staying under my roof, visited the place a few months
ago ; and I learn from his account that matters connected with the
temples there remain nearly in the same state in which they were
at the time of my visit.

" The town of Puttun is now in a condition very different from
that in which it was when it was assaulted by Muhammad of
Ghuzni. As mentioned by Sir John Malcolm, it is described by
Persian historians ' as being a lofty castle,' ' on a narrow peninsula,
with its three sides defended by the sea,' and it was famous as a
stronghold of power as well as the seat of a celebrated shrine. The
difficulties encountered by Muhammad in its attack clearly prove
that this was the case. At present, however, there is nothing connected with it deserving the name of a fortification, though part of
the town, which is very inconsiderable in point of size, is enclosed
within a wall. Veráwul, in its neighbourhood, is a port where
mercantile transactions are pretty extensive, and where a body of
respectable Banyas and Jain merchants are to be found.

" There are only two temples belonging to the Hindoos of any
consequence at Somnath. One of these is that built some fifty years
ago by Alya Báí, the famous Ránee of the Holkar family, of whom
such interesting accounts are published in Sir John Malcolm's *History of Central India*. The other is that which is declared by all
the natives of the place to have been the special object of the anti-
polytheistic ire of Muhammad. The latter is now utterly forsaken
by the natives as a place of worship. There was much filth accumulated in it when I saw it. It was traversed by the village swine, the
common scavengers of India, which were attracted to it by its being

occasionally a place of resort by the natives after their morning meal. The greater part of the building, which is of oolite sand-stone, is still standing ; and the remains of its external ornaments, though much defaced by the violence of the Mussulmans, bear wit-ness to a respectable state of advancement in the art of sculpture at the time that they were formed. The name of the temple, as well as its construction, indicates its connection with the god Shiva. The idol destroyed by Muhammad is declared by the natives to have been a *linga*, and of this fact there can be no doubt entertained by any person who attends to the form of the temple. The prin-cipal notices of the destruction of the idol taken by the Mussul-man historians are the following :—' The temple in which the idol of Somnath stood,' says the *Rauzat-as-Safa*, ' was of considerable extent, both in length and breadth, and the roof was supported by fifty-six pillars in rows. The idol was of polished stone ; its height was about five cubits, and its thickness in proportion : two cubits were below ground. Muhammad having entered the temple broke the stone Somnath with a heavy mace ; some of the fragments he ordered to be conveyed to Ghuzni, and they were placed at the threshold of the old mosque.' In the *Tabkat-Akbari*, a history of the Emperor Akbar, we have the following passage agreeing on the point referred to with that now quoted :—

" ' Muhammad,' says Ferishta, who is evidently guilty of gross exaggeration in his general account of Somnath, ' entered Somnath accompanied by his sons, and a few of his nobles and principal attendants. On approaching the temple he saw a superb edifice built of hewn stone. Its lofty roof was supported by fifty-six pillars, curiously carved and set with precious stones. In the centre of the hall was Somnath, a stone idol five yards in height, two of which were sunk in the ground. The king, approaching the image, struck off its nose. He ordered two pieces of the idol to be broken off and sent to Ghuzni, that one might be thrown at the threshold of the public mosque, and the other at the court door of his own palace. These identical fragments are to this day (now 600 years ago) to be seen at Ghuzni. Two more fragments were reserved to be sent to Mecca and Medina.'

" In the second of these extracts it is declared that the temple was ' levelled with the ground.' The *Rauzat-as-Safa*, the more respectable authority, however, does not notice this circumstance. The unanimous testimony of the natives of Somnath, so far as I could read it, is in favour of the representations of those who say that Muhammad contented himself with the destruction of the idol and the partial injury of the shrine.

" Sir John Malcolm, I may here mention, attributes the destruc-tion of the temple to Sultan Mahmoud Begoda, who came to the throne of Goojarat in the year 877 of the Hijra. ' He marched,' he says, ' against Somnath, razed the temple to the ground, and

with the bigoted zeal of a Muhammadan conqueror, built a mosque
on the spot where it stood.' He adds, 'The mosque has fallen into
ruin, and Alya Bái, the widow of a prince of the Maratha family of
Holkar, has lately erected a new temple on the exact spot where it
stood.' This last statement appears to me incredible, for Somnath
has remained in the hands of the Mussulmans ever since the days
of Mahmoud Begoda, and for long they were so much addicted to
obstruct the Hindoos in their worship that the British Government
begged on their behalf the freedom of pilgrimage from the Joonagurh State, to which the town of Somnath belongs. The natives
of Somnath, so far as I could learn, universally declare that the site
of Alya Bái's temple is *not* that of the ancient temple, and that the
temple to which I have already alluded as forsaken *is* the ancient
temple. In a case of this kind I am disposed to lay considerable
stress on the local tradition. Alya Bái's misguided zeal for Hindooism could find many spots near the ancient Somnath where it
could find its expression without its selecting the ruins of a mosque.
The whole neighbourhood, indeed, is sacred, according to the Hindoo
mythology. It is the reputed field of one of the most celebrated
engagements mentioned in the Mahábhárata. The god Krishna,
according to the Bhágawata, received his mortal wound at a spot not
very far distant from its enclosure.

"In the course of my reading I have found no notice in any of
the Mussulman histories of 'gates' having been taken from the
temple of Somnath. If such articles formed part of the trophies of
Muhammad of Ghuzni, it is probable that they were connected
with the ancient *fort* of the town, for it is not likely that the
Mussulmans would devote an article contaminated by idolatry to
an *ornamental* purpose connected with either their mosques or
tombs, though they might dispose of them for any purpose of
degradation that might occur to them. The author of the *Rauzat-
as-Safa*, as we have seen, says expressly that it was some 'fragments'
of the idol which were ordered to be sent to Ghuzni, and that
'they were placed at the threshold of the great mosque.' The
author of the *Tabkat-Akbari* speaks of one 'fragment' of stone
having been sent to Ghuzni, 'where it was laid at the threshold
of the principal mosque, and was there many years.' With these
testimonies that of Ferishta agrees. The story of the *gates* has
originated, it appears to me, with some of our late travellers ;
perhaps with erroneous information given to Mr. Elphinstone.

"The ancient temple of Somnath was devoted to *Shiva*. The
distinctive followers of this god in Kathiawar are now few and
uninfluential. There are no Brahmans in charge of the old temple
to which I have referred. That of Alya Bái is under the care of

APPENDIX. 371

the Sompada Brahmans, one of the smallest of the eighty-four sects into which the Goojarat Brahmanhood is divided, and who, are seldom met with elsewhere than at Somnath, from which they derive their name. The great body of the pure Hindoos in the province are now Vaishnavas. It is the legends relative to *Krishna*, who is one of the incarnations of *Vishnoo*, that principally attract the Hindoo pilgrims to Somnath, and neither the celebrity nor supposed sanctity of the old or the new temple. The Sompada Brahmans exist principally by the practice of mendicity. They are the Poojarees of the temple.

" Somnath, as I have already hinted, belongs to the Mussulman State of Joonagurh. That State has claims for *zortalabi*, or black mail, recognised by us, upon most of the petty States of the peninsula. It is at present particularly well affected to the British Government, as I saw last year when residing in Kathiawar, but it is jealous of the Gaikwar and some of the British and Baroda Hindoo tributaries. I question if it will cordially welcome the gates should they ever enter its boundaries. The Mussulmans throughout India will, I believe, be not a little hurt in their feelings by their public exhibition on their progress, and they, of all classes of the community, require to have their feelings most conciliated on this occasion.

" On reflecting on the present circumstances of Somnath, I see not how the gates can be conveniently disposed of, even should they reach Somnath, unless it be by planting them in some triumphal arch or monument entirely disconnected with any of the sacred edifices of the Hindoos. The Hindoos, so far as they would make any interpretation of their being presented to any of their temples, would conclude that the gift is the voluntary homage of the British Government to their religion, and a token of our espousal of their cause against the Mussulmans, their former foes. This cannot be the design of the Right Honourable the Governor-General. His grand object is to consecrate the *spolia opima* to the commemoration of British and Indian valour. From what I have observed of the Natives during the most intimate intercourse with them for fourteen years, I am led to the opinion that his Lordship's desires of benefit from the disposal of the gates can be accomplished only by their being kept entirely distinct from the *temples*. From his Lordship's late exemplary recognition of divine Providence in connection with our successes in Afghanistan and the preservation of our troops, and the bounty of God toward our native subjects in general, I am sure that his Lordship would revolt from inadvertently originating any measure which would appear to him to be in any way derogatory to our holy Faith, or adverse to that gradual divorce-

ment from superstitious observances which is now becoming apparent throughout the bounds of our Eastern Empire.

"I respectfully beg you to ask the Governor to pardon my
venturing on a single allusion extending beyond the inquiries of
your letter. It proceeds from one who has no common desire to
witness the continuance of the distinguished prosperity of my Lord
Ellenborough's administration—the blessing of peace which, under
God, his Lordship has been so instrumental in earning for us, and
his expressed determination nobly to consecrate the principal
resources of India to its own improvement and social and moral
elevation."

INDEX.

THE END.

Printed by R. & R. CLARK, *Edinburgh.*

OPINIONS OF THE PRESS ON THE FIRST EDITION.

The Life of John Wilson, D.D., F.R.S., for Fifty Years Philanthropist and Scholar in the East. With Portrait and Illustrations.   London : JOHN MURRAY, 1878.

Dr. Smith's life of the late Dr. John Wilson, of Bombay, is, without exception, one of the most valuable records of missionary work in India ever submitted to the English public, and equally worthy of its subject and its author. . .   Dr. George Smith's mature knowledge of Indian affairs has enabled him to give an admirable presentation of Dr. Wilson's life and labours in connection with the great public improvements and progress of the years, extending over two generations of official service, during which he resided in Bombay.   Dr. Smith has given us not simply a biography of Dr. Wilson, but a complete history of missionary, philanthropic, and educational enterprise in Western India, from the Governorship of Mountstuart Elphinstone, 1819–27, to that of Sir Bartle Frere, 1862–67.   He has arranged the many subjects with which he has had to deal and the materials placed at his disposal with great simplicity, clearness, and effect.—*The Times.*

Dr. George Smith has executed with skill and fine enthusiasm a work of rare difficulty.   While he has not failed to bring out fully the grand character of Dr. John Wilson, and the lofty spirit that from first to last sustained him, he has done much to make the general condition of Bombay and procedure of successive Governors clear ; and has thus, in a high and important sense, written a chapter of Indian history.—*British Quarterly Review.*

It is impossible to praise too highly the clear, dramatic, and instructive form in which Dr. Smith has arranged multitudinous and diversified incidents.   He has maintained throughout the vital unity of the volume, which reads as if it had been written at one sitting without wearying or abatement of the writer's interest in it. Yet Dr. Smith has presented us not only with the life of Dr. John Wilson, but with the social and civic history of Bombay ; while he has a word to say of every one of Dr. Wilson's contemporaries, European and Native, who has in any way made a name for himself.   It is a biography which will be widely read.—*The Athenæum.*

Dr. Smith has performed the task in compiling the memoirs with great industry and patience, and a cordial appreciation which makes him almost too uniformly laudatory.   This, however, is the way of biographers, and Dr. Smith has shown in one respect unusual skill.   He has brought out fully the specialty of his subject—his many-sidedness—and has allowed him to display himself in his own letters and papers, with an unusually modest self-effacement.—*The Spectator.*

The volume displays a masterly knowledge of Indian affairs.—*The Pall Mall Gazette.*

The biography cannot be praised too highly.   It is long, but it is too readable to be called too long ; and the entire sympathy between author and subject on all religious and political questions is not a fault, but the reverse.   It can only be doing justice in its eloquent description of Dr. Wilson's great qualities as a man, a philanthropist, and a missionary ; and it will, we hope, attract attention as a worthy tribute to a noble life.—T. W. Rhys Davids in *The Academy.*

In the hands of such a biographer the story of Dr. Wilson's life could not fail to be instructive. . .   This record of a truly apostolic life has been carefully, appreciatively, and conscientiously written.—*The Scotsman.*

Every chapter teems with incidents of the most instructive and suggestive kind. . . . Dr. Smith deserves the gratitude of Christians of all denominations alike for his admirable and lovingly-executed biography of a great missionary and a noble man.—*Edinburgh Daily Review.*

A work which must call forth the earnest gratitude of all the Churches and of all those who take an interest in India. We express our admiration of the literary grace and tact which Dr. Smith has shown in setting before us the life of Dr. Wilson. He tells fitly and well the story of a beautiful and heroic life.—*Aberdeen Free Press.*

An admirable presentation of the public life of the man, put together with great literary tact and sound judgment. In regard to Indian questions, which are naturally discussed at greater or less length in these pages, Dr. Smith may be said to be almost equal in authority to Wilson himself. His remarks indicate the sagacity of observant statesmanship. . . . This most interesting of missionary biographies.—*The Nonconformist.*

We are thankful for so admirable a record of a most useful life, which is fairly entitled to take rank with the best biographical memoirs of distinguished men.—*The English Independent.*

The author has taken the highest platform as a biographer, and has felt all the fervent enthusiasm of a kindred spirit for the elevating and benevolent pursuits in which Dr. Wilson's life was spent. Every library in India, and every Anglo-Indian's home library, must include Dr. Smith's Life of the eminent Scholar and Philanthropist.—*The Homeward Mail.*

The task of writing Dr. Wilson's Life could hardly have fallen into abler or more sympathetic hands than those of the well-known editor of the *Friend of India.* . . . The result is a book which it is difficult for any one interested in Bombay to lay down half-read, while to all it presents conspicuous literary merits. —*Bombay Times of India.*

We rise considerably edified from the perusal of this work. Dr. George Smith has accomplished his task admirably well.—*Indian Mirror.*

Dr. George Smith has done a service to the cause of Indian literature, progress, and humanity, by recording the life and career of such a truly good and great man. . . . Dr. Smith's splendid book is a fitting tribute to his glorious memory. It has other value than what it possesses as a biography.—*Hindoo Patriot.*

The Church of Scotland has furnished two eminent apostles for the Eastern world, who stand out pre-eminent for their talents, acquirements, and labours. These men were Dr. Duff in Eastern and Dr. Wilson in Western India. . . . Both are equally favoured in having one biographer.—Dr. E. D. G. Prime in *The New York Observer.*

All this and more has been accomplished by the learned and painstaking biographer.—*The Glasgow Herald.*

LONDON : JOHN MURRAY, ALBEMARLE STREET.

By the same Author.

The Life of Alexander Duff, D.D., LL.D. In Two Volumes. With Portraits by Jeens.
London : Hodder & Stoughton, 1879.

Memorials of the Rev. John Pourie, Minister of the Free Church of Scotland in Calcutta. W. Newman & Co., 1869.

India since the Mutiny. Serampore, 1874.

Annals of Indian Administration. Seventeen Volumes. Serampore, 1858–1874.

50, ALBEMARLE STREET, LONDON,
May, 1878.

MR. MURRAY'S

GENERAL LIST OF WORKS.

ABINGER'S (LORD Chief Baron) Life. By the Hon. P. CAMPBELL SCARLETT. Portrait. 8vo. 15*s*.

ALBERT MEMORIAL. A Descriptive and Illustrated Account of the National Monument erected to the PRINCE CONSORT at Kensington. Illustrated by Engravings of its Architecture, Decorations, Sculptured Groups, Statues, Mosaics, Metalwork, &c. With Descriptive Text. By DOYNE C. BELL. With 24 Plates. Folio. 12*l*. 12*s*.

———————— HANDBOOK TO. Post 8vo. 1*s*.; or Illustrated Edition, 2*s*. 6*d*.

———— (PRINCE) SPEECHES AND ADDRESSES, with an Introduction, giving some outline of his Character. With Portrait. 8vo. 10*s*. 6*d*.; or *Popular Edition*, fcap. 8vo. 1*s*.

ALBERT DÜRER; his Life, with a History of his Art. By DR. THAUSING, Keeper of Archduke Albert's Art Collection at Vienna. Translated from the German. With Portrait and Illustrations. 2 vols. 8vo. [*In the Press.*

ABBOTT (REV. J.). Memoirs of a Church of England Missionary in the North American Colonies. Post 8vo. 2*s*.

ABERCROMBIE (JOHN). Enquiries concerning the Intellectual Powers and the Investigation of Truth. Fcap. 8vo. 3*s*. 6*d*.

———————— Philosophy of the Moral Feelings. Fcap. 8vo. 2*s*. 6*d*.

ACLAND (REV. CHARLES). Popular Account of the Manners and Customs of India. Post 8vo. 2*s*.

ÆSOP'S FABLES. A New Version. With Historical Preface. By Rev. THOMAS JAMES. With 100 Woodcuts, by TENNIEL and WOLF. Poet 8vo. 2*s*. 6*d*.

AGRICULTURAL (ROYAL) JOURNAL. (*Published half-yearly.*)

AIDS TO FAITH: a Series of Essays on Miracles; Evidences of Christianity; Prophecy & Mosaic Record of Creation; Ideology and Subscription; The Pentateuch; Inspiration; Death of Christ; Scripture and its Interpretation. By various Authors. 8vo. 9*s*.

AMBER-WITCH (THE). A most interesting Trial for Witchcraft. Translated by LADY DUFF GORDON. Post 8vo. 2*s*.

ARMY LIST (THE). *Published Monthly by Authority.*

ARTHUR'S (LITTLE) History of England. By LADY CALLCOTT. *New Edition, continued to* 1872. With 36 Woodcuts. Fcap. 8vo. 1*s*. 6*d*.

ATKINSON (DR. R.) Vie de Seint Auban. A Poem in Norman-French. Ascribed to MATTHEW PARIS. With Concordance, Glossary and Notes. Small 4to, 10*s*. 6*d*.

AUSTIN (JOHN). LECTURES ON GENERAL JURISPRUDENCE; or, the Philosophy of Positive Law. Edited by ROBERT CAMPBELL. 2 Vols. 8vo. 32*s*.

———————— STUDENT'S EDITION, compiled from the above work, by ROBERT CAMPBELL. Post 8vo. 12*s*.

———————— Analysis of. By GORDON CAMPBELL. Post 8vo. 6*s*.

B

ADMIRALTY PUBLICATIONS; Issued by direction of the Lords
Commissioners of the Admiralty:—

A MANUAL OF SCIENTIFIC ENQUIRY, for the Use of Travellers.
Fourth Edition. Edited by Robert Main, M.A. Woodcuts. Post
8vo. 3s. 6d.

GREENWICH ASTRONOMICAL OBSERVATIONS, 1841 to 1847,
and 1847 to 1871. Royal 4to. 20s. each.

REENWICH OBSERVATIONS. 1848 to 1855. 20s. each.

MAGNETICAL AND METEOROLOGICAL OBSERVATIONS. 1844
to 1847. Royal 4to. 20s. each.

APPENDICES TO OBSERVATIONS.
1837. Logarithms of Sines and Cosines in Time. 3s.
1842. Catalogue of 1439 Stars, from Observations made in 1836 to
1841. 4s.
1845. Longitude of Valentia (Chronometrical). 3s.
1847. Description of Altazimuth. 3s.
Twelve Years' Catalogue of Stars, from Observations made
in 1836 to 1847. 4s.
Description of Photographic Apparatus. 2s.
1851. Maskelyne's Ledger of Stars. 3s.
1852. I. Description of the Transit Circle. 3s.
1853. Refraction Tables. 3s.
1854. Description of the Zenith Tube. 3s.
Six Years' Catalogue of Stars, from Observations. 1848 to
1853. 4s.
Plan of Ground Buildings. 3s.
Longitude of Valentia (Galvanic). 2s.
1864. Moon's Semid. from Occultations. 2s.
Planetary Observations, 1831 to 1835. 2s.
1868. Corrections of Elements of Jupiter and Saturn. 2s.
Second Seven Years' Catalogue of 2760 Stars for 1861 to
1867. 4s.
Description of the Great Equatorial. 3s.
1856. Descriptive Chronograph. 3s.
1860. Reduction of Deep Thermometer Observations. 2s.
1871. History and Description of Water Telescope. 3s.
1873. Regulations of the Royal Observatory. 2s.

Cape of Good Hope Observations (Star Ledgers): 1856 to 1863. 2s.
——————————— 1856. 5s.
——————————Astronomical Results. 1857 to 1858. 5s.
Cape Catalogue of 1159 Stars, reduced to the Epoch 1860. 3s.
Cape of Good Hope Astronomical Results. 1859 to 1860. 5s.
——————————— 1871 to 1873. 5s.
——————————— 1874. 5s.

Report on Teneriffe Astronomical Experiment. 1856. 5s.
Paramatta Catalogue of 7385 Stars. 1822 to 1826. 4s.

ASTRONOMICAL RESULTS. 1847 to 1875. 4to. 3s. each.

MAGNETICAL AND METEOROLOGICAL RESULTS. 1848 to
1875. 4to. 3s. each.

REDUCTION OF THE OBSERVATIONS OF PLANETS. 1750 to
1830. Royal 4to. 20s. each.
——————————— LUNAR OBSERVATIONS. 1750
to 1830. 2 Vols. Royal 4to. 20s. each.
——————————— 1831 to 1851. 4to. 10s. each.

BERNOULLI'S SEXCENTENARY TABLE. 1779. 4to. 5s.
BESSEL'S AUXILIARY TABLES FOR HIS METHOD OF CLEAR-
ING LUNAR DISTANCES. 8vo. 2s.
ENCKE'S BERLINER JAHRBUCH, for 830. *Berlin,* 1828. 8vo. 9s.
HANSEN'S TABLES DE LA LUNE. 4to. 20s.
LAX'S TABLES FOR FINDING THE LATITUDE AND LONGI-
TUDE. 1821. 8vo. 10s.
LUNAR OBSERVATIONS at GREENWICH. 1783 to 1819. Compared
with the Tables, 1821. 4to. 7s. 6d.
MACLEAR ON LACAILLE'S ARC OF MERIDIAN. 2 Vols. 20s. each.

ADMIRALTY PUBLICATIONS—*continued.*

MAYER'S DISTANCES of the MOON'S CENTRE from the PLANETS. 1822, 3*s.*; 1823, 4*s.* 6*d.* 1824 to 1835. 8vo. 4*s.* each.
————— TABULÆ MOTUUM SOLIS ET LUNÆ. 1770. 5*s.*
————— ASTRONOMICAL OBSERVATIONS MADE AT GOTTINGEN, from 1756 to 1761. 1826. Folio. 7*s.* 6*d.*
NAUTICAL ALMANACS, from 1767 to 1877, 80*s.* 2*s.* 6*d.* each.
————— SELECTIONS FROM, up to 1812. 8vo. 5*s.* 1834-54. 5*s.*
————— SUPPLEMENTS, 1828 to 1833, 1837 and 1838. 2*s.* each.
————— TABLE requisite to be used with the N.A. 1781. 8vo. 5*s.*
SABINE'S PENDULUM EXPERIMENTS to DETERMINE THE FIGURE OF THE EARTH. 1825. 4to. 40*s.*
SHEPHERD'S TABLES for CORRECTING LUNAR DISTANCES. 1772. Royal 4to. 21*s.*
————— TABLES, GENERAL, of the MOON'S DISTANCE from the SUN, and 10 STARS. 1787. Folio. 5*s.* 6*d.*
TAYLOR'S SEXAGESIMAL TABLE. 1780. 4to. 15*s.*
————— TABLES OF LOGARITHMS. 4to. 60*s.*
TIARK'S ASTRONOMICAL OBSERVATIONS for the LONGITUDE of MADEIRA. 1822. 4to. 5*s.*
————— CHRONOMETRICAL OBSERVATIONS for DIFFERENCES of LONGITUDE between DOVER, PORTSMOUTH, and FALMOUTH. 823. 4to. 5*s.*
VENUS and JUPITER: OBSERVATIONS of, compared with the TABLES. *London,* 1822. 4to. 2*s.*
WALES AND BAYLY'S ASTRONOMICAL OBSERVATIONS. 1777. 4to. 21*s.*
————— REDUCTION OF ASTRONOMICAL OBSERVATIONS MADE IN THE SOUTHERN HEMISPHERE. 1764—1771. 1788. 4to. 10*s.* 6*d.*

BARBAULD (MRS.). Hymns in Prose for Children. With Illustrations. Crown 8vo.

BARCLAY (JOSEPH, LL.D.). Selected Extracts from the Talmud, chiefly illustrating the Teaching of the Bible. With an Introduction. Illustrations. 8vo. 14*s.*

BARKLEY (H. C.). Five Years among the Bulgarians and Turks between the Danube and the Black Sea. Post 8vo. 10*s.* 6*d.*
————— Bulgaria Before the War; during a Seven Years' Experience of European Turkey and its Inhabitants. Post 8vo. 10*s.* 6*d.*
————— My Boyhood : a True Story. A Book for Schoolboys and others. With Illustrations. Post 8vo. 6*s.*

BARROW (SIR JOHN). Autobiographical Memoir, from Early Life to Advanced Age. Portrait. 8vo. 16*s.*
————— (JOHN) Life, Exploits, and Voyages of Sir Francis Drake. Post 8vo. 2*s.*

BARRY (SIR CHARLES). Life and Works. By CANON BARRY. With Portrait and Illustrations. Medium 8vo. 15*s.*

BATES (H. W.) Records of a Naturalist on the River Amazons during eleven years of Adventure and Travel. Illustrations. Post 8vo. 7*s.* 6*d.*

BAX (CAPT. R.N.). Russian Tartary, Eastern Siberia, China, Japan, and Formosa. A Narrative of a Cruise in the Eastern Seas. With Map and Illustrations. Crown 8vo. 12*s.*

BELCHER (LADY). Account of the Mutineers of the 'Bounty,' and their Descendants: with their Settlements in Pitcairn and Norfolk Islands. With Illustrations. Post 8vo. 12*s.*

BELL (SIR CHAS.). Familiar Letters. Portrait. Post 8vo. 12*s.*

BELL (DOYNE C.). Notices of the Historic Persons buried in the Chapel of St. Peter ad Vincula, in the Tower of London, with an account of the discovery of tha supposed remains of Queen Anne Boleyn. With Illustrations. Crown 8vc. 14s.

BELT (THOS.). The Naturalist in Nicaragua, including a Residence at the Gold Mines of Chontales; with Journeys in the Savannahs and Forests; and Observations on Animals and Plants. Illustrations. Post 8vo. 12s.

BERTRAM (JAS. G.). Harvest of the Sea : an Account of British Food Fishes, including sketches of Fisheries and Fisher Folk. With 50 Illustrations. 8vo. 9s.

BIBLE COMMENTARY. THE OLD TESTAMENT. EXPLANATORY and CRITICAL. With a REVISION of the TRANSLATION. By BISHOPS and CLERGY of the ANGLICAN CHURCH. Edited by F. C. COOK, M.A., Canon of Exeter. 6 VOLS. Medium 8vo. 6l.15s.

Vol. I. 30s.	GENESIS. EXODUS. LEVITICUS. NUMBERS. DEUTERONOMY.	VOL. IV. 24s.	JOB. PSALMS. PROVERBS. ECCLESIASTES. SONO OF SOLOMON.
Vols. II. and III. 36s.	JOSHUA, JUDGES, RUTH, SAMUEL, KINGS, CHRONICLES, EZRA, NEHEMIAH, ESTHER.	Vol. V. 20s.	ISAIAH. JEREMIAH.
		Vol. VI. 25s.	EZEKIEL, DANIEL. MINOR PROPHETS.

———————— THE NEW TESTAMENT. 4 VOLS. Medium 8vo.

Vol. I. 18s.	INTRODUCTION. ST. MATTHEW. ST. MARK. ST. LUKE.	Vol. III.	ROMANS, CORINTHIANS, GALATIANS, PHILIPPIANS, EFRESIANS, COLOSSIANS, THESSALONIANS, PHILEMON, PASTORAL EPISTLES, HEBREWS.
Vol. II.	ST. JOHN. ACTS.	Vol. IV.	ST. JAMES, ST. JOHN, ST. PETER, ST. JUDE, REVELATION.

BIGG-WITHER (T. P.). Pioneering in South Brazil; three years of forest and prairie life in the province of Parana. Map and Illustrations. 2 vols. Crown 8vo. 24s.

BIRCH (SAMUEL). A History of Ancient Pottery and Porcelain : Egyptian, Assyrian, Greek, Roman, and Etruscan. With Coloured Plates and 200 Illustrations. Medium 8vo. 42s.

BIRD (ISABELLA). The Hawalian Archipelago; or Six Months among the Palm Groves, Coral Reefs, and Volcanoes of the Sandwich Islands. With Illustrations. Crown 8vo, 7s. 6d.|

BISSET (GENERAL SIR JOHN). Sport and War in South Africa from 1834 to 1867, with a Narrative of the Duke of Edinburgh's Visit. With Map and Illustrations. Crown 8vo. 14s.

BLACKSTONE'S COMMENTARIES; adapted to the Present State of the Law. By R. MALCOLM KERR, LL.D. Revised Edition, incorporating all the Recent Changes in the Law. 4 vols. 8vo. 60s.

BLUNT (REV. J. J.). Undesigned Coincidences in the Writings of the Old and New Testaments, an Argument of their Veracity : containing the Books of Moses, Historical and Prophetical Scriptures, and the Gospels and Acts. Post 8vo. 6s.

———————— History of the Church in the First Three Centuries. Post 8vo. 6s.

———————— Parish Priest; His Duties, Acquirements and Obligations. Post 8vo. 6s.

———————— University Sermons. Post 8vo. 6s.

———————— Plain Sermons. 2 vols. Post 8vo. 12s.

BOSWELL'S Life of Samuel Johnson, LL.D. Including the Tour to the Hebrides. Edited by Mr. CROKER. *Seventh Edition.* Portraits. 1 vol. Medium 8vo. 12s.

BRACE (C. L.). Manual of Ethnology; or the Races of the Old World. Post 8vo. 6s.

BOOK OF COMMON PRAYER. Illustrated with Coloured Borders, Initial Letters, and Woodcuts. 8vo. 18s.

BORROW (GEORGE). Bible in Spain; or the Journeys, Adventures, and Imprisonments of an Englishman in an Attempt to circulate the Scriptures in the Peninsula. Post 8vo. 5s.

———— Gypsies of Spain; their Manners, Customs, Religion, and Language. With Portrait. Post 8vo. 5s.

———— Lavengro; The Scholar—The Gypsy—and the Priest. Post 8vo. 5s.

———— Romany Rye—a Sequel to "Lavengro." Post 8vo. 5s.

———— WILD WALES: its People, Language, and Scenery. Post 8vo. 5s.

———— Romano Lavo-Lil; Word-Book of the Romany, or English Gypsy Language; with Specimens of their Poetry, and an account of certain Gypsyries. Post 8vo. 10s. 6d.

BRAY (MRS.). Life of Thomas Stothard, R.A. With Portrait and 60 Woodcuts. 4to. 21s.

BRITISH ASSOCIATION REPORTS. 8vo.

York and Oxford, 1831-32, 13s. 6d.	Glasgow, 1855, 15s.
Cambridge, 1833, 12s.	Cheltenham, 1856, 18s.
Edinburgh, 1834, 15s.	Dublin, 1857, 15s.
Dublin, 1835, 13s. 6d.	Leeds. 1858, 20s.
Bristol, 1836, 12s.	Aberdeen, 1859, 15s.
Liverpool, 1837, 16s. 6d.	Oxford, 1860, 25s.
Newcastle, 1838, 15s.	Manchester, 1861, 15s.
Birmingham, 1839, 13s. 6d.	Cambridge, 1862, 20s.
Glasgow, 1840, 15s.	Newcastle, 1863, 25s.
Plymouth, 1841, 13s. 6d.	Bath, 1864, 18s.
Manchester, 1842, 10s. 6d.	Birmingham, 1865, 25s
Cork, 1843, 12s.	Nottingham, 1866, 24s.
York, 1844, 20s.	Dundee, 1867, 26s.
Cambridge, 1845, 12s.	Norwich, 1868, 25s.
Southampton, 1846, 15s.	Exeter, 1869, 22s.
Oxford, 1847, 18s.	Liverpool, 1870, 18s.
Swansea, 1848, 9s.	Edinburgh, 1871, 16s.
Birmingham, 1849, 10s.	Brighton, 1872. 24s.
Edinburgh, 1850, 15s.	Bradford, 1873, 25s.
Ipswich, 1851, 16s. 6d.	Belfast, 1874. 25s.
Belfast, 1852, 15s.	Bristol, 1875, 25s.
Hull, 1853, 10s. 6d.	Glasgow, 1876, 25s.
Liverpool, 1854, 18s.	

BROUGHTON (LORD). A Journey through Albania, Turkey in Europe and Asia, to Constantinople. Illustrations. 2 Vols. 8vo. 30s.

———— Visits to Italy. 2 Vols. Post 8vo. 18s.

BRUGSCH (PROFESSOR). A History of Egypt, from the earliest period. Derived from Monuments and Inscriptions. *New Edition.* Translated by the late H. DANBY SEYMOUR. 2 vols. 8vo. [*Nearly Ready.*]

BUCKLEY (ARABELLA B.). A Short History of Natural Science, and the Progress of Discovery from the time of the Greeks to the present day, for Schools and young Persons. Illustrations. Post 8vo. 9s.

BURGON (Rev. J. W.). Christian Gentleman; or, Memoir of
Patrick Fraser Tytler. Post 8vo. 9s.

BURN (Col.). Dictionary of Naval and Military Technical
Terms, English and French—French and English. Crown 8vo. 15s.

BUXTON (Charles). Memoirs of Sir Thomas Fowell Buxton,
Bart. With Selections from his Correspondence. Portrait. 8vo. 16s.
Popular Edition. Fcap. 8vo. 5s.

———— Ideas of the Day. 8vo. 6s.

BURCKHARDT'S (Dr. Jacob) Cicerone; or Art Guide to Painting in Italy. Translated from the German by Mrs. A. Clough. Post
8vo. 6s.

BYLES (Sir John). Foundations of Religion in the Mind and
Heart of Man. Post 8vo. 6s.

BYRON'S (Lord) LIFE AND WORKS :—

Life, Letters, and Journals. By Thomas Moore. *Cabinet
Edition.* Plates. 6 Vols. Fcap. 8vo. 18s.; or One Volume, Portraits.
Royal 8vo., 7s. 6d.

Life and Poetical Works. *Popular Edition.* Portraits.
2 vols. Royal 8vo. 15s.

Poetical Works. *Library Edition.* Portrait. 6 Vols. 8vo. 45s.

Poetical Works. *Cabinet Edition.* Plates. 10 Vols. 12mo. 30s.

Poetical Works. *Pocket Ed.* 8 Vols. 16mo. In a case. 21s.

Poetical Works. *Popular Edition.* Plates. Royal 8vo. 7s. 6d.

Poetical Works. *Pearl Edition.* Crown 8vo. 2s. 6d.

Childe Harold. With 80 Engravings. Crown 8vo. 12s.

Childe Harold. 16mo. 2s. 6d.

Childe Harold. Vignettes. 16mo. 1s.

Childe Harold. Portrait. 16mo. 6d.

Tales and Poems. 16mo. 2s. 6d.

Miscellaneous. 2 Vols. 16mo. 5s.

Dramas and Plays. 2 Vols. 16mo. 5s.

Don Juan and Beppo. 2 Vols. 16mo. 5s.

Beauties. Poetry and Prose. Portrait. Fcap. 8vo. 3s. 6d.

BUTTMANN'S Lexilogus; a Critical Examination of the
Meaning of numerous Greek Words, chiefly in Homer and Hesiod.
By Rev. J. R. Fishlake. 8vo. 12s.

———— Irregular Greek Verbs. With all the Tenses
extant—their Formation, Meaning, and Usage, with Notes, by Rev.
J. R. Fishlake. Post 8vo. 6s.

CALLCOTT (Lady). Little Arthur's History of England.
New Edition, brought down to 1872. With Woodcuts. Fcap. 8vo. 1s. 6d.

CARNARVON (Lord). Portugal, Gallicia, and the Basqu
Provinces. Post 8vo. 3s. 6d.

CARTWRIGHT (W. C.). The Jesuits: their Constitution and
Teaching. An Historical Sketch. 8vo. 9s.

CAMPBELL (Lord). Lord Chancellors and Keepers of the Great Seal of England. From the Earliest Times to the Death of Lord Eldon in 1838. 10 Vols. Crown 8vo. 6s. each.
———— Chief Justices of England. From the Norman Conquest to the Death of Lord Tenterden. 4 Vols. Crown 8vo. 6s. each.
———— Lives of Lyndhurst and Brougham. 8vo. 16s.
———— Lord Bacon. Fcap. 8vo. 2s. 6d.
———— (Sir George) Handy-Book on the Eastern Question; being a Very Recent View of Turkey. With Map. Post 8vo. 6s.
———— (Thos.) Essay on English Poetry. With Short Lives of the British Poets. Post 8vo. 3s. 6d.

CAVALCASELLE and CROWE'S History of Painting in North Italy, from the 14th to the 16th Century. With Illustrations. 2 Vols. 8vo. 42s.
———— Early Flemish Painters, their Lives and Works. Illustrations. Post 8vo. 10s. 6d.; or Large Paper, 8vo. 15s.
———— Life and Times of Titian, with some Account of his Family. With Portrait and Illustrations. 2 vols. 8vo. 42s.

CESNOLA (Gen. L. P. di). Cyprus; its Ancient Cities, Tombs, and Temples. A Narrative of Researches and Excavations during Ten Years' Residence in that Island. With Map and 400 Illustrations. Medium 8vo. 50s.

CHILD (Chaplin). Benedicite; or, Song of the Three Children; being Illustrations of the Power, Beneficence, and Design manifested by the Creator in his works. Post 8vo. 6s.

CHISHOLM (Mrs.). Perils of the Polar Seas; True Stories of Arctic Discovery and Adventure. Illustrations. Post 8vo. 6s.

CHURTON (Archdeacon). Poetical Remains, Translations and Imitations. Portrait. Post 8vo. 7s. 6d.
———— New Testament. Edited with a Plain Practical Commentary for Families and General Readers. With 100 Panoramic and other Views, from Sketches made on the Spot. 2 vols. 8vo. 21s.

CLASSIC PREACHERS OF THE ENGLISH CHURCH. St. James's Lectures, 1877. By Canon Lightfoot, Prof. Wace, Dean of Durham, Rev. W. R. Clark, Canon Farrar, and Dean of Norwich. With an Introduction by J. E. Kempe, M.A., Rector. Post 8vo. 7s. 6d.

CLIVE'S (Lord) Life. By Rev. G. R. Gleig. Post 8vo. 3s. 6d.

CLODE (C. M.). Military Forces of the Crown; their Administration and Government. 2 Vols. 8vo. 21s. each.
———— Administration of Justice under Military and Martial Law, as applicable to the Army, Navy, Marine, and Auxiliary Forces. 8vo. 12s.

COLERIDGE'S (Samuel Taylor) Table-Talk. Portrait. 12mo. 3s. 6d.

COLONIAL LIBRARY. [See Home and Colonial Library.]

COMPANIONS FOR THE DEVOUT LIFE. St. James' Lectures, 1875—6.

De Imitatione Christi. Canon Farrar.
Pensées of Blaise Pascal. Dean Church.
S. François de Sales. Dean Goulburn.
Baxter's Saints' Rest. Archbishop of Dublin.
S. Augustine's Confessions. Bishop of Derry.
Jeremy Taylor's Holy Living and Dying. Rev. Dr. Humphry.
Theologia Germanica. Can Ashwell.
Fénelon's Œuvres Spirituelles. Rev. T. T. Carter.
Andrewes' Devotions. Bishop of Ely.
Christia Year. Canon Barry.
Paradise Lost. Rev. E. H. Bickersteth.
Pilgrim's Progress. Dean Howson.
Prayer Book. Dean Burgon.

With Preface by J. E. Kempe, Rector. Crown 8vo. 6s.

COOK (Canon). Sermons Preached at Lincoln's Inn. 8vo. 9s.

COOKE (E. W.). Leaves from my Sketch-Book. Being a selection from sketches made during many tours. With Descriptive Text. 60 Plates. 2 vols. Small folio. 31s. 6d. each.

COOKERY (MODERN DOMESTIC). Founded on Principles of Economy and Practical Knowledge. By a Lady. Woodcuts. Fcap. 8vo. 5s.

COOPER (T. T.). Travels of a Pioneer of Commerce on an Overland Journey from China towards India. Illustrations. 8vo. 16s.

CRABBE (REV. GEORGE). Life and Poetical Works. With Illustrations. Royal 8vo. 7s.

CRAWFORD & BALCARRES (Earl of). Etruscan Inscriptions. Analyzed, Translated, and Commented upon. 8vo. 12s.

CRIPPS (WILFRED). Old English Plate : Ecclesiastical, Decorative, and Domestic, its makers and marks. Illustrations. Medium 8vo. 21s.

CROKER (J. W.). Progressive Geography for Children. 18mo. 1s. 6d.

———— Stories for Children, Selected from the History of England. Woodcuts. 16mo. 2s. 6d.

———— Boswell's Life of Johnson. Including the Tour to the Hebrides. *Seventh Edition.* Portraits. 8vo. 12s.

———— Early Period of the French Revolution. 8vo. 15s.

———— Historical Essay on the Guillotine. Fcap. 8vo. 1s.

CROWE AND CAVALCASELLE. Lives of the Early Flemish Painters. Woodcuts. Post 8vo, 10s. 6d.; or Large Paper, 8vo, 15s.

———— History of Painting in North Italy, from 14th to 16th Century. Derived from Researches in that Country. With Illustrations. 2 Vols. 8vo. 42s.

———— Life and Times of Titian, with some Account of his Family, chiefly from new and unpublished records. With Portrait and Illustrations. 2 vols. 8vo. 42s.

CUMMING (R. GORDON). Five Years of a Hunter's Life in the Far Interior of South Africa. Woodcuts. Post 8vo. 6s.

CUNYNGHAME (SIR ARTHUR). Travels in the Eastern Caucasus, on the Caspian and Black Seas, in Daghestan and the Frontiers of Persia and Turkey. With Map and Illustrations. 8vo. 18s.

CURTIUS' (PROFESSOR) Student's Greek Grammar, for the Upper Forms. Edited by DR. WM. SMITH. Post 8vo. 6s.

———— Elucidations of the above Grammar. Translated by EVELYN ABBOT. Post 8vo. 7s. 6d.

———— Smaller Greek Grammar for the Middle and Lower Forms. Abridged from the larger work. 12mo. 3s. 6d.

———— Accidence of the Greek Language. Extracted from the above work. 12mo. 2s. 6d.

———— Principles of Greek Etymology. Translated by A. S. WILKINS, M.A., and E. B. ENGLAND, B.A. 2 vols. 8vo. 15s. each.

CURZON (HON. ROBERT). Visits to the Monasteries of the Levant. Illustrations. Post 8vo. 7s. 6d.

CUST (GENERAL). Warriors of the 17th Century—The Thirty Years' War. 2 Vols. 16s. Civil Wars of France and England. 2 Vols. 16s. Commanders of Fleets and Armies. 2 Vols. 18s.

———— Annals of the Wars—18th & 19th Century, 1700—1815. With Maps. 9 Vols. Post 8vo. 5s. each.

DAVY (Sir Humphry). Consolations in Travel; or, Last Days of a Philosopher. Woodcuts. Fcap. 8vo. 3s. 6d.

———— Salmonia; or, Days of Fly Fishing. Woodcuts. Fcap. 8vo. 3s. 6d.

DARWIN (Charles) WORKS :—

Journal of a Naturalist during a Voyage round the World. Crown 8vo. 9s.

Origin of Species by Means of Natural Selection; or, the Preservation of Favoured Races in the Struggle for Life. Woodcuts. Crown 8vo. 7s. 6d.

Variation of Animals and Plants under Domestication. Woodcuts. 2 Vols. Crown 8vo. 18s.

Descent of Man, and Selection in Relation to Sex. Woodcuts. Crown 8vo. 9s.

Expressions of the Emotions in Man and Animals. With Illustrations. Crown 8vo. 12s.

Various Contrivances by which Orchids are Fertilized by Insects. Woodcuts. Crown 8vo. 9s.

Movements and Habits of Climbing Plants. Woodcuts, Crown 8vo. 6s.

Insectivorous Plants. Woodcuts. Crown 8vo. 14s.

Effects of Cross and Self-Fertilization in the Vegetable Kingdom. Crown 8vo. 12s.

Different Forms of Flowers on Plants of the same Species. Crown 8vo. 10s. 6d.

Facts and Argument for Darwin. By Fritz Muller. Translated by W. S. Dallas. Woodcuts. Post 8vo. 6s.

DE COSSON (E. A.). The Cradle of the Blue Nile; a Journey through Abyssinia and Soudan, and a residence at the Court of King John of Ethiopia. Map and Illustrations. 2 vols. Post 8vo. 21s.

DENNIS (George). The Cities and Cemeteries of Etruria. A new Edition, revised, recording all the latest Discoveries. With 20 Plans and 150 Illustrations. 2 vols. 8vo. 42s.

DENT (Emma). Annals of Winchcombe and Sudeley. With 120 Portraits, Plates and Woodcuts. 4to. 42s.

DERBY (Earl of). Iliad of Homer rendered into English Blank Verse. 10th Edition. With Portrait. 2 Vols. Post 8vo. 10s.

DERRY (Bishop of). Witness of the Psalms to Christ and Christianity. The Bampton Lectures for 1876. 8vo.

DEUTSCH (Emanuel). Talmud, Islam, The Targums and other Literary Remains. 8vo. 12s.

DILKE (Sir C. W.). Papers of a Critic. Selected from the Writings of the late Chas. Wentworth Dilke. With a Biographical Sketch. 2 Vols. 8vo. 24s.

DOG-BREAKING, with Odds and Ends for those who love the Dog and Gun. By Gen. Hutchinson. With 40 Illustrations. Crown 8vo. 7s. 6d.

DOMESTIC MODERN COOKERY. Founded on Principles of Economy and Practical Knowledge, and adapted for Private Families. Woodcuts. Fcap. 8vo. 5s.

DOUGLAS'S (Sir Howard) Life and Adventures. Portrait. 8vo. 15s.

———— Theory and Practice of Gunnery. Plates. 8vo. 21s.

———— Construction of Bridges and the Passage of Rivers in Military Operations. Plates. 8vo. 21s.

———— (Wm.) Horse-Shoeing; As it Is, and As it Should be. Illustrations. Post 8vo. 7s. 6d.

DRAKE'S (Sir Francis) Life, Voyages, and Exploits, by Sea and Land. By John Barrow. Post 8vo. 2s.

DRINKWATER (John). History of the Siege of Gibraltar, 1779-1783. With a Description and Account of that Garrison from the Earliest Periods. Post 8vo. 2s.

DUCANGE'S Mediæval Latin-English Dictionary. Translated and Edited by Rev. E. A. Dayman and J. H. Hessels. Small 4to. [*In preparation.*

DU CHAILLU (Paul B.). Equatorial Africa, with Accounts of the Gorilla, the Nest-building Ape, Chimpanzee, Crocodile, &c. Illustrations. 8vo. 21s.

———— Journey to Ashango Land; and Further Penetration into Equatorial Africa. Illustrations. 8vo. 21s.

DUFFERIN (Lord). Letters from High Latitudes; a Yacht Voyage to Iceland, Jan Mayen, and Spitzbergen. Woodcuts. Post 8vo. 7s. 6d.

DUNCAN (Major). History of the Royal Artillery. Compiled from the Original Records. With Portraits. 2 Vols. 8vo. 30s.

———— English in Spain; or, The Story of the War of Succession, 1834 and 1840. Compiled from the Reports of the British Commissioners With Illustrations. 8vo. 16s.

EASTLAKE (Sir Charles). Contributions to the Literature of the Fine Arts. With Memoir of the Author, and Selections from his Correspondence. By Lady Eastlake. 2 Vols. 8vo. 24s.

EDWARDS (W. H.). Voyage up the River Amazons, including a Visit to Para. Post 8vo. 2s.

EIGHT MONTHS AT ROME, during the Vatican Council, with a Daily Account of the Proceedings. By Pomponio Leto. Translated from the Original. 8vo. 12s.

ELDON'S (Lord) Public and Private Life, with Selections from his Correspondence and Diaries. By Horace Twiss. Portrait. 2 Vols. Post 8vo. 21s.

ELGIN (Lord). Letters and Journals. Edited by Theodore Walrond. With Preface by Dean Stanley. 8vo. 14s.

ELLESMERE (Lord). Two Sieges of Vienna by the Turks. Translated from the German. Post 8vo. 2s.

ELLIS (W.). Madagascar Revisited. Setting forth the Persecutions and Heroic Sufferings of the Native Christians. Illustrations. 8vo. 16s.

———— Memoir. By His Son. With his Character and Work. By Rev. Henry Allon, D.D. Portrait. 8vo. 10s. 6d.

———— (Robinson) Poems and Fragments of Catullus. 16mo. 5s.

ELPHINSTONE (Hon. Mountstuart). History of India—the Hindoo and Mahomedan Periods. Edited by Professor Cowell. Map. 8vo. 18s.

———— (H. W.) Patterns for Turning; Comprising Elliptical and other Figures cut on the Lathe without the use of any Ornamental Chuck. With 70 Illustrations. Small 4to. 15s.

ENGLAND. See Callcott, Croker, Hume, Markham, Smith, and Stanhope.

ESSAYS ON CATHEDRALS. With an Introduction. By Dean Howson. 8vo. 12s.

ELZE (Karl). Life of Lord Byron. With a Critical Essay on his Place in Literature. Translated from the German. With Portrait. 8vo. 16s.

FERGUSSON (James). History of Architecture in all Countries from the Earliest Times. With 1,600 Illustrations. 4 Vols. Medium 8vo.

Vol. I. & II. Ancient and Mediæval. 63s.

Vol. III. Indian & Eastern. 42s. Vol. IV. Modern. 31s. 6d.

———— Rude Stone Monuments in all Countries; their Age and Uses. With 230 Illustrations. Medium 8vo. 24s.

———— Holy Sepulchre and the Temple at Jerusalem. Woodcuts. 8vo. 7s. 6d.

———— Temples of the Jews and other buildings in the Haram Area at Jerusalem. With Illustrations. 4to. 42s.

FLEMING (Professor). Student's Manual of Moral Philosophy. With Quotations and References. Post 8vo. 7s. 6d.

FLOWER GARDEN. By Rev. Thos. James. Fcap. 8vo. 1s.

FORBES (Capt. C. J. F.S.) Sketches of Native Burmese; Life, Manners, Customs, and Religion. Crown 8vo. [In the Press.

FORD (Richard). Gatherings from Spain: Post 8vo. 3s. 6d.

FORSYTH (William). Hortensius; an Historical Essay on the Office and Duties of an Advocate. Illustrations. 8vo. 12s.

———— History of Ancient Manuscripts. Post 8vo. 2s. 6d.

———— Novels and Novelists of the 18th Century, in Illustration of the Manners and Morals of the Age. Post 8vo. 10s. 6d.

FORTUNE (Robert). Narrative of Two Visits to the Tea Countries of China, 1843-52. Woodcuts. 2 Vols. Post 8vo. 18s.

FORSTER (John). The Early Life of Jonathan Swift. 1667-1711. With Portrait. 8vo. 15s.

FOSS (Edward). Biographia Juridica, or Biographical Dictionary of the Judges of England, from the Conquest to the Present Time, 1066-1870. Medium 8vo. 21s.

FRANCE (History of). See Markham—Smith—Student's.

FRENCH IN ALGIERS; The Soldier of the Foreign Legion— and the Prisoners of Abd-el-Kadir. Translated by Lady Duff Gordon. Post 8vo. 2s.

FRERE (Sir Bartle). Indian Missions. Small 8vo. 2s. 6d.

———— Eastern Africa as a field for Missionary Labour. With Map. Crown 8vo. 5s.

———— Bengal Famine. How it will be Met and How to Prevent Future Famines in India. With Maps. Crown 8vo. 5s.

GALTON (FRANCIS). Art of Travel; or, Hints on the Shifts and Contrivances available in Wild Countries. Woodcuts. Post 8vo. 7s. 6d.

GEOGRAPHY. See CROKER—SMITH—STUDENTS.

GEOGRAPHICAL SOCIETY'S JOURNAL. (Published Yearly.)

GEORGE (ERNEST). The Mosel; a Series of Twenty Etchings, with Descriptive Letterpress. Imperial 4to. 42s.

———— Loire and South of France; a Series of Twenty Etchings, with Descriptive Text. Folio. 42s.

GERMANY (HISTORY OF). See MARKHAM.

GIBBON (EDWARD). History of the Decline and Fall of the Roman Empire. Edited by MILMAN and GUIZOT. Edited, with Notes, by Dr. WM. SMITH. Maps. 8 Vols. 8vo. 60s.

———— The Student's Edition; an Epitome of the above work, incorporating the Researches of Recent Commentators. By Dr. WM. SMITH. Woodcuts. Post 8vo. 7s. 6d.

GIFFARD (EDWARD). Deeds of Naval Daring; or, Anecdotes of the British Navy. Fcap. 8vo. 3s. 6d.

GLADSTONE (W. E.). Rome and the Newest Fashions in Religion. Three Tracts. 8vo. 7s. 6d.

GLEIG (G. R.). Campaigns of the British Army at Washington and New Orleans. Post 8vo. 2s.

———— Story of the Battle of Waterloo. Post 8vo. 3s. 6d.

———— Narrative of Sale's Brigade in Affghanistan. Post 8vo. 2s.

———— Life of Lord Clive. Post 8vo. 3s. 6d.

———— Sir Thomas Munro. Post 8vo. 3s. 6d.

GLYNNE (SIR STEPHEN R.). Notes on the Churches of Kent. With Preface by W. H. Gladstone, M.P. Illustrations. 8vo. 12s.

GOLDSMITH'S (OLIVER) Works. Edited with Notes by PETER CUNNINGHAM. Vignettes. 4 Vols. 8vo. 30s.

GORDON (SIR ALEX.). Sketches of German Life, and Scenes from the War of Liberation. Post 8vo. 3s. 6d.

———— (LADY DUFF) Amber-Witch: A Trial for Witch-craft. Post 8vo. 2s.

———— French in Algiers. 1. The Soldier of the Foreign Legion. 2. The Prisoners of Abd-el-Kadir. Post 8vo. 2s.

GRAMMARS. See CURTIUS; HALL; HUTTON; KING EDWARD; MATTHIÆ; MAETZNES; SMITH.

GREECE (HISTORY OF). See GROTE—SMITH—Student.

GUIZOT (M.). Meditations on Christianity. 3 Vols. Post 8vo. 30s.

GROTE'S (GEORGE) WORKS :—

HISTORY OF GREECE. From the Earliest Times to the close of the generation contemporary with the death of Alexander the Great. Library Edition. Portrait, Maps, and Plans. 10 Vols. 8vo. 120s. Cabinet Edition. Portrait and Plans. 12 Vols. Post 8vo. 6s. each.

PLATO, and other Companions of Socrates. 3 Vols. 8vo. 45s.

ARISTOTLE. 2 Vols. 8vo. 32s.

MINOR WORKS. With Critical Remarks. By ALEX. BAIN. Portrait. 8vo. 14s.

FRAGMENTS ON ETHICAL SUBJECTS. With Introduction. By ALEXANDER BAIN. 8vo. 7s 6d.

LETTERS ON SWITZERLAND IN 1847. 6s.

PERSONAL LIFE. Compiled from Family Documents, Original Letters, &c. By Mrs. GROTE. Portrait. 8vo. 12s.

HALL (T. D.) AND Dr. WM. SMITH'S School Manual of English Grammar. With Copious Exercises. 12mo. 3s. 6d.

―――― Primary English Grammar for Elementary Schools. Based on the above work. 16mo. 1s.

―――― Child's First Latin Book, including a Systematic Treatment of the New Pronunciation, and a full Praxis of Nouns, Adjectives, and Pronouns. 16mo. 1s. 6d.

HALLAM'S (HENRY) WORKS :―

THE CONSTITUTIONAL HISTORY OF ENGLAND, from the Accession of Henry the Seventh to the Death of George the Second. *Library Edition.* 3 Vols. 8vo. 30s. *Cabinet Edition,* 3 Vols. Post 8vo. 12s.

Student's Edition of the above work. Edited by WM. SMITH, D.C.L. Post 8vo. 7s. 6d.

HISTORY OF EUROPE DURING THE MIDDLE AGES. *Library Edition.* 3 Vols. 8vo. 30s. *Cabinet Edition,* 3 Vols. Post 8vo. 12s.

Student's Edition of the above work. Edited by WM. SMITH, D.C.L. Post 8vo. 7s. 6d.

LITERARY HISTORY OF EUROPE DURING THE 15TH, 16TH, AND 17TH CENTURIES. *Library Edition.* 3 Vols. 8vo. 36s. *Cabinet Edition.* 4 Vols. Post 8vo. 16s.

HALLAM'S (ARTHUR) Literary Remains; in Verse and Prose. Portrait. Fcap. 8vo. 3s. 6d.

HAMILTON (GEN. SIR F. W.). History of the Grenadier Guards. From Original Documents in the Rolls' Records, War Office, Regimental Records, &c. With Illustrations. 3 Vols. 8vo. 63s.

HART'S ARMY LIST. (*Published Quarterly and Annually.*)

HAY (SIR J. H. DRUMMOND). Western Barbary, its Wild Tribes and Savage Animals. Post 8vo. 2s.

HEAD'S (SIR FRANCIS) WORKS :―

THE ROYAL ENGINEER. Illustrations. 8vo. 12s.

LIFE OF SIR JOHN BURGOYNE. Post 8vo. 1s.

RAPID JOURNEYS ACROSS THE PAMPAS. Post 8vo. 2s.

BUBBLES FROM THE BRUNNEN OF NASSAU. Illustrations. Post 8vo. 7s. 6d.

STOKERS AND POKERS; or, the London and North Western Railway. Post 8vo. 2s.

HEAD (SIR EDMUND) Shall and Will; or, Future Auxiliary Verbs. Fcap. 8vo. 4s.

HEBER'S (BISHOP) Journals in India. 2 Vols. Post 8vo. 7s.

―――― Poetical Works. Portrait. Fcap. 8vo. 3s. 6d.

―――― Hymns adapted to the Church Service. 16mo. 1s. 6d.

FOREIGN HANDBOOKS.

HAND-BOOK—TRAVEL-TALK. English, French, German, and Italian. 18mo. 3s. 6d.
—————— HOLLAND AND BELGIUM. Map and Plans. Post 8vo. 6s.
—————— NORTH GERMANY and THE RHINE,— The Black Forest, the Hartz, Thüringerwald, Saxon Switzerland, Rügen the Giant Mountains, Taunus, Odenwald, Elass, and Loth-ringen. Map and Plans. Post 8vo. 10s.
—————— SOUTH GERMANY, — Wurtemburg, Bavaria, Austria, Styria, Salzburg, the Austrian and Bavarian Alps, Tyrol, Hun-gary, and the Danube, from Ulm to the Black Sea. Map. Post 8vo. 10s.
—————— PAINTING. German, Flemish, and Dutch Schools. Illustrations. 2 Vols. Post 8vo. 24s.
—————— LIVES OF EARLY FLEMISH PAINTERS. By CROWE and CAVALCASELLE. Illustrations. Post 8vo. 10s. 6d.
—————— SWITZERLAND, Alps of Savoy, and Piedmont. Maps. Post 8vo. 9s.
—————— FRANCE, Part I. Normandy, Brittany, the French Alps, the Loire, the Seine, the Garonne, and Pyrenees. Post 8vo. 7s. 6d.
—————— Part II. Central France, Auvergne, the Cevennes, Burgundy, the Rhone and Saone, Provence, Nimes, Arles, Marseilles, the French Alps, Alsace, Lorraine, Champagne, &c. Maps. Post 8vo. 7s. 6d.
—————— MEDITERRANEAN ISLANDS—Malta, Corsica, Sardinia, and Sicily. Maps. Post 8vo.   [In the Press.
—————— ALGERIA. Algiers, Constantine, Oran, the Atlas Range. Map. Post 8vo. 9s.
—————— PARIS, and its Environs. Map. 16mo. 3s. 6d.
—————— SPAIN, Madrid, The Castiles, The Basque Provinces, Leon, The Asturias, Galicia, Estremadura, Andalusia, Ronda, Granada, Murcia, Valencia, Catalonia, Aragon, Navarre, The Balearic Islands, &c. &c. Maps. Post 8vo. 20s.
—————— PORTUGAL, LISBON, Porto, Cintra, Mafra, &c. Map. Post 8vo. 12s.
—————— NORTH ITALY, Turin, Milan, Cremona, the Italian Lakes, Bergamo, Brescia, Verona, Mantua, Vicenza, Padua, Ferrara, Bologna, Ravenna, Rimini, Piacenza, Genoa, the Riviera, Venice, Parma, Modena, and Romagna. Map. Post 8vo. 10s.
—————— CENTRAL ITALY, Florence, Lucca, Tuscany, The Marches, Umbria, and late Patrimony of St. Peter's. Map. Post 8vo. 10s.
—————— ROME AND ITS ENVIRONS. Map. Post 8vo. 10s.
—————— SOUTH ITALY, Naples, Pompeii, Herculaneum, and Vesuvius. Map. Post 8vo. 10s.
—————— PAINTING. The Italian Schools. Illustrations. 2 Vols. Post 8vo. 30s.
—————— LIVES OF ITALIAN PAINTERS, FROM CIMABUE to BASSANO. By Mrs. JAMESON. Portraits. Post 8vo. 12s.
—————— NORWAY, Christiania, Bergen, Trondhjem. The Fjelds and Fjords. Map. Post 8vo. 9s.
—————— SWEDEN, Stockholm, Upsala, Gothenburg, the Shores of the Baltic, &c. Post 8vo. 6s.
—————— DENMARK, Sleswig, Holstein, Copenhagen, Jut-land, Iceland Map. Post 8vo. 6s.

HAND-BOOK—RUSSIA, St. Petersburg, Moscow, Poland, and
    Finland. Maps. Post 8vo. 18s.
——————— GREECE, the Ionian Islands, Continental Greece,
    Athens, the Peloponnesus, the Islands of the Ægean Sea, Albania,
    Thessaly, and Macedonia. Maps. Post 8vo. 15s.
——————— TURKEY IN ASIA—Constantinople, the Bos-
    phorus, Dardanelles, Brousa, Plain of Troy, Crete, Cyprus, Smyrna,
    Ephesus, the Seven Churches, Coasts of the Black Sea, Armenia,
    Mesopotamia, &c. Maps. Post 8vo. 15s.
——————— EGYPT, including Descriptions of the Course of
    the Nile through Egypt and Nubia, Alexandria, Cairo, and Thebes, the
    Suez Canal, the Pyramids, the Peninsula of Sinai, the Oases, the
    Fyoom, &c. Map. Post 8vo. 15s.
——————— HOLY LAND—Syria, Palestine, Peninsula of
    Sinai, Edom, Syrian Deserts, Petra, Damascus; and Palmyra. Maps.
    Post 8vo. 20s. *₊* Travelling Map of Palestine. In a case. 12s.
——————— INDIA — Bombay and Madras. Map. 2 Vols.
    Post 8vo. 12s. each.

ENGLISH HANDBOOKS.
HAND-BOOK—MODERN LONDON. Map. 16mo. 3s. 6d.
——————— ENVIRONS OF LONDON within a circuit of 20
    miles. 2 Vols. Crown 8vo. 21s.
——————— EASTERN COUNTIES, Chelmsford, Harwich, Col-
    chester, Maldon, Cambridge, Ely, Newmarket, Bury St. Edmunds,
    Ipswich, Woodbridge, Felixstowe, Lowestoft, Norwich, Yarmouth,
    Cromer, &c. Map and Plans. Post 8vo. 12s.
——————— CATHEDRALS of Oxford, Peterborough, Norwich,
    Ely, and Lincoln. With 90 Illustrations. Crown 8vo. 18s.
——————— KENT, Canterbury, Dover, Ramsgate, Sheerness,
    Rochester, Chatham, Woolwich. Map. Post 8vo. 7s. 6d.
——————— SUSSEX, Brighton, Chichester, Worthing, Hastings,
    Lewes, Arundel, &c. Map. Post 8vo. 6s.
——————— SURREY AND HANTS, Kingston, Croydon, Rei-
    gate, Guildford, Dorking, Boxhill, Winchester, Southampton, New
    Forest, Portsmouth, and Isle of Wight. Maps. Post 8vo. 10s.
——————— BERKS, BUCKS, AND OXON, Windsor, Eton,
    Reading, Aylesbury, Uxbridge, Wycombe, Henley, the City and Uni-
    versity of Oxford, Blenheim, and the Descent of the Thames. Map.
    Post 8vo. 7s. 6d.
——————— WILTS, DORSET, AND SOMERSET, Salisbury,
    Chippenham, Weymouth, Sherborne, Wells, Bath, Bristol, Taunton,
    &c. Map. Post 8vo. 10s.
——————— DEVON AND CORNWALL, Exeter, Ilfracombe,
    Linton, Sidmouth, Dawlish, Teignmouth, Plymouth, Devonport, Tor-
    quay, Launceston, Truro, Penzance, Falmouth, the Lizard, Land's End,
    &c. Maps. Post 8vo. 12s.
——————— CATHEDRALS of Winchester, Salisbury, Exeter,
    Wells, Chichester, Rochester, Canterbury, and St. Albans. With 130
    Illustrations. 2 Vols. Crown 8vo. 36s. St. Albans separately, crown
    8vo. 6s.
——————— GLOUCESTER, HEREFORD, and WORCESTER
    Cirencester, Cheltenham, Stroud, Tewkesbury, Leominster, Ross, Mal-
    vern, Kidderminster, Dudley, Bromsgrove, Evesham. Map. Post 8vo. 9s.
——————— CATHEDRALS of Bristol, Gloucester, Hereford,
    Worcester, and Lichfield. With 50 Illustrations. Crown 8vo. 16s.

HAND-BOOK—NORTH WALES, Bangor, Carnarvon, Beaumaris, Snowdon, Llanberis, Dolgelly, Cader Idris, Conway, &c. Map. Post 8vo. 7s.
———— SOUTH WALES, Monmouth, Llandaff, Merthyr, Vale of Neath, Pembroke, Carmarthen, Tenby, Swansea, The Wye, &c. Map. Post 8vo. 7s.
———— CATHEDRALS OF BANGOR, ST. ASAPH, Llandaff, and St. David's. With Illustrations. Post 8vo. 15s.
———— NORTHAMPTONSHIRE AND RUTLAND— Northampton, Peterborough, Towcester, Daventry, Market Harborough, Kettering, Wallingborough, Thrapston, Stamford, Uppingham, Oakham. Maps. Post 8vo.
———— DERBY, NOTTS, LEICESTER, STAFFORD, Matlock, Bakewell, Chatsworth, The Peak, Buxton, Hardwick, Dove Dale, Ashborne, Southwell, Mansfield, Retford, Burton, Belvoir Melton Mowbray, Wolverhampton, Lichfield, Walsall, Tamworth. Map. Post 8vo. 9s.
———— SHROPSHIRE, CHESHIRE AND LANCASHIRE —Shrewsbury, Ludlow, Bridgnorth, Oswestry, Chester, Crewe, Alderley, Stockport, Birkenhead, Warrington, Bury, Manchester, Liverpool, Burnley, Clitheroe, Bolton, Blackburn, Wigan, Preston, Rochdale, Lancaster, Southport, Blackpool, &c. Map. Post 8vo. 10s.
———— YORKSHIRE, Doncaster, Hull, Selby, Beverley, Scarborough, Whitby, Harrogate, Ripon, Leeds, Wakefield, Bradford, Halifax, Huddersfield, Sheffield. Map and Plans. Post 8vo. 12s.
———— CATHEDRALS of York, Ripon, Durham, Carlisle, Chester, and Manchester. With 60 Illustrations. 2 Vols. Crown 8vo. 21s.
———— DURHAM AND NORTHUMBERLAND, Newcastle, Darlington, Gateshead, Bishop Auckland, Stockton, Hartlepool, Sunderland, Shields, Berwick-on-Tweed, Morpeth, Tynemouth, Coldstream, Alnwick, &c. Map. Post 8vo. 9s.
———— WESTMORLAND AND CUMBERLAND—Lancaster, Furness Abbey, Ambleside, Kendal, Windermere, Coniston, Keswick, Grasmere, Ulswater, Carlisle, Cockermouth, Penrith, Appleby. Map. Post 8vo. 6s.
*** MURRAY'S MAP OF THE LAKE DISTRICT, on canvas. 3s. 6d.
———— ENGLAND AND WALES. Alphabetically arranged and condensed into one volume. Post 8vo. [In the Press.
———— SCOTLAND, Edinburgh, Melrose, Kelso, Glasgow, Dumfries, Ayr, Stirling, Arran, The Clyde, Oban, Inverary, Loch Lomond, Loch Katrine and Trossachs, Caledonian Canal, Inverness, Perth, Dundee, Aberdeen, Braemar, Skye, Caithness, Ross, Sutherland, &c. Maps and Plans. Post 8vo. 9s.
———— IRELAND, Dublin, Belfast, Donegal, Galway, Wexford, Cork, Limerick, Waterford, Killarney, Munster, &c. Maps. Post 8vo.
HERODOTUS. A New English Version. Edited, with Notes and Essays, historical, ethnographical, and geographical, by CANON RAWLINSON, assisted by SIR HENRY RAWLINSON and SIR J. G. WILKINSON. Maps and Woodcuts. 4 Vols. 8vo. 48s.
HERSCHEL'S (CAROLINE) Memoir and Correspondence. By MRS. JOHN HERSCHEL. With Portraits. Crown 8vo 12s.
HATHERLEY (LORD). The Continuity of Scripture, as Declared by the Testimony of our Lord and of the Evangelists and Apostles. 8vo. 6s. Popular Edition. Post 8vo. 2s. 6d.
HOLLWAY (J. G.). A Month in Norway. Fcap. 8vo. 2s.
HONEY BEE. By REV. THOMAS JAMES. Fcap. 8vo. 1s.
HOOK (DEAN). Church Dictionary. 8vo. 16s.

HOME AND COLONIAL LIBRARY. A Series of Works adapted for all circles and classes of Readers, having been selected for their acknowledged interest, and ability of the Authors. Post 8vo. Published at 2s. and 3s. 6d. each, and arranged under two distinctive heads as follows:—

CLASS A.

HISTORY, BIOGRAPHY, AND HISTORIC TALES.

1. SIEGE OF GIBRALTAR. By John Drinkwater. 2s.
2. THE AMBER-WITCH. By Lady Duff Gordon. 2s.
3. CROMWELL AND BUNYAN. By Robert Southey. 2s.
4. LIFE of Sir FRANCIS DRAKE. By John Barrow. 2s.
5. CAMPAIGNS AT WASHINGTON. By Rev. G. R. Gleig. 2s.
6. THE FRENCH IN ALGIERS. By Lady Duff Gordon. 2s.
7. THE FALL OF THE JESUITS. 2s.
8. LIVONIAN TALES. 2s.
9. LIFE OF CONDÉ. By Lord Mahon. 3s. 6d.
10. SALE'S BRIGADE. By Rev. G. R. Gleig. 2s.

11. THE SIEGES OF VIENNA. By Lord Ellesmere. 2s.
12. THE WAYSIDE CROSS. By Capt. Milman. 2s.
13. SKETCHES of GERMAN LIFE. By Sir A. Gordon. 3s. 6d.
14. THE BATTLE of WATERLOO. By Rev. G. R. Gleig. 3s. 6d.
15. AUTOBIOGRAPHY OF STEFFENS. 2s.
16. THE BRITISH POETS. By Thomas Campbell. 3s. 6d.
17. HISTORICAL ESSAYS. By Lord Mahon. 3s. 6d.
18. LIFE OF LORD CLIVE. By Rev. G. R. Gleig. 3s. 6d.
19. NORTH - WESTERN RAILWAY. By Sir F. B. Head. 2s.
20. LIFE OF MUNRO. By Rev. G. R. Gleig. 3s. 6d.

CLASS B.

VOYAGES, TRAVELS, AND ADVENTURES.

1. BIBLE IN SPAIN. By George Borrow. 3s. 6d.
2. GYPSIES of SPAIN. By George Borrow. 3s. 6d.
3 & 4. JOURNALS IN INDIA. By Bishop Heber. 2 Vols. 7s.
5. TRAVELS in the HOLY LAND. By Irby and Mangles. 2s.
6. MOROCCO AND THE MOORS. By J. Drummond Hay. 2s.
7. LETTERS FROM the BALTIC. By a Lady.
8. NEW SOUTH WALES. By Mrs. Meredith. 2s.
9. THE WEST INDIES. By M. G. Lewis. 2s.
10. SKETCHES OF PERSIA. By Sir John Malcolm. 3s. 6d.
11. MEMOIRS OF FATHER RIPA. 2s.
12 & 13. TYPEE AND OMOO. By Hermann Melville. 2 Vols. 7s.
14. MISSIONARY LIFE IN CANADA. By Rev. J. Abbott. 2s.

15. LETTERS FROM MADRAS. By a Lady. 2s.
16. HIGHLAND SPORTS. By Charles St. John. 3s. 6d.
17. PAMPAS JOURNEYS. By Sir F. B. Head. 2s.
18 GATHERINGS FROM SPAIN. By Richard Ford. 3s. 6d.
19. THE RIVER AMAZON. By W. H. Edwards. 2s.
20. MANNERS & CUSTOMS OF INDIA. By Rev. C. Acland. 2s.
21. ADVENTURES IN MEXICO. By G. F. Ruxton. 3s. 6d.
22. PORTUGAL AND GALICIA. By Lord Carnarvon. 3s. 6d.
23. BUSH LIFE IN AUSTRALIA. By Rev. H. W. Haygarth. 2s.
24. THE LIBYAN DESERT. By Bayle St. John. 2s.
25. SIERRA LEONE. By A Lady. 3s. 6d.

₄ Each work may be had separately.

c

HOOK'S (Theodore) Life. By J. G. Lockhart. Fcap. 8vo. 1s.

HOPE (T. C.). Architecture of Ahmedabad, with Historical Sketch and Architectural Notes. With Maps, Photographs, and Woodcuts. 4to. 5l. 5s.

—— (A. J. Beresford) Worship in the Church of England. 8vo. 9s., or, *Popular Selections from.* 8vo. 2s. 6d.

HORACE ; a New Edition of the Text. Edited by Dean Milman. With 100 Woodcuts. Crown 8vo. 7s. 6d.

—— Life of. By Dean Milman. Illustrations. 8vo. 9s.

HOUGHTON'S (Lord) Monographs, Personal and Social. With Portraits. Crown 8vo. 10s. 6d.

—— Poetical Works. *Collected Edition.* With Portrait. 2 Vols. Fcap. 8vo. 12s.

HUME (The Student's). A History of England, from the Invasion of Julius Cæsar to the Revolution of 1688. Corrected and continued to 1868. Woodcuts. Post 8vo. 7s. 6d.

HUTCHINSON (Gen.) Dog Breaking, with Odds and Ends for those who love the Dog and the Gun. With 40 Illustrations. 6th edition. 7s. 6d.

HUTTON (H. E.). Principia Græca; an Introduction to the Study of Greek. Comprehending Grammar, Delectus, and Exercise-book, with Vocabularies. *Sixth Edition.* 12mo. 3s. 6d.

IRBY AND MANGLES' Travels in Egypt, Nubia, Syria, and the Holy Land. Post 8vo. 2s.

JACOBSON (Bishop). Fragmentary Illustrations of the History of the Book of Common Prayer; from Manuscript Sources (Bishop Sanderson and Bishop Wren). 8vo. 5s.

JAMES' (Rev. Thomas) Fables of Æsop. A New Translation, with Historical Preface. With 100 Woodcuts by Tenniel and Wolf. Post 8vo. 2s. 6d.

JAMESON (Mrs.). Lives of the Early Italian Painters— and the Progress of Painting in Italy—Cimabue to Bassano. With 50 Portraits. Post 8vo. 12s.

JENNINGS (Louis J.). Field Paths and Green Lanes in Surrey and Sussex. Illustrations. Post 8vo. 10s. 6d.

JERVIS (Rev. W. H.). The Gallican Church, from the Concordat of Bologna, 1516, to the Revolution. With an Introduction. Portraits. 2 Vols. 8vo. 28s.

JESSE (Edward). Gleanings in Natural History. Fcp. 8vo. 3s. 6d.

JEX-BLAKE (Rev. T. W.). Life in Faith : Sermons Preached at Cheltenham and Rugby. Fcap. 8vo. 3s. 6d.

JOHNS (Rev. B. G.). Blind People; their Works and Ways. With Sketches of the Lives of some famous Blind Men. With Illustrations. Post 8vo. 7s. 6d.

JOHNSON'S (Dr. Samuel) Life. By James Boswell. Including the Tour to the Hebrides. Edited by Mr. Croker. 1 vol. Royal 8vo. 12s *New Edition.* Portraits. 4 Vols. 8vo. [*In Preparation.*

—— Lives of the most eminent English Poets, with Critical Observations on their Works. Edited with Notes, Corrective and Explanatory, by Peter Cunningham. 3 vols. 8vo. 22s. 6d.

JUNIUS' Handwriting Professionally investigated. By Mr. Chabot, Expert. With Preface and Collateral Evidence, by the Hon. Edward Twisleton With Facsimiles, Woodcuts, &c. 4to. £3 3s.

KEN'S (BISHOP) Life. By a LAYMAN. Portrait. 2 Vols. 8vo. 18s.
———————— Exposition of the Apostles' Creed. 16mo. 1s. 6d.

KERR (ROBERT). GENTLEMAN'S HOUSE; OR, HOW TO PLAN ENG-
LISH RESIDENCES FROM THE PARSONAGE TO THE PALACE. With
Views and Plans. 8vo. 24s.

———————— Small Country House. A Brief Practical Discourse on
the Planning of a Residence from 2000l. to 5000l. With Supplementary Estimates to 7000l. Post 8vo. 3s.

———————— Ancient Lights; a Book for Architects, Surveyors,
Lawyers, and Landlords. 8vo. 5s. 6d.

———————— (R. MALOOLM) Student's Blackstone. A Systematic
Ahridgment of the entire Commentaries, adapted to the present state
of the law. Post 8vo. 7s. 6d.

KING EDWARD VITH'S Latin Grammar. 12mo. 3s. 6d.
———————————— First Latin Book. 12mo. 2s. 6d.

KING (R. J.). Archæology, Travel and Art ; being Sketches and
Studies, Historical and Descriptive. 8vo. 12s.

KIRK (J. FOSTER). History of Charles the Bold, Duke of Burgundy. Portrait. 3 Vols. 8vo. 45s.

KIRKES' Handbook of Physiology. Edited by W. MORRANT
BAKER, F.R.C.S. With 400 Illustrations. Post 8vo. 14s.

KUGLER'S Handbook of Painting.—The Italian Schools. Revised and Remodelled from the most recent Researches. By LADY
EASTLAKE. With 140 Illustrations. 2 Vols. Crown 8vo. 30s.

———————— Handbook of Painting.—The German, Flemish, ard
Dutch Schools. Revised and in part re-written. By J. A. CROWF.
With 60 Illustrations. 2 Vols. Crown 8vo. 24s.

LANE (E. W.). Account of the Manners and Customs of Modern
Egyptians. With Illustrations. 2 Vols. Post 8vo. 12s

LAWRENCE (SIR GEO.). Reminiscences of Forty-three Years'
Service in India ; including Captivities in Cabul among the Affghans
and among the Sikhs, and a Narrative of the Mutiny in Rajputana.
Crown 8vo. 10s. 6d.

LAYARD (A. H.). Nineveh and its Remains. Being a Narrative of Researches and Discoveries amidst the Ruins of Assyria.
With an Account of the Chaldean Christians of Kurdistan : the Yezedis.
or Devil-worshippers; and an Enquiry into the Manners and Arts of
the Ancient Assyrians. Plates and Woodcuts. 2 Vols. 8vo. 36s.
  ₊ A POPULAR EDITION of the above work. With Illustrations.
Post 8vo. 7s. 6d.

———————— Nineveh and Babylon ; being the Narrative of Dis-
coveries in the Ruins, with Travels in Armenia, Kurdistan and the
Desert, during a Second Expedition to Assyria. With Map and
Plates. 8vo. 21s.
  ₊ A POPULAR EDITION of the above work. With Illustrations
Post 8vo. 7s. 6d.

LEATHES' (STANLEY) Practical Hebrew Grammar. With the
Hebrew Text of Genesis i.—vi., and Psalms i.—vi. Grammatical
Analysis and Vocabulary. Post 8vo. 7s. 6d.

LENNEP (REV. H. J. VAN). Missionary Travels in Asia Minor.
With Illustrations of Biblical History and Archæology. With Map
and Woodcuts. 2 Vols. Post 8vo. 24s.

———————— Modern Customs and Manners of Bible Lands in
Illustration of Scripture. With Coloured Maps and 300 Illustrations.
2 Vols. 8vo. 21s.

c 2

LESLIE (C. R.). Handbook for Young Painters. With Illustrations. Post 8vo. 7s. 6d.

———— Life and Works of Sir Joshua Reynolds. Portraits and Illustrations. 2 Vols. 8vo. 42s.

LETO (Pomponio). Eight Months at Rome during the Vatican Council. With a daily account of the proceedings. Translated from the original. 8vo. 12s.

LETTERS From the Baltic. By a Lady. Post 8vo. 2s.

———————— Madras. By a Lady. Post 8vo. 2s.

———————— Sierra Leone. By a Lady. Post 8vo. 3s. 6d.

LEVI (Leone). History of British Commerce; and of the Economic Progress of the Nation, from 1763 to 1870. 8vo. 16s.

LIDDELL (Dean). Student's History of Rome, from the earliest Times to the establishment of the Empire. Woodcuts. Post 8vo. 7s. 6d.

LLOYD (W. Watkiss). History of Sicily to the Athenian War; with Elucidations of the Sicilian Odes of Pindar. With Map. 8vo. 14s.

LISPINGS from LOW LATITUDES; or, the Journal of the Hon. Impulsia Gushington. Edited by Lord Dufferin. With 24 Plates. 4to. 21s.

LITTLE ARTHUR'S History of England. By Lady Callcott. New Edition, continued to 1872. With Woodcuts. Fcap. 8vo. 1s. 6d.

LIVINGSTONE (Dr). Popular Account of his First Expedition to Africa, 1840-56. Illustrations. Post 8vo. 7s. 6d.

———————— Second Expedition to Africa, 1858-64. Illustrations. Post 8vo. 7s. 6d.

———————— Last Journals in Central Africa, from 1865 to his Death. Continued by a Narrative of his last moments and sufferings. By Rev Horace Waller. Maps and Illustrations. 2 Vols. 8vo. 28s.

LIVINGSTONIA. Journal of Adventures in Exploring Lake Nyassa, and Establishing a Missionary Settlement there. By E. D. Young, R.N. Revised by Rev. Horace Waller. Maps Post 8vo. 7s. 6d.

LIVONIAN TALES. By the Author of "Letters from the Baltic." Post 8vo. 2s.

LOCH (H. B.). Personal Narrative of Events during Lord Elgin's Second Embassy to China. With Illustrations. Post 8vo. 9s.

LOCKHART (J. G.). Ancient Spanish Ballads. Historical and Romantic. Translated, with Notes. With Portrait and Illustrations. Crown 8vo. 5s.

———————— Life of Theodore Hook. Fcap. 8vo. 1s.

LOUDON (Mrs.). Gardening for Ladies. With Directions and Calendar of Operations for Every Month. Woodcuts. Fcap. 8vo. 3s. 6d.

LYELL (Sir Charles). Principles of Geology; or, the Modern Changes of the Earth and its Inhabitants considered as Illustrative of Geology. With Illustrations. 2 Vols. 8vo. 32s.

———————— Student's Elements of Geology. With Table of British Fossils and 600 Illustrations. Post 8vo. 9s.

———————— Geological Evidences of the Antiquity of Man, including an Outline of Glacial Post-Tertiary Geology, and Remarks on the Origin of Species. Illustrations. 8vo. 14s.

———— (K. M.). Geographical Handbook of Ferns. With Tables to show their Distribution. Post 8vo. 7s. 6d.

LYTTON (Lord). A Memoir of Julian Fane. With Portrait. Post 8vo. 5s.

McCLINTOCK (Sir L.). Narrative of the Discovery of the Fate of Sir John Franklin and his Companions in the Arctic Seas. With Illustrations. Post 8vo. 7s. 6d.

MACDOUGALL (Col.). Modern Warfare as Influenced by Modern Artillery. With Plans. Post 8vo. 12s.

MACGREGOR (J.). Rob Roy on the Jordan, Nile, Red Sea, Gennesareth, &c. A Canoe Cruise in Palestine and Egypt and the Waters of Damascus. With Map and 70 Illustrations. Crown 8vo. 7s. 6d.

MAETZNER'S ENGLISH GRAMMAR. A Methodical, Analytical, and Historical Treatise on the Orthography, Prosody, Ioflectioos, and Syntax of the English Tongue. Translated from the German. By CLAIR J. GRECE, LL.D. 3 Vols. 8vo. 36s.

MAHON (LORD), see STANHOPE.

MAINE (SIR H. SUMNER). Ancient Law: its Connection with the Early History of Society, and its Relation to Modern Ideas. 8vo. 12s.

———— Village Communities in the East and West. 8vo. 12s.

———— Early History of Institutions. 8vo. 12s.

MALCOLM (SIR JOHN). Sketches of Persia. Post 8vo. 3s. 6d.

MANSEL (DEAN). Limits of Religious Thought Examined. Post 8vo. 8s. 6d.

———— Letters, Lectures, and Papers, including the Phrontisterion, or Oxford in the XIXth Century. Edited by H. W. CHANDLER, M.A. 8vo. 12s.

———— Gnostic Heresies of the First and Second Centuries. With a sketch of his life and character. By Lord CARNARVON. Edited by Canon LIGHTFOOT. 8vo 10s. 6d.

MANUAL OF SCIENTIFIC ENQUIRY. For the Use of Travellers. Edited by REV. R. MAIN. Post 8vo. 3s. 6d. *(Published by order of the Lords of the Admiralty.)*

MARCO POLO. The Book of Ser Marco Polo, the Venetian. Concerning the Kingdoms and Marvels of the East. A new English Version. Illustrated by the light of Oriental Writers and Modern Travels. By COL. HENRY YULE. Maps and Illustrations. 2 Vols. Medium 8vo. 63s.

MARKHAM (CLEMENTS R.). The Introduction of Bark Culture into the British Dominions, containing a narrative of Journeys in Peru and India, and some account of the Chincona Plantations already formed. Illustrations. 8vo.

———— (MRS.) History of England. From the First Invasion by the Romans to 1867. Woodcuts. 12mo. 3s. 6d.

———— History of France. From the Conquest by the Gauls to 1861. Woodcuts. 12mo. 3s. 6d.

———— History of Germany. From the Invasion by Marius to 1867. Woodcuts. 12mo. 3s. 6d.

MARLBOROUGH'S (SARAH, DUCHESS OF) Letters. Now first published from the Original MSS. at Madresfield Court. With an Introduction. 8vo. 10s. 6d.

MARRYAT (JOSEPH). History of Modern and Mediæval Pottery and Porcelain. With a Description of the Manufacture. Plates and Woodcuts. 8vo. 42s.

MARSH (G. P.). Student's Manual of the English Language. Edited with Additions. By DR. WM. SMITH. Post 8vo. 7s. 6d.

MASTERS in English Theology. The King's College Lectures, 1877. By Canon Barry, Dean of St. Paul's ; Prof. Plumptre, Canon Westcott, Canon Farrar, and Prof. Cheetham. With Introduction by Canon Barry. Post 8vo. 7s. 6d.

MATTHIÆ'S GREEK GRAMMAR. Abridged by BLOMFIELD, *Revised* by E. S. CROOKE. 12mo. 4s.

MAUREL'S Character, Actions, and Writings of Wellington. Fcap. 8vo. 1s. 6d.

MAYO (LORD). Sport in Abyssinia; or, the Mareb and Tackazzee. With Illustrations. Crown 8vo. 12s.

MEADE (Hon. Herbert). Ride through the Disturbed Districts of
New Zealand, with a Cruise among the South Sea Islands. With Illustrations. Medium 8vo. 12s.

MELVILLE (Hermann). Marquesas and South Sea Islands.
2 Vols. Post 8vo. 7s.

MEREDITH (Mrs. Charles). Notes and Sketches of New South
Wales. Post 8vo. 2s.

MICHAEL ANGELO, Sculptor, Painter, and Architect. His Life
and Works. By C. Heath Wilson. Illustrations. Royal 8vo. 26s.

MILLINGTON (Rev. T. S.). Signs and Wonders in the Land of
Ham, or the Ten Plagues of Egypt, with Ancient and Modern Illustrations. Woodcuts. Post 8vo. 7s. 6d.

MILMAN'S (Dean) WORKS:—

> History of the Jews, from the earliest Period down to Modern
> Times. 3 Vols. Post 8vo. 18s.
>
> Early Christianity, from the Birth of Christ to the Aboli-
> tion of Paganism in the Roman Empire. 3 Vols. Post 8vo. 18s.
>
> Latin Christianity, including that of the Popes to the
> Pontificate of Nicholas V. 9 Vols. Post 8vo. 54s.
>
> Annals of St. Paul's Cathedral, from the Romans to the
> funeral of Wellington. Illustrations. 8vo.
>
> Character and Conduct of the Apostles considered as an
> Evidence of Christianity. 8vo. 10s. 6d.
>
> Quinti Horatii Flacci Opera. With 100 Woodcuts. Small
> 8vo. 7s. 6d.
>
> Life of Quintus Horatius Flaccus. With Illustrations.
> 8vo. 9s.
>
> Poetical Works. The Fall of Jerusalem—Martyr of Antioch
> —Balshazzar—Tamor—Anne Boleyn—Fazio, &c. With Portrait and
> Illustrations. 3 Vols. Fcap. 8vo. 18s.
>
> Fall of Jerusalem. Fcap. 8vo. 1s.

MILMAN (Capt. E. A.) Wayside Cross. Post 8vo. 2s.

MIVART (St. George). Lessons from Nature; as manifested in
Mind and Matter. 8vo. 15s.

MODERN DOMESTIC COOKERY. Founded on Principles of
Economy and Practical Knowledge. New Edition. Woodcuts. Fcap. 8vo. 5s.

MONGREDIEN (Augustus). Trees and Shrubs for English
Plantation. A Selection and Description of the most Ornamental
which will flourish in the open air in our climate. With Classified
Lists. With 30 Illustrations. 8vo. 16s.

MOORE (Thomas). Life and Letters of Lord Byron. *Cabinet
Edition.* With Plates. 6 Vols. Fcap. 8vo. 18s.; *Popular Edition*,
with Portraits. Royal 8vo. 7s. 6d.

MORESBY (Capt.), R.N. Discoveries in New Guinea, Polynesia,
Torres Straits, &c., during the cruise of H.M.S. Basilisk. Map an
Illustrations. 8vo. 15s.

MOTLEY (J. L.). History of the United Netherlands: from the
Death of William the Silent to the Twelve Years' Truce, 1609. *Library
Edition.* Portraits. 4 Vols. Post 8vo. 6s. each.

————— Life and Death of John of Barneveld,
Advocate of Holland. With a View of the Primary Causes and
Movements of the Thirty Years' War. *Library Edition.* Illustrations.
2 Vols. 8vo. 28s. *Cabinet Edition.* 2 vols. Post 8vo. 12s.

MOSSMAN (SAMUEL). New Japan ; the Land of the Rising Sun ; its Annals and Progress during the past Twenty Years, recording the remarkable Progress of the Japanese in Western Civilisation. With Map. 8vo. 15s.

MOZLEY (CANON). Treatise on the Augustinian doctrine of Predestination. Crown 8vo. 9s.

———— Primitive Doctrine of Baptismal Regeneration. Post 8vo.

MUIRHEAD (JAS.). The Vaux-de-Vire of Maistre Jean Le Houx, Advocate of Vire. Translated and Edited. With Portrait and Illustrations. 8vo. 21s.

MUNRO'S (GENERAL) Life and Letters. By REV. G. R. GLEIG. Post 8vo. 8s. 6d.

MURCHISON (SIR RODERICK). Siluria ; or, a History of the Oldest rocks containing Organic Remains. Map and Plates. 8vo. 18s.

———— Memoirs. With Notices of his Contemporaries, and Rise and Progress of Palæozoic Geology. By ARCHIBALD GEIKIE. Portraits. 2 Vols. 8vo. 30s.

MURRAY'S RAILWAY READING. Containing :—

WELLINGTON. By LORD ELLESMERE. 6d.	MAHON'S JOAN OF ARC. 1s.
NIMROD ON THE CHASE, 1s.	HEAD'S EMIGRANT. 2s. 6d.
MUSIC AND DRESS. 1s	NIMROD ON THE ROAD. 1s.
MILMAN'S FALL OF JERUSALEM. 1s.	CROKER ON THE GUILLOTINE. 1s.
MAHON'S "FORTY-FIVE." 3s.	HOLLWAY'S NORWAY. 2s.
LIFE OF THEODORE HOOK. 1s.	MAUREL'S WELLINGTON. 1s. 6d.
DEEDS OF NAVAL DARING. 3s. 6d.	CAMPBELL'S LIFE OF BACON. 2s. 6d.
THE HONEY BEE. 1s.	THE FLOWER GARDEN. 1s.
ÆSOP'S FABLES. 2s. 6d.	REJECTED ADDRESSES. 1s.
NIMROD ON THE TURF. 1s. 6d.	PENN'S HINTS ON ANGLING. 1s.

MUSTERS' (CAPT.) Patagonians ; a Year's Wanderings over Untrodden Ground from the Straits of Magellan to the Rio Negro. Illustrations. Post 8vo. 7s. 6d.

NAPIER (SIR WM.). English Battles and Sieges of the Peninsular War. Portrait. Post 8vo. 9s.

NAPOLEON AT FONTAINEBLEAU AND ELBA. A Journal of Occurrences and Notes of Conversations. By SIR NEIL CAMPBELL, C.B. With a Memoir. By REV. A. N. C. MACLACHLAN, M.A. Portrait 8vo. 15s.

NARES (SIR GEORGE), R.N. Official Report to the Admiralty of the recent Arctic Expedition. Map. 8vo. 2s. 6d.

NASMYTH AND CARPENTER. The Moon. Considered as a Planet, a World, and a Satellite. With Illustrations from Drawings made with the aid of Powerful Telescopes, Woodcuts, &c. 4to. 30s.

NAUTICAL ALMANAC (THE). (By Authority.) 2s. 6d.

NAVY LIST. (Monthly and Quarterly.) Post 8vo.

NEW TESTAMENT. With Short Explanatory Commentary. By ARCHDEACON CHURTON, M.A., and ARCHDEACON BASIL JONES, M.A. With 110 authentic Views, &c. 2 Vols. Crown 8vo 21s. bound.

NEWTH (SAMUEL). First Book of Natural Philosophy ; an Introduction to the Study of Statics, Dynamics, Hydrostatics, Light, Heat, and Sound, with numerous Examples. New and enlarged edition. Small 8vo. 3s. 6d.

———— Elements of Mechanics, including Hydrostatics, with numerous Examples. Small 8vo. 8s. 6d.

———— Mathematical Examples. A Graduated Series of Elementary Examples in Arithmetic, Algebra, Logarithms, Trigonometry, and Mechanics. Small 8vo. 8s. 6d.

NICHOLS' (J. G.) Pilgrimages to Walsingham and Canterbury. By ERASMUS. Translated, with Notes. With Illustrations. Post 8vo. 6s.

———— (SIR GEORGE) History of the English Poor Laws. 2 Vols. 8vo.

NICOLAS (Sir Harris) Historic Peerage of England. Exhi-
biting the Origin, Descent, and Present State of every Title of Peerage which has existed in this Country since the Conquest. By
WILLIAM COURTHOPE. 8vo. 30s.

NIMROD, On the Chace—Turf—and Road. With Portrait and
Plates. Crown 8vo. 5s. Or with Coloured Plates, 7s. 6d.

NORDHOFF (Chas.). Communistic Societies of the United
States; including Detailed Accounts of the Shakers, The Amana,
Oneida, Bethell, Aurora, Icarian and other existing Societies; with
Particulars of their Religious Creeds, Industries, and Present Condi-
tion. With 40 Illustrations. 8vo. 15s.

NORTHCOTE'S (Sir John) Notebook in the Long Parliament.
Containing Proceedings during its First Session, 1640. Edited, with
a Memoir, by A. H. A. Hamilton. Crown 8vo. 9s.

OWEN (Lieut.-Col.). Principles and Practice of Modern Artillery,
including Artillery Material, Gunnery, and Organisation and Use of
Artillery in Warfare. With Illustrations. 8vo. 15s.

OXENHAM (Rev. W.). English Notes for Latin Elegiacs ; designed
for early Proficients in the Art of Latin Versification, with Prefatory
Rules of Composition in Elegiac Metre. 12mo. 3s. 6d.

PALGRAVE (R. H. I.). Local Taxation of Great Britain and
Ireland. 8vo. 5s.
—————Notes on Banking in Great Britain and Ireland,
Sweden, Denmark, and Hamburg, with some Remarks on the amount
of Bills in circulation, both Inland and Foreign. 8vo. 6s.

PALLISER (Mrs.). Brittany and its Byeways, its Inhabitants,
and Antiquities. With Illustrations. Post 8vo. 12s.
————— Mottoes for Monuments, or Epitaphs selected for
General Use and Study. With Illustrations. Crown 8vo. 7s. 6d.

PARIS (Dr.) Philosophy in Sport made Science in Earnest ;
or, the First Principles of Natural Philosophy inculcated by aid of the
Toys and Sports of Youth. Woodcuts. Post 8vo. 7s. 6d.

PARKYNS' (Mansfield) Three Years' Residence in Abyssinia :
with Travels in that Country. With Illustrations. Post 8vo. 7s. 6d.

PEEK PRIZE ESSAYS. The Maintenance of the Church of
England as an Established Church. By REV. CHARLES HOLE—REV.
R. WATSON DIXON—and REV. JULIUS LLOYD. 8vo. 10s. 6d.

PEEL'S (Sir Robert) Memoirs. 2 Vols. Post 8vo. 15s.

PENN (Richard). Maxims and Hints for an Angler and Chess-
player. Woodcuts. Fcap. 8vo. 1s.

PERCY (John, M.D.). Metallurgy. 1st Division. — Fuel,
Wood, Peat, Coal, Charcoal, Coke. Fire-Clays. New Edition. With
Illustrations. 8vo. 30s.
————— 2nd Division.—Copper, Zinc, and Brass. New Edition.
With Illustrations. [In the Press.
————— 3rd Division.—Iron and Steel. New Edition. With
Illustrations. [In Preparation.
————— 4th Division.—Lead, including part of Silver. With
Illustrations. 30s.
————— 5th Division.—Silver. With Illustrations. [Nearly Ready.
————— 6th Division.—Gold, Mercury, Platinum, Tin, Nickel,
Cobalt, Antimony, Bismuth, Arsenic, and other Metals. With Illustrations. [In Preparation.

PHILLIPS' (John) Memoirs of William Smith. 8vo. 7s. 6d.
———— Geology of Yorkshire, The Coast, and Limestone District. Plates. 2 Vols. 4to. 31s. 6d. each.
———— Rivers, Mountains, and Sea Coast of Yorkshire. With Essays on the Climate, Scenery, and Ancient Inhabitants. Plates. 8vo. 15s.
———— (Samuel). Literary Essays from "The Times." With Portrait. 2 Vols. Fcap. 8vo. 7s.
POPE'S (Alexander) Works. With Introductions and Notes, by Rev. Whitwell Elwin. Vols. I., II., VI., VII., VIII. With Portraits. 8vo. 10s. 6d. each.
PORTER (Rev. J. L.). Damascus, Palmyra, and Lebanon. With Travels among the Giant Cities of Bashan and the Hauran. Map and Woodcuts. Post 8vo. 7s. 6d.
PRAYER-BOOK (Illustrated), with Borders, Initials, Vignettes, &c. Edited, with Notes, by Rev. Thos. James. Medium 8vo. 18s. cloth; 31s. 6d. calf; 36s. morocco.
PRINCESS CHARLOTTE OF WALES. A Brief Memoir. With Selections from her Correspondence and other unpublished Papers. By Lady Rose Weioall. With Portrait. 8vo. 8s. 6d.
PUSS IN BOOTS. With 12 Illustrations. By Otto Speckter. 16mo. 1s. 6d. Or coloured, 2s. 6d.
PRIVY COUNCIL JUDGMENTS in Ecclesiastical Cases relating to Doctrine and Discipline. With Historical Introduction, by G. C. Brodrick and W. H. Fremantle. 8vo. 10s. 6d.
QUARTERLY REVIEW (The). 8vo. 6s.
RAE (Edward). Country of the Moors. A Journey from Tripoli in Barbary to the Holy City of Kairwan. Map and Etchings. Crown 8vo. 10s. 6d.
RAMBLES in the Syrian Deserts. Post 8vo. 10s. 6d.
RASSAM (Hormuzd). Narrative of the British Mission to Abyssinia. With Notices of the Countries Traversed from Massowah to Magdala. Illustrations. 2 Vols. 8vo. 28s.
RAWLINSON'S (Canon) Herodotus. A New English Version. Edited with Notes and Essays. Maps and Woodcut. 4 Vols. 8vo. 48s.
———— Five Great Monarchies of Chaldæa, Assyria, Media, Babylonia, and Persia. With Maps and Illustrations. 3 Vols. 8vo. 42s.
———— (Sir Henry) England and Russia in the East; a Series of Papers on the Political and Geographical Condition of Central Asia. Map. 8vo. 12s.
REED (E. J.). Shipbuilding in Iron and Steel; a Practical Treatise, giving full details of Construction, Processes of Manufacture, and Building Arrangements. With Illustrations. 8vo.
———— Iron-Clad Ships; their Qualities, Performances, and Cost. With Chapters on Turret Ships, Iron-Clad Rams, &c. With Illustrations. 8vo. 12s.
———— Letters from Russia in 1875. 8vo. 5s.
REJECTED ADDRESSES (The). By James and Horace Smith. Woodcuts. Post 8vo. 3s. 6d.; or Popular Edition, Fcap. 8vo. 1s.
REYNOLDS' (Sir Joshua) Life and Times. By C. R. Leslie, R.A. and Tom Taylor. Portraits. 2 Vols. 8vo. 42s.
RICARDO'S (David) Political Works. With a Notice of his Life and Writings. By J. R. M'Culloch. 8vo. 16s.
RIPA (Father). Thirteen Years' Residence at the Court of Peking. Post 8vo. 2s.

ROBERTSON (CANON). History of the Christian Church, from the Apostolic Age to the Reformation, 1517. *Library Edition.* 4 Vols. 8vo. *Cabinet Edition.* 8 Vols. Post 8vo. 6s. each.

ROBINSON (REV. DR.). Biblical Researches in Palestine and the Adjacent Regions, 1838—52. Maps. 3 Vols. 8vo. 42s.

———————— Physical Geography of the Holy Land. Post 8vo. 10s. 6d.

———————— (WM.) Alpine Flowers for English Gardens. With 70 Illustrations. Crown 8vo. 12s.

———————— Wild Garden; or, our Groves and Shrubberies made beautiful by the Naturalization of Hardy Exotic Plants. With Frontispiece. Small 8vo. 6s.

———————— Sub-Tropical Garden ; or, Beauty of Form in the Flower Garden. With Illustrations. Small 8vo. 7s. 6d.

ROBSON (E. R.). SCHOOL ARCHITECTURE. Being Practical Remarks on the Planning, Designing, Building, and Furnishing of School-houses. With 300 Illustrations. Medium 8vo. 18s.

ROME (HISTORY OF). *See* LIDDELL and SMITH.

ROWLAND (DAVID). Laws of Nature the Foundation of Morals. Post 8vo. 6s.

RUXTON (GEO. F.). Travels in Mexico; with Adventrs. among Wild Tribes and Animals of the Prairies and Rocky Mountains. Post 8vo. 3s. 6d.

SALE'S (SIR ROBERT) Brigade in Affghanistan. With an Account of the Defence of Jellalabad. By REV. G. R. GLEIG. Post 8vo. 2s.

SCEPTICISM IN GEOLOGY; and the Reasons for It. An assemblage of facts from Nature combining to invalidate and refute the theory of "Causes now in Action." By VERIFIER. Woodcuts. Crown 8vo. 6s.

SCHLIEMANN (DR. HENRY). Troy and Its Remains. A Narrative of Researches and Discoveries made on the Site of Ilium, and in the Trojan Plain. With Maps, Views, and 500 Illustrations. Medium 8vo. 42s.

———————— Discoveries on the Sites of Ancient Mycenæ and Tiryns. With Maps and 500 Illustrations, Medium 8vo. 50s.

SCOTT (SIR G. G.). Secular and Domestic Architecture, Present and Future. 8vo. 9s.

———————— (DEAN) University Sermons. Post 8vo. 8s. 6d.

SCROPE (G. P.). Geology and Extinct Volcanoes of Central France. Illustrations. Medium 8vo. 30s.

SELBORNE (LORD). Notes on some Passages in the Liturgical History of the Reformed English Church. 8vo. 6s.

SHADOWS OF A SICK ROOM. With a Preface by Canon LIDDON. 16mo. 2s. 6d.

SHAH OF PERSIA'S Diary during his Tour through Europe in 1873. Translated from the Original. By J. W. REDHOUSE. With Portrait and Coloured Title. Crown 8vo. 12s.

SMILES' (SAMUEL) WORKS :—

BRITISH ENGINEERS ; from the Earliest Period to the death of the Stephensons. With Illustrations. 5 Vols. Crown 8vo. 7s. 6d. each.

LIFE OF A SCOTCH NATURALIST. With Portrait and Illustrations. Crown 8vo. 10s. 6d.

HUGUENOTS IN ENGLAND AND IRELAND. Crown 8vo. 7s. 6d.

SELF-HELP. With Illustrations of Conduct and Perseverance. Post 8vo. 6s. Or in French, 5s.

CHARACTER. A Sequel to "SELF-HELP." Post 8vo. 6s.

THRIFT. A Book of Domestic Counsel. Post 8vo. 6s.

INDUSTRIAL BIOGRAPHY ; or, Iron Workers and Tool Makers . Post 8vo. 6s.

BOY'S VOYAGE ROUND THE WORLD. Illustrations. Post 8vo. 6s.

SMITH'S (Dr. Wm.). DICTIONARIES :—

DICTIONARY OF THE BIBLE; its Antiquities, Biography, Geography, and Natural History. Illustrations. 3 Vols. 8vo. 105s.

CONCISE BIBLE DICTIONARY. With 300 Illustrations. Medium 8vo. 21s.

SMALLER BIBLE DICTIONARY. With Illustrations. Post 8vo. 7s. 6d.

CHRISTIAN ANTIQUITIES. Comprising the History, Institutions, and Antiquities of the Christian Church. With Illustrations. Vol. I. 8vo. 31s. 6d. (To be completed in 2 vols.)

CHRISTIAN BIOGRAPHY, LITERATURE, SECTS, AND DOCTRINES; from the Times of the Apostles to the Age of Charlemagne. Vol. I. 8vo. 31s. 6d. (To be completed in 3 vols.)

GREEK AND ROMAN ANTIQUITIES. With 500 Illustrations. Medium 8vo. 28s.

GREEK AND ROMAN BIOGRAPHY AND MYTHOLOGY. With 600 Illustrations. 3 Vols. Medium 8vo. 4l. 4s.

GREEK AND ROMAN GEOGRAPHY. 2 Vols. With 500 Illustrations. Medium 8vo. 56s.

ATLAS OF ANCIENT GEOGRAPHY—BIBLICAL AND CLASSICAL. Folio. 6l. 6s.

CLASSICAL DICTIONARY OF MYTHOLOGY, BIOGRAPHY, AND GEOGRAPHY. 1 Vol. With 750 Woodcuts. 8vo. 18s.

SMALLER CLASSICAL DICTIONARY. With 200 Woodcuts. Crown 8vo. 7s. 6d.

SMALLER GREEK AND ROMAN ANTIQUITIES. With 200 Woodcuts. Crown 8vo. 7s. 6d.

COMPLETE LATIN-ENGLISH DICTIONARY. With Tables of the Roman Calendar, Measures, Weights, and Money. 8vo. 21s.

SMALLER LATIN-ENGLISH DICTIONARY. 12mo. 7s. 6d.

COPIOUS AND CRITICAL ENGLISH-LATIN DICTIONARY. 8vo. 21s.

SMALLER ENGLISH-LATIN DICTIONARY. 12mo. 7s. 6d.

SMITH'S (Dr. Wm.) ENGLISH COURSE :—

SCHOOL MANUAL OF ENGLISH GRAMMAR, WITH COPIOUS EXERCISES. Post 8vo. 3s. 6d.

SCHOOL MANUAL OF MODERN GEOGRAPHY, PHYSICAL AND Political. Post 8vo. 5s.

PRIMARY ENGLISH GRAMMAR. 16mo. 1s.

PRIMARY HISTORY OF BRITAIN. 12mo. 2s. 6d.

SMITH'S (Dr. Wm.) FRENCH COURSE :—

FRENCH PRINCIPIA. Part I. A First Course, containing a Grammar, Delectus, Exercises, and Vocabularies. 12mo. 3s. 6d.

FRENCH PRINCIPIA. Part II. A Reading Book, containing Fables, Stories, and Anecdotes, Natural History, and Scenes from the History of France. With Grammatical Questions, Notes and copious Etymological Dictionary. 12mo. 4s. 6d.

FRENCH PRINCIPIA. Part III. Prose Composition, containing a Systematic Course of Exercises on the Syntax, with the Principal Rules of Syntax. 12mo. [In the Press.

STUDENT'S FRENCH GRAMMAR. By C. HERON-WALL. With Introduction by M. Littré. Post 8vo. 7s. 6d.

SMALLER GRAMMAR OF THE FRENCH LANGUAGE. Abridged from the above. 12mo. 3s. 6d.

SMITH'S (Dr. Wm.) GERMAN COURSE :—

GERMAN PRINCIPIA. Part I. A First German Course, containing a Grammar, Delectus, Exercise Book, and Vocabularies. 12mo. 3s. 6d.

GERMAN PRINCIPIA. Part II. A Reading Book ; containing Fables, Stories, and Anecdotes, Natural History, and Scenes from the History of Germany. With Grammatical Questions, Notes, and Dictionary. 12mo. 3s. 6d.

PRACTICAL GERMAN GRAMMAR. Post 8vo. 3s. 6d.

SMITH'S (Dr. Wm.) LATIN COURSE:—

PRINCIPIA LATINA. Part I. First Latin Course, containing a Grammar, Delectus, and Exercise Book, with Vocabularies. 12mo. 3s. 6d.
    ₊ In this Edition the Cases of the Nouns, Adjectives, and Pronouns are arranged both as in the ORDINARY GRAMMARS and as in the PUBLIC SCHOOL PRIMER, together with the corresponding Exercises.

APPENDIX TO PRINCIPIA LATINA Part I. ; being Additional Exercises, with Examination Papers. 12mo. 2s. 6d.

PRINCIPIA LATINA. Part II. A Reading-book of Mythology, Geography, Roman Antiquities, and History. With Notes and Dictionary. 12mo. 3s. 6d.

PRINCIPIA LATINA. Part III. A Poetry Book. Hexameters and Pentameters; Eclog. Ovidianæ; Latin Prosody. 12mo. 3s. 6d.

PRINCIPIA LATINA. Part IV. Prose Composition. Rules of Syntax with Examples, Explanations of Synonyms, and Exercises on the Syntax. 12mo. 3s. 6d.

PRINCIPIA LATINA. Part V. Short Tales and Anecdotes for Translation into Latin. 12mo. 3s.

LATIN-ENGLISH VOCABULARY AND FIRST LATIN-ENGLISH DICTIONARY FOR PHÆDRUS, CORNELIUS NEPOS, AND C.ESAR. 12mo. 3s. 6d.

STUDENT'S LATIN GRAMMAR. Post 8vo. 6s.

SMALLER LATIN GRAMMAR. 12mo. 3s. 6d.

TACITUS, GERMANIA, AGRICOLA, &c. With English Notes. 12mo. 3s. 6d.

SMITH'S (Dr. Wm.) GREEK COURSE:—

INITIA GRÆCA. Part I. A First Greek Course, containing a Grammar, Delectus, and Exercise-book. With Vocabularies. 12mo. 3s. 6d.

INITIA GRÆCA. Part II. A Reading Book. Containing Short Tales, Anecdotes, Fables, Mythology, and Grecian History. 12mo. 3s. 6d.

INITIA GRÆCA. Part III. Prose Composition. Containing the Rules of Syntax, with copious Examples and Exercises. 12mo. 3s. 6d.

STUDENT'S GREEK GRAMMAR. By CURTIUS. Post 8vo. 6s.

SMALLER GREEK GRAMMAR. 12mo. 3s. 6d.

GREEK ACCIDENCE. 12mo. 2s. 6d.

PLATO, APOLOGY OF SOCRATES, &c. With Notes. 12mo. 3s. 6d.

SMITH'S (Dr. Wm.) SMALLER HISTORIES :—

SCRIPTURE HISTORY. Woodcuts. 16mo. 3s. 6d.

ANCIENT HISTORY. Woodcuts. 16mo. 3s. 6d.

ANCIENT GEOGRAPHY. Woodcuts. 16mo. 3s. 6d.

ROME. Woodcuts. 16mo. 3s. 6d.

GREECE. Woodcuts. 16mo. 3s. 6d.

CLASSICAL MYTHOLOGY. Woodcuts. 16mo. 3s. 6d.

ENGLAND. Woodcuts. 16mo. 3s. 6d.

ENGLISH LITERATURE. 16mo. 3s. 6d.

SPECIMENS OF ENGLISH LITERATURE. 16mo. 3s. 6d.

SHAW (T. B.). Student's Manual of English Literature. Post 8vo.
7s. 6d.

———— Specimens of English Literature. Selected from the
Chief Writers. Post 8vo. 7s. 6d.

———— (ROBERT). Visit to High Tartary, Yarkand, and Kashgar
(formerly Chinese Tartary), and Return Journey over the Karakorum
Pass. With Map and Illustrations. 8vo. 16s.

SIERRA LEONE; Described in Letters to Friends at Home. By
A LADY. Post 8vo. 3s. 6d.

SIMMONS (CAPT.). Constitution and Practice of Courts-Mar-
tial. Seventh Edition. 8vo. 15s.

SMITH (PHILIP). A History of the Ancient World, from the
Creation to the Fall of the Roman Empire, A.D. 476. Fourth Edition.
3 Vols. 8vo. 31s. 6d.

SPALDING (CAPTAIN). The Tale of Frithiof. Translated from the
Swedish of ESIAS TEGNER. Post 8vo. 7s. 6d.

STANLEY'S (DEAN) WORKS :—

SINAI AND PALESTINE, in connexion with their History. Map.
8vo. 14s.

BIBLE IN THE HOLY LAND; Extracted from the above Work.
Woodcuts. Fcap. 8vo 2s. 6d.

EASTERN CHURCH. Plans. 8vo. 12s.

JEWISH CHURCH. From the Earliest Times to the Christian
Era. 3 Vols. 8vo. 38s.

EPISTLES OF ST. PAUL TO THE CORINTHIANS. 8vo. 18s.

LIFE OF DR. ARNOLD, OF RUGBY. With selections from his
Correspondence. With portrait. 2 vols. Crown 8vo. 12s.

CHURCH OF SCOTLAND. 8vo. 7s. 6d.

MEMORIALS OF CANTERBURY CATHEDRAL. Woodcuts. Post
8vo. 7s. 6d.

WESTMINSTER ABBEY. With Illustrations. 8vo. 15s.

SERMONS DURING A TOUR IN THE EAST. 8vo. 9s.

ADDRESSES AND CHARGES OF THE LATE BISHOP STANLEY. With
Memoir. 8vo. 10s. 6d.

STEPHEN (REV. W. R.). Life and Times of St. Chrysostom.
With Portrait. 8vo. 15s.

ST. JOHN (CHARLES). Wild Sports and Natural History of the
Highlands. Post 8vo. 3s. 6d.

———————— (BAYLE) Adventures in the Libyan Desert. Post 8vo. 2s.

SUMNER'S (BISHOP) Life and Episcopate during 40 Years. By
Rev. G. H. SUMNER. Portrait. 8vo. 14s.

STREET (G. E.) Gothic Architecture in Spain. From Personal
Observations made during several Journeys. With Illustrations.
Royal 8vo. 30s.

———————————————— Italy, chiefly in Brick and
Marble. With Notes of Tours in the North of Italy. With 60 Illustrations. Royal 8vo. 26s.

STUDENTS' MANUALS :—

     OLD TESTAMENT HISTORY ; from the Creation to the Return of the Jews from Captivity. Maps and Woodcuts. Post 8vo. 7s. 6d.

     NEW TESTAMENT HISTORY. With an Introduction connecting the History of the Old and New Testaments. Maps and Woodcuts. Post 8vo. 7s. 6d.

     ECCLESIASTICAL HISTORY. A History of the Christian Church during the First Ten Centuries; From its Foundation to the full establishment of the Holy Roman Empire and the Papal Power. Post 8vo. 7s. 6d.

     ENGLISH CHURCH HISTORY, from the accession of Henry VIII. to the silencing of Convocation in the 18th Century. By Rev. G. G. PERRY. Post 8vo. 7s. 6d.

     ANCIENT HISTORY OF THE EAST ; Egypt, Assyria, Babylonia, Media, Persia, Asia Minor, and Phœnicia. Woodcuts. Post 8vo. 7s. 6d.

     ANCIENT GEOGRAPHY. By REV. W. L. BEVAN. Woodcuts. Post 8vo. 7s. 6d.

     HISTORY OF GREECE ; from the Earliest Times to the Roman Conquest. By WM. SMITH, D.C.L. Woodcuts. Crown 8vo. 7s. 6d.
         * Questions on the above Work, 12mo. 2s.

     HISTORY OF ROME; from the Earliest Times to the Establishment of the Empire. By DEAN LIDDELL. Woodcuts. Crown 8vo. 7s. 6d.

     GIBBON'S DECLINE AND FALL OF THE ROMAN EMPIRE. Woodcuts. Post 8vo. 7s. 6d.

     HALLAM'S HISTORY OF EUROPE during the Middle Ages. Post 8vo. 7s. 6d.

     HALLAM'S HISTORY OF ENGLAND ; from the Accession of Henry VII. to the Death of George II. Post 8vo. 7s. 6d.

     HUME'S HISTORY OF ENGLAND from the Invasion of Julius Cæsar to the Revolution in 1688. Continued down to 1868. Woodcuts. Post 8vo. 7s. 6d.
         * Questions on the above Work, 12mo. 2s.

     HISTORY OF FRANCE; from the Earliest Times to the Establishment of the Second Empire, 1852. By REV. H. W. JERVIS. Woodcuts. Post 8vo. 7s. 6d.

     ENGLISH LANGUAGE. By GEO. P. MARSH. Post 8vo. 7s. 6d.

     ENGLISH LITERATURE. By T. B. SHAW, M.A. Post 8vo. 7s. 6d.

     SPECIMENS OF ENGLISH LITERATURE from the Chief Writers. By T. B. SHAW. Post 8vo. 7s. 6d.

     MODERN GEOGRAPHY ; Mathematical, Physical and Descriptive. By REV. W. L. BEVAN. Woodcuts. Post 8vo. 7s. 6d.

     MORAL PHILOSOPHY. By WILLIAM FLEMING, D.D. Post 8vo. 7s. 6d.

     BLACKSTONE'S COMMENTARIES ON THE LAWS OF ENGLAND. By R. MALCOLM KERR, LL.D. Post 8vo. 7s. 6d.

STYFFE (KNUTT). Strength of Iron and Steel. Plates. 8vo. 12s.

SOMERVILLE (MARY). Personal Recollections from Early Life to Old Age. With her Correspondence. Portrait. Crown 8vo. 12s.

——————— Physical Geography. Portrait. Post 8vo. 9s.

——————— Connexion of the Physical Sciences. Portrait. Post 8vo. 9s.

——————— Molecular and Microscopic Science. Illustrations. 2 Vols. Post 8vo. 21s.

STANHOPE'S (Earl) WORKS :—
>   History of England from the Reign of Queen Anne to the Peace of Versailles, 1701-83. 9 vols. Post 8vo. 5s. each.
>   British India, from its Origin to 1783. 8vo. 3s. 6d.
>   History of "Forty-Five." Post 8vo. 3s.
>   Historical and Critical Essays. Post 8vo. 3s. 6d.
>   French Retreat from Moscow, and other Essays. Post 8vo. 7s. 6d.
>   Life of Belisarius. Post 8vo. 10s. 6d.
>   Life of Condé. Post 8vo. 3s. 6d.
>   Life of William Pitt. Portraits. 4 Vols. 8vo. 24s.
>   Miscellanies. 2 Vols. Post 8vo. 13s.
>   Story of Joan of Arc. Fcap. 8vo. 1s.
>   Addresses on Various Occasions. 16mo. 1s.

SOUTHEY (Robert). Lives of Bunyan and Cromwell. Post 8vo. 2s.

SWAINSON (Canon). Nicene and Apostles' Creeds; Their Literary History ; together with some Account of " The Creed of St. Athanasius." 8vo. 16s.

SYBEL (Von) History of Europe during the French Revolution, 1789—1795. 4 Vols. 8vo. 48s.

SYMONDS' (Rev. W.) Records of the Rocks; or Notes on the Geology, Natural History, and Antiquities of North and South Wales, Siluria, Devon, and Cornwall. With Illustrations. Crown 8vo. 12s.

THIBAUT'S (Antoine) Purity in Musical Art. Translated from the German. With a prefatory Memoir by W. H. Gladstone, M.P. Post 8vo. 6s.

THIELMANN (Baron). Journey through the Caucasus to Tabreez, Kurdistan, down the Tigris and Euphrates to Nineveh and Babylon, and across the Desert to Palmyra. Translated by Chas. Heneage. Illustrations. 2 Vols. Post 8vo. 18s.

THOMS (W. J.). Longevity of Man; its Facts and its Fiction. Including Observations on the more Remarkable Instances. Post 8vo. 10s. 6d.

THOMSON (Archbishop). Lincoln's Inn Sermons. 8vo. 10s. 6d.

———— Life in the Light of God's Word. Post 8vo. 5s.

TITIAN'S LIFE AND TIMES. With some account of his Family, chiefly from new and unpubli-hed Records. By Crowe and Cavalcaselle. With Portrait and Illustrations. 2 Vols. 8vo. 42s.

TOCQUEVILLE'S State of Society in France before the Revolution, 1789, and on the Causes which led to that Event. Translated by Henry Reeve. 8vo. 14s.

TOMLINSON (Charles) ; The Sonnet ; Its Origin, Structure, and Place in Poetry. With translations from Dante, Petrarch, &c. Post 8vo. 9s.

TOZER (Rev. H. F.) Highlands of Turkey, with Visits to Mounts Ida, Athos, Olympus, and Pelion. 2 Vols. Crown 8vo. 24s.

———— Lectures on the Geography of Greece. Map. Post 8vo. 9s.

TRISTRAM (Canon) Great Sahara. Illustrations. Crown 8vo. 15s.

———— Land of Moab ; Travels and Discoveries on the East Side of the Dead Sea and the Jordan. Illustrations. Crown 8vo. 15s.

TWENTY YEARS' RESIDENCE among the Greeks, Albanians, Turks, Armenians, and Bulgarians. By an ENGLISH LADY. Edited by STANLEY LANE POOLE. 2 Vols. Crown 8vo.

TWISLETON (EDWARD). The Tongue not Essential to Speech, with Illustrations of the Power of Speech in the case of the African Confessors. Post 8vo. 6s.

TWISS' (HORACE) Life of Lord Eldon. 2 Vols. Post 8vo. 21s.

TYLOR (E. B.) Early History of Mankind, and Development of Civilization. 8vo. 12s.

———————— Primitive Culture ; the Development of Mythology, Philosophy, Religion, Art, and Custom. 2 Vols. 8vo. 24s.

VAMBERY (ARMINIUS) Travels from Teheran across the Turkoman Desert on the Eastern Shore of the Caspian. Illustrations. 8vo. 21s.

VAN LENNEP (HENRY J.) Travels in Asia Minor. With Illustrations of Biblical Literature, and Archæology. With Woodcuts. 2 Vols. Post 8vo. 24s.

———————— Modern Customs and Manners of Bible Lands, in illustration of Scripture. With Maps and 300 Illustrations. 2 Vols. 8vo. 21s.

VIRCHOW (PROFESSOR). The Freedom of Science in the Modern State. Fcap. 8vo. 2s.

WELLINGTON'S Despatches during his Campaigns in India, Denmark, Portugal, Spain, the Low Countries, and France. 8 Vols. 8vo. 20s. each.

———————— Supplementary Despatches, relating to India, Ireland, Denmark, Spanish America, Spain, Portugal, France, Congress of Vienna, Waterloo and Paris. 14 Vols. 8vo. 20s. each. *₄* An Index. 8vo. 20s.

———————— Civil and Political Correspondence. Vols. I. to VII. 8vo. 20s. each.

———————— Speeches in Parliament. 2 Vols. 8vo. 42s.

WHEELER (G.). Choice of a Dwelling ; a Practical Handbook of Useful Information on Building a House. Plans. Post 8vo. 7s. 6d.

WHITE (W. H.). Manual of Naval Architecture, for the use of Naval Officers, Shipowners, Shipbuilders, and Yachtsmen. Illustrations. 8vo. 24s.

WILBERFORCE'S (BISHOP) Life of William Wilberforce. Portrait. Crown 8vo. 6s.

WILKINSON (SIR J. G.). Manners and Customs of the Ancient Egyptians, their Private Life, Government, Laws, Arts, Manufactures, Religion, &c. A new edition, with additions by the late Author. Edited by SAMUEL BIRCH, LL.D. Illustrations. 3 Vols. 8vo.

———————— Popular Account of the Ancient Egyptians. With 500 Woodcuts. 2 Vols. Post 8vo. 12s.

WOOD'S (CAPTAIN) Source of the Oxus. With the Geography of the Valley of the Oxus. By COL. YULE. Map. 8vo. 12s.

WORDS OF HUMAN WISDOM. Collected and Arranged by E. S. With a Preface by CANON LIDDON. Fcap. 8vo. 3s. 6d.

WORDSWORTH'S (BISHOP) Athens and Attica. Plates. 8vo. 5s.

YULE'S (COLONEL) Book of Marco Polo. Illustrated by the Light of Oriental Writers and Modern Travels. With Maps and 80 Plates. 2 Vols. Medium 8vo. 63s.

BRADBURY, AGNEW, & CO., PRINTERS, WHITEFRIARS.